ASTD HANDBOOK

The Definitive Reference for Training & Development

Elaine Biech, Editor

ASTD Press is an internationally renowned source of insightful and practical information on workplace learning, training, and professional development.

Photo credits: Photo of editor, Elaine Biech, by Denis J. Anderson © 2014. Photo used with permission

ASTD Press
1640 King Street Box 1443
Alexandria, VA 22313-1443 USA

Ordering information: Books published by ASTD Press can be purchased by visiting ASTD's website at store.astd.org or by calling 800.628.2783 or 703.683.8100.

Library of Congress Control Number: 2014934637

ISBN-10: 1-56286-913-2
ISBN-13: 978-1-56286-913-7
e-ISBN: 978-1-60728-561-8

ASTD Press Editorial Staff:
Director: Glenn Saltzman
Manager and Editor, ASTD Press: Ashley McDonald
Community of Practice Manager, Learning & Development: Juana Llorens
Editorial Assistant: Ashley Slade
Cover Design: Lon Levy
Editorial, Design, and Production: Abella Publishing Services, LLC

Printed by Sheridan Books, Inc., Chelsea, MI, www.sheridan.com

Contents

Contents

Contents

Foreword

ASTD's mission is to "Empower professionals to develop knowledge and skills successfully." We do that by creating content, building connections, and bringing a myriad of resources to those who work in the training and development field.

What you are holding in your hands now, the second edition of the *ASTD Handbook,* is a world-class example of the profession-leading content that ASTD curates. This book, with contributions from more than 90 authors, is the most comprehensive, authoritative reference ever assembled for the profession.

The driving force behind this book is the incomparable Elaine Biech. She has my sincere thanks for the exceptional job she did in shaping and editing this incredible resource. An accomplished author of more than 50 books herself, Elaine is an outspoken advocate for ASTD and the profession of training and development. She has been recognized by ASTD for her passionate volunteer work. She is the recipient of the 1992 National ASTD Torch Award, the 2004 ASTD Volunteer-Staff Partnership Award, and the 2006 ASTD Gordon M. Bliss Memorial Award and was named a 2012 CPLP Fellow by the ASTD Certification Institute.

Why do so many experts agree to contribute to a book like this? I think the answer is two-fold. First, these authors are personally committed to the continuing growth and excellence of the training and development profession. They are passionate about the work of helping others achieve their potential—whether that person is a new hire just out of school or a new senior leader being groomed for the next step on the leadership path. Second, these thought leaders and practitioners trust ASTD to produce content that truly drives impact for the profession they love. We *all* owe a debt of gratitude to the outstanding contributors of the *ASTD Handbook*.

ASTD recently celebrated its 70th anniversary. For seven decades, ASTD has been a trusted voice in the training field. People look to ASTD to deliver vetted content that is solidly researched and readily applicable. They know that when ASTD identifies trends, it does so through the lens of positively affecting organizational results through employee development. ASTD's global reach and its vast network of members and practitioners around the world provide a perspective that is unmatched.

This second edition of the *ASTD Handbook* provides that perspective and that vetted content by the best and brightest thinkers in our field, masterfully woven into a single resource. From an overview of the training and development profession, including an analysis of the new competencies for practitioners, to a discussion of contemporary challenges facing all of us, you will find in these pages a comprehensive and definitive discussion that will inform your own thinking.

This is a book to come back to again and again. Whether you're faced with a new challenge or confirming your own knowledge, you will find a chapter here—there are 55 in all—that will have the answer you're seeking.

ASTD is privileged to bring the work of so many talented professionals to you. I believe you will appreciate the depth, breadth, and quality of this content—and I know your work will benefit from the time you invest in this book.

Thank you for engaging with ASTD.

—Tony Bingham
President and CEO, ASTD

Introduction to the *ASTD Handbook: The Definitive Reference for Training & Development*

The *ASTD Handbook for Workplace Learning Professionals* was published in 2008. Much has changed since then, and a new reference is due. The title of the second edition hints at something fresh and different: *The Definitive Reference for Training and Development*.

Compare the two handbooks and you will find similarities and differences. The intent of the first edition was to deliver all the basics of developing employees—assessment, design, development, implementation, evaluation—and to explore how to best manage the learning and performance function. The second edition expands on these same themes with a focus on the changes to the profession that have occurred in the last six years. While the first edition took a broad look at these topics and presented the basics, the second edition examines more topics from a narrower perspective and fine-tunes each. This means that the topics in the second edition are more specific in nature than those in the first.

What You'll Find in the New Edition

This *Handbook* takes a deeper dive into areas such as working with SMEs, the value of experiential learning, the global virtual classroom, and informal learning. It also introduces niche topics such as curation of content, integration of learning analytics, and the neuroscience of learning.

The *Handbook* is divided into nine sections that represent the major areas in our profession. These sections also represent the differences that have occurred in our profession over the past decade:

- The Training and Development Profession
- Assessing and Analyzing Needs

- Designing and Developing Effective Learning
- Delivering T&D Solutions That Make a Difference
- Transferring Learning and Evaluating Impact
- Expanded Roles of the T&D Professional
- Managing the Business of Training
- Developing and Leading Organizations: T&D's Role
- Contemporary Challenges

Each of these sections is introduced by a luminary—a unique individual who is a respected thought leader in our profession and who has had an active role in developing and leading the represented area. All of the luminaries are authorities in the sections they introduce. Two of our luminaries, Bill Byham and Elliott Masie, also received this distinction in the first *Handbook* edition.

The nine luminaries are internationally respected gurus. They have authored or co-authored more than 200 books, presented at thousands of conferences worldwide, and received multiple professional awards. We are delighted that they agreed to contribute their wisdom to the *Handbook*.

- Bill Rothwell is the luminary for "The Training and Development Profession." He has had a hand in helping to shape the field through his research, his writing, his global consulting, and his countless hours as a volunteer for ASTD.
- Dana Gaines Robinson is the luminary for "Assessing and Analyzing Needs." As a performance consulting leader, Dana's expertise reaches far and wide. We are delighted that she came out of retirement to provide her perspective for this section.
- Sivasailam "Thiagi" Thiagarajan is the luminary for "Designing and Developing Effective Learning." No one can dispute his rightful place as the master designer of learning solutions. We are delighted that he is the "resident mad scientist" at the Thiagi Group who develops solutions we all use. He wraps his typical Thiagi wit and humor into his introduction.
- Bob Pike is the luminary for "Delivering T&D Solutions That Make a Difference." He is truly a trainer extraordinaire and a model for most trainers around the world. He has certainly earned his "trainers' trainer" designation.
- Rob Brinkerhoff is the luminary for "Transferring Learning and Evaluating Impact." He is an internationally recognized expert on training effectiveness and evaluation, and you've probably either read one of his books or heard him speak at a conference. He offers a welcomed introduction to this section.

- Bev Kaye is the luminary for "Expanded Roles of the T&D Professional." No one knows more about the importance of professional development than Bev. Translated into 20 languages, the fifth edition of her bestselling book *Love 'em or Lose 'em* is living proof of that.
- Bill Byham is the luminary for "Managing the Business of Training." As the co-founder and CEO of DDI, he has forged important innovations in human resource systems that have had significant effects on organizations worldwide. Bill helps others manage successfully and puts into action all he knows with his own company.
- Ken Blanchard is the luminary for "Developing and Leading Organizations: T&D's Role." Leading is Ken's forte. Starting with *Situational Leadership* and the *One Minute Manager,* Ken's books have sold 20 million copies and have had an extraordinary impact on millions of people.
- Elliott Masie is the luminary for "Contemporary Challenges." Always on the cutting edge, always challenging us to consider the what-could-be, always first with the right questions, Elliott earns his luminary distinction for this section. As an internationally recognized futurist, researcher, and think tank convener, he often predicts the challenges before they exist.

You may have noticed that we have not listed a separate section for technology-enabled learning. We believe that is one of the shifts that has occurred since the publication of the first *Handbook*. We did not call out a separate section, believing that technology is a natural option for most T&D professionals today. Even though the many options grow daily, we do not need a reminder.

What We Asked of Our Authors

Each of the nine sections comprises a collection of four to 10 chapters written by experts in our profession. The first edition delivered 49 chapters written by 60 authors. In this *Handbook,* we juggled the expertise of 96 authors who wrote 55 insightful chapters. They are the elite of the "who's who" in training and development. All authors were asked to write about a topic about which they are most intimately knowledgeable. We asked them to deliver a chapter that was informative, practical, and thought provoking.

Authors were asked to reference the giants whose research shaped our profession and laid the foundation on which we base our assumptions and that many of us may take for granted: Benjamin Bloom, Robert Gagné, Malcolm Knowles, David Kolb, Kurt Lewin, Robert Mager, Abraham Maslow, and others. You will find names such as these woven into many of the chapters. Interspersed within the chapters are sidebars that also feature some of these distinguished leaders and the contributions they have made to our profession.

We asked our authors to challenge your thinking, and they did. Are you ready to challenge your e-learning beliefs? Are you willing to start your design with the last activity you want participants to be able to do? Are you prepared to ensure that the climate is right for informal learning? These are just a few of the ways our authors will challenge you.

The *Handbook* taps into the best minds in the field. Dozens of experts explore a multitude of topics. When woven together, the wisdom in these topics creates your professional persona. The new sections add content to explore potentially new roles. The expanded roles we experience and the contemporary challenges ahead of you will define you, your professional identify, and how you need to develop.

What You Can Expect

As you read the *Handbook,* these highlights may engage you more holistically.

Watch for Themes

Although we did not seek out specific themes, several emerged naturally. These were perhaps a sign of the times. You will find these themes running through different chapters: the need to focus on the business impact; the variety of meanings of experiential learning; and the need for delivering "the least amount" required by the learner.

Don't Miss the Collaborative Chapters

We are very excited about our collaborative chapters—those written from several viewpoints—for example, "The Importance of Certification," written from an employer's perspective and the employee's perspective; "Keep Participants Engaged," written from a classroom perspective and a virtual perspective; and "Developing Leadership Around the Globe," written from the perspectives of nine different countries or regions.

Prepare to Be Challenged

Are you wondering if the 70–20–10 learning principle really exists? Is SAM really better than ADDIE? Should you really begin evaluation with Level 4 first? Do new approaches actually exist, or is this all a rehash of Thiagi's old ideas?

Expect Differences

You have the benefit of the thinking of many experts, but as you might imagine, they do not all agree. The intention of the *Handbook* is to present numerous views on topics. They may be in contention with each other; they may disagree in theory. Do you believe that the concept of learning styles is myth? How do you define experiential learning?

What's Old Is Good

A couple chapters from the first edition are just too valuable, so we asked the authors to update and revise them. We have included these revised chapter topics in the new *Handbook:* the evolution of the profession, data collection, learning theories, legal aspects, and consulting on the inside.

Using the *Handbook*

The *Handbook* is meant to be practical. Go to it when you need content information. Think of it first as a resource, not as a book to be read cover to cover. The table of contents will be useful for finding broad general information about a topic such as evaluation or designing learning. The comprehensive index in the back of the book will be more useful if you require information about specific topics, such as a short biography of Malcolm Knowles or tips for finding a job in the profession. A glossary in the back of the book provides definitions to key words and concepts you may encounter in the *Handbook*.

We want everyone to go beyond reading this book; we want you to *use* it. It is filled with wisdom and tools to implement that wisdom. To enable this, we've included the tools on the website, so readers can download tools to help implement the concepts. We are happy to offer you a repository of almost 100 tools that accompany the chapters in the *Handbook*. These tools are located on the *Handbook's* website at www.astdhandbook.org. Each tool is referenced within its chapter, and you will also find a list of all the tools near the end of the book. Imagine a "Training Plan Worksheet" from Harold Stolovitch or a "Knowledge Management Organizational Assessment" from Marc Rosenberg. You will find checklists, activities, content resources, self-assessments, and more.

We are delighted to share this definitive guide and all its unique features with you.

We Are Thankful

The *ASTD Handbook* is certainly the definitive reference for all of us. It is an honor to once again edit this *Handbook*, but like every huge project, it is a team effort that includes many dedicated professionals. Thousands of hours went into its production, and this list is just a beginning:

- First and most essential to the project, my ASTD partner, Ashley McDonald. Without her enthusiastic and confident attitude, we would never have achieved the impossible deadline.

- The nine luminary guest contributors. Thank you for lending your name and your wisdom to a project that is on target to make a difference to thousands.
- The 96 authors who are vital to the *Handbook*. Thank you for accepting our impossible timeline and producing outstanding chapters that are practical, informative, and thought provoking. Your support is immeasurable and affirming. The benefit of having another reason to connect with and learn from you is incredible!
- The editorial advisory board included Halelly Azulay, Jean Barbazette, Justin Brusino, Pat Galagan, Jennifer Homer, Cindy Huggett, Jenn Labin, Jennifer Naughton, and Nancy Olson. They provided a great launch and were always there when we needed advice.
- Cat Russo for your practical counsel, pitch-hitting on demand, and problem solving in a flash.
- Tora Estep for defining, refining, and designing the tools.
- And of course, thank you ASTD and Tony for giving me another chance to grow and learn—one of the many reasons I continue to be a dedicated ASTD volunteer.

—Elaine Biech
May 2014

Section I

The Training and Development Profession

Shaping the Future of the Training and Development Profession

Luminary Perspective

William J. Rothwell

Neuroscience. Technology-assisted learning. Double-loop learning. Informal, social, and incidental learning. International and cross-cultural learning issues. These terms, and others, spark interest and attention in the training and development field today.

But in this introductory chapter, I would like to focus on several issues. First is the need to get back to basics in an innovative way, and the *ASTD Handbook* is an important tool in that effort. Second is the need to devote more attention to values and ethics. Third is the need to focus on learning competence and learning climate and not just trainer competence.

The Need to Get Back to the Basics With Innovation

What do we really know about current practices in training and development? Apart from limited information provided by ASTD and by *Training* magazine, the answer is "very little." Few, if any, governments in the world systematically collect detailed data about business and industry training practices. While sufficient funding exists to research the impact of Tibetan education on American classrooms, little or no information exists about current practices across all U.S. companies on training, development, on-the-job training, on-the-job learning, social learning, or other issues in the field. What information exists amounts to little more than wild guesses based on small sample sizes, low response-rate surveys, or specialized populations.

Consider: How do most organizations:

- Align learning with strategic objectives?
- Differentiate training from management needs?
- Assess and analyze training needs?
- Establish and measure instructional and performance objectives?
- Design training?
- Select, use, and blend technology to deliver training?
- Deliver training?
- Measure and evaluate reaction, learning, behavioral change, and transfer of learning to the job, results, return-on-investment, and business impact of training?
- Decide on ways to manage and budget for training?
- Manage training strategically?

These and other questions have no clear answers that are updated annually, based on research, around the world. Billions of dollars are spent annually on training and development with little known about how it helps organizations become (and remain) productive and helps individuals secure (and maintain) employment and advance in their careers.

To make matters worse, the training field itself has been accused—with some justification—of being too prone to focus on fads. Everyone, it seems, wants to know about the latest new innovation or gadget, and that is laudable. But what is not laudable is that few people want to first master the basics of training, even though they may have had limited training on training itself. Most trainers today are promoted from within, and few organizations provide systematic training on training itself. There is a bias for expensive technology-assisted learning methods but less interest in low-tech, but high-impact, approaches such as planned on-the-job training where the transfer of training is closer to 100 percent than the mere 8 percent transfer rate of classroom-based methods.

My advice? Government policymakers, private funders, and economists should devote more attention to exploring the basics. Everyone in the field needs to know what typical practice is, as well as best practice. Beyond that, academic researchers should devote more attention to truly practical data collection about typical and best practices on all training areas and explore innovative approaches to analyzing performance problems, assessing training needs, formulating learning and performance objectives, designing and delivering training, measuring the business impact of training, managing training effectively, aligning training with organizational strategy, and other topics of relevance to practitioners.

The Need to Devote More Attention to Values and Ethics

ASTD and other organizations have devoted attention to identifying trainer competencies. Those efforts deserve praise because they help to raise the general competence of practitioners in the field. But what is needed now is more attention to values and ethics. *Values* center around what is good or bad—or important or not important—to organizations; *ethics* center around right and wrong and the enormous continuum between them. Training and development professionals should care about values and ethics for three reasons.

The first reason is that training and development professionals often have responsibility for conducting instruction in their organizations on values and ethics. They need up-to-date information on how to measure and conduct research on values and ethics. These issues are too important for guesswork. Solid information is needed to shed light on these topics.

The second reason is that too little information exists on the values associated with top-performing organizations, training and development departments or functions, and individual training and development individuals. How are business priorities established, and how are they cascaded in organizations? How are values established and sustained in organizations? How are implicit values measured and compared to espoused or nominal values? These issues warrant further investigation.

The third reason is that ethics has emerged as a preeminent challenge for the future of the world. Corruption is an ethical issue, and its reach is global. As evidence, consider that the 2008 financial crisis in the United States was really an issue of placing performance above ethics because banks encouraged their workers to get profits at all costs and without regard to common sense or legal restrictions. Signing Codes of Conduct is not an effective way to deal with the problems that stem from such a complex issue. These Codes are written by lawyers and are intended to protect organizations from legal challenges, not address the issue of how ethical behavior may affect productivity and performance.

The training and development field is uniquely positioned in organizations to research genuine ethical challenges that stem from the daily work and to offer practical guidance to workers and managers alike on how to address those issues. But such an effort requires that the ethical standards of the training and development field are first researched and that trainers are themselves subject to rigorous, research-based, and not merely aspirational standards of ethical performance.

The Need to Focus on Learning Competence and Learning Climate

Training and development competence exists within a broader web of relationships. Demonstrating effective competence through research-based individual certification as a training and development practitioner is not enough. What is needed is information about what it takes for learners to be competent in their own learning efforts and what climate organizations must establish to facilitate learning to address real-world individual performer and organizational challenges.

Just as training and development competencies clarify the characteristics of successful or outstanding training and development practitioners, learning competencies clarify the characteristics of successful learners. Much research suggests that learning ability, which some call learning agility, is becoming the quintessential competence for everyone in the future. The reason is simple enough: All human knowledge now turns over every few years. Yet limited research exists on learning competence. That is much needed. As just one example, consider that about 80 percent of all e-learning is delivered without an instructor or facilitator, making the individual learner's ability to learn how to learn critical in the learning process.

But individual learning competence and trainer competence are also not enough by themselves. These competencies are enacted in organizational settings that may encourage (or discourage) learning. What are the characteristics of organizations that encourage learning to address real-world problems? What should be the standards for organizations to become true "learning organizations" that encourage individuals to learn, and to perform, to their peak potential? Answering that question is a challenge for the future. What is needed is a National Award for Learning and Performance Climate.

Conclusion

The introduction to this opening section has focused on some unique issues affecting the future of the training and development field. The sidebar presents questions you and your colleagues can explore around the issues that affect our profession. You can also download the questions in the form of a worksheet on the *Handbook's* website at www.astdhandbook. org. Addressing these issues may shape the future of the training and development field in contributing to individual career success and organizational performance and productivity.

Issues Affecting the Training and Development Profession

Use these questions to organize your thinking. There are no "right" or "wrong" answers in any absolute sense. Circulate your answers to other practitioners inside and outside your organization to spark discussion and stimulate thought.

1. How does your organization:

- Align learning with strategic objectives?
- Differentiate training from management needs?
- Assess and analyze training needs?
- Establish and measure instructional and performance objectives?
- Design training?
- Select, use, and blend technology to deliver training?
- Deliver training?
- Measure and evaluate reaction, learning, behavioral change, and transfer of learning to the job, results, return-on-investment, and business impact of training?
- Decide on ways to manage and budget for training?
- Manage training strategically?

2. How does your organization:

- Identify organizational values?
- Train workers and managers on organizational values?
- Identify organizational ethical dilemmas?
- Train workers and managers on how to address ethical dilemmas?

3. How does your organization:

- Identify individual learning competence?
- Encourage individuals to improve their learning competence?
- Identify and measure the organization's learning climate?
- Improve the organization's learning climate?

About the Author

William J. Rothwell, PhD, SPHR, CPLP Fellow, is president of Rothwell & Associates, Inc. (see www.rothwellandassociates.com) and professor of workforce education and development on the University Park campus of the Pennsylvania State University. A practitioner with 20 years of experience as a training director in business and in government before he became a professor, he has authored, co-authored, edited, or co-edited 85 books and 300 articles about training, learning, organization development, learning technology, training competence, and much more. In 2012, he earned ASTD's prestigious Distinguished Contribution to Workplace Learning and Performance Award, and in 2013, he was honored by ASTD by being named a Certified Professional in Learning and Performance (CPLP) Fellow. Active on the last five ASTD competency studies, he recently co-authored with Justin Arneson and Jennifer Naughton the *ASTD Competency Study: The Training and Development Profession Redefined.* He has delivered training and consulting in many nations, including 70 trips to China since 1996.

For Further Reading

Arbogast, S. (2013). *Resisting Corporate Corruption: Cases in Practical Ethics From Enron Through the Financial Crisis,* 2nd edition. New York: Wiley/Scrivener.

ASTD. (2012). *State of the Industry Report.* Alexandria, VA: ASTD Press.

Bedford, C. (2011). *The Role of Learning Agility in Workplace Performance and Career Advancement.* Ann Arbor, MI: ProQuest, UMI Dissertation Publishing.

Kraemer, H. (2011). *From Values to Action: The Four Principles of Values-Based Leadership.* San Francisco: Jossey-Bass.

Novak, J., D. Gowin, and J. Kahle. (2013). *Learning How to Learn.* Cambridgeshire, UK: Cambridge University Press.

Rothwell, W. (2002). *The Workplace Learner: How to Align Training Initiatives with Individual Learning Competencies.* New York: Amacom.

Chapter 1

The Evolution of the Training Profession

Kevin Oakes

············· **In This Chapter** ·············

- Learn how the training profession has developed over time.
- Understand the roots of training practices in use today.

It is somewhat ironic that the profession of training—which focuses so much on new initiatives and managing change—has never stopped undergoing rather dramatic change since its inception. Over time, the training profession has seen its initial focus on skills training evolve to focus on individual development to systems theory and organization development to learning and, most recently, to performance and talent management.

Today, corporate trainers and training and development departments are rapidly transforming from the sole creators of content and a sage-on-the-stage mentality to an environment where they are more facilitators than lecturers, editors than creators, and enablers of user-generated content throughout the enterprise. While more corporate executives and senior teams recognize the bottom-line business impact that training and learning can have, the identity of training is getting somewhat bifurcated by blurred roles, responsibilities, and titles. Today, the training professional is often called a learning and development professional, or talent development professional, or performance consultant, among many other titles. Over the last several years, the profession has become a component of the talent management wave, an important movement in organizations across the world but one that risks masking the critical significance of the training profession. As in the past, the training profession will adapt and change with an agility other professions can only envy.

To appreciate where the training profession is going, it's important to understand where it's been. What follows is an inclusive history of the training profession, going all the way back to medieval history through today's era of online, social, mobile, and performance-based learning programs.

Early Learning Models and Practices

Learning is as critical to human life as breathing. From the beginning, humans have relied on elders teaching the young how to find and recognize edible plants, hunt and process game, care for children, make weapons and tools from local materials . . . the list is endless. As humans evolved, so did our thoughts on learning. The advent of agriculture enabled societies to create a surplus of food, which in turn allowed people to become more specialized in their job roles. As a result, the need to train individuals in specific trades became more pressing. To meet this need, on-the-job training, apprenticeships, guilds, vocational and manual schools, factory schools, and vestibule training arose (see Figure 1-1 for a timeline of early training and learning practices).

On-the-Job Training

The earliest form of training was on-the-job training, and today it is still the most popular form of training. On-the-job training, which is defined as one-to-one training in which an experienced craftsperson shows a novice how to do a task (Sleight, 1993) is still popular, in part because of its simplicity; all that an organization needs to do is assign an experienced employee to show a new employee how to do the job. Furthermore, on-the-job training obviates any problems with transfer because training takes place in the job setting, so the learner has no problem in understanding how the learning applies to the work.

However, one drawback of on-the-job training is that the experienced employee is often unable to be as productive while he or she is providing training. In addition, being experienced at one's job is not necessarily an indicator of ability to teach or train well, and consistency in training is almost impossible to enforce. Lastly, on-the-job training generally isn't scalable; without capturing that training for reuse in the future, on-the-job training is a time-consuming exercise of continual repetition in an organization.

Apprenticeships

While on-the-job training was the earliest form of training, it was typically informal in nature. A more formal arrangement arose with the apprenticeship system. Although Steinmetz (1976) notes that rules governing apprenticeships appeared in the Code of Hammurabi (circa 1780 B.C.), apprenticeships really took root in the Middle Ages when jobs became too complex to master with just a few days of on-the-job training (Sleight, 1993).

Apprenticeships typically took several years. In exchange for work, the master trained a beginner in a craft. The beginner, who lived with the master and got no pay, became increasingly proficient in a particular craft and eventually became a journeyman or a yeoman. Although apprenticeships are generally thought of as applying only to artisanal crafts, they were not restricted to such jobs but could apply to medicine, law, and education (Steinmetz, 1976). Apprenticeships still exist today. In the United States, where apprenticeships are less common, apprentices are safeguarded by the U.S. Department of Labor, which ensures equality of access to apprenticeship programs and provides employment and training information to sponsors and the employment and training community.

In Asia and Europe, however, modern apprenticeship programs are more common. In Germany, they are an important part of the successful dual education system, which combines apprenticeships with vocational education. In India, the Apprenticeship Act, enacted in 1961, regulates the way apprentices are trained so that their training conforms with Central Apprenticeship Council standards and meets industry needs. The United Kingdom has more than 160 apprenticeship frameworks—including National Vocational Qualifications—which now extend beyond craft and skilled trades to other areas of the service sector without an apprenticeship tradition. Although apprenticeship declined in the United Kingdom in the early 2000s, the percentage of young people completing apprenticeships began to increase again in 2004 after the government established the Modern Apprenticeships Advisory Committee to make recommendations on the apprenticeship system.

Guilds

The guild system also developed in the Middle Ages in England before the Norman invasion of 1066. Guilds were "associations of people whose interests or pursuits were the same or similar. The basic purpose was mutual protection, assistance, and advantage" (Steinmetz, 1976). The guild system controlled the quality of products by establishing standards and regulating the people who were authorized to produce them. This also meant that apprenticeships came under the authority of the guild, which determined when a worker had reached a certain level of proficiency. Within the guild there were three levels of workers: the master, who owned the materials and directed the work; the journeyman, who worked for the master in return for pay; and finally the apprentice. Guild guidelines determined when a worker had reached a certain level of proficiency and was able to graduate to journeyman or master level.

Guilds also strictly regulated workers' hours, tools, prices, and wages and required that all workers have the same privileges and pursue the same methods. These conditions, coupled with the ever-growing capital investment required to start a workshop and the increasingly high standards set by masters, made it so difficult for journeymen to attain master status that they banded together in yeomanry guilds, which became the forerunners for today's labor unions (Steinmetz, 1976).

Vocational and Manual Schools

The guild and apprenticeship systems continued to dominate training and learning until the Industrial Revolution, which began in England, spread to France and Belgium, and then to Germany and the United States (Miller, 2008). However, the onset of industrialism started the acceleration of change in business that we see today as well as changes in training and learning practices. One of the new forms that learning took at this time was vocational and manual schools. These schools were intended to provide training in skills related to specific jobs. One of the earliest vocational schools was established by the Masonic Grand Lodge of New York in 1809; in 1824, Rensselaer Polytechnic Institute in Troy, New York, became the first technical college; and in 1828, the Ohio Mechanics Institute opened in Cincinnati, Ohio (Miller, 2008; Steinmetz, 1976).

Vocational schools—which lost popularity in the United States but have had a resurgence—have continued to be an important force in training, especially in Europe, which has included vocational training in the draft Constitutional Treaty establishing the European Community. To establish a vocational training policy that would apply to all members of the European Community, "two important schemes were devised: Europass-Training, which described skills acquired by training abroad, and Europass, which combines five documents aimed at providing a clear and simple picture of the qualifications and skills of citizens throughout Europe" (European Communities, 2007). Germany's successful vocational training program has also served as a model for Australia's vocational training program.

Manual training started in the United States around 1825. It started primarily as a correctional tool based on the idea that it was better to give idle hands something productive to do but then became widely established by the late 1880s. One of the greatest leaps forward in learning in the United States at this time was the passing of the Land Grant Act of 1862.

In signing this act, Abraham Lincoln provided a way for average people to get an education, which had previously been restricted to the wealthy.

Factory Schools

By the time that Hoe and Company in New York City started its factory school in 1872, classroom training had become the norm in education. The innovation was to attach the school directly to the factory and to develop the curricula based on tasks that were carried out in the factory. Sleight (1993) explains why factories turned to classroom training at this time:

> The machines of the Industrial Revolution greatly increased the ability of the factory to produce concrete goods quickly and cheaply, so more workers were needed to run the machines. The factory owners wanted the workers trained quickly because there was a large demand for the produced goods. Since the machines were much more complicated than the tools of the agrarian society of the past, and training needed to be accomplished quickly, the training methods of the past were inadequate.

The benefits of classroom training, compared with on-the-job training and apprenticeships, were that many workers could be trained at once and that fewer trainers were required. Also, learning was taken off the factory floor, minimizing distractions and leaving equipment in production. However, classroom training had some downsides as well. Learners needed to remember what they had learned until they got to work, and they also needed to transfer what they had learned back to the workplace. Furthermore, learners now had to learn at the trainer's pace and did not get the same level of feedback that they would have with on-the-job training and apprenticeships.

Vestibule Training

Around the turn of the 20th century, an innovation came about that addressed some of the problems of classroom training, namely vestibule training. Also called "near-the-job" training, vestibule training took place as close to the factory floor as feasible and contained the same equipment that the worker would use on the job. The trainer was an experienced employee in the company and would train six to 10 people at a time. This combined the benefits of classroom training (economy of scale, minimal distractions on the floor, equipment kept in production) with the benefits of on-the-job training (more hands-on, more feedback, fewer problems with transfer, fewer accidents). It did have some downsides, however. It was expensive, requiring duplication of the production line and full-time instructors, so it was restricted to situations in which many workers needed to be trained at once on unskilled or semiskilled tasks. Nonetheless, this form of training was popular through both world wars (Sleight, 1993).

The World Wars—Systematic Training

The world wars—especially World War II—saw the profession of training and learning begin a rapid maturation process. The wars brought on a massive surge in demand for products, at the same time that large numbers of experienced workers were enlisting. As a result, industry needed workers not only to fill positions left empty but also to fill new positions. Zuboff (1984), as quoted in Sleight (1993), summarizes the situation, "With the growing complexity and size of factories, expanding markets that exerted a strong demand for an increase in the volume of production, and a rising engineering profession, there emerged a new and pressing concern to systematize the administration, control, coordination, and planning of factory work."

In response to these conditions, Frederick Winslow Taylor proposed a method to shorten the amount of time it took to complete a task by studying workers and eliminating nonproductive time, which is referred to as scientific management. Another innovation conceived to speed up production was the assembly line. Training methods also had to be developed to train workers faster and more thoroughly than before. During World War I, Charles R. Allen put forward the show–tell–do–check method of training to train shipbuilders, which he adapted from the 18th-century German philosopher, psychologist, and educator Johann Friedrich Herbart's five-step framework for pedagogy. Herbart's framework included preparing the students, presenting the lesson, associating the lesson with ideas previously studied, using examples to illustrate, and testing pupils to ensure they learned (Clark, 1999).

Allen's work and Army research gave rise to several training principles. Sleight (1993) summarizes these principles:

- Training should be done within industry by supervisors who should be trained how to teach.
- Training should be done in groups of nine to 11 workers.
- The job should be analyzed before training.
- Break-in time is reduced when training is done on the job.
- When given personal attention in training, the worker develops a feeling of loyalty.

Although these principles were used in training, a systematic approach to training did not develop until World War II. At this point, large numbers of women and men over the age of 40 were entering the workforce to replace the men who had been called up for the war. These people needed training, but the supply of vocational school instructors ran out before the need was fully met (Shaw, 1994; Steinmetz, 1976). To supply much-needed trainers, the Training Within Industry Service of the War Manpower Commission developed the Job

Instructor Program, or JIT. The JIT's purpose was to teach first- and second-line supervisors how to teach their skills to others. These train-the-trainer programs came to be known as J programs and expanded to include topics such as human relations, job methods, safety, and program development. Influences on these topics included Abraham Maslow's "A Theory of Human Motivation" (1943) and Kurt Lewin's first experiments with group dynamics (1948).

In concert with systematic training came a systematic approach to instructional design. During World War II, the military applied a systems approach to learning design, which became the forerunner for today's instructional systems design (ISD). The research and theories of B.F. Skinner on operant conditioning affected the design of these training programs, which focused on observable behaviors. Training designers created learning goals by breaking tasks into subtasks, and training was designed to reward correct behaviors and remediate incorrect behaviors.

During the war, industry also came to recognize how important the training of supervisors had become. As Steinmetz (1976) puts it, "management found that without training skill, supervisors were unable to adequately produce for the defense or war effort. With it, new production methods were being established by the aged, the handicapped, and industrially inexperienced women." The need for leadership in training had become obvious, and so the title of training director became increasingly common in management hierarchies. In 1942, the American Society of Training Directors (ASTD) formed during a meeting of the American Petroleum Institute in New Orleans, Louisiana (for more on the history of ASTD, see the sidebar later in this chapter).

In addition to the development of leadership in the training function came the recognition of the need for development in leadership more generally. This led to the emergence of the first management development programs. According to Steinmetz (1976), these programs were sponsored and guided by universities and colleges, which offered college-level courses in management and technology.

The 1950s

After World War II, the economy boomed as the efficiencies that had been gained in industry to accommodate the demands of war production were harnessed for peacetime reconstruction. However, some of the methods that had been used to achieve those efficiencies—specifically, scientific management—were beginning to prove demotivating to employees. As a result, human relations training grew increasingly popular, and supervisors were often trained in psychology (Shaw, 1994).

B.F. Skinner

B.F. Skinner was a renowned behavioral psychologist and a major proponent of behaviorism, an influential school of psychological thought that was popular between World War I and World War II. Skinner, who is categorized as a neobehaviorist, believed that the best way to learn about human nature was to explore how an organism responds to stimuli, both from the external environment and from internal biological processes, in a controlled, scientific study. Skinner's scholarly interests were influenced by psychologists such as Ivan Petrovich Pavlov, Bertrand Russell, and the founder of behaviorism, John B. Watson. Skinner's major works include *The Behavior of Organisms* (1938), *Walden Two* (1948), and *Science and Human Behavior* (1953).

As a professor of psychology at Harvard University, Skinner devised experimental equipment to train laboratory animals to perform specific acts as tests of his behaviorist theories. One of his most famous experiments was teaching pigeons how to play table tennis.

These experiments led to the development of Skinner's principles of programmed learning. Skinner discovered that in most disciplines, learning can be most effectively accomplished when it is taught through incremental steps with instantaneous reinforcement, also known as reward, given to the learner for acceptable performance. Programmed learning should be implemented using teaching machines, which present the user with a question, allow the user to answer, and then immediately provide the user with the correct answer. Programmed learning as an educational technique has two major types: linear programming and branching. Linear programming rewards student responses that lead toward the learning goal; other responses go unrewarded. A correct response also moves the learner along through the program.

The branching technique uses an electronic program that provides the learner with information, asks a question based on the information, and then responds to the learner based on the answer. A correct answer results in a screen that reinforces the right answer then and moves the learner along in the program toward the learning goal. A wrong answer returns the learner to the original information or provides further tutorial.

Training departments had become widely established during the war. Businesses wanted to continue training their workers but at the same time lower the costs of training and increase its efficiency. In 1953, B.F. Skinner's book *Science and Human Behavior* was published, introducing behaviorism, which was built on the work he had done during the war. Behaviorism and the concept of job analysis formed the basis for a new form of training—individualized instruction—which would answer business's need for cheaper and more efficient training. Sleight (1993) describes the practice:

> *Individualized instruction in essence replaces the teacher with systematic or programmed materials. Programmed materials are instruction that has been divided*

into small steps which are easily understood by the learner. After each step is required an active response by the learner in the form of answering a question, drawing a graph, solving a problem, and so on. Immediate feedback is given after each response.

Individualized instruction was later automated through the use of teaching machines in the 1960s and also formed the basis for early computer-based training. It had the advantages of enabling learners to learn at their own pace, giving them privacy to correct mistakes, and reducing training time and error rates when back on the job. However, it could be expensive to produce, included only what the designer put into it, and required the learner to transfer knowledge back to the workplace.

Another development in ISD that occurred during the 1950s was the introduction of Bloom's taxonomy of educational objectives. In 1956, Benjamin Bloom presented this classification of learning objectives, which describes cognitive, psychomotor, and affective outcomes. Cognitive outcomes, or knowledge, refer to the development of intellectual skills. Psychomotor outcomes, or skills, refer to the physical movement, coordination, and use of motor skills to accomplish a task. Affective outcomes, or attitudes, refer to how people deal with things emotionally (ASTD, 2006). These categories are often referred to as KSAs (knowledge, skills, attitudes) and relate to the way learning objectives are written to specify the types of learning to be accomplished. For example, a knowledge objective might be to describe how the increased production needs of World War II affected the field of training and learning.

At the end of the decade, ASTD published Donald Kirkpatrick's articles about four levels of evaluation in *The Journal of the American Society of Training Director* (later *T+D*), which introduced a new theme into the field: measurement.

The 1960s

The introduction of measurement into the field of training tied closely with another theme that started to emerge in the 1960s: the need to understand the business. Already during the 1950s, more and more articles had appeared noting the importance of involving top management in training, and in 1960, Gordon M. Bliss, then executive director of ASTD, urged members to seek "wider responsibilities" and to understand "the vernacular which is used to report profits" (Shaw, 1994). To reflect this broader focus, ASTD changed its name to include the word *development* in 1964.

Timeline of ASTD's History

1942–1943: The American Society of Training Directors (ASTD) is formed on April 2, 1942, at a meeting of the American Petroleum Institute, in New Orleans, Louisiana. Fifteen training directors hold their first meeting on January 12, 1943, in Baton Rouge.

1945: ASTD publishes the first issue of *Industrial Training News*, a quarterly publication that is eventually to become *T+D* magazine. ASTD also holds its first national conference, on September 27 and 28, in Chicago, Illinois.

1947: *Industrial Training News* changes its name to *Journal of Industrial Training* and becomes a bimonthly periodical.

1951: ASTD opens its first permanent office in Madison, Wisconsin, the hometown of Russell Moberly, the secretary-treasurer who keeps all the records at the time.

1952: Membership reaches 1,517. There are 32 chapters across the country.

1954: *Journal of Industrial Training* changes its name to *The Journal of the American Society of Training Directors*.

1959: *The Journal of the American Society of Training Directors* publishes Donald L. Kirkpatrick's article establishing four levels of evaluation for training: reaction, learning, behavior, and results.

1961: ASTD begins publication of *Training Research Abstracts*, later incorporated into *Training & Development Journal*.

1963: *The Journal of the American Society of Training Directors* changes its name to *Training Directors Journal*.

1964: ASTD changes its name to the American Society for Training and Development.

1966: *Training Directors Journal* changes its name to *Training & Development Journal*.

1967: McGraw-Hill publishes the first edition of *Training and Development Handbook*.

1968: Membership reaches 7,422. There are 65 chapters.

1972: ASTD and the U.S. State Department sponsor the first international training and development conference in Geneva, Switzerland. Two hundred people from six continents attend.

1975: ASTD opens a branch office in Washington, D.C.

1976: ASTD holds White House Conference on HRD in the World of Work in Washington, D.C.

1978: In Washington, D.C., ASTD hosts the seventh annual conference of the International Federation of Training and Development Organizations. Membership reaches 15,323; chapters number 110. Following ASTD's efforts in Congress, the Employee Education Assistance IRS exemption is approved. ASTD publishes its first competency study, *A Study of Professional Training and Development Roles and Competencies*, by Pinto and Walker.

1979: ASTD elects its first woman volunteer president, Jan Margolis.

1980: Kenneth James Kukla becomes the 20,000th member of ASTD.

1981: ASTD moves its headquarters from Madison, Wisconsin, to Washington, D.C.

1983: ASTD publishes its second competency study, *Models for Excellence*, by Patricia McLagan.

1984: ASTD implements a new governance structure, resulting in a new leadership direction for the Board of Directors and the creation of a Board of Governors to look to the future. ASTD also launches *INFO-LINE*, a monthly publication designed to train the trainer in a broad array of topics.

1987: ASTD establishes a research function and receives a $750,000 grant from the U.S. Department of Labor. Research grants will reach almost $3 million by 1993. ASTD launches its second annual conference: National Conference on Technical and Skills Training.

1988: Membership reaches 24,451. There are 153 chapters.

1989: ASTD publishes its third competency model, *Models for HRD Practice*, by Patricia McLagan.

1990: ASTD and the U.S. Department of Labor publish *The Learning Enterprise* by Anthony P. Carnevale and Leila J. Gainer, as well as the more comprehensive *Training in America: The Organization and the Strategic Role of Training* by Carnevale, Gainer, and Janice Villet. Both publications establish the size and scope of the training enterprise in the United States. ASTD also launches a new magazine, *Technical & Skills Training*.

1991: ASTD publishes *America and the New Economy* by ASTD's chief economist, Anthony P. Carnevale, establishing the economic link between learning and performance. *Training & Development Journal* becomes *Training & Development*. The Benchmarking Forum is launched to benchmark learning and performance improvement processes, practices, and outcomes against the accomplishments of Forum members and to engage a worldwide network of high-level professionals and organizations.

1994: ASTD launches ASTD On-Line, an electronic information access service, and turns up on the Internet, where trainers are discussing the formation of a "cyberchapter" of ASTD. In addition, ASTD holds its 50th annual and first international conference in Anaheim, California.

1996: ASTD publishes its fourth competency study, *ASTD Models for Human Performance Improvement*, by William Rothwell.

1998: ASTD publishes its fifth competency model, *ASTD Models for Learning Technologies*, by George Piskurich and Ethan Sanders. The first Excellence in Practice Awards are given to recognize results achieved through the use of practices from the entire scope of workplace learning and performance. The first certificate program in human performance improvement is held. By 2007, ASTD offers 25 certificates. ASTD publishes the first annual *State of the Industry* report.

1999: ASTD publishes its sixth competency model, *ASTD Models for Workplace Learning and Performance*, by William Rothwell, Ethan Sanders, and Jeffery Soper. ASTD holds its first annual ASTD TechKnowledge Conference.

(continued on next page)

Timeline of ASTD's History (continued)

2000: ASTD starts a program to build a global community of practice, combined with local presence and action. By 2007, ASTD has 25 global networks. ASTD also launches its first online magazine, *Learning Circuits*, which covers topics related to e-learning.

2001: The ASTD Job Bank—a job site exclusively for workplace learning professionals—is launched. *Training & Development* magazine changes its name to *T+D*. The ASTD Certification Institute is established to govern certification and will launch certification for e-learning courseware in 2002.

2003: The first annual BEST Awards are held to recognize organizations that demonstrate enterprise-wide success as a result of employee learning and development.

2004: ASTD publishes its seventh competency model, *ASTD 2004 Competency Study: Mapping the Future*, by Paul Bernthal and others. This model forms the basis for certification.

2005: ASTD introduces Employee Learning Week, a global public awareness campaign to promote and celebrate the value of workplace learning and development.

2006: The ASTD Certification Institute formally launches its individual certification program, Certified Professional in Learning and Performance (CPLP).

2007: The WLP Scorecard debuts as an online decision support tool that allows organizations to monitor, evaluate, and benchmark critical areas of the learning function.

2008: ASTD publishes the first edition of the *ASTD Handbook for Workplace Learning Professionals*. The Learning Executive Confidence Index launches; it is a tool to measure the confidence of senior learning leaders and is modeled on CEO confidence indices used by The Conference Board and *Chief Executive Magazine*.

2009: ASTD acquires The Bureaucrat, Inc. and its quarterly journal *The Public Manager*, bringing ASTD's expertise to the public sector. ASTD publishes its first competency model for sales training, further strengthening the association's commitment to sales training effectiveness.

2010: *The New Social Learning* is the landmark book by ASTD CEO Tony Bingham and Marcia Conner that identifies the critical importance of using social tools for training and development.

2011: ASTD hosts first conference in Singapore with Singapore Training and Development Association (STADA), and launches new conference offering called LearnNow, focused on meeting the needs of practitioners focused on social, mobile, and informal learning.

2012: ASTD launches its Communities of Practice—networks of professionals with shared interests, knowledge, and expertise—through its new website.

2013: ASTD's new Competency Model is unveiled, adding focus on foundational competencies and technology literacy; the ASTD Learning System is revised to reflect the changes in the new Competency Model.

2014: ASTD launches new membership options reflecting more individual choice in selecting benefits. The new tiers are called Professional and Professional Plus. The second edition of the *ASTD Handbook* debuts at the ASTD 2014 International Conference & Exposition.

Another sign that the training profession was beginning to broaden its horizons at this time was the adoption of organization development (OD). According to the Organization Development Network, a professional organization for OD practitioners, "Organization Development is a values-based approach to systems change in organizations and communities; it strives to build the capacity to achieve and sustain a new desired state that benefits the organization or community and the world around them." Its roots lie in the behavioral sciences, using theories about organization change, systems, teams, and individuals based on the work of Kurt Lewin, Douglas McGregor, Rensis Likert, Richard Beckhard, Wilfred Bion, Ed Schein, Warren Bennis, and Chris Argyris (Haneberg, 2005). For more on OD, see the sidebar.

The wider focus on business results also related to the emerging field of human performance improvement (HPI) or human performance technology (HPT). Performance improvement is a systematic, systemic, results-based approach to helping organizations meet their goals through the work of people. The work of Thomas Gilbert, Geary Rummler, Donald Tosti, and Dale Brethower moved the field of workplace learning from a singular focus on training to a wide variety of activities that improve business results.

However, the general attitude toward business remained "let the adding-machine jockeys worry about the business." More popular were topics such as the psychology of influence, motivation, and attitude change. Topics related to the emerging American civil rights movement, such as workplace diversity, were also becoming more common.

In the areas of learning theory and design, the 1960s saw Jean Piaget, a Swiss developmental psychologist, create a model of cognitive development with four stages: the sensorimotor stage (birth to two years), the preoperational stage (ages two to seven), the concrete operational stage (ages seven to 11), and the formal operational stage (ages 11 and up). His theories form the foundation for the development of constructivism, which began to appear in the 1970s and 1980s.

Organization Development

Organization development work is, at its core, a purposeful and systemic body of work that improves how people and processes perform. Activities and initiatives represent a conscious and planned process to align the various aspects of the organization to meet its goals. Organization development professionals seek to improve the organization's capabilities as measured by its efficiency, effectiveness, health, culture, and business results. They do this by facilitating, consulting, coaching, analyzing, training, and designing.

There is some disagreement within the field about which practices and tools fit in OD. Some adopt a narrow interpretation that focuses on organization alignment and change intervention. Others see OD as a broader set of practices that includes leadership, diversity, and team training. There is some overlap of skills and practices among OD, training, human resources, project management, and quality improvement. To muddy the definition further, each company interprets these functional boundaries differently.

Warner Burke, an OD pioneer, said, "Most people in the field agree that OD involves consultants who try to help clients improve their organizations by applying knowledge from the behavior sciences—psychology, sociology, cultural anthropology, and certain related disciplines. Most would also agree that OD implies change and, if we accept that improvement in organizational functioning means that change has occurred, then, broadly defined, OD means organizational change."

These definitions, as well as the Organization Development Network's definition, share the notion that OD focuses on helping organizations get from point A to point B using a systemic approach based on knowledge of the behavioral sciences. The definitions also emphasize that OD work involves managing and implementing change.

Source: Haneberg (2005).

Meanwhile, Robert F. Mager proposed his model for instructional objectives in his 1962 book, *Preparing Objectives for Programmed Instruction*. This model indicates that objectives should have three components: behavior, condition, and standard. That is to say that the objective should describe the specific, observable behavior that the training should accomplish; indicate the conditions under which the behavior should be completed; and state the desirable level of performance. This type of objective is alternatively known as behavioral, performance, or criterion-reference objectives (ASTD, 2006).

Mager's theory of objectives was originally developed for use in programmed instruction. In the 1960s, programmed instruction became increasingly automated through the briefly popular use of teaching machines, which were electromechanical devices for delivering programmed instruction. Another development in technology at this time was the increasingly wide availability of minicomputers starting in 1965.

The 1970s

Sociotechnical systems theory became widespread in the 1970s (Shaw, 1994). The theory indicates that the interaction of both social and technical factors support or hinder the successful functioning of an organization. As Pasmore (1988) describes it,

> *The sociotechnical systems perspective considers every organization to be made up of people (the social system) using tools, techniques, and knowledge (the technical system) to produce goods or services valued by customers (who are part of the organization's external environment). How well the social and technical systems are designed* with respect to one another and with respect to the demands of the external environment *determines to a large extent how effective the organization will be. [emphasis in original]*

Thus trainers began to understand that to achieve peak performance, both the technical and the social aspects of organizations had to be considered and optimized together. This aligned with the broader focus for the field that OD and HPI had begun to establish in the 1960s.

At the same time, social movements, such as feminism, environmentalism, and the gay rights movement were having an effect on society as well as on how training took place in organizations. As a result, trainers increasingly turned their attention to social issues, such as pollution, racism, and discrimination against women.

Another popular training topic during the 1970s was sensitivity training—also known as the laboratory method—which was a form of human relations training that took place in groups and was designed to raise the attendees' self-awareness and understanding of group dynamics and enable them to modify their own behavior appropriately. The method was attacked by George Odiorne and others, who did not think it was appropriate for training to help "managers achieve authenticity and develop self-esteem," but its principal defender was Chris Argyris of the National Training Laboratories (Shaw, 1994).

Chief among new forms of training that developed during the 1970s was the case method, which had been used in business schools prior to this time but not in training programs. The case method involves the use of a case study to explore a topic. Trainers also began to teach management by objective, introducing expectancy theory as a way to predict employee behavior (Shaw, 1994).

The area of learning theory saw several developments. Malcolm Knowles's book *The Adult Learner: A Neglected Species* was published in 1973, which introduced adult learning theory. Although not the first to suggest that adults learn differently from children (already back in 1926, Eduard C. Lindeman challenged the notion that pedagogy was appropriate for adults in *The Meaning of Adult Education*), Knowles coined the term *andragogy* and presented six key principles that affect the way adults learn.

Malcolm Knowles

Malcolm Knowles is a key figure in adult education and is often regarded as the father of adult learning. Knowles made numerous contributions to the theory and practice of human resource development, but is best known for popularizing the term andragogy, which is the art and science of teaching adults. Andragogy recognizes that adults learn differently than children and, as a result, need to be treated differently in the classroom. In 1973, Knowles defined four assumptions about adult learning in his book *The Adult Learner: A Neglected Species*. These were expanded to the six listed below in a subsequent edition (1984):

- Adults need to know why it is important to learn something before they learn it.
- Adults have a concept of self and do not like others imposing their will on them.
- Adults have a wealth of knowledge and experience and want that knowledge to be recognized.
- Adults become ready to learn when they know that the learning will help them with real problems.
- Adults want to know how the learning will help them in their personal lives.
- Adults respond to external motivations, such as the prospect of a promotion or an increase in salary.

At about the same time, the nine events of instruction were presented for the first time in the 1974 book *Principles of Instructional Design*, by Robert M. Gagné and Leslie J. Briggs. Although Gagné originated from the behaviorist school of learning, the nine events represented a new theory in learning: cognitivism. While behaviorism focuses on outward behaviors, cognitivism focuses on how information is processed, stored, and retrieved in the mind.

Another learning theory that emerged in the 1970s is constructivism. With its roots in Piaget's theories about cognitive development, constructivism indicates that learning is a process of constructing new knowledge. Another important theorist related to constructivism, Jerome Bruner, saw learning as "a social process, whereby students construct new concepts based on current knowledge. The student selects information, constructs hypotheses, and makes decisions, with the aim of integrating new experiences into his existing mental constructs" (Thanasoulas, 2002). With the constructivist learning theory, the impetus in learning design is to create learning experiences that enable learners to discover and construct learning for themselves.

The 1980s

In the 1980s, productivity in the United States slowed down, while global economic competition became the biggest business challenge. Organizations in the United States underwent large downsizings, and many managers found themselves without jobs (Shaw, 1994). These events led organizations to look more closely at their training budgets, causing many training and development executives to focus more on training budgets and the bottom line and on proving the value that training brings to organizations. For this reason and others, cost-benefit analysis and the concept of return-on-investment (ROI) became increasingly hot topics.

At the same time, women entered the field of training and development at an unprecedented rate. By 1989, women made up 47 percent of ASTD's members. Assertiveness training flourished. Other popular training topics were behavior modeling, teamwork, empowerment, diversity, adventure learning, feedback, corporate culture, and trainers' competencies (Shaw, 1994).

The latter—trainers' competencies—were the topic of two competency models published in the 1980s that increasingly positioned the field of training and development as part of the broader field of human resources work. The first modern attempt to define training and development—*Models for Excellence: The Conclusions and Recommendations of the ASTD Training and Development Study*—captured this expansion of the role of training (McLagan, 1983). By 1989, career development and organization development had been added to the repertoire of training and development work, and the report titled *Models for HRD Practice* (McLagan, 1989) captured this new development by using Leonard Nadler's term for the field: *human resource development* (HRD). This report defined HRD as "the integrated use of training and development, organization development, and career development to improve individual, group, and organizational effectiveness." (For more on HRD, see the sidebar.)

Definition of HRD

HRD is the integrated use of training and development, organization development, and career development to improve individual, group, and organizational effectiveness.

- *Integrated* means that HRD is more than the sum of its parts. It's more than training and development, or organization development, or career development in isolation. It's the combined use of all developmental practices to accomplish higher levels of individual and organizational effectiveness than would be possible with a narrower approach.
- *Training and development* focuses on identifying, assuring, and helping develop, through planning learning, the key competencies that enable individuals to perform current or future jobs. Training and development's primary emphasis is on individuals in their work roles. The primary training and development solution is planning individual learning, whether accomplished through training, on-the-job learning, coaching, or other means of fostering individual learning.
- *Organization development* focuses on assuring healthy inter- and intra-unit relationships and helping groups initiate and manage change. Organization development's primary emphasis is on relationships and processes between and among individuals and groups. Its primary intervention is influence on the relationship of individuals and groups to affect the organization as a system.
- *Career development* focuses on assuring an alignment of individual career planning and organizational career management processes to achieve an optimal match of individual and organizational needs. Career development's primary emphasis is on the person as an individual who performs and shapes his or her various work roles. Its major solution is influence on self-knowledge and on processes that affect individuals' and organizations' abilities to create optimal matches of people and work.
- *To improve individual, group, and organizational effectiveness* means that HRD is purposeful. It is instrumental to the achievement of higher goals. Because of HRD, people and organizations are more effective and contribute more value to products and services: the cost-benefit equation improves.

Source: McLagan (1989).

In technology, the first electronic workstations came on the market in 1981. As laser discs began to be used for training with vivid video and immediate access to video segments, the training community became more enamored with the idea of multimedia's use as a way to engage the learner. By 1986, laptop computers emerged, and later smaller disk formats for interactivity and storing media (IBM's Ultimedia and CD-i by Philips, both of which eventually gave way to the CD-ROM). The rise of these technologies was about to change much of how learning was designed, delivered, and managed in organizations.

The 1990s

In the 1990s, technology exploded. Proponents of e-learning, computer-based training, and online learning proclaimed that classroom learning was over. Early e-learning followed the same behaviorist model that informed the programmed instruction of the 1950s and the learning machines of the 1960s in which a learner went through a sequence of steps, after which he or she responded correctly (or incorrectly) and then continued to the next learning element or doubled back as required.

The benefits were also similar: Learners could learn at their own pace, make mistakes and get feedback without being embarrassed, and repeat sections until they had mastered them. E-learning had the additional benefit of more branching capabilities than the old pro-grammed instruction and learning machines, which allowed learners to automatically bypass sections they already knew and focus more on problem areas. Multimedia capabilities also made e-learning more effective by stimulating more of the senses and appealing to different types of learners. And finally, e-learning allowed greater accessibility to training by minimizing costs associated with travel to training, time off from work to attend, and facilities.

However, e-learning did have some drawbacks. For one thing, it was hard to keep learners involved; learners frequently tuned out of poorly designed e-learning programs. While systems-based training took off in the format, e-learning did not work quite as well for training interpersonal skills. Keeping costs down and programs up-to-date was also an issue. In response, more organizations adopted blended learning, which combines e-learning with live classroom elements. One way to use blended learning was for learners to use e-learning elements to complete any prerequisite training so that all participants in a classroom session started from the same point, thus minimizing time spent to get everyone up to speed and maximizing time on the new skills and knowledge to be learned. Additionally, while asynchronous training became the early norm for e-learning, technology-based synchronous training gained in popularity, allowing students to mimic the classroom environment online, no matter where they were physically.

An alternate use for e-learning technologies that gained popularity at this time was their use as a performance support tool. Performance support tools in the form of job aids had been around since World War II in the form of printed cards with step-by-step instructions (Sleight, 1993), but technology allowed performance support to become more integrated into the work and more immediately accessible.

Another development in HRD in the 1990s was the introduction of the concept of the learning enterprise. In 1990, Peter Senge published his book *The Fifth Discipline*, which presented this concept. A learning organization commits itself to disciplines that will allow it to develop its learning capacity to create its future. Ideas underlying the learning organization are systems thinking, mental models, personal mastery, and shared vision and dialogue.

These last two topics—performance support and learning organizations—were popular training topics in the 1990s. Other popular topics included "reengineering, reorganization and transformation of work, customer focus, global organizations, 'visioning,' and balancing work and family" (Shaw, 1994).

This decade also saw training gain legitimacy in the public sector. President Bill Clinton was elected on a platform that endorsed training. Robert Reich, a strong proponent of training, became U.S. secretary of labor and established the Office of Work-Based Learning (Shaw, 1994).

The 2000s and Beyond

Since World War II, learning has evolved in many directions (see Figure 1-1 for a summary). In learning theory, behaviorism continues to have a strong influence on learning design, but cognitive and constructivist learning theories also have their effects through the use of Gagné's nine events of learning and discovery learning. Malcolm Knowles's theory of adult learning informs most training by emphasizing making learning relevant, using learners' experience as a platform for learning, and giving learners some say in how or what they learn.

In learning design, the basic ISD model has evolved; new models have developed that are applicable to different situations and have different emphases, such as rapid prototyping and learning modules. However, Bloom's taxonomy and Mager's model for learning objectives continue to influence the way learning objectives are written today by specifying first the type of learning—knowledge, skill, or attitude—and then the behavior, condition, and degree.

Measurement is another strong theme in the field of training and development. Kirkpatrick's classic four levels of evaluation—reaction, learning, behavior, and results—and the work of Jack and Patti Phillips in ROI still dominate the ways learning is measured and reported. There's still a ways to go for most organizations, however. A study conducted by ASTD and the Institute for Corporate Productivity (i4cp) in 2009 found that 92 percent of organizations say they use at least Level 1 of the model. But the use of the model drops off dramatically with each subsequent level, suggesting that managers may not fully grasp how the model should be used. In fact, only about one-quarter of respondents said they agreed that their organization got a solid "bang for their buck" from their training evaluation efforts (ASTD

Figure 1-1. Training and Development Timeline, World Wars to Present

Training

WWII	1950s	1960s	1970s	1980s	1990s	2000s–Present
Systematic training; train-the-trainer (J) programs; management training; foundation of ISD	Programmed instruction (chunking subject matter); Bloom's taxonomy; Kirkpatrick's four levels of evaluation	HPI/HPT; OD; Mager's model for training objectives; teaching machines	Case method; sensitivity training/ laboratory method (Chris Argyris)	Assertiveness training; cost-benefit analysis; electronic workstations and laptops; cross-cultural training; competency-based training	E-learning; the learning enterprise; learning organizations (Peter Senge)	Just-in-time learning; m-learning; skills gap; certification; community; collaboration; virtual classroom; big data

Theoretical underpinnings

Maslow's theory of human motivation; Lewin's group dynamics	B.F. Skinner; behaviorism; motivation theory	John Piaget's cognitive development; cognitivism; Richard Beckhard coined the term *organization development*	Malcolm Knowles's *The Adult Learner* (androgogy); Gagné's nine events of instruction (behaviorism); Jerome Bruner (constructivism)			

Societal influences

Industry shifts to war production; entry of massive numbers of women and men over the age of 40 into the workplace	Emergence of the idea of involving top management in training	Emergence of the civil rights movement	Sociotechnical systems; feminism; environmentalism; the gay rights movement	Large numbers of women enter the workforce; global economic competition; globalization		Rapid proliferation of new technologies; games; mobile devices; rise in social media platforms

Source: Compiled by ASTD.

and i4cp, 2009). Promising to help, initiatives, such as the Talent Development Reporting Principles (TDRp) produced by the Center for Talent Reporting, emerged to provide the learning profession with templates to operate more like a business.

TDRp, an industry-led, grassroots initiative, established internal reporting principles and standards for human capital. TDRp aimed to provide the same type of guidance for human resources that GAAP (Generally Accepted Accounting Principles) provides accountants in the United States or that IFRS (International Financial Reporting Standards) provides accountants elsewhere. This guidance includes a simple, yet comprehensive, framework for planning, collecting, defining, and reporting the critical outcome, effectiveness, and efficiency measures needed to deliver results and contribute to the success of the organization. TDRp answers the following commonly asked questions:

- What data should be collected?
- What measures should be used?
- How should the measures be defined?
- How should the measures be reported?
- What do leaders want to see?
- How do we show the value of human capital?

Measurement plays a big part in the drive to understand the business and to make the learning and performance function a strategic part of organizations.

Other significant developments in learning include the widespread use of social and informal learning throughout the enterprise and leveraging user-generated content. In an ode to the oft-cited 70/20/10 model, training departments have slowly evolved from being the sole providers and deliverers of content in their companies to a role that fosters sharing knowledge in the organization and connecting people. According to a 2012 study of 351 respondents by ASTD and i4cp, informal learning plays an acknowledged role to varying degrees in the organizations of nearly all the respondents (97 percent) to the survey (ASTD and i4cp, 2013b). More than one-quarter (27 percent) reported that informal learning represented more than half of the total learning taking place in their companies.

Technology has aided the progress. Easy-to-use content generation tools have enabled the workforce to share its knowledge and reinforce a performance-support-centered environment. Furthering the concept of performance support, the explosion of mobile devices, such as smartphones and tablets, has hastened the adoption of mobile learning and immediate access to information. In 2013, according to the International Telecommunication Union, "there are almost as many mobile-cellular subscriptions as people in the world" (ITU, 2013). That phenomenal number of subscribers, 6.8 billion, represents a population that, for the first time, has at its fingertips the mobile tools needed to achieve unprecedented access to resources and information.

A 2013 study by ASTD and i4cp found that the proportion of organizations that offer learning content via mobile devices is growing, but slowly: from 28 percent in 2012 to 31 percent in 2013. However, optimism runs high for the potential of mobile learning. More than half of survey respondents anticipate that mobile learning will bring improvement to overall learning in their organizations (ASTD and i4cp, 2013a).

Other technologies, such as simulations, virtual reality, and gamification, have begun to emerge in organizations as well. A 2013 study on gamification by ASTD and i4cp found that gamification is being used in 23 percent of organizations for learning. Of those using it, enthusiasm is high; 99 percent of respondents whose companies use gamification said it was effective, and more than half rated it highly so. Additionally, interest in gamification is strong, even among study participants whose organizations were not using it: More than four of 10 respondents said they weren't currently gamifying learning, but were considering doing so within the coming year (ASTD and i4cp, 2014).

The Talent Management Era

In 1997, the *McKinsey Quarterly* published a seminal paper titled "The War for Talent." The general premise was that organizations needed to compete on talent. This competition was quickly cooled by the slumping economy in the dot-com bust and recession of the early 2000s, but the concept of talent management was borne.

Human resources in most organizations runs in siloed departments, meaning that the different areas rarely share data between them or work cooperatively to have a more holistic view of talent. For example, these are some of the strategic areas that commonly exist in companies:

- recruitment (selection and assessment)
- total rewards (compensation, benefits)
- engagement
- leadership development
- learning/training
- performance management
- succession planning.

Organizations have moved swiftly to integrate these functions in order to have a more unified view of not only the talent in their organizations today but also for workforce planning: What are our talent risks, and how will we acquire, develop, and retain the right talent to be successful in the future?

In a book I co-authored with Pat Galagan, *The Executive Guide to Integrated Talent Management* (2011), we put forward a case that learning professionals often act as partners—teaming with others or working with function owners to support integration—or serve as facilitators who provide guidance and support for integration efforts. A 2010 study by ASTD and i4cp showed that the greatest percentage of respondents cited the partner role with regard to leadership development, high-potential employee development, employee engagement, and succession planning. Performance management as a function was found to be the most integrated function, and in efforts to integrate individual professional development, employee learning, and performance management, the largest proportion of respondents said that the learning function acts as a facilitator (ASTD and i4cp, 2011).

This shift in thinking presents an opportunity for training professionals who are well equipped to play leading roles in managing talent across an organization. Many see this as one more sign of increasing relevance for the profession.

The Future of the T&D Profession

The history of training and development reveals a recurring theme in the profession: expansion and growth. As organizations continue to recognize the importance of training to the overall expansion and growth of the business, the training professional will continue to rise in importance to the enterprise. This profession constantly creates new history, and the easiest prediction to be made for the future is that the training profession will continue to change and evolve in areas most can't imagine. Readers of this *Handbook*, however, will be more capable than most of not only imagining that future but also putting their own stamp on the history of the training and development profession.

About the Author

Kevin Oakes is the CEO and founder of the Institute for Corporate Productivity (i4cp), the world's largest vendor-free network of corporations focused on improving workforce productivity. Prior to founding i4cp, Kevin was the founder of SumTotal Systems, the world's largest learning management system company, when he merged Click2learn with Docent.

Prior to the formation of SumTotal, Kevin was the chairman and CEO of Click2learn. Kevin's most recent book is *The Executive Guide to Integrated Talent Management*. He was the 2006 chair of the national ASTD board of directors and is a frequent keynoter and author in the human capital field.

References

ASTD. (2006). *Designing Learning*. Module 1 of the ASTD Learning System. Alexandria, VA: ASTD Press.

ASTD and i4cp. (2009). *The Value of Evaluation: Making Training Evaluations More Effective*. Alexandria, VA: ASTD Press.

ASTD and i4cp. (2011). *Learning's Critical Role in Integrated Talent Management*. Alexandria, VA: ASTD Press.

ASTD and i4cp. (2013a). *Going Mobile: Creating Practices That Transform Learning*. Alexandria, VA: ASTD Press.

ASTD and i4cp. (2013b). *Informal Learning: The Social Evolution*. Alexandria, VA: ASTD Press.

ASTD and i4cp. (2014). *Playing to Win: Gamification and Serious Games in Organizational Learning*. Alexandria, VA: ASTD Press.

Bernthal, P.R., et al. (2004). *ASTD 2004 Competency Study: Mapping the Future*. Alexandria, VA: ASTD Press.

Chambers, E.G., M. Foulon, H. Handfield-Jones, S.M. Hankin, and E.G. Michaels III. (1997). The War for Talent. *The McKinsey Quarterly*, number 3.

Clark, D. (1999). World War I—Show, Tell, Do, and Check. *Knowledge, Performance, Training, & Learning*, www.nwlink.com/~donclark/hrd/history/war1.html.

European Communities. (2007). Vocational Training. *Europa Glossary*, http://europa.eu/scadplus/glossary/training_en.htm.

Gagné, R.M., and L.J. Briggs. (1974). *Principles of Instructional Design*. New York: Holt, Rinehart, and Winston.

Haneberg, L. (2005). *Organization Development Basics*. Alexandria, VA: ASTD Press.

International Telecommunication Union (ITU). (2013). The World in 2013: ICT Facts and Figures, www.itu.int/en/ITU-D/Statistics/Pages/facts/default.aspx.

Knowles, M.S. (1973). *The Adult Learner: A Neglected Species*. Houston, TX: Gulf Publishing.

Lindeman, E.C. (1926). *The Meaning of Adult Education*. New York: New Republic.

Lewin, K. (1948). *Resolving Social Conflicts; Selected Papers on Group Dynamics*, ed. G.W. Lewin. New York: Harper & Row.

Mager, R.F. (1962). *Preparing Objectives for Programmed Instruction*. Belmont, CA: Fearon Publishers.

Maslow, A.H. (1943). A Theory of Human Motivation. *Psychological Review* 50(4): 370-396.

McLagan, P.A. (1983). *Models for Excellence: The Conclusions and Recommendations of the ASTD Training and Development Study*. Alexandria, VA: ASTD Press.

McLagan, P.A. (1989). *Models for HRD Practice*. Alexandria, VA: ASTD Press.

Miller, V.A. (2008). Training and ASTD: An Historical Review. In *The 2008 Pfeiffer Annual Training*, ed. E. Biech. San Francisco: Pfeiffer.

Oakes, K., and P. Galagan. (2011). *The Executive Guide to Integrated Talent Management*. Alexandria, VA: ASTD Press.

Pasmore, W.A. (1988). *Designing Effective Organizations*. New York: John Wiley & Sons.

Senge, P. (1990). *The Fifth Discipline*. New York: Doubleday.

Shaw, H.W. (1994). The Coming of Age of Workplace Learning: A Time Line. *Training & Development* 48(5):S4-S12.

Skinner, B.F. (1953). *Science and Human Behavior*. New York: The Macmillan Company.

Sleight, D.A. (1993). A Developmental History of Training in the United States and Europe, www.msu.edu/~sleightd/trainhst.html.

Steinmetz, C.S. (1976). The Evolution of Training. In *Training and Development Handbook*, eds. R.L. Craig and L.R. Bittel. Sponsored by the American Society for Training and Development. New York: McGraw-Hill.

Thanasoulas, D. (2002). Constructivist Learning. *Karen's Linguistic Issues*, www3.telus .net/linguisticsissues/constructivist.html.

Zuboff, S. (1984). *In the Age of the Smart Machine: The Future of Work and Power*. New York: Basic Books.

For Further Reading

Arneson, J., J. Naughton, and W. Rothwell. (2013). *ASTD Competency Study: The Training & Development Profession Redefined*. Alexandria, VA: ASTD Press.

Oakes, K., and P. Galagan. (2011). *The Executive Guide to Integrated Talent Management*. Alexandria, VA: ASTD Press.

Chapter 2

ASTD's New Competency Model

Jennifer Naughton

········· **In This Chapter** ·········

- Learn how to use the new ASTD Competency Model for your career in training and development.
- Review the factors that led to driving changes in the T&D field in the past decade.
- Learn to create your own action plan if you are new to the T&D field.

"An organization's ability to learn, and translate that learning into action rapidly, is the ultimate competitive advantage."

—Jack Welch, former CEO, GE

Let's start with the *big deal*. Very simply, if implemented effectively, a well-defined competency framework can help to maximize employee performance and improve business results. But, as with most things, success requires action.

This chapter provides insights into the new ASTD Competency Model and ways you can use it for your own career development in training and development (T&D). In short, the new model captures current and emerging practices in T&D. It helps to answer the questions: What do you need to know and do to be successful in the T&D field? And where should you focus your development efforts to stay ahead of the curve?

Competency Approaches Through History

Three main schools of competency research and practice have been popular in the workplace since the Second World War: the differential psychology approach, the educational and behavioral psychology approach, and the management sciences approach. Each grew out of its own philosophical framework and has its own language and application focus. Here are brief descriptions of each and what distinguishes them:

The Differential Psychology Approach

This approach focuses on human differences, especially capabilities that are harder to develop. People who practice this approach tend to have psychology training. They emphasize intelligence, cognitive capabilities, hard-to-develop physical abilities, values, personality traits, motives, interests, and emotional qualities. That is, they focus on process capabilities and drives versus subject matter or knowledge. They also tend to single out those qualities that distinguish superior performers from average or typical performers. The bell-shaped curve is an important concept here, because the underlying belief is that human talents are distributed in a bell curve, with very few people at the top and bottom ends of the curve. Daniel Goleman, David McClelland, Richard Herrnstein, and Milton Rokeach are some thought leaders for this approach.

The Educational and Behavioral Psychology Approach

Although the differential approach emphasizes the unique and more innate abilities that people bring to work, the educational-behavioral approach is driven by the desire to shape and develop people so that they can be successful. The differential proponents also have this concern, but it is not their main focus. People who practice the educational-behavioral approach tend to have an education and training background. Their models and menus include subject matter and knowledge areas as well as some of the process and affective areas of the differential approach. Also, their models usually include *all* the competencies that are important to quality performance, whether they distinguish superior performance or not. Often, proponents of this approach also focus on the performance environment. They believe that the environment (including education) is often a more powerful determinant of behavior than genetics. For the differential practitioners, the emphasis would be reversed. Albert Bandura, B.F. Skinner, Thomas Gilbert, Geary Rummler, Benjamin Bloom, and David Krathwohl are chief proponents of aspects of this approach.

The Management Sciences Approach

This approach produces job descriptions and job evaluations. So, it mainly defines the *work* to be done, often spending a lot of time on work and task analysis and documentation. The models that emerge from this process include task and activity lists, and descriptions of tools and processes needed for effective performance. Knowledge, skills, and other personal characteristics needed to do the work may be added to the description, but are usually a secondary emphasis. Job evaluation consultants, personnel administrators and compensation specialists, re-engineering and total quality experts, and task analysts are the major purveyors of this approach. Frederick Winslow Taylor, Michael Hammer, and Elliott Jaques are some of the key thought leaders here.

The new ASTD Competency Model continues ASTD's 30-year-plus history of publishing groundbreaking models that have both defined and shaped the T&D profession. Like its predecessors, the study upon which it was based has identified key trends and drivers that are having the greatest impact on current and future T&D practices.

The Wake-Up Call

The last major ASTD Competency Model was published in 2004. Since that time, there have been unprecedented global changes. Looking at technology alone, Facebook was just a twinkle in Mark Zuckerberg's eye in 2004. The iPhone came out in 2007. And Twitter didn't even exist.

The T&D field has transformed substantially in the past decade. Four familiar factors have played a major role in driving the changes:

- economic uncertainty and volatility
- advances in digital, mobile, and social technology
- demographic shifts in the workforce
- increased globalization.

T&D trends—such as integrated talent management, employee engagement, crowd sourcing, and collaborative and mobile learning—have disrupted conventional notions of the T&D function and changed the competencies required for success. It comes as no surprise that T&D practitioners must also continue to adapt and develop if they want to remain relevant in this rapidly changing business environment.

Implications for T&D Competencies

Individuals in T&D should be prepared to address head-on some of the more recent shifts in the profession. In broad terms, this includes:

- staying abreast of new and emerging technologies and matching the appropriate technology to a specific learning opportunity or challenge
- moving beyond the role of deliverer of training to a facilitator of learning, content curator, information manager, and builder of learning communities
- fostering a culture of connectivity and collaboration around learning via mobile and social technology

- designing and presenting learning not as a discrete event—a training course—but as a process that engages learners in a variety of ways over time through formal and informal channels
- leveraging the learning styles and preferences of new generations entering the workforce and capturing the knowledge of those leaving it

Figure 2-1. The New ASTD Competency Model

- playing a role in integrated talent management so that learning informs all the processes and systems that create organizational capability and understanding the role and contributions of the learning function
- anticipating and meeting the T&D needs of an increasingly global workforce and contributing to talent development where the organization most needs it
- demonstrating the value and impact of learning by using metrics that are meaningful to business and using data analysis to measure the effectiveness and efficiency of T&D
- continuing to be business partners and leaders who align their activities to the organization's business strategies and goals and who demonstrate their return-on-investment, especially during challenging times.

The New Model Deconstructed

Let's explore the new ASTD Competency Model in greater depth. The new ASTD Competency Model identified six foundational competencies and 10 specific areas of expertise (AOEs). The foundational competencies are clusters of business and personal skills, which are the bedrock upon which to build more specific competencies (see Table 2-1). The AOEs are the specialized knowledge, skills, and behaviors that are required by specific roles in the T&D field (see Table 2-2). It is important to note that the foundational competencies are relatively generic and are needed across many professions, whereas the AOEs are unique and specific to the T&D profession.

Table 2-1. Foundational Competencies

Foundational Competency	Description
Business Skills	Demonstrate business understanding and drive business results and outcomes.
Global Mindset	Work effectively with people across borders, cultures, and generations.
Industry Knowledge	Maintain knowledge of relevant industries and industry segments.
Interpersonal Skills	Interact with others in a way that builds influence and trust.
Personal Skills	Demonstrate adaptability and continuous learning.
Technology Literacy	Demonstrate awareness of and proficiency in existing and emerging technologies.

Table 2-2. T&D Areas of Expertise

Areas of Expertise	Description
Change Management	Apply a systematic process to shift individuals, teams, and organizations from current state to desired state.
Coaching[1]	Apply a systematic process to improve others' abilities to set goals, take action, and maximize their strengths.
Evaluating Learning Impact	Use learning metrics and analytics to measure the impact of training and development solutions.
Instructional Design	Design and develop informal and formal learning solutions using a variety of methods.
Integrated Talent Management[2]	Build an organization's culture, capability, capacity, and engagement through talent acquisition and employee development.
Knowledge Management	Capture, distribute, and archive intellectual capital to encourage knowledge-sharing and collaboration.
Learning Technologies	Apply a variety of learning technologies to address specific training and development needs.
Managing Learning Programs	Provide leadership to execute the organization's people strategy; implement learning projects and activities.
Performance Improvement	Apply a systematic process for analyzing human performance gaps and for closing them.
Training Delivery	Deliver informal and formal learning solutions in a manner that is both engaging and effective.

[1]This information is based on the ICF (International Coach Federation) Code of Ethics and the ICF Core Coaching Competencies. Additional information can be found at ICF's website: www.coachfederation.org.
[2]Definition was adapted from the ASTD research publication *Learning's Critical Role in Integrated Talent Management*.

The new ASTD Competency Model includes important changes to the AOEs compared to the 2004 model. These changes reflect the growing influence of mobile and social technology, learning analytics, and integrated talent management (see Table 2-3).

It is important to note that the model is both broad and deep. The extent to which each individual needs to master the various competencies depends on a person's current role and future aspirations.

Table 2-3. AOE Changes Since 2004

2004 Name	2013 Name	Change
Designing Learning	Instructional Design	More emphasis on approaches involving mobile learning, social learning, informal learning, and rapid design
Delivering Training	Training Delivery	More emphasis on social media and informal learning tools and approaches
Human Performance Improvement	Performance Improvement	Minor updates
Measuring and Evaluating	Evaluating Learning Impact	Increased emphasis on learning analytics
Managing the Learning Function	Managing Learning Programs	Minor updates
Managing Organizational Knowledge	Knowledge Management	Increased emphasis on social learning and selecting learning management systems appropriately
Career Planning and Talent Management	Integrated Talent Management	Increased emphasis on talent management as an integrated system and learning's role in it; less focus on career planning
Coaching	Coaching	Minor updates
Facilitating Organizational Change	Change Management	Minor updates
	Learning Technologies	Highlights the importance of learning technologies and how to apply them appropriately

For example, functional specialists may wish to focus their development energy on mastering one or two of the AOEs. Business managers or leaders may wish to spend more time mastering a broad array of foundational competencies and ensuring that they have exposure across all of the AOEs. All training professionals need to know a bit of everything in the model, but the extent to which they need to focus and dive deep will vary by individual and the relevance of the competencies to the business in which they find themselves.

But, as with most things, success requires action—for you too. Using the tools that ASTD has provided is key to helping you realize the full value of the model. The sidebar, Creating Your Action Plan, is a good place to start as you begin to achieve your professional development and career aspirations. In addition, a high-level job aid is provided on the *Handbook's* website at www.astdhandbook.org to help with this task. Additional resources are listed at the end of this chapter.

Creating Your Action Plan

Especially if you are new to the T&D field, the key questions are: What areas should I develop? And where should I start? These are the main steps:

1. Review the list of foundational competencies shown in the model and rate their importance to your present job.
2. List your priorities for development of the competencies that are most important to your present job (those that will have the greatest impact).
3. Review the areas of expertise (AOEs) shown in the model and select those that are important to your present job and to future jobs you want to pursue.
4. List your priorities for development of your most important present and future AOEs.
5. Discuss your choices and priorities with your employer, mentor, coach, or supervisor. Begin developing your action plan.

As a member benefit, ASTD also offers the online ASTD Career Navigator tool at www.astd.org/careernavigator to help you identify your individual strengths and opportunities for development. This tool enables you to create a specific, individualized action plan to close your unique skill gaps and includes a list of pertinent, prioritized resources.

What are the benefits of going through this process? Let's say you work in a technical field and have been asked to develop a training initiative for that area. Or, you have been delivering training in a classroom for a long time and you want to begin using technology and social media tools to supplement that role.

In each of these situations, completing a self-assessment based on the model can help you identify the competencies and expertise needed to achieve your career goals. Furthermore, by involving your employer in the conversation, you can align your development in a way that will increase your value and relevance to the employer you serve.

If you are a training manager or supervisor, you can apply the same process to members of your team. You could even use it to guide nontraining managers who are responsible for workforce development in their business units.

Competencies and the Future

As the T&D field continues to evolve, competency models will be revised to reflect emerging practices. Align your development plans to the current and future models and prepare for the future faster so you can stay agile and ahead of the curve. Stay ahead of the game by knowing where you can locate what you need.

To Find	Go To
The research behind the new Competency Model and ways to put the Model into action	*The ASTD Competency Study: The Training & Development Profession Redefined* www.store.astd.org
Job aids and practical human capital planning tools that are aligned to the new Model	The ASTD Competency Model www.astd.org/model
An online assessment tool to help you or your team to develop a T&D developmental action plan	The ASTD Career Navigator www.astd.org/careernavigator

The new ASTD Competency Model captures new and emerging competencies needed for T&D professional practice. It is a lens for viewing the T&D profession from many angles. Use it to guide your own development or that of your team. Use it to get your bearings in a present job or create a road map for a future one. Use it as a benchmark for identifying strengths, weaknesses, and capabilities.

The ASTD Competency Model can serve as a guide to those who wish to enter the field, to deepen their understanding of the field and align their career development plans with emerging trends, or become certified via the ASTD Certification Institute's Certified Professional in Learning and Performance (CPLP) credential.

Quality Standards for the T&D Industry

The Institute for Credentialing Excellence (ICE) and ASTM International now offer quality standards for the training and development industry, with respect to assessment-based certificate programs. For further information about the related standards and accreditation processes, consult the following references:

ASTM E2659–09, Standard Practice for Certificate Programs: developed by ASTM International, a voluntary standards development organization.

ICE 1100: 2010 (E), Standards for Assessment-Based Certificate Programs: created by the Institute for Credentialing Excellence (ICE), an organization dedicated to setting quality standards for credentialing organizations.

About the Author

Jennifer Naughton is the senior director of Competencies & Credentialing for ASTD. In this capacity, she is responsible for providing the vision and direction for the ASTD Competency Model research and credentialing initiatives. She is a people system architect with more than 20 years of experience in the human resource and training field. Her passion is applying human resources strategies to address organizational challenges. She has authored numerous articles on the subject. She holds a master's degree in human resource development from the George Washington University. She is also an SPHR (Senior Professional of Human Resources) as recognized by the HR Certification Institute.

References

Arneson, J., W. Rothwell, and J. Naughton. (2013, January). Training and Development Competencies: Redefined to Create Competitive Advantage. *T+D*, 44-47.

Arneson, J., W. Rothwell, and J. Naughton. (2013). *ASTD Competency Study: The Training & Development Profession Redefined*. Alexandria, VA: ASTD Press.

ASTD and i4cp. (2011). *Learning's Critical Role in Integrated Talent Management*. Alexandria, VA: ASTD Press.

Bernthal, P.R., K. Colteryahn, P. Davis, et al. (2004). *ASTD Competency Study: Mapping the Future*. Alexandria, VA: ASTD Press.

ICF. (2011). ICF Core Competencies, www.coachfederation.org/icfcredentials /core-competencies.

Oakes, K., and P. Galagan. (2011). *The Executive Guide to Integrated Talent Management*. Alexandria, VA: ASTD Press.

Rothwell, W., J. Graber, and D. Dubois. (2013). *The Competency Toolkit*. 2nd edition. Amherst, MA: HRD Press.

Spencer, L.M., and M. Signe. (1993). *Competencies at Work: Models for Superior Performance*. Hoboken, NJ: John Wiley & Sons.

For Further Reading

Oakes, K., and P. Galagan. (2011). *The Executive Guide to Integrated Talent Management*. Alexandria, VA: ASTD Press.

Rothwell, W., J. Graber, and D. Dubois. (2013). *The Competency Toolkit*. 2nd edition. Amherst, MA: HRD Press.

Related Webcasts

ASTD Career Navigator: Create Your Personalized Learning Plan (http://tinyurl.com/pd4tcod), June 25, 2013.

Building Talent: Applying the ASTD Competency Model in Your Organization (http://tinyurl.com/mkwj3rh), September 15, 2013.

Training & Development Competencies: Redefined to Create Competitive Advantage (http://tinyurl.com/p37of86), March 27, 2013.

Chapter 3

The Importance of Certification

Kimo Kippen, Coline T. Son Lee, and Jeff Toister

In This Chapter

- Understand the value of certification and the CPLP specifically.
- Identify the value to the employer, the credential holder, and the T&D profession.
- Read about employer and candidate experiences.

Have you ever seen CPLP behind someone's names and wondered what it meant or if it meant anything at all? This chapter explores why certification in general (and the CPLP certification in particular) is such a big deal for individuals, employers, and the training and development profession.

The ASTD Competency Model (referenced in chapter 2 of this *Handbook*) is the content backbone upon which CPLP (Certified Professional in Learning and Performance) certification is based. CPLP certification is actually part of a larger competency-based ecosystem designed to equip training practitioners and training leaders with the tools they need to identify their skills gaps, demonstrate their competence, and ultimately increase their relevance and worth.

The ASTD competency-based ecosystem contains the following pillars: the ASTD Competency Model, the ASTD Career Navigator, and CPLP certification. The ASTD Competency

Model defines what knowledge and skills training and development professionals need to know and do to be successful. The ASTD Career Navigator is an aligned assessment tool that identifies related skills gaps and results in a professional development action plan to close them (by recommending relevant publications, educational courses, on-the-job experiences, and so on). CPLP certification enables individuals to validate their competencies through testing after closing those gaps.

CPLP certification not only requires passing rigorous exams, but also requires continuing education and renewal every three years to keep skills sharp and relevant.

What Is Certification?

Certification involves the comprehensive evaluation of skills that are measured against industry standards. Industry and trade associations, such as ASTD, CSTD (the Canadian Society for Training and Development), and CIPD (the Chartered Institute for Personnel Development), offer industrywide certifications that pertain to the training and development (T&D) profession, in particular.

What Is the Value of the CPLP?

ASTD and the ASTD Certification Institute first introduced the CPLP certification program in 2006. Today, thousands of training and development professionals across the globe have proudly earned this high mark of professional distinction. Furthermore, an even greater number of jobs have been posted as "CPLP preferred" on job announcements, including Fortune 500 organizations and those from all industry segments. One might even say that the market demand for CPLP jobs exceeds the supply of CPLP credential holders. It's indeed a hot commodity.

So, what does it take to earn it? CPLP certification is a rigorous evaluation process that includes the hurdles illustrated in Table 3-1.

Table 3-1. Requirements for CPLP Certification

Eligibility	Applicants must have five years of experience in the field.
Knowledge Exam	Candidates must pass a knowledge exam consisting of 150 multiple-choice questions focused on the 10 Areas of Expertise (AOEs) based on the ASTD Competency Model. Candidates must pass this exam before moving to the next phase.
Work Product Assessment	Candidates must submit a successful sample of work to earn the credential. The work sample must focus on one of four AOEs: Instructional Design, Training Delivery, Performance Improvement, or Managing Learning Programs.
Recertification	The CPLP credential is valid for three years. CPLP credential holders must accumulate 60 recertification points within the three-year recertification period to maintain their certification status.

Why Is Certification So Important?

The significance of certification extends far beyond just adding a few letters after someone's name. From a strategic perspective, certification benefits the entire profession and the employers for whom those professionals work. It creates industrywide standards and sets the bar for performance.

To break it down, certification sets performance standards for the profession. This defines where and how high the bar is with respect to professional practice. Through standards and testing, individuals have to demonstrate that they can meet those standards. This helps individuals to become better performers and contributors, which, in turn, helps to increase employee performance. This drives improved organizational results and ultimately elevates and increases the relevance of the industry and the professionals in it (see Figure 3-1).

Figure 3-1. The Importance of Certification

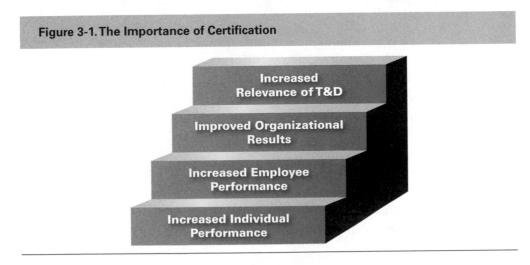

Whom Does It Benefit?

CPLP certification, in particular, enables credential holders to demonstrate their ability to strategically lead the training and development function, manage the projects within it, design and deliver training, and improve organizational performance. This can benefit hiring managers, employers, and credentialed individuals in the following ways:

- **Hiring managers:** Benefits for hiring managers include a faster way to screen applicants and make better hiring decisions. When an industry is flooded with self-proclaimed experts, certification helps hiring managers identify and select the right applicants.
- **Employers:** Benefits for employers include increased individual performance, increased employee performance, and a demonstration of commitment to the employee's development and to the field. This support and commitment often leads to increased loyalty and retention of top performers, not to mention the positive ripple effect it has on the organization as a whole.
- **Credential holders:** Benefits for credential holders include increased competence and confidence, greater opportunities for career advancement and increased earnings, and the sense of personal accomplishment. It also helps candidates stand out by providing a meaningful differentiator, especially in a competitive job market.

CPLP Case Stories

The real value of certification is demonstrated by the impact it can have on people's personal and professional lives and on the organizations they serve. The following section provides firsthand accounts about the value of CPLP certification, as told from the employer's and the credential holder's perspectives.

The Employer's Perspective:
Kimo Kippen, Chief Learning Officer, Hilton Worldwide

Our company is a leader in the industry and employs more than 300,000 staff worldwide across various business functions. In an effort to meet the needs of our growing business, we are committed to the development of talent as a key element of our global HR strategy. Our T&D team has made a similar commitment to the development of our learning staff by supporting the CPLP certification.

As part of our development strategy, we encourage our learning professionals to give serious consideration to CPLP certification. We have a dedicated team member who assists our learning professionals with career planning and development. We begin the process by administering the ASTD Career Navigator, a skills assessment tool based on the ASTD Competency Model, for all our learning professionals.

We work with our team to create customized development plans and encourage CPLP certification. Current CPLP credential holders coach new candidates through the study process by sharing advice and best practices. We support them throughout the process, encouraging them to pursue the CPLP together, as a team, and providing them with CPLP study materials, as well as a CPLP coach to support their efforts. We cover 100 percent of the cost for test preparation, along with 100 percent of the cost for exam registration.

We continuously check with our candidates throughout their course of study to further understand how we can support them. If they are struggling in a competency, we recommend someone who can coach them to improve their understanding in that particular focus area. We allow candidates to take time off to prepare for their exams, which our team found particularly helpful in the week leading up to their exam date. We also send motivational items to keep our team focused! Our goal is to provide study and test preparation support, while motivating and recognizing our team for their dedication and efforts to own their development.

Our success in increasing the number of CPLP holders (approximately 15 percent of our learning staff—and growing) is due to the learning culture and support provided by our senior leaders. The combination of mentoring, test preparation, financial support, and the possibilities for recognition and career advancement have created great excitement for the CPLP certification program and level of learning professionalism it brings to our organization.

CPLP holders are recognized in our learning organization as high-potential talent. We strategically shift their work focus toward projects that more effectively use the knowledge gained through the CPLP certification. Our current CPLP holders have been assigned more global work, high-level project management, and the opportunity to work closely with vendors and subject matter experts. One of our high-potential CPLP learning professionals was recently promoted from a senior manager to a key director-level role that will work with strategic business partners at top levels of the organization.

Our CPLP holders continuously add value toward meeting our organization's learning goals. Recent survey data show our training and development team to be more engaged and confident about their contributions and value in our organization after the program was introduced.

Their ability to speak with confidence about theory and practical application has landed our team roles managing enterprisewide learning initiatives. We have also seen an increase in trust of learning professionals from our internal business partners who work directly with our CPLP holders. This increase in trust has been particularly important as we continue to work toward transforming the perceived value that the T&D function adds to our organization.

The CPLP Credential Holder's Perspective:
Jeff Toister, CPLP Recipient, 2006

I earned my CPLP certification in 2006. At the time, my career was at a crossroads. I had just started my own training and consulting business and was trying to decide what I needed to boost my credibility.

CPLP seemed like a great alternative to going back to school. It represented an opportunity to be recognized for what I had already accomplished instead of investing two or so years in learning something new. I had earned another certification a few years prior and knew how much credibility a credential could lend. It was also exciting to know that the credential represented the future of our profession.

Earning my CPLP has really paid off. My credibility among clients and colleagues has certainly increased, but I've gained other unexpected benefits as well. Chief among them is the motivation to continuously reinvest in my own learning and access to the close-knit community of CPLPs. What follows is my perspective about each of these benefits as it relates to my credibility, continuous learning, and sense of community.

Credibility

Being a CPLP has helped me win business. The first time was when I bid on a large project not long after earning my credential. There were eight companies in the running. A little investigation revealed that none of my competitors had CPLPs on their team. I used that to my advantage by positioning the CPLP as a major qualification and told the client, "Even if you don't pick my company, be sure you select a company who has at least one person with the industry-standard certification."

I won the contract and my client later told me that being the only one who was certified was a major factor in their decision making.

CPLP lends a lot of credibility. It helps me build trust with existing clients and colleagues. Many people view certifications like mine as an industry seal of approval.

Continuous Learning

CPLPs must recertify every three years, which means that continuous learning is a must. The recertification requirement has caused me to be more deliberate about my own development. Some people are concerned about this requirement; I don't really see it has a burden. If I'm going to spend my days developing others, why wouldn't I take the time to develop myself?

For example, I've been coaching managers for as long as I can remember but haven't received any formal training. That led me to attend a two-day Coaching Skills certificate program. The course gave me skills I immediately used to help my clients. It also gave me 25 percent of the points I'll need for my next recertification once I combine the points received for taking the class with new on-the-job experiences.

Community

Far and away the best benefit of being a CPLP is the community. There's a group of us who met while volunteering for various CPLP projects and have become close friends. We all live in various parts of the country and may not have met if it weren't for the certification. Today, our relationship goes beyond training. We know each other's families and strategically plan business trips and vacations so we can see each other a few times each year.

Lifelong friendship is an amazing benefit, but I've also benefited professionally from my community of CPLP friends:

- Several of my CPLP friends are also my clients. I've earned their business because they know me, they trust me, and they know what it takes to be a CPLP.
- I found a publisher for my customer service book, *Service Failure*, through a connection made by one of my CPLP friends. (CPLPs are very well connected.)
- My CPLP friends are my most trusted advisors who I turn to whenever I need help tackling a complex training issue. They really know their stuff and give great advice.

There are also considerable benefits that come from being a member of the CPLP community as a whole. The CPLP LinkedIn group is a fountain of helpful information. There are amazing volunteer opportunities to help promote the CPLP. One of my favorite benefits is the rock star recognition and treatment from ASTD at ASTD's International Conference and Exposition, where CPLP credential holders have reserved front-row seating for the keynotes, allowing you to stroll in five minutes before showtime and nab one of the best seats in the house.

All the benefits of credibility, continuous learning, and community come together in one place. I am sharing a stage with some of the smartest people I know, who also happen to be very good friends. We are smart, enthusiastic, and ambitious training professionals who honor the spirit of continuous learning. And our efforts are supported by other CPLPs, who understand the importance of growing our community. It's awesome.

The CPLP: Is It Right for You?

Like many things of value, it requires commitment and perseverance. It's important to have a realistic self-assessment prior to embarking on the journey. Two self-assessments are available to you on the *Handbook's* website at www.astdhandbook.org. You may download one or both to conduct your self-assessment. The tools are the CPLP Candidate Self-Assessment and the Value of Certification Tool. These tools will help you decide if the program is right for you. Also factor in the following perspectives provided by CPLP candidates and study group leaders.

The Ideal CPLP Candidate:
Coline Son Lee, CPLP Recipient, 2010

The decision to pursue the CPLP certification should not be taken lightly. Each individual should take the time to evaluate his or her personal situation.

Willingness

First and foremost, individuals who choose to pursue the credential must have an intrinsic desire to earn the credential and stay the course. If you pursue the credential because it has been assigned or you have been tasked to do it, be aware that you might lose momentum.

Time Commitment

Second, factor in the investment of time in your decision-making process. It takes a substantial investment of time to achieve the CPLP designation. The CPLP credentialing process can take as little as six months from the time the candidate begins preparation to the time of results notification, or it can take much longer, depending on your results and preferred pace.

Ask yourself: Is there is anything going on in my life now or in the near future that will put my success at risk? For example, if you are dealing with a personal situation that requires much of your time and attention outside of work hours, then perhaps now is not the time.

Preparing for the knowledge exam, even at a minimum, still requires a commitment of time to study the breadth and depth of information that could be on the exam. As you evaluate your time constraints, give some consideration to your study habits and how long it's been since you were required to commit to studying. Perhaps you have not had to study for formal exams in years. Consider how long you may need to adjust to a new study routine. Being realistic and honest with yourself will help you make a better, more informed decision. What about your study habits? Do you have a photographic memory, or do you have to read something several times in order to grasp the concept? The answer to this too will help you estimate how much time you will need to invest.

Use the Countdown to CPLP Calendar in Figure 3-2 to help you plot your personalized study schedule. You can also find this tool on the *Handbook's* website at www.astdhandbook .org, where you can download it.

Support Network

Planning for success by taking an honest account of time constraints and obligations is one way CPLP candidates prepare themselves for success. Another is developing a trusted support group. Support can take a variety of formats and will only be successful with open and candid communication.

A support team can be helpful if they know what the goal is, what the goal means to you personally and professionally, what needs to be done to achieve it, and when to expect success. In other words, they need to know what's going, how they fit into the overall picture, and how they can support you.

Pursuing the CPLP credential is a long-term commitment. You want your support team to stay with you through the whole journey. Help them understand what you will be going through, what the process entails, what you need from them, what you will be doing less of at home or work while you prepare, and when the process is expected to conclude. Chances are they will keep cheering you on as long as you're staying on track with your study plans, honoring your commitments, and staying committed.

Figure 3-2. Countdown to CPLP Calendar

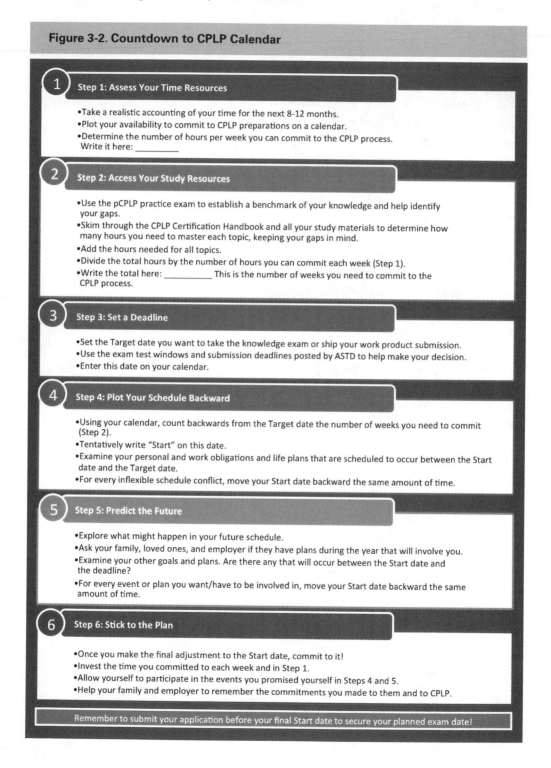

1   **Step 1: Assess Your Time Resources**

- Take a realistic accounting of your time for the next 8-12 months.
- Plot your availability to commit to CPLP preparations on a calendar.
- Determine the number of hours per week you can commit to the CPLP process. Write it here: _____

2   **Step 2: Access Your Study Resources**

- Use the pCPLP practice exam to establish a benchmark of your knowledge and help identify your gaps.
- Skim through the CPLP Certification Handbook and all your study materials to determine how many hours you need to master each topic, keeping your gaps in mind.
- Add the hours needed for all topics.
- Divide the total hours by the number of hours you can commit each week (Step 1).
- Write the total here: _____ This is the number of weeks you need to commit to the CPLP process.

3   **Step 3: Set a Deadline**

- Set the Target date you want to take the knowledge exam or ship your work product submission.
- Use the exam test windows and submission deadlines posted by ASTD to help make your decision.
- Enter this date on your calendar.

4   **Step 4: Plot Your Schedule Backward**

- Using your calendar, count backwards from the Target date the number of weeks you need to commit (Step 2).
- Tentatively write "Start" on this date.
- Examine your personal and work obligations and life plans that are scheduled to occur between the Start date and the Target date.
- For every inflexible schedule conflict, move your Start date backward the same amount of time.

5   **Step 5: Predict the Future**

- Explore what might happen in your future schedule.
- Ask your family, loved ones, and employer if they have plans during the year that will involve you.
- Examine your other goals and plans. Are there any that will occur between the Start date and the deadline?
- For every event or plan you want/have to be involved in, move your Start date backward the same amount of time.

6   **Step 6: Stick to the Plan**

- Once you make the final adjustment to the Start date, commit to it!
- Invest the time you committed to each week and in Step 1.
- Allow yourself to participate in the events you promised yourself in Steps 4 and 5.
- Help your family and employer to remember the commitments you made to them and to CPLP.

Remember to submit your application before your final Start date to secure your planned exam date!

Donna's Story

Donna was a working mother with two young children. She joined a CPLP Study Group for support with her study preparations for the knowledge exam. Donna studied while her children did their homework. This made her children feel like they were part of the process, and it encouraged them to study as well. She explained to them that if she could pass the test, she could get a better job and they would be able to do more things together if she made more money. She explained that she would need more quiet time away from them as she prepared. Donna also reassured them that their life would go back to normal after she completed the test. She attached a 12-month calendar to the refrigerator and circled her planned test date for the knowledge exam, her work product submission deadline, and anticipated results dates. She made a game of it during the final weeks as they counted down the days until Mommy's exam and work product submission.

Perseverance

A fourth component to success as a CPLP candidate is your ability to persevere through adversity. Murphy's Law states that if something can go wrong, it will; pursuing the CPLP is no exception. You can—and should—make your study plans, but something unexpected could happen along the way to derail those plans. You could find yourself suddenly in a personal transition or in a new job, and both can pull your attention from your CPLP studies. Perhaps a family emergency or a new high-profile project at work requires more energy. No matter the cause, things happen that can get in the way of success.

So, how do you deal with it? Some successful CPLP candidates use these adversities as opportunities. A new project gives them an opportunity to apply their new CPLP knowledge in a real-world setting. A new job opens the door to talk to leadership about the benefits that CPLP brings to organizations. A transition provides more flexible hours to study. There is a silver lining behind every cloud. The trick is to find the right mindset and to persevere.

Jose's Story

When Jose took his exam the first time, he realized that he was not prepared for the types of questions on the exam versus the ones he used to practice. He left the exam with valuable experience: Learn the material in order to apply it to specific situations. After returning to his study materials with his new mindset, he took the exam again. His score was higher, but not high enough. Nevertheless, he was determined to achieve his CPLP.

(continued on next page)

Jose's Story (continued)

He started the process once again, encouraged that his studies were on the right track and hoping that the third time would be the charm. On his third attempt at the knowledge exam, his car was broken into the night before the exam, and his state-issued ID was stolen. He was mortified. He knew a state-issued ID was required to take the exam.

He scheduled his fourth attempt. After 150 minutes, he submitted the exam for scoring and sat there blinking at the word on the computer screen. PASSED. Three months later, he submitted his work product. After more than two years of perseverance, persistence, and determination, Jose earned his CPLP credential.

Professional Consideration

Reading the email that announces that you have achieved the CPLP credential can be an incredibly exhilarating and rewarding experience. Whether you prepared for only a few months or it took two years to get that notification, the thrill is equal to the amount of sacrifice, commitment, and support you experienced during the journey.

Your decision to pursue the CPLP certification should not be taken lightly. Consider your personal, professional, and emotional situation carefully. Only you can decide on the best time to pursue the CPLP. The fact that you're reading this chapter demonstrates your commitment to training and development and everything for which the CPLP certification stands. You have already taken the first step!

It Is a Big Deal

The CPLP credentialing process is rigorous—and it's worth it. It's the benchmark of professional excellence in the training and development industry. Seeing those four letters following someone's name really IS a big deal.

About the Authors

Kimo Kippen, MS, is the chief learning officer at Hilton Worldwide, based in McLean, Virginia. Previously, Kimo was responsible for the Center of Excellence for Learning at Marriott International. Kimo led management engagement for the enterprise and in a previous role was vice president of Human Resources for Renaissance Hotels and Resorts, North America. He holds an MS in career and human resource development from Rochester

Institute of Technology, and a BS from the University of Hawaii. Kimo served as the chair of the board of ASTD in 2007. He is an adjunct professor at Catholic University of America for the university's master's program in human resources.

Coline T. Son Lee, CISA, PMP, CPLP, is the learning strategist and managing partner of Everest CS, working with Fortune 500 organizations to deliver custom programs that satisfy learner and business needs. Her approach links human performance with strategic goals through competency-based learning, e-learning, and web-based curriculum, video/interactive learning, and informal social programs. Coline holds a bachelor of science in information systems and is certified in project management (PMP), workplace learning and performance (CPLP), and IS auditing (CISA). Since achieving her CPLP, Coline has become a strong advocate for the credential, promoting its value to organizations and individuals, as well as mentoring and supporting candidates through the process.

Jeff Toister, CPLP, PHR, is the author of *Service Failure: The Real Reasons Employees Struggle with Customer Service and What You Can Do About It,* a book that reveals hidden obstacles to outstanding service. His company, Toister Performance Solutions, Inc., helps clients identify these obstacles so they can improve customer service. Jeff holds a Certified Professional in Learning and Performance (CPLP) credential from the ASTD. He is a past president of ASTD's San Diego Chapter, where he was a recipient of the WillaMae M. Heitman award for distinguished service.

Resources

ASTD Career Navigator: www.astd.org/careernavigator.
ASTD Competency Model: www.astd.org/model.
CPLP: www.astd.org/cplp.

Chapter 4

Take Charge of Your Career: Breaking Into and Advancing in the T&D Profession

Annabelle Reitman

.... **In This Chapter** ....

- Assess your current work and career situations.
- Create a professional development plan.
- Learn how to establish your brand.

Whether you are looking for your first T&D position, progressing along your career pathway, content with your status quo, or preparing to retire and planning to continue to use your expertise and experience, you do not know what the future holds for you. In today's uncertain and chaotic times, "be prepared" is a good motto to have.

It is not enough just to be prepared in terms of qualifications, such as certification requirements and awareness of qualifying competencies, to enter and remain competitive in the T&D field. Being successful depends on your initiative, assertiveness, motivation, ambition, and self-confidence—that is, taking charge of your career. Use strategies that, combined, form an integrated way to deliberately move you along your chosen career pathway.

Begin with two basic assessments: your current work situation and your current career situation. Without input from these evaluations, how can you plan the what, how, when, and where of your strategy to realize your T&D career goals?

Assess Your Current Work Situation

Review how your work interests and priorities have changed, remained the same, or shifted. What are your emerging passions/interests regarding how you would like to spend your working hours? Some basic questions to ask:

- Do you feel your work is meaningful and rewarding?
- Are your skills, knowledge, and abilities used to the fullest?
- Do you have some independence in how you do your work?
- What is the level of alignment between you and the organization's values and culture?
- How would you describe your relationship with your supervisor?
- How would you describe your relationship with your co-workers?
- Are opportunities for advancement available?
- Is your salary comparable for your position level and responsibilities?
- Do you have sufficient resources and budget to meet work goals effectively and efficiently?
- Are your efforts and achievements appreciated and recognized?

What is your assessment of your employment situation? What is your level of work satisfaction and fulfillment? Is it great, satisfying, tolerable, or poor? What are your thoughts regarding specific modifications that your next work opportunity should include? What revisions/updates do you need to make to a professional development plan that you are in the midst of carrying out? Do you have a written well-thought-out plan?

Assess Your Current Career Situation

Compare your current career situation with your ideal one and identify critical gaps. How have your preferences and focus changed or shifted? What do you see as your next challenge? Some basic questions to ask are:

- What do like about your chosen field, profession, or industry? Dislike? How is the balance scale in your present position?
- How satisfied are you with the niche you have developed within your choice? Why?
- Has commitment to your career grown more, stayed the same, or lessened in the last year?
- Have you reached a point in your career where you can or want to consider other T&D arenas (such as teaching or entrepreneurship)?

- Do you feel you need to grow further and expand your areas of practice?
- Do you have the professional development opportunities that you desire?
- Do you feel you are contributing to your career community?
- Have you reviewed the new ASTD Competency Model and given thought to how these changes may affect your future career decisions and job possibilities?
- Do you know how can you best achieve your career mission and ultimate ideal work situation?

What is the assessment of your career situation? How do you feel about its progress and development? Is it great, satisfying, tolerable, or poor? In what ways does the current situation match up to your ideal career image? Do you want to consider making a work modification? Why? A worksheet is available for you to explore what is most important to you with regard to your employment priorities on the *Handbook's* website at www.astdhandbook.org.

Work Modifications

It is not unreasonable to experience at least two major career movements or professional shifts and several minor ones. Some of these work modifications can be the results of: a) typical adult work experiences (move from staff to management); b) readjusted professional goals; c) personal milestones or situations (parenthood, spouse relocation); or d) external actions by others (downsizing).

Career movements are general and broad activities—modifications that occur more frequently or are more prevalent. Some examples of common career movements in the T&D field are:

- working for a new employer
- moving within your present organization
- transferring to a new geographic location
- retiring or entering semiretirement.

On the other hand, professional shifts are narrower and deeper in scope than career moves. This is where you refocus your specialized skills and knowledge, applying them in a different arena. Some common professional shifts are:

- starting your own T&D consulting business
- joining a consulting or contracting organization
- switching from one competency/specialization to another
- joining a teaching staff in a T&D or HRD graduate or certification program.

As you consider your next work undertaking, decide if it is a career movement or a professional shift. Work modifications can cause your career path to zigzag, or even to reverse itself. Determine how a specific action will influence or necessitate adjustments in your course of action, starting with your professional development plan.

A Professional Development Plan (PDP)

Have a deliberate course of action using a basic planning tool, a professional development plan (PDP). This tool reflects your awareness of T&D's future, workplace and economic trends, changing qualifications, your current strengths and weaknesses that influence its design, and specific steps and activities.

In *Career Moves*, we define a PDP as "a blueprint for how, when, and where to turn your dream into a reality. And just like an architectural project, you will revise, modify, reduce, or expand it, reflecting changes in your needs, interests, and circumstances" (Williams and Reitman, 2013). In actuality, this is a game plan that is constantly in motion and reactive to changes in the marketplace, business trends, and unforeseen opportunities.

By developing a PDP, you have a structure that:

- enables you to work out and refine a strategy to manage your career path and professional experiences
- gives you the means to develop a workable, comprehensive, practical action plan for accomplishing your professional goals
- empowers you to create a design reflecting what you want and when you want it, declaring your intentions to yourself and others
- spotlights what you need to do to eliminate gaps in your competencies, knowledge, and skills
- pinpoints a set of related tasks, allowing you to arrange them in logical order
- commits you to action by providing a format to turn your ideas and desires into substance
- targets priority tasks, placing them at the head of your to-do list
- serves as a measurement tool for monitoring progress and assessing needed revisions.

A PDP consists of seven basic components:

1. Summary of an ideal professional life—the vision you have of engaging T&D work that would serve to move you forward, energized into action. This image includes work responsibilities, tasks, workplace, colleagues/co-workers, and people served.

2. Long- and short-term goal declarations—present both the broader picture (three to five years) of accomplishment (for example, start your own T&D consulting practice) and the narrower one (12 to 18 months), for tasks needed to complete the broader picture (for example, take business courses and hire a business coach).

3. Established professional niche—consists of bundled specific Areas of Expertise, skills, knowledge, education, and achievements to form a unique professional image. These items can be regrouped, decreased, or expanded as often as a shift or move is being initiated and a revised professional niche is required.

4. Identified practical considerations—takes into account: a) personal and family life situations (for example, caring for younger children or an aging parent), b) needed resources (for example, graduate school financial support), and c) realistic limitations (for example, travel for work, cannot relocate due to spouse's work commitment).

5. Developed action plan—the heart of a PDP that lays out strategies for completing each of your short-term goals and keeping you focused on your target. This would include week-to-week tasks/activities, such as attending a professional meeting or revising a resume.

6. Interim benchmarks of advancement—the regular fixed checkpoints to monitor progress and determine if changes need to be made to your PDP. The recommendation is for quarterly reviews to be scheduled.

7. Needed adjustments and revisions—amendments to the PDP's action plan due to uncompleted tasks or missed deadlines (for example, unanticipated work projects or illness in your family).

Creating a PDP is a career management survival skill that allows you to be proactive for continuing professional growth and development, balancing work and personal lives, adapting to unexpected situations, recognizing relevant possibilities, and preventing things from falling through the grid. A PDP helps to center you in an uncertain and shifting workplace, maintain a positive mindset, and be a deterrent to feeling you have lost control over the path of your work life. With a PDP as your guide, you can manage your career and professional choices to arrive at your destination.

Transitions

No matter where you are on your pathway when it occurs, the transition process is an important step in a new beginning. How you handle this activity determines how successfully you will come through the transition. Being able to efficiently and effectively step into new or expanded roles and responsibilities is a characteristic of the ultimate professional. Whether you are in the process of making a career move or professional shift or are satisfied with the status quo, you need to be current in the T&D world and ready to take action.

An unexpected possibility may come your way, or your organization can decide to initiate changes that will affect you. How you respond to the specific event will depend on your flexibility, adaptability, and level of readiness to act.

A transition interval is the time to adjust your mindset, assess the effect of this change on your life, and gain a clearer perspective about the challenges that lie ahead of you. A temporary blank space exists that needs to be filled by establishing new perceptions of yourself or revising your self-image. Basically, you are reconfiguring reference points for yourself. These self-defining reference points are listed in *Career Moves*:

- **Changing identities:** How will your professional identity change?
- **Changing roles:** What will you be doing that will be new or performed in a different way?
- **Changing relationships:** In what ways will your interactions with colleagues, managers, friends, and family be altered?
- **Changing routines:** How will your present work, social, and family activities and practices be revised, decreased, expanded, or modified?

Think about the ideal professional image that you want to project today to advance you toward the future. This "branding" task needs to be done before initiating a marketing campaign. It is particularly crucial if you are undergoing a career change and transferring to the T&D field from, for example, the teaching field or the technology industry. The transition phase provides an opportunity to review, reflect, and plan how this change may affect your life and what the implications are for a revised image.

Use this downtime to create a statement and practice with your support group as the audience. Ask them what descriptive image words come to mind, and compare them to your new ideal professional vision. How did others see you? How did you think others saw you? Were their perceptions of you in sync with how you view yourself?

In a continuously changing, mercurial, and uncertain work world, with new issues, challenges, and opportunities, it is essential for your survival to know when, how, and where to position yourself for a targeted career move or shift that results in a successful transition outcome.

Establish Your Brand

Branding is a strategic tool to help you stand out from your competition, enabling people to value your unique T&D qualities and experiences and initiate a working relationship with you. Creating your own professional brand is one of the most important, if not the most important, promotional pieces you can use to establish your identity in the T&D industry.

The branding copy should be brief, concise, and targeted, telling your story in a few short phrases and including: a) the essence of your professional profile, b) your personality reflected through a projected image, and c) your strengths and expertise—the advantages for hiring, collaborating, or partnering with you.

All brands have carefully composed stories, with specific words and phrases projecting the passion, commitment, and genuineness of what you are marketing and to reinforce the bond between you and your audience. This action affects your success in achieving your goals. To ensure that you are telling the right story to the right audience, you need to stockpile a variety of stories from which you can choose. This story cache should be reviewed and updated regularly. Prepare for a networking event or other professional meetings, workshops, or conferences by selecting two stories that meet the above-listed reference points.

Purpose of a Branding Statement

The purpose of a branding statement is to:

- grab attention quickly and sustain interest in you
- allow you to stand out from other candidates
- focus on how you want to be seen.

A branding statement helps to maintain a current public presence and gives you a focal point for career fluidity, survival, and success. Therefore, it must be up-to-date and targeted in the message that it sends out. If you presently have a branding statement, now is the time to review it, have others look at it, and consider what needs to be taken out and what needs to be added for rebranding yourself. If you have never written one, do some research and talk with a marketing/promotional person before drafting this statement.

A basic branding statement characteristically:

- spotlights your unique professional niche—individualized combination of skills and savvy
- introduces a desired professional image—depicts an instantly recognized work identity and personality
- includes specific words and phrases—carefully chosen that attract your intended market/audience.

Branding is a powerful marketing tool. Think of products and services you use; why is the name so well known and remembered? What comes to mind when you think of a particular name? Now, think of how you would like to be known and remembered—the T&D professional who . . . or the person with T&D. . . .

How can you use branding for marketing situations other than just job searches? It can be used for promotions, team projects, repositioning yourself from one industry or specialization to another, moving from working for someone else to becoming your own boss, shifting from working for an organization to joining a consulting firm, and so on.

Think of a brand statement as a networking intro or a one-minute elevator speech. It should be brief, concise, targeted, and capture the essence of your professional image in a few short phrases, reflecting your personality in the projected image, as well as the strengths offered as benefits for developing a working relationship with you.

Thinking of yourself as a brand gives you a focal point for your professional success. How can your branding statement resonate with other people? How do you now want to spend your time earning your living? In what ways do you want to contribute to your organization's bottom line or become involved in the expansion of the T&D field? Create or revise your brand as a way to acknowledge anticipated new roles and responsibilities. This is essentially your new professional "skin." Think about how you would need to change your mindset if you were moving, for example, from a T&D practitioner to a professor in a graduate HRD program.

Why Stories? Branding the "New You"

Brands essentially tell stories to highlight and project a specific image (strengths, achievements, benefits, uniqueness, advantages, and so on). However, for a story to reflect your commitment, passion, creditability, and authenticity, its focus needs to be from today leading to the future, not looking back to the past. Stories are the core of establishing your brand. They can be quite powerful in engaging people's attention to want to learn about you or your products and services. Give serious attention to focusing on selecting the appropriate elements or qualities for your story that stress advancing yourself in a highly visible way by asking:

- Who should or needs to hear my story?
- What is the reason for someone to listen to my story?
- How do I select which story to tell to which individual or group?
- How do I ensure that my story leads to desired outcomes?

Stories work. They bring information alive. People can relate to them and react by telling their own stories. They can more clearly match required expertise to your experience, and therefore, a level of bonding takes place. For example, when interviewing for a position involving instructional design and training delivery, your stories would spotlight your achievements in these two expertise areas. Or, if presenting a rationale for a promotion, the focus would be on your accomplishments and initiatives within the organization.

Stories are the means to brag about the "new you," for you to be considered "wow," and, therefore, be the first choice for a new position, to join a consulting firm, or to be selected by a client to provide a needed service or product.

Marketing Yourself

Think of the image you presently project: visually, written, or orally. Now, envision your future image based on your changed self-defining reference points. In addition, ask colleagues, friends, and family members to give you their impressions of you and recommendations for improvement. Try to recall the last time you:

- expanded your networking circles
- reviewed your resume
- updated your LinkedIn profile
- read about trends or issues in your field or industry
- reconnected with colleagues or former co-workers
- attended a professional activity
- participated in a professional activity, such as volunteering, to increase visibility
- redid your business card, brochure, or website for a fresh look.

Select specific items from this list that you want to address or feel should be attended to at this moment. Can some of these changes occur by allotting two or three hours, for example, reading the *T+D* magazine? Do others require a major time commitment, such as a certification course? Do any items need a complete makeover or the start of a new initiative, such as updating your resume or expanding networking outlets for making connections? Do you need to do some review or self-assessing before moving forward, by selecting a beneficial professional activity to attend or targeting helpful colleagues to contact? Will you need to consult with or seek the services of a professional such as a career coach or fashion stylist? What actions will be costly, inexpensive, or free?

Sometimes, one activity, such as participation in a professional event, allows you to address several concerns simultaneously. For example, at a workshop, you can learn a new skill,

LEARN How to Break Into the Profession

By Elaine Biech

Are you reading this handbook because you are considering a career in the training and development field? Wondering how to break in? Looking for experiences that will connect you with either the content or the professionals who design, deliver, and evaluate it? Start with several of these ideas.

Learn About T&D

- Attend an ASTD Train-the-Trainer program.
- Partner with a trainer and tag along for the next training event.
- Take an adult learning class at a university.
- If you are a student, complete an internship through your graduate T&D program.
- For a thesis or final term project, identify and contact an organization to build a case study or obtain content.
- Offer to help a local training organization in exchange for an opportunity to "tag along" to some of their clients.

Experience T&D

- Volunteer to teach a class to a youth group.
- Teach a class at your community college.
- Volunteer to help with a class, either classroom or e-learning, for your company.
- Contact a community or nonprofit organization and offer to design and deliver a needed training workshop/course.
- Attend a pilot session in your organization and sit in on the review that follows.

Ask for Advice

- Either at work or through your ASTD chapter, ask someone to be your mentor.
- Conduct informational interviews with T&D department managers or directors.
- Take a trainer to lunch and pick his or her brain with questions such as:
    - What do you do in your position?
    - What do you like about the profession?
    - What's the greatest challenge of the profession?
    - How did you learn to do what you do?
    - What would you miss the most if you quit?

Read About T&D

- Read about the field in *Training* magazine, *CLO*, or several of the books at the end of this chapter, such as *Training for Dummies*.
- Subscribe to *T+D* magazine.
- Regularly check blogs of your favorite trainers.

- Subscribe to LinkedIn groups sponsored by ASTD, the eLearning Guild, training managers, or others.
- Read your "junk" mail:
  - email ads from your favorite T&D companies or suppliers
  - book catalogs from companies that publish T&D books, such as ASTD, Berrett-Koehler, Wiley, and others.

Network About T&D

- Attend ASTD's International Conference & Exposition and exchange business cards with other attendees.
- Join National ASTD and your local ASTD chapter.
- Volunteer as a leader or presenter in your local ASTD chapter.
- If an ASTD conference is held in your city, join the volunteer team provided by your ASTD chapter.
- Attend meetings of other related professional organizations, such as SHRM or ICF.

become aware of professional trends or issues, reconnect with old colleagues, and increase your networking contacts. Have you thought of looking up former classmates and colleagues on LinkedIn and connecting with them? Another option is joining LinkedIn's special interest groups that are related to your interests and work. Gain visibility by contributing to or initiating discussions.

Managing for Professional Success

To remain in charge of your career, commit to reviewing your professional image, tools, and activities every six months, particularly if in transition. You do not want to sense that you are in a rut. Keeping up your self-confidence and motivation is vital to moving ahead. One easy, quick way to feel your best is to give attention to your wardrobe. How you look plays a major role in the impression being made. A complete new set of professional clothing is not necessary; an older business suit can be refreshed with the latest accessories and a new, crisp blouse or shirt.

It is also important to make decisions about old habits, mindsets, and attitudes, and possibly be willing to take some risks. Experiencing fulfillment and engagement are indications of being successful. Whether in transition or satisfied with the status quo, you should always have one eye on future possibilities, opportunities, and changes. Be aware of your T&D options and the practical and realistic choices to progress toward your ideal professional goal.

One way to facilitate a desired move or shift in an established timeline is by integrating relevant success factors into your strategic action plan. Which factors from the following listing would you include?

- Take risks—be willing to gamble, think positive about the outcome.
- Face the unknown—as you step onto uncharted ground, lessen anxiety by preparing and picturing yourself in the new work arena.
- Direct yourself—make your own decisions, gather information to assess the situation.
- Express feelings about the changes—verbalize your emotions and sentiments, set up a support group.
- Deal with stress—manage tension and worry, do relaxing and energizing activities.

Whether you are experiencing a job plateau or burnout or are content with your employment, it is good career management practice to assess your work and career status once or twice a year. (Review the previously listed current work and career assessments.) Determine what you need from your work to feel challenged and acknowledged: Is it the same, or is it changing? How much progress has been made toward reaching your career objectives? Have you veered off course? Directing your course of action includes thinking about your ideal work situation, professional development and growth activities, maintaining motivation, and making plans—basically taking charge and deliberately managing your career pathway and direction.

Career Management Challenges

At times, responsibility for your professional life in addition to your personal one can be out of sync, perhaps even in conflict. In addition, experience and successes bring different perspectives to your professional needs, interests, and goals. At times, life demands and realistic barriers need to be faced and weathered. How do you keep your work–life balance, bounce back from a difficult situation, sustain self-confidence and motivation, resolve a problem or issue, or step back on track from setbacks?

Address challenges proactively by engaging in the following practices:

- Have and retain career fluidity. Be adaptable to workplace innovations, changes in job assignments or responsibilities, or trends influencing T&D.
- Prioritize career and professional management tasks and integrate them in your daily calendar, with your PDP as your cornerstone for efficient and effective tracking.

- Keep your brand visible. Review and update all means of your public presence, such as your LinkedIn profile, business cards, professional niche statement, and networking contacts.
- Maintain career health. Take preventive action and sustain upkeep for continued progression of your career by being alert to early warning signs that not all is well in your work world. Be ready to move or shift when required or a possibility arises.

In summary, taking charge of your career direction and designing your professional pathway is the way to fulfilling your potential, living your passion, and, most important, using your skills and savvy productively. It is your level of responsibility, assertiveness, initiative, and energy that make a difference to the quality of service and input provided to your clients, customers, organization, and the T&D profession.

Adapting the final paragraph of *Career Moves* reflects the core of the best career management philosophy: Be a realistic optimist—combine a positive mindset with a measure of reality. Have an array of career management skills to give you an advantage to proceed efficiently and effectively. Be persistent in following your dreams, and remain as enthusiastic and spirited as the day you started. May your work in the T&D profession match your vision of your future!

About the Author

Annabelle Reitman, EdD, with more than 35 years' experience in career coaching/counseling, specializes in resume development targeting clients' individualized professional stories and short-term coaching for clients in work transitions and changes. Annabelle's tagline, "possibilities without assumptions," summaries her philosophy and approach to working with people. An established writer and author, her latest publications are: "Talent Engagement Across the Generations," part of the *Infoline* series (ASTD Press, 2013), and, with Caitlin Williams, *Career Moves: Be Strategic About Your Future*, 3rd edition (ASTD Press, 2013). Since 2009, she has been the *Career Pathways* columnist for the Transition Network's newsletter.

References

Arruda, W., and K. Dixson. (2007). *Career Distinction: Stand Out by Building Your Brand*. Hoboken, NJ: John Wiley & Sons.
Biech, E. (2005). *Training for Dummies*. Hoboken, NJ: John Wiley & Sons.

Chartrand, J., et al. (2012). *Now You're Thinking: Change Your Thinking, Revolutionize Your Career, Transform Your Life*. Upper Saddle River, NJ: FT Press.

Jones, R. (2012). *Storytelling Pocketbook*. Alresford, Hampshire, UK: Management Pocketbooks.

Maruska, D., and J. Perry. (2013). *Take Charge of Your Talent: Three Keys to Thriving in Your Career, Organization, and Life*. San Francisco: Berrett-Koehler.

Williams, C., and A. Reitman. (2013). *Career Moves: Be Strategic About Your Future*, 3rd edition. Alexandria, VA: ASTD Press.

Worthman, C. (2006). *What's Your Story? Using Stories to Ignite Performance and Be More Successful*. Chicago: Kaplan Publishing.

For Further Reading

Bolles, R. (2014). *What Color is Your Parachute?* Berkeley, CA: Ten Speed Press.

Hoffman, R., and B. Casnocha. (2012). *The Start-up of You: Adapt to the Future, Invest in Yourself, and Transform Your Career*. New York: Crown Business.

Chapter 5

The Occasional Trainer: What You Must Know to Help Others Learn

Harold D. Stolovitch and Erica J. Keeps

"Maria, you're one of the best salespeople in this whole department. We're bringing on more new hires to keep up with increased business. We're also making you an on-the-job trainer. You'll be assigned new hires. Show them the ropes. Teach them the job and our systems. Get them up to speed as fast as possible."

"To speed up the internal audit process, we are asking you, as experienced internal auditors, to go out to the branches and help them prepare for audits. You have the expertise. You also know what the branches can do to reduce time and errors in an audit. For the next three months, you'll all be helping out to train branch personnel."

"Carlos, I don't know how to attach the cables and calibrate the new unit for running pressure tests. Can you help me figure it out? I'm expected to run a lot of these tests going forward."

"Now that you've been promoted to team lead, you'll be expected to monitor how each of your team members performs as members rotate through each station. In addition to your regular duties, you'll have to train them on operations, daily maintenance, sanitation, customer service, display case stocking. . . ."

These scenarios and others just like them occur daily somewhere in the workplace. Know how to do something well? Perform well? Sooner or later, you will be pegged to help others out. You may be "a doctor, a lawyer, a beggar, or a thief," but being good at what you do almost inevitably leads to having you "show" someone else how to do it. Translation: "Show" equals "train."

In fact, this is the most common way trainers are selected in the workplace. Superior performance is often a signal for assigning training responsibilities to an individual. Frequently, the training assignment is in addition to carrying out regular job duties.

Are you equipped to take on the training role? The purpose of this chapter is to have you respond to this question with an enthusiastic "yes." It is aimed at helping you become as competent an "occasional trainer" as you are a recognized high performer in your present work role. By the end of the chapter, you will be able to train "newbies," whom we define as anyone who has not yet acquired the skills and knowledge to perform in a given job, so they will be able to demonstrate desired performance to your, their, and other stakeholders' standards.

Occasional Trainer: What Is It?

Let's begin your journey as an occasional trainer with some basic vocabulary terms. These are useful to help you build up in your mind what it means to be an occasional trainer and why, to be successful, you will have to restructure a lot of your current doing and thinking.

Occasional Trainer (OT)

The OT is someone who, from time to time, finds him- or herself in the role of teacher or trainer. OTs do not usually start out seeking to become trainers as part of their careers. Often, because of work experience, practice, trial and error, and most important, successful on-the-job performance, the call goes out to someone like you. You know how to do something well. You are recognized for your competence. It is only a small, natural step to ask you to help others learn a piece or the entire competency repertoire you have acquired. The "occasional" in the term *occasional trainer* means that the teaching role will only be tapped infrequently and rarely on a regular basis.

Subject Matter Expert (SME)

A SME is someone who has mastered some area of expertise. It is a tricky but extremely important term—tricky because there is a huge distinction between knowing and doing. True SMEs are those who can successfully perform on the job at a high level. SMEs can be athletes, plumbers, salespersons, singers, scientists, software programmers, or restaurant servers. How they do their jobs and the results of their performance are judged to be of high quality.

There is a problem with SMEs, however. Most expert "doers"—ones who are truly competent in their jobs—are generally not able to explain *exactly* what it is they do to be successful. We refer to this as "unconscious competence." Some so-called SMEs, on the other hand, appear to *know* a lot and can speak intelligently about a topic or a task. Unfortunately, this does not necessarily mean that they can "do" it really well. The best OTs are SMEs who can perform (do) the task or job at a high level and can also provide meaningful explanations about the *why* and *how* of what they do. It is absolutely essential for you to understand and hold in your heart the difference between knowing and doing. They are not the same. Talk is insufficient and often confusing when it comes to helping people perform. SMEs who can make the transition to ideal OTs are ones who can correctly guide the performance of novices. As we continue along in this chapter, this will soon be you.

Tutor, Teacher, Trainer, Instructor, Educator, Coach, Helpful Colleague

All those named above have one common goal—to bring someone who lacks the capability (the required knowledge and skills) to perform to the point where they are able to achieve success. All are, to some degree, OTs. The key difference between them and you is that *you* have been deliberately selected, based on your track record, to fulfill the OT role in a very specific way.

Learner (a.k.a. Student, Trainee, Apprentice, New Hire, Lost Soul)

Last, but absolutely far from least (in fact, foremost), is the target of the OT's efforts—the learner. This is the person whom you have been tasked with the job of transforming. Your success as an OT is judged by one major measure—how well your learner or learners perform based your instruction. Going back to the opening scenarios of this chapter:

- Maria's success will be judged by how quickly and how much the new hires sell, as well as how successfully they do their jobs using the store's systems.
- The internal auditor OTs will be measured by the speed, efficiency, accuracy, and completion of branch audit preparations and, ultimately, improvement in the branch audit process.
- Carlos will be deemed successful as an OT if his young colleague is able to independently attach cables properly and calibrate the new unit so that his pressure tests run error free and according to technical standards.

■ The team lead will be judged as a success if her team members perform according to company standards at each station.

The learner is the central focus of the OT. It is not how well you, as an OT, can *transmit* information to the learner. It is the measured degree to which you have transformed the learner that is the ultimate criterion of his or her and your success.

Now for Some Learning Theory to Develop Your OT Mindset

Let's begin with some key concepts. If someone talks, do you necessarily learn? Perhaps sometimes and some bits, but it is unlikely that you will get all of it, right? So, what follows are a few key "theoretical" points about learning. (Note: Theory is, very simply, an explanation of how things work—of cause and effect. There is sufficient evidence to support the explanation, although it may require more testing to establish its full legitimacy.)

1. **The more learners do—that is meaningful to them—the more they learn and the better they feel about it.** The three key words here are *learners*, *do*, and *meaningful*. Remember, it's all about the learner. SME OTs tend to do a lot of doing and saying in their training roles rather than allowing the learners to become actively engaged right from the start. SME OTs also tend to use terms and provide explanations learners do not fully understand. If what the OT says is not meaningful to the learner, not much gets through. Having learners "do" early in the game and then shaping their behaviors as they try out things for themselves not only builds learning and performance more rapidly, but also it allows them to experience their own progress. They feel good about their successes.

2. **If learners feel competent and confident about the skills and knowledge they are acquiring, they will be more likely to use them in the real world.** This is self-explanatory. You do; you get feedback; you try again; you improve; you sense progress; you experience valued accomplishments. The result: You feel more capable of performing and your desire to apply what you have learned back on the job increases.

3. **Learning occurs most rapidly when instruction is organized according to the logic of the learner, not the content, and is focused on performance.** SMEs acquire their expertise over time, through trial and error, and by doing, not talking about what is to be done. Most of the time, SMEs acquire their skills and knowledge unsystematically. Events occur. They respond. They try things out. Eventually, they figure out or experience what works and what does not. The learning time is long.

Under your care as an OT, your learners are not given a long timeline to try out, experience, and assimilate. Your job is to take your learners from where they are to where they should be within a short timeframe. This means that you have to think like your learners, not like an expert. You have three critical responsibilities:

- To organize, from the chaos of your experience, activities that break down the task at hand into simple, logical steps that walk the learners from their starting points to where they eventually attain the targeted performance goal.
- To base all of your activities and explanations on how a *novice* thinks. You proceed based on learner logic rather than content logic. What you teach only makes sense if the learner is able to attach the new learning you provide with prior knowledge and experience.
- To focus on the doing, only bringing in explanations, terminology, and background content that reinforces learner actions. The rule is: Focus on the performance; do not dwell on the details.

4. **Experts process information differently than novices.** You ask a local for directions on how to get from Point A to Point B. Response: "Well, let's see. You can go about a mile, or maybe closer to two miles, along Oak Street. Well, actually, it used to be Steamboat Street, but the city council decided to use tree names— you know, eco-friendly, but that's another story—until you come to Phillips Tower. You'll recognize it because it's the only building in town with a weather vane on the top. Then, turn east until. . . ." Soon, you are lost and confused by the explanation. A final, "There's a shorter way, of course, if you just . . ." followed by, "Either way, you can't miss it," is when you know you are doomed.

Ask someone who only arrived in town the previous day and traversed from Point A to Point B a single time. More than likely, the explanation this newcomer gives will resemble this: "Go straight 15 blocks to Plum Street. Turn right and go five blocks until you see the McDonald's on your right. Turn left at the first corner just past Mc-Donald's onto Orchard Street. Point B is on the left about 10 buildings up." Makes a lot more sense, doesn't it?

As an OT, drop your SME persona. Become a learner with minimal acronyms and jargon. Assume a more general background and adopt the same fear of the unknown that your learners are experiencing. A frequent admonishment we give to OTs is: "Don't be a sage on the stage. Be a guide on the side." Be the support an anxious, untried, inexperienced learner requires.

A Universal Model for Structuring Training

Wouldn't it be wonderful if you had a simple, easy-to-use formula you could apply to any training situation, type and number of learners, content, and difficulty level and feel confident of achieving a high probability of success with your learners? The good news is that such a formula exists. We call it the 5-Step Model for Structuring Training. Let's examine it and then observe it in use. Figure 5-1 shows the model itself.

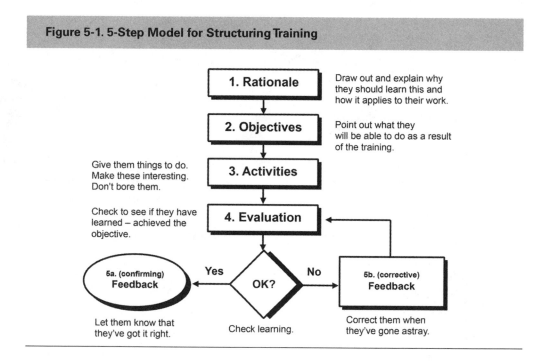

Figure 5-1. 5-Step Model for Structuring Training

Now for an explanation:

Rationale: Learners, especially adult learners, face a large number of competing priorities, all clamoring for attention. As an OT, you have to cut to the head of the line. You can best do this and grab their attention by providing a sound, *meaningful* reason (rationale) for focusing on what they will gain from their interaction with you. The more you engage your learner(s) in building the rationale, the more readily they will open their minds to you and learn.

Objectives: Give your learners a meaningful target to attain. It must be observable and achievable, and produce a valued end result. Here are several examples. Note that they always begin with "You will be able to. . . ."

- Complete the inspection report of the A3 engine, with every point checked off and annotated as required by the Safety Regulations Manual, p. 47.
- Discriminate between a flammable and an explosive material with 100 percent accuracy.
- Organize an office environment for a hiring interview so that it conforms to best practice standards in our HR Guidelines Manual.
- Adjust the ergonomic bus driver seat so that it conforms to your body at each of the seven key pressure points.
- Produce a proposal that contains all the information required by a given RFP, is fully accurate, and is considered convincing by your supervisor or trainer.

Notice that in every case, the burden is on the learner to demonstrate performance—"*You will be able to.* . . ." Nowhere do the words "I will show you . . . " "We will talk about . . ." or even "You will learn . . ." appear in the objective. You, as an OT, cut to the chase. You establish the contract. If the learners participate and engage in the session, they will be able to demonstrate real performance at a defined standard.

Activities: Now you embark on a series of instructional events that lead the learners from their current state of performance capability to the point at which they can demonstrate objective(s) accomplishment. The activities must be mentally engaging, meaningful (there we go again), and get the learners to demonstrate progress. There should be just enough challenge to motivate them to want to succeed and enough support that they do not feel threatened.

Bear in mind that each learner is unique. Each may require more or less challenge, encouragement or support, or practice based on the confidence each feels. Strike a balance between engendering under- and overconfidence (see Figure 5-2).

Evaluation: Along the way you, as an OT, continually encourage the learners to do things as they progress toward complete objective attainment. At each step of the way, you verify how well they perform. Continuous and final verification of performance with feedback is essential for helping learners meet the objective(s).

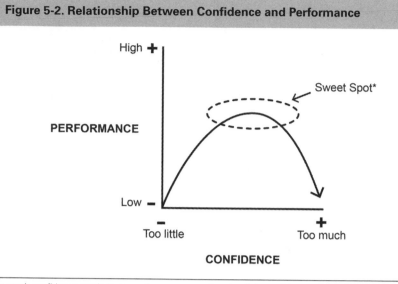

Figure 5-2. Relationship Between Confidence and Performance

*Too much confidence tends to generate more errors than too little confidence.

Feedback: Based on how each learner performs, you provide feedback, either *corrective*, to help the learner change behaviors, or *confirming*, to acknowledge that they have "got it." Important rule: You must always focus your feedback on the learner's performance and never on the person.

How Does This Work Out in Real Life?

Examine Figure 5-3: From Model to Training Plan. The 5-Step Model easily transforms itself from figure to worksheet. In planning your training, one-on-one or one-on-many, you select a straightforward title that encapsulates the lesson, name your learner (or learner group) by title or other meaningful descriptor, and then use bullet points to outline what you and your learners will be doing. You can add details as needed, but often key points are sufficient. Remember two absolutely essential rules:

- Every time you train, your session must be *learner centered* and *performance based*. Translation: It is all about the learners and their characteristics and capabilities. At every step of the way, the learners must be actively engaged and demonstrating performance. The opposite of learner centered and performance based is instructor centered and content based. Do not go there! Remember: Your success comes from their success. It is about their transformation, not your transmission.
- The less you do and the more they engage, the greater your success as an OT.

Figure 5-3. From Model to Training Plan

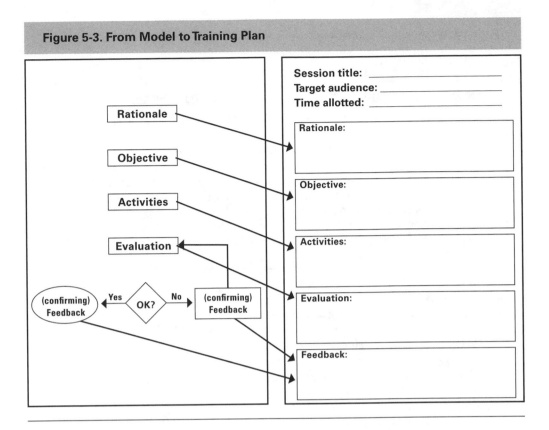

Figure 5-4 provides an example of a training plan (adapted from Stolovitch and Keeps, 2011, p. 88). You will find a blank copy for your use on the *Handbook's* website at www .astdhandbook.org.

Read through it. Imagine that you are conducting this training session. Picture what is happening during the session. Does it come to life for you? Can you see yourself running such a session, assuming that you possess the necessary subject matter expertise? (Some background: Once a year, the state fair opens for a month. Each year, organizers have to train off-the-street hires to work various operations of the event. One of the important groups is ticket sellers. Figure 5-4 is the training plan the OT assigned to train this new group of 25 part-timers has created. See if it incorporates all the key points we have presented so far in this chapter.)

Throughout the session, the OT draws learners into dialogue, building the rationale, clarifying objectives, engaging participation including requiring demonstration of performance, and verifying objective attainment.

Figure 5-4. Training Plan for State Fair Ticket Sellers

Training Plan

Session title: Selling tickets, collecting money, and giving change

Target audience: State Fair ticket sellers (15 participants per session)

Allotted time: Two hours, 30 minutes

Rationale:

- The most important and trickiest part of the job is selling tickets and making correct change.
- Despite background noise, if you've got the knack, you won't have problems.
- You are responsible for your errors up to $100. Learn the job right and you will be error free.
- Every day we have a bonus for the quickest and most accurate ticket seller.
- Some people get hostile when you are slow and make errors. This session will help you avoid the pain.

Objectives:

Overall objective:

Participants will be able to sell the exact number and type of tickets, collect the exact amount of money, and give the correct change for any customer without error and at an average time of 20 seconds per transaction (maximum group of eight people per transaction).

Specific objectives:

- Identify the exact numbers and types of admission tickets the customer requests.
- Calculate the exact total cost in 10 seconds with no errors.
- Collect the correct total amount with no errors.
- Give the customer the exact change with no errors.

Activities:

- Draw from participants what concerns them most about their new job.
- Show how this session helps decrease or eliminate those concerns.
- Present key points of rationale and discuss each one.
- Show ticket price/customer job aids and demonstrate use.
- Using different voices and admission requests, have participants determine exact request and cost.
- After several examples, time the exercise.
- Using play money and coins, have participants practice collecting money, issuing tickets, and giving change. This is a peer-pair activity.
- In simulated ticket booths, create a practice session putting all parts together. Loudly play audiotape of background noise.

Evaluation:

- Practice exercises with timing toward the end for each activity.
- Final evaluation: In the simulated ticket booths, each learner services 10 peer customers, each with different characteristics and requirements. An audiotape plays loud background noise. Peers talk.

Is Your Training Plan and Actual Training Session Likely to Produce Results?

Obviously, the proof of the pudding is in the eating. However, there is a way to check that you will achieve a high probability of success with your training plan. Figure 5-5, Training Plan Checklist, helps you test what you intend to do. You can also ask someone you trust, especially an experienced trainer, to observe you train using the checklist as a basis for feedback. Anytime a "no" is checked, a revision is necessary. By applying the checklist, you will soon find that your occasional training sessions hit the mark every time. You will find a copy of the checklist on the *Handbook's* website at www.astdhandbook.org.

Figure 5-5. Training Plan Checklist

Criterion	Yes	No
The rationale is presented in terms of the learner.	☐	☐
The learner participates and contributes in building the rationale.	☐	☐
The objectives are stated in terms of the learner.	☐	☐
The objectives are verifiable.	☐	☐
The objectives are appropriate to the learner and the content.	☐	☐
The activities are appropriate to the objectives (lead the learner to attain the objectives).	☐	☐
The activities require learner participation at least 50% of the time.	☐	☐
Learner can participate and contribute during the activities.	☐	☐
Evaluation is appropriate to the objectives.	☐	☐
Feedback is appropriate.	☐	☐
The session can be conducted within the allotted time.	☐	☐

Tying It All Together

When you get cast in the role of OT, either by accident or design, the most important thing you must hold in your mind and heart is that you are no longer the expert performer, no longer the SME. You are an educator—a drawer-out of performance. Whatever you know is of little value unless it contributes to verifiable, observable learner performance. You are the orchestra conductor. Your success is in how well the musicians play individually and, when needed, together.

The good news about being an OT is that you have the opportunity to help people in ways they and others value. We may not all love school, but we love to show how well we have learned and can perform. There is nothing more rewarding than seeing your learners' shining eyes and smiles—because of you.

About the Authors

Harold D. Stolovitch and **Erica J. Keeps** share a common passion—developing people. They have devoted a combined total of more than 80 years to make workplace learning and performance both enjoyable and effective. Their research and consulting activities have involved them in numerous projects with major corporations as well as government, military, and health organizations. Harold and Erica are the principals of HSA Learning & Performance Solutions LLC, specialists in the application of instructional technology and human performance technology globally. Their publications include 14 books and more than 200 articles and book chapters. They are the authors of *Telling Ain't Training, Beyond Telling Ain't Training Fieldbook, Training Ain't Performance*, and *Beyond Training Ain't Performance Fieldbook*, published by ASTD Press. Together, they are co-editors of the first two editions of the award-winning *Handbook of Human Performance Technology: A Comprehensive Guide for Analyzing and Solving Performance Problems in Organizations and Improving Individual and Organizational Performance Worldwide* and authors of the toolkit series, *Engineering Effective Learning*, and *Front-End Analysis and Return on Investment*, published by Jossey-Bass/Pfeiffer. They have won numerous awards for their contributions to the field of workplace learning and performance.

For Further Reading

Biech, E. (2005). *Training for Dummies*. Hoboken, NJ: John Wiley & Sons.

Goad, T.W. (2010). *The First-Time Trainer: A Step-by-Step Quick Guide for Managers, Supervisors and New Teaching Professionals*, 2nd edition. New York: American Management Association.

Stolovitch, H.D., and E. Keeps. (2011). *Telling Ain't Training: Updated, Expanded and Enhanced*, 2nd edition. Alexandria, VA: ASTD Press.

Stolovitch, H.D., and E. Keeps. (2004). *Beyond Telling Ain't Training Fieldbook*. Alexandria, VA: ASTD Press.

Chapter 6

What's on the Horizon for the T&D Profession?

Jane Hart

······················· **In This Chapter** ·······················

- ▦ Review the ways learning is evolving, including where it's been and where it's headed.
- ▦ Learn about the new tools being used and the emergence of social business.
- ▦ Discover the next-generation learning practices.

Workplace learning is changing! The Internet has dramatically changed the way we live, and it is now changing the way we learn. Businesses are transforming to social businesses and making use of new enterprise technologies to underpin knowledge sharing and collaborative ways of working.

All this also offers new opportunities for workplace learning professionals—if they are ready and willing to grasp them. But it will also require changes. The role of the training and development (T&D) profession will broaden from one that is focused on organising and managing knowledge transfer to one that involves working in partnership with managers to solve performance problems in a range of new ways, as well as enable and support the continuous performance improvement of their people through both knowledge sharing and collaboration in their teams and through independent professional learning.

To maintain authenticity of the author's original submission, this chapter is written using British spelling of certain words.

This chapter examines how workplace learning is changing and how the role of T&D is likely to evolve.

The Way It's Always Been

The training department has changed little since the first ones were set up in the latter half of the 20th century, when they were directed to control organisational learning. Harold Jarche reminds us that "this was part of the Taylorist industrial model that also compartmentalized work and ensured that only managers were allowed to make decisions. So in this context only training professionals were allowed to talk about training" (2012).

Although we have seen some changes since that time, notably a change of name to the learning and development department, the function has largely remained the same. And even though technological advances have automated training, first through computer-based training (CBT) and more recently through e-learning, the focus has still remained one of designing, delivering, and managing access to instructional content.

Certainly for most managers the T&D function is still seen as the function that creates, delivers, and manages courses to solve perceived training problems. But there are now an increasing number of people who no longer see the training room or corporate e-learning as the primary place where they learn.

Learning on the Social Web

Those who have been immersed in the social web for a number of years have developed new ways of learning. This has become clear from the annual Top 100 Tools for Learning survey (Hart, 2013b; now in its seventh year), which has identified a number of trends in the ways people are increasingly using social tools for their own professional learning:

- They are using social networks to build a trusted network of friends and colleagues (often referred to as a personal learning network, or PLN) where they can ask and answer questions of one another, exchange resources and ideas, brainstorm and solve problems, and keep up-to-date with what they are doing, as well as learn from one another, often without realising it.
- They are using social tools to "learn the new" and keep up with what is happening in their industry and profession.
- They are using social tools to find immediate solutions to their everyday performance problems.
- They are using social tools to participate in wider open educational opportunities online, such as MOOCs (massive open online courses).

- They are using social tools to share what they find, learn, create, and know with others.
- Additionally, work teams and other groups are using social tools to support collaborative working and learning.

All of this means that increasingly, individuals and teams are bypassing IT and T&D to solve their own training and performance problems quicker and easier by sharing their knowledge and collaborating with one another in powerful new ways.

For those active on the social web, "learning" will never be the same again, for it is a very different experience, whether it is continuous or on the fly, self-organised or autonomous. It is often unstructured—some even call it "messy" learning. It is certainly not the same way they learn in traditional training (and e-learning) events, where the content has been organised, structured, and "packaged" up for delivery in a very controlled way. For many on the social web, the lines between working, learning, and playing have become very blurred—and sometimes they don't even realize they are learning, because it happens serendipitously, accidentally, and often unconsciously.

The impact of learning in these new ways is that there is a growing frustration with current e-learning approaches, which Clark Quinn refers to as "knowledge dumps tarted up with trivial interactions" (Quinn, 2013). So the solution is not a matter of just adding new social tools into current e-learning, but rethinking learning practices in order to support workplace learning more widely and in more modern and relevant ways that appeal not only to Millennials entering the workplace, but also to those who have experienced new ways of learning on the social web.

The Emergence of Social Businesses

Another significant factor that is affecting organisational learning is the emergence of social networks and collaboration platforms to help build social businesses. Enterprise social networks (ESNs) are internal platforms, such as Yammer, Jive, or Socialcast, that are designed to foster collaboration and knowledge sharing among employees, and it is clear now that collaboration and conversation are becoming the next generation of working practices (Mitchell, 2013).

Deloitte (2013) predicted that by the end of 2013, more than 90 percent of Fortune 500 companies would have partially or fully implemented an ESN. Many of these networks have been "voluntarily adopted" by employees who saw the value of such a system for their own work and which have subsequently been formally adopted by their own companies.

But ESNs offer a big opportunity for T&D, because by integrating their own learning initiatives in the very same platform that is being used to underpin work processes, they can play a major part in inspiring, encouraging, supporting, and embedding learning, knowledge sharing, and collaboration throughout the organisation in ways that have never before been possible. This innovative approach brings a number of significant advantages:

- It means that thinking about "learning" is not constrained by a dedicated learning platform (or LMS) that underpins the traditional training approach.
- It means that all the knowledge and experiences shared in training are not locked away in a separate "learning" system.
- It means that it's not just about internal experts telling people what they should do or know but about peers sharing their thoughts and experiences and learning from one another.
- It means that "learning" is no longer seen as a separate activity from working, and that for the first time it can be truly embedded in the workflow.

Although some organisations are retiring their LMS in favour of an ESN, in others the LMS will continue to coexist with the ESN for the time being at least, where it will mainly be used to provide hosting for self-paced courses as well as tracking of compliance and regulatory training.

Next-Generation Learning Practices

It is not just new technology that is underpinning new practices in forward-thinking T&D departments, but a new mindset. Here are five ways that T&D departments are rethinking their learning practices in the age of knowledge sharing and collaboration, so that they can play a fuller part in the business and engage employees in learning in much more appealing and modern ways.

1. From a Focus on Learning to a Focus on Performance

This is about recognizing that learning and collaboration are simply means to an end, not the end goal, and that the end goal is improved performance. Although creating performance support solutions is part of this, it is a much wider concept than this. It means stop being "order takers" (that is, taking orders from a manager for courses) and working in closer partnership with them to support team and individual needs in the best and most appropriate ways by adopting a performance consulting approach. This involves carrying out performance analyses to find out the underlying causes of performance problems and identifying a range of ways that problems can be solved, rather than automatically assuming that training is the answer. (Note that a performance analysis is not the same as a training needs analysis, since to some the latter means that training is the solution.) It also means that the success of initiatives is measured in terms of performance outcomes rather than learning outcomes.

2. From a Focus on Training to Supporting Learning in the Workflow

This is about recognising that directed learning (such as training or e-learning) only accounts for a small percentage of how knowledge workers learn in the workplace, and that most of how people learn is self-organised, experiential, and social and takes place as individuals carry out their daily work. It involves using new workplace learning models, such as the 70:20:10 framework, to form the strategy for supporting learning more widely in the organisation (Jennings, 2013).

It is also about recognising that learning is not separate from work, but that "learning is the work" (Jarche, 2013). This means:

- helping to develop the right conditions for team learning, such as by supporting continuous learning through knowledge sharing
- helping teams to identify the sharing practices that are currently taking place and how these could be enhanced, built upon, or developed
- helping to ensure knowledge sharing becomes part of the daily workflow, so it is not seen as an extra initiative but an integral part of daily work
- helping to identify appropriate business performance metrics to measure the success of knowledge-sharing and collaboration activities
- recognising that you can't use command and control to "get" engagement (Zinger, 2013).

3. From a Focus on Teaching Old Skills to Modeling New Skills

This recognises the fact that working and learning together in the flow of work is not just about the use of collaboration technologies but about developing and applying a new set of personal and social business skills. It also offers T&D the opportunity to play a key role in helping to build these new skills by, for example:

- helping individuals to understand the value of sharing their knowledge and experiences—and what this means in practical terms within their work groups and teams
- helping teams collaborate purposefully and productively in order to get work done
- helping managers lead a connected team where they can manage complexity and build trust

- helping other work groups establish effective communities of practice that can support new working practices
- helping individuals manage their own professional learning and development in order to feed new ideas into their teams and work groups.

Developing these new skills, however, requires a new approach. It recognizes that "you can't train people to be social, only show them what it is like to be social" (Hart, 2013a). In other words, the traditional training model of telling teams how to work together is not appropriate in this context; instead, it involves working alongside teams, helping them develop these new skills as they do their work. This is the true social learning in action, and it is only through social learning that workers can learn how to become social learners themselves.

4. From a Focus on Packaging Content to Scaffolding Learning Experiences

It also appreciates that these new social skills can be stimulated through new learning activities, ones that lie between the structured, directed knowledge-transfer approach of current e-learning practices and the unstructured, self-directed knowledge-sharing approaches of work teams and groups, and which use a semidirected, semistructured approach that focus on building knowledge together. We might refer to this new design approach as connected learning. Connected learning design embodies the following five principles:

- **Scaffolding:** Rather than packaging e-learning content, it involves building a framework for learning to take place. This framework provides just enough structure, without constraining personal and social learning.
- **Self-governance:** It promotes and supports participation in the ways that individuals feel most comfortable and best suits them, and in doing so, it helps them take responsibility for their own learning.
- **Social first:** Social interaction lies at the heart of the connected learning experience, whether it is conversation, knowledge sharing, or collaboration in some other way so that participants can build their understanding together. In other words, it is not just about tacking on social interaction to content and (en)forcing it.
- **Content second:** Key resources are provided to get participants thinking, conversing, and doing, but participants are also encouraged to contribute to the knowledge base of relevant resources.
- **Performance oriented:** It is focused on what participants will be able to do as a result; it does not track the (inter)activity to use this as a measure of success. After all, activity doesn't equal learning, let alone performance. Performance might be assessed in a number of ways, through self-, peer-, or even manager evaluation, depending on the content and context.

Connected learning approaches might therefore include asynchronous learning activities such as online social workshops and synchronous learning activities such as backchannel learning, as well as new approaches to social onboarding and social mentoring.

5. From a Focus on Managing Learning to Building an Enterprise Learning Network

Whereas the traditional T&D function focuses on managing learning within an LMS, an ESN allows T&D to think in terms of building an enterprise learning network. By coordinating an ongoing set of learning activities (for example, live chats, hot seats, daily tips, or learning resources), T&D can engage employees in a continuous process of learning, which can in turn also help to foster connections and knowledge sharing across the organisation more broadly.

Figure 6-1 summarizes the key features of the next generation of workplace learning practices, as well as the type of new activities T&D might undertake.

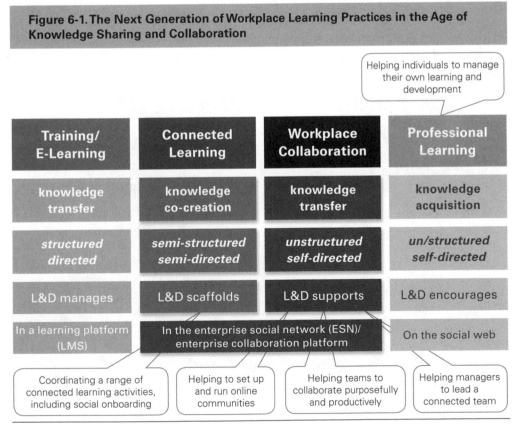

Figure 6-1. The Next Generation of Workplace Learning Practices in the Age of Knowledge Sharing and Collaboration

Source: © C4LPT. Reprinted with permission.

Are You Prepared for the Future?

This new generation of workplace learning practices will demand new T&D roles and skills. In particular, there will be need for specialists in performance consulting, connected learning design and facilitation, community management, collaboration, and professional learning. These new roles will focus on supporting individuals and teams as they learn in more self-organised and self-directed ways. Currently there are few formal programmes available to help develop these new emerging T&D roles and skills, but there are plenty of opportunities for self-development in order to get prepared for the future.

To find out if you are ready, ask yourself these five questions. If your answer to any of them is no, then read some advice on how to get started.

1. Do You Use the Social Web for Your Own Professional Learning?

Understanding social media is not just about learning how to use the tools themselves; it's about understanding the whole ethos of the social web, as well as developing a new set of personal skills to thrive there. It's also about building a personal learning network of colleagues and other contacts that bring you value, both personally and professionally. To be able to help others understand the value of the social web for professional learning, you will need to be an active user yourself. If you haven't already experienced the power of the social web, then just jump in and find out what it has to offer. There are no rules, and you'll learn more about it by just by being there.

2. Do You Work and Learn Collaboratively With Your Own Team?

The only people who can valuably help teams share their knowledge and work collaboratively will be those who themselves do so and can demonstrate the value of it for their own work teams. The quickest way to start, therefore, is for your own T&D team to begin to work and learn collaboratively; by doing so, you will develop your own understanding of the new social workplace skills that will be required for effective knowledge sharing and collaborative working.

3. Have You Participated in or Managed Any Online Communities?

Online community management is more than just setting up a private group space and letting the members get on with it. It takes time and skill to build and lead a successful community. One of the best ways to find out what makes for a good community is to participate in a range of communities and watch how the community leaders engage and stimulate the community. You won't be able to help others set up and manage online communities unless you have experienced what it is like to be a community participant yourself.

4. Have You Taken Part in Any Online Connected Learning Activities?

Many new learning activities that can be adopted within organisations can easily be experienced on the social web itself. For example, if you haven't already done so, take part in regular live Twitter chats to consider how these types of events might be used within your own organisation, participate in conference backchannels to find out about their value for both online and face-to-face events, and take part in MOOCs to experience social engagement in an online course.

5. Are You Familiar With Enterprise Social Networks (ESNs)?

If your organisation has already adopted an ESN, use it to set up a work group for your own team, create a community of practice on a cross-organisational topic, or open a private group space to try out some connected learning activities for your organisation. If your organisation doesn't yet use an ESN, it is easy to sign up for a free Yammer, Jive, or Socialcast account and find out for yourself what it's all about.

This self-assessment is also located at the *Handbook's* website at www.astdhandbook.org Yes, workplace learning is changing. This change offers new and challenging opportunities for you. Use the ideas in this chapter to learn about the opportunities for your organisation.

About the Author

Jane Hart is an independent adviser, writer, and international speaker on workplace learning trends, technologies, and tools. She is the founder of the Center for Learning and Performance Technologies, one of the most visited learning sites on the web and where, among other things, she runs an annual survey of learning tools, resulting in the popular "Top 100 Tools for Learning" list. Jane is the 2013 recipient of the Colin Corder award for Outstanding Contribution to Learning presented by the Learning and Performance Institute. Her website is www.C4LPT.co.uk.

References

Deloitte. (2013). 2013 Technology Predictions, www.deloitte.com/assets/Dcom-Brunei Darussalam/Local%20Assets/Documents/TMT%20Predictions%202013.pdf.

Hart, J. (2013a). Going Social? It's Not Just About New Social Technology; but About New Skills. *elearning age magazine*, http://c4lpt.co.uk/janes-articles-and-presentations-2 /going-social-its-not-just-about-new-social-technology-but-about-new-social-skills.

Hart, J. (2013b). Top 100 Tools for Learning 2013. Center for Learning & Performance Technologies, http://c4lpt.co.uk/top100tools.

Jarche H. (2012). Informal Learning, the 95% Solution. Life in Perpectual Beta, www.jarche.com/2012/01/informal-learning-the-95-solution.

Jarche, H. (2013). Learning Is the Work. Life in Perpetual Beta, www.jarche.com/2013/10/learning-is-the-work-2.

Jennings, C. (2013). 70:20:10 – A Framework for High Performance Development Practices. Learning at the Speed of Business, http://charles-jennings.blogspot.fr/2013/06/702010-framework-for-high-performance.html.

Mitchell, A. (2013). Conversation and Collaboration, the Next Generation of Working Practices. *Wired*, www.wired.com/insights/2013/10/conversation-and-collaboration-the-next-generation-of-working-practices.

Quinn, C. (2013). Yes, You Do Have to Change. Learnlets, http://blog.learnlets.com/?p=3232.

Zinger, D. (2013). 19 Antiquated Employee Engagement Approaches Contributing to Organizational Anxiety. David Zinger, www.davidzinger.com/xx-antiquated-employee-engagement-approaches-contributing-to-the-age-of-anxiety-16386.

For Further Reading

Hart, J. (2013). The Connected Workplace: Building the New Skills of the Networked Business. The Connected Workplace Consultancy, http://connectedworkplace.co.uk.

Hart, J. (2013). Enterprise Learning Networks. Center for Learning & Performance Technologies, http://c4lpt.co.uk/enterprise-learning-networks-how-to-embed-social-learning-in-the-workplace.

Hart, J. (2013). The Workplace Learning Revolution. Center for Learning & Performance Technologies, www.c4lpt.co.uk/blog/2013/05/07/the-workplace-learning-revolution-free-mini-e-book.

Section II

Assessing and Analyzing Needs

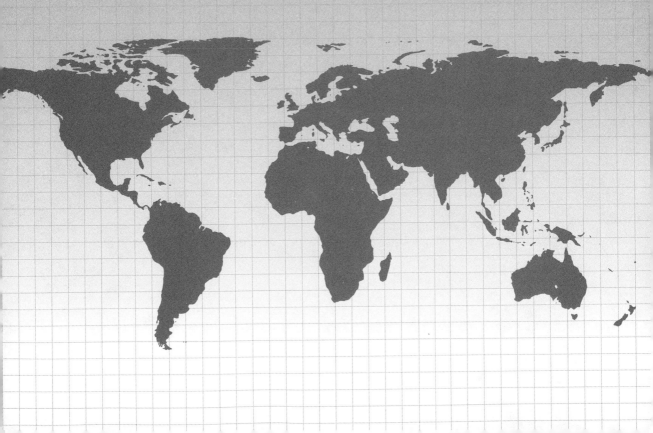

What I Know for Sure: Looking Through a Rearview Mirror

Luminary Perspective

Dana Gaines Robinson

January 2011 was an important month for me. That was the month when I officially re-tired and left the workplace learning and performance (WLP) field where I had worked for 35 years. Those years were times of discovery, learning, and challenges, which included both successes and disappointments. While in the throes of starting, growing, and manag-ing a consulting business, it was difficult to find time to reflect. In this new phase of my life, one that I refer to as my "redirected" life, there is time to identify lessons learned from those previous successes and disappointments. So in the spirit of looking back, through the proverbial rearview mirror, I share five principles I know for sure regarding needs analysis and the T&D professional.

Needs Analysis Is Not an Option

Too frequently I observed T&D professionals move directly from a client's request to solu-tion design and implementation, with the comment that there is no time to analyze the need. My response to this lament is actually borrowed from Peter Drucker, who said, "There is nothing so useless as doing efficiently that which should not be done at all." Investing the resources of time, money, and people into designing and delivering a learning solution that is either unnecessary or inaccurate in its focus is wasteful and leads to disappointment and frustration from those we are supporting. Jump-to-solution is not a tactic that we in the T&D field should be using.

Identifying Root Causes of Performance Gaps Is the Most Important Category to Analyze

Consider all the analyses that are possible to do: front-end analysis, task analysis, learning assessment, performance analysis, and content analysis, just to name a few. As T&D professionals, we are familiar with needs assessments designed to determine skill deficiencies. However, lack of skill is only one cause for performance issues. We are charged with the goal of enhancing human performance in support of business goals. It is wasteful to enhance skill and knowledge of people who then do not apply that capability on the job. And performance of people is almost never isolated to a single causal factor. Therefore, the most important analysis we do is to determine the causes for poor performance (if a problem exists) *or* the probable barriers to success (if working on a future opportunity). Once a skill deficiency has been identified, it may be necessary to do a task analysis or another analysis to obtain information required for instructional design. But first we must determine if lack of skill is truly evident—and what other root causes may be contributing to the problem.

The Gap Zapper in Figure A identifies the eight root cause categories that affect human performance and achievement of business goals. This tool first appeared in our book *Zap the Gaps: Target Higher Performance and Achieve It!*, which Jim Robinson and I co-authored with Ken Blanchard. It describes the three categories of root cause that have an impact on successful on-the-job performance required to achieve organizational and business goals. There are examples provided for each category. The examples are noted as enablers of performance; the absence of these factors becomes a barrier to performance.

As I reflect on the analyses I managed during my WLP career, some combination of three or more of these categories was typically identified. For example, a poor work process, coupled with insufficient on-the-job coaching and deficient skill, was a combination frequently determined as the causes for performance problems. Addressing only one of these would have yielded limited to no results.

Needs Analysis Is a Team Sport

Needs analysis begins a process that will, most likely, result in the implementation of one or more solutions. If solutions are to be implemented that ultimately bring about improved job performance, involvement of clients and other stakeholders is necessary. By *client*, I am referencing the person or people who are accountable for achieving the business and performance results supported by the initiative and who have authority to make things happen. Clients are also in the chain of command of the group(s) of employees being assessed. Usually, this means that one or more managers from the business unit will need to be actively

Figure A. The Gap Zapper

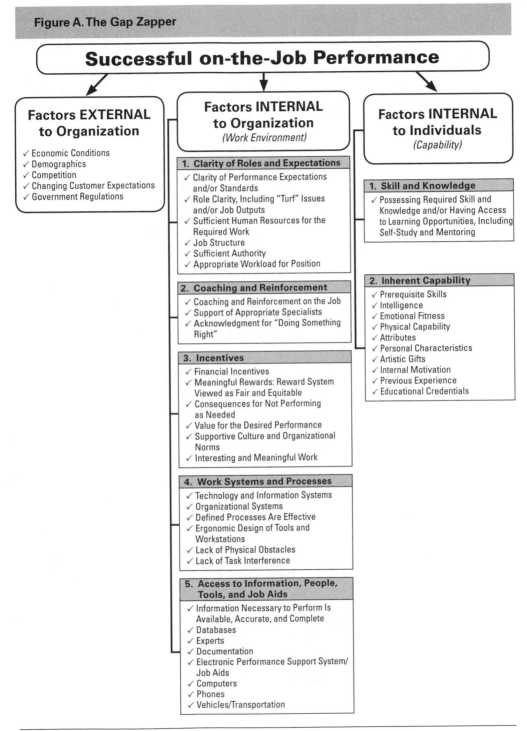

Successful on-the-Job Performance

Factors EXTERNAL to Organization

✓ Economic Conditions
✓ Demographics
✓ Competition
✓ Changing Customer Expectations
✓ Government Regulations

Factors INTERNAL to Organization
(Work Environment)

1. Clarity of Roles and Expectations

✓ Clarity of Performance Expectations and/or Standards
✓ Role Clarity, Including "Turf" Issues and/or Job Outputs
✓ Sufficient Human Resources for the Required Work
✓ Job Structure
✓ Sufficient Authority
✓ Appropriate Workload for Position

2. Coaching and Reinforcement

✓ Coaching and Reinforcement on the Job
✓ Support of Appropriate Specialists
✓ Acknowledgment for "Doing Something Right"

3. Incentives

✓ Financial Incentives
✓ Meaningful Rewards: Reward System Viewed as Fair and Equitable
✓ Consequences for Not Performing as Needed
✓ Value for the Desired Performance
✓ Supportive Culture and Organizational Norms
✓ Interesting and Meaningful Work

4. Work Systems and Processes

✓ Technology and Information Systems
✓ Organizational Systems
✓ Defined Processes Are Effective
✓ Ergonomic Design of Tools and Workstations
✓ Lack of Physical Obstacles
✓ Lack of Task Interference

5. Access to Information, People, Tools, and Job Aids

✓ Information Necessary to Perform Is Available, Accurate, and Complete
✓ Databases
✓ Experts
✓ Documentation
✓ Electronic Performance Support System/ Job Aids
✓ Computers
✓ Phones
✓ Vehicles/Transportation

Factors INTERNAL to Individuals
(Capability)

1. Skill and Knowledge

✓ Possessing Required Skill and Knowledge and/or Having Access to Learning Opportunities, Including Self-Study and Mentoring

2. Inherent Capability

✓ Prerequisite Skills
✓ Intelligence
✓ Emotional Fitness
✓ Physical Capability
✓ Attributes
✓ Personal Characteristics
✓ Artistic Gifts
✓ Internal Motivation
✓ Previous Experience
✓ Educational Credentials

engaged from the beginning of the assessment process through to the conclusion of the project. These managers have a stake in the initiative's success. They are also the decision makers; we are the influencers.

Consider this analogy. You and a client are in a car on a journey. The client sits behind the wheel because it is the client who ultimately determines the destination and route. You are seated in the passenger side of the car, influencing the decisions made regarding each of these. What if there is no client in the car? You have lost the opportunity to provide this influence and risk the loss of the client's support for the project. This support will be required for success and sustainability.

Data Must Be Converted Into Action, Otherwise It Is Only Research

In today's competitive and fast-moving world, organizations are too action oriented to tolerate collecting information that moves into the proverbial black hole, never to be seen or heard from again. Obtaining information that is never acted upon also generates skepticism among employees and managers who contribute their thoughts and time to the analysis and then learn that nothing happened as a result.

I think of the data conversion process as one in which we put the findings we have obtained through a funnel, as illustrated in Figure B.

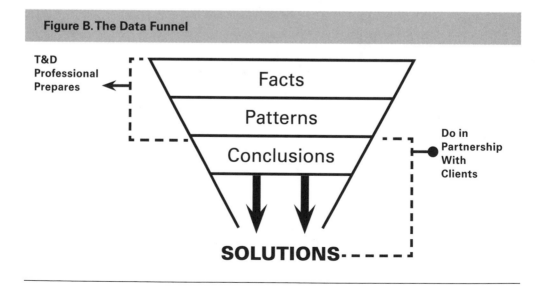

Figure B. The Data Funnel

T&D Professional Prepares

Facts

Patterns

Conclusions

Do in Partnership With Clients

SOLUTIONS

We begin with the hundreds, even thousands, of facts that we have obtained. These are the indisputable findings (for example, 62 percent of respondents indicate that they have insufficient skill in project leadership). In order to convert these facts into usable information, we must organize the facts into logical patterns. We are *not* interpreting the information; we *are* making it easier to interpret. For example, we could organize the findings by placing information in a table where one column lists those skills rated at or below 3.0 on a 5-point scale and a second column lists skills rated higher than 3.0.

Now we are ready to draw conclusions. A conclusion is a statement that combines multiple findings into a statement of meaning. There is not one correct or "right" conclusion; people will see things differently. Envision an eight-ounce glass that contains four ounces of water. Is that glass half empty—or half full? Each of these conclusions is accurate, but different. And different conclusions can result in differing opinions as to the solutions that will be required. Therefore, it is vital that the decision makers, or clients, for this initiative are actively engaged in drawing conclusions, increasing the probability that there will be agreement as to the required solutions. Given that a skill deficit is contributing to the problem, one or more learning solutions may be proposed. However, as I have already noted, lack of skill is rarely the only cause; other solutions need to be discussed and agreed upon. These other solutions will most likely address work environment challenges. And when decisions about solutions have been made, you have successfully facilitated the process of converting data findings into actions.

Needs Analyses Can Be Quick and Effective

One of the most frequently mentioned barriers to conducting any type of analysis is that it will take too much time. What I know for sure is that analysis does not need to take too much time. The actual investment made is dependent upon the thought put into the design. Here are just a few suggestions:

- **Have a narrow scope.** Limit the number of objectives for the assessment. Operate under the "less is more" principle. Purposes for an assessment should be narrow and specific.
- **Utilize automation.** The availability of technology and software is ubiquitous— and grows every year. Quick surveys, delivered to the workstations of employees with the data analyzed electronically, is one way to ensure a time- and cost-efficient approach.
- **Begin the analysis with a literature search.** There is a plethora of information available for any performance area we may need to assess, such as leadership, customer service, project management. Using what is already available, rather than

reinventing that content, is key to efficient analyses. With all the search engines available to us, obtaining information to leverage into a needs assessment has never been easier to do.

■ **Build something that generates discussion.** In essence, you develop a proto-type to stimulate thoughts, ideas, and suggestions from others. For people who have difficulty articulating ideas or scenarios, this approach can speed up the data collection process.

What I Know for Sure Looking Forward

As I indicated, I concluded my WLP career in early 2011; however, if you are reading this section's introduction in the *ASTD Handbook*, your career is probably full speed ahead. I want to acknowledge how fortunate you are to be part of a profession that truly makes a difference in the lives of people. I also want to acknowledge that you are in the field at a most opportune time because leaders and managers throughout the globe indicate through their words and behavior that *people* are the greatest competitive edge in an organization. Therefore, developing employees and managers is an investment that *must* be made. As a T&D professional, you have a responsibility to ensure that when this investment occurs, it is done for the appropriate reasons and with a high degree of certainty that the investment will yield enhanced human performance. Needs analysis is a key to delivering on this promise.

About the Author

Dana Robinson was the founder of Partners in Change, Inc., a consulting firm where she served as president for almost 30 years. During that time, she consulted with hundreds of organizations, supporting their efforts to define the performance required to achieve current and long-term business goals. Dana supported HR and learning functions in their transition from a traditional and tactical focus to one that is business-linked and strategic. With her husband, Jim Robinson, she co-authored six books, including *Performance Consulting* and *Strategic Business Partner*. Together with Jack and Patti Phillips and Dick Handshaw, the Robinsons are authoring the third edition of *Performance Consulting,* to be published in 2015. She has received numerous awards over her career, the most recent in 2013, when she and her husband received ISPI's Thomas Gilbert Professional Achievement Award. Dana and Jim live in Raleigh, North Carolina. Their retirement is active, including volunteer-ing with SCORE to support people who are starting businesses, traveling, taking university courses for personal enrichment, biking, and enjoying time with friends and family.

References

Robinson, D.G., and J. Robinson. (2005). *Performance Consulting: A Practical Guide for HR and Learning Professionals*, 2nd edition. San Francisco: Berrett-Koehler Publishers, Inc.

Rossett, A. (2009). *First Things Fast: A Handbook for Performance Analyses*, 2nd edition. San Francisco: John Wiley & Sons.

Rothwell, W.J. (2013). *Performance Consulting: Applying Performance Improvement in Human Resource Development*. San Francisco: John Wiley & Sons.

For Further Reading

Blanchard, K., D. Gaines, and J.C. Robinson. (2002). *Zap the Gaps: Target Higher Performance and Achieve It!* New York: William Morrow and Company.

Rothwell, W.J. (2013). *Performance Consulting: Applying Performance Improvement in Human Resource Development*. San Francisco: John Wiley & Sons.

Chapter 7

How Do Needs Assessments Align to the Bottom Line?

Roger Kaufman

In This Chapter

- Discuss needs assessment, strategic planning, and measurable success.
- Define Mega and what it means in regard to needs assessment and bottom lines.
- Review steps for conducting needs assessments for the bottom lines.

Needs assessments can align with a bottom line if done correctly. Furthermore, there are two bottom lines that are important:

- the conventional one displayed on a corporate profit and loss sheet
- the societal bottom line that documents what value has been added to individuals, the organization, and our shared society.

Both are important, but success can be further ensured by aligning and contributing to both bottom lines. This chapter identifies what needs assessment approaches are available, what each does and does not accomplish, and provides guidance on aligning needs assessments with bottom lines.

Defining and delivering success is the primary role of a needs assessment. A proper needs assessment—identifying and prioritizing gaps in results on the basis of the costs to meet the needs as compared to the costs to ignore them—can better ensure the continuing success of your organization. It provides evidence for strategic planning, decision making, design, development, implementation, evaluation, and continual improvement. To be certain that a needs assessment adds value to at least one bottom line and better to two bottom lines depends on which approach you use.

There is a choice of needs assessments approaches (Watkins, Leigh, and Kaufman, 1998), and which one you select from the options will determine what value you add and to whom the value is added. Select on the basis of what results you will get as compared to the usual "this is what others use and they say it is good." Only evidence-based approaches that have proven merit should be considered.

Needs Assessment, Strategic Planning, and Measurable Success

There are three levels of planning and thus three levels of needs assessment. Needs assessment will provide the basic evidence—data—for strategic thinking and planning. Which level you start with determines if you get results at the conventional bottom line or also at the societal bottom line. Every organization should ask several "commitment" questions, and the responses demonstrate three levels of results:

- societal results and contributions (Mega)
- organizational results and consequences (Macro)
- individual or team results and consequences (Micro).

The questions any organization should answer include these:

- Do you commit to deliver organizational contributions that add measurable value for your external clients and society? (Mega/Outcomes)
- Do you commit to deliver organizational contributions that have the quality required by your external partners? (Macro/Outputs)
- Do you commit to produce internal results that have the quality required by your internal partners? (Micro/Products)
- Do you commit to have efficient internal products, programs, projects, and activities? (Processes)

- Do you commit to create and ensure the quality and appropriateness of the human, capital, and physical resources available? (Inputs)
- Do you commit to deliver products, activities, methods, and procedures that have positive value and worth?
- Do you commit to deliver the results and accomplishments defined by our objectives?

These questions relate to the Organizational Elements Model to identify what every organization must consider if they are to deliver useful results for both the bottom line and the societal/Mega bottom line.

What Is Mega and What Does It Have to Do With Needs Assessment and Bottom Lines?

Mega is both an ethical as well as a practical imperative (Moore, 2010). If you are not adding measurable value to society, you are subtracting measurable value (Brethower, 2006). Societal value added can and should be measured. An Ideal Vision (Kaufman, 2011) has been suggested based on asking people, almost worldwide, "What kind of world do you want to help create for tomorrow's child?" Interestingly, responders did not routinely talk about means (hours of schools, number of beds in hospitals, spending on programs) but rather consistently about ends (the health, safety, and well-being of family; survival; and safety). From these responses, Kaufman (2012) identified Organizational Vital Signs that any organization may use in the same way a physician could calibrate one's physical health. The Ideal Vision is a definition of Mega, and the first level of Vital Signs provides measurable criteria variables in order that needs—gaps in results—may be assessed for selected variables. It defines a rational vision for any organization, and based on which Ideal Vision elements you select, you may identify needs for each and all. Examine the sidebar for a generic example.

Is the example in the sidebar ideal? Certainly. If one is not dedicated to moving toward perfection, where are they willing to stop, and how will they justify the triage in terms of human and social misery caused by not working to measurably improve the condition for all people?

Mega and the Ideal Vision are vital. Mega and the Ideal Vision focus on what value an organization adds outside itself. While it is convenient to look at the conventional bottom line alone, Drucker (Watson, 2002) advises that "all value is generated outside the organization; inside there are only costs." The conventional bottom line tends to capture one dimension of organizational survival and contribution.

A Generic Organizational Ideal Vision— Mega and Related Vital Signs

The Ideal Vision—Mega: There will be no losses of life, elimination or reduction of levels of well-being, survival, self-sufficiency, or quality of life from any source. Indicators or Vital Signs of success include:

First level—basic survival of all people:

- Zero pollution—there is no permanent destruction of our environment.
- No deaths or permanent disabilities result from what is delivered.
- No starvation and/or malnutrition resulting in death or incapacity.
- No partner or spouse abuse resulting in death or incapacitating physical or psychological damage.
- No disease or disabilities resulting in death or incapacity.
- No substance abuse resulting in death or incapacity.
- No murder, rape, crimes of violence, robbery, fraud, or destruction of property.
- No war, riot, or terrorism, or civil unrest resulting in death or incapacity of individuals or groups.
- No accidents resulting in death or incapacity.
- Citizens achieve and maintain a positive quality of life.

Second level—organizational survival:

- There is continued funding or profits based on measurable and demonstrated positive return-on-investment.
- Programs, projects, activities, and operations meet all performance objectives while not violating first-tier requirements.

Needs and Needs Assessment

Needs—gaps in results and consequences—should be collected at the three results levels of Mega/Outcomes, Macro/Outputs, and Micro/Products. Specifically, they may be assessed for each of the variables noted in the Organizational Vital Signs. That data allow strategic thinking and planning to move forward based on evidence, making useful and valid decisions and providing the basis for evaluation (Guerra-López, 2007, 2008).

It is vital that *need* is defined as a noun, as a gap in results, not as a gap in resources or processes, as show in Figure 7-1. Needs can and should be assessed at the three levels of results. Needs are gaps between current results and desired results at three levels (Mega, Macro, and Micro). Needs assessment is the identification and prioritization of needs for selection, elimination, or reduction. Needs may be prioritized on the basis of the cost to meet the needs, as compared to the cost of ignoring them.

Figure 7-1. Definition of Need

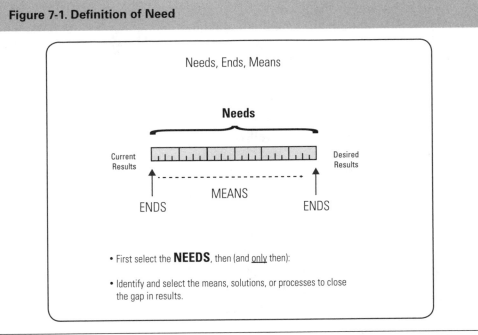

Source: Kaufman, R. (2011). *The Manager's Pocket Guide to Mega Thinking and Planning.* Amherst, MA: HRD Press.

When identified, needs can be captured in a summary form that identifies the gaps in results and also identifies possible means to close those gaps that should be considered after selecting the needs to be met (Table 7-1). These data allow useful strategic planning and decision making.

Table 7-1. Needs Assessment Summary Format

Current Results	Possible Means	Required Results	Related Ideal Vision Element	Need Level Focus		
				Mega	Macro	Micro

If you want to add to both bottom lines (conventional and societal), start at the Mega level. If you only intend to add to your organization's conventional bottom line, start at the Macro or Micro level and be aware that the limited focus may not add value to society or sustain your organization.

Ensuring That Needs Assessments Will Add Value to Bottom Lines

There are needs assessments for every whim and desire. We suggest that there are three needs assessments and one that, while called a needs assessment, is really a solutions assessment. Because a "need" is a gap in results, there are three types of needs assessments, as shown in Figure 7-2. These show the types of needs assessments as related to the Organizational Elements Model.

There are risks of starting strategic planning with an internal needs assessment or quasi-needs assessment. The internal ones might add to the conventional bottom line but not, over time, to the societal bottom line. According to Deming and Juran (cited in Kaufman, 2011), if you start with a "training needs assessment" (a quasi-needs assessment because training is a means, not an end), you will be wrong 80-90 percent of the time.

Figure 7-2. Three Types of Needs Assessments and One Quasi-Needs Assessment

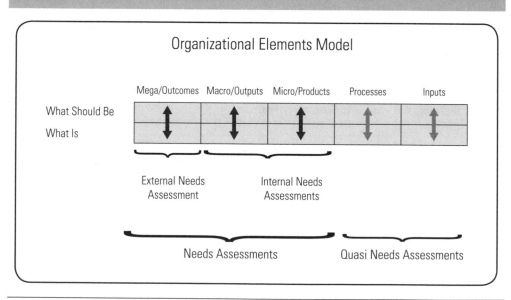

Source: Kaufman, R. (2006). *Changes, Choices, and Consequences: A Guide to Mega Thinking and Planning.* Amherst, MA: HRD Press.

Table 7-2 provides a guide for selecting a needs assessment that links the various levels of the needs assessments to the conditions that are associated with each of them. It also compares various well-known models. Use it to pinpoint where your organization requires and the analysis capability you desire from your needs assessment.

Table 7-2. Needs Assessment Levels and Frameworks

Level of Needs Assessment	Use It When the Organization	Relevant Needs Assessment Models	Analysis Capability
Mega	• Recognizes that what they use, do, produce, and deliver should be aligned and add value to internal and external clients, including society • Wants to ensure long-term survival and profitability • Is engaged in a strategic planning process • Adopts an ongoing strategic thinking culture • Is faced with significant change, threat, or opportunity	• Kaufman's OEM	• Kaufman's OEM uses a series of analysis tools to further understand gaps and solution requirements. • Analysis tools: – *Cost-Consequences* – *Methods-Means* – *SWOT*
Macro	• Recognizes that what they use, do, produce, and deliver should be aligned and add value to internal and external clients • Assumes (rather than ensures) what it delivers to clients adds value to them • Wants to ensure profitability in the short-term • Is engaged in a tactical planning process	• Kaufman's OEM • Rummler's AOP	• Rummler's AOP depicts a comprehensive analysis process that links the organizational or business issues to critical job issues and critical process issues, including causal factors.

(continued on next page)

Table 7-2. Needs Assessment Levels and Frameworks (continued)

Level of Needs Assessment	Use It When the Organization	Relevant Needs Assessment Models	Analysis Capability
Micro	• Recognizes that what the organization uses, does, and produces should be aligned and add value to internal stakeholders • Assumes (rather than ensures) that what is produced adds value to the organization and beyond • Introduces changes that will have an impact on job requirements • Is experiencing challenging symptoms related to particular jobs or performers • Is engaged in operational planning	• Kaufman's OEM • Rummler's AOP • Harless's FEA • Mager & Pipe's model	• Harless's FEA depicts a comprehensive analysis process that links human performance gaps to causal factors. • The Mager and Pipe model helps link human performance gaps to causal factors and potential solutions.
Quasi	• Recognizes that what the organization uses and does should be aligned • Assumes (rather than ensures) that what is used and done within the organization adds value to internal stakeholders and beyond • Is experiencing challenging symptoms related to processes or resources • Is about to implement a new process or resource • Is engaged in resource planning	• Kaufman's OEM • Rummler's AOP • Gilbert's BEM • Harless's FEA • Rossett's TNA • Mager & Pipe's model	• Gilbert's BEM is used after human performance gaps have already been identified and offers a systematic approach for analyzing causal factors contributing to those gaps, and potential solution requirements. • Rossett's TNA is primarily focused with analyzing training requirements, once training has already been identified as the required solution through a needs assessment.

So which one do you choose based on adding value to the bottom line? Table 7-3 provides a possible decision-making guide.

Table 7-3. Probability That a Needs Assessment Will Add Value to the Bottom Lines

Starting Point for Needs Assessment	Name of Needs Assessment	Probability of Adding Value to Societal Bottom Line	Probability of Adding Value to Conventional Bottom Line	Type of Planning Used	Sample Performance Indicators
Mega/ Outcomes	External	High	High	Strategic	Individual and group survival, self-sufficiency, quality of life, safety
Macro/ Outputs	Internal	Medium	High—short-term	Tactical	Conventional ROI, net profit, share value revenue (top line), brand value, intellectual capital
Micro/ Products	Internal	Medium	Medium—very short-term	Operational	Quality, passed test, competent staff, ISO certification
Processes/ Methods/ Activities/ Programs	Training or operational	Very low	Medium—very short-term	Efficiency	Training, planning, needs assessment, quality management, team building, collecting satisfaction data
Resources	Auditing	Very low	Low	Resources	Human capital, physical resources, buildings, equipment
Evaluation	Reactive assessment	Low	Low	Reactive	What worked and what didn't

If your organization intends to both survive and thrive, it should first start with the societal bottom line. It is both the practical and the ethical thing to do (Davis, 2005; Moore, 2010). But what to do with the boss who does not want to start with Mega and instead wants to start with the conventional business case—starting at Macro? One way to proceed is to use a strategic planning agreement process, as shown in Table 7-4. Here, several results and consequences questions are required of all planning partners to commit "yes" or "no" to each item.

Table 7-4. A Strategic Planning Agreement Requiring Commitment—Yes or No—to Each Question

	Commitment			
	Clients		Planners	
	Y	N	Y	N
1. The total organization will contribute to clients' and societal survival, health, and well-being.				
2. The total organization will contribute to clients' and societal quality of life.				
3. Clients' and societal survival, health, and well-being will be part of the organization's and each of its facility's mission objectives.				
4. Each organizational operation function will have objectives that contribute to 1–3.				
5. Each job/task will have objectives that contribute to 1–4.				
6. A needs assessment will identify and document any gaps in results at the operational levels of 1–5.				
7. Human resources, training, and/or operations requirements will be based on the needs identified and selected in step 6.				
8. The results of step 6 may recommend non-HRD/training interventions.				
9. Evaluation and continual improvement will compare results with objectives for 1–5.				

By getting the active response to each question, the series of nine questions gets people to begin to understand the implications of not starting with Mega and not basing decisions on an appropriate needs assessment. What happens if they persist? You have provided "informed consent," and the supervisor cannot blame you for the consequences. It is ethical and practical to help management understand what data should be used before jumping into a solution, such as training.

Lessons Still to Be Learned From the *Titanic*

In 1912, the HMS *Titanic* was the pride of the White Star fleet. It was designed to be unsinkable and thus the safest vessel afloat. (This intention was indeed Mega.) It was constructed by the Harland and Wolf shipbuilders, who applied the newest techniques to the construction (Processes and technology). The ship was divided into 16 bulkheads, which extended above the waterline with 11 vertically closing watertight doors that could seal off compartments in the event of an emergency (Products). The ship was outfitted with two 1.5 kW spark-gap wireless telegraphs for assured communication from the ship (Products). It was a state-of-the-art ship, which set the standard for safety (Mega) and luxury (Process).

It carried 20 lifeboats, which could accommodate only one-third of the 1,178 passengers. This was within regulations and followed what was legal and standard for ships of the day (benchmarking). The maiden voyage was to be the first of many cross-Atlantic journeys between Southampton, England; Cherbourg, France; Queenstown, Ireland; and New York. On April 10, 1912, *Titanic's* maiden voyage began at noon. It left Queenstown on a brisk and cloudy day, heading toward New York (Macro/mission). The crew was well trained (Processes) and all was proceeding well (Processes).

The first three days passed without incident, and then the crew began receiving a series of warnings from other ships (Inputs) of ice in the area of the Grand Banks of Newfoundland. Although the ship was not attempting a speed record (Product), time keeping was an overriding priority, and under prevailing maritime practices (Macro/mission), ships were often operated at close to full speed with the general belief that ice posed little danger to large vessels (benchmarking, best practice). Shipbuilding, it was thought, had gone beyond being concerned about foundering or sinking (Input).

At 22:40 on April 14, the bridge was alerted to steer around an obstacle. The ship was put into reverse (Process), but it was too late. The *Titanic* struck an iceberg at 02:20 and soon sank. Unthinkable. The ship was up to and beyond the standards of the day. The number of lifeboats, while not enough, met requirements, and yet it was a disaster where all conventional wisdom proved wrong. And everything went wrong in spite of the intention that it would be safe because all procedures and methods were "state of the art."

This scenario was derived from http://en.wikipedia.org/wiki/RMS_Titanic on October 1, 2013.

Aspiration vs. Accomplishment

Read the *Titanic* sidebar. It would seem that the owners of the *Titanic* had good intentions but did not start with measurable indicators of Mega but only the *intention* of Mega. None of the methods, procedures, activities, and resources was based on identifying the gaps between What Is and What Should Be for achieving real Mega. The owners benchmarked current best practice and built everything—the Products—to what was conventional and accepted. The operational mission was to get to its destination in good time, and that drove the journey, not "arrive alive." The crew was not ready to respond to the sinking, although each did his or her job to specification. While they were well trained in their routine jobs, none knew what to do in the actual emergency. Mega was more talked about than planned for, and since they did not have a measurable definition of safety and Mega, they had no way of assessing needs—gaps in results—during the ill-fated maiden voyage.

Blame, of course, was passed around, often to those not in direct command. The same thing evolved in the *Costa Concordia*, where the captain blamed his crew for the sinking. Even though the boss tells you to do something, if you don't provide informed consent, the blame will usually come back to you. Sample (2007) offers advice on how to avoid such personal legal threats.

Needs Assessments for the Two Bottom Lines

Once you know which needs assessment your organization will conduct, you can begin the steps to complete it.

Steps in Conducting a Mega-Level Needs Assessment

To ensure that a needs assessment will add measurable value at the societal bottom line, follow these steps and assign dates and individuals who will be responsible for each step.

- Determine the part(s) of the Ideal Vision your organization is committed to delivering and moving ever-closer toward, including indicators of its impact on the survival and quality of life of its external clients and society.
- Determine your organization's current status with regard to its impact on external clients' and society's survival and quality of life.
- Place Mega-level gaps (that is, needs) between your Ideal Vision and the current status, in a priority order, based on the cost to ignore versus the cost to successfully address the problem.
- Write an Ideal Vision–linked mission objective, that includes a specific sub-objective for each gap you decide to address (such as what you will have accomplished five or more years from now).
- Break down your mission objective to functional building block–block objectives.
- Present your Macro-level needs to your clients for concurrence.
- List alternative methods and means for addressing your Mega-level need(s) and identify the advantages and disadvantages of each.

A template and guide for doing a Mega-level needs assessment is located for you to download at the *Handbook's* website at www.astdhandbook.org.

Steps in Conducting a Macro-Level Needs Assessment

If your organization is focused on the conventional bottom line, follow these steps and assign dates and individuals who will be responsible for each step.

- Specify the desired quality of what your organization delivers to external clients. (Remember, starting here assumes that you have linked to the *Ideal Vision* level.)
- Determine the quality in performance terms of what your organization delivers to external clients.

- List the identified, agreed-upon need(s).
- Align the needs identified at the Macro level with the Ideal Vision and mission of your organization.
- Place Macro-level needs in a priority order, based on the cost to ignore versus the cost to address each identified need.
- Present your Macro-level needs to your clients for concurrence.
- List alternative methods and means for addressing your Macro-level need(s) and identify the advantages and disadvantages of each.

A template and guide for doing a Macro-level needs assessment are located for you to download at the *Handbook's* website at www.astdhandbook.org.

Figure 7-3 provides a job aid to guide you to define, select, and use needs assessments that will improve your chances for adding to both bottom lines, as well as examine the three levels of results while linking and aligning them. This job aid is located at the *Handbook's* website at www.astdhandbook.org.

Figure 7-3. Ensuring That a Needs Assessment Will Provide Valid Data for Adding Value at Both the Conventional and Societal Bottom Lines

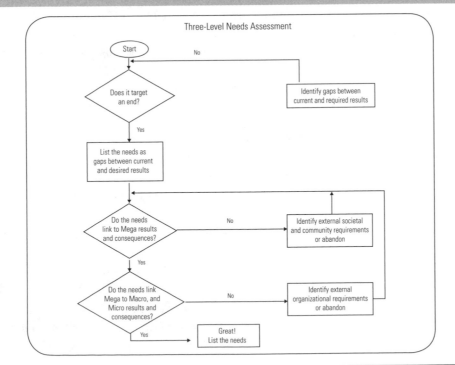

Source: Kaufman, R. (2013). *The Manager's Pocket Guide to Mega Thinking and Planning*. Amherst, MA: HRD Press.

Choices and Bottom Lines

You have a choice for finding the valid data for adding value to one or more bottom lines. If you choose to assume that the conventional—business-case—approach will serve you well and you are willing to live with the consequences of not providing sustainable results, choose a Macro-level needs assessment. If you want to better ensure that you and your organization both survives and thrives, then use a Mega-level needs assessment. The needs assessment choice is yours.

About the Author

Roger Kaufman, PhD, CPT, is professor emeritus, Florida State University, and Distinguished Research Professor at the Sonora Institute of Technology (Mexico). He received ASTD's Distinguished Contribution to Workplace Learning and Performance award. He is a founder, past president, honorary member for life, and Thomas Gilbert Award winner with ISPI. He has published 41 books and more than 285 articles on strategic planning, performance improvement, quality management and continual improvement, needs assessment, management, and evaluation. He consults worldwide with public, private, and NGO organizations. He created the Center for Needs Assessment and Planning at Florida State to conduct applied research and development. The literature often cites him as "the father of needs assessment." He is a Fellow of the American Psychological Association and of the American Educational Research Association.

References

Bernardez, M. (2009). Minding the Business of Business: Tools and Models to Design and Measure Wealth Creation. *Performance Improvement Quarterly*, 22(2):17-72.

Bernardez, M., R. Kaufman, A. Krivatsy, and C. Arias. (2012). City Doctors: A Systemic Approach to Transform Colon City, Panama. *Performance Improvement Quarterly*, 24(4),41-60.

Brethower, D. (2006). *Performance Analysis: Knowing What to Do and How*. Amherst, MA: HRD Press.

Davis, I. (2005). The Biggest Contract. *The Economist*, 375(8428):87.

Guerra-López, I. (2007). *Evaluating Impact: Evaluation and Continual Improvement for Performance Improvement Practitioners*. Amherst, MA: HRD Press.

Guerra-López, I. (2008). *Performance Evaluation: Proven Approaches for Improving Program and Organizational Performance*. San Francisco: Jossey Bass.

Kaufman, R. (1976). *Needs Assessment*. San Diego, CA: University Consortium for Instructional Development and Technology.

Kaufman, R.A. (1981). Determining and Diagnosing Organizational Needs. *Group and Organizational Studies*, 6(3):312-322.

Kaufman, R. (1991). *Strategic Planning Plus: An Organizational Guide*. Glenview, IL: Scott Foresman, Division of HarperCollins.

Kaufman, R. (1998). *Strategic Thinking: A Guide to Identifying and Solving Problems. Revised*. Washington, DC, & Arlington, VA: The International Society for Performance Improvement and ASTD.

Kaufman, R. (2000). *Mega Planning: Practical Tools for Organizational Success*. Thousand Oaks, CA: Sage Publications.

Kaufman, R. (2006). *Change, Choices, and Consequences: A Guide to Mega Thinking and Planning*. Amherst, MA: HRD Press.

Kaufman, R. (2011). *The Manager's Pocket Guide to Mega Thinking and Planning*. Amherst, MA: HRD Press.

Kaufman, R. (2012). Defining and Applying Organizational Vital Signs for Creating a Better Tomorrow. *Leader to Leader*, 65:21-26.

Kaufman, R., and I. Guerra-López. (2013). *Needs Assessment for Organizational Success*. Alexandria, VA: ASTD Press.

Moore, S. (2010). *Ethics by Design: Strategic Thinking and Planning for Exemplary Performance, Responsible Results, and Societal Accountability*. Amherst, MA: HRD Press.

Sample, J. (2007). *Avoiding Legal Liability for Adult Educators, Human Resources Developers, and Instructional Designers*. Malabar, FL: Krieger Publishing Company.

Watson, G.H. (2002). Peter F. Drucker: Delivering Value to Customers. *Quality Progress*, 55-61.

For Further Reading

Bernardez, M. (2009). Minding the Business of Business: Tools and Models to Design and Measure Wealth Creation. *Performance Improvement Quarterly*, 22(2):17-72.

Bernardez, M., R. Kaufman, A. Krivatsy, and C. Arias. (2012). City Doctors: A Systemic Approach to Transform Colon City, Panama. *Performance Improvement Quarterly*, 24(4):41-60.

Kaufman, R. (2011). *The Manager's Pocket Guide to Mega Thinking and Planning*. Amherst, MA: HRD Press.

Kaufman, R., and I. Guerra-López. (2013). *Needs Assessment for Organizational Success*. Alexandria, VA: ASTD Press.

Chapter 8

Data Collection and Assessment: Finding the Right Tool for the Job

Ethan S. Sanders

························· **In This Chapter** ························

- Learn the fundamental rules of data collection.
- Understand the whos, whats, and hows of measurement.
- Know the pros and cons of different tools.

The subject of data collection can best be captured in an old joke:

> *6th Grader: "Mom, I got a 100 on my math test."*
>
> *Mom: "That's wonderful."*
>
> *6th Grader: "Unfortunately, there were 200 questions on the test."*
>
> *Mom: "Oh, I'm sorry to hear that."*
>
> *6th Grader: "But it was the second highest score in the class."*
>
> *Mom: "That's wonderful."*
>
> *6th Grader: "But only two people were able to take the test that day."*

As with most things in life, children often exemplify what we see in the workplace. It is not uncommon to see "corporate statistics" that lack the type of relativity necessary to render a sound judgment on what the data mean. The first (and most important) rule of data collection is to only collect information that has a clear purpose and helps the organization to answer fundamental questions about its operation. The second rule is to always have a data collection plan that encompasses a sound data collection strategy. This chapter explores some of the fundamental rules of data collection and will highlight some of the principal considerations that must go into a data collection strategy. To effectively collect data, T&D practitioners must know what they are measuring, whom they are measuring, the pros and cons of different tools used for measuring, and how to analyze and present the data. Each of these topics is discussed in this chapter.

Know What You Are Measuring

"A strong conviction that something must be done is the parent of many bad measures."

—Daniel Webster

The Research Question

All good research begins with a fundamental question that the researcher (or organization) is trying to answer. The research question describes the who, what, where, why, when, and how of the investigation. In the social sciences, a research question might be, "Will low-income housing residents gain employment faster if they are provided additional education?" In the physical sciences, the research question might be, "Will the manipulation of proteins on the DNA molecule reduce the incidence of cancer cells forming?" When addressing T&D issues, the type of research being conducted is generally based in the social sciences. Therefore, the research questions tend to look like the former example. In addition, because organizations are complex economic and social systems, the more specific the research question is, the more focused the data collection effort will become. There are several components to a research question that must be covered:

- the *subject* of the assessment (that is, what relationship between two or more variables is being assessed?)
- the *source* of the data that will be used to measure the subject of the assessment (that is, according to what set or sets of data?)
- the *standard* for evaluating the subject (that is, by when, by how much, or by what quality measure is success being measured?).

One example of a good T&D research question is, "Does the new pay for performance system increase the number of loans processed by employees by 15 percent or more, as measured by the loan application reports?"

Joe Harless

Joe Harless, one of the early pioneers of human performance technology (HPT) and a student of Thomas F. Gilbert, followed Gilbert's diagnostic approach to performance, believing that the best way to find a solution is to first uncover the cause of the problem.

Harless found that most projects would benefit if analysis were done up front rather than at a project's end; he is credited with being the first person to coin the term *front-end analysis*. Like Gilbert, Harless derived his own performance equation.

Harless's equation states that performance (*P*) equals an employee's inherent capabilities (ic), skills and knowledge (*s, k*), motivation and incentives (m, i), and environmental supports (e); the equation is represented as $P = ic + (s, k) + (m, i) + e$. Harless was also one of the first to speak out about the power of job aids and was a proponent of using them as a training solution.

Harless's book *An Ounce of Analysis (Is Worth a Pound of Objectives)* (1975) outlined his performance improvement process, which stresses the importance of organizational alignment and continually measures training solutions to gauge their effectiveness in addressing performance gaps. The performance improvement process gave trainers what they needed to truly address performance issues.

In this example, notice that the subject of the research question is the effect that the "pay for performance system" is having on employees' productivity. The standard is "increase the number of loans processed by 15 percent," and the data source is "loan application reports."

Consider for a moment how much would change in data collection efforts if the research question were "Does the new pay for performance system increase the morale of the employees by 15 percent or more, as measured by the yearly employee satisfaction survey?"

Although the standard (15 percent) of the research question has not changed, and part of the subject remains the same (that is, it is still examining the effects of the new pay for performance system), there are considerable differences in these research questions. The latter research question focuses on the effects of the pay for performance system on employee morale rather than on productivity. The data source is an annual employee satisfaction survey. The difference will drastically affect the data collection strategy. The focus of the data collection effort now centers on validating employee opinions and attempts to link changes in perception to the pay for performance system. In general, the T&D professional will now address far more subjective and relative information than would be examined with the first research question. Although crafting clear and succinct research questions can be challenging, the data collection effort will be lost without a clear vision of what is being studied.

The Level of Performance

Goals within an organization are a funny thing. They tend to be multilayered and often float according to the perspective of the person examining the goals. As Geary Rummler (1990) highlights in his seminal work *Improving Performance*, there are three levels of goals within an organization: organizational, process, and individual. To achieve optimal performance, these three levels of goals must be aligned (see Figure 8-1).

For example, if an organization's goal is to "achieve 90 percent customer satisfaction," a fulfillment process goal might be "all products ready for shipping within 24 hours of receipt." An individual goal might be "complete form 1712 with 98 percent accuracy before shipping date occurs."

When conducting a data collection effort, it is essential to give careful consideration to which level is initially being measured and perhaps how many levels are being measured. For example, if the goal of a T&D project is to decrease the cycle time it takes to deliver a course to a customer, this would be a process-level goal (because what is being examined is an instructional design process). The types of measures that would typically be used are: 1) time to create the course outline, 2) time it takes to gain approval for the outline, 3) time it takes to develop the course, and 4) number of pilot sessions necessary to refine the course.

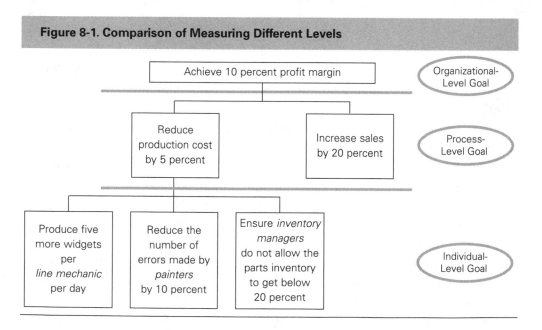

Figure 8-1. Comparison of Measuring Different Levels

In other words, the data collection effort would center on mapping out all steps in the design process and calculating how long each step takes. Conversely, if customer satisfaction or profits from a course are being examined (which is an organizational-level goal), the types of measures would be: 1) actual versus projected design budget for the course, 2) level 1 and level 2 evaluation results, and 3) gross sales of course materials. Table 8-1 highlights these distinctions. If the project involves aligning individual, process, and organizational goals, the number of variables (and the number of data sets) will increase.

Table 8-1. Sample Types of Measure and Data Collection Techniques

	Goal Statement	Typical Types of Measures	Data Collection
Organizational	"Solve world hunger"	• Number of people who do not have adequate food • Volume of food required to feed people • Number of organizations that currently provide food to feed the population • Tons of food required versus food available for population	• Examination of historical data related to food tonnage • Examination of operational capacity of various relief organizations • News articles, UN reports, etc., on food needs for the target population
Process	"All food inventories filled within one week of request."	• Number of steps currently in the process • Amount of time each step takes • Most time-consuming steps • Perspectives of team members on which steps are ripe for improvement	• Examination of operational manuals • Interviews with relief agency workers • Observation of various process steps • Examination of performance records • Focus groups with relief agency workers
Individual	"Reduce number of damaged goods during handling by dock workers by 50 percent."	• Damage rates by region, location, or individual • Perspectives of team members on causes for damage • Difficulty of tasks rating	• Examination of damage reports • Observations of exemplary versus average dock workers • Examination of damaged shipments • Conduct a job-task analysis

Standards and Measures

Once the T&D professional has a clear idea of the subject matter at hand and a general sense of which level of performance he or she is assessing (that is, individual, process, or organizational), the next step is to clearly define how the subject will be assessed. There are two elements that factor into this assessment: standards and measures. Measures describe how high the bar is being set; standards describe the bar itself. Table 8-2 describes the difference between absolute and relative standards, the differences between objective and subjective measures, and the intersection between measures and standards.

Table 8-2. Sample Absolute and Relative Standards and Objective and Subjective Measures[1]

	Absolute Standards *Example: "I want to build 10 widgets."*	Relative Standards *Example: "I want to build more widgets than my co-worker Bob."*
Objective Measures *Example: Average number of widgets built per hour.*	*Examples:* • Build 10 widgets per hour. • Call detachments within 24 hours of receiving coaching assignment. • Complete all HPI projects by deadline.	*Examples:* • Build 10 more widgets per hour than Bob. • Call detachments at least 1 hour faster on average than all the other coaches. • Complete projects faster then detachment average for a "5."
Subjective Measures *Example: Average customer satisfaction score on a survey.*	*Examples:* • Have 90 percent of Acme customers agree that they like our widgets. • Receive 80 percent approval rating from detachments related to coaching assignments. • Supervisor "strongly agrees" that all HPI projects are accurate.	*Examples:* • Acme customers are at least 15 percent happier than competitor customers. • Receive the highest satisfaction rating among all coaches to get a "5." • Receive the highest supervisor accuracy assessment among all detachments.

[1]Phillips, J. (1994, 1997, 2001). *Measuring Return on Investment*. Volumes 1, 2, and 3 of In *Action Case Study Series*. Alexandria, VA: ASTD Press.

A helpful way to think about standards and measures is to equate them to the legal concept of burden of proof. In the legal system, the burden of proof varies depending on the crime: in a criminal trial, the burden of proof is beyond a reasonable doubt; and in a civil trial, the burden of proof is a preponderance of evidence. As the seriousness of the crime increases, the burden of proof also increases. In T&D data collection, the same holds true depending on the ultimate decision that will be based on the data collection results. When the stakes are high and the implications are serious, stakeholders require more compelling and rigorous forms of data collection to base their decisions on. As Figure 8-2 illustrates, to have a high degree of rigor (and thus the ability to isolate the effects of the T&D program), you must use advanced evaluation designs (such as time-series or control groups) and you must measure results (either Kirkpatrick Level 4 or Phillips ROI). Table 8-3 defines the different types of evaluation designs that can be used to increase evaluate programs and increase the degree of rigor when needed.

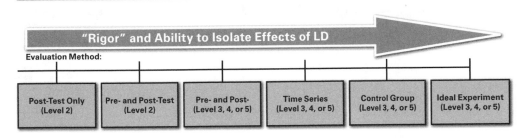

Figure 8-2. Identifying the Necessary "Burden of Evidence"

Table 8-3. Evaluation Designs

Evaluation Design	Characteristics
One-shot case study	• Single group • Only a post-assessment is conducted • Does not provide a baseline measurement
Single group, pre-post	• Single group • Pre- and post-assessments are conducted • Allows a measurable gain in knowledge and/or performance to be assessed
Control group	• Two groups • Participants already belong to a given group (e.g., comparing sales people in "region A" with salespeople in "region B" and the groups are fairly similar) • One group receives program and the other does not • Pre- and post-data gathered on both
Ideal experimental	• Two or three groups • Participants are randomly assigned to a select group • Only experiment group receives the learning intervention; the control group does not • Pre- and post-assessments are done on both groups
Time series	• One or two groups • May or may not include a control group • Multiple measures before and after program implementation provide initial and long-term results

Remember that all data collection efforts are trying to assess either "Did A cause B?" or "Does A have a relationship to B?" The assessment is trying to determine if some solution (or even a lack of a solution) has had the desired effect on some aspect of human performance. Depending on how serious the human performance issues are (or how expensive the solution is), the burden of proof will increase accordingly. For example, if the data collection effort is focused solely on determining employee satisfaction, relative standards and subjective measures will normally suffice. The data collection instruments may ask questions such as, "Are you happier working for this company today compared with a year ago?" This question is asking for a subjective measure of happiness and asking the respondent to make a relative comparison to a year ago. It may also ask for a relative comparison to other employees (for example, "Are you happier working here than most of your colleagues?").

If the ultimate intent of this data collection is to help the human resource manager decide if certain solutions aimed at improving morale should continue, the employee's subjective and relative responses are probably ample. However, if the intent is to determine the reason for excessive employee turnover, which is costing the company millions of dollars a year, simply capturing these subjective, relative responses will probably not suffice. The "burden of proof" has just increased and therefore a compelling case for change will require more absolute standards coupled with more objective measures. This might include actual turnover rates today versus those of last year (absolute standard, objective measure), a wage analysis to see how fairly the company is compensating employees (absolute/objective data), and then exit interview data (subjective data that tend to be more relative) to help triangulate the data.

Although it is impossible to have a measurement system that relies solely on absolute standards and objective measures, the aim should be to have a good mixture and to always attempt to find as much absolute and objective data as possible (see Figure 8-3).

Figure 8-3. Ideal Mix of Standards and Measures

Burden of Proof		Absolute Standards	Relative Standards
High	Objective Measures	#1 Choice	#3 Choice
Low	Subjective Measures	#2 Choice	#4 Choice

Know Who You Are Measuring

"I will prescribe regimen for the good of my patients according to my ability and my judgment and never do harm to anyone."

—The Hippocratic Oath

These words have endured in the medical community for thousands of years. Although T&D practitioners are not normally making life-and-death decisions with their data collection, the same principles must hold true. Collecting data on human performance issues requires a careful assessment of how much trauma the act of inquiry might have on the target population. For example, surveys are rarely seen as intrusive because the respondent always has the option of not participating in a survey. Likewise, requests for interviews and focus groups are normally not met with anxiety on the part of the respondent because respondents control what responses are given.

On the opposite end of the anxiety spectrum, however, observations and document analysis can have a profoundly traumatic effect if they are not handled properly. The act of being watched always carries with it some undertones of being spied on (even if the subject was notified that they were selected to be observed because they were identified as an exemplary performer).

Likewise, the act of rooting around in a performer's file cabinet looking for empirical evidence on a performance issue is sure to elicit some anxiety. In general, data collection efforts should always seek to gather the information in the least intrusive manner possible. This is not to say T&D practitioners should avoid observations and document analysis, just that great care must be taken when doing so.

The Target Population

There are numerous factors related to the target population that should be considered when creating the collection strategy. These include the demographics of the target population, the respondent's experience with similar data collection efforts in the past, the degree of anonymity required, the geographic dispersion of the target population, the particular sensitivities of the respondents around certain topics, and the logistical or technological realities. Table 8-4 summarizes some of the primary considerations.

Table 8-4. Primary Considerations for Target Populations

Factors	Questions to Consider	Comments
Demographics	• Is there a large range of ages in the target population? • If so, does this make a difference in how the data should be collected? • Is it necessary to distinguish supervisor, manager, executive, or individual contributor data? • Is it necessary to consider differences in race, experience, gender, or educational background?	Normally, a simple set of demographic questions at the beginning of the data collection instruments will suffice. Do not ask questions about race, gender, experience, etc., unless this information is needed for the analysis. Providing this information should be voluntary, and the instrument should explain why this information is necessary. Also consider a privacy act statement at the bottom of the instrument that specifically describes who will have access to the information.
Past Experiences	• What similar types of data collection efforts have occurred in recent years? • What became of those data (i.e., were there ever any recommendations, did the respondents ever see the results, etc.)? • Was the data collection process itself seen as valid, user friendly, and efficient? • Are the people who did the previous data collection still in the picture? • If yes, will they be receptive to the current data collection effort? • What were the client's perceptions of previous data collection efforts? • If negative, what are the specific things that should be avoided or changed this time?	Most data collection efforts fail due to inappropriate expectations being set with the client or the target population. Unfortunately, subsequent data collection efforts will experience guilt by association. It is essential to be aware of past attempts at data collection and to carefully plot a strategy that will serve to distinguish surveys.
Anonymity Required	• How important will anonymity of responses be to the target population? • Can all respondents be guaranteed anonymity? • If not, how will the data collection effort ensure that individual responses that might embarrass the respondent are not inadvertently provided to the customer?	Anonymity is a make-or-break issue for data collection. If the T&D practitioner is perceived at any point during the process as compromising confidentiality, participation in the effort will wane immediately. If they want to know the identity of each respondent and specifics of what they said, the WLP practitioner must convey to the respondents that all comments will be on the record.

Geographic Dispersion	• In how many locations does the target population reside? • Does it make more sense to gather the respondents in one location, or have the T&D practitioner travel to the various locations?	As the target population becomes more dispersed, the data collection effort will need to become more reliant on surveys and document analysis rather than observations, focus groups, and interviews. Remember that disruptions to productivity are normally not well received, so minimize the amount of travel time that participants will need.
Sensitivity	• Are there issues or topics within the organization (that are related to the data collection effort) that are taboo? • Are there any labor relations issues currently occurring that could affect the data collection effort (e.g., wage negotiations, EEO complaints, negative publicity about the company, etc.)?	Normally, a list of these issues can be generated by talking with the client or with an appropriate HR person. Although it is advisable to tread lightly on these subjects, they should not be avoided if they appear to be central to the larger issue being examined.
Logistics/ Technologies	• What are the working hours of the target population (i.e., do they all roughly work the same hours, or are there different shifts)? • Is there travel money available? • Do the various locations have private spaces for interviews or focus groups? • Do the respondents have access to computers, networks, or the Internet? • What policies does the organization have regarding storage of confidential data?	Modern technology has made data collection a lot easier and more efficient. Think carefully about the ultimate database that will be used to house the data (e.g., MS Excel, MS Access, SPSS, SAS, etc.). Try to find a way to collect survey data electronically, but make sure it is compatible with the chosen database. Be careful about where the data are stored and who has access to the data. In general, avoid putting data on portable devices such as laptops, smartphones, tablets, flash drives, etc.

Business Type

Just as every target population varies in terms of preferences, so too do different industries prefer certain types of data collection approaches. Highly regulated businesses, such as financial services, transportation, and pharmaceuticals, are usually driven by hard data. Over time, T&D practitioners learn that these clients will never accept recommendations that are based on an aggregate of options. Some types of businesses are fast paced and have little patience for data collection efforts that take months to complete. These types of businesses tend to go for less than perfect analysis, preferring to generate an educated opinion on the performance issue and then refine the solution as the implementation unfolds. Typically, this approach is found in high-tech companies, research and development firms, and military establishments. By contrast, many nonprofit, federal government, and educational institutions are more interested in having rich, qualitative data that may take more time to gather and analyze. Of course, these are all generalizations, and it is imperative that a T&D practitioner gets to know the specifics of each organization for which he or she works.

The Client

Clients are no different in terms of various preferences. There are many questions that should be addressed with a client before a data collection effort begins:

- What is the deadline for completing the effort?
- What resources will be available?
- Who is the advocate for this effort?
- Will he or she be able to help get access to the required data?
- What are the client's expectations in terms of the final report (for example, a presentation, a report, or a database)?
- What are the primary decisions that will be made based on the data?
- Will they be releasing the final analysis to the target population? If yes, how and when?
- What level of involvement will the client have in the data collection effort?
- How frequently does the client want status updates?
- What are some expected barriers to collecting the data or getting stakeholders to accept the recommended solutions?

This is a short list of questions to consider when determining the best way to work with the client. It is also helpful to ask the client if there are any questions that should have been asked but weren't.

Know the Pros and Cons of Different Tools

"Any tool is a weapon if you hold it right."

—Ani DiFranco

The tools used for data collection in a workplace setting are neither unique nor particularly modern. They are, however, the main interface between the data collection strategy and the target population. The most visible element to the respondent is the physical survey, the interview questions, the focus group format, or the test he or she is asked to take. If these tools are not well designed, thought provoking, aesthetically pleasing, and clearly written, the entire process will be called into question. Validity and reliability are the most vital factors to consider when building or buying data collection tools. To say a data collection tool is valid means that it is testing what it is designed to test. For example, if a teacher in a French language course gave a test to the students in German, it would not be valid.

To say a tool is reliable means that the results of the data collection using that tool should be repeatable. For example, if the French students received the same test on Monday morning and then again on Monday afternoon, the results should be about the same (assuming additional instruction was not provided between the tests). It is essential to remember that a tool could be reliable but not valid. For example, for the students taking French who took the test in German, the result would be reliable (that is, the students would fail the exam over and over again) until they were taught German. Table 8-5 details the pros and cons of the various tools, and provides some tips for ensuring validity and reliability. You will find an Evaluation Action Plan on the *Handbook's* website at www.astdhandbook.org that you may use to plan your next evaluation effort.

Table 8-5. Pros and Cons of Data Collection Tools

Tool Type	Pros	Cons	Tips on Validity and Reliability
Interview	• Collects rich, qualitative data. • Allows follow-on questions. • Allows observation of body language.	• Is time consuming. • Requires a lot of data synthesis. • Because data are subjective, normally requires corroboration of information from other sources.	• Write clear interview guide in advance. • Have a subject matter expert review and revise the form. • Tell the interviewee in advance what the purpose of the interview is and provide a general description of what types of information will be examined.
Observation	• Is the best way to see how work gets done. • Can often detect self-created job aids and other distinct advantages that exemplary performers possess. • Is the only method that allows the T&D practitioner to truly see the barriers that are present on the front line.	• The people being observed may adjust their behavior while being observed. • The people being observed may feel uncomfortable being observed. • It is a time-consuming method that will require a lot of data analysis later.	• Make sure the people being observed know in advance why they were selected and what information is sought. • Don't be perceived as a "spy" by standing over people while observing them. • The best way to get a feel for the job while observing is for the T&D practitioner to ask to try to do the job (assuming it is safe to do so).

(continued on next page)

Table 8-5. Pros and Cons of Data Collection Tools (continued)

Focus Group	• Allows respondents to build on each other's ideas. • Enables the consolidation of individual responses.	• It can easily deteriorate into a "whining session." • If working with an organization that has low trust, participants may refuse to speak in front of others. • It does not work well if participants feel intimidated by other participants (e.g., the "big boss" is in the room and no one wants to speak).	• Carefully choose participants according to a set of criteria. • Avoid mixing individual contributors with their supervisors. • Advise participants in advance about the ground rules (especially on confidentiality). Record session and use private room. • Have a recorder to take notes. • Use a structured approach, such as nominal group technique.
Survey	• Reaches a large population. • Automates data collection if online survey tools are used. • Tests assumptions over a large population.	• It is difficult to predict how the respondent will interpret questions. • It does not allow a lot of follow-on, probing questions. • It tends to have low response rates.	• Buy whenever possible. • Pilot test, review, revise, and test again. • Use a simple split-half reliability check.*
Test	• Is the best way to determine learning gains. • Is quick and easy to administer. • Carries a lot of weight when studying learning systems.	• It requires considerable skill to build a valid and reliable test. • Test anxiety may skew the results. • It is difficult to administer in situations where language is a barrier.	• Buy whenever possible. • Pilot test, review, revise, and test again. • Use a simple split-half reliability check.*
Document Review	• Is normally the only method for gathering hard data on performance issues. • Is difficult to argue with if the data come from valid performance records. • Is quick compared with more qualitative forms of data generation. • Is less subject to interpretation.	• Documents can be hard to access. • Documents must be true and accurate. • Review of some documents may be perceived as a violation of privacy.	• Only review documents that are directly linked to the research question. • Get written permission to review any sensitive documents. • Gather data on how much confidence the client and stakeholders have in the accuracy of these documents (e.g., ask employees if they believe that the standard operating procedure is accurate).

*A split-half reliability check allows the researcher to determine if the phrasing of the question has an influence on how the respondent answers the question. Two versions of the survey or test are provided. In one version, the questions are phrased in the affirmative, while in the other version, the questions are phrased in the negative. The responses are then compared to see if the way the questions were worded affected the responses.

Know How to Process the Data

"The only thing that counts is if you know how to prepare your ingredients. Even with the best and freshest ingredients in the world, if your dish is tasteless or burnt, it's ruined."

—Martin Yan

Collecting data is similar to grocery shopping. The process begins with a definition of the central ingredients. When grocery shopping, this takes the form of a recipe and then a shopping list. When collecting data, this takes the form of a data collection plan. But imagine spending the entire day shopping in the most exclusive grocery stores, driving to farmers' markets, and getting fresh milk from a dairy farm to throw all the ingredients into a microwave for a few minutes and see what comes out. The act of data collection has not met its pinnacle until the ingredients are properly prepared through a process of examination and contemplation.

The beginning of this process is normally intimidating. The sheer amount of data can often be overwhelming, and regardless of how much focus has been placed on the original research questions, extraneous data have a way of creeping in. Being able to address ambiguity early in the process of sifting through data is a key competency for T&D practitioners. It is not uncommon for the data to appear fuzzy early in the process. Processing data involves three distinct and important steps: synthesizing, displaying, and presenting.

Synthesizing Data

Depending on the type of research being conducted, synthesizing data can be done several ways. In general, the process involves the following steps. The first step is to become familiar with the data. This normally involves some initial frequency distributions to see if the data have initial face validity. To do so often means the data need to be coded. For example, if the research involved interviews, focus groups, or observations, the notes from these events must be placed into categories to spot trends. Table 8-6 provides an example of what this might look like.

In this example, notice that there are two nearly identical responses related to the broken phone system. Both responses are coded as R1. There is also another resource issue related to budgets that is coded R2. This coding will allow the T&D practitioner to understand how common these perceptions are and to place them in categories that potential solutions can be aligned to. Once the T&D practitioner is familiar with the data, the next step is to draw meaning from this information. It is essential to revisit the research questions and begin to run tests to see what answers the data provide. The original research question might have been "What are the primary causes for low customer retention rates?" The data set in Table 8-6 might provide part of the answer from the employee's perspective. Of course, employees can only see elements of the problem.

Table 8-6. Sample Results of Employee Focus Group: Why Are Customers Unhappy With Our Service?

Code	Response
R1	"My phone set doesn't work consistently, so the customers can't hear me."
K1	"I don't know how to use the customer database."
R1	"Phone sets do not work properly."
R2	"Shrinking budgets do not allow us to develop new products that the customer wants.
P1	"The fulfillment process is a mess. There are no standardized steps to follow."

Key:
R = Resource barriers
K = Knowledge barriers
P = Process barriers

The next perspective the T&D practitioner collects might be from company records on customer complaints. These data would provide the specific reasons that customers are unhappy. If these data also showed that customers were complaining about difficulty in hearing the employees over the phone, a much stronger case for changing the phone system would be made. Another source of data might be the number and type of product returns that have occurred. What's vital when synthesizing data is that a clear focus remains on telling a compelling story.

Remember that the goal of all data collection is to provide the client and stakeholders with the right information to use to make sound decisions. If they are not armed with persuasive data, the case for change will be difficult to make. Spend an appropriate amount of time determining which research questions can be answered with confidence, which ones seem to have some data to support the original hypothesis, and which ones really have no data to support or reject the original assumption. Remember that no data are data. If an important organizational issue is not being tracked in any meaningful way, this is a revealing element of the problem. In general, organizations track issues that are important to them.

Displaying Data

All clients have preferences when it comes to the look and feel of a presentation or report. It is important to establish the report guidelines up front. Some clients only want an executive summary and the supporting information in an appendix. Others expect to be walked through the entire set of findings. Some clients are visual and enjoy charts, graphics, and pictures of the performance environment. The following are some important guidelines to consider when drafting the report or presentation of the findings:

- Begin by walking the client through the methodology used for the data collection. Keep the description simple, but make sure there is enough information so that the client has confidence in the approach that was used.
- Point out strengths and limitations of the data collection approach.
- Do not drown the client in data.
- Summarize the data first without interjecting any interpretation of the data. Just stick to the facts.
- Next, highlight the data that clearly provide answers to the central questions. Do not give personal opinions of what the data say.
- Try to anticipate questions that the client may have and address them in the presentation.
- Include a distinct section that provides recommendations for change.
- Tie these recommendations to the data. Never stop using the data to justify the conclusions.
- Provide menus of options rather than a single approach toward addressing barriers.
- Include a section on "next steps," which might include a cost-benefit analysis or risk assessment.
- End with a strong set of conclusions. The client pays the most attention to the first and last pages of the report (or the first and last slides of the presentation).
- Use appendixes to back up the report and provide a clear table of contents for finding the information.

Presenting Data

Just as there are numerous ways to display data, there are numerous ways to present the data. Again, a lot depends on the client's preferences and the T&D practitioner's own comfort level with writing and speaking. A formal report carries a lot more weight than just a presentation. Even if the customer only requests a presentation, having a report to leave behind is advisable. Another possibility is to provide the report several weeks before the scheduled presentation, and then use the report as context during the presentation. During presentations, it is best to generate a discussion rather than give a lecture. If the customer has been provided with continuous status reports as the data collection effort was under way, there should not be any big surprises during the presentation. Instead, the presentation should provide a framework where learning occurs by reviewing the issues and collaborating on the ideas for moving forward. It is essential that the presentation of the data is not seen as a discrete event. There should be a lot of instances both before and after the formal presentation of the findings where the client is being educated. Also consider having multiple presenters if a formal presentation is given. It is quite powerful to have members of the target population help present the data. Their involvement can often be the most compelling testimony on the barriers, and their perspectives carry with them a certain credibility that the T&D practitioner can never have.

Conclusion

"You have to understand, my dears, that the shortest distance between truth and a human being is a story."

—Anthony de Mello, from *One Minute Wisdom*

Collecting and presenting data is a dance that combines solid reasoning, comprehensive research, and thoughtful conclusions. It is also a process of weaving a good tale. The most technically proficient data collection will still fail if it does not find a central message that resonates with the decision makers who are depending on it. Great storytelling is a process of finding authentic information that carries the true colors and flavor of the subject being described. Movies, books, and even songs feel contrived when they attempt to describe something that the author or musician does not really understand. A great literature professor once said, "If you are having trouble describing something in words, it is probably because you do not understand what you are trying to describe." When he or she crafts the final report, it will soon become apparent how well the T&D practitioner really understands the data. If the outline takes shape quickly and the words begin to flow, the story that needs to be told is probably there. If, however, there are fruitless starts and stops, the story is still hidden in the workplace. A great picture always begins with a blank canvas and a great idea. Use data collection as a process for discovering the elements that will be needed to paint that picture, and the customer will be captivated by the findings.

About the Author

Ethan S. Sanders is a senior fellow with ICF International's Organizational Research, Learning, and Performance Division. He is the former president of Sundial Learning Systems and director of organization development for the U.S. Navy's Human Performance Center. He was manager of instructional design for ASTD, where he led the research and writing of two major competency studies, redesigned several of ASTD's courses, and participated in high-profile research studies. Ethan is the co-author of *ASTD Models for Learning Technologies*, *ASTD Models for Workplace Learning and Performance*, *HPI Essentials*, and the ASTD courses on "Human Performance Improvement in the Workplace." He teaches several of ASTD's courses. He holds a master's degree in applied behavior science from Johns Hopkins University.

Reference

Rummler, G.A., and A. Brache. (1990). *Improving Performance: How to Manage the White Space on the Organization Chart*. San Francisco: Jossey-Bass.

For Further Reading

Kranzler, G., J. Moursund, and J. Kranzler. (1995). *Statistics for the Terrified*. Upper Saddle River, NJ: Prentice-Hall.

Mager, R.F., and P. Pipe. (1997). *Analyzing Performance Problems or You Really Oughta Wanna*. 3rd edition. Atlanta, GA: Center for Effective Performance.

Rossett, A. (1998). *First Things Fast: A Handbook for Performance Analysis*. San Francisco: Jossey-Bass.

Sanders, E. *ASTD Research Study: 2010 The Impact of Leadership Development Programs*. Alexandria, VA: ASTD Press.

Weisbord, M.R. (1978). *Organizational Diagnosis: A Workbook of Theory and Practice*. Reading, MA: Addison Wesley.

Zemke, R., and T. Kramlinger. (1982). *Figuring Things Out: A Trainer's Guide to Task, Needs, and Organizational Analysis*. New York: Addison Wesley.

Chapter 9

Analyzing Needs to Select the Best Delivery Method

Jean Barbazette

·· **In This Chapter** ··

- Learn how to determine the most appropriate class size for training.
- Understand the benefits and drawbacks of physical and virtual classrooms.
- Learn how to schedule training sessions for the best results.

How do you determine the best delivery method to achieve optimum learning results? You must take information from other types of needs assessments and identify how, when, and where you will deliver training. The best time to do this is when you are assessing and analyzing needs. You can compare different delivery mediums, as well as address scheduling issues and other logistics, in the context of the organization and the learning objectives. This chapter provides tools for comparing delivery options by class size, and explores the issues surrounding delivery in both physical and virtual classrooms.

How Will the Training Be Delivered?

Once you have identified the target population and the learning objectives, select the best medium or setting to deliver training to reach the objectives based on class size. Training can be delivered to a group of learners or one individual; it can be self-paced or on the job. For example, the learning objectives in interpersonal or supervisory skills training often require practice with other participants to achieve mastery. In this instance, group training in a physical classroom is more appropriate than self-paced training delivered over the Internet.

Group training can be delivered in a physical or virtual classroom. Individual or self-paced training can be delivered using a variety of high-tech (computer-based training) and low-tech (complete a workbook) options in a physical or virtual classroom. On-the-job training is usually delivered in the workplace and is often delivered by a supervisor to one learner or a small group of learners.

Determining Class Size

Table 9-1 shows five factors to consider when choosing the best class size for training: cost, consistency, delivery time, expertise of the trainer, and other considerations.

- Delivery cost is highest among the three options for on-the-job training since the time of the trainer or supervisor is repeated each time one person or a small group receives training.
- Consistency is maintained best when the entire group hears the same message and experiences the same training together. The more often training is repeated, the greater the opportunity for a variety of messages to be given and received. Consistency can diminish when several trainers deliver the same information, especially when a lesson plan is vague or unscripted. In self-paced training, consistency depends on the quality of the materials.
- Delivery time looks at how many people can be trained in a short period. If 200 people are trained in one group or eight smaller groups, the training can be accomplished quickly. Conversely, if 200 employees are required to take self-paced training, there are likely to be compliance issues. It will take the longest time to train 200 employees individually or in small groups.
- Expertise of the trainer must be high when the content expert meets with the group. The expertise of the trainer for self-paced training must be imbedded in the materials, since the individual reading the self-paced material usually does not have the opportunity to clarify understanding with the trainer. Expertise of the trainer for on-the-job delivery is rated medium, since most on-the-job trainers have subject matter expertise but little adult learning knowledge and skill.
- Other considerations include added travel costs if the target population needs to travel to join the group session. Self-paced training experiences a larger dropout rate than classroom training. Learners need to provide internal motivation to finish a self-paced course. On-the-job training consumes real materials and delays regular production work while the training occurs.

Table 9-1. Comparison of Three Delivery Options by Class Size

Delivery Option	Cost	Consistency	Delivery Time	Required Expertise of Trainer	Other Considerations
Group	Medium	High	Low	High	Travel costs
Self-paced	Medium	Medium	Medium	High	Dropout rate
On the job	High	Low	High	Medium	Waste and delay

Physical and Virtual Classrooms

After you have determined the most appropriate class size, decide whether a physical or virtual classroom is most beneficial to achieve learning objectives. Consider the physical location of the target population and whether the time away from the job to travel is excessive or more expensive than the virtual classroom option. There are two options for virtual training delivery: instructor-led or synchronous training (instructor and learners meet at the same time in different locations) and asynchronous training (the learner receives a one-way communication from a trainer through a recording). Here is an example: A U.S. federal government agency conducted a four-hour workshop via satellite for over 200 employees at 80 downlinks. This choice was more cost-effective than paying travel expenses for 200 employees to reach the same location.

Table 9-2 shows a comparison of physical and virtual delivery options. Consider these five factors when deciding whether a physical or virtual classroom is best to achieve learning objectives: location cost, travel cost, timely delivery, expertise of the trainer, and other considerations.

- Once a physical classroom is built, the only cost is the cost per square foot to use and maintain that space. Once a learning management system is purchased, the only cost is to use and maintain the system.
- Travel cost for a widely dispersed population, like the one in the previous example, can be high for physical classroom delivery. However, if the target population is not widely dispersed, travel cost is not a factor when comparing physical and virtual classrooms.
- Timely delivery of training depends on the availability of the physical classroom. The more training programs presented at a given facility, the greater the competition for that space. It is often easier to schedule virtual training than physical space.
- The requirement for trainer expertise is often higher when the trainer can physically see the participants. The virtual trainer must actively work to overcome the barrier of loss of sight to be effective.

- Distractions can plague both the physical and virtual classrooms. In the physical classroom, disruptive participants can start side conversations, enter and leave the classroom, use cell phones, and engage in all manner of other distractions. In the virtual classroom, the greatest distraction is multitasking by bored participants or dropping out before the conclusion of training.

Table 9-2. Comparison of Physical and Virtual Delivery Options

Delivery Option	Location Cost	Travel Cost for Widely Dispersed Population	Timely Delivery	Required Expertise of Trainer	Other Considerations
Physical	Medium	High	Medium ease	High	Distractions or disruptions
Virtual, instructor-led	Medium	Low	High ease	Medium	Distractions or disruptions
Virtual, asynchronous	Medium	Low	High ease	Medium	Dropout rate

Considerations for Physical Classrooms

If you will conduct group training in a physical classroom, decide whether the space available at the organization's location is appropriate for use as a classroom. Other physical classroom locations might include rented space at a hotel, conference center, or learning laboratory. Some workshops, like strategic planning and team building, are best held off-site to avoid interruptions and distractions of corporate classrooms. Table 9-3 compares four factors when conducting training on-site and off-site: location cost, ease of scheduling, quality of food and service, and other considerations.

- The cost of using existing training space is lower compared with that of a hotel or conference center.
- The ease of scheduling an internal facility is simpler when compared with external facilities where competition for space can be greater. However, if there is great competition for internal space, these ratings would change.
- Generally, the quality of catered food and service increases when using high-end facilities like conference centers. Obviously, there are exceptions to this statement.
- Other considerations for selecting a training site include fewer interruptions of participants at an external site. Weigh that against the travel time for participants to reach the external site. At conference centers and resort properties, sports, shopping, and other interests often compete with attending training.

Table 9-3. Comparison of Three Delivery Options by Location

Delivery Option	Location Cost	Ease of Scheduling	Quality of Food and Service	Other Considerations
On-site	Low	Variable	Variable	Interruptions
Off-site hotel	Medium	Medium	Medium	Travel time
Off-site conference center	High	Variable	High	Competing interests Travel time

Considerations for Virtual Classrooms

There are several options for virtual classroom delivery, including instructor-led (synchronous) training delivered via satellite, video or telephone conferencing, the Internet, or intranet via a local area network (LAN). The software program used to deliver training over the LAN is called a learning management system (LMS).

Asynchronous training (learners attend training alone at different times) is self-paced training delivered via the Internet, CD or DVD, or LAN. Also, asynchronous training can be attended by a group of individuals who learn the same material at different times. How asynchronous training is delivered often depends on the resources available in a given organization. For example, consider whether the target population has access to a desktop or laptop computer with a DVD drive, or Internet access with a high-speed connection via a tablet, iPad, or other mobile device. If the training has streaming video or complex graphics as part of the session, using a DVD or high-speed connection will allow smoother delivery than using a dial-up modem. If the target population is attending training in a virtual classroom that uses the Internet, consult with your organization's IT department about firewall and other access issues.

Table 9-4 compares virtual delivery options using six factors: cost of purchase, cost of delivery, consistency, timely delivery, expertise of the trainer, and class size. The first shows that the more sophisticated the technology, the higher the initial cost of purchase.

- Again, the cost of delivery for an individual training event decreases with the sophistication of the technology.
- The consistency of the training content is high in all delivery mediums for the virtual classroom. Everyone sees the same message.
- The timeliness of delivery depends on the availability of the technology and the schedules of the individuals who are to attend the training. Looking at the availability of the technology alone, it usually takes longer to schedule satellite delivery than video or telephone conferencing. Intranet (such as Skype or Google Hangout)

and CD or DVD delivery is controlled internally, so it is usually easier to schedule delivery. Internet-delivered training often depends on an external provider and is subject to the provider's schedule as well as internal schedules.

■ As for the expertise of the trainer, the synchronous delivery methods depend on the content and technical expertise of the trainer. The more a skilled physical classroom trainer practices with the virtual delivery medium, the greater the transference of the trainer's skills from the physical to the virtual classroom. Even the most expert physical classroom trainer requires technical help in getting the most from the virtual delivery medium. With the CD or DVD option, direct communication with the trainer is a greater challenge.

■ Optimum class size for each virtual delivery option is only limited by the technology. Including more than five video or telephone conference sites makes participation difficult.

Table 9-4. Comparison of Five Virtual Delivery Options

Delivery Option for Virtual Classroom	Cost of Purchase	Cost of Delivery	Consistency	Timely Delivery	Required Expertise of Trainer	Class Size
Satellite	High	High	High	Medium	Medium	Practically unlimited
Video conference	Medium	Medium	High	High	Medium	Best used with less than five sites
Intranet (LMS)	High	Medium	High	High	Medium	Practically unlimited
Internet	High	Medium to High	High	Medium	Medium to High	Practically unlimited
CD or DVD	Low	Low	High	High	Low	Individual

Blended Learning

Finally, consider if a blended learning option is appropriate to meet the learning objectives. Blended learning uses more than one delivery medium. For example, interpersonal skills like mentoring can be taught by starting with a self-paced component that requires learners to read background information about essential elements of mentoring programs or to complete a personal assessment (either hard copy or online). Next, a group discussion around mentoring issues and problems can be conducted in a physical classroom or synchronous session using the Internet. The target population can complete specific assignments to begin mentoring a protégé and report back to the group at the next meeting.

After deciding on the delivery medium, consider when to schedule the training.

When Will the Training Be Presented?

To schedule a training session, first consider the size of the target population and whether attendance is mandatory or voluntary. Decide whether a specific training session is a part of several sessions or independent of other training. Can individual sessions of a series be taken in random or sequential order?

What is the availability of skilled trainers to present the training? Are trainers internal employees or external contractors? What is the optimum size group to meet the learning objective and not exceed the physical space available? For example, an information briefing or update is easily conducted for a large number of participants. However, if skill development is part of the objective, practice and feedback are needed to develop a skill, and a class size of 12 to 20 will bring better learning results.

Finally, consider other restrictions that can affect training. Many organizations do not conduct voluntary training on Monday or Friday, since other work and personal issues compete for the learners' attention on those days. Often the beginning or end of a month is a difficult time to conduct training due to business needs and reporting requirements. Avoid holidays and peak vacation times.

Decide if training is conducted during work hours and employees are released from regular work to attend training. Some organizations conduct training before or after normal work hours and compensate employees by paying overtime or providing equivalent time off. Discuss workload considerations with supervisors to determine how many employees can be away from work to attend training as a group. Sometimes, it is difficult for employees to be away from work for more than a few hours, so a one-day workshop might need to be scheduled as two half-day sessions, or even four two-hour sessions. If employees must be replaced while attending training, you must also consider the availability of replacement personnel.

What Are the Other Requirements to Deliver the Training?

Some training requires that employees complete prework before attending training. Consider how this requirement can be met by the employees attending training. Will employees be given time away from their regular duties to complete prework, or are they to complete prework on their own time?

Some training requires practice between sessions. When and where will employees complete these practice sessions or homework assignments? If practice sessions include applying what is learned in the classroom to the job, what tools are provided for the practice? How will the employee's supervisor be involved in practice sessions? Will the learner use a checklist or skills observation sheet to report practice and progress between class sessions?

Consider if there are other requirements to deliver training. For example, if employees are union workers, some provisions in the labor contract might affect training. What type of record keeping for attendance at training is required? Be sure to consider these and other requirements when scheduling training sessions.

Wrapping Up

Let's consider an example of how, when, and where to present "Customer Call Training" for 120 customer service representatives (CSRs). Half of the 120 CSRs work from 7:00 a.m. to 3:00 p.m., and the other half work from 3:00 p.m. to 11:00 p.m. The learning objectives for this training include practice to develop interpersonal skills through discussions and role plays. Since all 120 employees work in the same place, group training in a physical (not virtual) classroom is most cost-effective and addresses the learning objectives for this mandatory training.

Supervisors request that the training sessions be delivered in two four-hour modules with no more than 20 CSRs attending training at a time. No training for this group is held on Mondays, since that is a peak call day. Conducting training before or after a shift would incur overtime expenses that the company is not willing to pay. Therefore, a schedule of six classes of 20 people each (three for the first shift and three for the second shift) for the first module and another six classes for the second module of training seems to meet this organization's needs. This organization has two classrooms that are shared with other departments that conduct training. The schedule for the next two months shows one classroom is available on each shift every Friday. For consistency, only two trainers will teach all the classes. One trainer is assigned to the first shift, and the other trainer is assigned to the second shift. The supervisors and the trainers will listen to live calls between the presentations of the modules to find out whether what was learned in the classroom transferred to the job.

Finally, the checklist in Table 9-5 is a tool that can remind you of all the requirements to consider when selecting the best delivery method for optimum results. You may download this checklist on the *Handbook's* website at www.astdhandbook.org.

Table 9-5. Delivery Method Checklist

How will training be delivered?
- ☐ Group
- ☐ Individual or self-paced
- ☐ On the job

Where will training be delivered?
- ☐ Physical classroom
  - ☐ Organization's site
  - ☐ Off-site at conference center, hotel, or learning laboratory
- ☐ Virtual classroom
  - ☐ Instructor-led training (same time, not necessarily same place), also called synchronous delivery
    - ☐ Satellite downlink
    - ☐ Video conference
    - ☐ Telephone conference
  - ☐ Asynchronous training (different times, different places)
    - ☐ Internet
    - ☐ CD or DVD
    - ☐ Local area network
    - ☐ Video
    - ☐ Printed workbook
- ☐ On the job
- ☐ Blended learning

When will training be presented? Consider these requirements or restrictions:
- ☐ Days of the week
- ☐ Workload
- ☐ Peak times during the month
- ☐ Organization holidays
- ☐ Peak vacation or leave times
- ☐ Space available
- ☐ Optimum size of the group
- ☐ Training during work hours or before or after work hours
- ☐ Number of hours permitted away from the job
- ☐ Compliance with collective bargaining agreement
- ☐ Prework options
- ☐ Practice required between workshop sessions
- ☐ Record keeping of attendance at training sessions
- ☐ Equipment and logistical support needed
- ☐ Number of instructors needed and available
- ☐ Willingness and ability of managers to provide coaching as needed

About the Author

Jean Barbazette is the founder of the Training Clinic of Seal Beach, CA. The Training Clinic is the leading train-the-trainer company in the United States. Her company conducts performance consulting, training function audits, and needs assessments; designs training programs; develops lesson plans, self-paced learning packages, games, and simulations; and presents seminars on over 30 different topics. Workshops include Training Trainers, e-Facilitation, New Employee Orientation, Communications, Management and Supervision, Interpersonal Skills, Sales and Customer Service, and Administrative Assistant Effectiveness. Twenty trainers in the United States, Canada, the Netherlands, Hungary, and Colombia present the workshops. Jean has authored eight books on various train-the-trainer topics and is a frequent presenter at ASTD's international conferences and *Training* magazine's conferences. You can reach Jean at jean@thetrainingclinic.com or visit the website at www .thetrainingclinic.com.

Reference

Portions of this chapter were adapted from *Training Needs Assessment: Methods, Tools, and Techniques* (Pfeiffer, 2006) and used with permission.

For Further Reading

Barbazette, J. (2006). *The Art of Great Training Delivery*. San Francisco: Pfeiffer.

Barbazette, J. (2006). *Training Needs Assessment*. San Francisco: Pfeiffer.

Barbazette, J. (2007). *Managing the Training Function for Bottom-Line Results*. San Francisco: Pfeiffer.

Barbazette, J. (2013). *How to Write Terrific Training Materials*. San Francisco: Pfeiffer.

Chapter 10

You Want It When? Balancing Time, Quality, and Expectations Before Designing

Jenn Labin and Halelly Azulay

.... **In This Chapter** ....

- Identify three specific methods for managing stakeholder expectations.
- Obtain four approaches to employee development outside the classroom.
- Consider four opportunities for high-impact approaches to design.

....

Employee development is increasingly being squeezed for high-quality output on shorter timelines and smaller budgets. This problem is not a new one; however, there are a growing number of inexpensive, quick, high-impact development opportunities you may not have considered that address constraint issues. The role of workplace learning professionals should encompass coaching stakeholders on expanding their definition of employee development and helping them think outside the classroom.

As new ways for delivering on employee development needs are added, workplace learning professionals must keep their focus on managing stakeholder expectations and solving critical issues for the organization instead of getting sidetracked by the latest new method or tool.

In the end, a successful employee development project meets or exceeds stakeholder expectations. This chapter will introduce methods for managing these expectations, describe specific time- and budget-saving approaches to development that expand your toolkit, and provide additional insight into how to take your employee development to the next level.

Managing Stakeholder Expectations

A large part of the success of employee development will depend on your ability to effectively communicate with the appropriate people at the right time. A workplace learning professional must be able to identify stakeholders, set expectations with each group, and communicate throughout the entire process. This section will look at how to create a stakeholder map, facilitate a project initiation meeting, and design an effective communication plan.

Stakeholder mapping is a critical step in managing expectations because it creates transparency across your target audience and organizational leadership and clarifies the people who need to be involved at each step of the process. The purpose of this tool is to clearly identify each group, role, or individual who needs to be considered when communicating, analyzing, designing, developing, or seeking approval throughout the project.

Figure 10-1 shows a partial sample stakeholder map that has been completed for a leadership development project with multiple layers of approval needed. This document helps everyone on the project team understand the relationship of key audiences and individuals and how they relate to the project.

When creating a stakeholder map, it is important to think through every group and individual who will need to be involved throughout the project. This helps to ensure that everyone is involved at the time they need to be and communicated with in ways that they expect. One outcome of this exercise is greater ownership over the process by people throughout your organization, as well as decreased resistance because of more effective communication.

Do not forget your employees' managers. One of the most overlooked groups of stakeholders is the people who supervise the target audience members. Consider how your proposed development solution will affect these supervisors and managers and how you can include them in the design process. By expanding their view of what options they may consider for their employee development needs, you will be better able to engage managers and win their support for your suggested solutions.

Figure 10-1. Stakeholder Map (Partial)

	Role in the Project	What Do We Need From Them?	Perceptions/ Expectations	Points of Engagement
CEO	• Final approval for big milestones • Inform monthly on progress	• Consult on philosophy of program • Approval at checkpoints	• Unhappy with candidate pool • Wants measurable improvement after 18 months	• Kick-off meeting • Monthly email communication • Hard copy deliverables for review
HR Director	• Project sponsor • Approval of all deliverables, communications • Inform progress weekly	• Makes critical decisions • Represents best interest of business • Provides resources	• Committed to CEO a successful leadership development program within 18 months	• Kick-off meeting • Weekly progress meeting • All deliverables for review • Bi-weekly meeting w/ CEO
High-Potential Employees	• Target audience	• Expectations for program • Review of content • Pilot group for content	• Excited about potential new program, want to be involved	• Kick-off meeting (representatives) • Quarterly email • Pilot group for testing and review
Managers of Target Audience	• Need buy-in for healthy adoption by target audience	• Expectations for program • Review/feedback for content	• Concerned about employee time away from work, hesitant	• Kick-off meeting (representatives) • Quarterly email • Pilot group for feedback
IT/HR	• Support functions for design and development	• Consult on legal and technological constraints and opportunities	• Feel like they are usually brought in too late on projects	• Kick-off meeting (representatives) • Monthly email • Involved in testing

A second method for managing stakeholder expectations is through the effective facilitation of a project initiation meeting. The purpose of the meeting is to share critical project information and ensure that there is complete transparency about the project goals, process, constraints, and expectations. At the conclusion of the meeting, everyone involved with the project should share the same vision for the end result of the project and how you will get there.

The project initiation meeting can be held in person or virtually, depending on the needs of your organization. It is not strictly required to hold the meeting prior to the project kick-off, but you certainly want to make sure it takes place before any significant amount of work is undertaken.

A project initiation meeting for a small, straightforward project can be fairly quick, while more complex projects may require a whole day set aside to work through all the important details. If you have completed a stakeholder map before you started work on the project, it should be clear whom to invite to this meeting. You will want to make sure that your project sponsor and project manager are present, as well as any stakeholders who were listed independently as approvers for the project (such as the CEO in Figure 10-1). In addition, be sure to invite representatives of groups of stakeholders listed in your map. You may want to ask for one or more participants from your target audience, management population, IT, marketing, finance, or other departments, all depending on the groups of people affected by your project.

Depending on the size and culture of your organization, you may have a difficult time scheduling a meeting that works for everyone. So, how do you get the right people together? It is essential to communicate the importance of the meeting and ensure that invited stakeholders understand the expectation that decisions will be made during the time together. Participants will have a hard time declining an invitation when they know that the outcome of the meeting will have an impact on their workload, development opportunities, budget, and so on.

It is also important that you provide an agenda prior to the meeting so that you appropriately manage expectations. Be sure to assess your stakeholder map to identify anyone who should review or approve the agenda before it is sent out. Figure 10-2 shows a sample agenda for a project initiation meeting.

After the conclusion of your meeting, it is important to send a summary of the meeting, minimally outlining key decisions and actions from your time together, to all stakeholders.

A third tool for managing stakeholder expectations is a communication plan. Well-designed communication plans are often the difference between projects that run on time and under budget and those that do not. A communication plan is built on the work done on the stakeholder map and during the project initiation meeting. Both previous tools will create outputs that help complete much of the communication plan for you.

The communication plan begins with identifying all stakeholders who will need to be communicated with throughout the life cycle of your employee development project. In some cases, you will need to break down your list of stakeholders into more specific and targeted groups for more effective planning. Once stakeholders has been identified, you will need to determine when they should be communicated with and by what methods. Figure 10-3 shows a partial communication plan to illustrate this point further.

Figure 10-2. Project Initiation Meeting Agenda

<table>
<tr><td colspan="4" align="center">Project Initiation Meeting: Leadership Development Program</td></tr>
<tr>
<td>Attendees</td>
<td>Karen Smith, CEO

Jane Doe, Rep of Hi-Po Group</td>
<td>Rob Hollisman, HR Director

Wilson Mackee, Rep of Manager Group</td>
<td>Sylvia Toms, HR Project Manager

Maria Rodriguez, IT
Daniel Webb, Legal</td>
</tr>
<tr>
<td>Meeting</td>
<td>Tuesday, May 6</td>
<td>8 a.m.–3 p.m.</td>
<td>Executive Conference Room</td>
</tr>
<tr>
<td>Agenda</td>
<td colspan="3">

8 a.m.–9:30 a.m.
- Project purpose and alignment to organizational goals (Karen Smith)
- Description of proposed project (Rob Hollisman)
- Project team members

9:30 a.m.–11:30 a.m.
- Goals and metrics of success
- Constraints on project
- Resources available for project

11:30 a.m.–12:30 p.m.
- Working lunch: creating a common vision for leadership development

12:30 p.m.–2 p.m.
- Project plan, milestones, timeline, deliverables
- Communication pan

2 p.m.–3 p.m.
- Next steps

</td>
</tr>
</table>

There are several benefits of a well-executed communication plan. Your stakeholders will feel engaged and have ownership in the process. You will have a proactive plan to check in periodically with stakeholders, rather than reacting as project obstacles arise. Team members and stakeholders will have appropriate expectations of when they will be communicated with and by what means.

All three of these tools—the stakeholder map, project initiation meeting, and communication plan—help effectively manage stakeholder expectations in order to set up your employee development project for success. Using these tools and events will create a strong foundation on which you can develop influential learning.

Figure 10-3. Communication Plan (Partial)

	Project Initiation and Planning	Progress Updates	Deliverable Reviews/ Approval	Pilot
CEO	• Facilitates kick-off meeting	• Monthly email • Bi-weekly meetings with HR Director • Periodic calls with project team	• Approves project documents and all deliverables • Reviews communications	• Participates in pilot offering
HR Director	• Facilitates kick-off meeting • Collaborates on project planning	• Weekly meetings, PM • Bi-weekly calls, project team • Periodic calls, leadership team	• Approves project documents and deliverables • Reviews status documents	• Observes pilot offering
Managers of Target Audience	• Representatives participate in kick-off meeting	• Monthly status updates • Pre-launch call	• Representatives review deliverables for feedback	• Representatives participate in pilot
IT/HR	• Representatives participate in kick-off meeting	• Bi-weekly project team calls • Weekly status updates	• Review deliverables for QA	• Observe pilot offering

Four Approaches to Employee Development Outside the Classroom

Another key aspect of managing expectations is defining the path for employee development. Regardless of the employee development needs you and the stakeholders have identified, one of the most common errors that managers, leaders, and workplace learning professionals make is focusing too narrowly when looking for the best ways to address those learning needs. As workplace learning professionals, our challenge is to expand their purview and increase awareness of the variety of solutions for knowledge and skills gaps they identified. There has been an explosion in the volume of information being shared recently about the wonders of informal learning methodologies, yet many of the end-users of employee development are unsure of how to effectively apply it.

There are many available informal learning options, and the number is only growing. This section will share a brief description of four ways to develop employees outside the classroom. It is by no means an exhaustive list. The four nontraining employee development methods described here are self-directed learning, mentoring, stretch and rotational assignments, and teaching others.

Self-Directed Learning

One of the oldest informal development methods, and the most basic, is self-directed learning, for which learners are "flying solo" on their development programs. Self-directed learning is a great option for developing employees anytime and almost anywhere. Solutions such as reading books or blogs, listening to podcasts or audiobooks, watching educational videos on TED or YouTube, or apprenticing and trying to practice a new skill with a master or a role model are but a few of the endless opportunities for self-directed learning. Libraries, online resources, and other employees are all examples of freely available resources that are readily accessible. Employees who are working on function-specific skills and competencies can use trade publications, conferences, or professional associations as resources. The competencies that can be developed through self-directed learning are virtually unlimited. Because it is so multifaceted and can be performed by anyone in almost any place, learning independently can be successfully achieved in almost any realm.

Help managers and other stakeholders assess their employees' learning needs, readiness, and style to see if self-directed development is appropriate. Self-directed learning encourages responsibility and ownership and puts learners in control of their experience. Therefore, to fully benefit, employees must be self-motivated and independent. Any employee, at any level, in any part of the organization, can benefit from self-directed learning because it can be tailored to suit one's individual learning level. However, employees who are not self-motivated, or who have significant concerns or inhibitions about the subject matter or their ability to be successful, would probably not find this kind of learning appealing.

It is important to note that learning in a vacuum is usually not enough to see real and significant performance improvement, regardless of the method, but this is especially true for self-directed learning. To take development to the next level, schedule follow-up meetings, book club discussions, email lists, or learning cohorts for enhanced learning. According to a study done by Brent Peterson of Columbia University, 50 percent of our ability to change and improve our behavior comes *after* a learning event. Therefore, an individual who reads a book on his or her own and never has the opportunity to discuss what he or she took away from it loses an opportunity to see growth. As discussed later in this chapter, it will be important to create follow-up and reinforcement opportunities to optimize the value that the learners can extract from these (and all) development methods.

Mentoring

Another common and important informal and inexpensive development method is mentoring. Whether acting in the role of the mentor or the protégé, participating in a mutually beneficial mentoring relationship (within or outside your organization) allows employees to develop a variety of new knowledge and skills and requires few resources (except a little bit of time). Employees can learn tricks of the trade and technical information, and can develop "softer" competencies such as leadership, networking and partnering, coaching, and listening skills. Formal mentoring programs match protégés with identified performance gaps to skilled mentors with strengths in those respective areas. Effective employee development is also found through informal mentoring relationships.

Mentoring relationships are most frequently conducted on a one-to-one basis. However, mentoring can also take place in groups or one-to-many arrangements. Finally, while most mentoring relationships last for a predetermined amount of time (usually nine months to one year), you can also arrange situational mentoring relationships to address a particular learning need or issue. The *Handbook's* website at www.astdhandbook.org includes a mentoring readiness tool for you to use.

The benefits to the employees, both mentor and protégé, are significant. Mentors can benefit by gaining a greater understanding of the barriers experienced at lower levels of the organization, and by enhancing their coaching, counseling, listening, feedback, and behavioral modeling skills. Mentors also are able to increase their generational awareness and benefit from an opportunity to help someone develop. Protégés, on the other hand, can gain skill and knowledge enhancement, as well as encouragement to stretch to new goals, overcome challenges, and explore novel career options. Also, their learning curve can be significantly shortened. One organization was able to accelerate the learning curve for a specific job role. It launched a mentoring program that reinforced classroom training for some individuals and compared them with another group that didn't receive the follow-up mentoring. The study showed that mentoring reduced the learning curve (the number of months it took a new hire to become "fully functional" in the role) by 28 percent, from 18 to 13 months. In addition, protégés gain career development opportunities, new or different perspectives and insights into business issues, and an opportunity to learn the organization's dos and don'ts and unwritten rules.

Mentoring programs create tremendous benefits for organizations as well. These include increased employee engagement, retention, higher productivity and performance, knowledge management, and the support of diversity and inclusion efforts within the organization.

The specific goals you set with employees to develop the selected competencies through participating in a mentoring relationship can be tracked in a variety of ways. Here are a few examples:

- A journal is one of the best tools that partners in a mentoring relationship can use to reflect on their progress and insights so they can glean developmental accomplishment.
- Employees who have prementoring feedback data from a 360-degree assessment or other sources can repeat the data collection at the end of the mentoring relationship to assess how well they progressed in demonstrating their chosen developmental competencies.
- Protégés seeking to expand their networks may choose to measure the number of new contacts they have gained as a result of the mentoring relationship.

Stretch and Rotational Assignments

A third way to develop employees outside the classroom and without incurring great expense is by placing employees in stretch and job rotation assignments. These kinds of assignments serve the purpose of taking employees out of their comfort zones and catalyzing development. In addition to learning new or enhancing existing skills, they must cope with the uncertainties and stress of a new setting or activity. This helps them to develop resourcefulness and resiliency in addition to new skills. Job rotation assignments involve assigning employees to different positions in the organization—usually lateral positions—so that the employees can learn new skills through immersion in the positions for an agreed-upon amount of time. A stretch assignment is a task or a project that employees undertake as part of their current position, but the task/project is beyond their job description and challenges and broadens their current skills.

Employees in job rotation or stretch assignments will need to have management support before, during, and after the assignment. It is critical to find the right balance of stretching employees a bit beyond their comfort zone, but not too far beyond it.

Job rotations and stretch assignments benefit both the employee and the organization in several ways. For the employee, such assignments help to not only build new skills, but also can reduce complacency, stimulate creativity, and increase both job satisfaction and engagement. For organizations, benefits include increased retention, greater leadership bench strength, alignment of competencies to organizational goals, and often more efficient and lower-cost learning.

Rotation Readiness

Before initiating a rotational assignment, consider these:

- The assignment will push the employee just beyond the current comfort zone.
- A plan is in place for meeting the business needs in the employee's current role during this temporary absence.
- The new team has the capacity to accept and assimilate the employee for the duration of the assignment.
- A plan is in place to ensure a smooth transition from one role to the other.

In preparing for a stretch or rotational assignment, the employee must be ready for the challenges inherent in the assignment. Track progress and results by determining the developmental goals the assignment helps address and the measures that will be used to track the employee's progress toward them. For instance, employees developing decisiveness can journal about their decision-making process and results. Being able to show increased speed and quality of those decisions will be a great way to show progress. Another idea to help sustain and promote success is building a community of practice (CoP) of employees who are taking part in these kinds of assignments. The CoP can be hosted online, with opportunities for group interaction, leadership, and support.

Teaching Others

A fourth development method to consider that allows employees to grow skills and competencies without any significant cost to the organization is encouraging them to develop or present learning programs for other employees (or in the organization's community). There's an old Japanese proverb that says, "To teach is to learn." If you want to help your employees develop quickly, give them an opportunity to teach others. It could involve taking a role of co-presenter or co-trainer at one of your on-site training programs, or it could be helping them find an opportunity to design, develop, and present a short workshop to their colleagues.

Any employee, at any level or from any department, can initiate, design, develop, or present a workshop or a brown bag session. Employees may be experts on a topic and want to share their knowledge with colleagues or may have a story of a challenge they faced and overcame so others also can benefit from the lessons they learned. Or, employees may want to learn more about a topic, issue, product, process, or anything else that may also be of interest to others in the organization, and might use an internal training (or brown bag lunchtime) session as a catalyst for learning as they prepare to teach about it.

Finally, this is a great developmental opportunity for employees whose development goal is to become better presenters or trainers, in which case the subject is irrelevant, because the benefit to the presenter is in the preparation for and delivery of the presentation itself. Additional benefits include developing a deeper understanding and knowledge about a topic of interest, as well as increasing the employee's visibility and reputation as an internal expert within the organization.

By engaging employees in the development and presentation of brown bag sessions or other short presentations, the organization can gain multiple benefits. First, they can now offer more learning sessions to staff participants at no cost. Also, the work performed by those who develop and deliver the teaching materials creates collaborative knowledge management and cross-training opportunities throughout the organization. Finally, organizations can realize shared problem-resolution strategies across teams/departments, as well as enhanced internal expertise and depth of understanding of organization-specific areas of focus such as products and services, internal systems, or operational procedures.

Consider Four Opportunities for High-Impact Approaches to Design

So far, we have described how to ensure you assess and manage your stakeholders' expectations and expand their thinking about employee development options. No matter what type of employee development method you choose, there are ways to increase the effectiveness before you begin designing the event itself. In this final section, we will share four ways you can design for a high-impact punch: work across organizational functional silos, engage leadership in all aspects of the project, optimize templates and materials for reuse and recycling, and build in opportunities for evaluation and reinforcement.

One way to increase the power of your employee development design is to use cross-functional efforts. "Nontraditional" methods for employee development require organizational savvy, business acumen, and a good network across the organization. However, involving individuals from across different roles and positions helps expand the credibility and perspective of any employee development project. Your employees will benefit from participating in development solutions with broader business implications and support.

Example: Lena is a branch manager, and her employee Ryan is developing his business acumen skills. Lena has been meeting regularly with other departments, so she knows there is a task force on competitor analysis being formed in the marketing department. She works with the leader of that team to incorporate Ryan into the team as a stretch assignment for a set amount of time each week. This development opportunity creates highly effective learning opportunities for Ryan, brings additional employee resources to the task force, and helps Lena develop her employee with few additional resources.

Another facet of cross-functional efforts is the development of non-ISDs to be more involved in the process of formal learning with an expanded role. When we are in instructional design mode, we frequently rely on subject matter experts (SMEs) for content. What if we enhanced the role of the SMEs to one that is specifically developmental for them? We could leverage the opportunity to create two-edged benefits to the organization by creating a mentoring or stretch assignment for the SMEs in which they learn instructional design competencies during their time as SMEs. These skills translate to a wide variety of project and people management competencies. Individuals who increase their knowledge of adult learning can use their new knowledge to be better leaders.

Example: Tariq knows the budget tracking technology thoroughly and is assigned to support Wanda as a SME on her ISD project for an online job support tutorial about the system. Wanda, in turn, allows Tariq to shadow her on some of her design work and walks him through her thinking process and design considerations. Wanda incrementally involves Tariq in the actual process and provides performance feedback. Tariq finishes the project with broader perspective on how to develop employees and can now use a systematic approach to managing projects and change.

A second method for high-impact design is engaging leadership. Solicit leaders in your organization who can help as mentors, lead stretch teams, assign individuals to be taught, and facilitate portions of workshops. The involvement of leaders in employee development solutions adds broad perspective, expands strategic thinking, and lends additional credibility to your project. Employees are able to learn about the business from the leaders of the business—and that is a great formula for success.

Be sure to underline the potential effect to leaders in this work. The leaders receive the benefit of increased transparency into the needs and strengths of their workforce. This method gathers additional buy-in from individuals in the organization, which often results in stakeholders seeing the need for a longer timeline or additional resources. This method also results in lower costs without the extensive use of formal facilitators. Finally, involving leaders, who would normally be only in an approval role in your stakeholder map, throughout more of the project speeds up workflow and reduces time to delivery.

A third way to make employee development even more effective is by reusing and recycling as much as possible so you can optimize the value that your work delivers. You do not need to, and should not, reinvent activities every time. Often, templates or activity "frames" can be reused in new contexts, and all you need to do is plug in new content. For example, a "stretch assignment guidelines" document can be repurposed for mentorship or self-development activities. In addition, you might find that checklists and guides that you use during a particular learning activity can then be recycled into performance supports that allow additional learning or reinforcement to continue after the learning program. A learner's manager or peers can employ an observation sheet used during a development program for a shadow or rotational assignment at intervals after the conclusion of the assignment to check for retention and skill level.

The fourth opportunity for increasing the effectiveness and significance of your employee development solutions is through reinforcement. As mentioned previously, the time following a specific learning event, when the learner synthesizes information into changed behavior, is a hugely valuable potential period for increasing performance. The opportunity for using follow-up methods should be considered during the design process as part of the overall plan for the project. Reinforcement methods can include scheduled group or individual calls with instructors, as well as articles and readings sent at intervals following the development. A highly effective method for involving stakeholders while reinforcing content is to provide participants and their managers with activities or prompted conversation starters each week or month following the employee development project. Another great way to reinforce learning without adding to your effort is to use portions of content, exercises and activities, or job aids during the follow-up to the development project.

Prior to the implementation of your employee development project (whether it is a book, stretch assignment, or so on), be sure to schedule time in your calendar for follow-up accountability. Prepare for the follow-up conversation with discussion questions, key points, and reflections.

Keep in mind that before designing your development program, you should have clarity on how you will evaluate the process and outcomes. Consider how you will evaluate both formal approaches (such as mentoring programs and in-person training) and informal or unstructured learning methods (such as self-development through reading or TED videos and individual stretch assignments).

Keep your evaluation approach simple to save money and time. Use a single tool for evaluating progress against individual development plan (IDP) goals multiple times throughout a mentoring relationship or stretch assignment. You can also combine questions on the process (level 1) and learning outcomes (level 2) into one tool. Finally, when implementing reinforcement techniques, consider setting up a cohort of individuals working together on the same competencies. The cohort also can be formed from individuals who have participated in the same type of alternative development method. These cohorts can be used as a community of practice, such as a group of individuals assigned to "best practices in self-development." Peer groups formed after going through a similar employee development experience can often create close-knit relationships, which reinforce key learning over an extended amount of time. You can also use a one-to-one or "learning buddy" version of this reinforcement technique to create deeper relationships. Cohorts can reinforce learning through teaching others, accountability, and reflection.

Creative and innovative approaches to employee development add high value with relatively low costs and effort. Gaining an awareness of the different possibilities of cross-functional collaboration, reinforcement, and the engagement of leadership throughout your project will help ensure highly effective employee development projects while saving your time and budget. In addition, thinking about developing your employees through alternative means, such as mentorship, self-development, stretch assignments, and teaching others, will reap considerable rewards for your organization without straining resources. Even with a creative approach, success of the project requires you to effectively identify your stakeholders and proactively manage their expectations.

Workplace learning professionals are expected to be consultative in the design of development opportunities and to align with the needs of the organization and leadership. Through creativity, innovation, and a systematic approach to employee development, your project can yield tremendous results while delivering under budget, on time, and exceeding expectations. So the next time you feel like responding, "You want it when?!" to an employee development design request, we hope you will feel empowered to say, "I can do that!" and know exactly how to provide the right results, on time, and under budget.

About the Authors

For more than 15 years, **Jenn Labin** has worked with organizations to improve workforce performance through leadership development and summits, formal and informal training, change efforts, and employee engagement programs. Jenn is the author of *Real World Training Design* (ASTD Press, 2012). She has also contributed articles to the Pfeiffer Annuals in

Consulting and Training, as well as other books and publications. Credentials include an MA in instructional systems design and certifications in DISC-PIAV, Kirkpatrick Four levels, Leadership Program Development, and Presentation Design. Jenn lives near Baltimore, Maryland, with her amazing family and two turtles.

Halelly Azulay is a consultant, facilitator, speaker, and author with more than 20 years of professional experience in workplace learning and communication. She is the author of *Employee Development on a Shoestring* (ASTD Press, 2012), a book providing managers and supervisors with hands-on tools and techniques for developing employees outside the classroom. Halelly is the president of TalentGrow LLC, a consulting company specializing in leadership, communication skills, team building, facilitation, and emotional intelligence with all organizational levels, including C-level leaders, frontline managers, and individual contributors. A sought-after speaker, Halelly is also a contributing author to numerous books, articles, and blogs. She blogs at www.talentgrow.com/blog.

Reference

Portions of this chapter were adapted from "Assessing Readiness for a Mentoring Partnership" in the *2013 Pfeiffer Annual, Consulting* (Pfeiffer, 2013) and used with permission.

For Further Reading

Azulay, H. (2012). *Employee Development on a Shoestring*. Alexandria, VA: ASTD Press.

Azulay, H. (2013, January). Learning Beyond the Comfort Zone. *T+D* 67(1):76.

Biech, E. (2008). *ASTD Handbook for Workplace Learning Professionals*. Alexandria, VA: ASTD Press.

Labin, J. (2012). *Real World Training Design*. Alexandria, VA: ASTD Press.

Russell, L. (2000). *Project Management for Trainers*. Alexandria, VA: ASTD Press.

Section III

Designing and Developing Effective Learning

Section III

Ideas for Designing and Developing Effective Learning

Luminary Perspective

Sivasailam "Thiagi" Thiagarajan

I was so flattered by the invitation to write this introduction that I forgot to read the small print. Only after I accepted the invitation did I realize that it is supposed to be practical and must deal with the "hottest innovation or the newest issue."

I have no problem keeping this practical because that is the only way I train, learn, design, and write. You will find several brief pieces of practical advice. These prescriptions or guidelines are deliberately listed in a random order without sequential numbering. My recommendation is that you not count the number of guidelines, but make each guideline count.

I am not sure about the mandate to deal with "hot innovations and latest issues." Most of the latest and greatest trends appear to be a rehash of my early days as a foot soldier in the Skinnerian revolution to teach twice as much in half the time. I have become a disillusioned skeptic.

One Thing Is Different Now

On further reflection, I see there is a significant difference between the good old days and today. When I started in the training design business, my colleagues and I packaged proprietary content and sold it to our clients. To mix metaphors, content was the king and we hoarded it carefully. Nowadays, content is available everywhere. With a few mouse clicks, you will probably have access to more content than what your subject matter expert (SME) knows.

Content and Activities

Recently, I have begun to focus on the learning activities rather than the content. I specialize in integrating activities with content. Many of the guidelines in the sidebar deal with this theme. However, the relationship between training content and activities deserves a more logical discussion.

Content is information, facts, demonstrations, explanations, stories, and so on. A trainer can deliver content through lectures, reading assignments, video recordings, text on the Internet, podcasts, slide sets, charts, and other such things.

An *activity* (more fashionably called *interactivity*) is a training exercise that requires the participants to interact with each other, with the content, and with the facilitator. A trainer can use games, simulations, puzzles, role plays, discussions, debates, experiential exercises, group projects, and other such events.

Content without activities produces inert knowledge. The learners store facts and information in a passive manner and regurgitate it mindlessly. They lack the ability to apply it to the challenges in their workplace and in the real world.

Activity without content is like requiring the learners to role-play headless chicken. The room is full of tumult and shouting, with people working intensely in teams and having heated debates. At the end of the activity, the participants are confused, wondering, "What was that all about?" For example, in online learning, one of the most popular activities is to click the mouse button. When you work this way, at the end of the online course you become an expert—in pushing mouse buttons. We forget that true interactivity is in the mind and not in the mouse.

Thiagi's Guidelines for Designing and Developing Effective Learning

☐ Reduce resistance. Use change management principles to reduce or remove resistance toward activities-based learning on the part of clients, trainers, and learners.

☐ Move from live to recorded. Begin your design activity by conducting a face-to-face training session with a live instructor. Record audio and video from the class. Gradually replace the instructor with these recordings.

☐ Design and develop follow-up activities. Plan and implement follow-up coaching to ensure workplace applications.

☐ Don't reinvent the wheel. Use suitable structures and templates for presenting different types of content.

☐ Organize an online community of your learners to share their applications of what they learned in the training session.

☐ Motivate the learners. Treat the training design process as an exercise in designing an intrinsic motivational system.

☐ Throughout your training session, ask the learners to recall and apply what they have learned earlier. Give appropriate feedback.

☐ Set up the room to encourage teamwork and discussion. Arrange the seats around tables. Avoid theater seating.

☐ Form a high-performance design team. Include subject matter experts, designers, writers, typesetters, graphic artists, and representative learners in this team. Make sure that everyone is involved in the design activity from the beginning.

☐ Space the training. Abandon the idea that training should be conducted in a continuous and self-contained session. Instead, plan for a series of short training sessions followed by structured application exercises. Repeat this process with cumulative units of learning.

☐ Supply assessment checklists and rubrics that help learners to conduct self-assessment and peer assessment.

☐ Remember that behavioral objectives don't give the big picture to the learners. Present a content outline instead.

☐ Integrate content into activities. Select suitable types of activities based on the types of content resources.

☐ Make the learners interact with the content, with each other, with the facilitator, with subject matter experts, and with the real world.

☐ Improve the total performance system. Use different types of human performance technology interventions to improve participants' learning performance and application of the learned skills.

☐ Keep in touch with managers of your learners. Ask for help in preparing, motivating, supporting, and coaching the learners.

☐ Blend everything. Blend content and activities; online and face-to-face; learning and performance; training and testing; motivation and instruction; and active and passive.

☐ Provide choices to the learners. Let them decide how they want to learn and how they want to be tested.

(continued on next page)

Thiagi's Guidelines for Designing and Developing Effective Learning (continued)

☐ Remember that adult learners have rich and relevant experiences. Use activities that lure them to contribute to the learning process.

☐ Present your training objectives in plain language. Don't clutter them up with unnecessary details that confuse the learners.

☐ Align everything. While designing a training package, repeatedly align content, activities, and assessment. Align all these elements with real-world results.

☐ Open minds with open questions. Require and reward higher-order thinking. Use alternative approaches for providing feedback for open-ended responses.

☐ Remember that training is not a one-shot activity. The prework before and the follow-up after are as important as the actual session.

☐ Let the inmates run the asylum. Empower learners to co-design the training package, generate training content, and conduct training activities.

☐ Make all lectures interactive. Add interactive interludes after each segment of the lecture.

☐ Encourage learners to create training content. Use structured approaches to help them share their best practices and their collective wisdom.

☐ Begin your training session with an activity that sets up the expectation of frequent interaction. Make sure this activity is relevant to the training goal.

☐ Be a grasshopper. While designing a training package, work on any of these elements in any sequence: content, activities, and assessment.

☐ Include representative learners in the design team. Use the agile design technique to test and modify your prototype materials while designing them.

☐ Train for real-world results. Begin your training design with a focus on business outcomes and personal accomplishments.

☐ Don't let video recordings, PowerPoint slides, flipcharts, and electronic whiteboards overwhelm your training session. Use them sparingly.

☐ Frequently vary the interaction pattern: Require learners to work alone, work with partners, and work in teams.

☐ At the end of your training session, conduct a review. Use an interactive exercise to do this instead of rerunning your lecture.

☐ Encourage learners to generate questions. Incorporate closed and open questions from learners in training activities.

☐ Encourage collaborative learning. Let the learners work with each other. But emphasize the need for individual mastery.

☐ Use different training methods for teaching facts, concepts, principles, and procedures. Select the appropriate method.

☐ Keep everything—activities, examples, test items, exercises, and problems—realistic and authentic.

☐ Save activities, change content. Use frames, shells, patterns, or templates to rapidly design learning activities.

- ☐ Transform trainers into facilitators. Encourage them to become agile and flexible learning guides.
- ☐ Empower your trainers. Specify the results you require, suggest suitable activities, and provide total freedom about how the results are achieved.
- ☐ Organize follow-up coaching sessions in which the learners pair up and support each other.
- ☐ Understand that all training involves changing your learners' behaviors. Learn and apply the skills of a change manager.
- ☐ Transform trainers into designers. Encourage them to apply local finish to the training package and to enhance the suggested activities. Use feedback from all trainers to improve the training package.
- ☐ Use playful and participatory approaches for analysis, design, and evaluation. Use playful and participatory learning activities during delivery.
- ☐ Build the airplane while flying it. Design training while delivering it.
- ☐ Integrate job aids in your training. Prepare a job aid that incorporates principles and procedures related to performing a task. Then, train the people to use this job aid.
- ☐ Modularize design activities. Use units of content, activities, or assessment to divide the training package into modules. During the design, feel free to jump from one module to another.
- ☐ Change the role of learners. Ask them to play the roles of trainers, coaches, and testers.
- ☐ Shift the "start" and "finish" lines. Make maximum use of pretraining activities. Cater for lifelong learning through follow-up activities and networking.
- ☐ Train with your mouth closed. In a training session, whoever talks the most learns the most. So shut up and encourage the learners to talk and learn.
- ☐ Make it safe for people to participate in the learning process. Better yet, make it rewarding to participate.
- ☐ Treat the training design process as a creative problem-solving exercise. Use creative training approaches; require learners to come up with creative responses.
- ☐ Don't present any content that is not used in a learning activity. Don't conduct an activity that does not incorporate the content.
- ☐ Encourage contextualized learning. Increase the effectiveness of learning and efficiency of transfer by creating a training environment that reflects the work situation as closely as possible.
- ☐ Use books, job aids, articles, and references to reinforce your training. Incorporate these text materials in suitable activities.
- ☐ Conduct training activities that involve your learners teaching each other and testing each other. This reinforces their learning.
- ☐ Make sure your training is relevant to the learner's job. Brandish this relevance throughout the session.
- ☐ Encourage the learners to share examples, challenges, questions, plans, and ideas that are relevant to the training objective.
- ☐ Conduct just-in-time analyses. Let analysis and design proceed simultaneously.

Blending Content and Activity

How exactly do we integrate content and activity? Where should we begin? What comes first: content or activity? Chicken or egg?

Here's a simple prescription for effective training: *Don't present any content that is not incorporated in a training activity. Don't conduct any activity that does not incorporate relevant content.*

You can present training content before an activity. Call it *briefing*. Present facts, principles, and procedures that can be immediately applied to an ensuing activity. You can present training content after an activity. Call it *debriefing*. Encourage the learners to reflect on their experience from the activity, gain personal insights, and share it with each other. And you can present content during an activity. Call it *coaching*. Place the activity on pause and present just-in-time, just-enough content so the learners can immediately use new tools, new principles, and new procedures.

Faster, Cheaper, and Better

The secret of effective training design is to do it faster, cheaper, *and* better. Conventional wisdom dictates that you can have only two out of the three standards. But my field experience around the world reveals that faster instructional design is cheaper (no surprise here). And faster and cheaper instructional design is better (in terms of effective learning, recall, and application).

Here are three practical guidelines for ensuring faster, cheaper, and better learning:

1. Use available sources of content.
2. Use templates to create activities.
3. Align the content with activities and both of them with the real-world results.

Take any workplace training topic. Do a Google search. You will discover hundreds of thousands of links. Do a search on Amazon.com. You will discover thousands of books. Spending time to design and develop your own content materials is insanity. It may feed the ego of your SME and ensure your job security, but it does not produce effective learning.

Finding the Content

Content exists in many different archived forms: text, video, audio, graphics, and the Internet. You can find the latest useful content in books, manuals, articles, job aids, tables, tests, questionnaires, samples, cases, graphics, infographics, and online databases. In case you are about to complain that your content does not yet exist in a document form, you can get the content from SMEs, practitioners, clients, consumers, informants, and fellow learners.

Finding the Activities

The secret for the rapid design of learning activities is to begin with the thousands of field-tested activities that currently exist. You need to isolate the structure of the activity and keep the activity and change the content. There are learning activities related to different content sources. For example, interactive lectures for content from SMEs, textra games for content from reading materials, double-exposure activities for content from video recordings, and the four-door approach for content from the Internet. You can also classify the activities in your toolkit according to different types of learning, different types of learners, and different types of learning outcomes.

In Summary

At the risk of redundant repetition, here is my latest prescription:

1. Use available sources of content.
2. Use templates to create activities.
3. Align the content with activities and both of them with the real-world results.

Let Me Walk the Talk

At the risk of spouting a cliché, this is just the beginning. Reading this section's introduction is only the first step.

One of the main themes in this introduction is that you don't learn through passive reading (or listening or watching). You learn through active participation. To walk the talk, I am going to insert active assignments at different places in this introduction. Take your time to interact with the content and complete the task. Otherwise, your brain will be filled with inert knowledge.

Here are four activities for you to do next:

1. Review the guidelines I presented in this introduction. Select the one guideline that is the most important for you. Once you have done that, select the one that you are effectively applying to your current design and development activities. You may also find this list on the *Handbook's* website at www.astdhandbook.org.

2. I made a provocative statement that faster and cheaper training design produces more effective learning. Can you humor me and come up with at least three different reasons this is true? After you have done this, you can be totally cynical and make sarcastic remarks about my unjustifiable statement.

3. I strongly recommend using existing sources of content, but I am not recommending pirating other people's intellectual property. How can you use existing content in an ethical and professional, justifiable fashion?

4. Did you come across jargon that you did not recognize or concepts that you would like to learn more about? Behave like my grandson and fire up your web browser.

About the Author

Sivasailam "Thiagi" Thiagarajan is the resident mad scientist of the Thiagi Group. He makes a living by playing games and facilitating other people to play games—to produce business results. He has been the president of the North American Simulation and Gaming Association (NASAGA) five times and has been elected the president of the International Society for Performance Improvement (ISPI) twice, 25 years apart.

For Further Reading

Thiagarajan, S. (2006). *Design Your Own Games and Activities: Thiagi's Templates for Performance Improvement*. San Francisco: John Wiley & Sons.

Thiagarajan, S. (2006). *Thiagi's 100 Favorite Games*. San Francisco: John Wiley & Sons.

Thiagarajan, S., and T. Tagliati. (2012). *More Jolts! 50 Activities to Wake Up and Engage Your Participants*. San Francisco: John Wiley & Sons.

Chapter 11

Design Models and Learning Theories for Adults

Darryl L. Sink

.... **In This Chapter** ....

- ▪ Define ISD models.
- ▪ Learn how to expand ISD models to meet current delivery systems.
- ▪ Understand how learning theories influence instructional design.

....

When an organization needs training solutions, the instructional designer must understand the business and individual needs that underlie the training initiative. This requires defining the business drivers for training program development and the organizational results needed or desired.

Once the designer has taken that critical first step, instructional design models and learning theories enter the picture to provide a systematic approach (or plan) for crafting effective and efficient training solutions that meet organizational and individual needs. These plans are referred to as instructional systems design (ISD) models.

Learning theories and the strategies and tactics (that is, lesson designs) derived from ISD models can help practitioners develop optimal instructional designs for learning—designs that support the learners as they acquire the knowledge, skills, experience, and motivation needed to produce results for themselves and their organizations.

The design phase of ISD models is the point where learning theories and their resulting strategies and tactics primarily come into play. This chapter will discuss ISD with emphasis on two popular approaches: ADDIE and the Dick and Carey model. It will focus on learning theories and their influence on the ISD model design phase.

ISD Models

ISD models are based on the systems approach; the output from one model phase provides the input for the next phase. ISD model origins can be traced to the application of a systems approach by the military starting in World War II. After the war, the military applied the systems approach to the development of training materials and programs.

During the 1960s, the systems approach began to appear in procedural models of instructional design in U.S. higher education and became widely taught through a college consortium including Syracuse, Michigan State, U.S. International University, and the University of Southern California (later joined by Indiana University). This work culminated in a joint project known as the Instructional Development Institute (IDI).

In 1973, the U.S. Department of Defense commissioned the Center for Performance Technology at Florida State University to develop procedures to substantially improve Army training. These procedures evolved into a model that was adopted by the Army, Navy, Air Force, and Marines called Interservice Procedures for Instructional Systems Development (IPISD).

The phases of this ISD model included analysis, design, development, implementation, and control. The control phase was later renamed evaluation and gave rise to the well-known acronym ADDIE. For a more complete history of ISD, see Molenda and Boling (2007).

The ADDIE Model

ADDIE remains one of the most popular ISD models and continues to be updated and used in many large organizations. Figure 11-1 shows the phases of the ADDIE model. The arrows illustrate the interactive nature of a systems approach.

Each phase of the model is made up of different procedural steps. For example, analysis typically includes needs analysis, learner analysis, context analysis, and content analysis. The output of the analysis phase is learning objectives, which serve as the input to the design phase. For an expansion of basic ADDIE phases into a more detailed procedural guide, see Gagné, Wager, Golas, and Keller (2005).

Figure 11-1. ADDIE Model

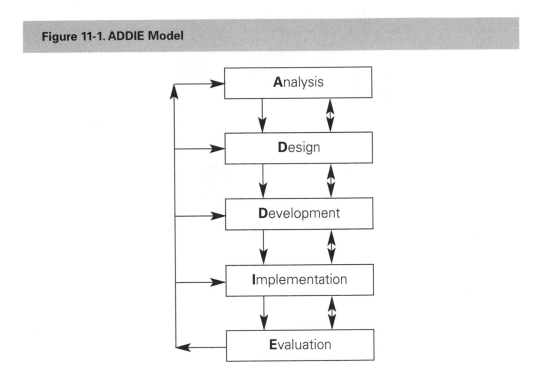

The Dick and Carey Model

Named for its developers, the Dick and Carey model (Figure 11-2) is the most widely known and used ADDIE-type model (Dick, Carey, and Carey, 2014). It is taught in most introductory college and university instructional design courses. Two of its characteristics are particularly noteworthy in our discussion of ISD models.

The model suggests creating assessments for learning objectives *before* designing and developing the instruction. This departure from the basic ADDIE model helps ensure alignment of learning objectives with the evaluation of success in achieving those objectives early in the development process. This sequence often results in an iteration of revising the objectives to better align with how they will be measured.

The Dick and Carey model also places increased emphasis on formative evaluation, or the evaluation of delivery formats and instructional strategies as they are being formed. Revision information gained from early try-outs of the instruction is fed forward in the training development process rather than waiting and facing the possibility of revising an entire program after it has been fully developed.

Figure 11-2. Dick and Carey Model of ISD

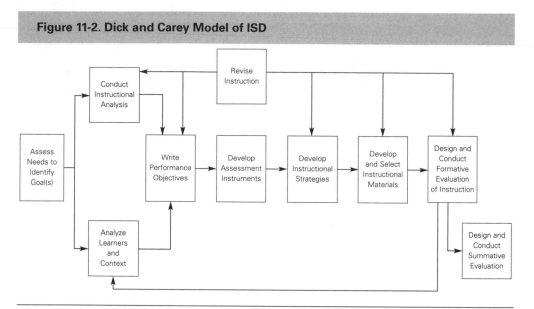

Source: Dick, Carey, and Carey (2008). *The Systematic Design of Instruction*. Pearson Education © 2008. Used with permission.

ISD Models, in General

Many ISD models have been developed and used over the last few decades. Models differ in terms of the number of steps, the names of the steps, and the recommended sequence of functions. Gustafson and Branch's (1997) *Survey of Instructional Development Models* includes 18 models. Their list is not intended to be exhaustive; rather it illustrates the various ways of implementing a systems approach.

Organizations typically use their own uniquely customized ISD model, often adapting or combining concepts from other models.

Expanding Models to Meet Current Delivery Systems

When an organization chooses a particular medium or delivery system, it is often necessary to expand, modify, and combine instructional design models with other models and considerations. Figure 11-3 shows one such adaptation for teaching e-learning training development (Sink, 2002).

The first part of the model depicts the basics of ISD, beginning with needs analysis to determine workforce training needs and matching solutions. If analysis confirms some sort of training is needed, the front-end analysis continues with audience, context, and content considerations. The results of these analyses enable a decision about whether e-learning is an appropriate delivery system choice.

Next, the model expands into three distinct paths that function simultaneously. The three paths are a programming model, an ISD model, and a model for project management. The programming portion of the model is needed to guide of the online learning content. An ISD model is needed to guide instructional program development. A model to guide project management is also needed due to increased project management responsibilities given the complexities of a delivery system that may involve so many different media, software programming, user-interface testing, and learning design strategies. Fairly large design and development teams may be required to provide all the different types of expertise needed.

The instructional design path in Figure 11-3 illustrates the basic components of a typical instructional design process. Additionally, the three-path model shows how and where the programming path and the instructional design or development path interact, and the checkpoints for project management and evaluation.

All these ISD models provide a road map or process for a systems approach with the goal of training outcomes that are results oriented. ISD models systematically strive to deliver the results individuals and organizations need and desire.

Learning Theories

Learning theories attempt to describe what is going on when people learn. Gagné (1997) puts it this way:

> [Learning theories] try to provide conceptual structures involved in the process of taking in information and getting it transformed so that it is stored in long term memory and later recalled as an observable human performance. This entire process, or set of processes, forms the basis of what I refer to when I speak of learning theory.

Learning theories give rise to learning strategies, tactics, experiences, and learning environments that support theory. Given the ISD models, instructional designers make the most use of learning theories and their resulting learning strategies in the design phase (see Figure 11-4).

Figure 11-3. ISD for E-Learning

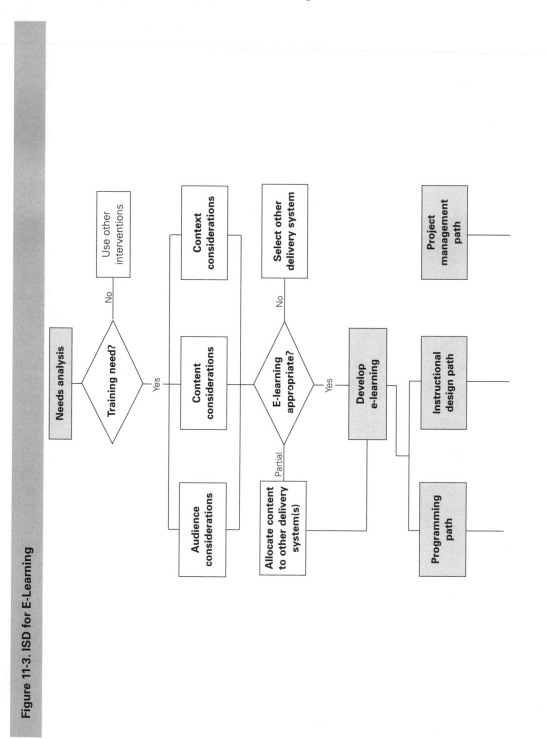

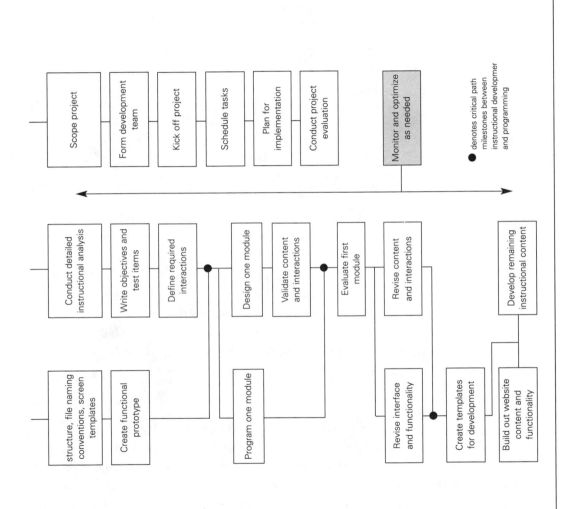

Scope project

Form development team

Kick off project

Schedule tasks

Plan for implementation

Conduct project evaluation

Monitor and optimize as needed

● denotes critical path milestones between instructional developmer and programming

Conduct detailed instructional analysis

Write objectives and test items

Define required interactions

Design one module

Validate content and interactions

Evaluate first module

Revise content and interactions

Develop remaining instructional content

structure, file naming conventions, screen templates

Create functional prototype

Program one module

Revise interface and functionality

Create templates for development

Build out website content and functionality

Figure 11-4. ADDIE Model and Learning Theories

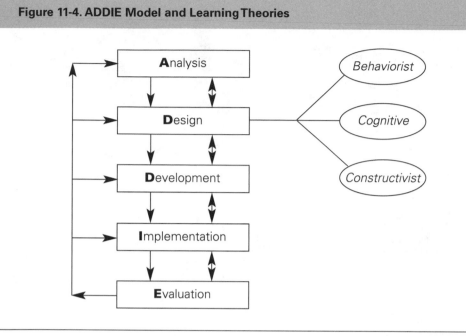

The different ways training courses may be structured and designed (as well as the structure and design of individual lessons, modules, or units of instruction in the course) usually have their origins in one or more learning theories (Molenda and Russell, 2005). The design phase of ISD has been heavily influenced by the behaviorist, cognitive, and constructivist learning theories.

Behaviorist Approach

Behaviorists concentrate their efforts on what is observable learner behavior and reinforcement. Drawing on the research and theories of B.F. Skinner on stimulus-response learning, behaviorist training programs focus on observable behavior. Main tasks are broken down into smaller tasks, and each small task is treated as a separate learning objective. Input and practice, followed by reinforcement (positive or corrective), are the base components of the behaviorist approach.

Behaviorist learning theory gave rise to teaching machines and programmed instruction, from which many practical and essential instructional design concepts are derived. Examples include:

- determining specifically stated descriptions of observable human performance (the objectives of the instruction)
- using objective-based testing rather than topic-based testing (later called criterion-referenced testing)
- using developmental testing of training material prototypes and approaches on members of the target learning populations for the purpose of improving the materials until learners can meet the preset criterion (a try-out and revision process)
- chunking instruction and designing and writing based on learning objectives and content types such as facts, procedures, concepts, processes, and principles.

Current Uses of the Behaviorist Approach

A behaviorist approach is useful in training that is intended to impart intellectual, psychomotor, and interpersonal knowledge and skills (that is, where the learner needs to gain fluency and automatic use of the knowledge and skills). A few examples will clarify the usefulness of this approach:

- Example 1: Teaching learners how to write user requirements for software development illustrates an instance when an intellectual skill should be practiced until learners can write user requirements in the context of their own work environments.
- Example 2: Teaching interpersonal skills related to conflict resolution requires repeated practice with feedback until learners gain enough confidence to use the skills in their own work environments.
- Example 3: Learning to drive a car is a psychomotor skill that must be practiced until certain sub-skills become automatic. Acquisition of automatic sub-skills enables learners to successfully drive without consciously focusing on each and every step in the procedure.

Another offshoot of the behaviorist approach was the research and development in the area of programmed instruction, which reached its peak in the 1970s. Instructional content was presented as prescribed in behaviorist instructional theory: in small chunks, followed by an interactive question or an activity to elicit a response from the learner, and concluded with corrective or confirming feedback.

Benjamin Bloom's (1968) philosophy and concepts revolving around *Learning for Mastery* also have their roots in the behaviorist approach. The learning for mastery model is based on Bloom's premise that perhaps 95 percent of the learner population can learn what we have to teach them and that it is our responsibility as designers and educators or trainers to figure out the means to help those learners master the content we have to teach. In particular, learning for mastery makes use of performance or behaviorally stated learning objectives and criterion-referenced testing. It also emphasizes diagnostic testing and remediation strategies. *Learning for Mastery* has been influential in public education and in military training.

Robert Gagné

As one of the founding fathers in the field of instructional design, Robert Gagné developed nine conditions of learning, which are instructional events that should be used in every complete act of learning. The conditions of learning are:

1. Gain the learners' attention.
2. Share the objectives of the session.
3. Ask learners to recall prior learning.
4. Deliver the content.
5. Use methods to enhance understanding, for example, case studies, examples, and figures.
6. Provide an opportunity to practice.
7. Provide feedback.
8. Assess performance.
9. Provide job aids or references to ensure transfer to the job.

Gagné was also instrumental in transferring his concepts of instructional theory to computer-based training design and multimedia-based learning.

Gagné was professor emeritus of educational research at Florida State University, where he played a leading role in the establishment and initial operation of the graduate program in instructional systems design. He was also director of research of the American Institutes for Research, where he supervised research programs on human performance, instructional methods, and educational objectives design.

Cognitive Learning Theory

While behaviorist learning theory is focused almost exclusively on external events and processes, cognitive theories focus on what is happening to learners internally. Cognitive learning theories try to understand understanding (Clark, 1999).

The cognitive approach has contributed what we know about internal cognitive processes to the field of instructional design. Cognitive theory helps us provide conditions that make it more likely that learners will acquire the thinking strategies necessary to improve their job performance. The cognitive view of how learning takes place is based on how information is processed, stored, and retrieved in the mind, rather than on how behavior changes (Foshay, Silber, and Stelnicki, 2003).

Cognitive approaches to training have given rise to in-depth strategies and tactics for helping learners acquire cognitive skills. Gagné's nine events of instruction (in the sidebar) are foundational for many cognitive training designs.

The cognitive training procedure suggested by Foshay, Silber, and Stelnicki (2003) juxtaposes the five tasks learners have to accomplish with the elements trainers and designers must put into lessons. Table 11-1 shows lesson elements associated with each of the five learner tasks consistent with the cognitive approach.

Current Uses of Cognitive Theory

The cognitive approach is well suited to helping learners recall new information, comprehend how things work, and remember and use new procedures (Davis and Davis, 1998). It applies generally to objectives in the cognitive domain, particularly to tasks at the lower and middle levels of complexity.

Instructional designers can use learning strategies and tactics from cognitive theory to build on the behavioral approach, thereby expanding their repertoire of strategies and tactics for how people acquire and learn cognitive skills.

Constructivist Learning Theory

Constructivist pedagogy emerged in the 1980s. It revolves around the notion that "knowledge is constructed by the learners as they attempt to make sense of their experiences" (Driscoll, 2000). Constructivist theory sees learning as knowledge construction and is based on the idea that learning occurs when a learner actively constructs a knowledge representation in working memory. According to the knowledge construction view, the learner is a sense maker; the teacher is a cognitive guide who provides guidance and modeling on authentic learning tasks (Mayer, 1999).

The constructivist learning experience is more discovery oriented, rather than expository oriented. Constructivist learning experiences involve carefully crafted activities, multiple perspectives, and learner-driven knowledge creation. These techniques result in tasks similar to those learners would encounter in the real world, with the natural complexities that surround those tasks.

With constructivist strategies, the aim is to make the learning experience reflect real-world experiences, enabling learners to transfer what they learn more efficiently and effectively to their jobs.

Table 11-1. Cognitive Training Model

Learners Must Do This to Learn	Trainers Put These Elements in Lessons to Help Learners
1. **Select the Information to Attend To.** Heighten their attention and focus it on the new knowledge being taught because that new knowledge is seen as important and as something that can be learned.	**Attention.** Gain and focus learners' attention on the new knowledge. **WIIFM.** Answer "What's in it for me?" for the learners. **YCDI.** Tell the learners "You can do it" regarding learning the new knowledge.
2. **Link the New Information With Existing Knowledge.** Put the new knowledge in an existing framework by recalling existing or old knowledge related to the new and linking the new knowledge to the old.	**Recall.** Bring to the forefront the prerequisite existing (old) knowledge that forms the base on which the new knowledge is built. **Relate.** Show similarities or differences between the new knowledge and old knowledge, so that the new knowledge is tied to the old.
3. **Organize the Information.** Organize new knowledge in a way that matches the organization of related existing knowledge to make it easier to learn, cut mental processing time, minimize confusion, and stress only relevant information.	**Structure of Content.** Present the boundaries and structure of the new knowledge in a format that best represents the way the new knowledge itself is structured. **Objectives.** Specify both the desired behavior and the knowledge to be learned. **Chunking.** Organize and limit the amount of new knowledge presented to match human information processing capacity. **Text Layout.** Organize text presentation to help learners organize new knowledge. **Illustrations.** Use well-designed illustrations to assist learners' organization and assimilation of new knowledge.
4. **Assimilate the New Knowledge Into Existing Knowledge.** Integrate the new knowledge into the old knowledge so they combine to produce a new unified, expanded, and reorganized set of knowledge.	**Present New Knowledge.** Using a different approach for each type of knowledge, present the new knowledge in a way that makes it easiest to understand. **Present Examples.** Demonstrate real-life examples of how the new knowledge works when it is applied.
5. **Strengthen the New Knowledge in Memory.** Strengthen the new knowledge so that it will be remembered and can be brought to bear in future job and learning situations.	**Practice.** Involve learners by having them do something with the new knowledge. **Feedback.** Let learners know how well they've done in using the new knowledge, what problems they're having, and why. **Summary.** Present the structure of content again, including the entire structure of knowledge. **Test.** Have learners use the new knowledge again, this time to prove to themselves, you, and their employer that they have met the objectives of the training. **On-the-Job Application.** Have learners use new knowledge in a structured way on the job to ensure they "use it, not lose it."

Current Uses of Constructivist Learning Theory

Constructivist pedagogy is now combined with the concept of performance-based training and has various names. Models that embrace performance-based training include problem-based learning (Nelson, 1999), goal-based scenarios (Schank, Berman, and MacPherson, 1999), and constructivist learning environments (Jonassen, 1999). In more general discussions, constructivist performance-based learning may be referred to as situated learning, authentic activities, or cognitive apprenticeship. Whatever name is used, the approach describes a learning experience that:

- has real-world relevance
- requires learners to define tasks and subtasks to complete activities
- enables learners to examine tasks and their deliverables from different perspectives
- provides the opportunity to collaborate
- allows for competing solutions and a variety of outcomes
- aims to create polished products or job-related tools valuable in their own right (Reeves, Herrington, and Oliver, 2002).

Adult Learning Theory

Adult learning theory and principles fit, according to our model, between the learning theories and the selection of macro or micro methods of instruction (see Figure 11-5). This sequence is suggested because the three learning theories described earlier are primary, as they apply to everyone. Once primary learning theories are considered, we can adjust our thinking more about selecting macro- and micro-level instructional strategies by considering adult learning theory.

Adult learning theory seeks to explain the concepts and differences of pedagogical and anagogical theories. Pedagogy is the art and science of teaching children. In its extreme, it assigns full responsibility to the instructor or teacher for making all decisions about what will be learned, how it will be learned, when it will be learned, and if it has been learned. It is instructor or teacher directed, leaving the learner only the submissive role of following the teacher's instructions.

In contrast, the andragogy model assumes that adults come to a learning situation with a greater volume and a different quality of experience than youths. These differences in experience then affect or should affect our strategies, instructional and otherwise, to facilitate learning for adults.

Malcolm Knowles (1990) identifies six principles of adult learning:

1. Adult learners *need to know* why they should learn something.
2. The learner's *self-concept*. Adults are internally motivated and self-directed.
3. The role of the learner's *experience*. Adult learners bring a wealth of experience to the learning situation.
4. *Readiness* to learn. Adults are most ready to learn those things that will help them right now or in the near future.
5. *Orientation* to learning. Adults are life-centered (or task-centered or problem-centered) in their orientation to learning.
6. *Motivation*. Adults are more internally motivated (chance for increased job satisfaction, self-esteem, or quality of life, and so on).

For instructional design and delivery suggestions related to these adult learning principles, see pages 35–48 of Elaine Biech's (2009) *10 Steps to Successful Training*. Also see the *Handbook's* website at www.astdhandbook.org for a checklist of sample strategies that the designer and instructor or facilitator may choose from depending on their learning outcomes and situation.

Figure 11-5. ISD Models, Learning Theories, Adult Learning Principles, Strategies, and Lesson Design

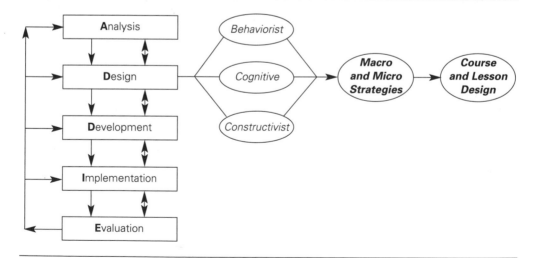

In conclusion, it is important to note that with adults, the *situation* still helps define our approach and strategies. Realistically, some situations may require a more pedagogical approach, at least at first. These include situations in which the learners may lack any experience or knowledge of the subject or job they are learning. In these situations, more directed approaches may be more appropriate.

An Eclectic Approach

Experienced instructional designers frequently take an eclectic approach when designing and developing training programs (see Honebein and Sink, 2012). One learning theory and its related strategies may dominate a particular course, but other theories and strategies may also be used in that same course. This diverse and flexible approach is usually more sensitive to the type and variety of content being taught, the learners, the context, and the results desired.

Figure 11-5 shows the connection among an instructional system design (in this case, ADDIE), the three leading learning theories, adult learning principles, learning strategies, and course design. The design provides the plan, and the learning theories and adult learning principles help instructional designers come up with plausible instructional strategies and tactics, which lead to course and lesson design.

Instructional designers and trainers can expand their approach to designing instruction by learning to pick and choose the strategies that work best for specific learning situations and goals (Reigeluth and Carr-Chellman, 2009). For example, in a course for IT professionals called "Gathering User Requirements," the overall approach was constructivist. The first day of the course, however, was dedicated to writing and validating good user requirements. This portion of the training used a more behavioral approach of intensive practice and feedback relative to the writing and identification of good user requirements. The course then shifted to constructivist approaches throughout a two-and-a-half day simulation, including readings relevant to the simulation and just-in-time interactive lectures (which also included practice and feedback). Each morning, learners received advanced organizers to clarify the mental schema for the day's learning experience. In addition, thought-provoking instructional games and JOLTS (short experiences to help learners think outside the box, from Thiagarajan and Tagliati, 2011) reinforced key processes and concepts.

Crafting a design that used strategies and tactics from different learning theories and adult learning principles ensured appropriate instruction while offering a variety of experiences that stimulated learners' full engagement in the training program.

Summary

Learning theories describe what's going on when people learn, which influences the ways that a learning designer approaches the design phase of ISD. Three learning theories are especially important in the context of learning design: behaviorism, cognitivism, and constructivism.

The behaviorist view focuses on observable behavior and suggests that learning occurs when a learner strengthens or weakens an association between a stimulus and a response. Thus, the theory influences learning design through the use of learning objectives, objective-based testing, and information chunking.

Cognitivism focuses on knowledge acquisition and is based on the idea that learning occurs when a learner places information in long-term memory. Learning designs that emphasize this theory consider how information is processed, stored, and retrieved in the mind, and frequently follow Gagné's nine events of instruction.

Finally, the constructivist view considers learning to be knowledge construction and is based on the idea that learning occurs when a learner actively constructs a knowledge representation in working memory. Thus, a constructivist learning design stresses activities that will enable learners to discover knowledge for themselves.

Adult learning principles must be applied also and must serve as an umbrella-like concept making the whole learning environment and experience work better for adult learners.

All three learning theories combined with adult learning principles have their strengths, depending on business and learner needs, which argues for an eclectic approach to instructional design. This is where instructional design professionals select best practices from all three theories; apply the best strategies based on the desired results; and create learning experiences that effectively meet organizational, business, and individual needs.

About the Author

Darryl L. Sink, EdD, is president of Darryl L. Sink and Associates (DSA). DSA has 32 years of experience designing and developing great learning experiences. His firm specializes in learning and performance consulting and custom training design and development. His graduate work was at Indiana University in Bloomington, where he specialized in instructional systems design and educational psychology. He is the author of six comprehensive guides to instructional design and development that are used with DSA's workshops to provide fundamental instructional design training and processes. These processes have been adopted and are being used by many Fortune 500 companies, public institutions, and nonprofit organizations. He is a contributing author to the International Society of Performance Improvement's (ISPI) *Handbook of Human Performance Technology* and to the *ASTD Handbook for Workplace Learning Professionals*. He is the recipient of ISPI's Professional Service Award and was three times awarded the Outstanding Instructional Product of the Year Award by ISPI.

References

Biech, E. (2009). *10 Steps to Successful Training*. Alexandria, VA: ASTD Press.

Bloom, B. (1968). *Learning for Mastery*. Los Angeles: The Center for the Study of Evaluation of Instructional Programs, University of California.

Clark, R.E. (1999). The Cognitive Sciences and Human Performance Technology. In *Handbook of Human Performance Technology,* 2nd edition, eds. H.D. Stolovitch and E.J. Keeps. Silver Spring, MD: ISPI.

Davis, J.R., and A.B. Davis. (1998). *Effective Training Strategies*. San Francisco: Berrett-Koehler.

Dick, W., L. Carey, and J.O. Carey. (2014). *The Systematic Design of Instruction*, 8th edition. Boston: Allyn and Bacon.

Driscoll, M.P. (2000). *Psychology of Learning for Instruction,* 2nd edition. Boston: Allyn and Bacon.

Foshay, W.R., K.H. Silber, and M. Stelnicki. (2003). *Writing Training Materials That Work*. San Francisco: Jossey-Bass/Pfeiffer.

Gagné, R.M. (1997). Mastery Learning and Instructional Design. *Performance Improvement Quarterly* 10(1):8-19.

Gagné, R.M., W.W. Wager, K.C. Golas, and J.M. Keller. (2005). *Principles of Instructional Design*, 5th edition. Belmont, CA: Thomson/Wadsworth.

Gustafson, K.L., and R.M. Branch. (1997). *Survey of Instructional Development Models*, 3rd edition. Syracuse, NY: ERIC Clearinghouse on Information and Technology.

Honebein, P.C., and D.L. Sink. (2012). The Practice of Eclectic Instructional Design. *Performance Improvement* 51(10):26-30.

Jonassen, D. (1999). Designing Constructivist Learning Environments. In *Instructional-Design Theories and Models: A New Paradigm of Instructional Theory, Volume II*, ed. C.M. Reigeluth. Mahwah, NJ: Lawrence Erlbaum Associates.

Knowles, M. (1990). *The Adult Learner: A Neglected Species*. Houston, TX: Gulf Publishing Company.

Mayer, R.E. (1999). Designing Instruction for Constructivist Learning. In *Instructional-Design Theories and Models: A New Paradigm of Instructional Theory, Volume II*, ed. C.M. Reigeluth. Mahwah, NJ: Lawrence Erlbaum Associates.

Molenda, M., and E. Boling. (2007). Creating. In *Educational Technology: A Definition With Commentary*, eds. A. Januszewski and M. Molenda. Mahwah, NJ: Lawrence Erlbaum Associates.

Molenda, M., and J.D. Russell. (2005). Instruction as an Intervention. In *Handbook of Human Performance Technology*, 3rd edition, eds. H.D. Stolovitch and E.J. Keeps. San Francisco: John Wiley & Sons.

Nelson, L.M. (1999). Collaborative Problem Solving. In *Instructional-Design Theories and Models: A New Paradigm of Instructional Theory, Volume II*, ed. C.M. Reigeluth. Mahwah, NJ: Lawrence Erlbaum Associates.

Reeves, T.C., J. Herrington, and R. Oliver. (2002). *Authentic Activities and Online Learning*. Milperra, Australia: HERSDA.

Reigeluth, C.M., and A. Carr-Chellman. (2009). Understanding Instructional Theory. In *Instructional-Design Theories and Models: Building a Common Knowledge Base, Volume III*, eds. C.M. Reigeluth and A. Carr-Chellman. Hillsdale, NJ: Lawrence Erlbaum Associates.

Schank, R.C., T.R. Berman, and K.A. MacPherson. (1999). Learning by Doing. In *Instructional-Design Theories and Models: A New Paradigm of Instructional Theory, Volume II*, ed. C.M. Reigeluth. Mahwah, NJ: Lawrence Erlbaum Associates.

Sink, D.L. (2002). ISD Faster Better Easier. *Performance Improvement* 41(7):16-22.

Thiagarajan, S., and T. Tagliati. (2011). *Jolts! Activities to Wake Up and Engage Your Participants*. San Francisco: John Wiley & Sons.

For Further Reading

Bell-Gredler, M.E. (2008). *Learning and Instruction: Theory Into Practice*. Upper Saddle River, NJ: Pearson Prentice Hall.

Biech, E. (2009). *10 Steps to Successful Training*. Alexandria, VA: ASTD Press.

Duffy, T., and D.H. Jonassen, eds. (1992). *Constructivism and the Technology of Instruction: A Conversation*. Hillsdale, NJ: Lawrence Erlbaum Associates.

Gagné, R.M., and K.L. Medsker. (1996). *The Conditions of Learning: Training Applications*. Fort Worth, TX: Harcourt Brace.

Gagné, R.M., W.W. Wager, K.C. Golas, and J.M. Keller. (2005). *Principles of Instructional Design*, 5th edition. Belmont, CA: Thomson/Wadsworth.

Reigeluth, C.M. and A. Carr-Chellman. (2009). Understanding Instructional Theory. In *Instructional-Design Theories and Models: Building a Common Knowledge Base, Volume III*, eds. C. M. Reigeluth and A. Carr-Chellman. Hillsdale, NJ: Lawrence Erlbaum.

Thiagarajan, S., and R. Thiagarajan. (2000). *Interactive Strategies for Improving Performance: 10 Powerful Tools*. Bloomington, IN: Workshops by Thiagi.

Chapter 12

SAM: A Practical, Agile Alternative to ADDIE

Michael W. Allen

···················· **In This Chapter** ····················

- Compare the original ADDIE model for instructional design to a more iterative process.
- Identify the actions that occur in the shorter SAM instructional design model.

Design and production of quality instruction are not easy tasks. There are many factors that interact with each other to determine success. An approach that is successful with one group of authors and developers may fail dramatically with another group teaching identical skills. Let me stress in opening that if you're happy with the process you're using—if it produces what you want to produce and does so within budget and schedule—it would be prudent to stay with it. You're fortunate, indeed. My experience, bolstered by observation and feedback from others, leads me to believe common practices may not be the best. As we've become more sensitive to the importance of the learning experience, not just the content to be delivered, the number of factors under consideration has risen.

The discussion in this chapter is much less about the legacy process ADDIE (an acronym for analysis, design, development, implementation, and evaluation) than about SAM (successive approximations model). There are many sources of information about ADDIE, but we'll review a few quick notes about this legacy process.

ADDIE in Retrospect

ADDIE is a process developed for the military to hasten production of training materials by persons having a less-than-thorough background in instructional design. As originally conceived, the model was a sequential or so-called "waterfall" model, indicating that each phase was to be completed before the next began (see Figure 12-1).

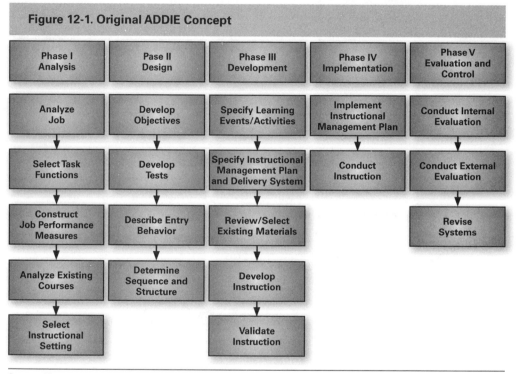

Figure 12-1. Original ADDIE Concept

Source: Allen, M. (2012). *Leaving ADDIE for SAM*. Alexandria, VA: ASTD Press. Adapted from Branson, Rayner, Cox, Furman, King, and Hannum, 1975 by Donald Clark, 2011. Figure courtesy of Donald Clark.

Although many have departed from the notion today, much was made of the importance of working through the phases in order. The justification was that each phase set directions and requirements for the next. If those requirements shifted as work was in progress, it created inefficiencies at best and potentially chaos with budget and schedule overruns. When I taught the use of ADDIE, as I did for years, I religiously stressed the frustration downstream workers have when, partway through their work, significant changes are made to input specifications. I had frequently seen it firsthand. Indeed, over the years as I used ADDIE and worked with teams using ADDIE, I witnessed considerable strife. Exhausted and annoyed team members would begrudgingly compromise in their requests for and acceptances of changes, but at some point, they'd resolutely refuse to make further adjustments. In the end, few people were proud of the resulting courseware. No one found the final product to closely approximate what he or she expected to produce at the outset, much less what was hoped for.

ADDIE is a logical and well-thought-out process. Those new to the design and production of instructional products would have trouble seeing fault with it, other than its onerous appearance in full disclosure. Indeed, it is an easily defended process that covers all the bases. But then it requires a great deal of time. Practicality requires taking shortcuts.

I'm a former advocate of ADDIE, but I now feel there are many changes in the workplace that require us to look beyond ADDIE. Change is difficult for us all—people tend to cling to the familiar and defend it. We can have trouble owning up to weaknesses in what we know and do, and sometimes just as much trouble appreciating the benefits of a different approach.

The success of content-centered design and development approaches, no matter how well organized and thorough, have become less satisfactory as we realize that successful instruction is so much more than transmission of information. It seems we are ever less patient and want our training developed faster, often by persons with less knowledge about instructional design and human learning. We need a simpler model. We need a faster and more collaborative model. We need a model that fosters creativity and is practical. For these and many other reasons, we searched long and hard for an alternative model with significant advantages.

Successive Approximations Model (SAM)

SAM is a derivation of several models, including ADDIE, and a product of extensive experimentation and revision. In many senses, it's a contemporary model not only because it's newer, but also because it has evolved in parallel with advanced models currently employed in engineering and software development where, perhaps surprisingly, many of the needs and challenges are similar. For example, all instructional designers have the need to meet the high hopes of clients that tend to waver, to meet actual needs clients have even when clients don't recognize them, to produce the product within restrictive budgets and schedules, and to serve end users who are not the client. Clients often have little appreciation for the many challenges projects have, yet need to be involved, have control, and be assured that their resources are being spent wisely.

Most simply put, SAM is an iterative prototyping process that evolves prototypes into the final product. It works through small steps, frequently taking measures to ensure that work is proceeding on the right path. It focuses far more on learning experiences, learner engagement, and learner motivation than it does on content organization, presentation of information, and summative post-tests, although these latter components get full and adequate attention when and where appropriate.

Let's look at the primary building block of SAM—the iteration (see Figure 12-2).

Figure 12-2. Basic SAM Iteration

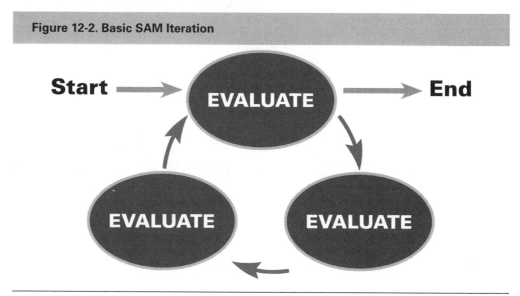

Source: Allen, M. (2012).

Evaluate

Note that the process is circular and has few components. It begins with an evaluation or analysis. As a project gets established, you'll probably know many things about the situation—the goals, the learners, the delivery platform—but in the first iteration, you should ask any of the following questions for which you don't have answers:

- What forms of delivery are available to us?
- Who are the learners, and what needs to change about their performance?
- What can they do now? Are we sure they can't already do what we want?
- What is unsatisfactory about current instructional programs, if any exist?
- Where do learners go for help?
- How will we know whether the new program is successful?
- What is the budget and schedule for project completion?
- What resources are available, human and otherwise?
- Who is the key decision maker, and who will approve deliverables?

Design

If you are familiar with the ADDIE process, this step may seem unusual. With a limited amount of analysis completed at this point, and with vital information surely lacking, the SAM designer is encouraged to use his or her instincts to guess at what might be a good solution and present it to stakeholders after little time or thought. In fact, the designer typically generates the first prospective design in a brainstorming project kick-off meeting, known in SAM parlance as a Savvy Start, with key stakeholders in attendance.

The plan, in contrast to typical processes, is to swap the question, "Why shouldn't we do this?" for the traditional question, "What should we do?" The latter question is so broad that it's hard for a team of people to answer it without an extended discussion that can be both time-consuming and not very productive. SAM is intended to be a fast process and can't afford drawn-out conversations. The former question, "Why shouldn't we do this?" is a narrower and more specific question. We need only discuss what's good and bad about the proposal, not what's good and bad about all the alternatives anyone can suggest. Assuming that the designer has based the design on some available information, the proposal will be somewhat on the mark. The conversation stimulated by this question will help fill in blanks in the project requirements and constraints. It will help the designer understand who is really in charge, what's important to the client/organization, where opportunities lie, what hidden agendas lie beneath the surface, who really knows the content, and so on.

The design should be visual—a quick, rough sketch. It's intended to be a disposable tool that helps the team consider alternatives. This first design will surely be replaced in subsequent iterations, so it should have only enough substance to identify strengths and weaknesses.

Develop

SAM is a process that depends on rapid prototyping to assist with ongoing analysis and design. In fact, development is more interleaved with design than subsequent to it. Design sketches are a form of prototype, or more often the basis of a prototype, as we usually refine sketches to aid subsequent appraisal and evaluation by the team. Prototypes need to be refined only to the point of minimizing miscommunication and clarifying what would be developed further, were the project to continuing building on the current design.

For e-learning, functional prototypes substitute for detailed documentation (in common with Agile processes, which call for minimal documentation) to be sure that time and effort are used most productively and to ensure the best communication. Written specifications take considerable time to construct, and even then are easily open to misinterpretation—especially when timing, logic, and the transitions of interactivity are involved. People can easily find that they've approved a written specification that led to something entirely different from what they thought was described. Prototypes used to facilitate face-to-face discussion suffer much less from these liabilities and are essential in SAM.

Repeat Two More Times

Upon completion of the first prototype, it's time to evaluate it. We are returned to the top of cycle, where we repeat the steps with some slight modification. In evaluation, we're now looking at prototyped solutions from the previous cycle and again asking why we shouldn't do this. Much hidden, incomplete, and inaccurate information is certain to be exposed at this time—information that might never have been revealed by even the most determined investigator in up-front analysis. Prototypes have a talent for flushing out information and doing so early before divergent expectations and understandings would be a disruptive surprise.

In the second iteration, it's wise to set aside the first design, even if it continues to have great appeal. Forcing yourself to come up with something entirely new is challenging and often seems both unnecessary and painfully difficult. But doing so nearly always reveals a superior design.

In the third iteration, design restrictions can be softened a bit. It's still wise to try for something completely new, but if the preceding evaluation yielded no contradiction and you cannot think of anything better, borrowing components from either or both the first and second designs is probably smart.

Contrasts

Some of the primary contrasts to ADDIE and many other models are these notions: 1) do very little analysis, guess where necessary to keep moving, and expect to get it right later, 2) assemble a Savvy Start team that includes not only the obvious members, but also the project financier, a performance supervisor, and one or more prospective learners, 3) design backward from the last instructional topics, that is, the most advanced skills, to the first, and 4) put forward a design proposal quickly and ask, "Why shouldn't we do this?"

Do Very Little Up-Front Analysis

In SAM, analysis is an ongoing endeavor. As designs are reviewed in functional prototypes, it's common to reconsider what might return the greatest impact to learners and the organization. Even such fundamental parameters as who should be trained and what the instructional goals should be are up for re-examination and potential revision as discovery work progresses, whereas with an analysis phase that is loaded up front, it's more likely these parameters would not be reconsidered.

Assemble a Mixed Team

The first three iterations, the Savvy Start, can usually be accomplished in one or two days. Sometimes many more than three iterations can be accomplished in that time. But for at least the first three iterations, it's important to have assembled the right team. Table 12-1 lists possible attendees together with their responsibilities for the Savvy Start team.

Table 12-1. Roles and Responsibilities

Role	Example Responsibilities
Budget maker	This person can explain budgetary constraints, knows the budget will be (or was) set, and understands assumptions made.
Person who owns the performance problem	This person will help to determine the organization's expectations for successful performance.
Person who supervises performers	Supervisors are closest to the real performance issues and will provide the most concrete examples of the performance problems that need to be solved.
Someone who knows the content (SME)	This person can provide insight into the content and direction for the instruction.
Potential learners	These people will support the ongoing development of the course through user testing and reviews.
Recent learners	Recent learners will help the team understand the strengths and weaknesses of current instruction, what is easy and hard to learn, and what may be best to learn on the job.
Project manager	This person will manage all the resources and schedules on the project.
Instructional designer	Designer(s) will select or create instructional treatments and keep the instruction focused on the learner.
Prototyper	This person will sketch and/or build prototypes to give the team the opportunity to visualize the team's ideas.

A large team can make the meeting difficult to manage, but not having key stakeholders represented can make the whole project difficult to delineate. There may be many more iterative sessions beyond the Savvy Start, depending on how many skills are to be learned and the complexity of them. It's unlikely that all such sessions can or even should command attendance by the initial group, but the Savvy Start will have set the tone, revealed expectations and biases, and let you know who is really in charge. That information will be of considerable help when you have to work without their direct involvement. It will also let you know who should receive periodic updates as the project progresses. By having attended the Savvy Start, recipients of your updates will have an easier appreciation of what is being reported and the progress that's being made.

Work Backward

Begin with the last instructional experience you would deliver before concluding an individual's instruction. What do you want learners doing before they attempt to work on their own? The answer, of course, is doing something that's as similar as possible to the required performance under the range of conditions the learner will encounter. This activity is better than an abstract discussion of what the learning goals should be to define goals in functional specificity. There should be little interpretive variance going forward and therefore no problematic surprises.

After learning experiences have been designed to ensure readiness of learners to perform the most challenging skills, design backs up to consider what preparation the learners need to be ready to engage in that final learning experience. Design iterations work to answer this question and, when done, another backup occurs until a learning experience is designed for which all expected learners are ready.

Ask Why Shouldn't We Do This?

As described above, it's easier to have a constructive conversation about why a proposed design wouldn't work than it is to have one to design the program considering all possible alternatives. In SAM, we propose a design almost immediately. Instead of lengthy, in-depth analysis, SAM suggests basing a knee-jerk design on easy-to-obtain information about the following parameters:

- learners—entry skills and variances, motivation
- performance needs—what exactly learners are expected to do after instruction and to what degree of perfection
- the conditions under which learners are expected to perform
- the frequency with which they will perform the task
- previous instructional successes and failures, if any.

If any of this information proves difficult to gather, guess. Speed is more important than accuracy. Evaluation of prototypes will correct faulty guesses and do so with helpful specificity.

SAM1 vs. SAM2

The basic SAM diagram in Figure 12-2 can actually serve as a complete process for smaller projects. It's simple, fast, and productive. Design and development interleave with evaluation, ensuring that the process is on the right path. But larger projects, especially those involving more than a few people and needing formal budgets and project plans or those in which development is completed by a separate team, perhaps even in a different facility or country, will need to use SAM2, as depicted in Figure 12-3. The major difference is that in SAM2, the project moves on to a development phase when design iterations have been completed, whereas in SAM1, the product is completed at the conclusion of these iterations.

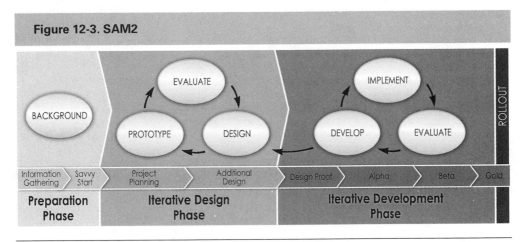

Figure 12-3. SAM2

Source: Allen, M. (2012)

SAM2

Work in SAM2 is divided into three phases: preparation, iterative design, and iterative development.

Preparation Phase

The preparation phase is the period for gathering background information, even before attempting to design the first solution, which we are eager to get into as quickly as possible. Backgrounding helps set the target, identify special issues, and rule out options. It prepares for the intensive design activities by narrowing focus. This is the time for actively exploring the performance problem in broad terms—its context within the organization's needs, goals, and outcome expectations.

Background information to be gathered includes:

- previous performance improvement efforts (if any) and their outcomes
- programs currently in use (if any)
- available content materials
- organizational responsibilities for training

- constraints such as schedule, budget, and legal requirements
- identity of the ultimate decision maker
- the definition of project success.

Key information-gathering objectives:

- Identification of the key players and their commitment to participate. Key players include decision and budget maker, opportunity owner, subject expert, performance supervisor, recent learner, target learner, and the organization's deployment manager.
- Identification of the organization's primary opportunity and its dependency on specifiable behavioral changes.

In SAM, preparation work is done quickly at first, taking paths of least resistance. It's not because this work is unimportant—it's critically important to base decisions on accurate information and avoid the risk of making unverified assumptions—but the model prescribes performing analysis in the context of considering alternative solutions. It explicitly avoids exhaustive research that will be inevitably incomplete anyway and might not even prove useful.

At the start of the process, much time can be spent collecting information that could be relevant, but turns out not to be very helpful. We need to get to the right questions—quickly. Perhaps it's surprising, but identifying the right questions comes most easily from iterative design where the context of alternatives makes them easier to consider. So we collect the information that's readily available and move right on to the Savvy Start, knowing that analysis is far from finished.

The Savvy Start

The Savvy Start is really the same process as SAM1—a brainstorming event in which the design team and key stakeholders review collected background information and generate initial design ideas. This phase of the design process begins with jumping into solutions that stakeholders may already have in mind. While it's important to get these on the table as soon as possible, whether they are destined to become part of the final solution or eventually abandoned, this activity proves invaluable for many purposes, not the least of which is determining who is really in charge and what outcomes are essential to success. Brainstorming solutions is an amazingly efficient way of determining what the main performance objectives are and simultaneously dealing with the organization's hierarchy that can so easily obscure the real goals.

Further information is discovered by design and review of rapidly constructed, disposable prototypes. These prototypes promote brainstorming and creative problem solving, help the team determine what really is and isn't important, and help align the team's values.

Savvy Start highlights:

- Design cycles are used to evaluate the direction suggested by gathered information, assumptions, and early ideas.
- Prototypes are rough and finished just enough to communicate and test ideas.
- Outcome performance objectives are listed along with the prototyped designs that will be used to help learners achieve them.
- Evaluation is done merely by discussion. Redefining and changing everything may be appropriate, including even the business problem to be addressed and the people to be trained.
- Speed is the key!

As in SAM1, design, prototyping, and evaluation continue to be done iteratively in small steps, but only exemplary samples of the instructional content are worked to completion. Additional content is created later, but even then, iteratively.

Iterative Design Phase

With larger projects or teams, documentation and coordination are prerequisites to success, but SAM pushes for minimal documentation. Only essential documents should be produced, and all should be questioned as to whether face-to-face communication or communication through prototypes would be better.

Note the additional activities along the bottom of the model diagram (see, for example, Figure 12-4). Project planning identifies tasks, when they will be completed, and who will hold responsibility for them. Additional design is produced later through more iteration, but by a smaller team focused on covering additional content, resolving inconsistencies among designs, or solving problems that arose along the way. These later design needs may actually be identified in the development phase as issues or opportunities are discovered.

Project Planning

As discussed before, a concept essential to successive iteration is that no project is ever perfect, but through repeated work, projects can evolve and become closer to perfection. This notion lends a great deal of practicality; it urges developers to put instruction into use and think of making future iterations based on feedback from the field. This is relevant to planning since there can be more certainty of project availability on a preset date than is possible with other approaches.

Figure 12-4. SAM2—Iterative Design Phase

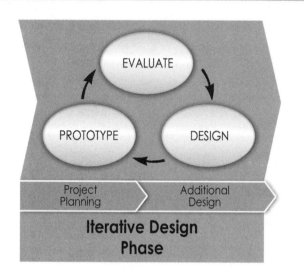

Source: Allen, M. (2012)

From the time functional prototypes are available, SAM projects always have courseware that can be used. The quality will rise continually, but at any point that it's necessary to begin instruction, the best product possible within the project's constraints will be available. To assist with this ultimate practicality, as tasks are listed, each is given a level of priority for the next iteration:

> *Threshold:* Must be completed in this iteration.
> *Target:* Expected to be completed in this iteration.
> *Future:* Will be held back until practical to implement.
> *Epic:* To be considered after this project has been put in use.

Based on the designs created or selected in the Savvy Start, it becomes possible to create a project plan that has integrity. Of course, there are typically many pressures to produce schedules and budgets before enough is known to do so with any credibility, but project planning really needs to be held off until after a Savvy Start. Once completed, content writing, media development, and programming can be estimated for the overall project plan.

Following is a list of project planning guidelines:

- The first step is to capture discussions and decisions by preparing and circulating a Savvy Start Summary Report.
- Initial Media and Content Style Guides can also be prepared, although they are likely to be incomplete until additional design cycles have been completed. It's easy and efficient to capture preferences as they spill out.
- An initial draft of a Content Development Plan can be prepared, indicating responsibilities for and estimates of what material will be needed. Remember to prioritize items by threshold, target, and future.
- The biggest risk lies with learning and performance objectives for which no solutions have yet been prototyped. There are likely to be some.

Additional Design

The Savvy Start session may take only a half-day, three full days, or sometimes even more. The length is as often determined by incidental factors, such as availability of people or meeting space, as it is by project parameters, such as quantity and complexity of content or variation in learner readiness. As intense (and fun!) as these sessions often are and should be, they are more properly considered brainstorming sessions rather than design sessions.

As good ideas and preferences spill out, the need for research and more information becomes apparent, and attractive instructional approaches emerge that need to be thoughtfully reviewed and refined, if not modified extensively or even replaced on closer examination. Furthermore, while the involvement of key stakeholders is essential to truly understanding boundaries and expectations, these people usually can't afford the time necessary to reach needed depth or cover all the content. Additional design work will be needed.

The additional design team will likely be smaller, and team members will likely be charged with preparing ideas in advance of meeting with others. It remains important, however, to follow the rule of *breadth before depth*. That is, it's important to consider all the content to understand whether a broad variety of instructional treatments will be necessary, or whether just one or a few will be appropriate for all content. This rule is harder to follow than it appears and can be the biggest liability of using SAM. With each iteration, design becomes more specific and reaches greater depth until all details are finalized. The temptation is to immediately follow up on ideas as they spring forth. This takes the team into great depth, potentially spending too much time on an unusual content segment and leaving too little time for more important needs and opportunities. Generally, no content area should receive more than three iterations until after all types of content have been worked for their three.

Prototypes

Prototypes continue to be important to test and communicate ideas. A usable prototype is better than any description, specification, or storyboard. It substitutes for many pages of documentation that can be both time-consuming to write and time-consuming to read. A prototype communicates specificity by example, making it easy for people to understand, ask constructive questions, and make detailed comments. Multiple types of prototypes may be developed following the Savvy Start, depending on the selected means of delivery.

- *Media prototypes* integrate media elements to demonstrate the desired "look-and-feel." Layout, colors, fonts, images, and samples of other elements are brought together to form a clear design example and set criteria for full product development.
- *Functional prototypes* are usually derived from Savvy Start prototypes by enhancing or adding details to make them testable with learners. In the case of e-learning, increased functionality provides a better sense of interactivity and usability.
- *Integrated prototypes* present the integration of functional and media prototypes along with representative content (that is, feedback text, sound, video, and so on).
- *Special-purpose prototypes* are created to test any technical or design components that must be finalized early in the process.

Guidelines for additional design tasks might include:

- The same iterative process of design–prototype–evaluation is used. The key decision makers should review and approve the new prototypes before development commences. Trusting they will be happy with how things are evolving is not a good practice.
- Except for small projects and those with a very narrow focus, there isn't enough time to create functional prototypes for all behavioral objectives. It's therefore important to review all content and organize it by similarities so that the smallest number of necessary treatments and prototypes can be identified.

Iterative Development Phase

The iterations that are so advantageous to the design process are equally powerful for development activities. They allow stakeholders to have a continuing means of evaluating decisions and making corrections within project constraints. The importance of this advantage cannot be overstated. Because a functional product becomes available quickly, before time-consuming refinements are made, stakeholders can get an invaluable glimpse of the design becoming real.

Figure 12-5. SAM2—Iterative Development Phase

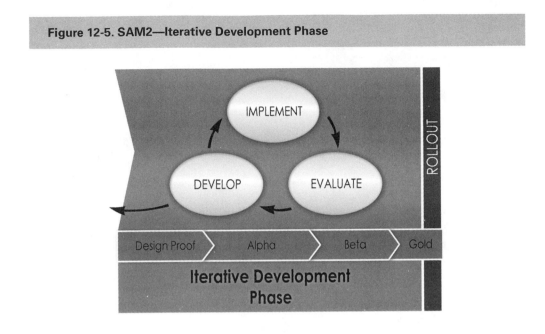

Source: Allen, M. (2012)

Design Proof

At the beginning of the development phase, a plan is made to produce a *design proof,* which is typically the product of the first development phase cycle. Projects with large amounts of content will require a cycle for each type of instructional approach. Approval or disapproval will determine whether:

- additional design work is needed (if so, the process returns to iterative design to produce needed designs)
- another development iteration is needed to make corrections
- iterative development can proceed to producing an *alpha* version of the final product.

The design proof is essentially a visual, functional demonstration of the proposed solution that integrates samples of all components to test and prove viability. It has greater functionality or usability than the design prototypes and is built with the same tools that will produce the final deliverable. In this way, it not only tests the viability of the design but also of the production system. If technology is involved, the design proof needs to run on the equipment and network to be used by learners and demonstrate functional communication with the learning management system, if one is to be used. If role playing, field demonstrations, or other activities are involved, trial runs are needed to be sure all details have been addressed to make activities run smoothly.

Design proof evaluation is a critical event in the process. Design proofs are used to scout out potential problems so they don't become last-minute crises. It's the big opportunity for the design team and the stakeholders to check how the course will function as a whole. At this point, it is possible to get the clearest sense of what the overall solution is becoming while still having time to note corrections that are clearly needed. Design proof highlights could include:

- The first production cycle produces the design proof, which provides an opportunity to confirm all design decisions by actually presenting and testing a functional application on the intended delivery platform.
- Design proofs test:
  — design viability
  — whether the design is in a form that communicates requirements effectively
  — the suitability of development tools
  — the ability to deliver required learning experiences reliably and repeatedly.
- Design proofs combine sample content, including examples of all components, with design treatments. Text and media are polished and representative of the final quality to be expected for all similar elements.

Alpha

The alpha is a complete version of the instructional application to be validated against the approved design. All content and media are implemented. If problems exist, and they well might because it is often important to begin evaluation before all issues can be rectified, those known problems are listed. No major, undocumented issues are expected to be found, but it's nevertheless common for them to surface despite everyone's best efforts.

Evaluation of the alpha release identifies deviations from style guides, graphical errors, text changes, sequencing problems, missing content, lack of clarity, and functional problems. Alpha highlights:

- The second production cycle (or set of cycles for large projects) produces the alpha from approved designs.
- Full content development integration occurs in this cycle. Samples no longer suffice.
- The alpha is nearly the final version of the complete instructional program to be validated against the approved design. All content and media are implemented.

- Completion and approval of the alpha signals the beginning of the validation cycles.
- Review of the alpha is expected to find only minor deviations from style guides, writing issues, graphical errors, and functional problems.

Beta

Because errors are nearly always found in alpha releases, a second cycle, called the validation cycle, is scheduled as part of the process to produce a second final product candidate, the beta release. The beta is a modified version of the alpha that incorporates needed changes identified during evaluation of the alpha. If all goes as expected and corrections are made carefully, the beta review should discover few errors, and those errors discovered should include only minor typographical errors or corrections in graphics. Beta highlights:

- The alpha release is modified to reflect errors identified in its evaluation. The resulting beta release is viewed as a first gold release candidate. There should be no functional errors at this stage. If there are, another iteration may be necessary to produce a second beta release and additional prospective releases if significant errors continue to be found.
- Not only subject matter experts but also actual learners representative of the target population should evaluate the beta release.

Gold

Construction of the gold release is the final phase of development. At this point, while no project ever reaches perfection, the courseware becomes fully usable within the parameters of previously approved project guidelines. Gold release highlights:

- If problems are identified, they must be rectified before the beta release can be given the gold crown. A modified version of a beta, "beta 2" (sometimes called "gold candidate 2"), and, if necessary, a succession of numbered candidates are produced until all problems are resolved.
- When the beta performs as expected and no additional problems are identified, it simply becomes the gold release without further development and is ready for rollout implementation.
- Hopefully, but all too rarely, the rollout signals the beginning of an evaluation study to determine whether targeted behaviors are actually achieved and whether these new behaviors secure the performance success expected.

Final Thoughts

Just as no project reaches perfection, no process is perfect; however, SAM is working better for me than ADDIE did. SAM is not all that new; it is something we've been testing and revising since the late 1970s, and in that time, many have given it a try, with positive results. The concepts have gained additional creditability in their commonality with Agile, rapid prototyping, and other contemporary processes devised to produce superior products efficiently. They are shared with only one purpose: to assist those making an earnest effort to produce the most beneficial learning experiences for others. A video on the *Handbook's* website at www.astdhandbook.org provides an overview of SAM and the deliverables at major steps in the process.

About the Author

Michael W. Allen, PhD, is the chairman and CEO of Allen Interactions and Allen Learning Technologies. He also serves as adjunct associate professor at the University of Minnesota. For more than 40 years, he has led research and development efforts to understand, invent, and implement means of helping individuals achieve their full potential. His custom e-learning studios at Allen Interactions have produced award-winning courseware for many prestigious organizations. His work includes projects funded by the National Institutes of Health, the National Science Foundation, and Control Data Corporation. He contributed to the first Internet-based solution demonstrated to reduce the spread of HIV, to reduction in school gang violence, and to academic success by those failing in traditional education. He has published seven books. He received ASTD's Distinguished Contribution to Workplace Learning and Performance Award and the Ellis Island Medal of Honor.

For Further Reading

Allen, M. (2003). *Michael Allen's Guide to e-Learning: Building Interactive, Fun, and Effective Learning Programs for Any Company.* Hoboken, NJ: John Wiley & Sons.

Allen, M. (2006). *Creating Successful e-Learning: A Rapid System for Getting It Right First Time, Every Time.* San Francisco: Pfeiffer.

Allen, M., and R. Sites. (2012). *Leaving ADDIE for SAM: An Agile Model for Developing the Best Learning Experiences.* Alexandria, VA: ASTD Press.

Buxton, W. (2007). *Sketching User Experiences: Getting the Design Right and the Right Design.* San Francisco: Morgan Kaufmann.

Chapter 13

Using Bloom's Digital Taxonomy to Flip the Classroom and Create the Best Blend

Jennifer Hofmann

································ **In This Chapter** ································

- Validate learning objectives and assessment techniques.
- Map learning objectives to delivery technologies using Bloom's Digital Taxonomy of Learning.
- Flip the classroom to maximize collaborative impact.

A s learning technologies practitioners, we are bombarded with new technologies and trends. It is hard to distinguish which are fads and which are worth investments of time and resources. The safest, and often most expedient, course of action is to continue to focus on the delivery technology that we know is not a fad—the traditional classroom. But to do so without incorporating any of the new technology options could come as a detriment to the learners. Instead of trying to fit all content into one type of delivery method, we should be working toward developing a more blended program that aligns certain content with the appropriate delivery method.

Planning for Blended Learning

As new technologies, such as the virtual classroom, e-learning, and social media, are introduced, we continue to play it safe by trying to make these technology experiences replicate the classroom. There are two issues with these assumptions:

- The classroom has been used for so long (centuries!) not because it is the most effective means of teaching, but because it was the technology available at the time. This setting is often the least optimal for delivering a particular piece of content.
- As the use of various learning technologies becomes commonplace in training departments, a perception has been building that implies you can force fit any content into any technology.

Benjamin Bloom

Benjamin Bloom was a noted educational psychology scholar who transformed the field with his influential Taxonomy of Educational Objectives, also known simply as Bloom's taxonomy. As head of a committee of cognitive psychologists at the University of Chicago, Bloom developed the idea of three learning outcomes based on three domains—cognitive (knowledge), psychomotor (skills), and affective (attitude)—and published his findings in the book *Taxonomy of Educational Objectives: Handbook 1, The Cognitive Domain* (1956). The three domains are the goals of the learning process. Trainers sometimes refer to the three domains as KSAs.

Bloom and his colleagues then created a hierarchical ordering of learning outcomes by subdividing the cognitive and affective domains beginning with the simplest behavior and working up to the most complex: knowledge, comprehension, application, analysis, synthesis, and evaluation. Each level builds on the previous level, which means that the learner must possess knowledge before comprehension, comprehension before application, and so on. This principle is used throughout the education community to assist in preparation of curricula and evaluation materials.

Bloom developed another influential educational philosophy in his book *Developing Talent in Young People* (1985), in which he explores the influence that environment exerts on human performance. Bloom proposes that attention and guidance from parents and educators, along with opportunity and effort on the part of the young person, play a greater role than genetics in achieving goals. It is the mission of educators, therefore, to provide students with an environment where their natural aptitudes can be discovered and then supported and cultivated.

Some highlights of Bloom's distinguished career include serving as the Charles H. Swift Distinguished Service Professor at the University of Chicago and as educational advisor to the governments of India and Israel, among others; aiding in the creation of the International Association for the Evaluation of Educational Achievement (IEA); chairing committees on the College Entrance Examinations Board; and serving a stint as president of the American Educational Research Association.

The question is: Can you teach ANY content using ANY technology? This seems to be the perception—a group purchases WebEx (or Articulate or some other software), so everything needs to be delivered in that way. There are fundamental problems with this perception:

- We are looking at entire programs (for example, project management or sales training) and attempting to force the entire program into one delivery modality.
- There's an implied assumption that all delivery modalities treat all types of content in the same way.

So what's the solution? From an instructional design perspective, we should be developing a blended program instead of trying to fit all content into one convenient delivery modality. Instead of making a design decision to teach project management via a specific tool, we break project management into its component learning objectives and match each learning objective to the best technology available.

To create successful blended training takes planning—a lot of planning, on paper (OK, digital paper), without developing any materials. The cost of poor planning for a blended learning solution is potentially higher than the cost for a poorly planned classroom program. Think about it: If you execute a poorly planned two-day classroom program, you'll know about it in two days; the cost of redevelopment is probably limited to leader guides and participant guides, and the affected audience is probably less than 20 participants.

If you execute a poorly planned blend with an equivalent amount of content, you may not know that the program isn't working for weeks, and multiple cohorts may have begun the learning process before you realize it isn't working. Changes may mean new storyboards, more programming, new technologies, or a dozen other actions. The more complex your blend is, the higher the cost of poor planning.

To plan your blend, take a three-step approach:

- Step 1: Validate learning objectives and assessment techniques.
- Step 2: Map learning objectives to delivery technologies using Bloom's Digital Taxonomy of Learning.
- Step 3: Flip the classroom to maximize collaborative impact.

Let's review each of these steps.

Step 1: Validate Learning Objectives and Assessment Techniques

When considering how to construct your blend and what technologies to use, you need to start with a clear definition of what it is you're teaching, why you're teaching it, how you will assess student mastery, and how much collaboration is required in order for the program to be successful.

A clear definition of what is being taught starts with a re-examination of your instructional goal. It's critical that the instructional goal be accurate and complete at the beginning; otherwise you may build the wrong class. For example, your instructional goal might be to develop a world-class sales team. This sounds straightforward, but it is not complete enough. You would use a different design to create a sales team that sells over the phone as compared to a sales team that needs to sell in a face-to-face environment. If you tell your instructional designers to create a world-class sales training program, it may include face-to-face presentation skills, how to dress, how to make a good first impression by shaking hands, and other physical interpersonal actions. None of these applies to a sales team that never meets face-to-face with a customer.

After the goal is determined, take a look at your performance objectives. The performance objectives indicate what learners will be able to do at the end of the training. Even if you are converting to a blend from a face-to-face environment, take this opportunity to validate your performance objectives to ensure that they are still valid.

Here's the key step in the planning process: How can you assess whether the learning objectives are being met? The reason this is so important is that the assessment techniques determine potential delivery technologies. There is generally a direct correlation between the type of assessment you will use and the type of technology you will use to deliver the content associated with that assessment. For example, if your assessment is a self-paced instrument that tests the students' recall of content, you can probably teach that content in a self-paced format. If students are required to collaborate with other students in order to be assessed, you will probably require a collaborative technology to deliver content. Collaborative technologies can be live (traditional classrooms and virtual classrooms) or not live (discussion board postings and some forms of social media). Remember, blended learning is not only about matching content to the most appropriate delivery medium, but also doing it at the learning objective level. It's the assessment technique that marries these two concepts.

You don't need to create the assessment instruments at this point. I'm not suggesting you create a 100-question test or design a role play. Just identify the types of assessments that could be used to ensure that the desired level of student mastery is being met. As you ascertain the different potential technologies (self-paced, live, collaborative), you are starting to identify the different modules in your blend.

Step 2: Map Learning Objectives to Delivery Technologies Using Bloom's Digital Taxonomy of Learning

Now that you have identified what you are teaching through the learning objectives, and how you might assess mastery, it's time to decide what technology fits best for each objective. The best approach I have found to match learning objectives to the most appropriate delivery technology is to use a new take on Bloom's Taxonomy. Originally developed in the 1950s, the intent of Bloom's Taxonomy was to categorize types of learning objectives to define a level of mastery in a classroom.

Using Bloom's Taxonomy, depending on the desired outcome, you would categorize your learning objectives into one of the six levels of learning, and then use appropriate activities that correspond to the levels of learning in order to achieve the desired level of mastery. For example, at the original knowledge level of learning, a student can recall knowledge by performing such activities as creating a list of defining features.

This really works. In fact, even those of us who have become instructional designers without prior training in the field can create effective programs using this simple, yet powerful, framework.

As content delivery moved out of the traditional classroom and into more collaborative learning technologies, Bloom's Taxonomy was badly in need of some reconstructive surgery. In 2009, Andrew Churches repackaged the taxonomy to take advantage of tools that can help us master different levels of learning in ways that were not previously possible. What follows is a high-level summary of each of the six levels of learning contained in Churches's Digital Taxonomy.

Remembering

"Retrieving, recalling, or recognizing knowledge from memory. Remembering is when memory is used to produce definitions, facts, or lists or recite or retrieve material."

Remembering is the level of learning where we become familiar enough with concepts that we can recognize when they are being used in another context. When we deal with the Remembering domain, we find ourselves using the tools available for self-directed learning. Web technologies like Google can help us to define terms. We can create an articulate storyline module that helps us to list important steps in a sequence. We can use books, PDF documents, and other web tools to read and then recall key concepts. Generally, we don't need to collaborate with other people to remember concepts. Since Remembering doesn't require collaboration, and testing to ensure that Remembering has taken place can occur in a self-paced format, learning objectives that use keywords like *recognize*, *list*, *identify*, *define*, and *locate* can be delivered in a self-paced format.

A conventional and inexpensive way to deliver knowledge-based content is via a virtual classroom webinar. We've all attended them (or pretended to attend them). A hundred people or more log on to the same virtual session at the same time, listen to what experts have to say, and, if permitted, ask questions where appropriate to verify understanding. The Remembering level of learning seemingly aligns itself well with these large-scale webinars. (I say "seemingly" because we are not conducting any sort of assessment to ascertain if content is actually being retained. With most webinars, we hope people will log in, pay attention, and remember what is said. "Hope" is probably not an effective measurement technique.)

We need to remember that this type of online session is not what we would traditionally define as "training." This is simply information dissemination. It's important. It's useful. But it rarely gets us beyond knowledge or perhaps bridging to the next level of learning.

Testing at this level of learning would most likely be objective. Assessment answers can be easily identified as correct or incorrect. Feedback on test responses is directive and instructional in nature.

Remembering Example

a) Learning objective: Identify common "slip and fall" areas on a college campus.
b) Assessment activity: Provide a campus map and have learners follow the map to the top five "slip and fall" areas.
c) Potential delivery technologies: A self-paced e-learning module that allows learners to interact with a campus map.

Understanding

"Constructing meaning from different types of function, be they written or graphic."

The Understanding level of learning occurs when the learner cannot only recall knowledge, but also can explain it in context to someone else. Paradoxically, the word *understanding* is one we typically try to avoid using when talking about learning objectives. The argument is that it is difficult to test for Understanding. How do we know what Understanding looks like? While we should not use the word as one of our learning objectives, we can use it to define this level of learning. The Understanding level of learning is taking what we recall and making that data meaningful. For instance, we take the definition of *project management* and apply it to a project manager job description.

When we have short, stand-alone e-learning modules that can be taken on demand, we may be in the realm of fostering Understanding. We are moving beyond mere recall and into connecting pieces of new knowledge together. Once again, self-paced formats are often more appropriate than live delivery mediums.

There is probably a higher level of discussion or structured thought in achieving Understanding than was present in getting to Remembering. It's not just a lot of data; the data suddenly become useful.

Understanding is not characterized by practicing a new skill or attempting to change behavior. It is a foundational understanding of key concepts that can be called upon and actually used later.

Understanding Example

a) Learning objective: Based on seasonal weather conditions, anticipate specific "slip and fall" hazards that are unique to a campus.
b) Assessment activity: Learners will photograph five "slip and fall" hazards on their campus and create a short presentation with the intent of informing the safety committee of these tests.
c) Potential delivery technologies: A discussion board where learners can get more information about the topic, post their individual presentations, and review the presentations posted by others.

What Comes First?

There is some debate as to whether Bloom's Taxonomy of Learning needs to occur in a linear fashion. For example, mastering the Applying level needs to occur before you can master the Evaluation level.

I consider Remembering and Understanding as foundational levels of learning and believe that they do need to come first. However, the next four domains (Applying, Analyzing, Evaluating, and Creating) may occur in any order, and we may not require an individual level of learning for a particular curriculum.

Applying

"Carrying out or using a procedure through executing or implementing. Applying refers to situations where learned material is used through products like models, presentations, interviews, and simulations."

The Applying level of learning takes us beyond foundational information and into the realm of training. Learners are starting to practice tasks, apply new skills, and correct mistakes. They can execute a checklist, create a table in Microsoft Word, enter data into a claims management system, or collaborate on a file in SharePoint.

Note that the verbs we are using are action oriented and can only be tested by the learner actually doing something. Generally, as we move into the Applying level of learning, we are starting to consider adding more collaborative activities to our learning plans. Activities such as discussions about how to apply key concepts, getting feedback on a presentation created, or working in breakout rooms to prioritize budget items support Applying.

Some start to see the social aspects of learning incorporated as we move out of Understanding and into Applying. While learning objectives in the Remembering and Understanding domains may have been delivered in a self-paced format or in a webinar format where interaction with others was limited and learners were expected to assimilate knowledge on their own, moving into Applying would often require live interaction.

Applying Example

    a) Learning objective: After identifying "slip and fall" hazards on your college campus, propose preemptive safety fixes to minimize the risk to students.

    b) Assessment activity: Learners will create a proposal that identifies the hazards, lists the cause of each hazard, and provides suggestions on how to mitigate the hazard risk.

    c) Potential delivery technologies: Learners will participate in a virtual classroom discussion to learn how to identify and mitigate potential hazards and how to create effective arguments that support that mitigation.

Analyzing

"Breaking material or concepts into parts and determining how the parts relate or interrelate to one another or to an overall structure or purpose. Mental actions include differentiating, organizing, and attributing, as well as being able to distinguish between components."

If the Applying level allows us to take new concepts and use them in a collaborative format, the Analyzing level starts to help us make cognitive decisions. Instead of just creating a budget and prioritizing budget items, Analyzing allows us to make decisions based on the data contained in that budget. We aren't just prioritizing items; we conduct and provide the analysis behind the decision making.

I'm sure you can see how this requires an activity that is more facilitated than, for example, Understanding objectives. Discussion boards, virtual classrooms, and live classrooms are often used for analysis.

Other learning technologies that can support analysis include simulations. For example, the military uses aircraft simulators to help pilots learn to make reliable decisions during combat situations. Similarly, we can use simulations to analyze data to determine whether or not to bring a drug to market. While simulations are not necessarily facilitated, the impact of not "passing the test" is significant. Learners can fail. The pilot can crash a plane. The pharmaceutical marketing trainee may bring a drug to market before it is ready. Or the financial trainee may create a budget that doesn't meet the needs of the department.

Creating and delivering training and assessments that meet the Analyzing level of learning take more time, more resources, and more quality control. If your objective is "Navigate a jet fighter in combat situations," then learners will need to practice those skills to successfully master that objective. Without the practice component, they will remain in the Remembering and Understanding levels at best.

Do We Blame Technology or Design?

This is where virtual program designs start to fall apart. We desire the outcome of the program to be at a high level. For example, we want learners to not only create a budget, but also we want them to be able to analyze the impact of that budget on the department. However, another common requirement is that the program be short in duration. These two outcomes are often mutually exclusive.

The end result is that the same content that took a full day in a face-to-face classroom is now delivered in less than half that time in the virtual classroom. How? Well, the practice opportunities, the collaboration, and the assessments were all removed. We meet the content requirements by filling the slides with words. However, by removing all those pieces, we are staying in the Remembering and Understanding levels of learning and therefore are not providing the structure necessary to facilitate the other levels of learning.

And then, when this doesn't work, we look at it as a failure in technology as opposed to a failure in design and implementation.

Analyzing Example

    a) Learning objective: Decide which hazard mitigation is most appropriate for a particular situation.

    b) Assessment activity: Learners will compare three "slip and fall" mitigation solutions and conduct a cost-benefit analysis to determine the best solution.

    c) Potential delivery technologies: The virtual classroom, combined with videos and job aids, provides background information on the various mitigation solutions.

Evaluating

"Making judgments based on criteria and standards through checking and critiquing."

Evaluating is a means of making a decision. A decision can be made individually or collaboratively as part of a group. Yes, ultimately, the learner can be making these decisions individually, in which case coaching or social media tools like discussion boards can be used effectively. If, however, the learner will eventually be collaborating on a decision as part of a group, this learning objective should be taught in a more collaborative format.

Evaluating is not about providing information to make a decision, but actually making that decision. The outcome is not the presentation of facts, but interpreting facts and applying them to make a judgment. (The process of a trial by jury is often used as an example of an evaluation activity.)

To get to the Evaluating level, obviously we need understanding of basic concepts and we need to be able to review and analyze facts. But do we need to actually create the presentation to analyze the facts? Probably not.

The objectives in leadership curricula often fall into the Evaluating level of learning. Leaders need to provide feedback based on facts and on the impact of particular actions on the organization as a whole. Managers need to make recommendations regarding promotions, team leadership roles, and raises.

Evaluating Example

    a) Learning objective: Determine the best vendor to mitigate identified "slip and fall" hazards.

    b) Assessment activity: Learners will research vendors and then make a recommendation to the safety committee based on their research.

    c) Potential delivery technologies: The virtual classroom, combined with videos and job aids, provides background information on the various vendors. Web searches, scavenger hunts, and referral checking will supplement the more structured training.

Creating

"Putting the elements together to form a coherent or functional whole; reorganizing elements into a new pattern or structure through generating, planning, or producing."

With all the tools that are readily available to learners today, the Creating level of learning can be a lot of fun. Learners can create videos, wikis, podcasts, and a variety of other "projects" using low-cost technologies organizations often have already available.

An argument made by many practitioners is that learning should start with Creating. For instance, allow people to create a presentation to explain their current understanding and their current point of view on a particular topic, and then use the other levels of learning to build on their ideas, identify misunderstandings, and really make sure the learning crystallizes.

The idea behind Creating is building something new, not regurgitating what was taught in class. This makes sense.

As we know, the classroom is a controlled environment. When learners go out into the real world and apply what they've learned, the situations aren't going to be as clean as the simulations or case studies we provided to them in the classroom. Allowing them to create something new that applies to personal situations is an exciting capstone to any curriculum.

Creating Example

    a) Learning objective: Design a hazard mitigation plan for the new student center on campus.
    b) Assessment activity: Create a hazard mitigation plan that includes budget, design, vendor recommendations, and evaluation protocols.
    c) Potential delivery technologies: The virtual classroom, combined with videos and job aids, provides background information. Web searches, scavenger hunts, and referral checking will supplement the more structured training.

Everything Old Is New Again

When I first discovered Bloom's Taxonomy (totally by accident, when trying to find a way to explain constructing learning objectives to a class participant), the simplicity of the model appealed to me. But I knew something was missing—the applicability to current learning technologies and industry trends.

The new Digital Taxonomy is not only transformational, in that it incorporates collaboration and new learning methods into its construction, but accessible. It is relatively easy to construct examples based on a particular curriculum to illustrate the need for a blend of technologies instead of creating a "one-size-fits-all" scenario and allows us to advocate for the best technological fit for our content. You can go directly to http://edorigami.wikispaces.com to learn more about the Digital Taxonomy. You will also find a tool that is a useful aid when creating objectives on the *Handbook's* website at www.astdhandbook.org.

Step 3: Flip the Classroom to Maximize Collaborative Impact

Finally, let's talk about flipping the classroom. The flipped classroom concept originated with K–12 educational systems, where traditionally students go to a class, learn from the teacher, and then go home to complete homework. Perhaps they build a model of a cell or write a report about the American Civil War. Because they are at home, they naturally turn to their parents and siblings for help. But the parents and siblings are not necessarily experts at biology or American history. Traditional homework doesn't set up the student for success. But the flipped classroom model attempts to solve this problem. It takes the lecture aspect of the classroom and turns knowledge-oriented content into self-directed work. The content might be delivered via an online video or a textbook or e-book. Students learn on their own and come to class to ask the expert questions about the content, complete project work, and apply knowledge.

Since project work isn't completed in a vacuum, we can kick it up a level. Students can collaborate in groups, with an expert to moderate, to create projects and interactions that reach a higher level of learning than they may have accomplished on their own.

How does flipping the classroom apply to blended learning? Remember, blended learning is not only about matching content to the most appropriate delivery medium, but also doing it at the learning objective level. If you follow the suggested process of using learning objectives and assessment techniques to determine the best delivery method for each objective, using a model like Bloom's Digital Taxonomy for guidance, you will be delivering a program that has students mastering knowledge-based objectives using self-paced technologies and moving toward more collaborative and live technologies as they move into application of skills, analysis of skills, and beyond.

Implementing a flipped classroom isn't a fad. When thoughtful instructional design is applied to a blended learning program, a flipped classroom is the result. You will find three tools on the *Handbook's* website at www.astdhandbook.org: Bloom's Digital Taxonomy tool, a tool to break the instructional goal into performance objectives, and a list of common challenges that could be faced when implementing a blended program with solutions. Each of these will help you flip your classroom.

About the Author

Jennifer Hofmann is a synchronous learning expert and the president of InSync Training, LLC, a consulting firm that specializes in the design and delivery of virtual learning. In the field since 1997, she has experience using all the major web-based synchronous delivery platforms. Jennifer is a recognized thought leader in the field of synchronous and blended learning. She is the author of *The Synchronous Trainer's Survival Guide, Live and Online!*, *Tailored Learning: Designing the Blend That Fits*, and *How to Design for the Live Online Classroom: Creating Great Interactive and Collaborative Training Using Web Conferencing*. Follow Jennifer on Twitter, @insynctraining; on her blog, www.bodylanguageinthebandwidth.com; and on Facebook, www.facebook.com/groups/insynctraining/.

For Further Reading

Aldrich, C. (2009). *The Complete Guide to Simulations and Serious Games: How the Most Valuable Content Will Be Created in the Age Beyond Gutenberg to Google*. San Francisco: Pfeiffer.

Bozarth, J. (2010). *Social Media for Trainers: Techniques for Enhancing and Extending Learning*. San Francisco: Pfeiffer.

Hofmann, J. (2003). *Synchronous Trainer's Survival Guide: Facilitating Successful Live and Online Courses, Meetings, and Events*. Alexandria, VA: ASTD Press.

Hofmann, J. (2004). *Live & Online! Tips, Techniques, and Ready-to-Use Activities for the Virtual Classroom*. Alexandria, VA: ASTD Press.

Hofmann, J. (2011). "Blended Learning," *Infoline*, number 1108. Alexandria, VA: ASTD Press.

Kapp, K. (2012). *The Gamification of Learning and Instruction: Game-Based Methods and Strategies for Training and Education*. San Francisco: Pfeiffer.

Chapter 14

Captivate Your Learners by Designing Effective Games, Simulations, and Activities

Tracy Tagliati, Becky Pluth, and Karl Kapp

·· **In This Chapter** ··

- Discover how to create engaging learning in the classroom.
- Learn to develop interactive exercises and address consistent needs in all delivery methods.
- Understand how to hold learners' attention during asynchronous, self-paced e-learning modules.
- Identify the differences, advantages, and disadvantages of each delivery method.

Immersion, interactivity, and engagement can be achieved regardless of the delivery medium, whether it's in a classroom, a synchronous virtual classroom situation, or an asynchronous self-paced e-learning module. Each environment provides the opportunity to include games, simulations, and activities. Often the three delivery methods employ similar techniques for engagement—but not always. Each delivery type has different affordances that the designer should leverage to provide the most interactivity for the learners. Table 14-1 provides an overview of some of the differences to consider.

Table 14-1. Differences Between Learning Delivery Types

	Classroom	Synchronous	Asynchronous
Learner Engagement Frequency	10 minutes	4 minutes	4 minutes
Maximum Content Length	8 hours a day	<3 hours	<20 minutes/module
Learner Feedback	Visual/Verbal	Emoticons/Polling	Visual
Replay-ability	None	On Demand (recorded session)	On Demand
Delivery Cost	Medium-High	Medium	Low
Learner Cost	Medium-High	Low-Medium	Low
Development/ Design Cost	Low	Low-Medium	High
Topic Variation	Highly varied	• Fact based • Problem solving • Test online; teach online	• Fact based • Procedures

This chapter provides examples of games, simulations, and activities in each of the three delivery formats. To provide an easy comparison of the three methods, a common topic, How to Open a Sales Call, is used in each section of the chapter.

Classroom Teaching

Classroom teaching allows a variety of ways to captivate your learners with games, simulations, and activities. This section of the chapter will describe how frame games can be included during each phase of classroom teaching, such as the opening and introductions, the delivery of content, the review and practice, providing feedback, and the closing activities.

What are frame games? Frame games are generic game templates that allow you to load your own content and instantly create customized instructional games. As mentioned before, the content used for the examples in this chapter will be derived from the topic How to Open a Sales Call; however, you can use the same frame game designs with any topic or content relevant to your areas of expertise.

Opening and Introductions: Knowing Your Audience

Before beginning a session, it is important to know something about your learners and for the learners to know something about one another. The traditional way to manage this situation is to have the learners introduce themselves one by one. Instead of using this traditional ritual that can sometimes be boring and drag on, try using a frame game. An effective frame game for this purpose is called Sudden Survey.

Here's how Sudden Survey was used in our example of How to Open a Sales Call:

> The instructor divides the participants into four groups and provides each group with a question. For example:
>
> Group #1: How many years of sales experience does everyone in the room have?
>
> Group #2: How could you maximize the benefits of attending this workshop?
>
> Group #3: What worries do you have about the opening a sales call?
>
> Group #4: What ground rules would you suggest to make the workshop more effective?
>
> The learners then spend the next three minutes interviewing each other to collect the data related to their question. This is followed with another three minutes of group work to analyze the data; finally, each group presents its findings to everyone in the class.

The benefits of using this type of opening activity are many. Not only does it serve as an engaging ice breaker, but also it allows the learners to get to know each other, provides an efficient approach for collecting relevant information, and gets the learners active and moving around. Perhaps the greatest benefit is that it sets the tone of the workshop right from the beginning and lets the learners recognize that they will play an active and interactive role throughout.

Delivering Content: Chunking Content

In a classroom, the next part of the agenda is typically providing the learners with content on the topic at hand. Content can come from recorded sources or live sources. Recorded sources include text materials, graphics, audio and video recordings, and real objects, while live sources depend on people delivering presentations such as lectures. Lectures have long been considered the norm for delivering content. However, lectures are a passive form of learning. An alternative approach is to use an interactive lecture format to deliver the content. Interactive lectures are delivered in seven- to 10-minute chunks and designed to have mini-summary activities (frame games) interspersed throughout.

Consider how interactive lectures were used in our example of How to Open a Sales Call:

> The instructor begins this section of the training by providing an overview of the six-step process for opening a sales call, and then begins her detailed lecture on Step 1, How to Develop a Professional Greeting. After 10 minutes, the instructor stops the lecture and inserts the frame game called Essence. Essence requires the learners to reflect on the lecture up to that point and work in small groups to reduce it to exactly eight keywords. Each group shares its eight-keyword summary and votes on the best.

> After the voting is complete, the instructor continues her lecture for another 10 minutes. This time she describes Step 2, How to Introduce Yourself and Your Company. When the 10 minutes are up, the instructor again stops the lecture and inserts another frame game called Artistic Summary. Artistic Summary requires the learners to individually draw a quick sketch that represents something they learned from the Step 2 portion of the lecture. They share and explain their drawings to the others in their group.

> When this is completed, the facilitator continues the lecture with Step 3, How to Express Gratitude to the Potential Client, and so on.

Interactive lectures are useful instructional design strategies that provide the learner with the opportunity to go beyond passively listening to large amounts of content. It instead facilitates two-way communication between manageable chucks of information.

Review and Practice: Building Fluency

After the content has been delivered, the next step is to help the learners develop their fluency with the content by providing the opportunity to practice. This can be achieved by using simulation-type frame games. Simulation games are designed to reflect the real-world workplace and enable the players to apply their new skills, concepts, and insights to their jobs.

Let's see how a simulation frame game was used in our ongoing example of How to Open a Sales Call:

> The simulation frame game activity in this portion of the session is called Rapid Role Play. During round one of Rapid Role Play, the learners are asked to find a partner. One partner is instructed to play the role of the salesperson,

and the other partner is instructed to play the role of the potential client. The learners are given two minutes to practice their techniques for opening a sales call with each other. After two minutes, they switch roles. The instructor debriefs the group to help identify the effective and ineffective behaviors for opening a sales call. During round two, learners find new partners and practice again using their new insights. The activity continues for a total of five rounds. Each round is followed by an instructor-led debriefing discussion to uncover the insights of the learners' experience up to that point.

The benefit of simulation games like Rapid Role Play is that they are low cost and yet still effective for learning skills. They also can be easily tweaked to replicate a variety of real-life workplace situations.

Feedback

As described, the simulation game Rapid Role Play and other simulation activities like it not only provide the learner with the repeated practice that's necessary to master a new skill, but also provide the opportunity for relevant feedback. In this case, the feedback was immediate, useful, and came from multiple sources, including the learners' peers, the instructor, and the learners' self-evaluations. The feedback can be further enhanced with rating scales, checklists, and other devices to ensure it is more objective and useful.

Use of Narrative

There may be times when it is difficult or impossible to facilitate a simulation activity. This may be because the room setup does not allow for it, there are not enough learners, or some other unpredicted reason. If a simulation activity cannot be facilitated, the narrative method may be just the right alternative option to reap similar benefits.

How does it work? Instead of conducting the simulation, use detailed storytelling techniques to describe what happened in the simulation with an actual or a fictional group. The simulation could be shared from the point of view of the different roles and paused at critical junctures to ask the learners for their input. When the story ends, the debriefing session could be conducted as in the actual simulation. This alternative method allows the learners to receive the same valuable insights, but instead of experiencing it themselves, they gain understanding vicariously by listening to the experience of the simulation group.

Closing

The closing of a training session provides another opportunity to include an activity. An effective closing activity used at this time serves the purpose of providing a review of the major learning points, planning for application, and celebrating the completion of the session.

The final activity for the How to Open a Sales Call workshop provides an excellent example of an effective closing activity.

> At the end of the session, the learners are experiencing cognitive overload from all the content presented during the day. Rather than provide a heavy review of the key learning points, the instructor facilitates a more playful and open-ended activity called Back-to-Back. In this activity, the learners are asked to stand back-to-back with another learner in the room. At the beginning of round 1, the instructor poses a question. When prompted, the learners turn around to face their partners and provide a response to the question within the minute allowed. During round 2, they find a new partner and respond to a new question. This continues for a total of three rounds. As evident in the list below, each question should be relevant and related to the training objectives:
>
> - Which step of the sales call did you find the most challenging, and why?
> - Which step of the sales process do you think you already use with ease?
> - Which step of the sales process do you most look forward to using?

The benefit of this activity is that the quick pace of the questions increased the energy in the room and provided for a social atmosphere that allowed for celebrating and networking as well as providing a memorable review of the session.

Classroom Teaching Summary

The instructional design of activities used in the classroom teaching method is in part determined by the number of learners and the planned duration for the training. Keep in mind that with a little creativity and flexibility on the designer's part, most of the activities can be easily modified to adjust for group size and shortened or lengthened to accommodate for changes in the duration of the training. Experiment with activities to suit your situation and personal preferences.

Synchronous E-Learning

Let's take the example of opening a sales call but this time looking at a synchronous e-learning module. *Synchronous* means same time. It means that you're in a webinar environment, also referred to as a "web-ex," or blackboard collaborate session, which requires using a platform that will allow you to be online, share your slides, interact and engage with the learner, and present your content. There are a lot of different things that we need to take into account as we begin designing. The challenge with the synchronous setting is that the instructor is unable to see what the learners are doing and to determine if they are really engaged or just pretending to be engaged. We really need to focus on creating an environment that provides maximum engagement to ensure the learners are engaged and learning. This requires us to design engagement into the virtual classroom ahead of time. Thinking that we can add interactivity "on the fly" just doesn't work. When designing interactivity into a session, we need to remember that learners can be logging in from all across the country and around the world. Culturalization is a key component in our design.

When determining what type of activity you want to include in a webinar setting, keep in mind the level of difficulty of the interactivity—both for the instructor and for the learner. If you are a brand new webinar facilitator/producer, then you need to consider using a "novice" activity. An example of a novice activity would be the use of a polling question. Create a scenario and have learners select the best option from a multiple choice list of ABCD. This interactivity provides you, the trainer, with an opportunity to know just how much the learners know about the topic by how they respond to the scenario. This is also an easy way to get interactivity for both the instructor and the learners.

After each of the learners has responded, you can publish the results of the poll for all to see and discuss. You can then go through each and every option to talk about why it is right or wrong. Perhaps there isn't a right or wrong and it's just a good–better–best situation. I really like when it's good–better–best because it allows learners to see if they selected the most effective answer or response to the scenario. An example scenario that I received from Jeb Brooks from the Brooks Sales Group is:

> In making contact via phone, your prospect's assistant says, "Ms. Johnson is not currently accepting phone calls from potential vendors." You should:
> A. Send an email to try to get the information in front of the prospect.
> B. Ask when she will be accepting calls from you or other vendors.
> C. Try calling back in a month, after she has had time to review the materials you sent.
> D. Ask the assistant to call you when Ms. Johnson is free.

The beauty of this type of scenario or situation-based polling is that you're able to talk about the most effective and least effective responses. It becomes an interactive debate/discussion. Because all answers are affected to some degree, you're coaching and teaching several positive solutions. Couple this with the text chatting feature for learners to be able to share why they selected a particular answer. Thus, this one small activity turns an online lecture into an activity. At the end of the session, you do want to give the correct answer to the group. You can have several different polling questions to create an entire engagement series. Have learners keep track of their scores, or have the questions and scenarios also in their handouts so they can reflect on the best answers later.

There are several other elements to also consider in an online synchronous course.

Feedback

In order for a game, simulation, or interactivity to be effective, we absolutely need to have feedback. Because you can't see your learners' faces, except for the situations where you have webcams, you need to make sure that participants are engaged with you and the content. Just because the instructor said it doesn't mean the learner caught it—especially in a synchronous learning environment with many available distractions.

There are several ways to give and receive feedback through the synchronous platform that will help you redirect your content as necessary. For example, in most webinar platforms, there is a way to have learners tell you if the pacing is good. Some platforms use emoticons, which come in the form of a smiley face; some have forward arrows indicating to speed up the pace or reverse arrows indicating the instructor should slow down. If you don't have the emoticon feature, use the polling or quiz tool. Ask, "How is the pacing?" A—just right, B—too fast, C—too slow.

Aside from wanting to know if your pacing is good, you also want to be able to correct learners in the moment. The simulation would be a good example of when to use this type of feedback. If I were teaching opening a sales call, I may have learners go to private breakout rooms and work on a situation. In their private breakout rooms, I would have them whiteboard responses to the scenario or the situation, and then copy their whiteboards back to the main room for everyone to review. Having them work alone in their private breakout rooms or even with a partner or two creates great engagement and opportunities to practice; however, we want to ensure they practice well. We do not want them walking away from the webinar with inaccurate information. By reviewing their group work or individual work as a large group, we are able to do just that. Caution: Be sure to tell the groups in advance of the breakout room that they will be sharing this back with the large group and receiving feedback. Give an example or demonstration of what that will look like so they are prepared. You can turn it into a game where other learners are asked to review the content learned and see if they can come up with an area that could be improved. When I forget to tell groups that their work will be shared or that they will receive feedback, I often face negative responses. On the other hand, I never have negative responses when I set the expectation prior to the breakout room.

Interactivity

After hosting hundreds of webinars and researching behaviors of learners on many webinars, the Bob Pike Group has found that learners begin dropping off and doing other things if not engaged every four minutes. Dr. William Glasser, in his research, found that having fun, freedom, power, and a feeling of belonging have a direct impact on retention and the ability to learn. How we do this in a webinar fashion is by ensuring the learners are active. They become part of the learning environment. This is done through polling, whiteboard activities, chat room exercises and activities, use of breakout rooms, application sharing, listening to audio/music, watching videos, playing games like Bravo! and Pronto! by C3Softworks, and listening to one another share. There are numerous ways to creatively use each on your platform. For example, I have a license from MP LC that allows me to stream video from a legal website or from my computer. I can application-share the video, streaming directly through, or send the link through the text chat area for individuals to watch on their own. This opens up a whole array of activities and exercises that can be done while watching the video clip or after the video clip is finished.

Use of Narrative

Storytelling has been a long-standing favorite form of learning. In a webinar format, have the learners share stories and examples so it adds a new voice, which is a re-engagement technique. In the book *Brain Rules,* author John Medina explains that the brain checks out at about the 10-minute mark unless something changes to grab the brain's attention. If you are telling the story, draw in the learners and place them in your story to grab their attention. For example, say, "Imagine you are four years old, and it's your first snowfall. . . ." Although it is your story, you have now just placed the learner inside the story.

Amount of Content

The webinar should be "need to know" content only. All other material should be in an appendix or an additional handout labeled "nice to know." So what equates to need to know content? Anything that will be used six times in the next 30 days is a need to know. If they are not using it, they are losing it. We follow the 90/20/4 rule. We never go longer than 90 minutes without a break of some sort. We chunk our content into bite-sized pieces of 20 minutes or less. In those 20 minutes, we have a little bit of content and some participation, then revisit the material. The four represents interactivity. We have some type of engagement every four minutes. Whether filling in the blank, highlighting on the whiteboard, or listening to a story, there is a re-engagement technique every four minutes. One way we extend the content beyond the webinar is by using what's called a "mindsetter." This product is a series of automated reminders based on the material presented. It is a great way to extend and help learners revisit the content once they're off the webinar.

Audience Size

It is often said that a small classroom size allows for a greater amount of personalizing, direct feedback, and attention. This is true; however, we've absolutely hosted webinars for hundreds at a time. Just remember, the interactivity needs to scale as the group size gets larger. If there are a hundred or more learners and you want to use a whiteboard activity, think about who will be writing versus allowing everyone to write.

Know Your Audience

It may not be possible for you to know who will be on your webinar at any given time. When you create sessions, begin with novice interactions until you learn how advanced your learners are. There is nothing worse than having frustrated learners give up and not participate. Provide plenty of opportunities for learners to practice using the tools at the beginning of the session. I like to take screenshots of the tools they'll be using so they can be successful each time. As you get to know your audience throughout the webinar, you can advance and progress to activities on the fly.

Record

Record your session every time. You never know when you may want to reuse the content, use it in an asynchronous e-learning module, or have learners who would like to review the session. It's a great way for you as an instructor to be able to enhance your program for the next session.

Asynchronous E-Learning Module

When teaching the content of opening a sales call with self-paced e-learning (asynchronous), the designer needs to take into account several factors to ensure effective instruction to engage the learner. The challenge with self-paced instruction is that there is no instructor to adapt to the needs of the learners in real time. The designer of the instruction must try to anticipate learner questions, needs, and level of knowledge. Well-designed self-paced e-learning has multiple paths through the content to help learners with different skills and knowledge levels gain the most from the content. This is not an easy task and requires careful consideration of the audience, nature of the content, levels of feedback, and amount of content.

One method of teaching a person how to open a sales call with self-paced e-learning would be through the use of a branching simulation. Another would be through a game teaching the concepts of opening and closing a sales call. Using a simulation, the e-learning software can present the learner with a situation such as being in an office of a potential client and trying to have an effective opening to continue with the call and, eventually, make the sale.

The branching simulation unveils a discussion between the learner, who would be playing the salesperson in the simulation, and a nonplayer character serving as a potential client. A number of questions are presented to the learner, and the learner is asked to select the best answer. Based on the answer by the learner, the e-learning simulation would branch toward getting closer to an effective opening or farther from the effective opening.

In many simulations, there is a coach feature. This is typically a character whom the learner can either "summon" by clicking on a coach button or who appears when the player is having problems. The coach provides a hint to the correct answer, guides the learner toward materials that would provide the answer, or, in some cases, gives the learner the answer.

Throughout the simulated sales call, the learner's choices are tracked and scored. Typically, at the end of an e-learning simulation, the learner is provided with feedback indicating what decisions or choices were appropriate, which decisions were incorrect, and what could be done differently the next time to reach a desirable outcome.

Following are various elements that are considered in a self-paced, online e-learning course.

Feedback

After taking an action in a simulation, the learner will receive some type of feedback. Feedback is of critical importance in an asynchronous learning environment because no adjustment can be made during the instruction. So, the reactions and actions of the learner must be anticipated and designed into the instruction.

In terms of the type of feedback, the learner can receive either authentic feedback or artificial feedback. The authentic feedback is feedback that would naturally occur, such as a potential customer smiling when the learner asks them about their children. Artificial feedback would be if text appeared on the screen telling the learner that the customer is not happy with a particular line of questioning. The learner would never see floating text in the actual environment.

The feedback can be immediate or delayed, and it can be positive or negative. One great element of self-paced learning in a simulation is that the amount of feedback provided can be consistent and evident for every action a learner takes. If a learner walks into a virtual room without knocking, the nonplayer character might get upset and end the sales opportunity. An online module can provide a "happiness meter" that can turn red if the potential customer is getting angry or losing interest, and the learner can adjust immediately. In online, self-paced learning environments, it is possible to craft continual, immediate feedback through the entire learner's experience.

Interactivity

Research strongly indicates that what makes an interactive learning experience effective is the level of activity of the learners as they participate in the activity. If learners are engaged, they learn more and retain the knowledge longer. If the asynchronous learning module has a large number of passive elements and the learner is forced to observe for much of the module, the learning is limited. Online learning has the opportunity to have continual interactivity. The learner can be interacting with the content by dragging and dropping items or clicking to find information. The use of good–better–best types of questions is a great way to encourage the learner to think about the content and to apply newly learned knowledge.

The learner can continually be making decisions and seeing firsthand the consequences of those actions and activities. Online learning events allow for the learners to practice the skills they just learned and to be active in learning.

Use of Narrative

An effective tool for gaining and maintaining a learner's attention in a self-paced online learning course is to draw your learner into a story or narrative. The story provides the context for the learning and creates a schema in the learner's mind to place the lessons learned for easy retrieval in the future. Researchers have found that the human brain has a natural affinity for narrative construction. People tend to remember facts more accurately if they encounter them in a story rather than in a list. Additionally, the story provides the initial "hook" for the learners and carries them through the content to the end.

Amount of Content

In an online, self-paced course, an important element to remember is to not overload the learner with too much content. One method of chunking the content is to place a minimal amount of content on each screen without scrolling. This can be done by having content "revealed" when a learner rolls over a particular area of the screen or having them click on something for more information.

Audience Size

For an online, self-paced course, the number of audience members does not factor into the design. It is possible to make the course more social by building in elements that allow learners taking the course at different times to post notes or messages but, by and large, the need to consider audience size is minimal. Most of the time, the designer creates an asynchronous online course considering only one learner taking the course at a time.

Know Your Audience

With a self-paced e-learning module, it might be possible to know the audience through an audience analysis conducted before designing and building the online module, but it is also possible to create the e-learning in such a way as to have it adapt to the different needs of learners. A simple example is to have different entry points into the instruction. You could make three levels of instruction within the module and target the module based on whether a learner self-selects as a novice, intermediate, or expert in the subject matter being taught. Another technique is to pretest the learner on the content and then only present the learner with the content he or she got wrong in the pretest. An asynchronous e-learning module can even be created to adapt to learner skill levels on the fly by looking at the learner's level of comprehension, efficiency of strategy help needed, and response time and adapt accordingly. Not many e-learning programs currently have these capabilities, but the industry is moving in that direction.

Final Considerations

There are a number of elements of self-paced online learning that should be considered when determining the use of self-paced games, simulations, or activities.

Start/Stop

Self-paced learning allows learners to stop viewing the content or playing the game or simulation anytime they would like. Most good designs allow for saving points and bookmarking, so the learners can come back to the exact spot they left when returning to the online game, simulation, or activity. This means if learners get tired, their minds start to wander, or if they need to get up for a bio break, they do not have to miss anything. They simply pause or stop the game, simulation, or activity and come back to the exact same spot whenever they are able.

Pacing

Closely related to the ability to stop and start the game, simulation, or activity anytime a learner would like, pacing also gives the learner the ability to move through the content as quickly or slowly as desired. A learner can spend 10 minutes on one screen reviewing possible answers or contemplating a next move before proceeding. The pace of the instruction is learner centered. The learner does not need to try to keep up with classmates or an instructor. The learner sets the pace.

Replay-ability

Well-designed simulations and learning games provide the learner with many paths through the content. For example, in our branching simulation, the learner can attempt to get all the right answers for the simulation, but if he or she misses a correct answer, the opportunity exists to go back to the simulation, and replay by taking another path. When a simulation is over because a learner took one path, other paths are still open and will potentially reveal new and different information, and that can encourage the learner to go through the content again, which provides another opportunity for practice and learning of the content.

Anywhere/Anytime

Because the course is self-paced, the learner can usually access the content whenever or wherever he or she happens to be at that point in time. Learners do not need to travel to a specific location for classroom instruction, nor do they have to be online at a designated hour. If they want to review the course at 4:00 a.m. because they can't sleep, they can log in to the course and review the content. There is no waiting for an instructor or driving to a physical location. Often, many learning management systems have an "offline" mode where learners can download a course while they have Internet access and then review the course on a laptop or tablet, even when they don't have Internet access.

Acceptability of Embedded Testing

One element of self-paced, online learning that is highly effective is the ability to quiz the learner at any time and to track his or her performance on that quiz. Although classroom instruction and synchronous virtual classrooms have the ability to quiz students at any time, that seems to be a seldom-practiced phenomenon in those environments. In self-paced, online learning, it has become acceptable to frequently quiz the learner both with questions embedded into the instruction and with end-of-module quizzes.

Summary

In summary, classroom, synchronous, and asynchronous delivery methods each provide a variety of opportunities to enhance the learning experience with games, simulations, and activities. Table 14-2 provides some additional considerations for each method. You can download a copy of this chart at the *Handbook's* website at www.astdhandbook.org to help you remember the unique considerations for each method when you are designing a learning experience.

Table 14-2. Additional Considerations for All Delivery Methods

Considerations	Classroom	Synchronous	Asynchronous
Instructor able to monitor group and modify the activity in the moment.	✓		
Instructor able to monitor learners during activities and provide individual feedback in the moment.	✓		
Learners can participate in activities at the same time while in different locations.		✓	✓
Activities provide the opportunity for learners to build personal relationships with instructor and with each other.	✓		
Learners are more aroused when a quick response is expected.	✓	✓	
Learners can replay and review activities as often as needed.			✓
Learner has time to read and reflect before responding to questions and activities.			✓
Requires technological coordination and reliability. Bandwidth may also be an issue.		✓	✓
Communication during activities is largely dependent on written communication methods. Students who rely on oral skills may feel disadvantaged.		✓	✓
Ability to record all interactions and provide for frequent testing.			✓

About the Authors

Tracy Tagliati, MS, CPLP, knows how to engage the learner. As training manager at MOVE, Inc., she develops and facilitates customized learning using a rapid instructional design approach. Her specialty is activities-based training in both instructor-led and web-based environments. She has co-authored three books on topics relating to interactive learning techniques and has presented at numerous international conferences. Her mission is helping people improve their performance effectively and enjoyably.

Becky Pluth, MEd, CSP, MPCT, is the president and CEO at the Bob Pike Group. A published author of four training industry books, she has presented around the world and online to groups of 1,600 learners and standing-room-only sessions at ASTD for the past seven years. Becky achieved her CSP (Certified Speaking Professional) designation in 2013, the highest designation in the speaking industry. In 2012, she was named one of *Training* magazine's Top 40 Under 40 Trainers and is an active member of ASTD MN, the Instructional Systems Association, and the National Speakers Association.

Karl M. Kapp, EdD, CFPIM, CIRM, is a full professor of instructional technology at Bloomsburg University in Bloomsburg, Pennsylvania. He serves as the assistant director of Bloomsburg's Institute for Interactive Technologies. Karl has authored or co-authored six books, including the bestselling learning book *The Gamification of Learning and Instruction* and its accompanying how-to book *The Gamification of Learning and Instruction Fieldbook: Theory Into Practice.* You can catch up with him at his widely read blog, Kapp Notes, at http://karlkapp.com/kapp-notes/.

References

Brooks, J., and W. Brooks. (2011). *Perfect Phrases for the Sales Call: Hundreds of Ready-to-Use Phrases for Persuading Customers to Buy Any Product or Service.* New York: McGraw-Hill.

Glasser, W. (1999). *Choice Theory: A New Psychology of Personal Freedom.* New York: HarperPerennial.

Medina, J. (2008). *Brain Rules: 12 Principles for Surviving and Thriving at Work, Home, and School.* Seattle: Pear Press.

For Further Reading

Aldrich, C. (2005). *Learning by Doing: A Comprehensive Guide to Simulations, Computer Games, and Pedagogy in eLearning and Other Educational Experiences.* San Francisco: Pfeiffer.

Kapp, K.M. (2012). *The Gamification of Learning and Instruction: Game-Based Methods and Strategies for Training and Education.* San Francisco: Pfeiffer.

Kapp, K.M. (2013). *The Gamification of Learning and Instruction Fieldbook: Theory Into Practice.* San Francisco: Pfeiffer.

Pluth, B. (2007). *101 Movie Clips That Teach and Train*. Minneapolis: Pluth Consulting.

Pluth, B. (2010). *Webinars With Wow Factor: Tips, Tricks and Interactivities for Virtual Training*. Minneapolis: Creative Training Productions.

Pluth, B. (2014). *SCORE! Super-Openers-Closers-Revisiters-Energizers for Enhanced Virtual Training*. Minneapolis: Creative Training Productions.

Thiagarajan, S., and T. Tagliati. (2012). *Interactive Techniques for Instructor-Led Training*. Bloomington, IN: The Thiagi Group.

Thiagarajan, S., and T. Tagliati. (2013). *More Jolts! Activities to Wake Up and Engage Your Participants*. San Francisco: John Wiley & Sons.

Chapter 15

Creating Media Learning Content That's Fabulous, Fast, and Affordable

Jonathan Halls

.... **In This Chapter** ....

- Discover why video is the new flipchart.
- Learn how to create fabulous learning content.
- Acquire tips for video, editing, audio, text, and equipment.

Twenty years ago, train-the-trainer programs taught newcomers to our profession how to write on flipcharts. They talked about what color pens to use, how large the lettering should be, and even how to turn the page in a way that least distracted the learner. The flipchart has been an indispensable tool for facilitators. That's about to change.

Video Is the New Flipchart

For many trainers, the indispensable tool will soon be multimedia. Future train-the-trainer programs will talk about how to seamlessly integrate media into learning as well as how to create it. And job descriptions will include "media production experience" in their selection criteria.

There are many reasons for learning professionals to be excited by media. One compelling reason is it enables us to extend our learning beyond the classroom so anyone can engage anytime and anywhere. This sounds like learning autonomy to me—classic adult learning principles. Malcolm Knowles would be proud.

Media also allows classroom trainers to bring content into the classroom from the outside world that would otherwise be relegated to boring diagrams on PowerPoint slides. Why show a diagram of how to change a tire when you can show a real-time video complete with close-ups and slow-motion replays? And why not record subject matter experts on video so they are part of every class rather than once or twice a year?

As new technology makes media much cheaper and easier to produce, some learning professionals may be reluctant to embrace it out of fear. Yes, making good content is complex and can be hard work. But more than any other profession, I think learning professionals start out with the best set of foundational skills.

What's Fabulous Media?

Media has traditionally referred to radio, television, and print such as newspapers and magazines. *Media* is plural for *medium*, which suggests that it is a tool that mediates between two people. Five hundred years ago at classic universities, the lecturer was the medium. Thousands of years ago, the medium might have been a papyrus scroll. While we traditionally think of media as being radio, television, and newspapers, a medium could also refer to posters, postcards, and any other objects through which a message passes, such as workbooks and job aids. And, yes, the Internet.

Traditional media is driven by communication. Communication is the process of creating shared understanding. Producers manipulate information and form it into digestible packages that are quick and easy to understand. The documentary you see on the Discovery Channel has been packaged to be easily understood. When you listen to the news on the radio, radio professionals structure it so you are not left scratching your head confused.

Does this work sound familiar? You do this as a trainer, although you have a few extra responsibilities. Learning professionals aim to make the topic not only easy to understand, but also easy to remember and apply. Media communication is about shared understanding. Learning is about understanding, retention, and application. This is why many learning professionals find it easy to pick up media skills.

Many of the instructional design principles that were drilled into you when you started as a trainer happen to be the perfect foundation for creating media content. It's on this foundation that learning professionals need to add production and editorial skills. Some of these skills are general to all media. Some are specific. For example, making television programs draws on a range of skills that apply across radio and television, but there are some specific skills that are exclusive to it.

Traditional media included the three mediums of radio, television, and print. In today's new world, we have the Internet. And when we consume audio, video, and text on the Internet, they are no longer mediums in their own right. By virtue of media convergence, these are now communication methods that exist on the medium of the Internet. For the rest of this chapter, we'll refer to them as methods rather than mediums.

The Internet supports other communication methods too. These include graphics, animation, and data. Many are familiar with graphics and animation. However, data are less talked about. Data refer to dynamic applications that tell a story based on data. The actual story changes automatically when the data are updated. In the media world, it is referred to as data journalism. Examples include Flash sites that tabulate and display real-time election data on election night.

In this chapter, we will focus on audio, video, and text. This begs the question: What makes fabulous or engaging media content? Good learning content—whether it is video, audio, or written text—should be quick to understand so it is easily remembered and applied to the real world. To achieve this, we need to ensure the planning is robust and the production is disciplined.

How Do We Create Fabulous Learning Content?

One of the secrets to creating powerful video is planning. If you're not spending roughly 40 percent of your overall production time on planning, there is a good chance you'll end up wasting time in the edit stage, fixing mistakes or catching up with something you forgot earlier. Planning is equally important for audio and video.

The first step to creating engaging learning content is to establish a learning objective. The objective focuses you as you start brainstorming your content and provides you a yardstick to review your success. Mager's principles for criterion-referenced instruction are just as relevant for learning media as they are for a classroom, as is Bloom's Taxonomy.

Once you have a learning objective, you need to consider what method of communication is best suited to your topic.

Rapid Video Workflow

Follow this workflow to speed up your video production:

1. Establish the learning objective.
2. Determine whether audio, video, or screen text is best to facilitate it.
3. Break the learning objective into chunks.
4. Use the chunks to create a structure that makes the objective easy to understand.
5. Draw a storyboard based on the structure.
6. Write your script based on the storyboard.
7. Shoot your video.
8. Edit your video.
9. Review your video.

As a general rule, video is excellent for any learning that has visual action. If you have action and interesting pictures, the topic will work well for video. Video, however, is not strong on details or complex learning points, so use it for declarative tasks that do not require the learning of lots of new details.

Audio is good for narrative learning. It appeals to the listener's imagination and draws on their long-term memory to create meaning. However, it's lousy for conveying detailed information, such as statistics, in anything other than a very general form. So don't use it for HR compensation policies, but use it to share sales strategies and leadership lessons.

Screen text is excellent for detail and complexity. It is easier for the learner to pause and reread a sentence than to pause and rewind a video. However, it is not so good when action is involved. For example, video can show you how to change a tire in a minute or so. It would take a lot of words to capture as much detail as the picture.

Once you have determined whether your learning is best facilitated by audio, video, or text, it's time to break it down into chunks of information and arrange it into a pattern that is easy to understand. Everyone has a different way of doing this, so if you're an instructional designer, follow what works best for you.

If you're struggling, look at your learning objective and ask yourself, what knowledge do I need to perform this task? Write it down. What skills do I need to perform this task? Write them down. Are there any attitudes to adopt that may help the learner perform this task better? Write them down. These chunks of information need to be formed into a structure that's easy to understand.

How do you do this? Often, when you work with the information chunks, a pattern will emerge. You may see how the chunks tell a story, and that becomes the structure you use, or a process may emerge and you create a step-by-step structure.

When a structure has been formed, you need to consider how you will use your communication method to facilitate the learning. If it is video, what pictures will you use? If audio, will you use interviews, role plays, or a monologue? If it's text, how will you structure it?

One of the classic principles of learning is that memory retention is aided by rehearsal. This process of rehearsal is how we learned our times tables in grade school. It's how actors learn their lines. And it's how soldiers learn their skills. Media doesn't allow us to rehearse the learning because it's a one-way medium. But we can use repetition. As you work through your plan, look for opportunities to engage in creative repetition of your key points to ensure retention.

Once you have planned your content, you're ready to decide how it will work with your chosen communication method. Let's look at this in detail. First, we'll discuss video, then move on to audio and screen text.

Using Video for Learning

Video is primarily a visual method of communication. Viewers tend to watch first and listen second. That's why people tend to remember the radar pictures and graphs when they watch the weather forecast on television but rarely do they remember the words of the meteorologist.

Video relies on (moving) pictures to convey a message. The first step in creating video learning is to draw a storyboard. Instead of using words to explain your topic, you need to think of pictures that convey your message. The other elements of video are layered on top of the pictures and work to support the pictures in carrying the message.

Planning your message in pictures is hard work if you are a seasoned writer who has never worked with video before. Photographers pick it up quicker but still need to learn about movement and sequencing shots. The good news is that communicating with pictures is a skill that can be learned.

Let's say you needed to convey the idea that Paul is late for a meeting with John. Using the written word, we'd simply write a sentence such as, "Paul is late for a meeting with John, who was frustrated because he had a tight schedule that day." If you were conveying this information in video, you might shoot a wide shot of Paul dressed in a business suit rushing down a street. You might then cut to a close-up of Paul's perspiring face. Paul would display a facial expression of stress. Then you could cut to a mid-shot of John in a conference room looking annoyed. Then cut to a close-up of John tapping a pencil on a conference table or looking at his watch.

This is how video works—pictures carry the message. Once you have chosen pictures that carry your message, you can think about other message layers that add to the message and plug information gaps left by the pictures. For example, you could get John to record a voice-over with a touch of reverb so it sounds as if we are hearing the thoughts in his head. He could say, "Paul is late again!" Likewise, we could do the same for Paul. He could say, "John's going to kill me—I know he's tight on time today. . . ." To add more power to the message, we could then add some music behind the shots of Paul running. Music is great for influencing mood, so we could choose music that sounds stressful.

The more we think about how pictures carry the message, the better our video will look. This is why it's important to always storyboard your video before writing a script. You will find an example of a storyboard and a template you can use to create your own storyboard at the *Handbook's* website at www.astdhandbook.org.

One of the important principles of video is to keep changing the shot. That's why our example of Paul and John works; the shots keep changing, and each shot conveys a message. If we hold one shot too long, the viewer quickly gets bored. That's why videos of seminars and lectures are generally not effective. It's why typical "talking head shots" are not suited to video. Your viewer's mind will start wandering within about 15 seconds.

However, we don't always have the luxury of time to shoot lots of engaging shots. The boss may ask you for a video of a lecture or speech and you have little opportunity to influence her of its ineffectiveness. So what do you do? Sometimes you have to get a message out to a learning community and literally have no time to set up a great production. In these cases, think creatively about adding slides and changing the shot sizes on a regular basis so your viewer sees the screen changing. For example, if you are shooting a lecture, shoot it in wide and then use the crop tool in the editing program to cut between a wide shot and a close-up.

The bottom line for video is to consider how you can use pictures to convey your message. The more you plan them, the better they will be.

Shooting Your Video—Making Video Fast

One of the aims of this chapter is to consider how to make media content fast. Doing a storyboard is proven to speed up video production because it focuses your energies. Another way to speed up your production is to follow good production discipline.

A lot of hours are wasted in the edit stage of production because the video someone has shot is poor quality. It may be overexposed or underexposed (too light or too dark). An object may need to be cropped out of the shot because the camera operator missed it. Video shot without a tripod requires time to apply a special effect that removes the shaky camera experience.

Mistakes are often made because we try to shoot the action too fast. Sometimes, two extra minutes checking your environment and camera settings is all that is needed to prevent common problems that take hours to fix in the editing process.

When you shoot your video, make sure there is plenty of light. And make sure it shines on the person you have in the shot or the object on which you are focusing. Do not shoot into the light or position a talking head in front of a window. Get into the habit of mounting your camera on a tripod so you don't have shaky footage. If your camera has manual functions, use them rather than auto focus, auto exposure, and auto sound. If your camera only has auto functions, set your camera on wide so the auto focus does not get confused. If you need a close-up, physically move closer to the object and resist the temptation to use the zoom control.

Although video is primarily about pictures, lousy audio can ruin your video. So pay attention to the audio. Professionals use external microphones. However, if you have a lightweight camera with a built-in microphone, get close when you are recording someone talking. And avoid recording in areas with background noise. It's very difficult to fix lousy sound while editing. There are tricks to hide lousy sound, but it presents some serious challenges.

Editing

The editing process is where you take all your video footage, music, sound effects, and other audio elements and turn them into a completed package. These elements are generally referred to as media assets. During the edit, you might also add visual effects to correct poorly shot assets or add an effect to support the narrative. And you add transitions, which is the way one shot changes to another, much like an animation in PowerPoint.

You can read many books about editing technique. The gist of it is that you should cut pictures so they flow together naturally in a way that conveys your message without distractions. It can be tempting to add lots of special effects and transitions, but be careful because they draw attention to your technique rather than your content. Special effects should be saved for only special occasions.

There are many video editing software packages on the market today. They all have their strengths and weaknesses. It's important to choose one that you are comfortable using. It's also important to remember that good video is not the result of the editing software. It is the result of the decisions you make about how to cut pictures together. So learn the craft of editing before you learn the software. Professional picture editors will still create a masterpiece on an entry-level software package.

Audio

Just as good learning video starts with a clear learning objective, so does an audio package. Having broken your learning objective into chunks and structured it so it makes sense to your learner, it's time to plan your audio piece.

Once again, planning is important. Audio communicators have three storytelling tools available to them. They are spoken word, music, and sound effects. Spoken word content is important for conveying details. Music is good for affecting mood and influencing the listener's energy level. Sound effects are great for building powerful pictures in your listener's mind.

The key difference between communicating with video and audio is that video pictures exist on a screen. It could be a computer, mobile, or data projector screen. Audio pictures reside in your listener's mind. What makes audio more powerful is that your listeners create these pictures using their imagination and drawing on experiences in long-term memory.

Audio is an incredibly powerful method of communication in its own right. If you create a podcast, you can create role plays for leadership training that are far more powerful than anything we can do in video. And you can take your listener anywhere in the world. Instead of carting a film crew to a baseball match, a few well-chosen sound effects can take the listener directly to the game. Drawing on their own memories, listeners can experience the game with more color and passion than anything on video.

Audio is an important component in e-learning that often supports slide shows created in programs like Camtasia. While we don't address that form of audio in this chapter, many of these principles apply.

Audio offers a wealth of options for getting your message across. You could create a simple learning monologue. You could conduct a series of interviews with subject matter experts. You could record role plays and create drama much as they did in the 1950s with radio soap operas.

Before you pick up a microphone or tape recorder, plan the structure of your podcast. That means setting a sequence of elements and working out how much time you need for each one. You might start with a spoken introduction and then cut to an interview with a subject matter expert. You might then transition to a role play. The more voices you include, the more dynamic and engaging it is. Make sure each element is faithful to your learning objective. Think about using music and sound effects to transition between elements.

Once you have a structure, plan your production. As a general rule, it will be more efficient to record each element of your podcast separately before combining them. So record the role plays. Record the interviews separately. And then record any commentary such as an intro and outro.

Once you have recorded all these, assemble them in an audio editing software program. You should use a program that offers multitracking so you can layer all the elements and add music beds for voice-overs. Just as with video, there are many audio editing programs on the market. If you like cheap and cheerful, Audacity works very well, and it's a free download from the Internet. (Google *Audacity* and you'll find it's the first listing.)

Podcast Equipment

Many people spend hours scouring the web looking for the right equipment to create audio learning podcasts. Equipment will always change and be updated so we won't get into specific models, but here are a few things to watch out for. The most important tool is your microphone. If you record podcasts and audio in Camtasia using a headset microphone, it will always sound like you're using a headset microphone. These are good for gaming and Skype conversations, but not the best for audio podcasts.

Invest in a studio condenser microphone. Your podcast will instantly sound much more professional. You will sound as if you are sitting next to your listener. With a headset microphone, you will always sound as if you're on a Skype call. You can pick up a USB studio condenser from Amazon for $60; it will be your best investment.

Podcast Equipment

You can produce a podcast or piece of audio with just a microphone and a set of headphones. However, more equipment can give you more options. Here's a list of the bare essentials and nice-to-haves.

Essentials

- Computer: You need this to record and edit your audio.
- Microphone: Avoid headset mics. Consider a USB studio condenser mic.
- Headphones: Get good-quality headphones that are comfortable to wear.
- Audio editing software: Audacity is free, but Adobe has Audition, Sony has Sound Forge, and there are other great packages available.

Nice-to-Haves

- Digital audio recorder: Great for recording interviews with subject matter experts (SMEs) in the field. Don't use an office Dictaphone recorder; the quality is not good enough.
- Telephone hybrid: This is a box that sits between your telephone and computer and enables you to record telephone interviews. Great if you can't visit SMEs in person for an interview. A cheaper alternative is to use telephone recording software with Skype, although the quality is not as good.
- USB mixer: If you plan to record panel discussions, you can get a USB mixer to mix multiple microphones. You will need to buy analogue microphones for this though.

Some microphones, and especially headset mics, come with the tantalizing feature of "noise removal." They promise to reduce background noise such as air-conditioning or people talking. The only way to get good audio is to find a quiet room. Noise-removal technology removes other parts of your recording, making it sound artificial. Avoid recording in rooms that have parallel surfaces such as a square room or room with lots of glass. This creates a distracting echo. Instead, find a room with soft furniture that absorbs and reflects acoustic noise. If you have curtains in the room, draw them to reduce echo.

When you create a podcast, you'll find it is quicker to write a script and read it on the microphone than to ad lib. There are a number of important principles for writing media scripts that apply to both audio and podcasts. See the sidebar for details.

---■---

Media Writing

Writing an audio or video script requires a different approach than writing for paper. That's because we are writing to speak, not writing to read. Here are some tips for your script:

- Write in a conversational tone. Write as if you are speaking to only one person. Referring to "my audience" kills rapport.
- Use phrases. That means one clause per phrase and no subordinate clauses. Write in the active voice. And make sure the words, when spoken together, do not give off another meaning. For example, *attacks on senior citizens* can sound like *a tax on senior citizens* when spoken aloud.
- Always go for the short words. Monosyllables are best. For example, *start* is better than *commence. End* is better than *conclude.*
- Use concrete descriptive words that are visual. *Cut* or *slash* is better than *reduce.* Watch out for words like *it* or phrases such as *these things.* Replace them with the object to which you're referring.

---■---

Screen Text

The final area of media skills that learning professionals need to understand is writing text for the screen. Writing for the screen is a different discipline than writing for the page because people read screen text differently. The screen is a very different medium. On paper, our eyes read under reflected light. On screen, the light is beamed into our eyes. Despite terrific developments in screen technology, screens still create eye fatigue.

As a result, screen readers tend to be distracted and lazy, scanning text looking for keywords rather than reading carefully as they would with a book. Often, they will not read to the end of a sentence. Screen readers get impatient, especially when reading on mobile devices such as phones. If you write the way you were taught in school, it's highly likely people will not read your content. So what do we do to create text that's engaging and makes reading on the screen easier? Here are some tips:

- Structure: Keep online text as short as possible. Use headings and subheadings to guide the reader. Provide a summary paragraph at the beginning so the learner knows what to expect.
- Tone: Write in a conversational but respectful tone.
- Paragraphs: Readers skip heavy blocks of text. Long paragraphs create heavy blocks. Aim for two sentences per paragraph, and make sure you have a line space between paragraphs.

- ■ Sentences: Keep them short. Avoid subordinate clauses. Write in the active voice. Favor verbs over abstract nouns.
- ■ Words: Short words are always preferable to longer words. Make sure they are familiar, and avoid technical jargon.
- ■ Large blocks of content: Use lists and tables to package lots of content. This is easier to scan. If you have a list of information with additional points, use tables.

Learning Professionals as Media Professionals

As we transition to the post-industrial world where everyone is a media producer, learning professionals will rely on media communication with audio, video, and text as they have relied on the trusty old flipchart. Media will empower us to deliver learning anywhere, anytime, and for anyone. Using it effectively means embracing the instructional design processes we have learned as a profession and adding to them the craft of using these new methods in a way that draws on their strengths and plays to the needs of learners. Additional tips for success can be found on the *Handbook's* website at www.astdhandbook.org.

About the Author

Jonathan Halls authored *Rapid Video Development for Trainers* and has taught media and learning in 20 countries for more than 20 years. Today he divides his time between media training and organizational development work. He consults with corporate clients and is an adjunct professor at George Washington University in Washington, D.C. Jonathan has worked across television, radio, and newspapers and was a learning executive at the BBC, where he ran its prestigious television, radio operations, and new media training department. He has worked as a talk show host, journalist, and media executive. Jonathan has a bachelor's degree and a master's degree in adult education.

For Further Reading

Begleiter, M. (2001). *From Word to Image*. Studio City, CA: Michael Wise Productions.

Friedmann, A. (2010). *Writing Visual Media*. Burlington, MA: Focal Press.

Halls, J. (2012). *Rapid Video Development for Trainers*. Alexandria, VA: ASTD Press.

Malamed, C. (2009). *Visual Language for Designers*. Beverly, MA: Rockport Publishers, a division of Quayside Publishers.

Ratcliffe, M., and S. Mack. (2007). *Podcasting Bible*. New York: John Wiley & Sons.

Chapter 16

Working With SMEs

Chuck Hodell

························· **In This Chapter** ·························

- ▦ Learn five types of SMEs.
- ▦ Select and evaluate SMEs.
- ▦ Review best practices with SMEs.

In the world of training, there are few, if any, more important strategic relationships than those we create and nurture with subject matter experts, or SMEs as they are commonly called. Paradoxically, there is also an almost total vacuum of available best practices and "rules of the road" with these valuable assets, and it is time to move the utilization of SMEs front and center in our training endeavors.

As the process of instructional design has become more professional and the world of training has become more complex, the need for a more thoughtful and enlightened approach to integrating SMEs has evolved. We now have the foundation for categorizing, assessing, and evaluating our content experts in a way that goes beyond subjective intuition and resides in objective classifications of different types of SMEs, meaningful standards for assessment of SME candidates, and evaluations of performance for all of our SME family.

Let's consider five categories of SMEs, the standards that assist in assessing potential SMEs, and how we can evaluate and best work with SMEs in the training function.

Five Types of SMEs

While SMEs hold countless different responsibilities in the world in general, in our training world SMEs play specific roles that merit our attention and focus. For our purposes, we divide them into five categories: technical, hybrid, instructional, functional, and sentinel SMEs. Each of these classifications has specific characteristics and contributes to our work in unique ways. Not all SMEs are created equal, and this is a real advantage for trainers.

Technical SMEs

First in our categories of SMEs is the technical SME. This group is primarily focused on technical content and isn't overly involved or concerned about other aspects of the instructional design process such as implementation. Technical SMEs are brought into the process to provide content knowledge and to make sure that every detail related to content is correct. These SMEs often work in groups, and the larger the scale of a project, the more of these experts you can expect to be involved.

Examples of technical SMEs include OEM (original equipment manufacturer) representatives, engineers, scientists, lawyers, medical professionals, skilled trades workers, and many others. This group is expected to have documented proficiency in the content area, and these SMEs usually have certifications, degrees, or other professional standing.

Hybrid SMEs

This unique category of SME embodies someone who is both a content expert and an implementation expert. These SMEs are expected to provide support both in the content of a course or program and in the best ways to deliver it. This, of course, assumes substantial documented expertise in both areas.

In most but not all cases, this combination is a very good thing, but there are exceptions that you need to be aware of as you consider a SME's qualifications. For example, a college professor who has never taught or designed a course for online implementation may not be a good choice for both content and implementation expertise if you are designing online college courses. In fact, a SME's combination of depth in content and lack of applicable implementation knowledge can be a source of friction when designing implementation, since his or her views will likely not resonate with the views of the more experienced design team members relating to online course design. Be careful in these situations.

Instructional SMEs

The roles of facilitator, mentor, coach, and teacher are all included in the instructional subject matter expert category. While this group may possess some degree of subject matter expertise, its primary role is to enhance the instructional aspects of the training during implementation. It is likely that someone who does not participate in the design, development, or management of the training will teach a technical course. Having this group's input about the best way to implement the content is often valuable.

Examples of instructional SMEs include a teacher who has considerable online course experience but doesn't possess any relevant content knowledge. There are also a number of talented skilled trades instructors who can assist with classroom and shop-level implementation course development. Both of these experts offer considerable value to the course design process.

Functional SMEs

Within your design team, you often have experts in areas who are not content or implementation related, but are nonetheless vital to your project. This might include programmers, software designers, photographers, artists, writers, and a wealth of other noncontent expertise. In most cases, we don't consider these valuable assets as SMEs, but they are in every way subject matter experts in their professions. To treat them in the same manner as our content experts will almost always work to the design team's advantage.

Sentinel SMEs

The final classification of SMEs is reserved for those in our world who manage and monitor many of our projects, yet may possess less relevant or dated content knowledge. These sentinel SMEs are most often members of governing boards, grant committees, or high-ranking organizational leaders, or they may sit on oversight or technical committees. While they may not be contributing directly to the content, they may feel compelled to comment on various aspects of the technical side of a content area.

Sentinel SMEs may sit in judgment of programs and courses and expect their knowledge to influence content decisions. Their input may be a distraction to the process if they insist on making their influence felt on decisions that the design team and other SMEs are in a better position to make. In other situations, technical and hybrid SMEs may sit as sentinels on projects to which they can serve as a real plus in moving positive momentum and direction from the perspective of both a technical expert and a sentinel leader for the project.

As you identify the different types of SMEs in your work, don't get trapped into thinking that one individual can only play one SME role in your work. There are the rare and talented individuals who are perfectly capable of contributing in multiple ways. Just be sure you have identified their roles in each situation to best use their abilities.

Selecting and Evaluating SMEs

The selection and evaluation of SMEs are generally parallel activities since they are based on a set of criteria related to several key observable and measurable standards expected in SMEs. To even a greater degree than in some choices made in the design process, making sure you have articulated your expectations, in both securing and evaluating your SME, is a necessity.

SME qualifications are best divided into two general categories: content specific and noncontent specific. This allows a thorough and comprehensive 360-degree scan of both the professional criteria associated with content knowledge and the numerous noncontent skills deemed necessary for SMEs in the design environment.

Content-Based Criteria

When looking at content knowledge, you need to be more than one-dimensional in your assessment of SMEs. Content knowledge is a complex and often confusing set of skills that rests atop a foundation of five multidimensional aspects of achievement.

You will need to review and determine the level of expertise based on at least these five elements of subject matter knowledge in each SME:

- relevance of experience
- depth of experience
- timeliness of experience
- location of experience
- training/teaching experience.

While on the surface these may not seem to be related to an extent that really allows discretionary judgment of an individual SME, drilling down into each of the criteria nets a wealth of information on which to base valid and documented decisions.

Relevance of Experience

While this may seem deceivingly obvious on the surface, relevance is the first obstacle that each SME must pass through to be considered qualified. Hopefully you don't assume that every SME in a content area is qualified for your specific content needs in a project. One size does not fit all, or perhaps even most, of your content knowledge needs; don't allow yourself to be lazy in this judgment.

Relevance in our SME assessment is the ability of a content expert to share content knowledge in a specific content area with relative ease. To be considered to have relevant experience, a SME must also have a documented body of work in the specific content area you are working in. For example, you might need a content expert in a specific engineering process, and while an engineer with experience in a related field might be easier to secure, you need to determine if a particular candidate can cover your content without compromising your expectations.

Depth of Experience

When looking at depth of experience in a SME, it may be tempting to think that depth and relevance might seem like a difference without a distinction, but this is a costly mistake. Depth in SMEs is fundamentally their ability to drill down to the lowest point of detail necessary for your content requirements. For example, if you are working on a project related to the printing business and color selection, the candidate who knows that a professional color chart contains 1,114 colors is preferable to one who thinks that the primary colors of red, green, and blue are all you really need to know about color. This same principle applies to all issues associated with depth—how deep can a SME go into the details?

Timeliness of Experience

Our third area of assessment in choosing SMEs is sometimes one of the most important to you as an instructional designer because having dated content appear in a new course or program is one of the cardinal sins of training. Ensure that you have the most recent and relevant content by working with SMEs who are current in their knowledge.

The shelf life of your content is something you need to determine quickly. Well-established and stable content that only changes incrementally over time is less affected than state-of-the-art content that may change on an hourly basis. If your knowledge base is considered "just in time," then your SMEs need to be operating at that same speed. Determining the criticality of timeliness for your needs is the first decision to make.

Imagine you are working on a project that requires the most recent statistical data such as economic reports relating to unemployment, job creation, and productivity. Choosing a SME with a PhD who teaches economics at a major university, but has little knowledge of this week's employment numbers would not be a better option than choosing an economist working with the data as they are released. By the same token, your college professor acting as a SME may be best suited for a course in economic theory.

Location of Experience

Thinking about geography when selecting SMEs might seem puzzling, until you consider that even minute changes in location can have a major effect on content. Depending on your project, failing to account for the location of an expert's experience can either marginally or completely affect your work. Let's look at several examples.

If you are working on a project to train paramedics that has a regional or national scope, each jurisdiction potentially has different skill requirements, licensure requirements, and clinical requirements for participants. Some may require 180 hours in clinical practice, and some may require 80. This is a huge difference in terms of designing training. Knowledge of and input from these differing standards are critical.

When designing technical and skills training, geographic location can be a critical element. The elements of geography that affect content include weather variables like temperature ranges and humidity; soil and ground condition variables like clay versus sand; and earthquake, hurricane, flood, and other natural disaster potential. To an outsider looking in, these variables may seem minor at best, or even unimportant, but nothing could be further from the truth. A content expert who has only worked in a warm climate has no relevant information for cold weather climate situations, and building codes are certainly different in quake-prone areas compared to others with little, if any, quake activity. These are just examples, but depending on your situation, there could be many differences that you need to represent on your committee.

The other regional variation that often comes to the surface in SME committees is jargon. This not only applies to tools and equipment, but also comes up in the names of processes and procedures that are exactly the same, but called one thing in California and another in Connecticut. This may be a major problem down the line if it isn't addressed early in the process. You can't have a large percentage of your end-user population trying to figure out your terminology because you didn't allow for regional variations in your SME group.

One indirect consideration here is that a budget may not allow for the cost of bringing in dispersed committee members. You may have to choose members who can represent the locational variations within the committee or use remote conferencing options.

Training/Teaching Experience

If you are working on a project that has a training deliverable, having a SME with training experience can be a valuable asset to the process. Knowing what works and doesn't work during implementation can be a critical added dimension. At times, it is this SME who eventually teaches the content, and having the connection at this stage of the process may lessen the disconnect issues from the design to implementation stages. Someone possessing these skills is your ideal candidate as a hybrid SME.

It will be useful to determine if the training and teaching experiences are relevant to the content and eventual implementation choices. A career as a classroom teacher may not work to your benefit if you are designing online learning using a learning management system (LMS) since the approaches are different.

There are also variations in teaching approaches and philosophy, for example, in higher education versus more general technical training. Having the correct fit is important since experienced teachers and trainers may be set in their views on implementation or they may not work well with your content and population.

Noncontent-Based General Skills Criteria

In addition to the SME content-based criteria, you should be familiar with your SME's general skills competencies. In a world of equals in terms of content expertise, you may find the noncontent skill set useful in assessing and evaluating your SMEs. While there are a number of criteria you could use in this regard, you may find the most important general skills criteria to consider include:

- communications ability
- writing ability
- sociability.

Communication Ability

Having an expert who can communicate with you and the other committee members is nothing short of critical. At some point, we all have experienced experts who obviously know the content but are less willing or able to efficiently and effectively communicate this information when needed, creating a bottleneck in the process. On the other hand, overly verbal experts can drown the content in minutiae and slow things to a crawl. This is an admittedly subjective criteria, but this can become a momentum stopper that can have unintended results.

Writing Ability

A real plus in a committee member is the ability to write content-related supplemental materials. There are times when an expert can more effectively reduce a process to writing than a team of instructional designers or technical writers. Even the ability to sketch an outline can save hours and days in writing.

How someone writes is also a consideration, since many academic and technical SMEs write in academic and technical styles, which may not be appropriate for your work. It is sometimes more work rewriting their submissions than anticipated, since the translation from formal to less formal styles is not an easy transition for some.

While it may not be expected that a SME is a good writer or can pull research together for the project, the occasional content expert who enjoys doing this work can make your project more efficient and usually increases the quality of the product. If at some point you can determine who likes to write and is actually pretty good at it, you may find a resource that is worth the effort to encourage and to integrate into the team.

Sociability

While this criterion is also subjective, we need to guard against a committee member who won't make an effort to get along and work with the team. Better to select on the basis of caution if possible. However, there are some indispensable experts you may just have to live with.

Best Practices With SMEs

The utilization of SMEs in the training community has evolved to the point where it is now possible to assemble a series of "best practices" related to their selection, evaluation, and retention. These general guidelines of best practices may be modified to fit particular situations and environments, but they serve as a strong starting point in making sure SMEs are a contributing asset in your work.

Show Appreciation

One of the easiest, yet most effective, ways to bring and keep SMEs in your design family is to show them how much you appreciate their participation. More than any other group you work with, content professionals often feel disassociated and unappreciated as they contribute to your project's success. Make every effort to see that every SME who works with you knows how much you appreciate his or her work.

Provide Clear Guidelines on Roles and Responsibilities

Nothing is more confusing to SMEs than not knowing what is expected of them and where they fit in the design process. This also includes the roles and responsibilities for the instructional design team. Taking the time at the first available moment to explain everyone's roles and responsibilities will clear up any misconceptions and allow everyone, especially your SMEs, to concentrate on the work that falls in their field of responsibility.

Make SMEs Part of the Design Team

The integration of your SMEs into your design team is critical to having a successful relationship with the professionals. If you have provided information on the roles and responsibilities for everyone on the project, the next logical step is to make sure your SMEs feel like they are part of the design team and not just adjuncts to the process. This doesn't have to be complicated, but making everyone feel as equal partners provides a number of both tangible and intangible benefits to the project, not the least of which is a shared experience of both responsibility and appreciation.

Pay Attention to the Needs of Your SMEs

SMEs, like any busy professional, will require some special attention to allow them to best support your project. This might be scheduled meetings that need to be moved, a place to work if they are away from their usual location, assistance with copying or accessing materials, or any number of unique support issues. The more you can accommodate these reasonable and expected needs, the more your SMEs can concentrate on their work for you.

Celebrate Project Milestones

One of the most often neglected best practices with SMEs is making the time and taking the effort to celebrate with SMEs the milestones in a project they are supporting. While it may seem trivial to some, to SMEs who have invested their knowledge, time, and effort into a project, anything from a simple certificate of appreciation to a lunch or dinner celebration is both highly valued and serves to build a strong foundation for future efforts where they might play a crucial role. A small investment in time and resources will almost always pay off somewhere down the road.

Conclusion

Finding the best ways to work with your SMEs is no longer just a hit-or-miss proposition. There are now objective ways to categorize, assess, and incorporate best practices in all our work with SMEs. Using this knowledge base as a foundation, your work with SMEs will become more productive and efficient.

About the Author

Chuck Hodell, PhD, is the author of *SMEs From the Ground Up*. He is also the author of the bestselling book *ISD From the Ground Up*, and he writes for *T+D* magazine, several *Infolines*, and other publications for ASTD. He is presently Associate Director of the Graduate Program in ISD at the University of Maryland, Baltimore County (UMBC). He holds a BA from Antioch University and an MA and a PhD from UMBC.

For Further Reading

Hodell, C. (2011). *ISD From the Ground Up,* 3rd edition. Alexandria, VA: ASTD Press.

Hodell, C. (2013). *SMEs From the Ground Up*. Alexandria, VA: ASTD Press.

Hodell, C. (2013, October). Five Considerations for Selecting SMEs. *T+D*.

Chapter 17

Curation of Content

Ben Betts

······························· **In This Chapter** ·······························

- Define the role of the curator.
- Understand how curation can be used in learning.
- Learn the four roles for digital curation:
  inspiration, aggregation, integration, and application.

M y favorite place of learning is the Natural History Museum in London, England. As you wander the neo-gothic halls, you come across fascinating stories, told through objects collected over hundreds of years. A curator will rummage through the archives to find fossils, video footage, paintings—anything that will help to tell a story. By transforming these very different objects into a compelling story, curators engage the audience in a journey that helps them to make sense of the individual pieces in a wider context. Individually, the objects tell a minor part of the story. Collectively, they are worth more than the sum of their parts. What's more, different curators can reuse the same objects in different ways. By bringing a particular lens of expertise and experience, each curator can weave a different story from the same content.

I like to bring this analogy out of the museum and onto the web. Here we are collectively producing millions of "objects" in the form of videos, blogs, news articles, research, debate, tweets, pictures, and more. As the barriers to content creation have fallen, the amount of content that is created has vastly increased. This has left us with a problem. Information is piling up everywhere.

Content Rich, Context Poor

We are undoubtedly content rich. A Google search for *curation* brings 4.3 million results. *Information overload* brings 18.2 million results. In this mix is a world of rich content. Of course, there is also a lot of trash. Google has been termed the "fast food" of knowledge sharing by curation guru Robin Good; it gets you answers quickly, but it comes with a health warning. If you want quality information, on whose substance you can rely, you need to go via a personal recommendation. What you need is a curator.

Google recognizes this problem. Using both the Google+ platform and Google Author tools, the search engine now allows for named authors to display their pictures alongside content in search results. By associating expertise with authoritative authors, Google is legitimizing certain pieces of content over others. We're now being given personal recommendations of exactly who endorses what content. It's not a stretch to see the Facebook Social Graph or LinkedIn being used on a wider scale for this exact purpose. However, giving a recommendation is only a minor part of the role a curator plays. At the micro level, this action is the curator merely authorizing an object as being worthy for some purpose or another. It does nothing to tell a story or build a collection in and of itself. It is in the lens of context that curators bring real value to content.

Imagine two curators; we'll call them Jill and Jeff. Both Jill and Jeff are accountants by training. Both specialize in tax. Both use social media extensively to promote themselves and their work. Jill runs a small business specializing in helping high-net-worth individuals to be as tax efficient as possible with their earnings. Jeff works for the Internal Revenue Service (IRS). When a new piece of legislation hits the marketplace, both Jill and Jeff are quick to pounce, blogging op-ed pieces and tweeting out the link to the published article. As a follower of Jeff's curation activities, my frame of reference for how to interpret the new legislation will be very different from my interpretation following Jill. Jill sees opportunities everywhere; her wider collection of links and blogs all frame her perception of the legislation and how to take advantage. It's no hassle for Jill to pick out the pieces of the article she wishes her readers to view and to ignore the pieces that Jeff might highlight. She can literally use a tool to quote verbatim from the published article and put it in a different context in her own articles. In this case, Jill actively transforms the article, without necessarily changing the words written on the screen. Increasingly, we are publishing smaller and smaller, bite-sized chunks of information. These are even easier to take out of their original contexts. Tweets, pictures, and short videos are easier to re-blog, embed, and share around the Internet. Now, if I were a high-net-worth individual (ha, I wish!), my first stop on the Internet would often be Jill's website or maybe her newsletter digest that she emails each week. I would know that Jill's interests align with my own; she's a better and more relevant source of information because of the context she brings.

The Role of the Curator

The role of the curator has been valued for centuries, but it has been somewhat reserved for a chosen few professionals who practice their dark art in the confines of the world's museums and galleries. To suggest that digital curators all bring the same depth and breadth of knowledge as a professional curator might be somewhat missing the point. Curation, when it comes down to it, is all about creating value from collection building. The Internet allows for a more granular approach to collection building than can be taken in the world's museums. You don't need to appeal to hundreds of thousands of visitors, just a handful of like-minded folk. Building collections for niche audiences is becoming increasingly common; you only need to see the rise of websites like Pinterest to know that the popularity of curated content is soaring.

Before getting into the logistical process of curation, curators first need to define their areas of interest. A digital curator will have a particular personal lens with which they seek information. It is in this context that digital curators start to add value; they approach objects with an agenda, not only asking if a particular piece of content connects with their field of interest, but also deciding how this will frame their personal opinions and how it helps tell a wider story. Extreme examples show us how this lens can be all-encompassing; 9/11 conspiracy theorists, for example, can make quite compelling arguments, but only when ignoring the much larger masses of rational evidence on the other side of the story.

Collecting information can be somewhat haphazard, but the best curators treat it like a science. Curators, such as *Inside Learning Technologies* editor Annie Garfoot, set up processes and systems to have information delivered directly to their inboxes. Annie does this with Google Alerts, giving her information often hours before it shows up in normal search results. This fits with Annie's workflow as a curator of the learning technologies world. As an alternative to Google Alerts, many curators use RSS feeds to receive information from publishers as it is published. These automated newsfeeds "push" news to subscribers as it occurs. Others perform similar actions using Twitter. It is possible to "follow" keywords or hashtags using a Twitter client on a smart device or desktop computer. I do this myself, keeping the occasional eye on the "tweet stream" to see what articles are being published and talked about. Some curators merely dedicate part of their days to scouring the corners of the Internet for tidbits of information they would like to share, frequenting content aggregation websites and industry portals for updates.

Regardless of their methods of receiving new information, all curators perform three basic actions: they store, they transform, and they share. Where and how curators store information is again largely personal preference. It is possible to streamline (to the point of complete automation) the process such that the program that collects information also stores it, transforms it, and shares it. "Personal newspaper" applications like Paper.li do this for thousands of users on a daily basis by inspecting the links that curators tweet and retweet and formatting them into a "newspaper" layout. However, this automation can also yield questionable results. We use a curator to get a personal context on content; if this portion of the process is also automated, it is worth questioning the true value of the curation piece. Curators add value; they create a story, but they don't just pass things on. For this to happen, the curator must be able to store information in a repository for easy access in the "transform" component of the process. For some people, this might be favoriting tweets; for others, it could be bookmarking, adding to Google+ or Facebook, or subscribing to a feed of information. It could be as simple as an Excel spreadsheet, for that matter. As long as the storing process allows the curator to revisit the content at a later time, it doesn't matter. Knowing that our end goal is to "share" should shape your decision at this stage; it's much easier to share with a web-based bookmarking tool like Digg than it is with Excel.

With information gathered, the digital curator sets about transforming the parts into a wider story that is more useful as a whole. Adding value comes in many forms, but it usually manifests in collection building or remixing content. As collections build, curators have the opportunity to demonstrate more evidence for their assertions, gathering not just a single blog, but several videos and other objects to back up a point or opinion. This process is actually a useful learning exercise in and of itself. In fact, remixing or transforming someone else's work into something new is an established pedagogical practice. Seymour Papert and his theory of constructionism—the act of constructing and reconstructing as a process of learning—would suggest that getting your learners to do the curating is a sound method of deepening understanding.

The final role of the digital curator is sharing. Having stored a range of content and added value through collection building and remixing, it is up to the curator to spread the message through social media. Following a prolific curator can be all that is needed to keep you personally abreast of what's going on in your industry. Career bloggers like Chris Brogan and Darren Rowse have made highly profitable lifestyles out of curating content on a daily basis. Websites like Pinterest have shown the popularity of curated content sharing; it was the fastest social media website yet to reach 10 million registered users. Sharing brings with it some risks; content that is curated without attribute treads a thin line between sharing and stealing, especially when you stand to make money out of it. Knowing copyright law and being able to readily cite sources are key skills in the mission to become a successful curator.

Curation in Learning

As discussed so far, we've seen curation in a fairly broad context, used to bring a personal perspective to the world of information that exists on the web. We can now focus our thoughts on the application of curation to training and development.

For this purpose, we can think of digital curation as being useful to us in four broad roles that we call inspiration, aggregation, integration, and application. Inspiration is how we term curation that is done by other people on your behalf, outside a formal learning environment. Aggregation is the same thing, but done in a formal learning context. Integration is a more personal curation process; it is how individuals blend new learning experiences with existing thoughts. And finally, application is how individuals apply new insights in the real world—how we individually manage knowledge on a day-to-day basis. We capture this flow in a simple matrix (Figure 17-1) that demonstrates how the four types of curation can flow into each other in a continuous learning cycle.

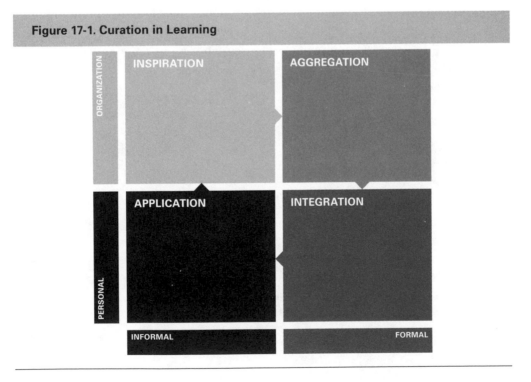

Figure 17-1. Curation in Learning

Inspiration

With the proliferation of content on the web, it should come as no surprise that we are in increasing need of systems to sort, maintain, and repurpose content in a systematic manner. For a while now, we've been making do with search as a primary means of sifting through the pile. But increasingly, we are turning to named experts to act as our filter to content. Where these experts spend time storing, transforming, and sharing resources with the world, they are in fact playing the role of the curator on our behalf. These experts have appeared in every industry. In our own industry, content curators are plentiful, and many have become well known for their curation efforts. Chances are that if you've attended a conference in the last three years, you've benefited from the backchannel curation skills of David "LnDDave" Kelly. Kelly stores an event's tweets, blogs, and presentations and brings them together on one webpage for easy reference. By following curators like Kelly, we can draw inspiration from a set of content that we know is going to be relevant to our work. It's like having the best insights into an industry hand-delivered straight to your mailbox.

Organizations can, of course, benefit from this approach. Here, the role of the digital curator is that of a guardian of resources; someone who stores, transforms, and shares in the context of the strategic needs of the company. Some companies do this internally; curating insights onto social intranet pages or moderating communities of practice for the best thoughts. Others do it externally, for the benefit of their customers. Companies like Spiceworks, the IT support company, base their business models around their communities, from which they curate the best questions and answers to help promote a collaborative and consistently helpful service.

Aggregation

Increasingly, we are being challenged to deliver "more with less" in the learning department. Curation potentially holds an interesting answer to some of the constraints we're facing in time and cost. Why build new content when you can curate?

In the context of a formal learning intervention, organizations can use curation to aggregate content as part of the learning design process. This can mean using insights gathered from both inside and outside the organization as a baseline of content from which to develop new courses. Sometimes these resources will be rewritten and transformed; other times it is enough to use the resources in their original form. With the increasing quality of online educational content, it is becoming somewhat redundant to always make new material. You aren't going to make a "better" TED video than the real deal. It is no longer necessary to create new learning content each time a demand passes down the line. Blending resources from the outside world with a selection of resources from inside the firewall can increase your speed to delivery and cut costs dramatically for the T&D department.

Taking this further, some organizations are beginning to advocate a "resources not courses" strategy. Here T&D looks beyond providing highly structured courses and toward individual resources. BP adopts this approach. Led by Nick Shackleton-Jones, director of Online and Informal Learning, BP focuses on producing high-quality performance support tools, videos, and infographics delivered through simple but effective portal-type websites. They do not develop traditional courses at all; the aggregation and presentation of resources have proven to be far more successful than any previous course ever was.

Integration

Curation can and should be used as a tool of teaching and learning itself. It is not enough for us to simply present content and imagine that it will be so compelling that our audience will instantly change its behavior. The learning process is a complex one that, especially in experienced learners, requires a process of integration between new and old experiences. In many ways, when we seek to "teach" people, what we are really seeking to achieve is "integration" between old and new experiences. For most individuals, this will be a process of curation: storing ideas, transforming them to fit with existing experiences and mental models, and, at some point in the future, sharing them through behavior. Thought of in this light, we can suggest that curation is a key part of the learning process, a key digital literacy that will be required for all current and future knowledge workers. It is not enough to be told; that's grade school stuff. In the current working landscape, it is constantly necessary to problem solve and innovate. That requires critical thought.

Taking this approach, we can seek to produce pedagogical frameworks in our formal learning activities that encourage individuals to cast a critical eye over knowledge and to be more reflective in their approach to learning. In these circumstances, learners articulate their grasp of a subject area by storing, transforming, and sharing their understanding. If we don't allow for these processes, we are short-changing learners. Static, anti-social online learning activities are repeat offenders here; presenting experienced learners with an online PowerPoint presentation and expecting them to have a meaningful, lasting learning experience simply isn't going to cut it. Learners have to be able to curate formal learning to integrate new insights with existing experiences, and to demonstrate back to you, the teacher, how they are going to change.

Application

Moving beyond the classroom and into the world of day-to-day work, we can envisage curation as a tool of continuous personal learning. Here curation helps individuals to capture information that is important to them and to wrap it in a context that gives more meaning than the message alone would impart. Many of us do this in blogs, in tweets, and in other collections of knowledge that we share with the world. Increasingly, we are seeing the rise of this concept in the form of personal knowledge management (PKM; see Harold Jarche's website, www.jarche.com/pkm, for more information). According to Jarche, individuals seek, sense, and share as they seek to explicitly state their understanding of the world. This process could be seen as the fundamental driver to user-generated content—more and more people are willing to share content to inspire others. This process is more than just bookmarking or collection building. For many individuals, their curated insights represent a "learning locker," which allows for reflection as well as a demonstration of what they know. It is these individuals who seed the world of content that organizations often seek to curate. And so as we encourage the adoption of PKM tools and techniques, so we see a rise in the overall amount of content available for curation. The cycle begins again.

Curation Cheat Sheet

To get started curating, Table 17-1 shows a fantastic list of websites and resources you can use, free of charge, to develop yourself or your "baseline of content" for your next teaching requirement. You can also download this list from the *Handbook's* website at www.astdhandbook.org.

Table 17-1. Websites and Resources to Develop a Baseline of Content

Name	URL	Description
OER Commons	www.oercommons.org/browse/general_subject/business	Links to more than 1,000 business-related learning content objects
Learning Resource Exchange (for schools)	http://lreforschools.eun.org/	Open and free teaching resources across many subjects at grade school level
Stanford Business School	www.youtube.com/user/stanfordbusiness	Stanford Business School videos
Harvard Working Knowledge	http://hbswk.hbs.edu/	Great papers across the range of management topics from some of the key experts in the field

Udemy	www.udemy.com/	Free video-based courses on a wide range of topics
ERI HR Distance Learning	http://dlc.erieri.com/?FuseAction =Main.Home#List	Virtually every aspect of HR covered, for free
YouTube Education	www.youtube.com/education	Curated videos across all levels of learning, covering many topics
Open Course Library	http://opencourselibrary.org/	Free to use courses that you can download, edit, and use for teaching
TED Ed	http://ed.ted.com/	TED videos made into meaningful lessons with discussions and MCQs
Times 100 Business Case Studies	http://businesscasestudies.co.uk/	Free business case studies with text, mp3s, and more
MIT Open Courseware	http://ocw.mit.edu/	The original open educational resources website; free courses and lessons from MIT
Khan Academy	www.khanacademy.org	Khan Academy specializes in math tuition but has hundreds of video lessons on other subjects
PhET, University of Colorado	http://phet.colorado.edu/	Free, interactive simulations, mostly on science topics at grade school level
Open Library	https://openlibrary.org/	Free books with detailed descriptions and e-copies
Coursera	www.coursera.org/	Number-one provider of massive open online courses (MOOCs)
Learn CPR	http://depts.washington.edu/learncpr/	A free public service run by the University of Washington School of Medicine

Summing Up

Curation comes in many forms, even in a small niche like training and development. We can use it at an organizational level to help inspire our employees and our customers or to help us design and deliver more formal learning experiences using a wide range of content. We can use curation at a personal level too, to help us develop our understanding in a formal learning process and to help us demonstrate our knowledge and insight from our day-to-day work. Truth be told, it is early days for curation in our world. Although the practices are old, the technologies are often new, and as we come to grips with the possibilities that new technologies bring us, it's easy to see that more opportunities for storing, transforming, and sharing resources will become apparent. Curation, as a skill, is on the verge of becoming a key differentiator for employees; knowledge workers could well be expected to bring their curated insights with them to their next job roles. People are making names for themselves as industry experts by the ways in which they curate other people's work. Telling a story like those I find so interesting at the Natural History Museum is most certainly a skill, but increasingly, it is becoming easier for each of us to become the curator.

About the Author

Ben Betts, PhD, is an entrepreneur, technologist, and social learning geek. He is CEO of HT2, where he specialises in the use of game-based and social learning approaches for corporate learning. Clients include Accenture, BP, Barclays, Pearson Education, Duke CE, Oxford University, and others. Ben recently completed his doctorate at University of Warwick, researching new methods of workplace e-learning with a particular focus on the role of curation. He speaks around the world at conferences and teaches on various academic programmes in the United Kingdom and United States.

For Further Reading

Bingham, T., and M. Conner. (2010). *The New Social Learning: A Guide to Transforming Organizations Through Social Media*. Alexandria, VA: ASTD Press.

Rosenbaum, S. (2011). *Curation Nation: How to Win in a World Where Consumers Are Creators*. New York: McGraw-Hill.

Chapter 18

The Legal Aspects of Training: Protect What Is Yours and Avoid Taking What Belongs to Someone Else

Linda Byars Swindling and Mark V.B. Partridge

······················· **In This Chapter** ·······················

- ▨ Get a blueprint for converting your intellectual property to protected property.
- ▨ Understand key intellectual property rights.
- ▨ Learn to use legal rights to protect your intellectual property.
- ▨ Avoid infringing on others' rights.

Most training professionals, whether working in large organizations, sole proprietorships, or any business entity in between, would agree they need to know the basics of human resource law to prevent discrimination or harassment while training or consulting. Most would agree that they should know about the basics of contracts, entering agreements, and clarifying the expectations of the other parties. Those smart training professionals often speak with their internal legal counsel or their own attorneys to review agreements they are drafting and signing. Many even want to understand liability, risk avoidance, and insurance when it comes to preventing property loss or injury, especially when clients require insurance or indemnity agreements to work with them. Remarkably, however, many training professionals fail to invest the time in understanding their most important assets—their intellectual property.

What is intellectual property (IP)? *Wikipedia* defines intellectual property as "an umbrella term for various legal entitlements which attach to certain names, written and recorded media, and inventions."

More simply put, we are talking about the ideas, information, and innovations associated with your business. For most learning professionals who provide services, the biggest asset in our business is not equipment, inventory, or employees; it is our knowledge and expertise and how we deliver it. Therefore, protecting your intellectual capital assets is critical for building and maintaining your business. For internal learning professionals, ensuring you have the proper ownership of materials and are properly using others' materials is paramount in protecting your organization and your own reputation.

Intellectual property exists when those intangible assets and intellectual capital of your business—your brand, content, data, information, website, innovations, systems, and methods—are converted into protected property. This protection occurs through the effect of certain legal rights—patent, trademark, copyright, and trade secret—collectively referred to as intellectual property rights. These legal rights are the tools that convert your intellectual capital into property that can be protected from infringement, sold and licensed for profit, and leveraged to increase the value of your business.

This chapter provides a blueprint for converting your intellectual capital to protected property, discusses the key intellectual property rights that shape success in your business, and shows how to use those legal tools to protect and enforce your rights in the critical assets. It also shows how to avoid infringing on the protected works of others.

Brands

Your brand is the ultimate symbol of your business. It represents who you are and how you perform business. It may be embodied in a name (such as Ford or Disney), a symbol (the Nike Swoosh), a slogan ("You deserve a break today"), a sound (the Law and Order "thunk thunk"), a color (the color pink for Owings-Corning fiberglass), or any other device that identifies a particular source.

The primary legal tool to protect a brand is trademark law. Trademark law is designed to prevent confusion and mistakes in the marketplace.

Creation of Rights

A trademark is entitled to protection when it is used in commerce and is distinctive of a particular source. In fact, *distinctiveness* as a term of art means the ability to serve as an indication of a particular source. Distinctive terms or devices—such as coined names like Exxon or Kodak or arbitrary names like Apple for computers or Camel for cigarettes—may be protected immediately upon use in commerce. Other terms—such as a surname like Ford or Disney, a descriptive term like *Sports Illustrated* magazine, or a geographic term like California Pizza Kitchen—can only be protected if they have been used enough so that they acquire a second meaning in the public mind that is associated with a particular source.

Rights in trademarks are not a monopoly. They cannot prevent all other businesses from using the name. The name must be associated with particular goods or services involved. Marks used for unrelated goods or services may coexist without conflict; for example, Ritz Hotels, Ritz Crackers, and Ritz Camera stores. While all use the same name, each is distinctive for the product or service it represents.

The Benefits of Federal Registration

Trademark rights can be established based solely on use. However, federal registration has added benefits. For example, federal registration creates nationwide rights and creates notice of rights as a matter of law. This notice may discourage infringers.

Registration is obtained through the United States Patent and Trademark Office. Applications can be filed online at www.uspto.gov for a governmental filing fee of approximately $280 (effective 2014). A valid application requires identification of the applicant, a drawing of the proposed mark, a description of the applicable goods or services, and a statement of current use or of a bona fide intention to use the mark in commerce.

The application process involves several steps:

- *Filing the application*. Applications can be filed online. Required information includes identification of applicant, description of mark, description of goods or services, date of first use in commerce, or statement that applicant has a bona fide intent to use the mark in commerce.
- *Examination by a trademark office examiner*. The trademark examiner reviews the application to determine if the information is complete and specific, that the mark is distinctive, and that it does not conflict with an existing application or registration.

- *Publication for opposition by others*. If approved by the examiner, the application will be published to allow other parties to object if they believe they will be damaged by registration of the mark.
- *Final approval of application (if there is no successful opposition)*. If there is no opposition during publication, the application will be allowed for registration. If it was a used-based application, it will proceed directly to registration. If the application was based on an intent to use the mark, the applicant is required to file a statement of use before registration will issue.
- *Issuance of the registration certificate*. When all the steps are cleared, the registration will finally issue. The entire process is likely to take 18 to 24 months or more, but the rights under the registration are based on the filing date.

International Registration

Protecting your brand overseas may be advisable. The Unites States has been a party to the Madrid Protocol since 2003. With the filing of a single application, you can obtain protection for your brand in multiple member countries. International registration is completed under the Madrid Protocol through the same process as a federal registration. Although each country retains the rights to reject local registration of a trademark, the Madrid Protocol provides an efficient mechanism to obtain rights internationally. It is also possible to file directly in foreign jurisdictions, but that is a less efficient process.

Licensing and Assignment

Trademarks may be sold or licensed. Common examples include the licensing of university or sports logos for caps and apparel or franchise names like McDonald's or Burger King. You might have seen a news story about the confiscation of sporting goods at a ballgame when the vendors did not have the license to use the team's registered logo. This violation of a trademark owner's rights is known as infringement.

Infringement

Trademark rights are infringed when a junior party or someone who didn't use the mark first subsequently uses an identical or confusingly similar mark for identical or related goods or services in a manner that is likely to cause confusion, mistake, or deception in the marketplace. The typical relief available in court is an order to prevent use of the infringing mark and an award of the actual damages caused by use of the mark. When a mark has been properly registered with the federal government, those damages and relief may increase.

---◼---

Case Study

In 1985, L'Oreal determined that young people craved pink and blue hair. To meet the anticipated demand, L'Oreal created a line of hair cosmetics named Zazu. Apparently, young people had better taste than expected. The product flopped, but not before spawning a federal lawsuit. The trial court awarded the plaintiff, the Zazu hair salon in Hinsdale, Illinois, more than $2 million in damages plus $76,000 in attorneys' fees. Obviously, a trademark can have incredible value, even to a small business.

Unfortunately, the story continues. L'Oreal appealed, claiming the hair salon had insufficient use to create nationwide rights. The appellate court agreed, taking away the award. The Hinsdale salon was left with nothing but a large bill for attorneys' fees. The story demonstrates the importance of small things. The Hinsdale salon had failed to seek trademark registration. If they had, at an expense of a few hundred dollars, the salon could have established nationwide rights that would have avoided this sad outcome.

As a training professional, be careful that you have proper permission *before* creating posters, t-shirts, or training products displaying someone's brand. Also be careful about using the brands of others to attract traffic on the Internet. Certain fair uses of another's trademark are permissible, but the line between what is permitted and what is infringing can be hard to draw. When in doubt, consult a legal advisor. If you or your company has a brand, don't put your valuable rights at risk by failing to take appropriate action early to secure the intellectual property in your brand.

---◼---

Content

Your content is key to conveying your knowledge and information to the world. For trainers, speakers, and consultants, content typically takes the form of books, articles, newsletters, workbooks, CDs, DVDs, media recordings, software, podcasts, and websites. Each of these may be a revenue source or a work distributed freely for promotional purposes. In either event, the author will want to control the use, receive credit, prevent unauthorized copying, and stop others from profiting improperly from using his or her material in undesirable ways. The principal tool for protecting content and transforming it into protected property is copyright law.

Copyright can create incredible value for you and your business. And misusing the copyrighted works of others can lead to disaster. In 1996, motivational speaker Anthony Robbins created a new financial course complete with a 300-page workbook. A jury found that two key phrases in the workbook were copied from a book by Wade Cook, the author of the *Wall Street Money Machine*, and awarded Mr. Cook more than $650,000 in damages. While the result may be extreme, this situation is not unusual.

Think of how often some trainers "borrow" materials from another source. They copy a cartoon they like into a handout, post a motivational phrase on a social media account, play an upbeat popular song, take a snippet from a movie, or tell someone else's story. Many times there is no reference to the author. Other times, training professionals forget where the materials originated. Some even begin to believe the materials are their own. This "borrowing" of another's work is also unethical. Several professional organizations, such as ASTD and the National Speakers Association, have prohibited the practice in their Code of Ethics, and violation can even result in a loss of membership.

Unauthorized use of work belonging to another may constitute copyright infringement or plagiarism. The terms are often used interchangeably, but it is more accurate to recognize *infringement* as the violation of a legal right, while *plagiarism* is unethical conduct or dishonesty. Put another way, infringement is stealing someone's property. It doesn't make it right to tell the world whose property you've taken. Plagiarism is academic dishonesty— claiming something is yours when it's not. The concepts overlap; an unauthorized taking may be both infringement and plagiarism. Either way, the risks are significant.

The Subjects of Copyright

Copyright protects original, tangible expression. Copyright does not protect concepts, ideas, or facts. This means that protection is available for the actual expression embodied in a work, such as an article, audio or video recording, or software program, but it is not available for ideas or concepts behind that tangible expression. Copyright protection also does not extend to short phrases such as simple trademarks or book titles.

Creating and Owning Copyright

Copyright exists from the moment of creation and belongs to the author of the work. Although beneficial for the reasons discussed later, copyright notice or registrations are not required to create a copyright in your content.

Determining authorship is important to your rights. If the work is created by an employee in the scope of his or her employment, usually the author or owner is the employer. But if you hire an outside vendor to create a work for you—a photographer, website designer, or ghostwriter—he or she owns the copyright in the work unless there is a written work-for-hire agreement or other written transfer of rights. If two people create a work together, they both own an undivided interest in the whole, unless there is a written agreement making other arrangements. That means, if you are working with or relying on others to create work for you, such as a marketing piece or a website, it is critical that you have a clear understanding about ownership and the rights to use the work created. And make sure your creative person has the ability to use photographs, images, music on a website, and so on in that mode. Using unlicensed music or pictures that aren't royalty free is one way that unethical or uneducated graphic artists save money.

Useful Links

www.uspto.gov
United States Trademark Office. Search and register trademarks online.

www.uspto.gov/trademarks/law/madrid
International trademark registration and Madrid Protocol

www.copyright.gov
United States Copyright Office. Obtain forms and guidelines for copyright registration.

www.allwhois.com or www.betterwhois.com
Provide domain name registration records. Check ownership records for domain names.

www.wipo.int
World Intellectual Property Organization. File complaints against cybersquatters using infringing domain names.

www.aipla.org
American Intellectual Property Law Association. Locate attorneys who handle patent and other intellectual property matters.

www.inta.org
International Trademark Association. Trademark protection information.

www.bmi.com and www.ascap.com
Music licensing societies. Obtain permission for public performance of music to enhance seminars and training.

www.PartridgeIPlaw.com/partridge-blog
The Partridge IP Law blog. Obtain current intellectual property information and articles by co-author Mark Partridge and other members of Partridge IP Law.

If you are purchasing materials, make certain you understand the rights you are purchasing. Determine if you can reproduce the materials freely, if you or others can present the information without the creator's presence, or if the materials are developed for your organization alone. You don't want to pay a large sum to have materials developed for your team, only to find that the trainer plans to use the same course with your competitors.

If you are an outside vendor, it is now common practice for some companies to contract for all works created to become their property. Before you sign such an agreement, make sure you understand the rights you are giving and any limits on your ability to use the materials in the future. Many times, organizations will negotiate if you take the time to explain your hesitation with an agreement. For instance, some companies are concerned primarily about you protecting their trade secrets and not giving their competitors inside information. If you explain you have similar concerns that one of your competitors or an inside trainer might use your materials without permission, savvy business professionals will understand.

Often clients are flexible and may agree to use your published materials or you as a presenter for programs you create. However, you have to recognize and ask for those exceptions. Before you sign, check that the agreement doesn't conflict with other agreements you have. For example, your agreement with a publisher might require permission to use materials found in the book you authored. Those answers may determine how willing you are to do the work as well as the price you charge.

Exclusive Rights

Copyright provides the copyright owner a bundle of exclusive rights, including:

- the right to make copies and reproductions
- the right to create modifications and derivative works
- the right to public performance or display.

The scope of rights includes the right to control copies that are identical as well as those that are substantially similar to the protected expression contained in the original. Substantial similarity is judged by whether or not the similarities would cause an ordinary observer to conclude that the infringing work was copied from the original.

Term

Copyrights have a long life. The actual term of copyright protection has changed over time and depends on when the work was created. Generally, for works created after 1978, protection lasts for the life of the author plus 70 years. For anonymous works or works made for hire, the term is 95 years from first publication or 120 years from creation, whichever expires first.

Questions to Ask a Prospective Lawyer

Seek the advice of a competent attorney regarding any of the issues in this chapter. Here are several questions to ask a prospective lawyer:

- Do you specialize in the area of law related to my problem?
- Have you handled this type of problem before?
- Have you worked for others in my industry?
- How long will it take to complete the work?
- Is this a simple matter, or will you need to do research?
- What are your hourly rates?
- Is there a set fee or flat fee for this work?
- Can you give me the best case and the worst case scenarios on timing and expense for a matter like this?
- Is a retainer required?
- Who else will work on the project? What are their rates?
- If a professional with a lesser billing rate can do work such as research, will you use that person?
- What extra costs will I need to pay (copying, delivery, filing fees, and so on)?
- Do you charge me for every phone call?
- How will you communicate with me? How often?

Notice and Registration

As mentioned previously, you are not required to use a copyright notice or register your copyright to have rights. However, both provide important benefits and are simple and inexpensive to do.

A proper copyright notice includes a claim of copyright, the date of creation, and the name of the owner: © 2014 Jane Doe. One of the myths about copyright is that works can be freely copied if there is no copyright notice. This is false, but since it is commonly believed to be true, using a copyright notice can help to deter infringers. Copyright notice may also help you avoid claims of innocence if you are forced to take legal action against an infringer. In addition, a good practice is to include your contact information, such as your phone number and website, on every page in case someone wants to contact you about using your materials: © 2014 Jane Doe. All rights reserved. Doe & Associates, www.doeassociates .com; 972-555-1212.

Registration is also relatively simple to obtain by submitting a two-page application form and specimen of the work to the United States Copyright Office. The current application fee for a basic claim is $35 (effective 2014). The process is explained at the Copyright Office website at www.copyright.gov.

Registration before an infringement occurs provides two key benefits. First, it is required to recover the statutory amount of damages specified in the Copyright Act, which is up to $150,000 per work infringed. Without prior registration, the copyright owner is limited to recovery of actual damages or profits. Second, registration prior to infringement permits the copyright owner to seek recovery of attorneys' fees from the infringement. Otherwise, the usual rule is that each party is responsible for its own attorneys' fees. Attorneys' fees in intellectual property litigation can be very high. A 2011 survey by the American Intellectual Property Law Association found that the average litigation cost for copyright infringement trials was more than $350,000 when less than $1,000,000 was at stake, and went up dramatically from there.

Obtain Permission for Use of Music for Seminars and Workshops

The situation: Music motivates, so Amway Corporation conventions and videos used music to inspire its distributors, featuring popular songs by the likes of the Beatles, Michael Jackson, Whitney Houston, Gloria Estefan, and Michael Bolton—more than 100 songs in all.

The problem: Unfortunately, Amway and its agents failed to secure permission.

The result: A lawsuit in 1996 seeking more than $10 million in copyright damages.

The lesson: Public performance of music requires permission.

The cure: Obtain a license from a music licensing society, such as BMI or ASCAP.

The ability to recover statutory damages and attorneys' fees can be the difference in whether the copyright owner is able to protect his or her property. For example, a trainer finds that 10 of her articles have been used without her permission by a competitor in a book. The actual monetary damages are likely to be low (the royalty value of the articles or a portion of the royalties earned by the competitor from the book) and considerably less than the legal cost to pursue the claim. Although she has a claim, it could be financially unreasonable to pursue it. If, however, the trainer had registered her right before the infringement occurred, she would be in a position to seek up to $150,000 per article and to recover the cost of pursing the claim, obviously enough to justify the cost of registration and the legal action to protect her rights.

Fair Use

Fair use is an exception to the exclusive rights of the copyright owner, which permits another party to use the copyright holder's work for purposes such as commentary, news reporting, and education. Whether such use is permitted depends on consideration of four factors:

- The nature of the infringing work. Uses that transform the original into something new are more likely to be permitted. Noncommercial use is more likely to be permitted than commercial use.
- The nature of the original work. Factual works receive less protection than expressive works such as poems or songs.
- The amount of the taking. The quality and quantity of the taking are important. Even a small taking may be an infringement if it is qualitatively important and "goes to the heart" of the original.
- The effect on the market for the original. An infringement is not likely to be permitted if it supplants market demand for the original.

Determining fair use in a particular case can be difficult. Some examples of uses allowed as fair use include:

- a hip hop parody of Roy Orbison's song "Pretty Woman"
- the use of thumbnail copies of Grateful Dead posters in a history book about popular music culture
- a portion of a photograph used in a collage by the artist Robert Rauschenberg.

Uses that were not permitted include:

- George Harrison's song "My Sweet Lord," which was found to be too similar to the song "He's So Fine"
- a parody about O.J. Simpson based on "The Cat in the Hat"
- video clips of Elvis in a documentary.

When in doubt, the best course of action is to seek permission from the owner of the original or a noninfringement opinion from a qualified attorney. Watch out for a common misconception among training and development professionals. The term *education* is narrowly defined. For example, you cannot get around a copyright-protected piece by claiming it was for corporate education or education for a trade association program.

Important Checklists

Trademark Checklist
- ☐ Protects distinctive names, logos, designs, other devices designating source
- ☐ No protection for generic terms
- ☐ Rights arise from use
- ☐ Registration provides nationwide rights and enhanced damages
- ☐ Infringement based on likelihood of confusion

Copyright Checklist
- ☐ Protects original expression
- ☐ No protection for facts, concepts, or ideas
- ☐ Rights arise from creation
- ☐ Registration provides right to recover attorneys fees and statutory damages
- ☐ Infringement based on copying of protected expression

Domain Names Checklist
- ☐ Protects brand identity on the Internet
- ☐ Available on a first-come basis
- ☐ Rights are created by contract with a domain name registrar
- ☐ Infringement based on bad faith use or registration

Patent Checklist
- ☐ Protects inventions and business methods
- ☐ Only available if invention is novel and nonobvious
- ☐ Rights arise only through registration
- ☐ Twenty-year term of protection
- ☐ Infringement based on use within scope of claims covered by patent

Trade Secret Checklist
- ☐ Protects business secrets, information, and data
- ☐ Only available if information is maintained as a secret
- ☐ No registration
- ☐ Infringement based on misappropriation of secret information

Online Protection

Online works are protected by copyright just as any other work of original expression. It is a serious error to conclude that works freely available on the Internet can be freely copied and used for a commercial purpose. As indicated previously, notice is not required for protection. The lack of a copyright notice does not mean the work can be freely taken. Most websites hosting content also have terms restricting use. For example, YouTube has terms and conditions that prevent unauthorized commercial use of the material posted on the website. Unauthorized commercial use of YouTube content may thus be a violation of contractual rights as well as copyright.

Special procedures are available to help copyright owners stop unauthorized online use of copyrighted works. The Digital Millennium Copyright Act (DMCA) creates a safe harbor for online service providers such as Google and YouTube who post content of others. If the copyright owner finds infringing works posted online, he or she may be able to submit a DMCA complaint to the service provider demanding that the work be taken down. If the service provider honors the demand, it will not be liable for copyright infringement. Because of this "safe harbor," most service providers have posted take-down procedures that comply with the DMCA. These procedures can be an inexpensive way to police copyrights online.

International Protection

Registration with the United States Copyright Office can also help protect your content internationally. Under the TRIPS Agreement, all World Trade Organization member countries are required to protect the rights of copyright owners of other member countries. Although these rights exist, enforcement can be difficult.

Domain Names

For many speakers and trainers or training companies, a website is an important marketing and product delivery tool. Thus, domain names—the addresses for finding websites—have become critical business assets.

Rights in domain names are created by a contract with a domain name registrar, such as Verisign or GoDaddy. Domain names are typically renewed on an annual basis, so it is important to ensure that your registration information is up-to-date and results in the receipt of renewal notices by someone who will respond. Otherwise, valuable domain names may lapse and be snapped up by others, a common occurrence afflicting small and large businesses alike. (This happened to Microsoft—twice!) Registration records can be checked for accuracy with the domain name registrar or at information sites such as www.allwhois.com or www.betterwhois.com. In addition, when acquiring a domain name from a company or person selling "popular" names, clarify whether you have actual ownership or just the rights to use that name for a period of time.

The importance of domain names in the marketplace has inspired a new industry involving the registration and use of domain names similar to the names of others. Bad faith use and registration of a domain name that is confusingly similar to another's trademark—cyber-squatting—is a violation of the domain name registration contract and of the trademark laws in the United States. Victims of cybersquatting have several options for recovering the infringing domain name.

- A demand letter to the registrant of the domain name may result in a voluntary transfer of the domain name to resolve the dispute. Typically the registrant will want some payment to cover its expenses.
- A complaint may be filed under the Uniform Dispute Resolution Policy (UDRP) incorporated as part of the domain name registration contract. The UDRP is an administrative procedure to resolve cybersquatting disputes without court action. The procedure is available for disputes on a global basis. Thus, a trainer located in the United States may use the procedure to challenge a domain name held by a registrant in China. There is no live hearing or trial. The dispute is decided based on written submissions by a neutral party appointed by the dispute resolution service provider. The only relief provided is a transfer or cancellation of the disputed domain name. More information is available from the United Nations' World Intellectual Property Organization, www.wipo.int.
- A lawsuit may be filed in the United States under the Anti-Cybersquatting Consumer Protection Act (ACPA), a provision contained in the U.S. Trademark Law. Litigating in federal court can be expensive and lengthy, but may be the right choice for extreme cases of cybersquatting, particularly when serial infringement is involved. The ACPA can result in recovery of attorneys' fees plus $100,000 per infringing domain name. The ACPA may also be used to recover domain names from distant cybersquatters if the relevant domain name registry is located in the United States, which is the case for .com, .net, and .org domain names.

Starting in 2013, the Internet expanded to encompass new generic top-level domains (gTLDs), the part of the name to the right of the "dot." This expansion to ".anything" opens up many opportunities for online marketing, as well as potential problems of infringement. A focused strategy is important for brand owners to define and protect their identity in this new space.

Data and Information

A successful training business often rests on accumulated contact information about clients and prospects. Many training assignments may also involve access to client information that is subject to nondisclosure agreements. In other instances, training methods may be proprietary and only disclosed to clients under confidentiality agreements. Each of these situations involves data and information that may be protected under trade secret law.

A trade secret is any information that is 1) sufficiently secret to derive economic value, actual or potential, from not being generally known to other persons who can obtain economic value from its disclosure or use; and 2) the subject of efforts that are reasonable under the circumstances to maintain its secrecy or confidentiality. A trade secret can take any number of forms—a formula, a database, a customer list, blueprints, technical data, or a manufacturing process. One of the most famous trade secrets is the formula for Coca-Cola.

Trade secret law does not protect against the independent creation of the trade secret by a third party. Rather, it protects against the misappropriation or the unlawful taking of the trade secret by another. Generally, a court will find trade secret misappropriation in one of two circumstances, either 1) the trade secret was stolen from the company or obtained by improper means, or 2) a trade secret lawfully obtained was used or disclosed in violation of a confidential relationship. Damages may be awarded in trade secret cases, and in appropriate cases, a court may order the offending party to cease any further use or disclosure.

To determine if something is protectable as a trade secret, a court will typically look at whether the information is known outside the business, what safeguards are in place to protect its secrecy, how valuable it is to the business and its competitors, how difficult and expensive it was to develop the information, and how easy it would be to duplicate by lawful means.

Unlike trademark and copyright law discussed previously, there is no agency that registers trade secrets. Ownership and protection is a function of the actions taken by the company to restrict access.

The owner of a trade secret must take affirmative action to protect a trade secret's confidentiality. It is important that employees who have access to a trade secret take steps to prevent its unauthorized disclosure, whether on the Internet, by word of mouth, or otherwise. All proprietary materials should be marked as such, denoting that they should be kept confidential and are considered proprietary. Access to the trade secret should be limited to those individuals with a need to know. Procedures for maintaining confidentiality °should be implemented and enforced. If disclosure to employees and third parties is necessary, those who are granted access to trade secrets should execute nondisclosure and confidentiality agreements.

When you are hiring training professionals, it is a good practice to make sure they are not prevented from doing your work by a trade secret, noncompete, or nondisclosure agreement. Many organizations have begun asking whether an agreement would prevent the applicant from working with them. Some ask the applicant to sign a document that makes it clear that the hiring organization does not want the new employee to do anything that would violate a protective agreement or infringe on the rights of another company. Agreements may require consultants to protect trade secrets in their own companies, including taking special measures to keep information password protected, in a separate file cabinet, and to avoid discussing with employees and subcontractors.

Systems and Methods

It is common to think of patents as applicable to technical inventions—a better mousetrap—and not applicable to the business of speakers, trainers, and consultants. In fact, the scope of patent protection is far broader and may cover systems and methods developed by training professionals. For example, patents have recently been issued on tax preparation methods. It is easy to imagine how such protection could extend to training methods.

A patent is a government grant of exclusive rights provided in exchange for disclosure of an invention. The grant involves the right to exclude others from making, using, selling, or offering to sell the invention for a period of 20 years. After that, the invention enters the public domain.

The narrow view of patents being limited to technical inventions began to fade away about 15 years ago when the leading court responsible for patent claims acknowledged that "anything under the sun made by man is patentable." That court extended the protection of patent law to business methods, holding that any method or process that produces a "useful, concrete, and tangible result" is potentially protectable. Although this ruling has been controversial, numerous business methods have been patented, including Amazon.com's "one-click" method and the Netflix method of renting videos.

For a business method to be patentable, it must be novel (not in the prior art) and nonobvious (to someone skilled in the art in view of the prior art). In the United States, patent protection must be sought within one year of disclosure. The process of obtaining a patent can be complicated and expensive. A patent is best pursued with the help of an experienced patent attorney with knowledge about the subject matter of the patent. Qualified attorneys can be located through the American Intellectual Property Law Association in Washington, D.C., or through local patent law associations.

Four Key Ways to Use Intellectual Property to Make More Money

Intellectual property discussions often focus on legal rights: patents, trademarks, copyrights, trade secrets. These are important, of course, but they are merely legal tools for protecting key business assets. The starting point for training professionals should be the underlying assets: information, innovation, content, brands, names, reputation, websites, and more.

Applying intellectual property rights to these key assets can create value in four key ways.

1. **Charge a Premium for Your Goods and Services**
   Consider generic cola versus Coca-Cola. Why is one worth more? Coca-Cola has used intellectual property to enhance the value of a simple commodity. It receives a premium because it has a secret formula and a distinctive, well-known brand. Generic cola has a formula, too, but it's not secret; it also has a name, but it is not distinctive. Anyone can make cola and use the cola name. Intellectual property keeps Coca-Cola from being copied. The formula is protected as a trade secret, and the brand is protected as a trademark.

2. **Earn Additional Revenue**
   Consider the average software developer versus Microsoft. The software developer is a knowledge worker paid for his or her labor. If the developer doesn't work, he or she can't make any money. Without his or her work, the developer's business has no value. Microsoft uses intellectual property to turn the product of many knowledge workers into property that can be licensed and sold. Once that is done, Microsoft can make money without further time and effort from the knowledge worker. Copyrights and patents are the intellectual property rights that keep others from copying Microsoft's products.

3. **Increase Market Valuation**
   The value of a commodity business is typically the book value of its hard assets. The market value of an S&P 500 company is usually several times book value. The difference is largely the value of intellectual property. The same principal applies to training professionals who can leverage intellectual property rights to increase business value beyond mere book value.

4. **Create Marketable Assets**
   Markets exist for the resale of intellectual property rights. Brands and domain names can be sold or used as collateral for loans. David Bowie raised $57 million selling bonds backed by the royalties in his recordings. These financial strategies let intellectual property owners cash in on intellectual property assets.

In all the areas discussed, it is always in your best interest to seek the advice of a competent attorney to help you understand your rights and how to avoid infringing on the rights of others. The cost of a phone call, a contract review, or an office visit could save a multiple of 100 times that amount in later representation or help you walk away from deals that don't serve you. When seeking legal counsel, remember that lawyers, like doctors, have specialties. You would not go to an eye doctor for heart surgery. Likewise, your local real estate attorney is unlikely to be the best choice for your intellectual property needs. Lawyers generally charge by the hour, and the rates of experienced, specialized professionals are likely to be significantly higher than the rates of less experienced, general attorneys. You are likely to get the most value by working with an experienced, specialized attorney who has handled similar problems. You won't have to pay for the attorney's learning curve, and he or she knows where to pay the most attention and knows areas where things might go wrong. The sidebar suggests questions to ask a prospective attorney. You may also download this checklist at the *Handbook's* website at www.astdhandbook.org.

Talk to other training professionals who have attorneys, and ask about their experience and legal representation. A training professional's chief asset is intellectual capital. Protecting that property and having clarity around your use of others' property is an essential part of being a professional.

About the Authors

From the courtroom to the boardroom, **Linda Byars Swindling,** JD, CSP, is an authority in high-stakes communications, negotiating workplace drama, and influencing decision makers. Her specialty is negotiation strategies that drive high performance. Linda first addressed employment and workplace communication issues as an attorney and a mediator. After co-authoring *The Consultant's Legal Guide* with Elaine Biech, Linda left her legal practice to focus full-time on Journey On, her Dallas-based professional development company. In addition to training and consulting, Linda delivers keynote speeches on her recent book: *Stop Complainers and Energy Drainers: How to Negotiate Work Drama to Get More Done.* For more information, visit www.JourneyOn.com or www.StopComplainers.com.

Mark V.B. Partridge is an internationally recognized expert in intellectual property law with more than 30 years of experience representing major corporations, business owners, and creative professionals. A Harvard Law School graduate, he is the managing partner at Partridge IP Law, a boutique law firm with a global practice helping businesses defend brands, content, and ideas. The author of many articles and four books on intellectual property law, he has been recognized as one of the 250 top IP strategists in the world. For more information, visit www.PartridgeIPLaw.com.

For Further Reading

Biech, E., and L. Byars Swindling. (2000). *The Consultant's Legal Guide: A Business of Consulting Resource*. San Francisco: Jossey-Bass/Pfeiffer.

Blaxill, M., and R. Eckardt. (2009). *The Invisible Edge: Taking Your Strategy to the Next Level Using Intellectual Property*. New York: Portfolio/Penguin Group.

Charmasson, H., and J. Buchaca. (2008). *Patents, Copyrights & Trademarks for Dummies*. Hoboken, NJ: John Wiley & Sons.

Chisum, D., et al. (2011). *Understanding Intellectual Property Law*. LexisNexis.

Eyres, P.S. (2006). *The Legal Handbook for Trainers, Speakers, and Consultants: The Essential Guide to Keeping Your Company and Clients Out of Court*. New York: McGraw-Hill.

Ginsburg, J., and R. Dreyfus. (2006). *Intellectual Property Stories*. New York: Foundation Press.

Partridge, M. (2003). *Guiding Rights: Trademarks, Copyright and the Internet*. Bloomington, IN: iUniverse.

Ward, F. (2007). *Staying Legal: A Guide to Copyright and Trademark Use*. Alexandria, VA: ASTD Press.

Section IV

Delivering T&D Solutions That Make a Difference

Delivering T&D Solutions That Make a Difference

Luminary Perspective

Bob Pike

Reread the title for this section of the *Handbook*. There's one word that stands out for me. What's your guess? If you guessed *difference*, you're right. And where do you think the word *difference* came from? It might have come from a variety of places, but it is used most often and, in my opinion, most significantly in Don Kirkpatrick's four levels of evaluation model. Here is his model—and my interpretation of it:

	Kirkpatrick	**My Interpretation**
Level 1	Reaction	Did they like it? (smile sheets)
Level 2	Learning	Did they learn it? (testing)
Level 3	Behavior	Did they use it? (on-the-job observation)
Level 4	Results	Did it make a difference? (pre-/post-intervention benchmarking)

About 10 years ago, I wrote an article saying that we needed to turn Kirkpatrick upside down. What I meant by that is that most practitioners tend to put too much emphasis on Level 1, and most practitioners ignore Level 4. What Don (and his son and daughter-in-law, Jim and Wendy) would say is that if you want training to make a difference, each level is necessary, but not sufficient for the next level. In other words, if people like it, they are more likely to learn. If they learn, they are better able to use. If they use, it is more likely to make a difference. And I would agree with that wholeheartedly.

The reason I said we should turn Kirkpatrick upside down is that in my experience, we often attempt to use training to solve problems that have nothing to do with a deficiency of knowledge, skill, or execution. So if we want to make a difference with our training and development solutions, we need to start with level 4. And applying level 4 begins before we ever begin to think of what a solution might look like—by clearly identifying the problem.

Essentials to Ensure Your Training "Makes a Difference"

Here are some essential thoughts that will help us to focus on making sure that the training we deliver makes a difference:

- Training is a process, not an event. It begins before that training ever starts and continues until we see results in the workplace.
- The only purpose of training is to deliver results.
- When performance is the question, training is the sixth answer.

Why is training the sixth answer? Because there are many sources of performance problems—and training only resolves a handful of them. I developed a "performance solutions cube" that helps trainers ensure they are really designing and delivering training that makes a difference. Two parts of the cube are important for our discussion here. Side one is identifying performance needs, and there are basically three.

1. There is a problem or deficiency. High performers are doing things low performers are not.
2. There is an opportunity for improvement. Tom Peters, in his book *Thriving on Chaos*, said, "If it ain't broke, fix it anyway." What he means is that the best time to get better is when you are choosing to—not when you are reacting to outside forces. This section of the *Handbook* deals with delivering results using a variety of delivery mediums, some classroom based, others virtual. Think about tools and technologies that were shining stars but now no longer exist. They were, as Frank Sinatra put it, "King of the hill and top of the heap." WordStar was king— and got crushed by MS Word. Lotus 1-2-3 was the dominant spreadsheet—until Excel. Facebook, Twitter, LinkedIn, and YouTube are dominant social media players today, but just a few years ago it was Geocities, theGlobe, Sixdegrees, and MySpace. Some of these may still exist, but are largely irrelevant. Why? Because they didn't improve and evolve rapidly enough (or at all). And something better came along. There were search engines long before Google and Bing, but can you name any of them? Archie (shortened from Archive) was the first search engine in 1991, followed by Veronica and Jughead. Boomers will instantly recognize where

these names came from; otherwise, just Google it (LOL). These were followed by Excite, Infoseek, and Altavista. Do you even recognize any of these names? They were once front runners in the search engine arena. Enough said—if we do not continuously improve, we are in danger of being irrelevant at the least and obsolete and extinct at the worst.

3. Future planning. Something new is coming along, and we need to get some or all of the organization ready for it. It could be as simple as a new phone system or software update, or more complex like moving to a new location or launching a new product or service.

Six Performance Solutions

The other side of the "performance solutions cube" that will help you gain the most from this section is side three—the six performance solutions. Presented here is the order in which I use them when I work with clients:

1. **Systems.** Do the systems that you have in place support the performance that you want, or does this system itself actually affect performance? For example, all webinar delivery systems are not alike. Many times, people will attend one of our webinars and participate in voice over IP (VoIP) breakout groups where they talk to others rather than text chat and say, "But we can't do that." It may be a feature they are unaware of or don't know how to use, or the platform may not have that feature available. If it's not available and is something you see as valuable to delivering participant-centered webinars, you have a systems problem, and no amount of training will overcome it. On the other hand, if your platform does have it, you may have a performance need that can be solved with either coaching or training.

2. **Policies and/or procedures.** Sometimes policies and procedures prevent or punish performance rather than enabling and rewarding performance. If people are rewarded for doing great work by being handed more work that they know came from people who are not performing, it may not be too long before their results decline because they don't want to be doing someone else's work all the time. No amount of training is going to improve performance when people feel punished for doing a great job. They may be inclined to simply do a good job or to go to an organization that rewards outstanding performance.

3. **Recruitment.** Sometimes we are so eager to fill a head count that we hire anyone and then assume that training will straighten them out. In many parts of the world, it is becoming more and more difficult to fire someone once they have been hired. So developing a better recruiting strategy based on real skills, knowledge, and competency needed to do the job can be critical. A major fast food restaurant client of

mine applied this strategy when it moved into a new market. Past experience told them that they needed to hire for the skills and aptitudes of the job above the one they were hiring for because people wanted the opportunity for growth. But in the area they were moving into, they were finding it hard to hire people on that basis. They could fulfill the role of a front counter person, but didn't have the math and reading skills needed for the next level. For two years, they bused people in from nearby areas who had the knowledge, skills, and competencies to be promoted. At the same time, they offered free education to people in the local community to build the math and reading skills needed to be hired with the potential for promotion. In the past, they had ignored the "hire for the second level" guideline. The result was that people hired earlier resented people hired later who got promoted because they had the reading and math skills needed at that next level. Earlier, they had a recruitment problem—but not anymore.

4. **Placement.** Sometimes we hire great people and put them in the wrong jobs. We take someone who is naturally outgoing and put him or her in a job that does not provide social contact. Or we hire people who prefer to focus on individual tasks they can do alone and put them in face-to-face contact–intensive jobs. Both of these situations cause the people involved to be drained in energy throughout the day, rather than ending the day energized. No amount of training is going to rewire someone's natural preferences.

5. **Coaching.** Sometimes people need a little coaching, not an entire training program. The question to ask here is: Have we prepared people in the work environment to be coaches? Most of us have never had someone coach us, and we may not realize that coaching is one the requirements of our job. When I was writing the very first edition of my *Creative Training Techniques Handbook* back in the mid-1980s, I was using a state-of-the-art word processing program called WordStar. We did not yet have mouses (some of you reading this are thinking, you're kidding, right?) and automatic word wrap did not exist. I was editing a chapter of the book and had added a few lines to a paragraph and found that my sentences were running off the screen. So I cursored over and did a carriage return. This corrected the line I was on, but now the next line ran off the screen. I continued this until, near the end of the paragraph, my administrative assistant asked what I was doing. After I explained, she said, "Why not do this?" She took over the keyboard and put the cursor inside the paragraph and tapped Control and Q at the same time. The entire paragraph smoothed itself out. I said, "What did you do?" She said, "I used the 'reformat' command." I didn't even know there was a reformat command. I became 25 percent more productive immediately. I didn't need an entire training program. I needed some just-in-time coaching.

6. **Training.** When I've finished the diagnostic I've just outlined, 95 percent of my performance needs will have been met—and anything left will probably be met with some type of training. But training today is both the same and different than when I first started in 1969. How adults learn is the same, because we have not rewired our brains. But what is available to help me learn what I need to know, and need to be able to do for my job, has changed radically.

As I wrote this section introduction, I made use of infographics to remind myself of the various technologies and timelines I wanted to mention. Many of us are now creating apps that people can use on their smart devices (both phones and tablets) to get just-in-time instructions, diagrams, video clips, and other supporting materials that can help us do our jobs faster, better, and easier.

We are using adaptations of social media internally (such as wikis) to collect the knowledge we gain both as subject matter experts and the people who spend the most time performing a task to pool our knowledge about best practices, answers to frequently asked questions (FAQs), and other content leads.

My best advice to you as you read this section, prepared for you by 15 of the best and brightest in our profession, is to keep asking these simple questions (assuming you've landed on training as a solution):

- How does my target audience learn best?
- What parts of this can be taught online? Hint: If you can test it online, you can teach it online.
- How frequently does content need to be updated?
- Have I remembered to build in time to learn how to use the learning tools? Most people know how to function in a classroom, but there are a host of little things that make the difference in a virtual learning environment. For example: How do I raise my hand? How do I use the whiteboard? How do I ask a question? How do breakout rooms work? These are just the tip of the iceberg.
- How online savvy is my target audience? Not everyone is on Facebook, LinkedIn, or Twitter, or uses Pinterest, Instagram, or Foursquare, or cares about what their Klout score is (though some companies now use it as a hiring guide). We can use these things to foster learning, but we may need to get people up to speed in order to have them using these sites.

Use these as a guideline to get the most from this section, and I believe that you'll find this section filled with immediately practical and useable ideas.

About the Author

Bob Pike, CSP, CPAE, CPLP Fellow, has long been described as the "trainer's trainer." More than 150,000 trainers on five continents have attended his Creative Training Techniques (CTT) Train the Trainer (TTT) program. With more than 300,000 copies sold, his *CTT Handbook* is the bestselling TTT book ever published. He is the author or co-author of more than 30 books in the field. He has been named an Instructional Systems Association Thought Leader, and Training Industry Inc. named him one of the 20 most influential people globally in the human resource development field. Bob keynotes at dozens of conferences worldwide each year and has been one of the five top presenters in both attendance and evaluations at the ASTD International Conference & Exposition for more than 25 years.

Chapter 19

Evidence-Based Training: The Most Recent Research for Delivery

Ruth Clark

······························· **In This Chapter** ·······························

- ▨ Define evidence-based training.
- ▨ Discuss research questions regarding the use of delivery media, graphics, text, and audio.
- ▨ Consider the value of general instructional strategies.

Review Figure 19-1, which is a storyboard from an e-lesson on identity theft. Decide which statements you think are true:

- ▨ The storyboard is effective because it includes a visual, text, and audio for all learning styles.
- ▨ The storyboard will generate interest because the visual is engaging.
- ▨ The storyboard will be especially helpful to novice learners because it includes a lot of detail.

This chapter focuses on what evidence tells us about three fundamental modes used to communicate training lessons: graphics, text, and audio. In Figure 19-1, the delivery technology was digital. But it also could have been a slide for a classroom context. Let's begin with a brief description of delivery and summarize evidence on the benefits of different delivery media. Because this chapter focuses on evidence, we will explore the kind of evidence and the psychological basis for that evidence in terms of cognitive load. Turning to the different modalities, we will review the latest evidence on the following questions: Do graphics benefit learning? Do some learners gain more from graphics than others? Are some types of graphics more effective than others? Is it better to explain a graphic with text or with audio narration?

Figure 19-1. A Storyboard From an E-Lesson on Identify Theft

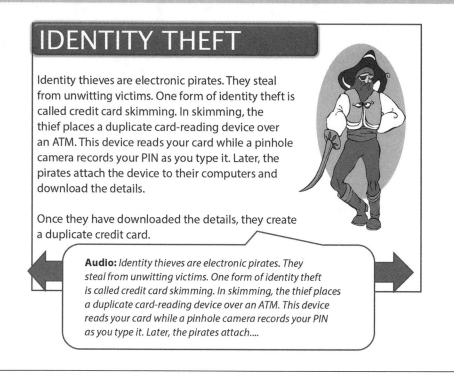

What Is Delivery?

Delivery refers to the presentation of instructional content and instructional methods to learners. There are multiple technologies for delivery, such as computers to deliver self-study or instructor-led virtual classes, in-person classroom delivery typically augmented with slides or video, and print-based handouts or job aids. Most delivery media offer trainers the opportunity to display graphics (on slides, screens, or pages) and to explain those graphics with text or audio or both text and audio. Audio may take the form of instructor explanations in classrooms or narration to support computer self-study lessons. This chapter focuses on the research of best practices in the use of graphics, audio, and text in any training delivery environment.

What Is Evidence-Based Training?

I define evidence-based practice as the application of data-based guidelines when making decisions regarding the design, development, and delivery of instructional environments designed to optimize individual or organizational goals. As training professionals, you routinely have to juggle multiple constraints in your work, such as time to prepare training, time allocated to deliver training, delivery technologies, budget, and so forth. Evidence is but one element to consider as you prepare and deliver training. Although we have evidence regarding all of the major stages of our work, this chapter will focus on delivery and specifically on the use of graphics, text, and audio in delivery. Although there is a considerable amount of instructional research available, most practitioners lack the time to search, read, and interpret that evidence. Therefore, this chapter bridges the divide between academic evidence and practitioner decisions.

What Is Experimental Evidence?

There are a number of different types of evidence, including surveys, case studies, and qualitative research. For our purposes, however, I will rely primarily on experimental research. In experimental studies, a group of learners (most often college students) are randomly assigned to two different lessons that are the same, except for the instructional method of interest. For example, 25 subjects are assigned to a lesson that uses text only and a different 25 subjects are assigned to a lesson with the same text but with graphics added. After a study period, all subjects are tested for either their recall or comprehension of the lesson content. Because workforce learning depends primarily on application rather than recall, the data I include here reflects comprehension or problem-solving tests. Next, the averages and standard deviations from the test results of the two groups are subjected to statistical tests to determine that they are significantly different from one another (that is, unlikely to have occurred by chance alone) and that they are meaningful (in other words, large enough to have practical implications).

In some situations, sufficient research studies have been conducted on a specific instructional method that the multiple results can be aggregated into a research summary called a meta-analysis. Meta-analyses are useful because they reflect the results of many experiments and because often the research team subdivides those experiments into smaller groups to help us understand under what conditions a given instructional method works best. For example, a meta-analysis on graphics would give overall effectiveness data but would also provide data subsets such as experiments that involved children versus adults, different types of subject matter, or still graphics versus animations. Based on these subsets, we can begin to define the conditions under which graphics are most effective.

Evidence and Cognitive Load

While evidence is useful, it is also helpful to have a theoretical basis to aid in the interpretation of that evidence. Cognitive load theory is a current and practical model for this purpose. Cognitive load theory is based on the limits of our working memory. You have probably heard the expression "seven plus or minus two." Basically, we know that working memory can hold only limited amounts of information, and when working memory fills, its ability to process (learn, think, or solve problems) is degraded. There are good and bad forms of cognitive load. The form most relevant to this chapter is called *extraneous cognitive load*. Extraneous cognitive load is mental work imposed on working memory that impedes learning. In this chapter, we will focus on extraneous load imposed by flawed use of graphics, text, and audio. Your goal as a T&D professional is to minimize extraneous load to free up limited working memory capacity for learning.

Having defined delivery and evidence-based training, the remainder of the chapter will focus on the seven research questions most relevant to the decisions you face regarding the use of delivery media, graphics, text, and audio.

Research Question 1: What Delivery Media Are Best?

Starting with radio and film (way before your time), each new technology introduced as an instructional delivery medium reignites the question: Is this a better technology for learning than traditional classroom instruction? The U.S. Army conducted one of the first published media comparison studies in 1947 to determine whether learning was better from film compared to an instructor-led classroom session. In its study, the Army compared learning a basic procedure from a film, a print-based handout, or a classroom session. All three delivery environments used the same words and visuals, except the film and instructor versions included motion in their demonstration while the print version used still graphics.

Which group learned best? Surprisingly, learning was the same from all three versions. Since that groundbreaking study, many media comparison experiments have been reported, most comparing some form of electronic mediated lesson to an instructor-led version of the same lesson. A meta-analysis reported by Bernard et al. in 2004 found that overall there was little difference in learning from classroom compared to electronic media when the lessons used the same instructional methods. A more recent meta-analysis from the U.S. Department of Education published in 2010 found that compared to pure instructor-led training or pure computer-based training, blended learning environments that use a mix of media lead to best learning. The advantage of blended learning stems from leveraging the different features of diverse media effectively over a series of instructional events. For example, self-study computer prework can be followed by a face-to-face classroom event, which in turn can be followed by a virtual classroom session. Rather than spend classroom time dispensing information, that function can be off-loaded to a self-study medium such as computer tutorials or books. Then a classroom session can be devoted to hands-on activities, discussions, or role plays that cannot as readily be accommodated in other delivery environments. Follow-up sessions to discuss and guide learners as they transfer new skills to the job can be delivered by virtual sessions. In this way, the strengths of each delivery medium can be leveraged to optimize learning and transfer.

Research Question 2: What Are Value-Added Instructional Methods?

Rather than comparing different media, more recent research refocused on what instructional methods can be added to a basic lesson that will improve learning. For example, if you add graphics to a text explanation, will learning be improved? This stream of research goes beyond general questions such as "Are games good for learning?" and asks instead "What elements can we add to a basic game to optimize learning?"

Do Graphics Improve Learning?

To answer this question, an experiment tests two versions of a lesson: one with and a second without graphics. This is what Dr. Richard E. Mayer did in a series of experiments that focused on topics such as How a Bicycle Pump Works, How Brakes Work, or How Lightning Forms. In some experiments, the words were presented in text and the graphics consisted of a series of still visuals. In other experiments, the graphics were animated and the words were delivered by audio narration. In all experiments that compared lessons with and without graphics, the versions with graphics led to better learning (Clark and Mayer, 2011).

Research Question 3: Do Some Individuals Benefit More From Graphics Than Others?

You may be familiar with the idea of learning styles. Three popular learning styles are visual, audio, and kinesthetic. According to the learning styles concept, visual learners would learn best from a graphics-intensive environment compared to auditory learners, who would benefit more from lessons that emphasize listening. A lot of resources have been invested in learning styles with efforts such as learning style inventories, learning style classes, and lessons tailored to multiple styles.

The learning style idea reflects one form of individual difference. Individual difference research tests the effects of a given instructional method on individuals with different attributes such as different learning styles or different levels of background knowledge. What have we learned about individual differences when it comes to graphics? Experiments that used different methods to measure learning styles have shown no correlation among the different measures (Kratzig and Arbuthnott, 2006).

However, when it comes to prior knowledge, we see a different picture. The experiments that compared lessons with and without visuals described in the previous section involved subjects who were unfamiliar with the topic of the lesson. To determine the effects of graphics on novice versus experienced learners, the same experiments were repeated with two different groups of students: those unfamiliar with the topic and those with experience in the topic. You can see the results in Figure 19-2. How do you interpret these results? Which of these statements applies?

- Novice students profited more from graphics than experienced learners.
- Learning of experienced students was degraded by graphics.
- Novice student performance was raised to the level of experts by graphics.

Figure 19-2. Learning of Novice and Experienced Students From Lessons With and Without Graphics

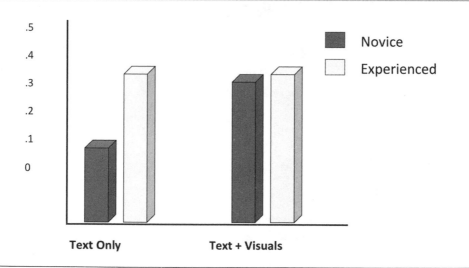

Note: Based on data from Mayer and Gallini, 1990.

From experiments like these, we conclude that it is more important to provide graphics for novice learners than for learners with topic background. Experienced learners can usually form their own images as they read the words. Therefore, additional graphics do not add much value. Our previous conclusion about graphics can be modified to state that you should add graphics to lessons designed for novice learners.

Research Question 4: Are Some Types of Graphics More Effective Than Others?

Adding graphics to lessons benefits novice learners the most. Are all graphics equally effective? In this section, we will review evidence on decorative versus explanatory graphics and on stills versus animations.

Decorative vs. Explanatory Graphics

Decorative visuals are added to make lessons more interesting and hopefully more motivating. Harp and Mayer (1998) compared two different versions of a lesson on how lightning forms. The basic version included simple explanatory graphics and text to explain the process. The spiced-up version added some interesting facts and visuals about lightning. For example, there was a visual of an airplane struck by lightning accompanied by a discussion of the effects of lightning on airplanes. Which version led to best learning: the basic version, or the basic version with interesting facts and visuals added?

The basic version was much more effective. Note that the facts and visuals in the spiced-up version were related to the topic of lightning but were irrelevant to the instructional goal, which was to learn how lightning formed. Because they were highly interesting, the anecdotes and visuals distracted learners from the main objective.

Rather than decorative visuals, I recommend explanatory visuals that illustrate relationships described in the text. For example, a tree chart or flow diagram can show qualitative summaries of concepts in the text. Maps use colors to indicate temperatures in different geographical areas. An interactive map can show temperature changes over seasons as the viewer selects different months. Science lessons are good sources for explanatory diagrams.

Are Animations More Effective Than Still Graphics?

Suppose you wanted to prepare a short computer-based lesson on how a toilet flushes or on how some equipment works. You could illustrate the description with an animated visual or with a series of still visuals. Which would be better for learning?

Although it seems intuitive that an animated visual would provide a more realistic rendition than a series of still visuals, evidence showed that stills were generally more effective than animations. Recall our previous discussion of cognitive load. Animations project a great deal of visual information that is transient. To make sense of the information, memory must hold previous images as new images appear. Therefore, animations impose much more cognitive load than a series of still graphics.

There are some exceptions. If your goal is to teach how something works, as in the research described in the previous paragraph, stills are probably a better choice. However, if you want to teach a procedure, such as how to perform a task, we have limited evidence that animated visuals are better. What if your goal is performance support rather than learning? Would a job aid to guide workers assigned to an assembly task be more effective if instructions were provided in text, in a series of still graphics, or by animations? Watson et al. (2010) compared time to build a small piece of equipment using these different formats for guidance. They found that on the first assembly attempt, text was least efficient and either stills or animations more efficient. After several rounds of building the same equipment, all three types of directions were equally effective, as the performers learned the procedure and relied less on the aids. Your choice of modes for performance support might depend on how often workers will apply the procedure, as well as what type of display the environment will support. Based on the above study, a series of stills might be the most cost-effective.

If you are going to use animation, recent research has focused on ways to help learners process them. Visual cueing is one approach. You can add visual cues by highlighting the important elements of an animation or by using a colored line to illustrate the progress of an animation in a piece of equipment. Additionally, be sure to provide controls that allow the learner to pause and replay as needed. We are still learning about when and how to best use animations. For now, however, keep in mind that a series of still visuals in many cases can be equally or more effective for learning than an animated version.

Research Question 5: What Is the Best Way to Explain Graphics?

Typically, your visuals will need to be explained. Is it better to explain a visual with text, with audio, or with a combination of text and audio?

To answer this question, you would test two or three versions of a lesson that included graphics. One version would explain the visual with audio narration, a second with on-screen text, and a third with both. Many experiments of this type have yielded consistent results: Learning is best when a complex graphic is explained by audio narration. Working memory has two storage areas: one for visual information and a second for auditory. Lessons that explain a complex graphic with text overload the visual center and fail to leverage the auditory storage area. In contrast, in a lesson with a complex visual, such as an animation, the eyes are free to view the visual while the ears listen to the explanation.

Exceptions to Audio Narration

There are situations, however, in which audio alone is *not* the best way to explain a visual. First, if the visual is quite simple or learners are familiar with the topic, there is less cognitive load and learning would be as good from a text explanation. Second, if the explanation is quite long, text would be more effective because audio has a shorter shelf life in memory. Research has shown that text is best for explanations that exceed four to five sentences. Third, sometimes learners need to refer back to instructional explanations multiple times. For example, directions to a practice exercise or feedback to a response may warrant repeated or slow review. Finally, factors regarding your audience or delivery medium may preclude audio. If learners are working in a secondary language or if you are working in print media, text may be your better or only option.

When to Use Audio and Text

Evidence concludes that using audio to narrate identical text on a slide or screen depresses learning. However, research has shown that using a visual accompanied by short text phrases, which are then expanded with audio narration, does not compromise learning.

Research Question 6: Where Should Text Be Placed?

Have you ever been reading a book in which an important graphic explained on one page appears on the back of that page? You need to flip back and forth to make sense of the information. The frustration most of us feel is our working memory complaining about the extra load of having to hold information in memory. This is one example of what psychologists call split attention. Split attention occurs in any layout that requires the learner to hold some elements of the instruction in memory while reviewing other elements. For example, a scrolling screen that places text at the top and a graphic at the bottom can lead to split attention. Even placing text at the bottom of a slide or screen containing an important visual can lead to split attention. In general, it's best to place text close to the relevant portion of the graphic. You might use word wrap or callouts to ensure the text is co-located with a graphic.

Research Question 7: Should You Use Formal or Informal Language?

As you write out explanations, you can assume an informal tone with phrases that include *I, you,* or *we.* Alternatively, you can use a more formal approach. Does the tone of your explanations make a difference to learning? The answer is yes. In comparisons of multiple explanations, including some in games or in tutorials, Mayer consistently found that a more conversational tone that uses first- and second-person phrases and polite language led to better learning than a more formal version. Mayer calls this a "personalization effect" and attributes it to basic human social communication instincts.

Evidence-Based Instruction: No Yellow Brick Road

When it comes to evidence-based training methods, there are few absolute guidelines. As we reviewed the research on graphics, we saw that the benefits of graphics on learning depend on the type of graphic used, the prior knowledge of the learner, and the instructional content. We also saw that while often learning is better when a graphic is explained by audio, there are important exceptions. Graphics and audio are not unique in this regard. When considering the value of any general instructional strategy, such as graphics, games, or social media, you will find few universal guidelines. Instead, you will need to consider:

- What is the prior knowledge of the learner? Individuals familiar with the topic are less subject to cognitive overload.
- Do the specific features of the method or technique impose an extraneous mental load on learners?
- Is the method or technique designed to align with the learning objectives?
- Is the method or technique more efficient than a more traditional approach?

A checklist for you to use to plan effective use of graphics, text, and audio in delivery is located at the *Handbook's* website at www.astdhandbook.org.

Is Figure 19-1 Effective?

At the start of this chapter, you reviewed Figure 19-1 and answered the statements that followed. Review the figure again now that you have read the chapter. Which statements do you now think are true?

- The storyboard is effective because it includes visuals, text, and audio for all learning styles.
- The storyboard will generate interest because the visual is engaging.
- The storyboard will be especially helpful to novice learners because it includes a lot of detail.

Based on evidence to date, neither the first nor third statements are true. The pirate visual is basically eye candy. Although loosely related to the topic, it does not contribute anything to the instructional goal of understanding the process of credit card skimming. Second, the explanation is presented in text and identical narration. Finally, novice learners will be overwhelmed by so much detail presented all at once. However, many learners will rate screens like this higher than a screen with an explanatory graphic or with no graphic, even if their learning is degraded. In a number of research studies, the lesson version that was least effective was rated higher than the more effective version. Overall, there is a low correlation between what learners like and what is most helpful to learning. Therefore, while student ratings are important, keep in mind that you cannot use them to assess the instructional effectiveness of your class.

About the Author

For more than 30 years, **Ruth Clark,** PhD, has helped workforce learning practitioners apply evidence-based guidelines to the design and development of classroom and e-learning instruction. Ruth has written seven books that translate important research programs into practical training guidance, including *e-Learning and the Science of Instruction* with Dr. Richard E. Mayer and *Scenario-Based e-Learning.* Her book, *Evidence-Based Training Methods,* is the main resource for this chapter. A science undergraduate, Ruth completed her doctorate in instructional psychology/educational technology in 1988 at the University of Southern California. She is a past president of the International Society of Performance Improvement and was honored with the 2006 Thomas F. Gilbert Distinguished Professional Achievement Award.

References

Bernard, R.M., P. Abrami, Y. Lou, E. Borokhovski, A. Wade, L. Wozney, P. Waller, M. Fixet, and B. Huant. (2004). How Does Distance Education Compare With Classroom Instruction? A Meta-Analysis of the Empirical Literature. *Review of Educational Research* (74):379-439.

Clark, R.C. (2013). *Scenario-Based e-Learning.* San Francisco: Pfeiffer.

Clark, R.C., and R. Mayer. (2011). *E-Learning and the Science of Instruction,* 3rd edition. San Francisco: Pfeiffer.

Harp, S.F., and R. Mayer. (1998). How Seductive Details Do Their Damage: A Theory of Cognitive Interest in Science Learning. *Journal of Educational Psychology* (90): 414-434.

Kratzig, G.P., and K. Arbuthnott. (2006). Perceptual Learning Style and Learning Proficiency: A Test of the Hypothesis. *Journal of Educational Psychology* (98):238-246.

Mayer, R.E., and J. Gallini. (1990). When Is an Illustration Worth Ten Thousand Words? *Journal of Educational Psychology* (88):64-73.

U.S. Department of Education, Office of Planning, Evaluation, and Policy Development. (2010). Evaluation of Evidence-Based Practices in Online Learning: A Meta-Analysis and Review of Online Learning Studies. Washington, DC.

Watson, G., J. Butterfield, R. Curran, and C. Craig. (2010). Do Dynamic Work Instructions Provide an Advantage Over Static Instructions in a Small Scale Assembly Task? *Learning and Instruction* (20):84-93.

For Further Reading

Clark, R.C. (2010). *Evidence-Based Training Methods*. Alexandria, VA: ASTD Press.

Clark, R.C. (2013). *Scenario-Based E-Learning.* San Francisco: Pfeiffer.

Clark, R.C. (2014). Multimedia Learning in E-Courses. In *Cambridge Handbook of Multimedia Learning,* 2nd edition, ed. R.E. Mayer. New York: Cambridge Press.

Clark, R.C., and C. Lyons. (2011). *Graphics for Learning,* 2nd edition. San Francisco: Pfeiffer.

Clark, R.C., and R. Mayer. (2011). *E-Learning and the Science of Instruction,* 3rd edition. San Francisco: Pfeiffer.

Hattie, J., and G. Yates. (2014). *Visible Learning and the Science of How We Learn*. New York: Routledge.

Chapter 20

Keep Participants Engaged

Cindy Huggett and Michael Wilkinson

In This Chapter

- Learn five facilitation tactics to keeping participants engaged.
- Acquire strategies that ensure successful facilitation in both an in-person and virtual workshop.

Whether you are leading an in-person or virtual workshop, if you don't grab your participants' hearts and minds right from the beginning, and then keep them engaged through to the end, your chances of gaining the outcomes and the learning transfer you desire are seriously jeopardized. How long does it take for your audience to conclude whether what you are doing, and how you are doing it, will be worth their time? It should be no more than 15 minutes and sometimes only two or three minutes.

The Key to Engaging Participants Is Facilitation

How do you engage participants from the beginning? We believe facilitation is the key. *Facilitate* comes from the Latin word *facilis,* which means to make easy. Great training workshop leaders don't just "deliver" training, they "facilitate" learning transfer. While some trainers seek to be the "sage on the stage," we believe that the most effective trainers seek to be the "guide on the side" who helps participants discover insights and how to apply them. When participants discover their answers, they understand them, they accept them, and they are much more likely to apply them once the training is over.

While there are many definitions of facilitation, for our purposes, we define facilitation as *"the act of engaging participants in creating, discovering, and applying learning insights."* Training delivered in a facilitated method frequently results in significantly higher levels of participant engagement, buy-in, and commitment to action following the training.

Five Keys to Great Facilitation

Between us, we have trained more than 20,000 people in facilitation-related skills. Based on that experience, we've learned that effective training facilitators focus on five keys in both virtual and in-person training:

- define success
- prepare relentlessly
- start with impact
- engage throughout
- manage dysfunction.

This chapter provides strategies for each of the five keys for use in both in-person and virtual settings.

1. Define Success

Having participants engaged during a training session is good. However, having them engaged in activities designed to achieve a specific purpose is even better. Effective facilitators define the purpose of a training session and ensure that every module, and every engagement in every module, is designed to achieve the desired goal. There are four related questions that help a facilitator clearly define success:

- What is the end goal or desired outcome of the training?
- What are the symptoms that indicate that the training is needed?
- How will the participants use the training?
- As a result of the training, what must the participants be able to do that they aren't able to do today?

The definition of success will also help determine the type of training session—whether it should be in-person or online and whether it should be a large group presentation-style seminar, one-on-one coaching, or a small group corporate training class. Each of these session types serves a specific purpose, so you will make choices based on what is most appropriate for the desired outcome.

If you will facilitate online, it is also important to determine your organization's exact definition of virtual training, since people frequently have different views of what it actually is. Some people assume that any type of remote learning can be considered virtual training, while others believe it's a more narrow definition. Getting clear on what your organization means by "virtual training" allows you to plan ahead and set appropriate expectations for the experience with all stakeholders.

One definition of virtual training is *"a highly interactive, synchronous, online, instructor-led training class, with defined learning objectives, that includes participants from geographically dispersed locations who are individually connected using a web-based classroom platform."*

Virtual training classes typically include 10-15 people per session with 60- to 90-minute training modules and interactivity every four to five minutes. In comparison, a 60-minute marketing webinar might have 50-200 participants with some limited interactivity, while a 30-minute presentation-style webcast might have thousands of participants with very little interactivity.

2. Prepare Relentlessly

You have probably heard the familiar adage attributed to Bob Pike, "Proper preparation prevents poor performance," which can be applied to almost any situation, including facilitation. The most effective facilitators spend an immense amount of time preparing for each and every session. Top-notch facilitators prepare relentlessly in four specific areas: content, knowledge of participants, environment, and self. Let's look at each one in turn.

Content

How do you get participants to take what they have learned and change their behavior once the training is complete? We have found that the best way to influence behavior change is to give participants what we call "the what, the how, the why, and the engagement."

Table 20-1. The What, How, Why, and Engagement of Facilitation

The What	The concept, tool, or technique participants need to learn
The How	The steps that a participant takes to use "the what"
The Why	The value to participants of using "the what"
The Engagement	How the facilitator will engage participants in learning "the what"

Good facilitators cover both "the what" and "the how." But these two alone are generally not enough to bring about behavioral change outside the classroom. Great facilitators are intentional about explaining "the why" and using a variety of engagement strategies to maintain interest. "The why" helps participants see the high value of "the what" and makes it worth their while to take the time to learn and to apply their learning after the class is complete. Therefore, during your preparation, be sure to define the what, the how, the why, and the engagement for each of your training modules. Below is an example of the what, the how, the why, and the engagement for a training topic called "The Starting Question."

Table 20-2. An Example of the What, How, Why, and Engagement

The What	The Starting Question: How to ask a question that yields a bonfire of responses, nearly every time.
The How	• Start with an image-building phrase. • Expand the image with at least two phrases that guide participants to "seeing" their answers. • Ask the direct question.
The Why	• Ask, "How many of you have asked an important question in a training class and have gotten complete silence?" • Explain that the problem may have been the way the facilitator asked the question, because when you ask a "Type B" question, you will nearly always receive a bonfire of responses.
The Engagement	• Provide a scenario and the two ways to ask the same question (Type A and B). • Have participants indicate which question type they prefer and why. • Show them the power of the Type B question and how it gets participants to see an image of their answers. • Give the three steps in building a Type B question. • Provide practice opportunities for participants to build their own Type B questions and gain feedback.

You may also download a worksheet at the *Handbook's* website at www.astdhandbook.org that will help you prepare for your next training session.

Knowledge of Participants

Second, effective facilitators learn as much as they can about the participants ahead of time. There are many ways to do this, from querying the stakeholders, to surveying participants, to making personal phone calls. If participants are geographically dispersed, then an email message requesting a response might work well. If facilitators are not able to communicate with participants ahead of time, then they at least do their homework to investigate as much as they can with questions such as:

- What kind of learners might attend this session?
- What might they already know about the topic?
- What questions might they ask?

The more a facilitator knows about the participants ahead of time, the better the facilitator can anticipate and prepare for the session.

Environment

Third, effective facilitators prepare their environment—the classroom and technology. They also put back-up plans in place as necessary.

All facilitators must ensure the following:

- An appropriate classroom is selected and appropriately set up. A physical room is required for in-person classes, while a virtual classroom platform is needed for online ones.
- Adequate supplies are available based on "the what" and "the how." In-person class participants might need markers, chart paper, and sticky notes, while virtual class participants might need electronic handouts and telephone headsets.
- Electronic devices are all set and ready to go. In-person classes often use projectors and sound systems, and both types of classes can use computers or mobile devices.
- System redundancy is in place, such as extra printed handouts or an alternative method to share visuals, should the technology fail.

In addition, for virtual classrooms, effective facilitators go above and beyond by ensuring the following:

- Every technology component has been tested and prepared.
- The facilitator's audio is crystal clear, Internet connection is solid, and a back-up laptop or connection device is easily available.
- Participants' technology has been tested and is ready to go.

Virtual facilitators make it easy for learners to join in a session and use the platform tools. In essence, they recognize that the technology should fade into the background while the session learning objectives remain the focus.

The Power of the Producer

Producers are the technical experts who assist a facilitator during a live virtual session. Some producers specialize in technology-only assistance (working with participants who need help connecting or using the platform), while other producers co-facilitate sessions along with the facilitator. In some cases, a producer may be called a host or session moderator.

Since facilitators and producers must work seamlessly together during a virtual session, it's critical for them to interact ahead of time to determine who will do what. Some facilitators like to control the technology while they communicate with participants; others prefer the producer to stay involved. In the case of co-facilitation, each person needs to know how to smoothly transition at the appropriate times.

Self

With all the other major items prepared, the final step is to prepare yourself to be ready to excel. Give special attention to several items.

- **Timing:** Be sure to create and print a time estimate for each module in the training agenda. During the session, this will allow you to know if you are ahead, behind, or on track.
- **Opening words:** Outline the opening words you will say to start the session.
- **Practice:** Practice your delivery of the training to ensure that you are comfortable with the content and your engagement strategies.
- **Roll call list:** If your training is virtual, prepare a list of participants' names that you can use to check off as you engage people; this will help ensure that you engage the entire group fairly evenly.

3. Start With Impact

There are many activities to perform at the start of a training session. But which activity is the most important to do first:

- Introduce people if they don't know each other? Important, but not first.
- Review the agenda? A very common error.
- Go over the ground rules for the training session? Not yet.

Participants typically attend any training, in person or virtually, with two questions. They want to know:

- Is this going to be worth my time?
- Am I going to get something that's going to help me?

Therefore, it is important to answer these questions right at the beginning before diving into other areas. To help answer these questions, use the acronym IEEI as a reminder of the things to include in your opening words to the participants.

- **Inform:** Let the participants know the purpose of the training and the outcome they will receive: "The purpose of this training session is. . . . When we are done you will walk away with. . . ."
- **Excite:** Explain the benefits and why the session should be important to them: "This is exciting because. . . ."
- **Empower:** Describe the role the participants will play or the authority that has been given to them in the session: "During this session, you are empowered to. . . ."
- **Involve:** Get them involved immediately through an engagement question requesting their personal objectives or requesting other information that furthers the training session's purpose: "Before we get started, let's find out. . . ."

Facilitators often do a great job of informing. And while empowering and involving sometimes don't happen well, the excite segment is the part of IEEI that is most often overlooked by facilitators. So, let's focus on this segment in particular.

You excite by making statements that answer the "What's in it for me?" question for the participants. Compare these two sample openings. Which one does the better job of exciting?

> **Excite Sample I:** *"Good morning; it's a pleasure to be with you. Let's start by reviewing why we are here. The purpose of this training session is to provide tools for running better meetings. Through this session, everyone in the organization will have tools for making meetings more effective. This course provides strategies for preparing for meetings, starting, keeping them focused, managing dysfunction, resolving disagreements, and closing effectively."*

> **Excite Sample II:** *"Good morning; it's a pleasure to be with you. Let's start by reviewing why we are here. The purpose of this training session is to provide tools for running better meetings. Think about all the time you spend in useless, unproductive, and unnecessary meetings. This class will give you tools for cutting the number of meetings you attend by 20-50 percent. You*

will learn the questions to ask to avoid having a meeting, and for those meet-ings that are necessary, you will have techniques for ensuring that they are highly effective, even when you are not leading the meeting! This is your opportunity to gain the techniques for making sure that the time you spend in meetings is highly effective and highly productive."

Most would agree that the second sample is by far the better one in terms of exciting the participants because it does a better job of describing the benefits to them. But did you notice the number of times the words *you* or *your* show up in the two excite statements? There are none in the first one and eight in the second. A key secret, therefore, for ensuring that your opening statement explains what is in it for the participants is to include the words *you* or *your* at least four times in the excite portion of your IEEI.

When Does a Training Class Begin?

If you think a training class begins at the scheduled start time, reconsider. A class begins the mo-ment a participant walks into the in-person classroom or logs in to the virtual classroom.

Actually, backing up a little, participants will begin to form impressions about the class when they first encounter the description and receive communication about the class. Therefore, the invitation, the welcome, and the instructions play an important part in how the training is perceived.

When the class begins—at the moment participants walk into the room or join online—participants should be engaged immediately in some type of activity. The engagement could be something sim-ple such as answering a question related to the training topic. In the virtual classroom, it could be responding to a poll question, writing on the whiteboard, or using the status indicators. The purpose is to set the tone for an interactive, engaging virtual class. The secondary purpose of engaging im-mediately is to teach the participants the virtual platform, if that's needed. The time is not used for learning new content related to the topic, but instead to establish an engaging learning atmosphere. The engagement activity also begins to empower participants so they get involved during the train-ing session and use any technology tools with ease.

You may also download a list of ideas for how to start with impact at the *Handbook's* website at www.astdhandbook.org.

4. Engage Throughout

How do you keep participants fully engaged in a 60-minute virtual training or a full-day in-person workshop? We use four key principles of engagement in our design and delivery to help keep the learner focused:

- **Variety:** Plan a variety of different learning experiences to keep the interest high.
- **Involvement:** Have a high degree of learner involvement by using questions, role plays, practice exercises, and other strategies that keep the session interactive.
- **Sharing:** Provide opportunities for learners to share their experiences and learn from one another.
- **Relevance:** Ensure that the content is relevant through examples and case studies related to the real-world and workplace experiences of the participants.

To help ensure engagement, for many long courses we break our training into 60- to 90-minute modules and start each one with an engagement question that gets participants immediately involved. By starting each module with an engagement question, we honor the wisdom of the group by having participants share what they already know about the topic. This technique also gets participants mentally ready to add new approaches to their toolboxes.

Table 20-3 provides examples of the engagement question used for three of the modules of a course on facilitative consulting skills. These questions could be answered individually by participants or in small breakout groups for even more engagement. This technique works for both in-person and virtual classes.

Table 20-3. Engagement Question Examples

Module	Module Engagement Question
Consulting: What Is It?	In which of the four scenarios (e.g., description of an independent software expert called in to fix a problem) is the person serving as a consultant?
Relationship Management	What is the difference between a project manager and a relationship manager across each of the following dimensions (e.g., definition of success)?
Defining the Need	A potential client has asked you to meet with members of the executive team to learn about their problem and come back a week later with a proposal. What are the questions you will ask?

After opening the training module with an engagement question, use a variety of strategies to keep participants engaged. Less effective facilitators often use a presentation–question–answer format. The facilitator presents and then asks for questions; participants ask questions; the instructor answers and then moves on to the next topic. This process happens over and over again with each module.

Effective facilitators know the importance of having a full toolbox of engagement strategies and using a variety of them to keep training engaging and participants motivated to learn.

With in-person, instructor-led training, your goal is to have a meaningful engagement activity every 15-20 minutes. And, as indicated earlier, in virtual training your goal is interactivity every four to five minutes. See the "For Further Reading" list at the end of the chapter for books that include engagement strategies you can add to your toolbox.

One distinguishing factor of a virtual class is that participants typically come together without eye-to-eye connections. Therefore, an effective facilitator has to engage with an unseen audience. In addition, since learners usually remain at their own desks to participate, the facilitator needs to keep the session more interesting than any distractions around them. An effective facilitator engages participants in a way that keeps them involved in the class instead of tempted to direct their attention elsewhere.

You Know You Have Engaged Well When Participants Say . . .

In-person training: "I never doodled once!"

Virtual training: "You kept me so engaged that I didn't have time to check my email during the session."

(These are actual comments received by the authors.)

5. Manage Dysfunction

Whether in a virtual or in-person training, dysfunctional behavior can have a great impact on success. We define dysfunctional behavior as *"any activity by a participant that is consciously or unconsciously a substitution for expressing displeasure with the training purpose or content, the training method, or outside factors. Dysfunctional behavior is a symptom, not a root cause."*

There are many different types of dysfunctional behavior that can occur in a training session, ranging from dropping out and not participating to verbally attacking someone and leaving the virtual or in-person training room in disgust. In managing the variety of dysfunctions, consider the following three steps: conscious prevention, early detection, and clean resolution.

Conscious Prevention

The best dysfunctions are those that don't occur at all. Therefore, we recommend that you take action in advance of the training to consciously prevent dysfunctional behavior from occurring. Based on information you gain about participants during preparation, consider dysfunction prevention strategies such as adding ground rules, assigning teams, interacting with certain people in advance of the session, and having private chats during the breaks.

Early Detection

Should dysfunction occur, you will want to address it early to avoid it getting worse. Accordingly, we recommend that you actively look for the early signs of dysfunction and take action immediately should you detect any of them. Early signs may include:

- participants who are not speaking
- participants who complain or object publicly to the group
- participants whose outward expressions seem to indicate that they are not buying in
- participants whose body language seems to indicate uneasiness with the session, such as folded arms.

One of the challenges in virtual training is that you typically cannot see the expressions or body language symptoms that would be evident in an in-person training. Therefore, virtual trainers have to work doubly hard to keep people engaged so that those not engaged become more readily obvious.

Clean Resolution

How you respond to a dysfunction depends on the dysfunction and other factors, including when it occurs, the number of people affected, and the probable root cause. However, consider the following general formula:

- Approach privately or generally. Either do a private chat with the people during a break or address the behaviors generally to the group without singling out any individuals.
- Empathize with the symptom. Praise an appropriate aspect of their behavior or express concern about the situation they find themselves in.
- Address the root cause. Make an effort to get at the real issue by asking a question that will yield a response that confirms the issue.
- Get agreement on the solution. Get agreement on how the situation will be handled going forward. Be sure that the solution addresses the root cause of the dysfunction and not just the symptom.

Technology Dysfunction

Unforeseen challenges can occur during virtual classes: a participant may disconnect, an activity might not pan out as planned, or a distraction in the workspace might need to be addressed (such as a co-worker interruption or a barking dog in the audio background).

Effective facilitators expect one or more of these challenges to arise; it's part of the territory in virtual training. Handled gracefully, challenges are an opportunity for facilitators to stay calm, take care of the issue, and return their focus to the learning as quickly as possible.

Of course, effective facilitators who apply the second principle, prepare relentlessly, will be able to quickly rely on their back-up plans for any unexpected technology challenges. If they lose Internet connectivity, they switch to their backup provider. If they disconnect from the audio, they quickly re-join the call. If an activity doesn't work exactly as they had planned, they respond with flexibility and switch to something else. Their back-up preparation pays off in these situations.

When the challenge occurs unexpectedly and is one that would not be prevented with preparation, then an effective facilitator will still respond with ease. They stay calm, manage the situation, and move on. More specifically, they:

- stay calm and take a deep breath
- let participants know what's going on (if appropriate)
- use back-up plans
- spend just a moment or two troubleshooting
- take a short break to deal with the situation.

If it's a situation that affects the entire virtual class and it's not possible to continue, then the facilitator keeps participants informed, takes a short break if necessary, and regroups when possible. Fortunately, most challenges are temporary and can be easily overcome.

Based on our own experiences, when you use the five keys described in this chapter to define success, prepare relentlessly, start with impact, engage throughout, and manage dysfunction, you will be rewarded by most of your participants rating the training as "the best" or "one of the best" they have ever experienced.

About the Authors

Cindy Huggett, CPLP, has more than 20 years of experience as a consultant, speaker, instructional designer, facilitator, and author who specializes in workplace training and development. She is the author of *The Virtual Training Guidebook* and *Virtual Training Basics* and the co-author of two ASTD Press *Infolines*. She holds a master's degree in public and international affairs from the University of Pittsburgh, and a bachelor's degree from James Madison University. Cindy is a past member of the ASTD National Board of Directors and was one of the first to earn the Certified Professional in Learning and Performance (CPLP) designation.

Michael Wilkinson is the managing director of Leadership Strategies, Inc. – The Facilitation Company, the largest provider of professional facilitators and facilitation training in the United States. He is a national leader in the facilitation industry. Michael is the author of five books, including *The Secrets of Facilitation* and *CLICK: The Virtual Meetings Book*. He is a board member of the International Institute for Facilitation and was named Facilitator of the Year in 2003. He is the founder of the FindaFacilitator database. Michael has provided training to hundreds of organizations across a variety of industries and in more than 15 foreign countries.

For Further Reading

Huggett, C. (2010). *Virtual Training Basics*. Alexandria, VA: ASTD Press.

Huggett, C. (2013). *The Virtual Training Guidebook: How to Design, Deliver and Implement Live Online Learning*. Alexandria, VA: ASTD Press.

Pike, R.W. (2002). *Creative Training Techniques Handbook,* 3rd edition. Amherst, MA: HRD Press.

Wilkinson, M. (2012). *The Secrets of Facilitation: The SMART Guide to Getting Results with Groups*. San Francisco: Jossey-Bass.

Wilkinson, M. (2013). *CLICK: The Virtual Training Book*. Atlanta, GA: Leadership Strategies Publishing.

Chapter 21

The Value of Experiential Learning

Robert (Bob) W. Lucas and Kris Zilliox

······················· **In This Chapter** ························

- ■ Define the many varieties of experiential learning.
- ■ Understand the process required to ensure successful experiential learning.
- ■ Consider elements that enhance experiential learning.

Experiential learning means different things to different people and is applied to a variety of learning opportunities—all referencing "experiences" in some way. It may be an "experience" that is created in a classroom or a simulation on a computer. Experiential learning may also occur informally on the job when a colleague provides a solution, or it could be a "stretch assignment" defined by a supervisor. Higher education is getting in the game as well, especially in business schools, where employers prefer that graduating students have skills in "professionalism" acquired in the workforce. In all of these cases, the essential features of experiential learning include:

- ■ **An experience:** Some action or event must occur, preferably a meaningful incident that leads to a change in knowledge, skill, or attitude. The learner must be engaged or must do something.
- ■ **An opportunity for reflection:** Time must be available to allow the learner to think about the experience and to interpret the effect. In many instances, the learner "publishes" or shares what happened, why it happened, and what was

learned. Reflection on the emotion and feelings about what was learned also plays an important part in experiential learning.

■ **A future action:** The learner must use analytical skills to conceptualize the experience and decide either consciously or unconsciously to apply or not apply what was learned. The key is that the learner makes a decision.

Experiential learning capitalizes on the life and work knowledge, experiences, and abilities of participants to learn and grow so that they are prepared for new situations they encounter in real life. The learner plays a pivotal role in ensuring that learning is taking place and transfer of knowledge and skills follow. Experiential learning may be known by other names, such as discovery learning, interactive learning, transformational learning, active learning, action learning, or brain-based learning.

When learners engage in activities and work through various issues, challenges, and problems, they identify potential options and gain new knowledge and insights that help them develop their own solutions. To some extent, learners facilitate their own learning and recognize solutions or develop strategies for applying what they learned.

The Theory Behind Experiential Learning

Numerous bodies of research support experiential learning and how to best aid individuals in their quest for knowledge, skills, or perspectives that influence their attitudes. Additional research and theories related to the importance of group dynamics and the impact of the environment on people and learning (ed. note: see chapter 53 in this *Handbook*) also contribute to the concepts behind experiential learning today. Prominent ideas exist in works by many past and current adult learning practitioners and educators, including David Kolb, Jean Piaget, John Dewey, Kurt Lewin, Robert Mager, Peter Jervis, and Malcolm Knowles. For example, Knowles referred to andragogical (the art and science of teaching adults) assumptions, which state that adults or andragogical learners:

■ are essentially self-directing
■ enter any learning experience with a great deal of prior experience
■ are ready to learn when they perceive a need to perform more effectively in some aspect of their lives
■ are problem centered in their learning
■ want to immediately apply what they have learned.

All of these proponents of adult learning advocate active involvement during the learning process in order to maximize learning potential and transfer of knowledge and skills to the workplace or the next real-world situation. This idea has been supported and expanded upon through dozens of studies and research projects dealing with brain-based learning and how the brain best gains, retains, recalls, and uses what it encounters.

According to Baker, Jensen, and Kolb (2002), experiential learning theory "provides a holistic model of the learning process and a multi-linear model of adult development." Experiential opportunities are major factors in helping people learn new knowledge and skills. They do this by comparing new information, data, processes, or whatever they are involved in during a learning event to their current knowledge and experience. They assimilate the new material to come up with effective ideas, thoughts, strategies, or conclusions that address their current situation. Ultimately, they transfer this new understanding or comprehension from the learning event to the real world and benefit from the lessons learned.

Kolb was a key advocate of experiential learning and created the Experiential Learning Theory (ELT) Model. He looked at the learning process as a cycle that could begin at any point in the model, but often starts with a Concrete Experience. Kolb's ELT model describes approaches through which people acquire new knowledge or skills.

Concrete Experience

According to Kolb, an experience in the form of data, information, activity, or whatever provides the platform for learner observation and reflection on what they encounter. In a training session, this experience might take the form of a small group activity in which learners work together to address a challenge, issue, or problem; a discussion of a workplace dilemma they face; or an exercise in which the outcome can be related to a real-world issue. For example, in the case of the latter, learners who work for a financial firm that advises clients might be asked to play a customized version of Monopoly. In the game, participants experience the importance of financial planning, managing money, strategies for investing, how to deal with adversity and its impact on finances (for example, going to jail, having to deal with unexpected obstacles like taking a detour back to a place where an unexpected tax is incurred), and a multitude of other life lessons.

Reflective Observation

During this phase of the model, learners reflect on the experience and analyze it by comparing to similar things that they already know in an effort to compare their experience to their previous knowledge or skills. Reflective observation can be either directed by a facilitator, with other learners, or working through it on their own. Asking the right questions to encourage reflection, comparisons, and analysis is critical. In the Monopoly scenario, participants might be asked what happened and how they felt.

Abstract Conceptualization

Successful reflection on the experience allows learners to consider new ideas or a modification of an existing behavior, thus assimilating the experience and the potential to create new strategies, techniques, and ways of using what they have learned in real-world settings. Personal preferences (for example, learning styles, personality, or other factors) play an important role in the approach that an individual prefers. In the Monopoly experience, participants might be asked to compare the experience with what happens in real life.

Active Experimentation

The conclusions and learning from the previous step readies the learner to test or try out new options or, if not immediately able to do so, to create a plan that can be implemented in the future. They can use the Monopoly experience as a basis to develop a plan for working with clients, identifying what they will do differently in the future to be more successful or to be more helpful to their clients.

Figure 21-1. Kolb's Experiential Learning Theory (ELT) Model

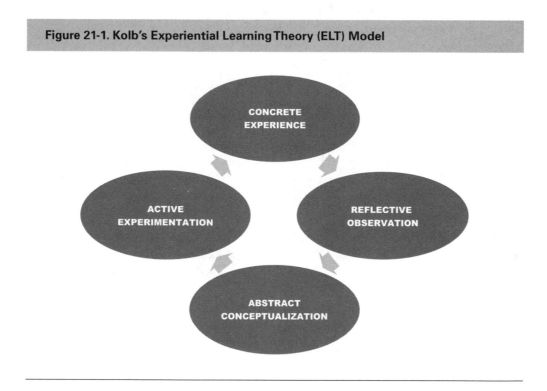

Effective learning occurs when a learner progresses through Kolb's four stages. These four stages can be summarized as follows:

- **Concrete Experience:** Doing something—having the experience.
- **Reflective Observation:** Reviewing what happened—thinking or talking about the experience.
- **Abstract Conceptualization:** Coming to conclusions—learning from the experience.
- **Active Experimentation:** Planning next steps—trying out what was learned from the experience.

Exploring the Experiential Learning Process

With many advocates for experiential learning in the learning and performance profession, it is little wonder that there are numerous process models from which a facilitator might choose when designing and developing an effective learning environment.

Pfeiffer and Jones Experiential Learning Cycle

One popular model is the Pfeiffer and Jones five-stage Experiential Learning Cycle. You will recognize similarities to Kolb's ELT model. The unique element of this model is that Pfeiffer and Jones focused on the questions that could be asked in each phase. These questions were developed specifically for an experiential learning activity (ELA) designed for classroom or online learning but are also a good example of how to facilitate discussions with a colleague you are coaching, an employee you are supervising, or even your child. Facilitation can be challenging, but asking the right questions that guide reflective conversations throughout the experience can be very powerful.

1. Experiencing

This is the activity phase, where learners perform the task or activity with little or no assistance from the facilitator. It is an active stage in which learners personally experience a process or learning event, an activity, or demonstration; solve a problem; or perform some other defined task in which they become active participants. The goal of the experience is to replicate or represent a life event from which the learners will gain knowledge or skills or will change their attitudes. The facilitator avoids revealing the expected outcome to allow the learners to experience the AHA!

If the process ends here, all learning is left to chance. However, precise, well-crafted questions in the next four steps ensure that the experience leads to learning. The questions build on each other, promoting critical reflection, valuable discovery, and ultimate learning.

2. Publishing

In this step, learners share their reactions and observations to what they experienced during the activity or training. As Kolb notes, feelings are equally important and are explored. Questions for this step include:

- What happened? What did you observe?
- What occurred during the activity?
- How did you feel?

3. Processing

Step three provides an opportunity for learners to examine and discuss the dynamics and any patterns they may have experienced. Questions for this step encourage learners to test hypotheses and may include questions such as:

- Why do you think that may have occurred?
- What did you learn? What did you learn about yourself?
- What principles may be true based on this experience?

4. Generalizing

During the fourth step, learners identify any similarities that relate to personal application, on the job or in other aspects of the learner's life. This step is sometimes called the "So what?" step. During the debrief of the activity, a facilitator draws out these lessons through specific questions that might include:

- How does this relate to. . . ?
- What does this suggest to you about. . . ?
- How does this help you understand. . . ?

5. Applying

The final step of the model represents the "Now what?" step. The questions help learners apply generalizations to actual situations. Learners develop action plans or effective ways to implement the learning, to make changes in their behaviors, or to put the knowledge to use in real life. Questions that help to bring learners around to this point include:

- What will you do differently as a result of this experience?
- How will you transfer this learning to the workplace?
- How can this help you in the future?
- What's next?

HRDQ's Experiential Learning Model

HRDQ Press, a publishing house in Pennsylvania, developed a more intricate experiential learning model. HRDQ's model sports seven phases.

1. **Focusing:** Engaging the learner is unique to this model and is a step that is needed in the classroom and on the job. Prepare the learners, whether it is making them feel comfortable or letting them know that the facilitator is there to support them.

2. **Experiencing:** Similar to the other models, the learner must experience something. HRDQ emphasizes that the experience must be both engaging and meaningful.

3. **Reflecting:** HRDQ emphasizes a need to provoke critical thinking skills so that learners can recall previous situations or examples.

4. **Thinking:** Adding a discussion, theoretical in nature, to help understand the experience is a reflection of the Kolb model.

5. **Modifying:** While this step is similar to other models, the HRDQ model boldly emphasizes that the learner should consider feedback and discussion to decide what to change.

6. **Practicing:** Other models do not openly advocate practicing, but it is a natural step when the experiential learning is occurring on the job.

7. **Integrating:** This step is also unique to the HRDQ model, encouraging learners to rediagnose their changes at some later date. Learners explore to what extent they have learned or used new skills, knowledge, and attitudes.

You can download more about this model on the HRDQ website at www.HRDQ.com.

Figure 21-2. HRDQ Experiential Learning Model™

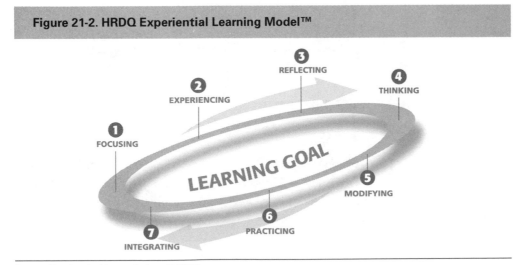

Source: Reprinted with permission of HRDQ.

Whether you use Kolb's four-step model, HRDQ's seven-step model, or something between, or whether you are working in a classroom with 25 participants or in a plant one-to-one with your employee, following the steps, asking the right questions, and allowing the learner to experience, reflect, and discover ensures successful experiential learning.

Following are some additional reminders make the effort easier and more effective.

Reminders to Make Experiential Learning Easier and More Effective

Experiential learning can occur in a classroom or on the job. On the job, the experience occurs naturally (ed. note: see chapter 25 in this *Handbook*). However, when experiential learning is intended for a classroom or online experience, it must be designed to be as realistic and valuable to the learner as possible. Experiential learning environments focus on engaging participants throughout the learning process so that they become an integral part of the event and act to facilitate their own attainment of knowledge, skills, or attitudes. Designers and facilitators consider several aspects in order to ensure successful experiential learning.

Make Learning Contextual

Help learners put the content they experience into terms of their life or workplace in order to recognize how they can immediately apply what they learn. When you only provide information, facts, data, and tools without helping learners see the relationship and importance to them and their jobs, the learning connection is often missed. A key role of a facilitator in the experiential learning environment is to act as a conduit to reinforce how the learning that occurs applies to the workplace. This may be done through well-chosen questions, feedback, coaching, or reminders of lessons learned. By encouraging reflection and consideration of content, facilitators can aid learners in their efforts to see application of theory and practices.

Address All Learning Modalities

Remember that you will typically have a combination of visual, auditory, and kinesthetic learners in your sessions. In designing session content and format, remember to create activities and materials that will add value for all participants. Experiential learning environments offer opportunities where support materials and activities tie to multiple modalities throughout the session so that learners can maximize their learning potential. The ConAgra Foods case study later in this chapter is an excellent example of this.

Create a Positive Learning Environment

Learning is encouraged and facilitated better in an environment that is relaxed yet stimulating socially, emotionally, physically, and mentally. When learners can feel comfortable and safe in their environment, they are free to experiment; try new things; open up with ideas, questions, and concerns; and freely explore options that are offered or developed throughout the event.

Encourage Learner Collaboration

Adults gain more in environments where they can easily and frequently collaborate and share ideas. In the classroom, find ways that allow learners to interact in groups or activities by providing an ongoing collection of activities and exercises designed to bring learners together to learn. Some of the techniques used might include brainstorming, groups, buzz groups, project work teams, role plays, small groups, or simulations. In the workplace, encourage teamwork, social networking, and peer coaching.

Encourage Active Learner Participation

Malcolm Knowles stated that a major difference between the way children and adults learn is that adults have more experience and knowledge and can thus contribute more actively to achieving their learning outcomes. When you engage adults in training and make them active players in the learning process, they typically assume more responsibility for stated learning outcomes. Since experiential learning tends to be more action based, rather than content or information based, participants become engaged mentally and physically. Brain-based learning research shows that in such environments, the brain often becomes more stimulated and then better processes information and concepts; forms new dendrites; and starts making key connections to current memories, knowledge, and skills. Thus, through engagement, learners can more likely assimilate learning and form cognitive connections related to application of what they learn to the workplace. The result is a higher degree of transfer of learning from training to the learner's real-world environment(s).

Use Self-Assessments

Self-graded manual or computer-generated reports based on personal elements like communication, leadership, and behavioral styles offer personal insights that can be easily used as the "experience." Self-assessments can also be used to create personal action plans for implementing what was learned during the experiential learning cycle.

Help Track Progress

Introduce the concept of keeping a journal. Maintaining a written record of the learning events and lessons learned provides participants something that they can later reference.

It also helps reinforce the learning as they review session notes and content in the future. This increases the likelihood of using the lessons learned from a training experience or to remember tips on the job.

Incorporate Brain Research Findings

Brain research supports the use of techniques and learning strategies that have an impact on all five human senses to improve the chance that learners will better remember and act upon what they experience. Learners are provided with many opportunities to make associations with knowledge and skills that they already possess while forming new patterns and making additional connections. These connections are strengthened by the use of analogies, simulations, metaphors, stories, examples, and various interactive techniques. When designing a brain-based learning environment, material and instruction must be learner centered and delivered in a manner that is fun, meaningful, and personally enriching. There must also be ample opportunities for participants to have time to process what they experience in order for them to make mental connections, form memories, master session content, and plan ways for implementation of lessons learned. The ConAgra Foods case study later in this chapter describes the creative approach the company used to ensure a valuable experiential learning event.

What's Unique About Experiential Learning?

An important thing to remember about experiential learning is that individuals are charged with responsibility for their learning by matching content and activities to their personal knowledge and experiences. They are encouraged to make decisions on how to assimilate new material and techniques into their daily performance and are challenged to analyze learning content, identify solutions, and create plans to apply what they learn to their personal workplace and life situations. As a result of being an active participant in their own learning, they are more likely to gain, retain, recall, and be able to use what they experience.

The key is that participants play a significant role in learning outcomes. Unique features of experiential learning include the following:

- Content is uncovered by the learners, sometimes not until after the experience has been debriefed.
- Learning is dependent on questions that encourage learners to reflect and discover.
- Environment can be located anywhere.

■ It is probably the most personalized learning. On the job, it is responsive to what is needed here and now; in the classroom, participants glean what they need, which may be different for different learners.

Growth of Experiential Learning

Experiential learning has been gaining momentum in the past two decades and now is moving along at a dizzying pace for a number of reasons.

More Learning and Performance Professionals Embrace It

As knowledge about the value and results of experiential learning spreads through the adult learning and education profession, facilitators and instructional designers are building elements of it into their training design. They are also striving to educate themselves on the research that supports the tenets of experiential learning and working to find ways to build it into all their learning events. As mentioned earlier, colleges and universities readily see the benefits of creating opportunities for students to participate in experiential learning. The sidebar briefly describes how one university is offering experiential learning to its students. Rather than simply studying business, students at Long Island University (LIU) are learning about business firsthand: marketing, advertising, accounting, making wise business decisions, and other skills. Kim Cline, president of LIU, states, "We want to make sure the students can put the experience on their resumes."

Technological Advances

There have been monumental strides in technological developments of training aids and equipment that can be used to supplement classroom instruction. Examples of this technology include electronic games, e-learning platforms and solutions, online access to training and record keeping, innovative intelligent computer simulations, video, and much more. Training can also now be delivered directly to an employee's desktop or handheld device and make the need to travel to distant training sessions a thing of the past.

Learner Abilities and Preferences Have Changed

Because employees from Generation X and beyond have had access to technology most of their lives and are comfortable with its use, creating experiential learning applications to address their learning preferences and needs is a natural progression. Using a practical hands-on approach to training in which the learners control the pace and level of their content makes sense, especially if it is in the form of games, activities, or other formats that they enjoy and often embrace. Technology-based content can provide a means of engaging the three primary learning modalities described in the next section of this chapter.

Experiential Learning in Higher Education: Giving Students an Essential Experience

By Kimberly Cline, President, Long Island University

Integrated experiential learning is an emerging practice in higher education, enhancing the traditional classroom experience through innovation and entrepreneurial activities. Long Island University (LIU) is an early adopter, offering students opportunities to create and operate businesses on campus, from a clothing store to an art galley gift shop to a computer store. Student committees manage and operate ventures that complement their areas of study. They gain valuable experience for their resumes, and all profits are returned to scholarships and to capital funds for future student ventures.

Students become skilled in planning, critical thinking, and problem solving as they build businesses. An added benefit is that future employers value this conscious linking of knowledge and practice. Typically, college students gain experience through internships, but the practice of conceptualizing and running a business offers a greater level of experience that cannot be achieved through normal internship routes.

LIU is moving forward. The evolution of managing student-run businesses to the development of their own companies is a natural one. To facilitate this transition, LIU has partnered with high-tech companies who are in the incubation stage. In addition to forming campus-based businesses, LIU students have the opportunity to work alongside proven entrepreneurs, such as the founder of companies like Fatwire. This full integration of experiential learning creates a challenging and innovative learning environment where students continually learn by doing. LIU graduates are workforce ready.

Costs Have Decreased

While front-end costs are still high, depending on the types of experiential paths you want to follow, overall costs can be less than classroom training if you want to create your own activities and materials and have the technical resources to design and develop them.

Information Is Readily Available

With all the research that has been done into brain-based learning and the effectiveness and process of creating experiential learning materials, activities, and content, facilitators and organizations now have an inexpensive way to learn the value of and a process for creating learning that results in higher impact through active learner engagement. There are hundreds of articles and books available to explain how to develop experiential activities and strategies for use in the classroom or in electronic format.

An Experiential Learning Activity Worksheet is located on this *Handbook's* website at www.astdhandbook.org and can be used to create your own experiential learning exercise.

Experiential Learning Beyond the Classroom

Experiential learning allows learners to own and master the content when and where they need it. Most learning occurs outside the classroom. In the classroom or through an e-learning event, facilitators and designers play a key role in creating opportunity for reflection and application to enhance what they learned. A well-designed practice session can often be almost as effective as the real-life event if it is realistic and provides opportunity to use models, simulations, and equipment that mirror on-the-job activity. Pilots successfully learn skills in how to land and take off in various weather conditions through the use of flight simulators without the added cost or potential safety risks of doing so in an actual airplane.

Once learners are back on the job, supervisors and team leaders assume the role of facilitator in order to ensure that learners use and benefit from lessons learned in training. We have an obligation to ensure that these supervisors are good coaches and understand the steps in experiential learning. This includes providing them with tools to help learners perform tasks that use their new knowledge and skills on the job, then receive productive performance feedback and constructive correction if improvement is needed.

In an ideal world, supervisors and team leaders will experience the same content as their employees in a learning environment so they know what learners have experienced. They can then more effectively emphasize, support, and guide employee application of concepts and experiences.

Supervisors assist employees by discussing how the learning objectives and content can be applied on the job. From this discussion, the employee can work with their supervisor or team leader to develop an action plan and performance goals. On the job, the supervisor's role is one of observation, resource, and support, as well as providing regular performance feedback. They may also conduct just-in-time skill training, connect employees with experts, or engage them in role plays.

Online or technology-based support systems are another excellent means of reinforcing and supporting previous learning. If it is not available to the organization, there are myriad free webinars and podcasts or other content on a variety of workplace topics free through various websites and blogs. For example, if you type in the term *customer service* on the YouTube website, there are dozens of short videos related to service skills that could be used to introduce or reinforce knowledge or skills. Supervisors might use such materials as discussion vehicles when working with employees. Once the employees view the materials, the supervisors could guide a discussion and create opportunities where the employees could practice the skills they learn.

All learning experiences should be valid and relevant in order for them to see value and embrace the effort required to learn and use the information or skills. The ConAgra Foods case study provides a creative experience that is meaningful and relevant.

From Farm Gate to Dinner Plate: Experiential Learning at ConAgra, Kris Zilliox

ConAgra Foods Manages Enterprise Learning

One of the greatest struggles for learning professionals is how to make learning solutions engaging and impactful for the participants. We often feel limited by time and budgets, which can impede the level of innovation and creativity we are able to infuse into our training events. Many of our classroom training sessions are executed in a conference room via PowerPoint presentations with the time broken up by small group exercises and breaks. Although this format of classroom training can be effective and even necessary for some subject matter, we are facing stronger competition than ever for the attention of our participants in today's age of constant digital connectivity. Like many of our peers, we at ConAgra Foods have struggled to find ways to make learning more engaging and more memorable, and to have strong learning transfer to the participant's job—until recently. In 2013, we set out to redesign our executive leadership development program by integrating learning events that were minimally structured and experience based. We sought to provide our leaders with an experiential, big-picture view of our business—literally from farm gate to dinner plate.

Leadership Development Need

With tremendous growth comes tremendous challenge. ConAgra Foods has grown from a grain milling and livestock feed business that was founded in 1919 to one of North America's largest food companies. Acquisitions have been the core of the ConAgra Foods growth strategy, which has been extremely effective, but also comes with its share of challenges. Acquisitions start as a financial transition, but they soon become a human transaction. Making and closing the deal is easy; the real job is making the deal work. We have not had the luxury of a long history to cultivate a single organizational culture, as we are a melting pot of numerous cultures. Change has been constant, and each new acquisition brings new people, policies, and philosophies. In 2011, the ConAgra Foods senior leadership team, led by CEO Gary Rodkin, introduced our "Recipe for Growth"—a five-year, strategic road map for how we operate our business and deliver shareholder value with a goal to become the fastest-growing food company by 2017. The incredible growth experienced in the organization in the past five years validated the tremendous need to develop the leaders of our organization. We derive our competitive advantage by the imaginative ways that our leaders accomplish business results. As we integrate acquired businesses, enter new markets, and build relationships with new customers, we must constantly improve our leaders' ability to resolve extraordinary challenges and address unanticipated business conditions.

Overview of the Leadership Excellence Series Redesign

As ConAgra Foods has changed and evolved the past five years, it became evident that our leadership development programs were not keeping pace with the developmental needs of ConAgra Foods' leadership. Leadership Excellence Series (LES), our executive leadership development program, was the first to have its curriculum reviewed and revised. The first step was to determine what we were trying to solve. Senior leaders were interviewed to identify what our current leadership misses were and how we could best develop our leaders for the future of the consumer packaged goods industry. Additionally, we had recently completed an organization-wide engagement survey and used that topline data to identify key organizational challenges that related to leadership. One opportunity area that continued to surface was to help our leaders better see the big picture by viewing the business in a more holistic way. We kept the original framework of the program, which included three, three-day sessions, with each session focusing on a different level of leadership development: developing an improved understanding of self, leading others, and leading growth in the business. The curriculum followed the ConAgra Foods Enterprise Learning's "Learn, Apply, Sustain" methodology. Participants were guided to *learn* through prelearning assignments that included both individual reading and work done in assigned cohort groups. Next, they *apply* what they have learned in the live classrooms sessions by participating in interactive and often hands-on activities and discussions to help drive behavior change and learning transfer. Finally, they *sustain* their learning through guided self-reflection and follow-up work in their cohort groups.

The newly redesigned LES was launched in the spring of 2013 with 45 cross-functional leaders representing every aspect of the ConAgra Foods business. This group completed their LES journey in late August 2013 with rave reviews and tangible ideas to improve themselves as leaders, their teams, and the organization as a whole. We concluded the series with a final session that was heavy in experiential learning activities and proved to be a valuable learning experience for our participants.

Leadership Excellence Series: Session 3—Leading Growth

The greatest change in the LES curriculum occurred during the final session, which focused on developing a strategic understanding of the business. As we identified early in our analysis phase, we needed to help our leaders see the business holistically. Like many large organizations, we have challenges where the different functions may not understand or appreciate the roles the other functions play in "delivering everyday foods in extraordinary ways" (ConAgra Foods Purpose Statement), which can cause conflict, inefficiencies, and redundancies. Many of our vice presidents (core audience for LES) are experts in their functional area, whether it is information technology, human resources, supply chain, research, or quality and innovation, but most have limited understanding in how the other functions enable the Recipe for Growth within the organization. Keeping the goal of helping our leaders see the big picture, we completely redesigned the final session of the LES. We went back to the drawing board and eliminated the previous design. We shifted our mindset from telling our participants about our business challenges to immersing them into the challenges from the source. We sought to provide our leaders with an experiential, big-picture view of our business—from farm gate to dinner plate.

ConAgra Foods is one of North America's largest packaged food manufacturers, with branded and private branded food found in 99 percent of America's households, as well as a strong commercial foods business serving restaurants and foodservice operations globally. Our product cycle begins on a farm and ends on a plate—either as part of a home-cooked meal or at a restaurant. Consumers vote for our products by purchasing or not purchasing our food. As mentioned earlier, our purpose statement is that we deliver everyday food in extraordinary ways. When our employees appreciate food manufacturing from the farm to the plate, they develop better business acumen and stronger relationships with internal and external stakeholders. Before the design process, we interviewed several ConAgra Foods leaders and asked them about what issues the food industry, and specifically ConAgra Foods, were facing today and what we would continue to face in the future. The answers we received identified issues that were both internal and external to our organization. Consumers have rising concerns about genetically modified organisms (GMOs) and animal welfare. Manufacturing plant employees feel disconnected from "corporate" as reflected in their lower engagement survey scores. Finally, our shoppers' purchasing behaviors are rapidly changing and competition for their dollars is as fierce as ever, so our business relies on our ability to better connect with shoppers. These issues inspired the farm gate to dinner plate design for our final LES session, which included a farm tour, plant tours, an immersive shopping exercise, and a cooking experience.

Farm Tour

The work we do delivering everyday foods in extraordinary ways would not be possible without production agriculturalists growing the raw materials that we manufacture into the food our consumers love. The learning objective of the farm tour was to increase the agricultural literacy of our LES participants. Agricultural literacy includes an understanding of agriculture's history and current economic, social, and environmental significance. This understanding includes knowledge of food and fiber production, processing, domestic and international marketing, and how it all affects our business at ConAgra Foods. This knowledge prepares our leaders to have fact-based conversations with key stakeholders.

Although the design of the farm tour may have appeared minimal to the participants, there was quite a bit of behind-the-scenes preparation that took place to ensure that our learning objectives were met. The first step was to find a diverse farm that raised both crops and animals to facilitate both the GMO and animal welfare discussions. Additionally, we needed to find a farm that was in close proximity to our hotel and that was willing to host our leaders on a tour. Ultimately, we collaborated with a dairy and crop farm, which was helpful in making the connection to our manufacturing plant tours, as the greatest raw material for one of the plants was milk. We had several pre-tour calls and an on-site visit with the farm owner prior to our tour day. We used this time to explain our learning objectives of the tour and align for the best way to execute the tour to meet those objectives.

In addition to the farm owner/operator and his family, several agricultural industry experts who represent both plant and animal agriculture joined us on the tour. We found that the agriculturalists are very connected and eager to share their story, as representatives of the state university, government, and various agricultural groups joined our tour. These experts were present to network with our leaders and to create common ground between food production and food manufacturing. Ultimately, we share the same consumer and the same goal: to produce and manufacture safe and affordable food.

Sticking with the Learn, Apply, and Sustain methodology, the participants were prepared for the farm tour by completing prereadings about the various viewpoints surrounding GMOs and animal welfare. They also reviewed a presentation about how ConAgra Foods procures milk and the many federal and state laws that regulate the dairy industry. Additionally, the participants were provided a participant guide with pre- and post-tour reflection questions plus space to write notes along the way. Our leaders applied their prelearning knowledge on the tour by appreciating firsthand what it takes to run a dairy and crop farm and asking educated questions along the way. Our participants saw corn, soybeans, and hay growing in the field and asked questions about GMOs, pesticides, herbicides, and organic farming. They saw all stages of the dairy operation, from the calving pens to the milking parlor, and asked questions about separating calves from their mothers, dehorning, a cow's diet, and the milking process. The questions asked by participants during the tour were answered either by the farmer or by another agricultural expert. Like many of our consumers, most of our participants had never been on a farm before and had no idea what farming was like or how a farm operated. They learned a tremendous amount about the business of farming, a farmer's perspective of key agricultural issues, and the many laws and regulations that regulate the industry. They *sustained* their learning by completing a writing reflection exercise and debriefing the experience with the larger group the next day. Overall, the learning objectives were met and the leaders left the tour in awe and inspired by the hard work of an American farm family.

Plant Tours

The next step follows the raw agricultural products to our manufacturing facilities, where they are made into the food our consumers love. ConAgra Foods is a food manufacturer with more than 80 food processing plants throughout the world. We turn raw agricultural products raised on farms and ranches into safe, marketable products. The learning objectives of these tours were to make our leaders appreciative of the processes, capabilities, and roles played at our manufacturing facilities. Manufacturing plants are the core of our business, yet many of those in leadership positions have never been to one of our facilities. Many leaders make decisions each day about how we manufacture our products to improve our top and bottom lines, but they may have little to no connection to the people at those locations. Improving plant engagement is a high priority at ConAgra Foods.

Plant tours are a critical part of the LES experience. We selected the geographic location for this session based on the proximity to two manufacturing plants. One plant was a food processing facility, and the other produced packaging for several lines of our products. Safety and minimal disruption to the plant were our first priorities on these tours, so although the participants were unable to work on one of our manufacturing lines in the plants, they were able to complete full tours and visit with employees on the line about what they do. Each of the tours began with an overview session about the plant, its employees, its accomplishments, and its investment in the local community. Plant employees candidly and respectfully shared some of the challenges of the plant environment and were open to answering questions from our leaders.

Continuing with the Learn, Apply, and Sustain methodology, the participants were prepared for the plant tour by completing *prelearning* about each of the plants, including plant history, facts, leadership, safety requirements, operational overviews, and employee roles at each location. This knowledge was *applied* on the tours as they saw the facilities, processes, and people they read about come to life before their eyes. The learning was *sustained* by completing a reflection exercise and debriefing the experience with the larger group. As they were for the farm tour, the participants were provided with a guidebook with pre- and post-tour reflection questions and space to write notes along the way. The learning objectives were met as the participants gained an appreciation not only for the big picture of the manufacturing process from beginning to end, but also for the people who make it happen 24 hours a day, seven days a week.

Shopper Immersion Exercise

At the beginning of our 2014 fiscal year, CEO Gary Rodkin challenged our employees to "be perfect at retail to win with shoppers and consumers." This challenge was integrated into the LES learning design through an immersive shopping experience. The learning objective of this experience was for our leaders to learn how Shoppers' Lifestages drive their behavior at retail and how they could relate their learning to the bigger picture at ConAgra Foods.

The learning design was simple, yet impactful. Prior to the session, our participants completed their *prelearning* by watching a video about the Shopper Lifestages, research completed by the ConAgra Foods Shopper Insights team regarding the unique behaviors of shoppers during different periods of their lives. This knowledge was *applied* during the immersive shopping experience. Our participants were divided into groups and were told that they would be completing the weekly grocery shopping for a specific lifestage. Each group was assigned a realistic, unique shopper profile that represented a family in a specific Shopper Lifestage and their budget. It was critical for the experience that they immerse themselves in their shopper profile—shopping where their assigned shopper would shop and buying what their shopper would buy, all within their shopper's budget. Every decision made had to be reflective of their shopper's profile—from where they would shop, how much time they were given to shop, whether or not they used coupons, whether they bought private label or name brands, and so on. The groups were provided with a card preloaded with their shopper's weekly grocery budget. This shopping experience was hectic and eye opening for many of our executives, especially for those shopping as larger families on very limited budgets. When the groups returned to the hotel, they set up their purchases along with their shopper profiles at tables, and then preceded to "gallery walk" the other groups' purchases. Finally, the group began the *sustain* process by completing one of the most impactful debrief discussions from the entire LES. We found that when our leaders immersed themselves into someone else's weekly shopping trip, they were able to see what was important from their perspective—brand, price, convenience, packaging, promotion, and so forth. The participants compared what they learned to some of our current business strategies and discussed why they did or did not make sense with their new perspectives. Leaders were eager to bring their learning during this immersive shopping experience back to their teams. In alignment with the ConAgra Foods mission to end child hunger, all of the food purchased for this exercise was donated to a hunger relief organization.

Cooking Experience

A food company teaching how food is grown and made would be remiss without including a hands-on cooking experience for participants. The final evening our LES participants were together, we gathered at a small culinary school for a hands-on cooking experience that combined camaraderie and culinary education and resulted in a wonderful dinner. Although our only learning objectives were to make an amazing meal out of ConAgra Foods' products and to have fun, it was a valuable addition to the experiential learning journey of the final session of the LES.

LES Conclusion

At the conclusion of the third session of the LES, our leaders had increased their agricultural literacy to be better prepared to have conversations about industry issues, they gained appreciation for the work that happens in our plants and the capabilities and imagination of our plant workers, and they were inspired to develop and market products that will better connect with consumers. We have identified ways to improve this session for the next group of Leadership Excellence Participants and are looking forward to continuing this journey with our leaders. Our ambition to become the fastest-growing food company will not happen unless we build a highly skilled leadership population that can deliver against the ever-changing demands of our customers and markets. Experiential learning experiences like those within the LES will help fuel our innovation pipeline, yield new products that meet the needs of today's consumers, and keep us at the forefront of our industry.

Why Is Experiential Learning So Important?

As learning and development professionals, we often talk about how it is better to facilitate learning instead of just presenting information. By facilitating, we strive to support learners on their paths, but not give them all the answers. I believe that experiential learning is the epitome of facilitated learning. The learning and development professional provides the proper guardrails to learners, but learners drive their own learning.

Experiential learning can provide a new way of thinking about an old way of teaching. Hands-on learning is anything but new, as laboratories have been an essential component of many educational philosophies. Historically, hands-on learning has been essential to train task- or skill-heavy jobs. Few of us would want to ride with someone who learned to drive a car from a PowerPoint presentation any more than we would want to have brain surgery performed by a surgeon who has only experienced surgery through computer simulations. It is obvious that experiential, laboratory-type training is necessary for some fields, but I urge you to continue to think outside the box. The laboratory should no longer be limited to the usual suspects of science, medicine, and vocational skills. When designing learning, we need to think far beyond the standard instructor-led classroom session. What experiences can you provide the learners to guide them to accomplish the learning objectives? How can we as learning and development professionals truly facilitate the learning process in a learner-centric way?

As our participants' attention spans get shorter and their expectations for entertainment get higher, we will continue to struggle to keep them engaged and have the greatest learning impact. It is more important than ever that we break loose from the binds of the typical classroom and embrace experiential learning where it can add the most value. As facilitators of experiential learning, we can evoke curiosity and emotion in the learner, which increases their intrinsic motivation to learn, ultimately transferring learning to their job.

Summary

Experiential learning is not the cure-all for learner and organizational needs. It does, however, provide one potential tool for ensuring that time, money, and effort are well spent when providing knowledge and skills training to employees. By actively engaging participants in the learning process, facilitators and designers can more effectively tap into the wealth of information and life experiences possessed by adult learners. This ultimately leads to enhanced absorption, comprehension, and application for all that is learned.

The venerable Chinese philosopher Confucius (551–479 B.C.) may have described the advantages of experiential learning best: "By three methods we may learn wisdom: First by reflection, which is the noblest; second, by imitation, which is the easiest; and third by experience, which is the bitterest." Sometimes learning by experience can be painful; it is our job as workplace learning professionals to allow maximum learning with minimum bitterness.

About the Authors

Robert (Bob) W. Lucas, BS, MA, CPLP, an internationally known author and learning and performance expert, has four decades of experience in workplace performance-based training and consulting. He has trained thousands of participants in trainer development, customer service, communication, and management programs in organizations and at international conferences. Bob applies experiential and brain-based learning elements to help ensure that participants are actively engaged and to help them take ownership for their own learning. Bob has written and contributed to 32 books and compilations and is listed in *Who's Who in the World* and *Who's Who in America*. He writes three blogs, including one on creative brain-based learning strategies at www.thecreativetrainer.com. He can be reached at www.robertwlucas.com.

Kris Zilliox, BS, MA, is a learning and development manager at ConAgra Foods, Inc. with a passion for food . . . from the farm to the fork. As a member of the ConAgra Foods Enterprise Learning team, she works to activate and enable the ConAgra Foods business strategy through the development of people. Additionally, she serves as the vice president of educating for American Agri-Women, a nonprofit coalition of farm, ranch, and agribusiness women with more than 50 state, commodity, and agribusiness affiliate organizations throughout the country. She resides in Omaha, Nebraska, with her husband Tim.

References

Baker, A., P. Jensen, and D. Kolb. (2002). *Conversational Learning: An Approach to Knowledge Creation.* Westport, CT: Quorum.

Biech, E. (2005). *Training for Dummies.* Hoboken, NJ: John Wiley & Sons.

Glaser, R., and B. Roadcap. (2007). *Designing Experiential Learning in Adult Organizations.* King of Prussia, PA: HRDQ.

Jacobson, M., and M. Ruddy. (2004). *Open to Outcome.* Oklahoma City: Wood 'N' Barnes.

Lucas, R. (2003). *The Creative Training Idea Book: Inspired Tips and Techniques for Engaging and Effective Learning.* New York: AMACOM.

Lucas, R. (2007). *Creative Learning: Activities and Games That Really Engage People.* San Francisco: Pfeiffer.

Lucas, R. (2010). *Energize Your Training: Creative Techniques to Engage Learners.* Alexandria, VA: ASTD Press.

Pfeiffer, W., and J. Jones. (1975). *A Handbook of Structured Experiences for Human Relations Training.* La Jolla, CA: University Associates.

Silberman, M. (2007). *The Handbook of Experiential Learning.* San Francisco: Pfeiffer.

For Further Reading

Glaser, R., and B. Roadcap. (2007). *Designing Experiential Learning in Adult Organizations.* King of Prussia, PA: HRDQ.

Lucas, R. (2010). *Energize Your Training: Creative Techniques to Engage Learners.* Alexandria, VA: ASTD Press.

Silberman, M. (2007). *The Handbook of Experiential Learning.* San Francisco: Pfeiffer.

Chapter 22

A Serious E-Learning Manifesto

Michael W. Allen, Julie Dirksen, Clark Quinn, and Will Thalheimer

In This Chapter

■ Review a rationale for the urgency to refocus
e-learning on quality learning experiences.

Although e-learning has been in research, development, and use for nearly half a century, advances in technology continuously refresh interest and opportunities. While advancing capabilities contribute to the steadily widening use of e-learning, some of them have also defocused the field from its primary mission. It appears that serious consideration of instructional design principles are increasingly ignored in a rush to serve up content for passive absorption. It appears that more concern is given to authoring time than the quality of learning time. It appears that unique and exceptionally valuable capabilities of learning technology are subjugated to delivering content without sensitivity to the learner's readiness and needs.

These and many other observations have led to serious concern among the authors of this chapter. We believe it is time for a concerted effort to return focus to the need for quality, taking disruptive action—even disruptive action that includes the construction of the Serious E-Learning Manifesto. This Manifesto is presented here and also available online at seriouselearningmanifesto.org. We hope you, our readers, will agree with our values and principles and pledge along with us to exert our influence to produce better learning experiences.

Figure 22-1. The Serious E-Learning Manifesto to All Training and Development Professionals

Michael Allen, Julie Dirksen, Clark Quinn, and Will Thalheimer

We believe that learning technology offers the possibility for creating uniquely valuable learning experiences.

We also believe, with a sense of deep sadness and profound frustration, that past and current e-learning methods have failed to fully live up to their promise.

We further believe that current trends evoke a future of only negligible improvement in learning design—unless something radical is done to bend the curve.

Finally, we have concluded that the only way to elevate e-learning to the height of its promise is to begin with a personal commitment to a new set of standards.

Through continuous assessment of learner performance, the learning experience can optimize use of the learner's time, individualize the experience for full engagement, address needs, optimize practice, and prepare for transfer of learning to performance proficiency.

Through our work in developing e-learning experiences and helping others do the same, we have identified the following requirements for quality learning experiences and concerning practices that need to be curtailed:

Serious E-Learning Requirements	Concerning Practices
♦ Creates real impact	♦ Content focused
♦ Meaningful to learners	♦ Emphasis on authoring speed
♦ Emotional engagement	♦ Passive engagement
♦ Authentic contexts	♦ Knowledge delivery
♦ Realistic decisions	♦ Testing facts in lieu of skills
♦ Individualized challenges	♦ One size fits all
♦ Spaced practice	♦ One-time events

Supporting Principles

1. **Learning is *not* always the answer.** We do not assume that a learning intervention is the solution.

2. **E-learning is *not* always the answer.** When learning *is* required, we do *not* assume that e-learning is the only (or the best) solution.

3. **Learning should tie back to organizational impact.** We will couple the skills we are developing to organizational needs.

4. **Improved performance is the goal.** We will help our learners achieve performance excellence, enabling them to have improved abilities, skills, confidence, and readiness to perform.

5. **Realistic practice is required.** We will provide learners sufficient levels of realistic practice, including simulations, scenario-based decision making, case-based evaluations, and authentic exercises.

6. **Authentic contexts are required.** We will provide learners with sufficient experience in making decisions in authentic contexts.

7. **Guidance and feedback are essential.** We will provide learners with guidance and feedback to correct their misconceptions, reinforce their comprehension, and build effective performance skills.

8. **Provide realistic consequences.** When providing performance feedback during learning, we will provide learners with a sense of the real-world consequences.

9. **Adapt to learner needs.** We can and should use e-learning's capability to create a learning environment that is flexible or adaptive to learner needs.

10. **Relate to learner goals and motivate engagement.** We will provide learners with learning experiences that are relevant to their current goals or that motivate them to engage deeply in the process of learning.

11. **Long-term impact is the goal.** We will create learning experiences that have long-term impact—well beyond the end of instructional events—to times when the learning is needed for performance.

12. **Interactivity prompts deep engagement.** We will use e-learning's unique interactive capabilities to support reflection, application, rehearsal, elaboration, contextualization, debate, evaluation, and synthesization—not just in navigation, page turning, rollovers, and information search.

13. **Post-training follow-through is critical.** We will support instruction with the appropriate mix of after-training follow-through, providing learning events that reinforce key learning points, marshal supervisory and management support for learning application, and create mechanisms that enable further on-the-job learning.

14. **Diagnose root causes.** When given training requests, we will determine whether training is likely to produce benefits and whether other factors should be targeted for improvement. We will also endeavor to be proactive in assessing organizational performance factors, not waiting for requests from organizational stakeholders.

(continued on next page)

Figure 22-1. The Serious E-Learning Manifesto to All Training and Development Professionals (continued)

15. **Use performance support.** We will consider providing job aids, checklists, wizards, sidekicks, planners, and other performance support tools in addition to—and as a potential replacement for—standard e-learning interactions.

16. **Measure organizational results.** Ideally, we will measure whether the learning has led to benefits to the organization.

17. **Measure actual performance results.** Ideally, approximately two to six weeks after learning, we will measure whether the learner has applied the learning, the level of success, the success factors and obstacles encountered, and the level of supervisor support.

18. **Measure learning comprehension and decision making during learning.** At a minimum, during the learning, we will measure both learner comprehension and decision-making ability. Ideally, we will also measure these at least a week after the learning.

19. **Measure meaningful learner perceptions.** When we measure learners' perceptions, we will measure their ability to apply what they've learned, level of motivation, and the support they will receive in implementing the learning.

20. **Iteration is necessary.** We won't assume that our first pass is right, but we will evaluate and refine until we have achieved our design goals.

21. **Support performance preparation.** We will prepare learners during the e-learning event to be motivated to apply what they've learned, inoculated against obstacles, and prepared to deal with specific situations.

22. **Support learner understanding with conceptual models.** We believe that performance should be based upon conceptual models to guide decisions, and that such models should be presented, linked to steps in examples, practiced with, and used in feedback.

23. **Use rich examples and counterexamples.** We will present examples and counterexamples, together with underlying thinking.

24. **Mistakes can be good.** Failure *is* an option. We will, where appropriate, let learners make mistakes so they can learn from them. In addition, where appropriate, we will model mistake making and mistake fixing.

We acknowledge that this is an important, but not exhaustive, list.

You can find a copy of the Manifesto in its entirety, as well as a checklist to remind you of how you can implement each of the supporting principles, at the *Handbook's* website at www.astdhandbook.org.

Comments From the Authors

In support of this team effort, the authors of the Manifesto have attested to the urgency of refocusing e-learning on quality learning experiences. Their personal statements follow.

Michael W. Allen, PhD

Too much of today's e-learning falls short. I hope I'm not becoming (or already have become) a grumpy old man. I have been working on e-learning for about 45 years and doing so with great enthusiasm. I'm eternally enthusiastic because of the personal benefits I've seen e-learning deliver to individuals.

I've seen students failing even under the close, caring mentorship of teachers, suddenly make great progress when given a chance to work with adaptive e-learning. I've seen violent gangs reform completely as they found unrecognized intellectual strengths with the help of e-learning and became winners in mathematics competition. I've seen adults who considered themselves incapable of learning new skills become euphoric, almost obsessive learners with e-learning that matched their needs. And I've seen sales teams sell with dramatically greater success when they had the benefit of well-designed e-learning, despite having been given excellent prior training.

But I'm feeling grumpy because so many of my examples, while representative of the work many were doing in the early days of e-learning, are exceptions today. They could be quite easily replicated for different learner populations and different content and skills. Instead, we see so many thinly veiled page-turning presentations pretending to be instructionally interactive. Learners aren't challenged. They don't practice enough. They don't have the opportunity of seeing the consequences of errors and mistakes. So many opportunities are missed.

Design Matters

The key to success, of course, regardless of delivery means, is design. Our industry is suffering through an introspective phase in which some have even questioned whether instructional design has any relevance. It's a silly conversation unless the question is whether anyone is even attempting it anymore. That's a serious issue. Looking at the preponderance of courseware delivered today, one has to conclude that there's very little informed design going on.

Why is this? Is it just so difficult to deliver effective instruction that we are willing to waste every learner's time in order to bypass a serious design effort? Are designers just not exposed to effective designs and therefore emulating what they see so much of?

Just Tell Me How to Do It

Some years ago, I was asked to deliver, at one of America's largest and most prestigious corporations, an intensive one-day course on instructional design for e-learning. I was somewhat overcome when I was led into a very large, nearly opulent auditorium with state-of-the-art electronics. The room and even the balcony filled, and I began showing as many examples of excellent courseware as I could squeeze in. I dissected the design, explaining the key principles employed. It seemed from the ardent note taking, that even though this wasn't a very interactive experience (ironic, I know), I seemed to be on target.

About an hour before we were scheduled to wrap up, shouts from somewhere in the balcony indicated that there was a question from someone obscured by stage lighting. Thank goodness—a question. But then this: "I suspect no one told you, but we've just gone through a major reorganization." That, I knew. "Until last Friday, we all had business cards that read 'software engineer.' This Monday, we received new cards that read 'instructional designer.' We don't have a lot of time left. Are you going to tell us just how to do this design stuff?" Speechless—and yet so much to say.

Boring Is Bad

Long before this disturbing event, I had made many efforts to identify core instructional design concepts that would lead reliably to highly successful designs. The impetus for this work was my observations that many who had advanced degrees from reputable institutions could enter into impressive discussions of human learning and instructional design, but could not design even a few minutes of interesting instruction, or at least they weren't doing it. It seemed that being conversant was quite different from being skilled.

It took me some years to discover, because it seems quite hard to believe, that the majority of traditionally schooled instructional designers never considered the notion that boring instruction is bad, ineffective instruction. The issue of boring versus engaging wasn't a professional issue; it wasn't discussed, perhaps left for the concern of entertainment designers. No, in the shadow of skills hierarchies (where all the interesting content comes way back at the end of a course) and of formally structured behavioral objectives (that couldn't interest most students less), getting a design right had little to do with actually connecting with learners.

Way Back to 1966

It wasn't always true that designers of e-learning had so little recognition of their obligations and of the means of meeting them. In fact, e-learning was spawned under hopes for a new science of instruction. It's hard to hold enough factors of instructor-led learning constant for meaningful comparisons of pedagogy. But with e-learning, there were new, practical opportunities for control and outcome measurements.

A prolific scientist, physicist, mathematician, and educator, Patrick Suppes has performed numerous experiments showing how basic algorithms could readily adapt instruction to individual students. His 1966 paper published in *Scientific American* might be seen as awakening contemplation of computers as teachers. The foundational notion was that through iterative scientific investigations, we could not only evolve the effectiveness of our courseware but also identify critical components of instructional design. As with no other form of instruction, we could envision highly effective learning experiences for everyone.

The Internet Ruined Everything

Working with early instructional systems, we could only dream of transmitting high-definition graphics, animation, sounds, and video. We probably weren't even imaging the speed of computation minimal devices have today. Mobility? (What?) Ubiquitous, cheap, worldwide access? (Science fiction!) But even with none of these capabilities, we were seriously studying and developing some amazing learning experiences. Much time and effort went into each, to be sure, but learners truly benefited. The costs (and they were high) were worth it.

With the multimedia and computational capabilities available today, we would have thought that instructional designs would be similarly advanced and be developed using amazing software tools that made meaningful, memorable, motivational learning experiences much easier and faster to produce. Be careful what you wish for. With everything we hoped for and much more available, how are we using technology? I'm chagrined to admit we're taking too little advantage of our opportunities.

Disruption Team

I'm indebted to my co-authors, who have not only been commiserating with me for years, but have also said enough is enough. They didn't say somebody has to do something, they said *we have to do something—we have to be disruptive!*

We have all been doing our best to demonstrate better ways of helping learners. We have been sharing in every way we could think of. We've been writing, speaking, and consulting. We've said, "If there's anything in our work that you think would improve the learning experiences you provide, please take it and use it." But now we're making one more effort—perhaps a somewhat desperate effort—because we really want to be part of a movement that improves the learning opportunities everyone has. Things have to change.

The Manifesto

Working enthusiastically, earnestly, and exhaustively, our band of authors has tried to set down what we believe is required to use instructional technology as professionals—what is required to earn the right to absorb the learner's time. We know e-learning can be a valuable experience, but it isn't valuable because technology is present; it's valuable only if technology is harnessed to do beneficial things. So we've enumerated those things that need to be done.

But setting forth principles does not a revolution start. So we've gone further. We've turned the Manifesto into a pledge. By putting forth this Manifesto, we pledge to do specific things whenever and wherever we possibly can. We realize there are constraints, and we realize some of us work for clients who may not permit some of the design components we know are important. But as professionals, we will do our best to find the means to produce learning experiences—regardless of constraints—that are truly beneficial to learners.

We invite you to join us in your work and at www.seriouselearningmanifesto.org.

Julie Dirksen, MS

The field of e-learning is fundamentally broken. That's a big claim, I know, but let me explain why I think so.

There are many symptoms of this; the biggest is that e-learning isn't getting better, and it is probably getting worse. I've been working in the field for at least 20 years, and with some exceptions, there was frequently better and more innovative work going on in the computer-based CD-ROM courses of 1993 than much of what is happening 20 years later in the web-based world of this millennium.

There are several reasons I think this is the case, but the primary issues I see are an absent feedback loop, a disconnect with the academic literature, an absence of design guidelines, and a tendency to let the design follow the technology rather than making the technology fit the design.

Reason 1: The Absent Feedback Loop

Anyone who has read Malcolm Gladwell's *Outliers* is familiar with the idea of the 10,000-hour rule. This is the idea that real mastery of something requires 10,000 hours of deliberate practice. This idea is used to explain the mastery of Tiger Woods, who started playing golf in the womb, and the Beatles, who played thousands of hours in German nightclubs before returning to the UK and hitting it big.

While the actual number may or may not be exactly right, the idea of mastery stemming from significant time and practice seems to be supported.

It would follow that someone who had been doing e-learning design for decades would be the Tiger Woods of e-learning design, right? Well, maybe not.

The problem comes with the phrase *deliberate practice*. Deliberate practice involves a robust feedback loop that allows the person practicing to judge how successful an attempt has been and adjust accordingly. This feedback can come from visible performance, audience reaction, or expert coaching.

If you sit down in an instructor-led class, you know right away whether you are in the hands of an expert facilitator or not. The tone of the instructor's voice, level of confidence, the easy and clear explanations, and movement from topic to topic are all evidence of a high level of mastery.

If you've ever taught a live class, you know it doesn't take long at all to find out what works or what doesn't when you are actually in front of students. It's immediately apparent if something isn't working—if the instructions for an activity aren't clear or an explanation isn't making sense. If that happens, then you adjust as needed.

E-learning frequently lacks this kind of feedback loop. In fact, e-learning frequently lacks any kind of meaningful feedback at all for the designer. All too frequently, an e-learning course is loaded on the LMS (learning management system) and never looked at again. When I was recently on a panel at an e-learning industry conference, I asked the room how many of them get to see people use what they build, and less than half of the room raised their hands. LMS reporting is almost worthless as a feedback mechanism for designers, comprised primarily of completion status, scores, and possibly time on task.

So, not being able to see the effectiveness of a design means that 10,000 hours may or may not move a designer toward mastery. Typically, people get better at what they can see, so e-learning people typically get better at the development process as they obtain more experience with what is visible to them. Unfortunately, someone can create e-learning for a decade and not be creating designs that are any more effective than when they started.

The result is that we have a feedback system that makes e-learning instructional designs better at the *process* of producing e-learning, but not better at the *design* of e-learning. The absence of feedback loops also makes it incredibly difficult for instructional designers to show the value of their contributions to the organization.

Reason 2: A Disconnect With the Academic Literature

I don't know that e-learning is any worse than any other field in its disconnect with the academic literature. I suspect it's a common problem in many fields, but I rarely see academic research making its way into the practice of frontline e-learning designers. And in most cases, I really don't think that's their fault. With a few notable exceptions, like Ruth Clark and Will Thalheimer, there are an insufficient number of people acting as translators to help practitioners navigate the dense world of academic research.

Aside from the obvious benefit of being able to design better learning, a knowledge of research is an invaluable tool for establishing credibility. Some professions use exams and certifications as mediums for credibility, but even e-learning designers with advanced degrees find themselves treated like order takers rather than experts in human performance and learning.

Reason 3: An Absence of Design Guidelines

Instructional design was largely founded on process models. When large numbers of people were recruited or drafted into the military in World War II, there was a recognized need for a more systematic process for training people quickly and efficiently.

As a result, something like ADDIE gets referred to as a design model, when it's really a *process* model, a series of steps to follow. The steps of ADDIE can be used to build everything from a sandcastle to a fighter jet; there is nothing there that is inherently germane to instructional design.

Many people are good instructional designers, but they've had to intuitively feel their way into it, without having good design frameworks that could move them along quicker. And without the necessary feedback loop described in Reason 1, the design frameworks that have been proposed within the industry frequently aren't getting the kind of rigorous trial and revision necessary to make them more useful.

A significant part of what constitutes a profession is an accumulation of knowledge, rules, guidelines, practices, and experience. Leadership in the area of instructional design owes it to the field to provide better, more current, empirically validated design guidelines and practices.

Reason 4: A Tendency to Make the Design Fit the Technology, Rather Than Requiring the Technology to Accommodate the Design

As I mentioned above, when I first started working in e-learning (although we called it computer-based training then), some really nice work was being done using technologies, such as Authorware and Director, involving rich multimedia. Then along came the web, and we were lucky if we could display a decent-size image or maybe a rollover. After a while, the technology got a little better and the relatively ubiquitous presence of the Flash plug-in meant that some interesting things were starting to be created for online learning. Then several companies developed rapid authoring tools, and the quality and types of interactivity in e-learning was severely curtailed. The rapid authoring tools eventually started to get better, but by then the emphasis on mobile had begun, and most of the tools publishing to Flash had to be taken back to the drawing board.

The field of e-learning has been marked by this cycle where gradual waves of improvement get rolled back by some other development, causing designers to have to begin again, fostering an unfortunate but understandable learned helplessness. Add an adherence to the reporting limitations of the way that the SCORM was implemented (we basically traded interoperability for such a tiny view of user behaviors that we might as well be peering at our target audiences though a drinking straw), and we are left with the frustrating feeling of pushing the e-learning boulder up a hill for a long time without much noticeable improvement.

There have been some glimmers of hope and innovation in areas of social media for learning, but those have largely been due to the use of more mainstream technologies. If we'd all been forced to wait for social learning features to be implemented into e-learning technologies, like authoring tools and LMSs, many of us would still be waiting.

So How Does the Manifesto Help Us?

From conversations with Michael Allen, Clark Quinn, and Will Thalheimer, I know I'm not the only one to feel frustrated that a field I've worked in and loved for many years isn't further along. Action needs to be taken.

I may see the issue a little differently than my colleagues, but I don't believe the problem is one of attitude or motivation. I teach instructional design workshops several times a year to e-learning designers who care deeply about their work, and I want to do better. I also hear from them about the limitations they are forced to deal with in terms of technology and resources. People want to do better work, and they are also frustrated by their inability to do so. I see a desire to do better, but it is difficult to focus without better guidelines to follow.

I do see the Manifesto as a first step toward changing things, though. I see it as having real and tangible benefits in the following ways:

- It is based on the best science that we know and provides guidelines that are empirically validated.
- It sets a baseline that we can start evaluating against, which is necessary in any feedback system.
- It provides a tangible rallying cry not only for practitioners but also leadership about what e-learning can and should be.

Clark Quinn, PhD

My work passion has been the application of new technologies to support human endeavors, particularly achieving goals of learning and performance. And I have been fortunate to be able to work and play at the cutting edge of technology for learning for more than three decades, leading design and development of solutions across the space of games, mobile, adaptive systems, performance support, content architectures, and more. Along the way, I have spent (and continue to spend) considerable time getting to know what leads to learning, gaining insight into technology capabilities to be able to cut through the hype and see what the real opportunities are and investigating processes of design that optimize outcomes as well as the organizational systems to implement these processes. It should not be surprising that I have been an advocate for good learning design throughout my career, but there is a pressing need for the Serious E-Learning Manifesto. Let me place my concerns in context.

I undertook a PhD in cognitive psychology because I wanted to understand how our brains work. I went further and looked at behavioral learning, social learning, even *machine* learning! I have looked beyond the traditional learning horizon, investigating affective and conative (read: emotional and intentional) aspects of learning, as well as meta-learning (learning to learn). And we have a pretty good handle on the elements that are necessary, given that our wetware hasn't changed over millennia, and are pretty well understood.

As I was lucky to get into computing at the beginning of my career, I have had the experience of designing and developing for mainframes, minicomputers, microcomputers, handhelds, and the web. I've explored programming languages, artificial intelligence, computer architectures, algorithms, networking standards, and more. I've led the development of adaptive systems, mobile solutions, and interactive computer games. While I no longer program myself, I have a pretty deep understanding of what technology can do to support learning, and there are real advantages to doing so.

I have also spent a lot of time investigating design, in the interest of continual improvement. I have taught interface design and instructional design, seeing the similarities and differences. I've also looked at the psychological literature on design, to see what is known about what works. I've even looked into design processes in other fields, including architecture, software engineering, and industrial design, to see what might inform better outcomes.

To top it all off, I have looked at how organizations function, particularly how they design, develop, and deliver learning solutions. More and more of my work is at the strategic level, helping organizations achieve learning goals whether internal or for their customers and clients. While I've learned that the barriers are not always with our understanding, but also in structural issues like processes and practices, I have also seen and created solutions.

I regale you with this litany to help you understand that when I came out of my academic and organizational roles and started attending corporate learning and technology events, I had some pretty strong ideas of what could be, and I was *really* excited. Here I was finally going to have an opportunity to leverage what we knew about learning with folks who had the resources to apply the latest technology to meet real needs. Despite the downturn, the Internet was still growing in capability, and we had a lot of new opportunities in technology as well as deep understandings of how learning worked. This was going to be great!

Imagine my dismay, then, as I slowly grew to realize that what was being done in organizational learning was less than optimal (to be diplomatic). Alone and with partners, I went into companies where the request was to take PDFs and PPTs and turn them into courses. There was little appetite for learning *experiences*; what they expected and wanted on the cheapest possible cost was, essentially, content dump and knowledge tests. They wanted it flashy, but were not interested in depth.

What I continue to see is e-learning that *looks* good, but is fundamentally lacking in design: content that is not designed to have an impact on real organizational needs, content that is *not* going to lead to any meaningful changes in behavior, and content that is well produced (if not *over*produced) but underdesigned. I have seen award-winning e-learning products that are a waste of time and money. I have had the dubious pleasure of critiquing client content, pointing out systematically why content they valued was really not any good. I even built a workshop on advanced learning design because it was so obviously needed, when I'd rather have been talking about strategy and concepts like immersive design, semantic technologies, advanced systems, and other elements that support really advanced learning experiences.

When hanging out at yet *another* learning conference exposition hall, commiserating with my colleagues yet *again*, I could no longer countenance not doing *something*. Seeing the same old tired concepts, but with new window dressing, was just too onerous. We noted more tools to convert "content" (PDF/PPT) to knowledge dump and knowledge test, more ways to tart up an inherently meaningless interaction, and more ways to track content access instead of looking at whether any learning outcomes were achieved.

What we didn't see, with few exceptions, were people talking about how to find the real business impact and create learning experiences that would actually achieve outcomes. We weren't seeing people talking about the need for iterative design and evaluation, about meaningful practice, or about alignment between objectives and content. Except for the wrapping, the core of the exposition halls could have come from a decade ago or more.

I understand many of the forces that oppose change. However, that does not mean I have to tolerate them. It's easy to be in "order-taking" mode rather than focusing on performance and organizational impact. I don't assume all designers have a grasp of the necessary learning sciences. I recognize that there are time and money concerns. And I know that our tools can constrain our thinking. What I also know is that there are known solutions, and if we do not transcend these problems, what we create is not going to have any impact. We will ultimately doom ourselves to irrelevance.

Understand that I have been favored; my clients bring me in when the task is to go beyond the ordinary, focusing on architectures and processes that really deliver on the promise of technology. And I have been able to work on some truly exciting projects like a content-sensitive performance support system, deep games, an overarching content model, mobile applications, and strategies and learning solutions where they were willing to let me lead truly good design. Yet I have seen how rare this is, and what is happening in most of the industry is a different story. And it does not need to be this way!

We know better. In addition to our own writings, there are an increasing number of efforts trying to document the existing research on how we learn and how to design learning. Yet, somehow, the impact has not reached critical mass. And the end result is a concern; we have e-learning that people avoid and that has no impact, yet the industry spends lots of money to achieve this end!

We need better learning. Our learning effectiveness needs to increase or we risk being outpaced by the changes to which we need to adapt. Please read and understand the Manifesto, and I encourage you to join us in working to make learning that matters.

Will Thalheimer, PhD

Why me? Why now? Why am I one of the originators of the Serious E-Learning Manifesto?

"Where will e-learning go from here? Not far, not far,
if we keep circling the forest looking at eaglets."

—From the iPad musings of Eeyore[1]

Introduction

I'm 55 years old and have worked in the workplace learning and performance field for almost 30 years. I haven't actually met Eeyore, except existentially, but I have walked a long way through the forest. I've been a trainer, instructional designer, simulation architect, project manager, product manager, researcher, and consultant. I joined the field in 1985 at the dawn of the personal computer age. In my first job, I had a 30-pound *portable* computer with two colors: green and black. I was around soon after the first commercial e-learning program was created and a few years before the e-learning industry began to bloom.

Of course, none of this qualifies me for much of anything, except another trip to the optometrist—to help me see more clearly. On the other hand, I do remember the early hallowed hopes for e-learning, the soaring promises, and the unrestrained optimism. I also remember intimately the early challenges and successes. I was the project manager for the first commercially viable PC-based leadership simulation, where we had fun while making a ton of mistakes. The stuff we created then—ugly and unglamorous by today's standards—garnered rave reviews. The industry loved our stilted efforts. Our learners loved our simulations too—and they learned more than they would have without the e-learning component. It was one big rave, one big party! An endless e-learning bacchanal.

About 10 years ago, as a research-driven learning consultant, I was called into a major pharmaceutical company to teach its standup trainers about e-learning. At the end of my workshop, the trainers said to me, "Will, we are so grateful. We thought you were here to ram e-learning down our throats. This e-learning stuff actually makes sense."

Within the past five years—while teaching a workshop on e-learning at a conference of social scientists—the reaction was very different. My learners weren't resistant to e-learning but were eager to learn what e-learning could contribute to learning.

Certainly, e-learning has come a long way with myriad advances, including wikis, blogs, social media, performance support, mobile learning, MOOCs, and so on. The best e-learning developers are creating great e-learning, but the great mass of e-learning still

---

1   With apologies to A.A. Milne; no such communication exists.

hasn't advanced that much from its earlier days. And frankly, the slow curve of improvement doesn't bode well for the field and our overall effectiveness. Something fundamental is missing, and we must grasp it before we can bend the curve of e-learning upward toward full effectiveness.

The Thing That's Missing

Why have I helped initiate the Serious E-Learning Manifesto? Because the gap between e-learning promise and execution has gnawed at me for years! Because really, it's so easy to see what we need to do better. I'm eternally naïve and optimistic that the collective can learn quickly and easily—and can remember and integrate new skills into a continuing behavioral repertoire. I am a fool for learning!

But alas, the world doesn't work that way. I learned this the hard way when I started Work-Learning Research in 1998. I thought it would be relatively easy to compile research on learning, spread the word about it, and see learning practices change. I was wrong. First, compiling the research is very difficult. Second, conveying validated information in a way that persuades is difficult. But more difficult still is getting people to remember what they understand, integrate such wisdom into their practices, and maintain their new understandings and skills over time against the wind of others' perceptions and beliefs.

This has been my life for the past 15 years—attempting to combine research and practice—so I've seen how difficult it is to change practices in the e-learning field. But this work has enabled me to see—I think—what's missing. What's missing is that we in the learning and performance field don't really have a common body of knowledge that we all buy into. Well, we sort of, a little bit, buy into it—but we don't take responsibility for doing learning right. Almost all training fails to sufficiently support learners in remembering. Almost all training fails to plan and use after-training follow-through. Perhaps worst of all, lots of training gets done where there's no causal link between training and desired results.

I've offered my list of the 12 most important learning factors—The Decisive Dozen—with the idea of helping people stay focused on critical factors that can improve learning. I've used simple metaphors like the learning and forgetting curves to convey information. And, while I stand firmly behind my work, it obviously has not been enough to move the field toward better e-learning. My conclusion? We in the field need a multifaceted approach to our own self-improvement. The Serious E-Learning Manifesto is important to all of us.

The Importance of the Serious E-Learning Manifesto

Since the dawn of the e-learning age, it's been obvious that most e-learning is poorly constructed. Page turning has been a consistent boogeyman. PowerPoint conversion is ubiquitous. We present, quiz, iterate, and irritate (our learners). What is less obvious is that even award-winning e-learning often fails to provide learners with the scaffolding needed to build learning results. We use too little realistic practice. We fail to space learning over time. We don't integrate job aids into our e-learning. We don't prepare learners for after-training application. E-learning is suboptimal in too many ways!

I support the Serious E-Learning Manifesto because individual members of the field need to know what great e-learning looks like—and we in the field need to take personal responsibility for making our e-learning as good as it can be. The Manifesto's 24 principles very clearly identify what world-class e-learning should look like. Of course, not every e-learning intervention will meet each principle. But most e-learning will benefit if we are mindful of the target principles—and stretch to meet them. With the Manifesto as a guide, the following are more likely to occur in the e-learning field:

1. E-learning developers will have a clearer, more potent benchmark to aim for in their e-learning designs.
2. E-learning purchasers will have a much better idea of what to ask for from e-learning providers.
3. E-learning vendors will more easily be able to guide clients and potential clients toward good e-learning designs.
4. E-learning professionals will be better able to educate their organizational stakeholders about what constitutes effective e-learning.
5. Business leaders and organizational managers will have a set of principles to guide their understanding of e-learning design—to enable them to make better decisions and see beyond any hype, propaganda, and marketing messages they encounter.
6. Graduate schools are more likely to examine and improve their curriculum to align with the Manifesto's principles.
7. Professors and e-learning instructors will have a potent set of guidelines to share with their students.
8. Graduate students will have a clear set of guidelines toward which to aim.
9. Certification programs will have clear target goals.
10. Trade associations will be better able to select programs, speakers, books, and materials to guide e-learning professionals.
11. Employment lawyers will have guidelines to suggest to clients for the design of effective training, including compliance training.

12. Lawmakers at the federal, state, and local levels will have guidelines that will help them draft laws that more effectively guide the deployment of e-learning.
13. Policymakers and advocates will have a set of principles to guide their work.
14. Marketers are more likely to emphasize the aspects of their e-learning products and services that align with the Manifesto's principles.
15. E-learning vendors are more likely to invest in practices, procedures, and tools that enable the high level of design suggested in the Manifesto's principles.
16. Industry awards are more likely to be given to those who develop e-learning that aligns with the Manifesto's principles.
17. Employers are more likely to hire recruits who can demonstrate that they can build Manifesto-aligned e-learning.
18. Job seekers are more likely to get jobs if they demonstrate that they can build e-learning that aligns with the Manifesto's principles.
19. Researchers will have hypotheses to test and experiments to run to better enable the field to engage in a virtuous cycle of continuing improvement.
20. E-learning professionals will have a starting point for discussions with each other—and as time goes by, the principles in the Serious E-Learning Manifesto will be discussed, dissected, debated, and ultimately improved as we learn more from research and practice and as technology enables additional capabilities.

Of course, this is probably too much to hope for from a few words on a page. Then again, the power of words may be something we hold as a self-evident truth, giving us the energy to join together against the current reign of mediocrity.

I am involved in the Manifesto not because I think we can easily achieve the highest levels of perfection outlined here, but because I know we can achieve much better e-learning than we are aiming to do now, and we owe it to our learners, our organizations, and ourselves to make the effort.

About the Authors

Michael W. Allen, PhD, is the chairman and CEO of Allen Interactions and Allen Learning Technologies. He also serves as adjunct associate professor at the University of Minnesota. For more than 40 years, he has led research and development efforts to understand, invent, and implement means of helping individuals achieve their full potential. His custom e-learning studios at Allen Interactions have produced award-winning courseware for many prestigious organizations. His work ranges from projects funded by the National Institutes of Health, the National Science Foundation, and Control Data Corporation. He contributed to the first Internet-based solution demonstrated to reduce the spread of HIV, to reduction in school gang violence, and to academic success by those failing in traditional education. He has published seven books. He received ASTD's Distinguished Contribution to Workplace Learning and Performance Award and the Ellis Island Medal of Honor.

Julie Dirksen, MS, is an author, speaker, and instructional designer with more than 20 years' experience creating interactive e-learning experiences for wide variety of clients. She wrote the book *Design for How People Learn* and has been an adjunct faculty member at the Minneapolis College of Art and Design. She's also a big learning geek. You can find her at www.usablelearning.com.

Clark Quinn, PhD, has been helping organizations develop strategic learning technology solutions for more than three decades. Clark combines a deep background in the learning sciences with broad experience in technology applications, which he applies to the corporate, government, education, and not-for-profit sectors. An internationally known consultant, speaker, and author, he's the author of *Engaging Learning: Designing e-Learning Simulation Games, Designing mLearning: Tapping Into the Mobile Revolution for Organizational Performance, The Mobile Academy: mLearning for Higher Education*, and a forthcoming title on learning and development strategy. Clark can be found at www.quinnovation.com, and he blogs at www.learnlets.com.

Will Thalheimer, PhD, is president of Work-Learning Research, Inc. He is a learning expert, researcher, instructional designer, business strategist, speaker, and writer. He was the project manager for the first commercially viable computer-based leadership simulation. He has trained managers to be leaders at numerous Fortune 500 companies. In 1998, he founded Work-Learning Research to bridge the gap between research and practice, to compile research on learning, and to disseminate research findings to help work-learning professionals build more effective learning and performance interventions and environments. Will holds an MBA from Drexel University and a PhD in educational psychology, human learning, and cognition from Columbia University. He can be found at www.work-learning.com and www.willatworklearning.com.

References

Suppes, P. (1966). The Uses of Computers in Education. *Scientific American* (215):206-208, 213-220.

For Further Reading

Allen, M. (2003). *Michael Allen's Guide to e-Learning: Building Interactive, Fun, and Effective Learning Programs for Any Company.* Hoboken, NJ: John Wiley & Sons.

Bransford, J.D., A. Brown, and R. Cocking. (2000). *How People Learn: Brain, Mind, Experience, and School.* Washington, DC: National Academies Press.

Dirksen, J. (2012). *Design for How People Learn.* Berkeley, CA: New Riders Press.

Koedinger, K.R., A. Corbett, and C. Perfetti. (2012). The Knowledge-Learning-Instruction (KLI) Framework: Bridging the Science-Practice Chasm to Enhance Robust Student Learning. *Cognitive Science* 36(5):757-798.

Quinn, C.N. (2005). *Engaging Learning: Designing e-Learning Simulation Games*. San Francisco: Pfeiffer.

Thalheimer, W. (2013). *The Decisive Dozen: Research Background Abridged*, http://willthalheimer.typepad.com/files/decisive-dozen-research-v1.2-1.pdf.

Chapter 23

The Global Virtual Classroom

Darlene Christopher

·· **In This Chapter** ··

- Explore the challenges of delivering virtual training to an international audience.
- Learn the skills required to deliver successful virtual training globally.
- Learn how to create a successful global virtual classroom by analyzing participants, attending to logistics, and adjusting content and exercises.

More organizations than ever are using virtual classrooms to bring individuals and teams together for learning events in an increasingly global business environment. Whether it's a global sales team connecting from several country offices or managers separated by multiple time zones, the ability to easily connect people and train them in the same virtual classroom is one of the main benefits spurring the increased use of virtual learning.

Virtual classroom training is training that takes place in a virtual environment via the Internet. As compared to face-to-face training, where facilitators and participants come together in the same physical space, in the virtual classroom, facilitators and participants come together in real time via computers connected to an Internet-based classroom.

Designing and delivering virtual classroom training to a global audience requires careful preparation and planning. Simply reusing presentation slides and other materials intended for in-person training for a global audience in the virtual classroom will result in a poor learning experience for the participants. The content and exercises need adjusting to work properly in a virtual environment. Furthermore, offering virtual classroom training designed for a national audience to an international audience with no adjustments to facilitation techniques, content, or exercises will not meet the needs of international participants. The global virtual classroom facilitator needs to think about *every* aspect of the training from the learner perspective and make adjustments geared to those perspectives.

The Global Virtual Classroom Team Skills and Competencies

The global virtual classroom presents the facilitator accustomed to face-to-face training with a variety of challenges. For example, teaching in the global virtual classroom challenges facilitators to overcome their reliance on body language since you cannot see your participants and they cannot see you. Also, facilitators may find that the additional complexity of technology required to facilitate training in a virtual environment works better if you partner with an additional person—a producer—to help.

If you already facilitate in the virtual classroom and you are ready to add global participants, then you will need to focus on language and cultural awareness. In either of these cases, the global virtual classroom facilitator builds on the facilitation techniques that he or she already uses and adjusts to the unique needs of an international audience that is physically separated. Failing to adjust runs the risk of confusing and alienating global participants. Let's examine the skills needed for the two key roles in the global virtual classroom: the facilitator and the producer.

The Facilitator

The global virtual classroom facilitator has skills that span many areas in addition to general facilitation skills and subject matter expertise as described below.

Cultural Skills

Our native culture has an impact on how we communicate with others and how we work together cooperatively and collaboratively, and informs the assumptions we make about others. That's why a deep understanding of our own cultural assumptions is important for global facilitators. For example, if you were raised, were educated, and work in the United States, some of your cultural assumptions may include the following:

- Speaking directly and openly is best.
- Praising an individual is a way to encourage someone.
- Productivity improves when we work together to reach a solution.

And in other parts of the world, participants may assume that:

- It's wrong to ask questions of an instructor.
- Being singled out and praised is bad.
- The value of the common greater good is more important than valuing one's own needs.

Culturally self-aware facilitators understand that their cultural assumptions are their own and that participants from other cultures have their own cultural assumptions.

A skilled facilitator also uses "international" English, meaning English language that is free from country-specific idioms ("keep your nose to the grindstone" or "put your ducks in a row"), colloquialisms ("I need my coffee fix" or "beats me"), or slang expressions ("y'all" or "my bad"). The same guideline of "internationalizing" your language applies if the session is being delivered in German, Arabic, or any other language.

Communication Skills

In a face-to-face setting, learners can rely on body language, gestures, facial expressions, and a bit of lip reading to fill in language gaps. In a virtual classroom, these nonverbal cues are limited or absent for participants, so facilitators need to make their speeches even more clear and precise to help convey the message. The global virtual facilitator should focus on making deliberate word choices, such as, "Sally, use the phone and tell us your answer to number 6" or "Turn to page 9 and spend two minutes reflecting on the text. When you are done, type your response to the question in the chat box." As the virtual facilitator, you can also help the nonnative speakers of your language by slowing down the pace of your speech to give them more time to process your words.

Tip

Practice the pronunciation of participant names in advance. Even if your pronunciation is not perfect, participants will appreciate your effort.

Multitasking Skills

There are many moving parts in a virtual classroom: the presentation sharing area, ongoing chat, and instant feedback where participants may raise their hands and indicate that they have a question or have stepped away. The successful facilitator can quickly jump from one task to the next and keep an eye on the various parts of the screen where activity may be taking place.

Technology Skills

The global virtual classroom facilitator should be comfortable with virtual classroom technology so he or she can focus on the subject matter when facilitating training—rather than the technology. A good understanding of how all the features of the virtual classroom work will help in planning how you will deliver content and interact with participants. Many facilitators choose to partner with a producer (described below) who is a technology expert.

The Producer

Delivering training in the virtual classroom is best accomplished as a team rather than as a single individual. Typically, the facilitator partners with a producer who provides a full range of technical expertise to support the virtual classroom facilitator and has the following skills.

Technology Skills

The producer should have expert knowledge of the virtual classroom tool and should understand how all the features work. During a live session, the producer troubleshoots technical problems, including specific problems that participants experience.

Multitasking Skills

Since the producer's job is to ensure all elements of the course are coordinated effectively, multitasking skills are essential. This "ringmaster" may be chatting with an individual participant to solve a technical problem, troubleshooting connectivity issues, launching polls, or preparing a screen for the next exercise.

Understanding of Basic Adult Learning Techniques

While the facilitator(s) will be the main speaker in the session and should have a superior knowledge of the subject matter as well as how to teach adults, the producer should also understand key adult learning techniques.

Fast Typing Skills

The producer typically manages the chat area and answers questions when possible and refers others to the facilitator. This activity requires quick, accurate typing while monitoring the screen, so touch typing is essential (two-finger, hunt-and-peck typing is not really an acceptable skill level).

Global Participant Analysis

Before you begin designing your virtual classroom training session, gather some background information on your remote participants so that you can tailor your training accordingly. Some potential sources for audience information might include local site managers and human resource personnel, members of the local site learning team and IT staff, or even members of the target audience. Here's a look at four important core areas and the impact of making these course adjustments.

Language

Determine the languages spoken by the participants and whether the group shares fluency (and what level of fluency) in a common language such as English. In addition, ask if the participants have experience attending virtual training delivered in English. This information will help you determine to what degree you need to adjust and simplify your spoken language and text on the materials provided.

Cultural Differences

In a global training environment, participants bring an added dimension of expectations tied to cultural differences, including what is expected of the instructor and the participants.

Determine if the audience is familiar with typical corporate training techniques common in the United States and what expectations participants have of the facilitator and of each other. Likewise, check to see what gender or religious issues should be considered.

Previous Experience With Virtual Classrooms

Determine if participants have experienced training in a virtual classroom and offer a brief orientation for participants who have no virtual classroom training experience. The purpose of such an introductory session is to ease any anxiety participants may have about using the technology and to clarify the expectations for participants during the live session. If participants are not available for a live training, send a recording of an orientation session that demonstrates key features or a document that includes screen shots for the training and explanatory notes and tips.

Environment

Investigate the virtual participants' physical environments (including the availability of computers, telephones, and headsets) in advance of the virtual training to allow time to mitigate any potential disruptive issues. For example, if participants are joining the session from an open office environment and plan to use a microphone and headset, make sure that nonparticipating co-workers and managers understand that the learners are involved in a company-sponsored training event. And, double-check with the remote site IT personnel to ensure that enough bandwidth is available for the virtual training session you've designed (that is, use of video or other bandwidth-draining features incorporated into the design).

Attend to Logistics

Training in the global virtual classroom means you leave behind some of the traditional logistical worries associated with traveling long distances and obtaining visas to get to your destination. However, a new set of logistical concerns arises from coordinating different workweeks, public and religious holidays, and time zones.

Select a Date for Your Training

First, make sure the day(s) you plan to hold your virtual training event matches the work-week where the targeted participants will take the training. In many countries around the world, including the United States, Brazil, and China, the typical workweek is Monday through Friday. However, in countries such as Egypt, Iraq, and Libya, the workweek is Sunday through Thursday.

Next, check for public and religious holidays and find out when most people in the target countries typically take vacations. For example, scheduling a training event in the United States on Thanksgiving Day would pretty much guarantee that you'd have a solo virtual training event. Other countries have similarly important national holidays, so avoid scheduling these holidays for virtual training.

Resources to Help With Global Logistics

TimeandDate.com
   www.timeanddate.com

World Time Server
   www.worldtimeserver.com

Worldwide Daylight Saving
   www.webexhibits.org/daylightsaving/g.html

Worldwide Public Holidays
   http://qppstudio.net

Workweek

http://en.wikipedia.org/wiki/Workweek

Mobile Apps

In addition to web resources, check the appropriate app store on your mobile device. Business apps such as Global Time and Global Holidays are examples of helpful resources.

Select a Time for Your Training

After you've identified the appropriate date(s) for your training, focus on selecting what time to offer your training. The easiest way to ensure you select the right time to offer your session is to create a ranking of target locations based on proximity to your own time zone. Next, do some research (either through Internet searches or conversations with local colleagues and associates) to make sure you understand the typical business hours for participants and whether any hours of the days should be avoided due to observance of certain religious practices or typical lunch break times.

Adjusting Content and Exercises

An exciting aspect of a global audience is the diversity in the virtual classroom. People raised and educated in different parts of the world will come to your virtual classroom with a variety of learning styles and perceptions about what is expected of the instructor and the participants. Hopefully you've gained valuable knowledge and audience expectations based on your participant analysis as described earlier. Set expectations beforehand with clear instructions about how the session will run and the types of exercises participants will encounter. Provide an emphasis on how the participants will benefit from the session. Then match diversity of participants with diversity of exercises by offering participants a variety of exercises and giving them options for responding, such as typing in a chat or verbalizing on the phone. Participants will select what feels right for them. Use polls and instant feedback tools to engage participants and overcome shyness around speaking or typing in a nonnative language.

There is no magical solution for addressing culturally diverse learning styles. What *is* important is the facilitator's awareness of cultural differences and the incorporation of a range of activities to meet the diverse needs of a global audience. For more information, Geert Hofstede has done significant research on cultural differences: http://stuwww.uvt.nl/~csmeets/.

Adjusting your content will improve your virtual classroom training with global participants. Like a classroom setting, a variety of options ensure that the class will be effective and enjoyable for your participants. Consider the following ideas.

Presentation Slides

A virtual classroom session needs well-designed slides to serve as a backdrop for the course content. If the training that will be delivered in the virtual classroom has already been delivered in person, then a good starting point is the slide deck from a previous in-person training session. However, several adjustments are needed to optimize the slides for a global virtual classroom.

First, review your slides and other support material, such as handouts, and adjust or remove culturally inappropriate content or examples. All participants, even those from other countries, expect to see content that makes sense to them as well as examples they understand. Remove sports, political, or entertainment references such as popular national television shows, performers, or any other limited pop culture references. If your slides include images of people, make sure nothing about the images might be offensive to your own careful sensibilities, and then ask someone familiar with the target culture to advise you on the images.

For exercises and interactivity, your participants need verbal and written instructions. Add slides with brief instructions to clearly describe what is expected. Tell participants how the exercise will work, how long it will last, which interactive features they are expected to use, and any materials they need to complete an exercise.

Simplified Text

Simplify the vocabulary on slides and handouts to make it easier for nonnative speakers to understand the content. Simplified means that you make the text concise, ensuring every word on the slide is necessary to convey the concept. Simple text will also help your nonnative speaking participants to review concepts by looking up key words in a dictionary or online translation tool when needed.

Translation

If course materials will be translated into one or more languages, concise and precise terminology will yield more accurate translations. Once translated, ask a native speaker from your target country who is also familiar with the content or concepts presented to review the translated content. Keep in mind that language meaning and usage varies among countries. For example, using a Mexico City–based translation firm to translate materials into Spanish for a course being taught in Madrid would not be the optimal translation option.

Furthermore, if participants share a common language but come from different countries, ensure that the translation represents an "international" version of the language.

Adjusting the Use of Virtual Classroom Features

Keeping participants engaged is vital to a successful virtual class, so well-planned exercises that offer sufficient interactivity every few minutes are essential. Exercises designed for use by classroom facilitators need adjusting for use in a virtual classroom. This can be done by using all the available features in your virtual classroom tool. Refer to Table 23-1.

Table 23-1. Adjusting Exercises From Face-to-Face to Virtual Classroom

If you do this in your face-to face training:	Try this in the virtual classroom:
Verbal quizzes	Polls
Small group work	Small group work in breakout rooms
Raising hands	Instant feedback
Writing on flipchart or whiteboard	Digital whiteboarding
Open-ended questions	Chat

Suggestions abound to maximize learning transfer and create a positive learning experience for global participants. Several listed here enhance efficiency and effectiveness and require only small adjustments in the way you may currently use virtual classroom features.

Chat

Global audiences benefit from using chat to support verbal comments. To do this, the producer types key messages, summaries, and emphasis points in chat as the facilitator speaks. Nonnative speakers benefit from this written confirmation of their understanding. To make this tool run smoothly, prepare a text file with the key messages in advance. The producer will cut and paste these messages into the chat area as the facilitator speaks. Native speakers will also benefit from this practice!

Polling

Polls engage participants and overcome nonnative speaker shyness about speaking or typing in a nonnative language. Let participants know that their responses are anonymous if that is the case for your virtual classroom tool. Make sure the question-and-answer set for the poll is concise and easy to understand and gives an international audience extra time to answer.

Instant Feedback

For many facilitators, their first attempt at online facilitation makes them realize the extent to which they rely on visual cues, such as body language, in the physical classroom—a fact they may not have even been aware of until they facilitate online. Use the instant feedback tool to make up for the lack of eye contact. To learn if everyone has finished reading a document or is ready to move on, ask participants to select "agree" in the instant feedback tool. To solicit a volunteer to read aloud, ask participants to use the instant feedback tool to "raise hand" and select the first person to raise a hand.

Tip

If your session will take place in a language other than English, check the language settings of your virtual classroom tool. Some tools allow you to change the language for the user interface.

Video

Provide a transcript of any video provided in the training so nonnative-speaking participants can follow along using the written transcript. The transcript helps with comprehension and gives participants a tool for later reference.

Breakout Rooms

Some participants are uncomfortable with individual exercises and prefer collaborative group work. Consider using breakout rooms for small group work to complement individual exercises and to add variety to your session. If possible, divide participants by language. If the common language of the session is English and you expect participants to share their work from the breakout rooms, ask the groups to take notes in English.

Rehearsing Is More Critical Than Ever

Prior to delivering your virtual classroom training with a live audience, spend time rehearsing—this point cannot be overemphasized. Even if you've mastered the course material through numerous face-to-face deliveries, it's important to rehearse. Rehearsing is also one of the easiest ways to identify and correct culturally unsuitable content in a global training program. In addition, it gives you the opportunity to test bandwidth constraints in target countries.

Rehearse in the environment where you will deliver the actual training. If the facilitation team will be in a conference room for the live event, rehearse in the conference room.

Select a room that is quiet and has multiple Internet connections and proper audio capability. If the facilitator team will deliver the session from home, rehearse from home. You should also rehearse with the computer or laptop you will use for your live session. Some virtual classroom tools require an application download, and you don't want to discover just before your session begins that you need to wait for an application to install or, even worse, that your computer is blocked from the installation. A three-step process provides ample time to rehearse and to eliminate as many concerns and potential problems as possible.

Step 1: Rehearse With Facilitation Team

Start by practicing with the facilitation team and get used to the team roles and responsibilities. Agree on who will say what and who will do what to ensure an effective learning event. Your facilitator guide should contain this information and should be followed as you rehearse. Note what may be missing and what is unclear in the guide as you rehearse and make any necessary additions.

Step 2: Rehearse With a Mock Audience

Engage the mock audience fully so that you can get used to the interactive features of the virtual classroom. Include participants from the target country or countries, and instruct them to listen and look for items that are not culturally appropriate or that won't have meaning for a global audience. Ask them for feedback on response times of the virtual classroom tools, especially if you plan to show a video or use a webcam.

If you can't rehearse with someone from the target country, look for someone who has experience living or working in the target country. As a last resort, rehearse with someone who did not grow up in the same country as you. This person will be able to spot the most egregious errors.

Keep in mind that there are two key areas to focus on in the mock rehearsal: the first three minutes of the session and the exercises. If you are pressed for time and cannot rehearse a full session, practice the first three minutes so they are flawless and energetic, in order to set a positive tone for the session. Also, focus on rehearsing the exercises and the interactive parts of the session, as you want to make sure that instructions are clear, that you are comfortable with the interactive features of the classroom, and that the time allocated is sufficient.

Step 3: Incorporate Feedback

After rehearsing, gather the facilitation team to review the feedback you solicited. Feedback will come from the rehearsal feedback forms as well as notes from the facilitation team.

Whenever possible, schedule time to incorporate feedback from the rehearsal immediately after the mock rehearsal. Otherwise, you may not remember what your notes meant or you may lose valuable information gathered.

Conclusion

Globalization trends coupled with the increasing need to deliver training efficiently means that training departments need qualified staff to develop courses that can be delivered in a global virtual classroom. If you don't know where to start in the global virtual classroom, find a short course with relatively simple content. Allow plenty of time not only to adjust the content and exercises but also to rehearse delivery of the course to get used to the absence of a physical audience. Table 23-2 will guide you as you prepare. You may also download the table on the *Handbook's* website at www.astdhandbook.org.

Table 23-2. Global Virtual Classroom Planning Form

Topic	Action
Facilitation Team	Identify a facilitator with global virtual facilitation skills and a producer to partner with.
Logistics	Select a date and time that is convenient for participants' time zones.
Environment	Find out if participants have access to proper equipment. Check with IT about bandwidth constraints.
Language	Select language(s); if English, use international English and adjust your pace.
Cultural Considerations	Determine participant expectations of the facilitator. Offer diverse exercises to match diverse participant needs.
Presentation Slides	Use culturally appropriate images and simplified text.
Exercises and Interactivity	Adjust exercises for virtual classroom delivery and plan for interactivity every few minutes.
Translation	Ask a native speaker from the target country to review.
Virtual Classroom Features	Adjust virtual classroom feature use for a global audience (for example, type key messages in chat as the facilitator speaks).
Rehearsal	Rehearse with someone from the target country.

The successful facilitator adjusts delivery style, language, and content to meet the unique needs of a global audience, while at the same time taking advantage of all of the interactive features of the virtual classroom. By accounting for the global participants' perspectives and making adjustments based on them, you will make participants feel included, maximize learning transfer (regardless of their location or cultural background), and entice them to be eager for more.

About the Author

Darlene Christopher has designed and delivered virtual training programs for global audiences for 10 years and has authored numerous articles and a book, *The Successful Virtual Classroom,* on the subject. She is a knowledge and learning officer for the World Bank in Washington, D.C., where she directs regional learning programs for staff and provides technical leadership on distance learning programs for international government institutions. Previously, Darlene held technology development and management positions at Disney Internet Group, 3Com, and Nextel. Darlene has an MA in international management from the Monterey Institute of International Studies and a BA in Spanish from the University of California, Davis. Darlene blogs at www.darlenechristopher.com and can be followed on Twitter @darlenec.

Reference

Portions of this chapter are adapted from chapter 1, Introduction; chapter 4, The Virtual Classroom Team and Roles; and chapter 8, Working With Global Participants, from *The Successful Virtual Classroom* by Darlene Christopher (AMACOM, 2014). Used with permission.

For Further Reading

Christopher, D. (2014). *Real-Time Online Training.* New York: AMACOM.

Edmundson, A. (2010). "Training for Multiple Cultures," *Infoline* number 10 volume 2. Alexandria, VA: ASTD Press.

Huggett, C. (2014). *The Virtual Training Guidebook.* Alexandria, VA: ASTD Press.

Lewis, R.D. (2006). *When Cultures Collide.* Boston: Nicholas Brealey International.

McClay, R., and L. Irwin. (2008). *The Essential Guide to Training Global Audiences.* San Francisco: Pfeiffer.

Chapter 24

Pervasive Learning: Formal, Informal, and Social

Dan Pontefract

In This Chapter

- Define pervasive learning.
- Explore the 70–20–10 and 3–33 models.

*"Knowledge is of two kinds. We know a subject ourselves,
or we know where we can find information on it."*

—Samuel Johnson

Reread that opening quotation again. When you stop and think about it, isn't he right? Samuel Johnson, the famous poet, essayist, and speaker, is credited as having said this on April 18, 1775, while visiting his colleague Richard Owen Cambridge's library (Boswell, 1993). Johnson was intent on perusing the contents of the library shelves at his friend's new home, and after Cambridge asked Johnson why his interest level was so high, he uttered this famous passage. More than 235 years later, it still rings true. Where we find information, knowledge, and help still comes via the library, although in 2014 the library is a metaphor for access via people and the Internet.

How prophetic, in spite of Nicholas Carr's (2011) objections in his book, *The Shallows: What the Internet Is Doing to Our Brains,* in which he attacks the usefulness of easy and quick access to information and knowledge. Although I learned a lot from reading his book, I'm not of the same mindset as Carr. In this age of the connected leader, we either have competence in a subject matter—with varying degrees of depth—or, via our networks and social collaboration tools, we know how to find it. We learn at the speed of need. Johnson is right. Carr is, well, a tad cataclysmic in his thinking about the web, people, and quicker access to information. Kudos to British Columbia's Ministry of Education, which recognized this exact paradox and now aims to undo decades of "sage on the stage" teaching and of rote memorization expectations of its students. In a report titled "Transforming B.C.'s Curriculum," it states:

> [The curriculum] tends to focus on teaching children factual content rather than concepts and processes—emphasizing what they learn over how they learn, which is exactly the opposite of what modern education should strive to do. In today's technology-enabled world, students have virtually instant access to a limitless amount of information. The greater value of education for every student is not in learning the information but in learning the skills they need to successfully find, consume, think about and apply it in their lives. (B.C. Ministry of Education, 2012)

The arc of this chapter is to define pervasive learning. More important, it articulates the modes a leader should utilize to enhance the behaviors of connecting, participating, and collaborating through pervasive learning itself. Unfortunately, some leaders have a premeditated view of learning; they still believe it occurs solely in a classroom from some resident expert. They unconsciously link classroom training to rigid forms of leadership. Why is that?

It's my belief we are conditioned as children—through the hierarchy of a centuries-old schooling system—to believe the oldest person in the room (the teacher) is the smartest. That works only for so long. We are further conditioned to believe that when we're extremely smart, we'll be recognized by the highest authority—the school principal—through commendations and "bravos" on our report cards. Conversely, when things go awry, the teacher (or perhaps the manager in a corporate comparison)—and/or the principal (the vice president or CEO in a corporate comparison) may sternly call us out for unruliness, poor grades, or anything in between. Do you remember the absolute fear of being called into the principal's office? You were probably particularly fearful if you hadn't a clue as to why you were being summoned to the office via the PA system, an office administrator, or a student runner. Now *that* was stressful—and it was not unlike an archaic, antiquated, and classically hierarchical annual performance review in today's organization.

We are conditioned at a very young age, through the kindergarten–to–higher education continuum, to believe that it is our individual accomplishments that allow us the chance to achieve great things in life. But success in today's world is not merely about academic prowess or individual accomplishments alone. Success is not about power, greed, and stockpiling knowledge in a vault. Success can't be found by proficiently ruling in a silo. Nor is success found through a hierarchical, command-and-control philosophy.

If we're trained as children and teenagers to believe that it is the school system of master and apprentice that breeds success, is there any hope for a more collaborative work experience after high school or higher education? Is there any hope for a more creative, innovative, and open-thinking organization? As Ralph Waldo Emerson (1860) once said, "You send your child to the schoolmaster, but 'tis the schoolboys who educate him."

I dislike the word *training*. Each and every time I type those eight letters, they hark back to endless drills during my soccer (football) training sessions as a youth—those boring, repetitive tasks that are meant to enhance or augment a skill. Google returns more than 2 billion hits on the term *training*. Training as we know it and live it is to invoke the brilliance of Carol Dweck (2006); it's a fixed mindset, not a growth mindset.

To further assist leaders and organizations, I propose a concept called pervasive learning: the switch from a "training is an event" fixed mindset to a "learning is a collaborative, continuous, connected, and community-based" growth mindset.

I liken it to moving from "sage on the stage" to "guides and strides from all sides." Think of it as my friend Dennis Callahan does through the simple yet powerful graphic he devised in Figure 24-1.

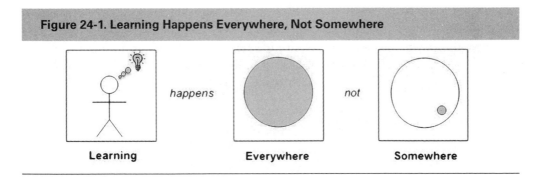

Figure 24-1. Learning Happens Everywhere, Not Somewhere

That's right—learning happens everywhere. It's like it functions through osmosis; it floats around and fills whatever volume it needs to. It should be encouraged. John Seely Brown, in his book *The Social Life of Information* (co-authored with Paul Duguid, 2000), writes, "People learn in response to need. When people cannot see the need for what's being taught, they ignore it, reject it, or fail to assimilate it in any meaningful way."

Put another way, "I learn at the speed of need." Everywhere. Anywhere. I learn through you, with you, and around you.

Does Organizational Learning Matter?

Santiago Budría, from the Universidade da Madeira, and Pablo Swedberg, from St. Louis University, published research in 2010 under the title "The Shadow Value of Employer-Provided Training." By using the European Community Household Panel data set (ECHP)—a survey of households and individuals containing labor market characteristics—the researchers took into account 17,632 observations of organizational learning in various forms. They set out to prove whether organizational learning actually mattered—that is, whether there was any benefit to it. Their results didn't surprise me. Four key points surfaced from their work:

- Taking part in organizational learning opportunities can be equivalent to a 17.7 percent increase in earnings.
- Short learning opportunities are particularly relevant for job satisfaction.
- Formal learning courses attended on a part-time basis are roughly as rewarding as those attended full-time.
- Organizational learning is particularly rewarding among dissatisfied workers and, when targeted to this audience, has a large effect on the average job satisfaction level in the organization (Budría and Swedberg, 2010).

Cagri Bulut and Osman Culha would agree with Budría and Swedberg's findings. In a research paper also published in 2010 titled "The Effects of Organizational Training on Organizational Commitment," they set out to determine if organizational learning was in fact beneficial to the organization itself. Based on research on four- and five-star hotels in Izmir—the largest city on the Aegean in Turkey—they make four key observations:

- The willingness of employees to participate in organizational learning has a positive effect on organizational commitment.
- Employees tend to work harder, attach themselves to their organizations, and display organizational citizenship when there is access to learning and they feel their organizations have been willing to invest in them.
- Employees who expect benefits from their participation in organizational learning activities are more committed to their organizations.
- Employees feel more attached to the organization when they receive support for organizational learning from their direct managers (Bulut and Culha, 2010).

In both cases mentioned above, we might argue that yes, organizational learning does in fact matter. Does it matter anywhere else?

At TELUS, a similar positive pattern emerged. Employee engagement sat at 53 percent in mid-2008, but by the end of 2013, it had jumped to 83 percent. Interestingly, a similar spike in both the career development and learning subdrivers tied to employee engagement occurred over this five-year period, reaching approximately the same levels. As TELUS added more organizational learning opportunities to the mix, the level of engagement rose. This may not be causal, but there are indirect implications. Over this period, formal learning opportunities rose by 85 percent, informal learning opportunities rose by 200 percent, and social learning interactions went from zero to more than 800,000 unique interactions.

To be sure, TELUS continued with in-depth formal courses, but the addition of shorter bursts of learning and short social user–generated nuggets helped to drive up—in Budría and Swedberg's language—job satisfaction. When organizational learning is shifted in its definition and deployment—and it is positioned in any form imaginable—it becomes a critical piece to the company's sustainable competitive advantage. Organizational learning is an investment in a company's people. By continuously improving on the modes, methods, and opportunities involved in organizational learning, an improvement in both financial performance and employee engagement (and productivity) is realized. This is the case at TELUS. Voluntary attrition is down, financial metrics are up, and a deep sense of organizational commitment is in motion. The story at TELUS confirms what the researchers from above posit.

70–20–10 or 3–33?

Karen Kocher is one cool corporate leader. As the chief learning officer of CIGNA—a global healthcare management company with $20 billion in revenue and more than 30,000 employees globally—her job is to ensure CIGNA employees are smart, capable in their roles, and adapting to the challenges that surface—however and whenever. Karen believes flexibility in learning and a sharing mentality are key. In fact, her email signature says it all: "Let's GO SOCIAL . . . collaborate, grow, and learn from each other!"

What's so cool about Karen and her organization? CIGNA believes learning and collaboration practices have a unique impact on overall employee engagement. "The working assumption by the majority of the population," she said to me, "is that performance will likely be enhanced when working and learning with and through others." Karen doesn't believe everyone has to collaborate or employ shared learning all the time, but she does believe "active listening, positive collaboration, and continuous learning will improve employee engagement." CIGNA believes learning comes from myriad sources including instant messaging, blog posts, and tweets, as well as multiday online employee jams and face-to-face events. There is no one way or right way at CIGNA to learn.

Karen said to me that achieving superior business performance on a consistent basis requires not only that the organization be a learning organization, but also requires that the learning be actively applied to generate improved performance. If employees are not engaged, it is not only less likely that they'll learn, but also much less likely they'll apply the learning and perform.

Karen as the chief learning officer, and CIGNA as an organization, have no time for a classroom-only learning strategy; it's important but not the sole way in which learning, engagement, and performance are going to manifest. CIGNA has a learning culture that empowers and aligns to a model we might call the 3–33, as shown in Figure 24-2.

Figure 24-2. Pervasive Learning (3–33)

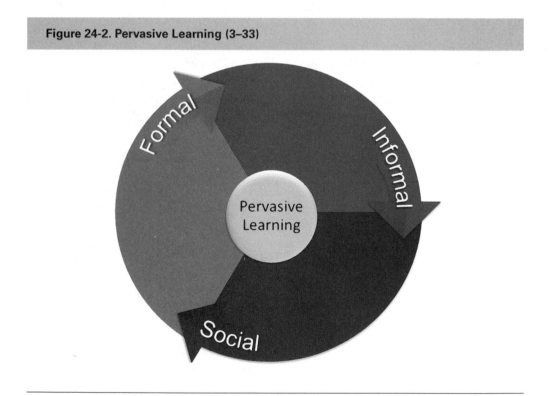

The pervasive learning model suggests that learning happens in three equally divided ways:

- 33 percent formal learning
- 33 percent informal learning
- 33 percent social learning.

Pronounced "three thirty-three," this model aims to highlight my personal belief surrounding the validity of the "70–20–10" model put forward by Robert Eichinger and Michael Lombardo from the Center for Creative Leadership in the 1980s. The 70–20–10 model is broken down as follows:

- 70 percent learning from on-the-job experiences
- 20 percent learning from others
- 10 percent learning from formal courses (Lombardo and Eichinger, 1996).

To get to the 70–20–10 model, Eichinger and Lombardo interviewed senior executives and asked them to reflect back on their careers and denote where they believed meaningful learning, development, or competence improvement came from, in the context of leadership. This could have been for themselves, their teams, or their organizations. In essence, the research focuses on how these executives actually managed or led. Somehow, along the way, the learning profession has taken over the model to depict how workplace learning occurs. This is puzzling to me. D. Scott DeRue and Christopher G. Myers (2012) echo my puzzlement as they write, "There is actually no empirical evidence supporting this assumption [that learning maps to the 70–20–10 rule] yet scholars and practitioners frequently quote it as if it is fact."

The executives being interviewed by Eichinger and Lombardo were reflecting on their leadership styles and how they learned to be leaders. To me, basing today's learning model on research that focuses solely on executives' learned leadership styles is incomplete. First off, the research was conducted in the 1980s, when the Internet was something only the military knew about, and it certainly wasn't deployed in organizations where the studies were conducted. Secondly, the 1980s seem to carry with them the weight of command-and-control leadership practices. Let's forget the Cold War rhetoric for moment and think back to the era of Ronald Reagan, Margaret Thatcher, Lee Iacocca, Jack Welch, and Roger Smith—not exactly a collaborative leadership decade in my books. Organizations are therefore basing a learning model on executives from the 1980s. It's time to evolve.

TELUS investigated this exact concept through the implementation of an updated performance model that linked learning and leadership. Over the course of two years, the company asked its team members, across the organization on a quarterly basis, if they were learning in formal, informal, or social ways. On the whole, 80 percent said they were learning through formal modalities, 82 percent through informal means, and 55 percent using social methods. By reviewing the amount of time spent learning, however, TELUS found that each of the modalities equated to roughly 33 percent of time. That is, if a team member confirmed that he or she spent 120 hours learning per year, 33 percent was through formal means, 33 percent through informal means, and 33 percent through social means. That's 40 hours each in this example.

When asked if their leadership performance increased as a result of each mode individually, TELUS team members stated the following:

- As a result of formal learning, 82 percent saw a leadership performance increase.
- As a result of informal learning, 84 percent saw a leadership performance increase.
- As a result of social learning, 56 percent saw a leadership performance increase.

When averaged together, the return on performance increased from 62 percent in 2010 to 74 percent in 2013. But when leaders were specifically asked how they spent their time learning, not surprisingly, the breakdown of formal, informal, and social was roughly divided equally, which is to say, TELUS team members believe their performance varies between formal, informal, and social modalities (as does their learning participation rate), but the way they spend their time learning is roughly the same. It's a 3–33 model.

Informal Learning

Anatole France once said, "Nine-tenths of education is encouragement." This is a perfect way to begin the exploration of informal learning within the pervasive learning model. With such a fervent quest by many to predict that formal classrooms will become extinct and that learning will exist solely in a digital format, we forget learning often occurs via the vehicle known as motivation, or, as France insists, by encouragement. Informal learning is the key link between formal and social learning. It is often overlooked.

Review the informal modalities in Figure 24-3. Consider one of the informal learning modalities—mentoring. Chief learning officer of Success Factors, Karie Willyerd, co-authored the book *The 2020 Workplace: How Innovative Companies Attract, Develop, and Keep Tomorrow's Employees Today* (2010) with Jeanne Meister, in which they state that Millennials actually prefer to learn through mentoring than any other formal, informal, or social learning type. So much for the digital-native assertion that people in this age bracket prefer to do everything online. In fact, Willyerd believes mentoring is quickly becoming an extremely important element in the workplace given this cohort is about to make up 50 percent of the actual workforce. Mentoring, like the other informal learning opportunities, are nonformal ways—devoid of any web-based interaction—to motivate, encourage, assist, and educate an individual, team, or organization. What it lacks in depth, it makes up for in personal interaction. What it lacks in formality, it makes up for in creativity. Regarding mentoring specifically, we might define it as an informal relationship between two people—not in a manager–team member lineage—where the mentor helps the mentee through various issues, change situations, or objectives. It really is an informal encouragement opportunity for both parties to learn.

Figure 24-3. Pervasive Learning: Informal

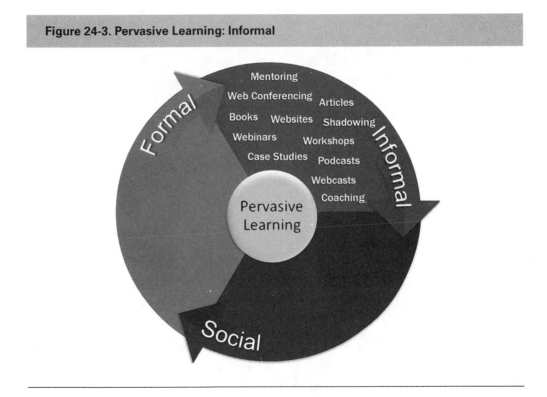

For purposes of our pervasive learning model, we define informal learning as "an opportunity without conventionalism that provides guidance, inspiration, expertise, or acumen in a nonformal environment."

Coaching is also a key action in the informal learning triad. Coaching is an ongoing informal conversation with the employee that focuses on providing the following:

- counsel on current objectives and actions to categorically improve the result
- feedback concerning their progress or improvements on behaviors
- advice on personal and career advancement or opportunities.

Coaching is different from mentoring. Coaching is an attribute that functions between members of a team. Mentoring, on the other hand, is an opportunity to obtain counsel and advice from others in the organization not situated within the same span of leadership. Both are important.

Other modalities, such as webcasts, webinars, and podcasts, provide opportunities to record information, content, and thoughts on any subject matter, making it available to everyone in the organization. These should be short pieces of content that can be easily shared. They can vary from an update regarding quarterly financials to thoughts on a recent acquisition or a thought-provoking concept that would help employees be more efficient. Whatever the content area, it's an opportunity to motivate through interesting, short nuggets of content.

Informal learning offers many ways for leaders to play a role in organizational learning. Have your leaders read an interesting or thought-provoking article or book lately that could be shared with the team? Have they discussed a website that might help the team understand the nuances of your business? Could they share a case study about one of your competitors that could help team members understand both your industry and the makeup of your competitor?

Web conferencing is another opportunity for informal learning. Employing services such as Cisco WebEx, Adobe Connect, or Microsoft products such as Live Meeting or Skype to conduct catch-up meetings is useful in many ways. Any of these could motivate employees, and each is an example of informal learning. You don't have to go to a classroom, and there is no e-learning course to sign up for. It's a simple and enthusiastic action to encourage the competency growth of all employees.

I love what Louis Franzese, vice president of Labor Relations and Human Resources practices at Hertz Corporation, told Jathan Janove for a piece in the June 2012 issue of *HR Magazine*. When discussing the aspect of job shadowing, he says to his employees, "Wash cars. Spend time behind the counter. Get a real sense of what work life for employees truly is." TELUS employs the exact same sentiment with its Closer to the Customer program. Spending time in other roles for a few hours once or twice a year keeps team members aligned with what's really going on in the organization. Why can't a university chancellor spend time with those in the IT support team to see what it's like assisting thousands of students and faculty every day? Can't a vice president of marketing and his team shadow frontline retail agents in the stores where their marketing plans are alleged to sell more products? Shadowing is culture building, and it's a critical element of informal learning.

Socratic Learning

Pervasive learning also leans heavily on Socratic learning, which itself is based on the idea that human beings have faculties that can be awakened through questioning, exploration, collaboration, and self- or cross-examination.

Based on our learning requirements (individual, team, organizational, and so on), we must continuously connect the need that has to be filled to the learning modality, be it formal, informal, or social. We have to question and explore which modality provides the appropriate amount of breadth and depth juxtaposed with the speed at which we need the information or new knowledge. How each can be utilized in parallel should always be at the forefront of your learning strategy.

Close your eyes and think of a capital letter *T* for a moment. If the top were considered breadth and the stem depth, you'd have a relatively good depiction of how learning should be thought of in your organization, and it might look like the visual in Figure 24-4. Breadth comes in the form of most social learning in addition to informal opportunities. The depth certainly comes from formal learning with spots of informal and social as well. Let's refer to it as the educational *T*.

Figure 24-4. Educational *T*

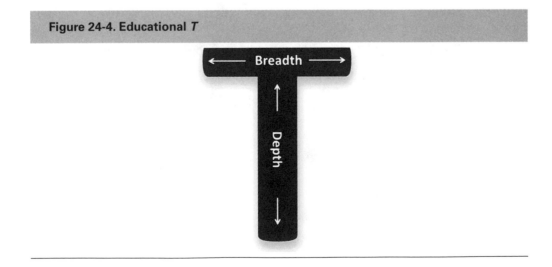

What would this look like if it occurred in an organization?

Matthew Wilder is an engineer at TELUS. He looks after myriad different technology innovations that affect TELUS customers and employees. One problem Matthew faced was something called IPv6, the next iteration of Internet addresses. It turned out the world was running out of Internet addresses, and it was Matthew's job not only to sort out what had to be done for the organization to overcome the issue, but also to figure out how to educate various TELUS team members as well. Taking a look around at what was occurring at TELUS, Matthew decided to first build an open wiki that outlined what IPv6 was all about. From there, he created a discussion forum, a microblogging channel, and a video channel, along with links to articles, books, and webcasts. To complement the site, Matthew listed a series of formal learning opportunities too. He certainly didn't offer a formal-only learning strategy to the organization. He had breadth and depth. He had formal, informal, and social learning packaged together nicely. I had the chance to ask Matthew about his decision to go this route, and he replied, "Dan, it just made sense. How else should we be learning and leading at TELUS these days?" If Matthew can be successful at generating understanding of something as complicated as IPv6 through both the pervasive learning model and the metaphor of the educational *T*, shouldn't we be able to employ this tactic for any type of learning requirement in an organization?

Pervasive learning should not be treated as a commodity; rather, it should be treated as a way of being. Matthew didn't build a training course. You don't go to training; you learn wherever, whenever, and however. T&D leaders should employ this model and all its modalities as shown in Figure 24-5 in an attempt to build engaging teams who also want to learn. This model can be found on the *Handbook's* website at www.astdhandbook.org.

Paying homage to John W. Gardner (1995), author of the book *Self-Renewal: The Individual and Innovative Society,* leaders need to become interested in pervasive learning, not become interesting to others.

Figure 24-5. Pervasive Learning

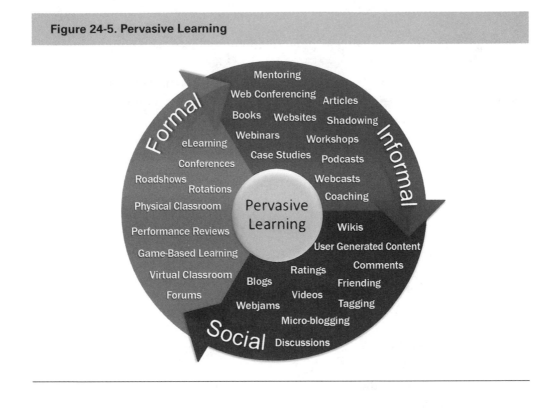

About the Author

Dan Pontefract is author of *Flat Army: Creating a Connected and Engaged Organization* (2013, Wiley) and is also head of TELUS Transformation Office, an organizational culture change consulting firm. Much of this chapter is adapted from his book. Previously, he led the leadership development, learning, and collaboration technology strategy at TELUS, where he introduced the TELUS Leadership Philosophy, an open and collaborative-based leadership framework for all 40,000+ TELUS employees, in addition to a litany of social tools and the pervasive learning model. Engagement improved from 53 percent to 83 percent in five years. A renowned speaker and practicing futurist, Dan believes that today's organizations could be so much more if only they thought about employee engagement first.

References

B.C. Ministry of Education. (2012, August). Transforming BC's Curriculum, www.bced.gov.bc.ca/irp/transforming_curriculum.php.

Boswell, J. (1993). *The Life of Samuel Johnson.* New York: Everyman's Library.

Brown, J.S., and P. Duguid. (2000). *The Social Life of Information.* Boston: Harvard Business Review Press.

Budría, S., and P. Swedberg. (2010). The Shadow Value of Employer-Provided Training. *Journal of Economic Psychology* 33(3).

Bulut, C., and O. Culha. (2010). The Effects of Organizational Training on Organizational Commitment. *International Journal of Training and Development* 14(4).

Carr, N. (2011). *The Shallows: What the Internet Is Doing to Our Brains.* New York: W.W. Norton & Company.

DeRue, D.S., and C. Meyers. (2012). Leadership Development: A Review and Agenda for Future Research. In *Oxford Handbook of Leadership and Organizations*, ed. D.V. Day. Oxford: Oxford University Press.

Dweck, C.S. (2006). *Mindset: The New Psychology of Success.* New York: Random House.

Emerson, R.W. (1860). *The Conduct of Life.* Boston: Ticknor and Fields.

Gardner, J.W. (1995). *Self-Renewal: The Individual and the Innovative Society.* New York: W.W. Norton & Co.

Janove, J. (2012). To Know the Business, Start in the Trenches, *HR Magazine* 57(4).

Lombardo, M.M., and R. Eichinger. (1996). *The Career Architect Development Planner.* Minneapolis: Lominger.

Willyerd, K., and J. Meister. (2010). *The 2020 Workplace: How Innovative Companies Attract, Develop, and Keep Tomorrow's Employees Today.* New York: HarperBusiness.

Portions of this chapter were adapted from *Flat Army* (Wiley, 2013) and used with permission.

For Further Reading

Clow, J. (2012). *Work Revolution: Freedom and Excellence for All.* Hoboken, NJ: John Wiley & Sons.

Grant, A. (2013). *Give and Take.* New York: Penguin Group.

Gratton, L. (2011). *The Shift: The Future of Work Is Already Here.* New York: HarperCollins.

Logan, D. (2008). *Tribal Leadership: Leveraging Natural Groups to Build a Thriving Organization.* New York: HarperCollins.

Shirky, C. (2010). *Cognitive Surplus: How Technology Makes Consumers Into Collaborators.* New York: Penguin Group.

Chapter 25

Learning Informally in Your Workscape

Jay Cross

················· **In This Chapter** ·················

- Describe informal learning.
- Consider the growing importance of informal learning in the workplace.
- Explore the challenge to measure the intangible of intellectual capital and to discover how it feeds the organization's informal learning efforts.

Informal learning is the primary way people learn to do their jobs. Study after study has found that people acquire the skills they use at work informally—talking, observing others, trial and error, and simply working with people in the know. Formal training and workshops account for only 5-20 percent of how people learn.

Informal learning is the unofficial, unscheduled, impromptu way most people learn to do their jobs. Informal learning is like riding a bicycle: The rider chooses the destination and the route. The cyclist can take a detour at a moment's notice to admire the scenery or help a fellow rider.

Like learning to ride a bicycle, most informal learning is experiential and occurs naturally. Think of informal learning as *natural* as opposed to lackadaisical or haphazard; *natural* is a better way to think about it. Most corporate learning is experiential and occurs naturally.

Refer to Table 25-1 for some examples of informal learning interventions tht can occur on the job.

Informal Learning Is Not Entirely Informal

Informal learning is guided by the learner. There is no curriculum. Rather, the learning is *pull*. The learner is in charge. Formal learning is the opposite. The curriculum is often accompanied by an instructor, a schedule, and an ending assessment. Formal learning is *push*. Someone other than the learner is calling the shots.

All learning is part informal and part formal. Think of a college course in philosophy. It's quite formal, with lectures, exams, and a textbook, but the learning doesn't end there. The formal, push component is complemented by late-night bull sessions in the dorm and perhaps sneaking a peak at CliffsNotes.

Similarly, think of learning to sell. The learning comes through apprenticeship, mimicking experienced salespeople, or the school of hard knocks, all informal activities. The career salesperson will probably supplement his or her informal learning with courses from Miller-Heiman, SPIN, or Consultative Selling. The sales manager may assign readings from Zig Ziglar or Og Mandino. The formal joins the informal.

The issue is not whether a learning experience is formal or informal but rather in what proportion. Often, informal is more effective and less expensive than formal learning, but a combination of both is ideal.

Embracing Informal Learning Is Vital

John Hagel and John Seely Brown (2012) explain how unpredictability changes the game in corporate processes from push to pull. Consider a typical manufacturer in the mid-20th century. The company would predict future demand and build inventory to suit it. Then the company would sell (that is, push) its products on consumers.

The world is no longer so simple. Everything is becoming connected to everything else. Nothing happens in isolation any more. Complexity takes over. The future becomes unclear. Manufacturers can no longer predict future demand. Instead of building inventory, sustainable companies create flexible processes that enable them to deal with surprises and build to order. Customers demand (that is, pull) the products they desire.

Table 25-1. Specific Informal and Individual Learning Interventions That Support Common Learning Needs on the Job

Orient Workers to the Technical Aspects of a Job	Onboard Workers to the Culture and Values of the Group	Expand the Scope of Assignments a Worker Can Handle	Build Workers' Proficiency	Help Workers Address Undocumented Challenges	Update Workers' Skills and Knowledge	Help Workers Choose Career Goals	Prepare Workers for Their Next Jobs	Address Ongoing Initiatives
• Documentation • Guided tours	• Advertising • Case Studies • Mentoring	• Advertising • Case Studies • Developmental assignments • Documentation • Gaming simulations • Guided tours • Independent research and study • Mentoring • Performance support • Tips and tricks • Trial and error	• Advertising • Case Studies • Developmental assignments • Documentation • Gaming simulations • Guided tours • Independent research and study • Mentoring • Performance support • Tips and tricks • Trial and error	• Advertising • Case Studies • Documentation • Gaming simulations • Guided tours • Independent research and study • Mentoring • Performance support • Tips and tricks • Trial and error	• Advertising • Case Studies • Documentation • Guided tours • Mentoring • Performance support • Tips and tricks	• Advertising • Case Studies • Developmental assignments • Documentation • Gaming simulations • Guided tours • Independent research and study • Mentoring • Trial and error	• Developmental assignments • Documentation • Gaming simulations • Independent research and study • Mentoring • Tips and tricks	• Advertising • Case Studies • Documentation • Gaming simulations • Guided tours • Performance support • Tips and tricks

Source: Carliner, S. (2012). *Informal Learning Basics*. Alexandria, VA: ASTD Press, p. 147.

Hagel and Brown draw analogies to the software industry. Platforms (environments) replace programs (stand-alone entities). Once upon a time, software manufacturers delivered stand-alone programs (Microsoft Word, for example). That old push model is fast becoming obsolete. Increasingly, manufacturers supply apps that plug in to an existing platform (TCP/IP, in the case of the Internet). Users can swap new apps in and out of the platform without changing the whole shooting match.

Because the platform provides standards, individual applications can be attached with an application program interface (API). This provides a path to greater capabilities without acquiring a whole new program.

This transition from programs to platforms is an inevitable part of a large movement from stocks to flows, from push to pull, from institutional control to personal freedom, and from rigid industrialism to flexible, more human work environments.

Business overall is becoming more networked. Each new node on a network creates value disproportionate to its size because it can connect to all previous nodes. As a result, networks multiply quickly. The denser a network's interconnections, the faster its cycle time becomes. Hence, the pace of business is accelerating.

These two factors—the unpredictability of business and its increasing velocity—are making it impossible for push training programs to keep up with the rate of change.

Training departments have traditionally provided push training. They deliver courses, workshops, and conferences. To stay abreast of the pace of progress, training and development departments must reconceptualize what they do. In many cases, there's no time to churn out push courses for new learning. Instead, T&D must prepare and nurture pull learning platforms. Such a platform is the organization's learning ecology.

"Learning in advance" doesn't work in a real-time world, so learning and work have converged. Learning is simply an aspect of getting the job done. Learning new things—sometimes by inventing them—is an obligation of corporate citizens. Most of this learning takes place in the workplace. Thus, the learning platform is the organization itself, not some separate entity.

The work is learning, and learning is the work.

Creating a Workscape for Learning

The learning platform of an organization is its workscape. A workscape is a metaphorical space. The workscape includes the water cooler, the Friday beer bust, the conversation nook at the office, Wi-Fi in the cafeteria, the enterprise culture, in-house communications, access to information, cultural norms around sharing and disclosure, tolerance for nonconformity, risk aversion, organizational structure, worker autonomy, and virtually any aspect of the company that can be tweaked to enable people to work smarter.

Think of a workscape as a garden. (The "scape" is a reference to landscape.) Gardeners clear the land and move some dirt around. They remove rocks and prepare the soil. Eventually they may plant seeds, and then they water or fertilize occasionally. No one can force plants to grow or people to learn.

There are always a few surprises when the plants come up. Gardeners may need to move some plants to a more appropriate spot and uproot the inevitable weeds. They may mourn the seeds that never sprout and continue to tend the garden, tweaking it to make it look splendid. The plants, like learners in the organization, grow on their own.

Most organizations are chock full of fertilizer, so workscape gardeners need not worry about that. Green thumb learning gardeners need to pay attention to creating an environment and culture that support these principles:

- Most learning is self-directed. The workscape should give people the freedom to chart their own courses. As Winston Churchill said, "I love to learn, but I hate to be taught." Make sure resources are readily available and easy to find.
- Set high expectations, and people live up to them. Help people make sense of and prosper in the world and the workplace. Facilitate social networks that enable people to compare their situation to others'.
- Conversations are the stem cells of learning. Foster open, frequent, frank conversation both virtually and in person. Praise courageous conversation.
- People learn by doing. Encourage experimentation.
- Ensure that managers and mentors understand the impact of stretch assignments. Learning is experiential, and stretch assignments give learners new experiences.
- Teach people the least they need know to tackle things on their own.
- Make it drop-dead simple to access people in the know, the lessons of experience, how-to information, and performance support.
- Learning is social. Encourage participation in communities. Make collaboration the norm. Narrate your work, and share with others. Communities and guilds

create knowledge as well as consume it. If you don't have a vibrant social network, create one.

- More than half of us work part of our time outside the office. The workscape must be mobile.
- We want what we want, no more. Whenever possible, provide choices. Give employees the pieces to create personalized learning experiences.
- Learning is for everyone, not just novices and up-and-comers. You can't expect to prosper without it. Make sure everyone's covered.
- Learning takes reinforcement in order to stick. Seek feedback. Blog, tweet, and otherwise share your reflections. Revisiting what you learn fixes it in memory.
- Innovation is born of mashing up concepts from different disciplines. Encourage looking outside the box.
- Provide feeds for what's going on in the team, the department, the company, the industry, and technical disciplines.
- People confuse learning with schooling. Build lessons on learning how to learn into the workscape itself.

Download these 15 tactics from the *Handbook's* website at www.astdhandbook.org.

---

10 Ways to Promote Informal Learning: Setting Up Employees for Success

By Saul Carliner

Much learning does not happen in a classroom or online. It happens informally among colleagues and on the job. Your organization's enterprise learning system (LMS or LCMS) most likely has the capability to support your employees and engage them in informal learning activities that you may not have thought about. These 10 tactics suggest ways to expand knowledge and skills and increase your employees' chances for success.

1. Encourage learners to continue learning after formal courses. Most enterprise learning systems provide a variety of communication capabilities in the context of a course that share administrative information about the course and course materials, and that facilitate informal learning after the course. Communication capabilities include:

- Preset reminder notes, which can remind employees to apply skills taught in training at times when instructors anticipate that employees might need reminders.
- Distribution of resource materials, such as supplementary readings, references, job aids, and similar materials that employees could consult on the job.
- Ongoing discussions among participants in which they can share challenges of transferring learning to the job.

2. Provide a space for "communities" within an organization. Because they allow learning professionals to distribute information and promote conversation among participants in a course, most enterprise learning systems allow learning professionals to set up "groups" with the same capabilities. Within these groups, learning professionals can promote conversations among occupational communities, demographic communities, or interest-based communities.

3. Provide self-assessments. Self-assessments help employees assess their interests and skills and apply that self-awareness to what is available in the organization. The self-assessments can be written internally or acquired through third-party sources.

4. Maintain skills profiles for key job categories. Enterprise learning systems provide a number of capabilities for using skills effectively within organizations, called skills management. The first of these capabilities are tools for maintaining profiles of the skills (competencies) needed in particular jobs. Skills profiles are challenging to develop because the underlying research is often as thorough as an in-depth needs assessment and, to ensure that the profiles are accurate, require a validation process. Even with a rigorous process, devising the profiles is daunting because organizations can list either a limited number of broad competencies, which could be too general to be useful, or a larger number of specific competencies, which often feels restrictive and exceeds 100 competencies, too many to be useful in some situations.

Most large professional services organizations invest heavily in skills management. So do many larger and more established government agencies and technology companies. Because informal learning focuses on the development of competencies, skills management provides a means of both guiding competency development and, once it happens, recognizing it.

5. Assess skills that employees currently possess. Some enterprise learning systems assess employees' skills against job profiles. Employees can use this analysis to determine their individual training and development needs. Employees can review a list of competencies needed in each particular job and, for each, indicate their perceived skill level. The system matches the skills and the level of each employee with a generalized profile of employees in that job and generates a list of skills gaps—areas where the skill level of the employee falls below that of a competent person in the position.

6. Track skills development. If organizations can link the competencies developed through training to the competencies in one or more skills profiles, the system can automatically update that employee's skills profile to reflect the new skills acquired after programs. Most systems also allow manual skills profile updating to reflect competencies developed through informal learning. Ideally, the system should require that employees demonstrate to a manager that they can perform a skill before updating the profile. Otherwise, employees could receive recognition for skills they may not have.

7. Assist with career planning. Career road maps, which identify skills needed in a particular career, allow employees to assess their current qualifications and link those skills to developmental opportunities to fill the gaps, including informational interviews, training, developmental assignments, and professional organizations.

(continued on next page)

---

10 Ways to Promote Informal Learning: Setting Up Employees for Success (continued)

8. Tailor information to the needs of a particular employee. Called dynamic publishing, such capabilities provide employees with the information they are likely to need based on their particular work contexts. These systems maintain profiles for each employee and match employee characteristics with labels on content that authors included when they stored the content on the system. Emerging systems hope to offer additional levels of tailoring, much like Amazon.com and e-commerce systems that pinpoint content based on previous use of the system.

9. Record informal learning activities. Because most informal learning happens outside an internal event or some similarly measurable activity, people usually need to manually track it. Managers and employees might add participation in conferences, completion of university and other third-party courses, completed books, leadership roles in nonprofit organizations, and similar activities. Doing so increases the likelihood that others will recognize the employee for skills acquired informally.

10. Track progress toward a particular goal. Just as enterprise learning systems can track informal learning activities, they can also track activities focused on a larger goal. For example, a company that makes custom hearing devices certifies new employees who custom-fit the devices through a combination of classes and supervised fieldwork. The system automatically records course completions. Later, managers manually record completion of each supervised field activity in the system. When employees complete all the required activities, they receive certification.

Using These Capabilities

If you want to increase the availability of and participation in informal learning in your organization, try to use these capabilities. In many cases, you're probably already paying for them. Find out which ones your systems offer, then start by choosing one; when the organization embraces it, add another.

Saul Carliner is an associate professor and Provost Fellow for e-learning at Concordia University in Montreal, as well as author of eight books, including the recently published *Informal Learning Basics* (ASTD Press, 2012). Portions of this article appeared in *Chief Learning Officer*, October 2013 and are used here with permission.

Get Out of the Pink Box

Should you paint the walls of your call center pink? Don't think of it. In the late 1970s, scientists discovered that certain shades of pink calmed people who were agitated or angry. Walking into a pink room sapped the energy of difficult prisoners. Police painted holding cells pink. Some football coaches repainted visiting team dressing rooms pink. (Painting locker rooms pink is now banned from professional sports.)

The tiniest thing can confuse people and hinder their ability to learn. Consider:

- People come up with twice as many innovative uses for a paper clip after a picture of a light bulb is shown to them, even when it flashes by too quickly for recognition.
- People contribute more to victims of a hurricane if their own name starts with the same letter as the name of the storm.
- Tell teachers that certain students are "academic bloomers," and those students' IQs rise 10 to 15 points over the course of a year.
- Show an Apple logo to people subliminally and they think more creatively than people who are shown an IBM logo.
- Mount a photograph of peering eyes in the coffee room, and fewer people cheat the honor-system money cup.
- When the Japanese mounted blue lights in train stations, crime rates dropped and suicides ceased.
- Olympic wrestlers are more likely to win a medal if they are wearing red.
- People think it's easier to drive south because it's down, not up, on the map.
- People reflect more intently on messages in difficult-to-read fonts.
- People are more aggressive in hot weather and amorous in cold.

Like it or not, environmental factors such as these have a huge impact on how well or poorly people learn. Improving learning effectiveness goes beyond instructional design to color theory, psychology, group dynamics, social networks, information architecture, workplace design, value network analysis, and dozens of other things that T&D professionals had not considered part of the job. Wise managers invest in factors that once seemed superfluous to learning.

It's not your responsibility to boil the ocean, but it *is* your responsibility to make and execute wise choices even when they are unconventional. We live in extraordinary times.

Solutions and Results

I've worked in learning and development since 1976, but I am not a "learning guy." My background is business. My first job out of college was selling computers the size of a half-dozen refrigerators. Later, I became a market researcher. My MBA is in marketing. I see the world through a business lens.

From my viewpoint, the only results that matter are business results. That goes for formal and informal learning. I'll take an unpopular program that generates profits over a popular program that produces no results every time. When using the Four Levels of Evaluation, Level 4 is all that matters to business. Unfortunately, T&D does not have the yardstick for measuring level four; that belongs to the people managing the business functions. What business results are we seeking? Increased revenue, lower costs, better customer service, innovation, and sustainability come to mind.

Managers want people who can not only perform today but also perform even better tomorrow. They want continuous improvement and stick-to-itiveness. They want people who can work smarter. Learning is a long-term investment. Only a fool demands immediate results.

When I began proselytizing informal learning, and e-learning before that, people asked, "How can you prove this is as effective as traditional learning?" My response was to ask how they evaluated traditional learning.

The school system has conditioned us into thinking that testing and grades were the proof of learning. A look at the research suggests that this is not the case. Grades have no bearing on anything outside the school system. You'd think that receiving strokes for being "an excellent student" would give you the self-confidence to outshine the flunkies. You'd be wrong.

The honor students are no more happy, wealthy, or well than the students who almost flunked out. Tests measure neither street smarts nor how to get along with other people. Most testing is bogus.

Ask people how they learned life's important lessons, and you'll join me in extolling informal learning.

What Really Matters

I don't advocate throwing investments in learning to chance; the gardening I'm talking about comes with a price tag. I'd like to see the budget justification taken to a higher level. Convince T&D's sponsors with logic, coherence, and results.

When I call for results, I'm not talking about accounting results. The business world is hamstrung with a system of accounting that doesn't account for what's important.

Some consultants advise people to disregard intangibles. This is like throwing away the banana and keeping only the skin. The intangibles are the most important part—and they are what experiential learning feeds.

In his marvelous book *Intellectual Capital*, Tom Stewart asked, "What's new? Simply this: Because knowledge has become the single most important factor of production, managing intellectual assets has become the single most important task of business." In the last 20 years of the 20th century, Wall Street investors changed the way they determined what a company was worth. That's why return on intangibles is the most important metric in the T&D's toolkit.

In the Industrial Age, tangible assets produced wealth, so investors put their money on plant and equipment. In the Network Era, know-how, innovation, and relationships became the keys to profitability, and investors began to value these invisible things more than physical assets. Things you couldn't see (intangibles) became more valuable than things you could see and touch (tangibles).

In 1980, tangible assets accounted for 80 percent of the market cap of companies in the S&P 500. In a scant two decades, an amazing flip-flop took place. By 1999, intangible assets accounted for 80 percent of the value of the market. Instead of relying on investing in expectation of a continuation of a stable past, investors began betting on the future.

That change in what investors value is fundamental to understanding return-on-investment, but many T&D managers are saddled with outmoded, mid-20th-century notions and procedures that don't value intangibles at all.

Mechanically, intellectual capital is a company's market capitalization (its value on the stock market) less its book value (the value reported on its balance sheet). When I attended business school in the 1970s, nobody had this anomaly figured out. Shouldn't stockholders' equity be marked to market? The historical figures on the balance sheet failed to report what a company was worth.

Intellectual capital is largely a matter of mind and relationships. It's impossible to measure directly, but you know in your heart that it's real. What's more important: the plant or the people? Where's the real value to come from? The biggest upside is improving know-how, relationships, and processes; that's what gives investors the confidence to up their ante.

Businesspeople love the security of firm numbers; they feel objective, even when they're not the right numbers. The downside of leaving intangibles out of the equation is that it almost guarantees that they will not receive the attention they deserve, leading to unbalanced and suboptimal decisions.

Most business managers recognize that they're managing a living organization, not a balance sheet, but many managers of T&D are still in a fog. Why? Because they've learned a narrow view of return-on-investment, namely, ROI as seen through the eyes of a bank loan officer.

As a T&D professional, pay attention to leveraging the intangibles because that's where the big upside resides. Determine what your role is in facilitating learning in your organization. How can you ensure that environmental factors are in place so your organization's talent can thrive and grow? The intangibles feed the informal learning that occurs in your organization.

About the Author

Jay Cross, a change agent and author whose philosophies of informal learning and network have altered the world of organizational learning, believes his calling is to help people improve their performance on the job and satisfaction in life. Cross is a graduate of Princeton University (BA, sociology) and Harvard Business School (MBA) but says experience is a better teacher. Cross designed the first business degree program for the University of Phoenix. An early champion of taking learning online, he was the first to use the term *e-learning* on the web and served as the first CEO of eLearning Forum. He and four colleagues founded the Internet Time Alliance to help organizations work smarter. Their *Working Smarter Fieldbook* posits that knowledge work and learning are indistinguishable. He lives in the hills of Berkeley, California, with his wife Uta and their longhaired dachshund.

References

Carliner, S. (2012). *Informal Learning Basics*. Alexandria, VA: ASTD Press.

Cross, J. (n.d.). *Where Did the 80% Come From?* Informal Learning blog, http://www.informl.com/where-did-the-80-come-from.

Cross, J. (2013, October). Return on Intangibles. *CLO.*

Hagel, J., and J. Brown. (2012). *The Power of Pull.* Wiley.

Stewart, T. (1997). *Intellectual Capital: The New Wealth of Organizations.* New York: Doubleday.

Portions of this chapter were adapted from columns that appeared in the August 2013 and October 2013 issues of *Chief Learning Officer* magazine and used with permission.

For Further Reading

Cross, J. (2006). *Informal Learning: Rediscovering the Natural Pathways That Inspire Innovation and Performance.* San Francisco: Pfeiffer.

Cross, J., and L. Dublin. (2009). *Implementing eLearning.* Alexandria, VA: ASTD Press

Cross, J., J. Hart, H. Jarche, C. Jennings, and C. Quinn (2011). *Working Smarter Fieldbook.* Raleigh, NC: Lulu Press.

Chapter 26

M-Thinking:
There's an App for That

Clark Quinn

G iven that almost everyone now has a mobile device, the question becomes one of what to do with that capability. In this case, we are curious about how training and development can, and should, use these devices to facilitate the desired performance outcomes for the organization.

This chapter looks at mobile from a systematic perspective. The first section clarifies the meaning of mobile devices and mobile learning. The second section looks at designing mobile solutions, while the third section supports design by discussion development. The fourth section takes a step up to consider mobile strategy. The fifth section looks forward to what will be coming.

Thinking M-Learning

If you ask people, "How do you use your mobile device to make you smarter?" you are likely to hear answers such as:

- to look up information, such as a word or phrase used in a meeting, product information in a store, or the weather forecast
- to use an application to help with a task, such as using a calculator to split a bill or figure out how much to tip, to set a timer for your tea, or get navigation instructions
- to record information such as taking a note, making a to-do list, or setting an appointment
- to contact someone for an answer with a text message or a call
- to take pictures of situations to get help with something, such as an odd installation of a product or to see if a piece of clothing fits, or to remember things, such as a parking spot or hotel room number
- to find out where there's a restaurant, coffee shop, hotel, or subway station nearby.

Note that if you subsequently ask, "How much of that is a course?" the answer will be, "None." Contextual performance support is the essence of mobile—using the device to help at the moment of need. And this is the opportunity for m-learning—to help employees be more effective whenever and wherever they are (Quinn, 2011).

It is *way* past time to start thinking about mobile (Quinn, 2012a); the devices are out there, tablets are on a pace to outsell computers, and *everyone* has a mobile device on them at pretty much all times. The only remaining question is how to take advantage of this to meet your organization's training and development needs. And the short answer is by thinking outside the course.

To get on top of m-learning, we need a bit more definition. We need to be clear about what a mobile device is and what isn't. We also want to be clear about what m-learning is and is not.

M-Devices

One of the ongoing debates has been around the definition of a mobile device, and more particularly, is a laptop a mobile device? This becomes more complicated as we begin to see mobile devices covering a continuum of capabilities, not just categories.

The prototypical mobile device was what we can call a "pocketable," a device that could fit in a reasonably large pocket, whether it was a cell phone, smartphone, or personal digital assistant (PDA). The emergence of the tablet and the netbook has complicated the picture. How do we make sense of the differences?

One early proposal was on usage, where Palm research (PalmSource, 2003) noted that laptop use tended to be a few times a day for long periods of time, whereas PDAs tended to be used

---

Apps at ASTD

By Justin Brusino

We live in a mobile world. We're all accustomed to having access to information where and when we need it. ASTD is committed to providing its members and customers a quality mobile experience. ASTD's events app provides conference goers with the most up-to-date conference and session information and much more; the *T+D* app gives readers a mobile-optimized version of the magazine that includes bonus content not found anywhere else.

Conference apps for the ASTD International Conference & Exposition, TechKnowledge, and the ASTD Chapter Leader's Conference allow attendees to build schedules, send tweets, review speakers, and access session materials on mobile devices and tablets.

The *T+D* app offers a condensed version of each issue of the magazine, plus bonus app-only content such as podcasts, sidebars, pictures, and links to extra resources. In the app, you can read magazine articles, listen to podcasts, read interviews from the popular Long View and At C Level series, and share articles with friends and colleagues. The free tablet app is available for iPad, Android, and Kindle.

---

many times a day but for short periods of time. However, as devices and form-factors have proliferated, these distinctions are blurring. Another proposal might be whether the device is doing something *because* of where and when you are, as opposed to doing something that you can do anywhere, arguing that a laptop is just a portable desktop, not really a mobile device.

To provide a meaningful differentiator, I propose that a mobile device is one that can be used as a handheld without support in a natural way. I don't mean holding up a laptop or a netbook with one hand and pecking with the other, but instead being able to use the full capabilities with one or two hands while standing or moving. This restricts mobile devices to pocketables and tablets. So, how do we make sense between them?

The distinction proposed here is that the prototypical mobile device is the pocketable; when you look at how devices are used, the pocketable is the one that people are most likely to have with them *everywhere*. Folks are less likely to take a tablet shopping or to a party, but their pocketable will definitely be there.

When does a tablet make sense? There are three situations when a tablet is the preferred answer:

- The first is when the amount of data necessary to be presented to the user at one time is more than can be displayed on a pocketable. The strength of our cognitive architecture is pattern matching and meaning making, and there are times when we need significant data to make a decision. This might happen in a content- or data-intensive environment, such as medicine.

- The second is when our mobility is not that constrained. A person is not likely to use a tablet when hopping in and out of a cab or on a crowded elevator. On the other hand, in a more spacious environment, such as a hospital or factory floor, or where the user is more settled, such as in a cockpit, the tablet is likely to be used.

- The third situation is when the device is being shared simultaneously. When individuals are viewing the device together or are collaborating, a larger screen is desirable. Sales presentations are a prototypical example.

Having characterized mobile devices, then what is m-learning?

M-Learning

This chapter makes the case that m-learning is not about courses. To be fair, courses may make sense on tablets, given the content-intensive nature, but they really do not make a lot of sense on pocketables. Jason Haag (2012), mobile lead of the Advanced Distributed Learning initiative of the U.S. government, has distinguished between m-learning and mobile e-learning: The latter is putting courses on a mobile device, while m-learning is taking advantage of the inherent nature of mobile devices. So, if we're not talking about mobile e-learning, what *are* we talking about?

The proposition here is that there are four categorical uses of mobile devices to support organizational performance (Quinn, 2013a):

- *augmenting* formal learning
- providing performance support
- connecting to people
- contextually specific versions of the above.

We need to distinguish between these elements. We have two separate dimensions: whether we're talking formal learning or performance support, or whether we're talking social or content.

Table 26-1. Opportunities for Mobile Devices to Support Organizational Performance

M-Learning	Content	Social
Augmenting Formal	Concepts, examples, practice	Explanations, feedback
Performance Support	Job aids, wizards	Answers, pointers

The first important distinction here is between *delivering* formal learning and *augmenting* formal learning. The case has already been made that m-learning is *not* mobile e-learning, so what is meant here? Learning is more effective if the content is reactivated over time; spaced learning is more effective than massed practice. There are several ways we can extend formal learning, including presenting new representations of the concepts involved, conveying new examples of the concepts in new contexts, and providing new practice opportunities. Each of these can reactivate and extend the learning outcomes. Mobile, while not naturally suited for concerted content presentation, is precisely the delivery vehicle for small chunks of additional content and experiences. Mobile can also be used *within* formal learning. As Jane Bozarth (2010) has made clear in *Social Media for Trainers*, mobile devices can be used to promote learning interactions in the classroom as well as extend them outside and beyond. This is extending mobile e-learning, not delivering it.

However, the prototypical use of mobile is for performance support. If you look at how people use their mobile devices as we did above, most of that can be characterized as performance support. While, like augmenting formal learning, it is accessing content and interactivity, now it is to meet immediate needs, not long-term learning. And we are (or should be) more concerned about having an impact on organizational effectiveness than just whether something is learned, and many times the best solution is not to try to get information to the user, but to have it available as needed. Our brains really are not good at remembering arbitrary bits of information, but digital technology can do so with ease. Similarly, we often will perform better with external support than we will with just what is in our heads.

The other main thing we do besides access information in the moment is connect to people. Formally, we can be getting feedback on our performances. For the other needs, we are likely getting answers or pointers to people or content that may help. We may use text messages (SMS), voice, email, VoIP, or various social media apps (Twitter, LinkedIn, Facebook, or their corporate equivalents). Social can be used both to augment formal and to support performance support, but it is worth it to separate out social from either one, conceptually. The ability to get answers to questions quickly and help at the time of need is another form of performance support, with the caveat that it's typically on the fly, not preproduced. However, the statement that the value we bring to the organization is no longer just what is in our heads, but who is in our network, the value of leveraging that network at the point of need is a real benefit.

Each of these is an m-learning solution: both augmenting formal and for performance support, whether content or connecting to people. These opportunities are valuable, but are not unique to mobile. You can access content and your network from your desktop, whether for formal learning needs or performance support. Having that capability at hand wherever and whenever needed is, however, a valuable extension, and by itself makes the case for mobile. There is another unique opportunity for mobile, however. What can be done is to deliver formal learning *and* performance support, both content and social, because of the *context* of the individual.

The context of an individual can be because of either where they are or *when* they are. Devices increasingly have global positioning system (GPS) chips, which can determine location. Another mechanism for taking advantage of location is via proximity, whether using wireless network, Bluetooth connections, or radio frequency identification (RFID) to recognize where a device is. Alternatively, a device can use calendar and clock capabilities to know what a learner is doing, because of his or her scheduled activities. In either case, serendipitous usage can be supported, either by leveraging contextually available resources or providing contextually relevant information.

Table 26-2. M-Learning Solution Options

Contextual	Content	Social
Augmenting Formal Learning	Contextually relevant or alternate experiences	Directory of or contact from local or contextually aware mentors
Performance Support	Contextually relevant or augmented resources	Directory of local or contextually aware collaborators

So, for example, we could provide specific information about local resources or activities that extend learning experiences relevant to learning goals (for example, an alternate reality game). For performance support, specific information relevant to the current context could augment what is available, pointers could be provided to local resources, or even augmented reality could be available. For the social side, directories of appropriate people, whether formal mentors or performance collaborators, could be provided. In the case of a particular event that has happened, a mentor could even be automatically connected. While a more complicated proposition, there is potentially considerably more value to be found.

To take advantage of this, however, requires rethinking our design processes.

Thinking M-Design

With this characterization of m-learning, we now need to look at how to systematically take advantage of these opportunities. We do so by asking the question, "Where's the need?" We want to address organizational needs where the performance gaps are occurring. You need a two-pronged approach.

Focus on Performance Support First

On an editorial soapbox, the suggestion here is that the first focus should be performance support. The pattern of quick access for short periods of time more appropriately maps to quick help rather than extended learning. Of course, this is part of a larger shift to incorporate performance support into the T&D department's agenda.

The initial point is to focus on performance that is not operating at the desired level of outcome *and* is happening away from the desktop. Begin to think of yourself as a mobile worker. When you are in a meeting, on a site visit, or away at a conference, you are a mobile worker, just as you are if you are a field sales representative or engineer. People are expected to be in touch and capable of work wherever they are located.

A key here is to look for metrics that indicate what the current performance is and statements about what it could and should be. Your analysis should identify not only the need but also the root cause and measurable ways to determine any impact of your mobile interventions. This isn't unique to mobile but is worth reiterating.

From there, if the problem is a skills gap, a learning intervention may make sense. You want to add mobile to your repertoire of solutions, not as the main delivery, but for extending the learning experience and possibly leveraging subsequent performance situations to turn into learning experiences. So, for every course you subsequently develop or retrofit, you should be thinking about the mobile augments that can and should be included.

If the problem is a knowledge gap, it may make sense to create a performance solution. Conrad Gottfredson and Bob Mosher's *Innovative Performance Support* (2011) provides guidance for thinking through workflows and the types of potential support, though their focus is not mobile in the first instance. The rigor in their work, however, can guide the steps once performance support is chosen.

Ideally, the approach is to design *backward*, starting with an exploration of what an optimal *augmented* performance would be, and then develop that. As mentioned, our brains are not good at rote memory or complex calculations, but are good at pattern matching and meaning making. Fortuitously, digital technology is the reverse. Together, our abilities are greater than the sum of the parts. This has been the advantage that led to the personal computer revolution and is now driving the adoption of mobile.

Our performance solutions should posit a virtuous distribution of tasks between the human and technology system. Particularly in the situation where we are expecting context-driven needs, we should be looking for context-driven solutions. From a specification of what support we need to provide, we can design the technology solution (whether a job aid, app, or connection to an appropriate social network) and finally design a learning experience that incorporates the technology solution (for example, Quinn, 2013b).

The Importance of Iterative Testing

Another component of good design is regular iterations on testing. The process that guided interface design evaluation for decades needs to be adopted for learning technology: iterative, formative, and situated. That means you prototype, test, refine, and repeat. Your testing should start with those close to you and be easy or cheap to get. Your prototype should gain fidelity, as should your testing. You will want to test in the real context before you are done.

And, of course, the one rule to bind them all is "the least assistance principle." You need to ask yourself, "What's the least I can do?" Instead of being rude, it is pragmatic *and* user-friendly. Users don't want everything you could do; they want to do what they need to do. The least you can give them that gets them back to their task successfully is the best option. It's also pragmatic, in that you are assigning your resources in the most efficient approach possible.

The key to mobile design is to focus on the need wherever and whenever it is, to look to a minimal solution, and to iteratively test and refine your design. And talking about prototyping slips over into mobile development.

To guide you in the future, this section is summarized in a downloadable tool on the *Handbook's* webpage at www.astdhandbook.org.

Thinking M-Development

At the design stage, your prototypes should start as low-tech. You should bounce ideas around on the back of napkins or with sticky notes. Eventually, you might whip up prototypes and print them out with a graphics package or even with templates for presentation

---

ASTD Trainer's Toolkit App

By Justin Brusino

The ASTD Trainer's Toolkit provides activities, exercises, and tools for classroom and online facilitators. Activities contributed by more than 40 authors, speakers, and experts were curated, tagged, and organized by Elaine Biech. In addition to activities, the app contains *T+D* articles and other content related to facilitation, as well as a tool for creating your own original activities. Additional features include a built-in timer to keep you on schedule and the ability to create notes and bookmark your favorite activities. New features and activities are added regularly. This free app is available for Android and Apple devices. Additional activities packs are available for in-app purchase.

---

software. One of my early design mantras was "postpone programming and prefer paper" (Quinn, 1995). It still holds. Once development starts, you likely will still want to work on a minimalist basis.

For mobile, one of the easiest ways to develop is via mobile web. Essentially, all mobile devices are equipped with browsers. Consequently, developing for the web allows you to create an easily hosted and revised solution. In addition, using good web design (using Cascading Style Sheets [CSS] and eXtensible Markup Language [XML]) means that the web pages can resize depending on the screen size and orientation of the device. More careful design can mimic the look and feel of an app.

The fact that HTML5, the newest proposal for HTML5 standards (still in process), is converging on a standard means that even interactivity will be deliverable on mobile devices, opening the door for formal learning and performance support interactions. Similar developments in e-book standards mean that there are increasing mechanisms for delivering content on mobile devices. Web applications can similarly interface with databases and application programming interfaces (APIs), meaning that social and richer functionalities can be supported. E-learning and development tools are increasingly capable of HTML5 output, though as yet the output can be idiosyncratic, but this is rapidly changing. While rote content delivery is not the essence of m-learning, content and interactivity can be used to deliver the core m-learning capabilities of augmenting formal learning and performance support.

A new approach, called responsive design, is specifically focused on creating an interface that elegantly resizes across screens. Going beyond just web pages, this approach uses mobile web to create real interfaces with typical elements such as fields, buttons, and other controls. Still undergoing work to create specific recommendations, the responsive design approach is definitely worth investigating for principles that can improve the portability of your solution across platforms.

In many cases, mobile web may be suitable for your final solution. The advantages of mobile web are that if the data is volatile, you need not revise the app or deal with the complexities of data incorporation in an application. There are trade-offs, of course. Mobile web is less elegant and does require an Internet connection to work. In some locations, such as underground, under water, or in remote areas, connectivity may be a problem. In those cases, an application may be required.

Even when an app is required, however, there are three major categories of options. The usual expectation is the development of a custom-coded application specific to the operating system and perhaps even to the device. The full development option provides the most elegant solution, at a higher initial cost and potentially more expensive revisions. A second option that is available is to take a mobile web solution and localize it with a "wrapper" that brings the functionality to the device. The "wrap" approach removes the requirement for data access, though such access can be made and is advisable if some of the data may be subject to change or is sufficiently large and only a small selection is needed at any one time to make it more sensible to request as needed. Yet a third option is a third-party solution where you use a provided tool to enter data into a system and use the provider's application on the mobile device.

Again, there are trade-offs. The custom application provides full access to the hardware capabilities of a device such as sensors for contextual usage, the fastest operation, and the most seamless interface. Coming with that capability is a higher cost and longer development time. The "wrap" option offers access to a selection of the most common hardware capabilities, localized operation, and a less onerous development process. The outsourced application has only content development costs, but limits capabilities to what the provider hosts.

Depending on the importance of the outcome, such as business critical or serving an external audience, an application—regardless of mechanism—may be justified. However, prototyping in mobile web is a justifiable interim step in many situations. The ability to iterate quickly and test, as advised above, can serve as a rapid way to improve and finalize a design. Once a design is tried and tested, the "wrap or app" decision can be considered.

Ultimately, a justified question about any technology solution across T&D, indeed across the enterprise, will be, "Is your solution mobile enabled?" In 2010, Google announced they were going "mobile first" (Gundotra), and many, if not most, providers of enterprise software are making their capabilities accessible by mobile. This includes social software, performance support, and learning management systems (LMSs). Mobile will be ubiquitous in more ways than one, and the inability to access most functionality via mobile will increasingly be a deal breaker. This suggests that mobile plans become a strategic decision, not just a tactical one.

Thinking M-Strategy

At the core, mobile is a platform, just as the desktop is. Consequently, just as desktops came onboard initially for specific capabilities and blossomed from there to now be the workhorse of the office, so too will the initial use of mobile devices end up being suborned for more usage. Thus, while you should be making a first mobile initiative, you should simultaneously be developing your mobile strategy. There are a number of entailments that accompany this perspective.

The first thing you need to ensure is that your mobile strategy aligns. An m-learning strategy needs to align with the learning strategy *and* the mobile strategy, just as an e-learning strategy needs to align with the learning strategy and information technology (IT) strategy. Ultimately, your m-learning strategy has to align with the overall organization strategy.

This also implies the benefits of partnerships. A mobile learning strategy ultimately will have an impact on the IT strategy. Consequently, IT will be a fundamental partner. In general, there are two types of partners: those fundamental to your strategy and those who are organizationally placed to be able to facilitate, or hinder, your success. You will want to engage these individuals, to understand and address their issues. Those that can be convinced to support you will be strategic partners.

One essential element to strategy is governance, and this provides a potential mechanism to secure needed support. You will want oversight as well as assistance on your strategy, and a governance board provides this function. By including amenable strategic partners as well as your fundamental partners, you inform them of your plans, involve their input, and secure their participation in execution. Typically, they will have valuable input from their perspectives that will improve your plan.

There is still the possibility of resistance to mobile. One of the ways to address this issue is to ask stakeholders the same question as at this chapter's start: "How do you use your mobile device?" It's a sure bet that they do use mobile devices. Once everyone is aware of the extent that these devices empower us personally, it becomes easier to consider the benefits to the organization.

The rest of the elements of a mobile strategy are not unique. The need to establish a vision, sell a value proposition, budget accordingly, anticipate risk factors and be prepared for problems, align rewards with desired behaviors, celebrate successes, and so on are all elements of organizational change that come into play (Cross and Dublin, 2002). A mobile initiative is an organizational change, and it needs to be implemented as such.

A fundamental area not unique to mobile, but that plays a uniquely important role, is that of content strategy (Udell, 2012). The need for concise content separate from e-learning, but related, suggests the value of beginning to think of content engineering—a concerted effort to be more detailed about content development. This effort at being more systematic in content development pays off in several ways. One is a reduction in content development. A second is a more manageable content archive. The longer-term benefit is the foundation for more advanced capabilities.

The necessary steps are to develop a content model (Quinn, 2012b); revise content development processes in association with the model; start using content management, such as via a content management system; and start assigning roles and responsibilities around the content life cycle.

With the ubiquity of mobile, the need for a mobile strategy is not a question of if, but when. The future is here, which is not to say that there isn't more to come.

Thinking M-Future

The potential of mobile is already impressive, but there are considerable advances still to come. We are seeing continued technology advances, and the growing ubiquity of mobile has implications as well.

The integration of sensors in these devices is just beginning. Location sensitivity is already being exploited, but the use of the calendar and clock is just in its infancy. Other capabilities, such as knowing what (and who) is near and leveraging temperature, altitude, weather changes, and more are on the horizon. What these sensors provide is the ability to know considerable information about not just where the individual is, but also what that person is doing and what is currently nearby. Customizing information on that basis will allow us to fulfill the potential originally coined by Wayne Hodgins (2002) about the "right stuff," bringing the right capability to the right person at the right time and the right place in the right way on the right device.

This context sensitivity will require additional effort on the content model discussed above, leveraging semantic web technology to pull content on the fly. The necessary steps are understanding and employing semantic tags on content to support rule-driven content access as opposed to hard-wired content access (Tozman, 2012; Quinn, 2012c). While capitalizing on this will require a design approach as well as the initial work, understanding and laying the foundations now is an important strategic step to empowering the workforce going forward.

Our understanding of design for mobile is still embryonic. We haven't yet developed a learning design strategy that really addresses the possibility of an extended learning experience, let alone context sensitivity. The possibility of taking simulation games (Quinn, 2005) and extending them into the world via alternate reality games is only just being explored (Pagano, 2013).

Ultimately, the "m" will disappear. Learning will be ubiquitous and seamless, taking advantage of where we are and what digital technology is at hand to leverage our actions, add unique value to what we are doing, make us more effective in the moment, and develop us over time. The ability to access and deliver content, capability, and collaborators can provide the necessary components that organizations need: the ability to support both optimal execution in the moment and continual innovation on an ongoing basis. There is, or will be, an app for that, and you should be preparing to capitalize on the opportunity. Are you ready?

About the Author

Clark Quinn, PhD, has been helping organizations develop strategic learning technology solutions for more than three decades. Clark combines a deep background in the learning sciences with broad experience in technology applications, supported with practical experience in management, which he applies to the corporate, government, education, and not-for-profit sectors. He has previously worked as an academic and in learning technology organizations. An internationally known consultant, speaker, and author, he's written three books with another on the way, along with numerous chapters and articles, and has been invited to keynote around the world. Clark can be found at http://quinnovation.com, and he blogs at http://blog.learnlets.com.

References

Bozarth, J. (2010). *Social Media for Trainers.* San Francisco: Pfeiffer.

Cross, J., and D. Dublin. (2002). *Implementing eLearning.* Alexandria, VA: ASTD Press.

Gottfredson, C., and B. Mosher. (2011). *Innovative Performance Support: Strategies and Practices for Learning in the Workflow.* New York: McGraw Hill.

Gundotra, V. (2010). *Barcelona: Mobile First,* http://googlemobile.blogspot.com/2010/02/barcelona-mobile-first.html.

Haag, J. (2012). *Mobile eLearning Is Not Mobile Learning,* http://www.adlnet.gov/from-adl-team-member-jason-haag-mobile-elearning-is-not-mobile-learning.

Hodgins, W. (2002). Are We Asking the Right Questions? *Transforming Culture: An Executive Briefing on the Power of Learning.* Charlottesville, VA: University of Virginia: The Batten Institute at the Darden Graduate School of Business Administration.

Pagano, K.O. (2013). *Immersive Learning: Designing for Authentic Practice.* Alexandria, VA: ASTD Press.

PalmSource. (2003). *Zen of Palm,* http://www.cs.uml.edu/~fredm/courses/91.308-fall05/palm/zenofpalm.pdf.

Quinn, C.N. (1995). Designing the Design Process. *Proceedings of the Australian Computers in Education Conference.* Perth, Australia.

Quinn, C.N. (2005). *Engaging Learning: Designing e-Learning Simulation Games.* San Francisco: Wiley.

Quinn, C.N. (2011). *Designing mLearning: Tapping Into the Mobile Revolution for Organizational Performance.* Pfeiffer: San Francisco.

Quinn, C.N. (2012a). *Mobile Learning: The Time Is Now.* The eLearning Guild Research.

Quinn, C. (2012b). Content Systems: Next Generation Opportunities. *Learning Solutions,* http://www.learningsolutionsmag.com/articles/976/content-systems-next-generation-opportunities.

Quinn, C. (2012c). The Next Step for Learning: Practical Contextualization. *Learning Solutions,* http://www.learningsolutionsmag.com/articles/1028/the-next-step-for-learning-practical-contextualization.

Quinn, C. (2013a). Mobile Learning. In R. Hubbard (ed.), *The Really Useful eLearning Instruction Manual: Your Toolkit for Putting eLearning Into Practice.* Chichester, UK: Wiley.

Quinn, C.N. (2013b). *Redesigning Learning Design,* http://eli.elc.edu.sa/2013/sites/default/files/abstract/Dr.%20C.%20Quinn%20FULL%20FINAL%20PAPER%20TH2.pdf.

Tozman, R. (2012). *Learning on Demand: How the Evolution of the Web Is Shaping the Future of Learning.* Alexandria, VA: ASTD Press.

Udell, C. (2012). *Learning Everywhere: How Mobile Content Strategies Are Transforming Training.* Nashville, TN: RockBench Publishing.

For Further Reading

Quinn, C.N. (2011). *Designing mLearning: Tapping Into the Mobile Revolution for Organizational Performance.* Pfeiffer: San Francisco.

Quinn, C.N. (2014). *Revolutionize Learning & Development: Performance and Innovation Strategy for the Information Age.* San Francisco: Wiley.

Udell, C. (2012). *Learning Everywhere: How Mobile Content Strategies Are Transforming Training.* Nashville, TN: RockBench Publishing.

Chapter 27

Effective Social Media for Learning

Jane Bozarth

In This Chapter

- Identify social media tools and ways to use them.
- Understand the relationship between social learning and social media.
- Learn how to use social tools to extend formal training and choose the one that best suits your needs.

The emergence of popular social tools, coupled with the proliferation of handheld devices like smartphones, has brought us to a new awareness of the power of connections in supporting social and collaborative learning. We've come a long way from the early days of e-learning, when long conversations were held about what to do for those employees who did not have access to computers at work, due to the work itself or the worker's location in a vehicle or out in the field. We're also moving past the age of traditional knowledge management practices: We know that asking workers to write down everything they do isn't very effective, but we haven't had better ideas. Using new approaches to capture and share real work, and learning in work rather than just at work helps to connect talent pools and cross silos, reduces meetings and duplication of effort, helps us transition as new people move in and out of work units, and extends our ability to document institutional knowledge.

The social age presents exciting, myriad opportunities for T&D professionals to extend their practice and for the T&D function to extend its reach.

Social *Learning* Is Not New; Social *Media* Helps It Happen on a Larger Scale

The advent of new tools has helped to surface and extend learning as it was already happening: through people talking to each other, sharing what they know, and helping each other. Social learning is how you learned to speak your native language: by living in the world, moving in your environment, listening to your parents and siblings, and responding with your own newly emerging language. Hunters on the ancient veldt talked about ways to make sharper arrowheads. New employees learn to navigate the political waters of a new worksite with new bosses and colleagues by talking with and watching others.

Social media are tools that help to broaden learning across organizations and disciplines and continents. When considering why and when to use social tools (or otherwise look to support social and informal learning in the workplace) ask, "What problem do I want to solve?" Do you want to extend the traditional classroom experience beyond the confines of a classroom or calendar? Stay in touch with learners as they go back to the job and work to use their new skills? Position yourself as a partner and advocate for management? Or is it something related to productivity? How many times have you finished a project only to find that someone else had already done something similar, or had a degree in the thing you've struggled to learn, or knew someone who knew someone who could speed it up? All of these would be good reasons for exploring options. But wanting to "do social" isn't a strategy, and you will have trouble selling and supporting and sustaining efforts.

Extensive past research on social and situated learning, particularly around apprenticeship, comes to us from Jean Lave and Etienne Wenger; Wenger has since emerged as one of the world's best-known authorities on communities of practice and recently produced a new conceptual framework for assessing the value of online interactions (see the reading list at the end of this chapter). Likewise, John Seely Brown, in association with colleagues such as Paul Duguid and Allen Collins, published a robust body of work on social learning, situated cognition, learning in communities, and learning culture that informs much of our understanding today. More recently, Jane Hart and I, via publications, conference presentations, workshops, and webinars, have done considerable work to explain and promote the use of new social tools to support formal as well as informal learning in the workplace.

What Is Social Media?

The *Wikipedia* definition of social media is: "The means of interactions among people in which they create, share, and/or exchange information and ideas in virtual communities and networks." For T&D, social media are tools that can help extend social learning. Where before workers in different locations communicated by occasional phone calls, serendipitous encounters, and formal, scheduled face-to-face or virtual meetings, new tools give us access to one another all the time, every day, in real time, through voice, text, photos, videos, music, and various combinations of these. Some people, encountering resistance to the soft effect the word "social" can have, are increasingly calling these "collaborative media" and "collaborative tools."

Popular tools today include profile sites like Facebook and LinkedIn; microblogging tools like Yammer and Twitter; collaboration tools like wikis and Google Docs (in Google Drive); photo tools like Flickr and Instagram; pinboard tools like Pinterest; and even collaborative music-sharing tools like Spotify. And, of course, some organizations use their own internal tools, from SharePoint to homemade products to inside-firewall versions of products like Yammer and social tools built into learning management systems (LMSs). As tools, users, and devices like smartphones mature, more capabilities emerge and existing tools combine. While it's difficult to predict what will catch on with users, it is clear that they have embraced photo sharing. Right now, languages and accents create limitations, but as voice-to-text software is fine-tuned, it's easy to imagine a near future in which people can readily post to social sites by just speaking into a phone.

What Can You Do With Social Tools?

Let's start by considering how you can use social tools.

- **Publish:** One-way communication out to a defined or unknown audience. These can take many forms, but are often seen as blog posts or newsletters inviting little feedback; Facebook pages with updates about training department activities or today's featured class; or a marketing-focused Twitter account that shows little interaction with anyone else. They can also take the form of things like course assignments, readings, or suggested videos. The problem? You can use the tools to publish, but it's not very social, and the payoff will likely be marginal.
- **Talk:** Conversation, one-on-one or in communities. Unlike an email conversation, one-on-one conversation with a social tool is available for others to see and perhaps join. (It's been said that "email is where organizational knowledge goes to die.") Rather than just publishing, look for ways to create conversation or ask for feedback. Rather than just broadcasting blog posts, end them with a question or recruit

some guest bloggers to write a paragraph or two. Rather than just saying, "Please look at the video at www.yyyyy.com," invite comments by asking: "What would you have done differently?" or, "How do you think the customer will react?" or, "What are three things this supervisor could do to help this employee feel valued?"

- **Share:** Profiles, links, images, slides, documents, and so on. Depending on the platform (as with Slideshare, for instance), sharing can include conversation and comments.
- **Collaborate:** Accessing and working online in real time with tools like wikis or Google Docs (in Google Drive).

Using Social Tools to Support Workplace Learning: Formal Training

As noted earlier in this chapter, "social" isn't new. The most obvious uses of social tools to T&D practitioners are, naturally, ways of using them to extend formal training. We already do a good many "social" things in our work, including group activities, games, case studies, book clubs, and in-class or online discussions. Good virtual classroom facilitators invite learners to engage with one another via whiteboard and chat tools and breakout rooms. Social tools can be used to replicate all these sorts of activities, and in most cases, a decision about the tool itself is really a matter of what the learners like and the organization already uses or will allow. You could, for instance, host a time management book club using a blog, Yammer, LinkedIn, or a wiki or other collaborative document. Shift traditional group work to a wiki or other collaborative tool. Class participants could share and explore their own images of customer service issues with any tool that allowed for photo uploads with commenting, such as a wiki, a profile tool, a pinboard tool, or one of the photo-sharing sites. During class sessions, invite those who like to take notes to use a shared document for everyone to have as a takeaway; encourage participants to post "aha" moments, key points, and takeaways using their phones. After training ends, invite learners to share one example of when they applied something from class, discuss an unexpected complication they encountered, or offer a lesson learned that might be useful for the next incoming class.

A decision: Will you use a tool or two for one-off activities, or do you want to build something more holistic? While participants who will be meeting in a three-day class face-to-face might just want to introduce themselves on the company's internal messaging channel, those enrolled in a multiweek program might benefit from participating in a more comprehensive online community.

Choosing Social Tools

With myriad tools available, it can be difficult to choose which of them suit your needs best. Consider carefully what you are trying to achieve and what will make the most sense for the learners, the organization, and the type of content with which you are dealing. Because tools constantly evolve and are acquired or added to others, it's important to step back and get a big picture of what a tool really is. For instance, a blog is, at its root, a very simple webpage creation tool with comment functionality. Table 27-1 displays a chart that provides an overview of types of tools and their uses. Go to the *Handbook's* website at www.astdhandbook .org where you will find the same chart to download for your personal use.

Table 27-1. Choosing Social Tools

Tool	Examples	Description	How Used	Limits	Important to Know
Microblogging	• Twitter • Yammer • SocialText	Tool for posting, usually to a group or to the public, quick comments	Quick, often loosely structured discussions; good for quick thinkers	Can be chaotic; reflective thinkers can struggle; most tools have character limits (Twitter = 140), which most see as an advantage	Structure questions or comments so that they can be answered within space/character constraints
Blog	• Blogger • Wordpress • SharePoint (internal)	Easy-edit webpage creation tool	Online journals, post-and-respond conversations, course support	Typically limited use for conversation; of all the social tools, offers the highest level of privacy and most control	Can be difficult to keep in front of users; anecdotally, expectation is that blog is the most "formal" of the tools
Social Profiles	• Facebook • Google+ • LinkedIn • MySpace	Individual's interests, career, education, status updates, groups	Building connections and relationships; participating in communities; locating others with similar skills or interests	Learners may need help understanding limits of personal/ professional connections, using privacy settings	Most tools have different levels of groups (for instance, Facebook groups can be public, private, or secret); invest time in learning about these features and using privacy settings

(continued on next page)

Table 27-1. Choosing Social Tools (continued)

Tool	Examples	Description	How Used	Limits	Important to Know
Wiki	• PB Works • Seedwiki • Google Docs	Shared documents	Tools for collaboration and co-creation; can be shared in real time	Limited use for conversation	Simplest form of wiki is a shared document such as a Google Doc
Photo Sharing	• Flickr • Pinterest • Instagram	Online library or aggregator for user-generated or other image-focused solutions	Documenting machine repairs, organizational culture issues; narrating work, great potential for low-literacy workers or those with different languages	Effective searching depends on effective tagging	• Easy to use; adult Internet users comfortable with photo sharing • Explore group capability; users need to be in agreement on tags to use • Great potential for connecting with learners at all levels, abilities, different languages
Social Bookmarking	• Diigo • Delicious	Easy-access web-based library of selected links; can be shared with group or made public	Sharing online resources; curating resources around a work interest or topic area	As with photo sites, success rests largely with effective tagging	As with photo sharing, explore group capability; users need to be in agreement on tags to use
Video Sites	• YouTube • Vimeo	Web-based library of public and/or user-generated video	Distributing information; requesting learner response to situation or scenario; inviting learner-generated submissions; narrating work		Explore potential for strategic/instructional use of comment feature; note that Google Hangouts offer real-time video chats

Source: Adapted from Bozarth, J. (2013). "Social Media for Government Learning," *Infoline* number 13 volume 14. Alexandria, VA: ASTD Press.

One of the challenges confronting T&D practitioners is that of extending formal learning past scheduled events and into the spaces in between. This is the critical time when learners are working to implement their new learning. Consider some of these ideas:

- An online leadership book club to sustain learning beyond the confines of the organization's structured leadership academy; consider inviting all organization leaders rather than only class attendees.
- A networking group for graduates of a particular course can be a great way of supporting transfer of new learning from the classroom event.
- Can the training department help to host a FAQs page for new hires, created by new hires? Tips from top sales staff?
- Create a wiki for group projects; for a dynamic, evolving FAQs page created by new hires; or as a repository for collective participant course notes.
- A site for critical incident discussions related to training topics like customer service or ethics.
- A microblog-based scheduled live chat for all the leaders in your organization, or all leaders in the pharmaceutical industry, or all leaders everywhere.
- Assign a Twitter hashtag to your training sessions and ask participants to tweet out key points and takeaways to those who were unable to attend. Bonus: Managers can get a better idea of what's covered in the training, a constant struggle for many practitioners.
- One area ripe for expansion is performance support. T&D is perfectly positioned to leverage social media tools to deliver job aids, and provide real-time mentoring and coaching. Helping to establish and nurture communities for recent course graduates and new hires is an excellent way to build and reinforce ties between learners and learning.
- Find ways for learners to support each other and showcase their work. For instance, when a stellar salesperson closes a big sale, Google's Julia Bulkowski recommends asking that employee to share her presentation, narrating key points, objections, responses, and what she considered critical to the sale. Publish this with a sharing tool or company site as a support tool for others.
- As mentioned earlier, many instructors choose to create communities for learners such as graduates of the leadership academy, or all employees of the customer call center, or all the bank tellers. Discussions could offer additional materials, such as readings or videos related to the course content.
- Watch for opportunities to do things we couldn't do 10 years ago. Bring in the CEO via a tool like Skype video or a Google Hangout for a 10-minute live welcome to new hires during orientation. Invite an author to a half-hour Skype chat or include

them in your Twitter-based book club. Invite user reviews and star ratings in your training course catalog. Offer real-time access to expertise.

Tips for Success

Ready to get started? Learn from others' experience. These tips will help create a smooth start:

- **Don't over-govern or over-manage.** Use your existing organizational communication policies. If someone is posting inappropriate comments, deal with the individual; if an employee abuses the telephone, we don't take all the phones out of the building. Be realistic: Rarely are full-scale social media disasters caused by one rogue employee. What is the cost of *not* using social tools?

- **Make it as public as possible.** Consider the value of learners being able to talk to everyone in a global company doing work similar to theirs, or all new supervisors anywhere, across industries. Use your communication policies to decide what is truly confidential or proprietary. Teach learners to recognize when a matter is in fact private and would be better moved to a channel like email, and to recognize when a conversation has become heated and should be taken offline.

- **Get it into the workflow.** We did it with email, and we can do it with newer tools. Choose tools that require a minimum of additional effort to locate and use. More URLs and passwords will only serve as more hoops for learners to jump through. Always suggest better ways of working. Is a group struggling with planning a project? Create a wiki for them. Are there too many people complaining about trying to work via too many reply-all email chains? Help them set up a private online group. And set an example by using tools yourself. Be the change.

- **Help people find each other; help them connect.** T&D practitioners are uniquely positioned to know where talent and interests reside. Help people make meaningful connections. Use social platforms to support ongoing, in-the-moment learning and interaction. Encourage organizations to provide space as well as time to facilitate connecting.

- **Recruit ambassadors.** Organizations successfully using social media for learning report that a critical factor is having social media–using staff in place to help. This is not just identifying champions who will talk up the efforts. Look around for learners who are already blogging, or are fluent on Twitter, or are enthusiastic wiki users. They can help you choose tools, craft conversations, and influence others.

- **Beware of myths.** There are plenty of examples of social learning support and use of social tools for learning across all industries, including government, finance, healthcare, military, and regulatory fields. Recent examples include the U.S.

Department of Defense, the Centers for Disease Control, the U.S. Department of Veterans' Affairs, the Mayo Clinic, and Suntrust Bank. Remember: Your competition is already doing this. Often, "can't" is more a failure to offer a rationale, provide a strategy, and articulate real needs. Work to have meaningful conversations with executives, your IT department, and other stakeholders.

- **Help learners learn to learn, and be more mindful of their learning.** So much learning is informal, and much of it unconscious. Use social channels to ask, "What did you learn today/this week/this month?" "How did you learn that?" "Can you teach me to do that?" Help them tie this back to the ways they learned it, especially if that learning happened through social interactions.
- **You can't *make* anyone do anything: What do they want to talk about?** The corollary is that you can't convince someone they're having fun when they're not. People will participate if it's meaningful and enjoyable. According to Wenger, enjoyment is one of the reasons people participate.
- **Look at your own skills.** What do you need to work on to help organizations move forward and stay current in the field? Assess your abilities at roles like curator and community manager. Demand for those is only going to grow.
- **Stay current.** New tools are emerging all the time. There are tools for building shared online murals with images and text; tools for collaborating using virtual sticky notes that can be arranged by color and placement; tools that allow you to add a voice clip to points on a map; tools like a new write-on iPad cover that sends your notes and doodles directly to the iPad.
- **Be careful of rules that will only shut down conversation.** Long lists of guidelines for posting and rules for participation only send the implicit message: "We don't really want you to talk." Remember: Trust is cheaper than control.

The Two Best Things You Can Do Right Now

So you want to get started. What can you begin to do now?

Listen. People talk about their work all the time. People talk to other people all the time. What do they want to talk about? What conversations will have meaning for them? A well-known example that appears in *Social Media for Trainers* (Bozarth, 2010) showcases a private Facebook group created and self-managed by a community of prison guards. A key theme in their conversations is getting ahead in the organization. They want to talk about training and job roles and developing competence in new areas and learning more about career progression. Who is *not* part of the conversation? The training department. Those of us in T&D are masters at pushing content and facilitating discussions according to some preset agenda. But "social" works both ways, and it involves far more than layering a social tool on top of some existing silos. What do they want to talk about? Listen.

Participate. You can't nurture a community by standing apart from it, and you can't learn about Twitter by reading books about Twitter. Supporting social learning means you will need to be a partner in learning, not a stand-apart facilitator grading discussion comments. Using social tools for learning will require that you learn to use them yourself, so that you can understand their functionality, their nuances, their typical and unusual uses, and their privacy settings—and make choices about what to use when. Nurturing and growing a community will require you to be a visible member of that community—even if it should happen that you can step away later. You can't "do social" by yourself. Participate.

What's the *Real* Change?

Apart from web-based tools and hardware, we've seen another huge change elsewhere: in the learners themselves. You'd be hard-pressed to find anyone in the workforce who has not learned something from YouTube, whether it's home plumbing or auto repair, a craft, or executing a task in a software program. Learners are identifying their own learning needs and seeking out their own solutions, for example, choosing from 900 videos on faucet repair the three that are most useful to them. They realize that learning can often come in bits and doesn't require a full-day course costing hundreds of dollars. They belong to online communities filled with people they can turn to for help. In other words, we are increasingly faced with supporting a workforce of people who know what they need and want it now, in a bite sized just for them. And they know how to get it.

Finally, remember that the focus for using social tools should be on helping people talk to each other in easy, natural ways. We want to help extract learning from work, not just add more work to the pile.

About the Author

Jane Bozarth, MA, PhD, has been a training practitioner for more than 20 years and holds both master's and doctorate degrees in training and development. She is the author of *eLearning Solutions on a Shoestring*, *Better Than Bullet Points*, and *From Analysis to Evaluation: Social Media for Trainers*, and the forthcoming *Show Your Work* (co-published by ASTD Press). She additionally designed *The Challenge Continues* workshop package and articles in ASTD's *T+D*. She is the recipient of a LOLA award, a *Training* magazine

Editor's Pick Award, NASPE's Rooney Award for innovation in government service, and an NC State University Distinguished Alumni Award. Jane lives in Durham, NC, and can be contacted via her website www.bozarthzone.com and via Twitter @JaneBozarth.

References

Bozarth, J. (March 2012). From Traditional Instruction to Instructional Design 2.0. *T+D* 65-68.

Bozarth, J. (2013). "Social Media for Government Learning," *Infoline* number 13 volume 14. Alexandria, VA: ASTD Press.

For Further Reading

Bingham, T., and M. Conner. (2010). *The New Social Learning*. Alexandria, VA: ASTD Press.

Bozarth, J. (2008). The Usefulness of Wenger's Framework in Understanding a Community of Practice. NSCU Libraries, http://repository.lib.ncsu.edu/ir/handle /1840.16/4978.

Bozarth, J. (2010). *Social Media for Trainers*. San Francisco: John Wiley & Sons.

Hart, J. "Learning in the Social Workplace" blog at http://www.c4lpt.co.uk/blog/.

Pastoors, K. (2007). Consultants: Love-Hate Relationships With Communities of Practice, *The Learning Organization* 14(1):21-33.

Wenger, E., B. Trayner, and M. DeLaat. (2012). *Promoting and Assessing Value Creation in Communities and Networks: A Conceptual Framework*. Heerlen, Netherlands: Ruud de Moor Centrum. Also available at http://wenger-trayner.com/resources/ publications/evaluation-framework/.

Chapter 28

Supporting Worker Performance in the Workplace

Patti Shank

······················· **In This Chapter** ·······················

- Review the relationship between training and performance.
- Examine a list of factors that may cause performance problems.
- Review T&D's role in identifying and implementing performance solutions.

> *"Good judgment comes from experience.*
> *Experience comes from bad judgment."*
>
> —Anonymous (true no matter who said it)

T&D professionals have traditionally seen themselves as designers and facilitators of instruction. The growth of corporate networks and the Internet has changed how and where some instruction is delivered, but instruction is still seen as the primary deliverable. But businesses don't value instruction; they value performance.

From Training to Performance

What's the difference between training and performance? The Venn diagram in Figure 28-1 shows the relationship between training and performance and provides a concise definition of each. This chapter explains the relationships in more detail and the reason for the question marks. But for now, let's simply say that training is one of the things we do to affect performance, but it's certainly not enough to affect it fully, and that's a problem we need to face—and the sooner we face it, the better.

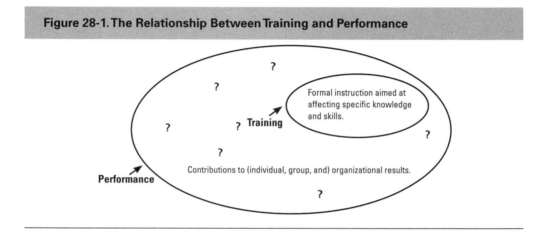

Figure 28-1. The Relationship Between Training and Performance

Actually, businesses only value the *business results* that performance enables. So, performance is valued to the degree that it enables production of business results that customers are willing to buy at a price that provides an adequate return-on-investment. An adequate return-on-investment is dependent on what businesses pay for materials, performance (salaries and benefits, contractor costs, and so on), and administrative costs (utilities, office supplies, hardware and software, building costs, and so on).

Business leaders may not believe that training doesn't deliver the desired return-on-investment or results that they desire. That is one reason training departments may be given limited authority and budgets.

It's not that training doesn't work; *it's that training alone is very rarely a solitary solution to performance problems*. But when used in conjunction with other *performance* interventions, training often can provide good results. We must stop seeing our role as providers of instruction and start looking at ourselves as performance-problem preventers and solvers.

Let's consider an example to get used to thinking about performance rather than only training.

A large company that manufactures small kitchen appliances (blenders, food processors, waffle irons, toaster ovens, and the like) recently experienced problems with one popular toaster oven model. In the last few months, the number of purchaser calls, complaints, and returns has risen dramatically. The main complaint is that the oven is burning toast and other items, even when set to lower temperatures or times.

Executives believe production workers may not be seating the heating element in accordance with production quality standards and has asked the training group to provide training on meeting production quality standards.

Of the following 10 tasks, pick two that you think should be done **first**.

1. Determine what content is available.
2. Review production quality standards.
3. Determine which trainers will deliver the course.
4. Find a SME.
5. Talk to production line workers.
6. Review calls, complaints, and returns.
7. Determine if the course can be online.
8. Determine if workers can seat the heating element in accordance with production quality standards.
9. Ask the executive committee what outcomes are needed.
10. Watch workers work.

Now let's consider the tasks that have more of a training focus and the tasks that have more of a performance focus. Tasks 1, 3, 4, and 7 in Figure 28-2 have more of a training focus. The others have more of a performance focus. Remember, a performance focus is a wider focus. Why start with a wider focus? It encompasses more possible solutions. It could be that the materials are at fault or that something gets in the way of doing the work the right way. If we assume training is the solution from the start, we too often miss the bigger picture with a more lasting solution. Look at the performance tasks and ask yourself what kind of information you could gain through each of these activities.

Figure 28-2. A Training Focus Versus a Performance Focus

Training/Performance Focus

1. Determine what content is available.
2. Review TR195 production quality standards.
3. Determine which trainers will deliver the course.
4. Find a SME.
5. Talk to TR195 production line workers.
6. Read through calls, complaints, and returns.
7. Determine if course can be online.
8. Determine if workers can seat the heating element in accordance with production quality standards.
9. Ask the executive committee what outcomes are needed.
10. Watch workers.

The Performance System

One of the reasons that training doesn't fix all performance problems is that it can only have an impact on *knowledge and skills*. But the reasons people don't perform well go far beyond knowledge and skills. Think of all the reasons people at the front desk of a hotel might not be able to answer customer questions. Sure, they might not know the answers. And if that's the case, they *might* need training. But there are many other possible reasons. They may not have adequate tools to answer questions they're asked (for example, their computer system might not have updated, correct, or adequate information). They may be understaffed and simply be unable to handle the volume of calls and questions well. Management may have set improper expectations or hired people who are not customer focused. None of these problems can be fixed with training or training alone.

Figure 28-3 displays the factors that often have an impact on performance and, therefore, the attainment of needed business results through performance. Table 28-1 explains these factors in more detail.

Figure 28-3. Factors That Most Often Have an Impact on Performance

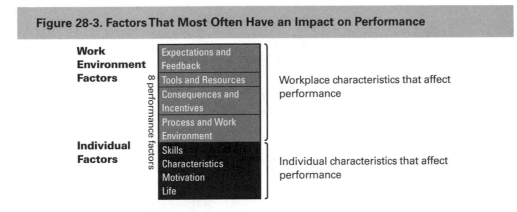

Source: Adapted from Carl Binder's (1998) Six Boxes™ model, *Performance Improvement,* 43(8).

Table 28-1. Examples of How Performance Can Be Affected

	Factors	Description
Work Environment	1. Expectations and feedback	Clear standards of what performance is expected, how it is to be accomplished, and timely feedback on performance.
	2. Tools and resources	Access to tools and information needed to perform, including hardware and software, reference materials, and help.
	3. Incentives and consequences	Monetary and nonmonetary consequences and incentives, intended or not, for performing in one manner over another. Intended consequences may include recognition, rewards, promotions, work assignments, and penalties. Unintended consequences and incentives may include negative consequences for doing a good job and positive consequences for doing a poor job.
	4. Process and work environment	Process factors, including time, complexity, obstacles, and barriers. Setting and ergonomic factors, including lighting, noise, work stressors, and impediments.
Individual Performance	5. Skills	The skills that an individual uses on the job that contribute to desired organizational results.
	6. Characteristics	The personal and professional characteristics that an individual brings to the work, including personality, aptitude, preferences, and limitations.
	7. Motivation	The value an individual places on doing a good job. Includes mood, attitudes, compensation, recognition, and so on.
	8. Life	Conditions and situations outside of work such as sleep, diet, family, personal problems, and personal stressors.

Source: Adapted from Carl Binder's (1998) Six Boxes™ model, *Performance Improvement,* 43(8).

Robert F. Mager

Robert F. Mager made many significant contributions to the field of human performance technology (HPT) and set the standard for measurable objectives. In his seminal 1962 book, *Preparing Objectives for Programmed Instruction* (later retitled *Preparing Instructional Objectives*), he developed behavioral learning objectives with three key elements: what the worker must do (performance), the conditions under which the work must be done, and the standard, or criterion, that is considered acceptable performance.

Another significant contribution Mager made was to develop criterion-referenced instruction (CRI). CRI is a framework around which training can be designed and delivered, which includes identifying what needs to be learned, defining performance objectives and how to measure them, and developing learning based on the specified performance objectives.

Together with his colleague, Peter Pipe, Mager also developed a human performance equation that found that performance *(P)* was a result of resources *(r)* plus consequences *(c)* plus skills and knowledge *(s, k)* plus the difficulty of the task *(t)*, or $P = r + c + (s, k) + t$. Mager and Pipe also developed a human performance model that involves determining the importance of the problem and the results of either solving or ignoring it. If the problem is deemed important, the next step is to determine if a skill deficiency is involved.

To better understand these factors, consider how each of the performance factors could be creating the gap between desired performance and actual performance:

- **Business issue:** Customer returns are higher than expected. We have determined that one unexpected part of the problem is that we are shipping the wrong item to customers.
- **Performance requirement:** We must correctly pull, package, and ship the items that the customer orders.
- **Current performance:** 3.27 percent of the items sent to customers are the wrong item (data from customer returns).
- **Details:** For each order, a form showing item(s) and shipping information is sent to the warehouse from accounting. A computer inventory program shows where each item is stocked in the warehouse and how many are available. The warehouse clerk looks up, finds, and then pulls each item. The warehouse clerk then boxes the item(s), prepares and applies a shipping label, and places the package, according to final destination and shipping type, in the proper location for shipper pickup. Old-timers teach new folks how to do the job. A monthly report details picking and shipping errors based on returns.

How can each factor have a negative impact on performance? Two examples are listed.

	Factors	How This Factor Might Have an Impact on Performance
Work Environment	1. Expectations and feedback	
	2. Tools and resources	The warehouse inventory program could contain inaccurate data.
	3. Consequences and incentives	
	4. Process and work environment	
Individual Performance	5. Skills	
	6. Characteristics	
	7. Motivation	
	8. Life	Workers may have had too little sleep.

We do not expect to affect every aspect of these factors. For example, we are unlikely to have a direct impact on the last factor. You may also download this list as a reminder at the *Handbook's* website at www.astdhandbook.org.

Performance Factor Alignment

When analyzing the reasons that actual and desired performance do not match, people may tend to latch onto a specific factor as *the* "cause." We see, when looking at systems behavior, that a system's characteristics are emergent, arising from the interaction of the system's components. The performance system works the same way; most performance problems arise from interactions among and alignment of these factors. Another way to say this is that performance is commonly the result of multiple factors, and therefore, multiple factors must be taken into consideration and aligned to close the gap between actual performance and performance requirements. Here are two examples.

1. We train nurses and nursing aides in a hospital on a new system that tracks patient medications (in order to eliminate medication errors). The system requires the person giving the medications to scan in patient data, but there is only one scanner

per unit. Many times the scanner is at the other end of the unit, and nurses and nursing aides don't have time to keep running back and forth to get it. So the scanner sometimes isn't used.

2. Deandra expects billing staff to key in a minimum of 60 charges per hour. The training department built job aids to help billing clerks perform their jobs like the most productive people in the department. But the performance analyst who built the job aids warned Aisha that there were disincentives for working faster, such as being assigned more work than other staff.

The point here is that it is a good idea to look beyond the obvious as there may be more than one factor at work. Many times quite a few factors are at work, such as when tools are poor, there are negative incentives for good work, the environment makes it hard to perform well, *and* people don't have adequate training. When fixing performance issues, you may need to fix more than one problem.

Factor Interventions

While this chapter is not intended to discuss *how* to implement interventions, Figure 28-4 shows the interventions that align with each of the factors.

Figure 28-4. Performance Factor Interventions

Work Environment Factors	Expectations and Feedback	Provide clear and achievable performance standards, timely feedback
	Tools and Resources	Furnish adequate tools and resources
	Consequences and Incentives	Align consequences/incentives with desired performance
	Process and Work Environment	Reduce barriers and supply favorable environment (lighting, noise, etc.)
Individual Factors	Skills	Provide training and support
	Characteristics	Hire the right people
	Motivation	Don't demotivate, make work rewarding
	Life	Don't add unneeded stressors

Source: Adapted from Carl Binder's (1998) Six Boxes™ model, *Performance Improvement*, 43(8).

Some T&D professionals might look at this list of interventions and think, "That's not my job!" but I hope you'll answer the call differently. Analyzing performance problems, determining which interventions need to be put into place, and designing them are exactly what we need to be doing. As you can see, training and support are a small part of the performance puzzle. Who is going to put the whole puzzle together for our organizations if we don't?

Think, "What's The Least I Can Do?"

Many training professionals instantly think of training when they are asked to support performance problems, but at this point, you should be able to see that this is often overkill (because it is too much effort and may not solve the problem). Instead, we should be asking ourselves, "What's the least I can do (to solve the particular performance problem)?" Even when there is a skill need, most people learn *best* by doing, not through courses (see Ebbinghaus's forgetting curve at http://en.wikipedia.org/wiki/Forgetting_curve for one of the reasons why doing is so important to learning).

Consider learning to work with headings in Microsoft Word. You may take a course to learn to work with Microsoft Word, but where do you *really* learn and remember how to use headings? That's right—*you learn while doing it over and over.* And if you ask people how they really learn the bulk of their job skills, it's on the job, not in a course. It's not that courses aren't useful, but many times, people need to know how to do something right away, on the job, and the course they took (or will take) is not at their fingertips. Something has to be at their fingertips so they can perform right now!

As a result, one of the things we should be providing is performance support. Performance support is a learning resource that is available to the worker *at the moment they need it*, typically embedded in the workflow. For example, if I'm working at a cash register in a grocery store and need to know price look-up (PLU) codes, I don't have to remember my course materials on PLUs (which, of course, would be impossible). I can use the PLU job aid or the PLU button on the cash register. Both of these are performance support tools. Notice that tools and resources are some of the work environment factors that affect performance, and remember that multiple factors often affect performance.

What Is Performance Support?

Performance support can be paper based or electronic. We typically call paper-based performance support job aids or quick references. What's interesting is that you'll often see people create their own quick references (look on their monitors or next to their desks). Electronic performance support provides access to information or guidance to assist job performance at the time the task is performed. These days, information or guidance is often online, and more and more people are counting on mobile assistance as well.

Gloria Gery

Gloria Gery is considered a pioneer in the field of e-learning and performance support systems due in large part to her groundbreaking work in defining the field of electronic performance support systems. An electronic performance support system, commonly referred to as an EPSS, is a computer application that runs simultaneously with another application, or is a component of a software package, used to guide workers through a task in the target application. Examples of EPSSs are tutorials or hypertext links. EPSSs deliver just-in-time information with minimum staff support.

EPSSs are unique in that they have a performance-centered design, which aims to train workers to be more productive with less effort.

As early as 1976, Gery was beginning to experiment with and implement various forms of e-learning tools while she worked at Aetna Life & Casualty. Based on her previous training experience, she noted that much of the task-oriented training given prior to performing a task did not help much when a worker was faced with the intricacies of executing the actual task. This served as her inspiration to write *Electronic Performance Support Systems* (1991), which "serve[d] as a rallying call to examine whether a new alternative of providing direct support of work processing by technology would be a more powerful alternative to traditional training." This book is now considered a classic in the training and development field because it sparked the EPSS movement.

Gery also developed the three levels of performance support: external support, extrinsic support, and intrinsic support. External support is the most basic type of help or support system. It is usually developed after the fact to help with a deficiency in the system. Some examples are job aids and help desk documentation. Extrinsic support is a help system that does not require a user to stop work to get support but does require the user to decide how to use certain features, such as an online database or help center. Intrinsic support is an intelligent help system that has the ability to adapt to a user's needs based on patterns. Examples are Microsoft Word help resources and certain toolbars.

Examples of performance support include looking up information about a patient's healthcare coverage at a doctor's visit, getting help diagnosing a car's problems, looking up prices at stores, and downloading maps and directions. The information may be text, graphics, audio, or video. The information and guidance may include:

- **information,** such as contract numbers, error codes, prices, warehouse locations, names, addresses, and so on
- **assistance,** such as a decision tree, an expert system that asks questions and then suggests the best course of action, and so on

- **instructional support,** such as a link to a video showing how to do the task, a simple list of steps to take, a practice simulation, and so on
- **tools,** such as spreadsheets, databases, online calculators, company programs used for a specific purpose, and so on

Typically, the workers determine when they need help, and they typically have a present need that is determined by the task at hand. This means that the performance support must be:

- easily available and findable (or it won't be used)
- only the specific information needed at that instant (or it won't be used)
- correct and up-to-date (or it will be incorrect)
- easy to maintain (or it will be incorrect)
- different for different levels of user knowledge (so it's tailored to workers' needs)
- different for different users (so it's tailored to workers' needs)
- friendly for different types of access (mobile, online, offline)
- possibly user maintainable so local experts can add or maintain information.

Conclusions

This chapter is a primer on thinking about addressing performance solutions. The next time you think of training as a solution, consider performance support first. The next time someone asks you to fix a problem, reflect on other causes and options. One of the reasons training gets a bad rap is that we often use training to fix problems that training can't and was never meant to fix.

Training is an expensive fix, even for skill-related problems. In those instances, there are many other, less expensive options, such as performance support and the use of social media, to get the answers you need. In many of today's jobs, knowledge often changes too quickly to train people. So knowledge often cannot remain in one's head. What we can train people to do is to know how to use performance support and social support.

We must analyze the root causes of the performance problem. Although stakeholders often ask us to implement training (an individual performance solution) before we know anything about the reasons for performance problems, it isn't professional or wise to solve problems in this way. Just as in medicine, *you must diagnose before prescribing*.

Research clearly shows that the cause of most performance problems is related to workplace environment. Even if you find a skill-related problem, thinking, "What's the least I can do?"

will ensure you aren't using an overkill approach to solving the problem. In fact, this approach is often more effective.

About the Author

Patti Shank, PhD, CPT, is the president of Learning Peaks LLC, an internationally recognized instructional design consulting firm that provides learning and performance consulting and training and performance support solutions. She is the research director of the eLearning Guild, is listed in *Who's Who in Instructional Technology*, and is an often-requested speaker at training and instructional technology conferences. Patti is quoted frequently in training publications and is the co-author of *Making Sense of Online Learning* (Pfeiffer, 2004), editor of *The Online Learning Idea Book* (Pfeiffer, 2007, 2011), co-editor of *The E-Learning Handbook* (Pfeiffer, 2008), and co-author of *Essential Articulate Studio '09* (Jones & Bartlett, 2009).

References

Binder, C. (1998). The Six Boxes™: A Descendent of Gilbert's Behavior Engineering Model. *Performance Improvement* 37(6):48-52.

Fuller, J., and J. Farrington. (1999). *From Training to Performance Improvement: Navigating the Transition.* San Francisco: Jossey-Bass.

Gilbert, T. (1996). *Human Competence: Engineering Worthy Performance,* 2nd edition. Silver Spring, MD: International Society for Performance Improvement.

Gottfredson, C., and B. Mosher. (2010). *Innovative Performance Support: Strategies and Practices for Learning in the Workflow.* New York: McGraw Hill.

Hale, J. (1998). *The Performance Consultant's Fieldbook.* San Francisco: Jossey-Bass/ Pfeiffer.

Mager, R.F., and P. Pipe. (1997). *Analyzing Performance Problems.* Atlanta: The Center for Effective Performance.

Martin Ryders' Performance technology links, http://carbon.cudenver.edu/~mryder /martin.html.

Road Maps: A Guide to Learning System Dynamics, http://www.clexchange.org/curriculum /roadmaps/.

Robinson, D.G., and J. Robinson. (2008). *Performance Consulting: Moving Beyond Training,* 2nd edition. San Francisco: Berrett-Koehler Publishers.

Rossett, A., and J. Gautier-Downes. (1990). *A Handbook of Job Aids.* San Francisco: Pfeiffer.

Rossett, A., and L. Schafer. (2006). *Job Aids and Performance Support: Moving from Knowledge in the Classroom to Knowledge Everywhere,* 2nd edition. San Francisco: Pfeiffer.

Rummler, G.A., and A. Brache. (1995). *Improving Performance: How to Manage the White Space in the Organizational Chart.* San Francisco: Jossey-Bass.

Stolovitch, H.D., and E. Keeps. (2004). *Front-End Analysis and Return on Investment.* San Francisco: Jossey-Bass.

Sweeney, L.B., and D. Meadows. (1995). *The Systems Thinking Playbook: Exercises to Stretch and Build Systems Thinking Capabilities.* Sustainability Institute.

Teodorescu, T., and C. Binder. (2004, September). Competence Is What Matters. *Performance Improvement* 43(8).

For Further Reading

Robinson, D.G., and J. Robinson. (2008). *Performance Consulting: Moving Beyond Training*, 2nd edition. San Francisco: Berrett-Koehler Publishers.

Section V

Transferring Learning and Evaluating Impact

Section V

The Growing Importance of Measuring Results and Impact

Luminary Perspective

Robert O. Brinkerhoff

Anyone who has had anything to do with training and development (T&D) for more than a few months, much less years, knows this simple truth: Sometimes training works, and sometimes it doesn't. In my four-plus decades of evaluating T&D—from leadership development to technical skills, in dozens of settings from foundations to corporations to government agencies—I have seen many instances where training had tremendous impact, helping drive new performance that led to highly worthy organizational outcomes worth many multiples of the cost of the training. And I have seen an almost equal number of instances of training failure, producing no learning at all, or producing new learning that never gets deployed in on-the-job performance.

It is not the case that some programs are so good that they produce 100 percent success while others are so bad that they have no success at all. In any one program, you are virtually assured of finding a wide range of success and failure among the hundred or so employees who participated in that program. In more successful programs, you'll find a higher proportion of successful performance improvement, and in the poorer programs, a smaller ratio. But on average, the rate of success across training and development programs is not high.

If we define success (impact) as *sustained behavior change that is aligned with organization performance improvement goals,* then almost all T&D initiatives score less than 50 percent success, and many are a good bit lower than that; our evaluation experience shows that 20-25 percent is most typical. But some—a distressingly low number—achieve far greater success rates. As I have presented it to audiences in the past, the typical T&D endeavor invests a pound of learning for an ounce (or less) of impact.

In my view, evaluation should be focused on a simple and single purpose: to turn this formula around, so that T&D initiatives regularly invest a few ounces of learning for many pounds of impact. And I believe this effort is not only advisable but also vital. Why? Organizational success relies on it.

Why T&D Success Matters

All training is not the same. Some T&D investments are aimed at helping employees improve job performance and, in the highest and best instances, to produce the skills and knowledge that will foster the execution of strategic initiatives. T&D programs of this type demand the best and most thorough evaluation efforts. Other T&D initiatives aim at lesser goals and do not warrant such intense evaluation. Knowing when and why to evaluate training is a vital and strategic competency.

Those T&D initiatives that warrant little in-depth evaluation effort are aimed at what I like to call *staff benefit* outcomes. For example, no one can run a successful organization without including enough T&D opportunities to recruit and retain employees. So some T&D is all about recruitment and retention. And no one can run a successful complex organization without offering T&D to help employees advance and have a fair shot at promotion. Other T&D investments are made to avoid legal risk exposure or to meet regulatory requirements that demand certain numbers of hours in training in certain topics. These sorts of T&D investments do not need to produce sustained behavior change to pay off and are simply table stakes in today's marketplace. You can't run an organization without them. They are a required overhead, much like a parking lot for employees, insurance coverage, tuition subsidies, and such. They are necessary but not sufficient for organizational success and do not warrant evaluation efforts beyond checking in now and then to see if people value them and whether they are well designed and efficiently administered.

But strategically imperative T&D investments go beyond simply a license to play in the competitive organizational marketplace. This is T&D that helps organizations thrive, grow, and win; T&D that drives production and performance to new levels and establishes disruptive competitive advantage. This highest and best purpose for T&D is *to accelerate the execution of strategic initiatives.* These T&D initiatives are driven by another organizational truth: Most organizations fail not because they are aimed along the wrong path, but they fail because employee workplace performance does not follow the strategy path. By many research and expert estimates, as much as 70 percent of organizational failures are due to failures to adequately execute the intended strategy.

And strategy needs not just to be executed, it must be executed quickly. In many industries, competitors adopt almost identical strategies. The national pharmacy chains (Walgreens, CVS, and Rite Aid, for example) have all adopted a similar growth strategy that includes providing more basic medical services such as flu shots and strep tests. The winning competitors will be those who execute best and execute the fastest.

This is where T&D comes in. The need for quick adoption of the changes that new strategies demand arrives immediately, as soon as the new strategic imperative is decided upon. But the execution of the strategy takes time, since it always calls for new workplace behaviors that, at a minimum, require learning to understand their details and rationale, and often also require new skills and knowledge to be able to execute them effectively. The ideal scenario is shown in Figure A.

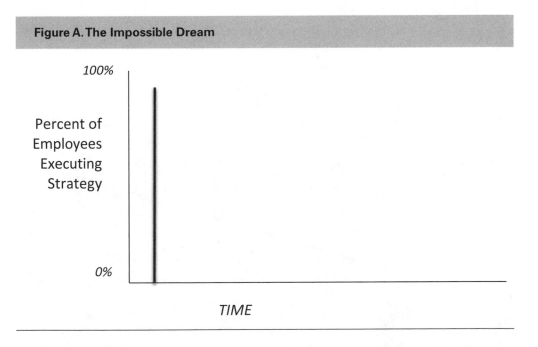

Figure A. The Impossible Dream

This chart shows time on the horizontal axis and the percentage of employees executing a change on the vertical axis. The impossible ideal is that an organization could announce a new strategic change on Monday, and by Tuesday morning, 100 percent of employees would be working in the new ways required to execute that strategy—a hopeless fantasy.

Figure B shows the reality that adoption of change takes considerable time, beginning with early adopters, and moving through several phases of trial and error until a critical mass of employees has adopted the workplace behaviors and performance outcomes that the new strategy requires to deliver intended results. And too often, by the time this critical mass of employees is working in alignment with the new requirements, the strategy is obsolete, new strategic goals must be adopted, and thus the cycle must start anew.

Figure B depicts the value-add that effective T&D provides, steepening the adoption slope and accelerating the effective execution of the strategy, shortening the timeline to achievement of a sufficient critical mass. This is where the payoff lies: the difference between accelerated performance that aligns with and executes strategy versus the slower adoption curve that fails to serve customers soon enough and allows competitors to surge ahead, leading eventually to the death of the organization.

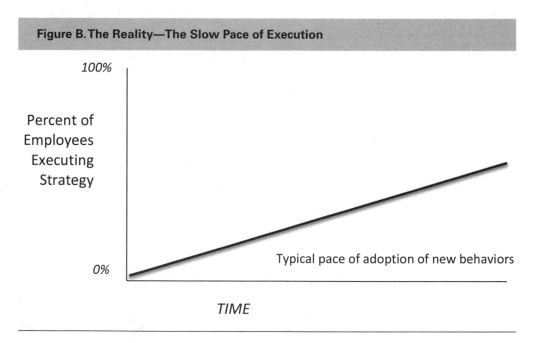

Figure B. The Reality—The Slow Pace of Execution

Evaluation: How We Learn to Make Training Work

The T&D business-as-usual approach that achieves performance improvement rates of around 20 percent or so is too slow to fulfill the value premise laid out in Figure C. Organizations that can achieve only these meager rates of translating learning into workplace performance will not thrive and may not survive. We as T&D professionals, the organizations we serve, and the countries we live in have to do better. Companies and other organizations have to outlearn to outperform their competitors. The pace of change in technology, markets, innovations in products and services, and demands of customers and clients pose needs for ever-evolving and more frequent strategic shifts and thus, far faster migration of new learning into workplace performance.

Figure C. Accelerated Rate of Execution

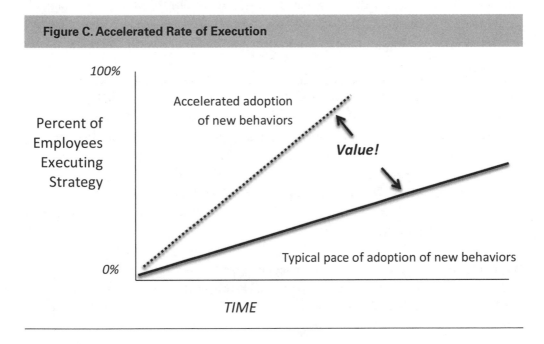

As I noted earlier, T&D organizations in some companies I have worked with that do far better than average. When it comes to mission-critical training that is meant to help employees change their behavior to execute strategy (the definition of mission-critical), these few exemplars achieve success rates of 80 percent and better. They have done this in part by managing their T&D processes more effectively; for example, by getting managers of trainees to truly prepare employees before training, integrating performance support tools into learning initiatives, helping managers set expectations for applying learning in their jobs, and following up with coaching and other performance support. In short, they have transformed their organizations into true learning organizations, where getting results from training is whole-organization accountability, where trainees, their mangers, senior leaders, and the T&D function all play an integrated part in turning new learning quickly into new performance.

Use Evaluation to Tell the Story, and Tell It to the Right People

The other part of their "secret sauce" for making this transformation has been evaluation. They don't just measure training; they measure how well training is working to turn learning into performance. They measure how and when managers support training, they measure how and when trainees use their learning, they measure the obstacles trainees encounter in trying to use their learning, and they measure who and what facilitates or impedes learning and the process of turning learning into performance improvement.

The evaluation process boils down to a simple recipe. When training works, they notice, applaud, and nurture; when it doesn't work, they notice and figure out who has to do what to make it work, and they tell the involved audiences what worked and what didn't. So if, for example, employees who struggled with applying their learning encountered little manager support, this fact gets reported, not just to the T&D function, but also to audiences up and down the chain of command. When the value of training that worked is made clear, and when the money that was left on the table when training failed to work is made clear, and when who did what or did not do what to help it work is made clear, people take action to change things.

In sum, evaluating training and transferring learning to workplace performance go hand in hand. You cannot get to truly effective training without measuring how well things are working now and telling the truth about why it works when it works and why it does not when it does not. Every T&D initiative presents an opportunity to learn how to make the next one more effective. As you uncover and report—loudly and clearly—what is happening in your organization that accelerates performance, and what is happening that slows it down, your organization learns to excel. Evaluation is organizational learning. You are just the right person to make it happen.

About the Author

Robert O. Brinkerhoff, PhD, is an internationally recognized expert in evaluation and training effectiveness and winner of the ASTD 2007 Exceptional Contribution to Workplace Learning and Performance award and the 2008 Neon Elephant award for creative contributions to workplace learning. Brinkerhoff is creator of the Success Case Method for evaluation of training, author of numerous books on evaluation and training, global consultant, keynote speaker, and presenter at hundreds of conferences and institutes worldwide. In addition to 30 years as university professor, he has been an officer in the U.S. Navy during the Vietnam era, carpenter, charter boat mate in the West Indies, grocery salesman in Puerto Rico, and factory laborer in Birmingham, England.

For Further Reading

Broad, M. (2005). *Beyond Transfer of Training.* San Francisco: Pfeiffer.

Brinkerhoff, R.O. (2007). *Telling Training's Story.* San Francisco: Berrett-Koehler.

Kirkpatrick, D. (2006). *Evaluating Training Programs,* 3rd edition. San Francisco: Berrett-Koehler.

Mooney, T., and R. Brinkerhoff. (2010). *Courageous Training.* San Francisco: Berrett-Koehler.

Chapter 29

Implement the Four Levels of Evaluation to Demonstrate Value

Jim Kirkpatrick and Wendy Kayser Kirkpatrick

··· **In This Chapter** ···

- ▦ Explain the origins of the Kirkpatrick Model and the New World Kirkpatrick Model.
- ▦ Learn how the dimensions in the New World Kirkpatrick Model relate to each of the four levels of evaluation.
- ▦ Implement the four levels of evaluation.
- ▦ Understand the five Kirkpatrick Foundational Principles.

··

The purpose of all training is to enhance on-the-job performance through consistent application and to affect organizational results. The Kirkpatrick Model, often referred to as the four levels, is one of the primary methods used to ensure that training is being applied and is contributing to results.

The most effective way to apply the Kirkpatrick Model is to consider all four levels during the training design and development process. If you wait until after training to determine how trainees will apply the learning on the job and how you will measure impact on the business, it is likely that neither of these activities will occur reliably.

In this chapter, you will learn the four levels and how they have been enhanced with the New World Kirkpatrick Model. The Kirkpatrick Foundational Principles describe guidelines for effective application of the four levels.

The Kirkpatrick Model

The Kirkpatrick Model was developed by Dr. Donald Kirkpatrick in the mid-1950s as he was writing his PhD dissertation. His goal was to effectively measure the impact of the management development programs he was teaching at the University of Wisconsin Management Institute.

Dr. Kirkpatrick Sr.'s work became known and later was published by a trade journal in the late 1950s. Over the following 50 years, worldwide use grew organically. Today, the Kirkpatrick Model, illustrated in Figure 29-1, is the most highly recognized, used, and regarded method of evaluating the effectiveness of training programs.

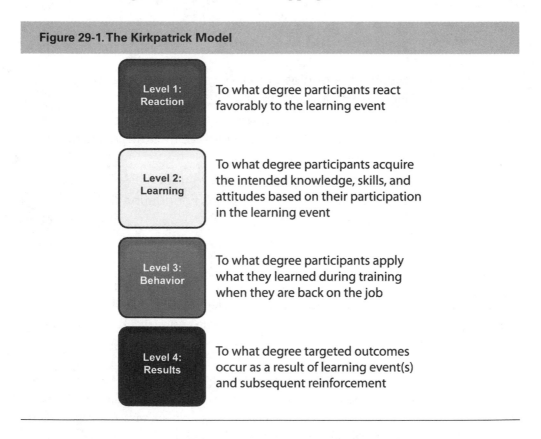

Figure 29-1. The Kirkpatrick Model

Level 1: Reaction — To what degree participants react favorably to the learning event

Level 2: Learning — To what degree participants acquire the intended knowledge, skills, and attitudes based on their participation in the learning event

Level 3: Behavior — To what degree participants apply what they learned during training when they are back on the job

Level 4: Results — To what degree targeted outcomes occur as a result of learning event(s) and subsequent reinforcement

Donald L. Kirkpatrick

Donald L. Kirkpatrick is considered the father of training evaluation. Renowned for developing the four levels of evaluation, he first presented his ideas on the topic in the article "How to Start an Objective Evaluation of Your Training Program," which appeared in the May–June 1956 issue of the *Journal of the American Society of Training Directors* (later *T+D*). These ideas were then compiled into his seminal book, *Evaluating Training Programs: The Four Levels* (1994). Kirkpatrick's four levels of evaluation are as follows:

Level 1: Reaction

Level 1 evaluation focuses on the reaction of participants to the training program. Although this is the lowest level of measurement, it remains an important dimension to assess in terms of participant satisfaction.

Level 2: Learning

This level determines whether the participants actually learned what they were supposed to learn as a result of the training session. It measures the participant's acquisition of cognitive knowledge or behavioral skills.

Level 3: Behavior

Level 3 focuses on the degree to which training participants are able to transfer learning to their workplace behaviors.

Level 4: Results

The last level moves beyond the training participant to assess the impact of training on organizational performance.

In 2010, Dr. Kirkpatrick Sr.'s son, Jim, and daughter-in-law, Wendy, enhanced the Kirkpatrick Model to accomplish the following goals:

- Incorporate the forgotten or overlooked teachings of Dr. Kirkpatrick Sr.
- Correct common misinterpretations and misuse of the model.
- Illustrate how the model applies to modern workplace learning and performance.

The New World Kirkpatrick Model, depicted in Figure 29-2, honors and maintains the time-tested four levels and adds new elements to help people to operationalize them effectively.

The New World Kirkpatrick Model: Levels 1 and 2

Levels 1 and 2 of the New World Kirkpatrick Model are referred to as *effective training*. These levels measure the quality of the training and the degree to which it resulted in knowledge and skills that can be applied on the job. These measurements are useful primarily to the training function to internally measure the quality of the programs they design and deliver.

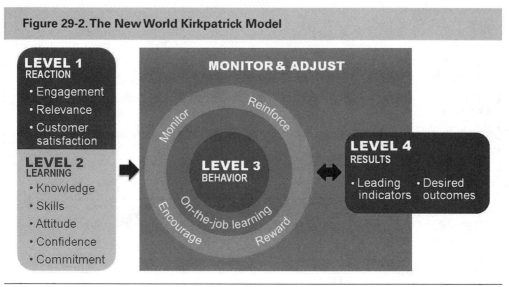

Figure 29-2. The New World Kirkpatrick Model

Level 1: Reaction

Level 1 Reaction is the degree to which participants react favorably to the learning event.

Approximately 78 percent of training events measure Level 1 Reaction in some fashion. The current investment in gathering this type of data is far greater than the importance this level dictates. This investment occurs at the cost of measuring Levels 3 and 4, which would yield data more meaningful to the business; these levels are only measured 25 percent and 15 percent of the time, respectively (ASTD, 2009).

The New World Kirkpatrick Level 1 Reaction has three dimensions: engagement, relevance, and customer satisfaction.

Engagement

Engagement refers to the degree to which participants are actively involved in and contributing to the learning experience. Engagement levels directly relate to the level of learning that participants attain.

Personal responsibility and program interest are both factors in the measurement of engagement. Personal responsibility relates to how present and attentive participants are during the training. Program interest is more commonly the focus, including how the facilitator involved and captivated the audience.

Relevance

Relevance is the degree to which training participants will have the opportunity to use or apply what they learned in training on the job. Relevance is important to ultimate training value because even the best training is a waste of resources if the participants have no application for the content in their everyday work.

Customer Satisfaction

The original definition of Level 1 measured only participant satisfaction with the training. Dr. Kirkpatrick Sr. referred to this as the customer satisfaction measurement of training.

Tips for Implementing Level 1

- Level 1 evaluation efforts should be matched to the degree of the course or program's importance to the organization.
- Level 1 is the least important to stakeholders, so keep it as brief and efficient as possible.
- Use a variety of methods to measure Level 1, including formative (that is, during the class) observation. Save survey and interview questions for the higher, more important levels.

Level 2: Learning

The original definition of Level 2 Learning is the degree to which participants acquire the intended knowledge, skills, and attitudes based on their participation in the learning event. The New World Kirkpatrick Model has two new dimensions in this level: confidence and commitment. These dimensions help to close the gap between learning and behavior, and to prevent the cycle of waste when training is repeated for people who possess the required knowledge and skills but fail to perform appropriately on the job.

Knowledge and Skill

Knowledge is the degree to which participants know certain information, as characterized by the phrase, "I know it."

Skill is the degree to which they know how to do something or perform a certain task, as illustrated by the phrase, "I can do it right now."

Many organizations make the common and costly mistake of inaccurately diagnosing poor performance as a lack of knowledge or skill. Underachievers are continually returned to training with the belief that they do not know what to do when, in reality, the more common cause of substandard performance is a lack of motivation or other environmental factors.

Only about 10 percent of learning transfer failure (that is, a training graduate failing to perform new skills on the job) is due to training; 70 percent or more of such failure is due to something in the application environment (ASTD, 2006).

Attitude

Attitude is the degree to which training participants believe it will be worthwhile to implement what is learned during training on the job. Attitude is characterized by the phrase, "I believe it will be worthwhile to do this in my work."

Confidence

Confidence is the degree to which training participants think they will be able to do what they learned during training on the job. It is characterized by the phrase, "I think I can do it on the job."

Addressing confidence during training brings learners closer to the desired on-the-job performance. It can proactively surface potential on-the-job application barriers so they can be resolved.

Commitment

Commitment is the degree to which learners intend to apply the knowledge and skills learned during training to their jobs. It is characterized by the phrase, "I intend to do it on the job." Commitment relates to learner motivation by acknowledging that even if the learner masters the knowledge and skills, he or she must still put forth effort to use the information or perform the skills daily.

Tips for Implementing Level 2

- Level 2 is primarily measured during the course using quizzes, activities, demonstrations, and discussions.
- Use pretests and post-tests only when the program will be modified to fit the pretest results or when stakeholders specifically request this information.
- Keep Level 2 measurement focused so resources stay in line with its relatively low importance compared to Levels 3 and 4.

The New World Kirkpatrick Model: Levels 3 and 4

Levels 3 and 4, referred to as *training effectiveness*, encompass:

- on-the-job performance and subsequent business results that occur, in part, due to training and reinforcement
- demonstration of the value that the training has contributed to the organization.

Level 3: Behavior

Level 3 is the degree to which participants apply what they learned during training when they are back on the job. The New World Level 3 Behavior consists of critical behaviors, required drivers, and on-the-job learning.

Critical Behaviors

Critical behaviors are the few specific actions that, if performed consistently on the job, will have the biggest effect on the desired results.

There are perhaps thousands of behaviors a given employee might perform on the job; critical behaviors are those that have been identified as the most important to achieving organizational success.

Required Drivers

The New World Kirkpatrick Model adds required drivers to Level 3. Required drivers are processes and systems that reinforce, monitor, encourage, and reward performance of critical behaviors on the job.

Organizations that reinforce the knowledge and skills learned during training with accountability and support systems can expect as much as 85 percent application on the job. Conversely, companies that rely primarily on training events alone to create good job performance achieve around a 15 percent success rate (Brinkerhoff, 2006).

Required drivers are the key to accomplishing the desired on-the-job application of what is learned during training. They decrease the likelihood of people falling through the cracks or deliberately crawling through the cracks if they are not interested in performing the required behaviors.

Active execution and monitoring of required drivers are perhaps the biggest indicators of program success for any initiative.

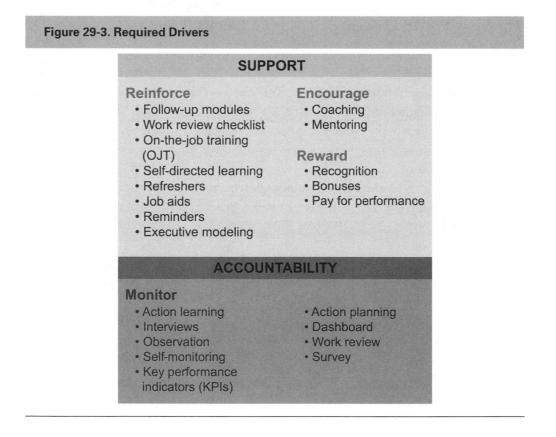

Figure 29-3. Required Drivers

SUPPORT

Reinforce
- Follow-up modules
- Work review checklist
- On-the-job training (OJT)
- Self-directed learning
- Refreshers
- Job aids
- Reminders
- Executive modeling

Encourage
- Coaching
- Mentoring

Reward
- Recognition
- Bonuses
- Pay for performance

ACCOUNTABILITY

Monitor
- Action learning
- Interviews
- Observation
- Self-monitoring
- Key performance indicators (KPIs)

- Action planning
- Dashboard
- Work review
- Survey

On-the-Job Learning

The New World Model also adds on-the-job learning to Level 3 in recognition of two facts in today's workplace:

- Up to 70 percent of all learning takes place on the job.
- Personal responsibility and motivation are key partners to external support and reinforcement efforts for optimal performance.

By creating a culture in which individuals are expected to maintain the knowledge and skills to enhance their own performance, organizations can empower employees and encourage them to be accountable. On-the-job learning provides an opportunity for employees and their employers to share the responsibility for good performance.

Tips for Implementing Level 3

- Have a pretraining conversation with the managers of the people who will attend training. Jointly determine the critical behaviors that need to occur on the job for them to view the training as time well spent.
- Design learning objectives around the critical behaviors.
- Create job aids that assist training participants in performing the critical behaviors on the job. Introduce the job aids during training, and use them during hands-on activities.
- Design post-program follow-up as you design the training materials. This will ensure accomplishment of this task. Take advantage of technology to schedule and automatically send reminders, refreshers, and encouraging messages.
- Make a note in your calendar (or set up automatic reminders for yourself) to check in with some or all of the training participants after they have had a reasonable amount of time to try the new behaviors on the job. Ask them how it is going and whether they need any additional resources or support to be successful.
- Make it part of your training design and development process to create the post-program implementation and support plan. Building this structure increases the likelihood that the resources that go into training actually will produce a measurable increase in performance.

Level 4: Results

Level 4 holds the distinction of being the most misunderstood of the four levels. It is the degree to which targeted outcomes occur as a result of the learning event(s) and subsequent reinforcement.

A common misapplication occurs when professionals or functional departments define results in terms of their small, individual area of the organization instead of globally for the entire company. This creates silos and fiefdoms that are counterproductive to organizational effectiveness. The resulting misalignment causes layers upon layers of dysfunction and waste.

Clarity regarding the true Level 4 Result for an organization is critical. By definition, it is some combination of the organizational purpose and mission. In a for-profit company, it means profitably delivering the product or service to the marketplace. In a not-for-profit, government, or military organization, it means accomplishing the mission.

Every organization has just one Level 4 Result. A good test of whether the correct Level 4 Result has been identified is a positive answer to the question, "Is this what the organization exists to do, deliver, or contribute?" While this definition of results is straightforward, frustration with the seeming inability to relate a single training class to a high-level organizational mission is common. Business results are broad and long-term. They are created through the culmination of countless efforts of people and departments, and by environmental factors. They can take months or years to manifest.

Leading Indicators

Leading indicators help to bridge the gap between individual initiatives and efforts and organizational results. They are short-term observations and measurements that suggest that critical behaviors are on track to create a positive impact on the desired results. Organizations will have a number of leading indicators that encompass departmental and individual goals, each contributing to the accomplishment of the highest-level results. Common leading indicators include:

- customer satisfaction
- employee engagement
- sales volume
- cost containment
- quality
- market share.

While leading indicators are important measurements, they must be balanced with a focus on the highest-level result. For example, a company with excellent customer satisfaction scores could go out of business if they do not maintain profitability, comply with laws and regulations, and keep their employees reasonably happy. Note that customer satisfaction is an example of a goal that does not provide an affirmative answer to the question, "Is this what the organization exists to contribute?" No organization exists simply to deliver customer service alone.

Tips for Implementing Level 4

- At the beginning of any initiative or training program, start by considering the highest-level result your organization is charged with accomplishing. Use this Level 4 Result as your target for any and all efforts in the initiative. If you cannot describe how the intended training would in some way positively affect your overall result or mission, you are not on the right track.

- Every major training initiative should be tied to the highest goals and key directives of the organization. Here are a few ways to discover them:
  - Read the *about us* section of the organization's website.
  - Look at mission and vision statements, as well as what types of messages are posted on the walls of the office.
  - Ask your boss about the highest priorities or directives for each department this quarter or year.
  - If appropriate, request to attend strategy and planning meetings, even if just as an observer to start. Or, ask your boss for a summary of what was discussed.
- Once you are clear on the key initiatives and goals, look at the training programs that are consuming the most time, money, and resources. Is there a direct link between them? If not, re-evaluate whether training resources are being properly allocated.

The Kirkpatrick Foundational Principles

The Kirkpatrick Foundational Principles were developed in 2009, the 50th anniversary of the publication of the works that have become known as the Kirkpatrick Model. Because the Kirkpatrick Model had developed organically over the prior 50 years, cases of misuse and misinterpretation existed. The principles illustrate the meaning that Dr. Kirkpatrick Sr. intended when he published his first works. These are the five Kirkpatrick Foundational Principles:

1. The end is the beginning.
2. Return-on-expectations (ROE) is the ultimate indicator of value.
3. Business partnership is necessary to bring about positive ROE.
4. Value must be created before it can be demonstrated.
5. A compelling chain of evidence demonstrates your bottom-line value.

Kirkpatrick Foundational Principle #1: The End Is the Beginning

Effective training and development begins before the program even starts. Don Kirkpatrick (D.L. Kirkpatrick and J.D. Kirkpatrick, 1993) said it best:

> *Trainers must begin with desired results (Level 4) and then determine what behavior (Level 3) is needed to accomplish them. Then trainers must determine the attitudes, knowledge, and skills (Level 2) that are necessary to bring about the desired behavior(s). The final challenge is to present the training program in a way that enables the participants not only to learn what they need to know but also to react favorably to the program (Level 1).*

Figure 29-4. The End Is the Beginning

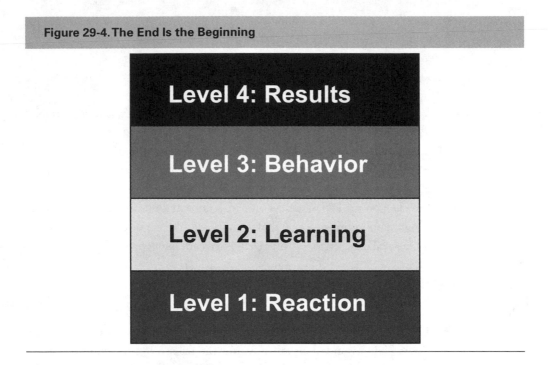

It is important that the results are at the organizational level and are defined in measurable terms so that all involved can see the ultimate destination of the initiative. Clearly defined results will increase the likelihood that resources will be used most effectively and efficiently to accomplish the mission.

Attempting to apply the four levels after an initiative has been developed and delivered makes it difficult, if not impossible, to create significant training value. All four levels must be considered at every step in the program's design, execution, and measurement.

Kirkpatrick Foundational Principle #2: Return-on-Expectations (ROE) Is the Ultimate Indicator of Value

ROE is what a successful training initiative delivers to key business stakeholders demonstrating the degree to which their expectations have been satisfied. When executives ask for new training, many learning professionals retreat to their departments and begin designing and developing suitable programs. While a cursory needs assessment may be conducted, it is rarely taken to the extent to which expectations of the training's contribution to Level 4 Results are completely clear.

Stakeholder expectations define the value that training professionals are responsible for delivering. Learning professionals must ask the stakeholders questions to clarify and refine their expectations on all four Kirkpatrick levels, from leading indicators to the Level 4 Result.

Determining the leading indicators upon which the success of an initiative will be measured is a negotiation process in which the training professional ensures that the expectations are satisfying to the stakeholder and realistic to achieve with the resources available.

Once stakeholder expectations are clear, learning professionals then need to convert those typically general wants into observable, measurable leading indicators by asking the question, "What will success look like to you?" It may take a series of questions to arrive at the final indicators of program success.

Agreement surrounding leading indicators at the beginning of a project eliminates the need to later attempt to prove the value of the initiative. It is understood from the beginning that if the leading indicator targets are met, the initiative will be viewed as a success.

Kirkpatrick Foundational Principle #3: Business Partnership Is Necessary to Bring About Positive ROE

As noted previously, training events in and of themselves typically produce about 15 percent on-the-job application. To increase application and therefore program results, additional actions must be taken before and after formal training.

Historically, the role of learning professionals has been to accomplish Levels 1 and 2, or just to complete the training event alone. Not surprisingly, this is where learning professionals spend most of their time. Producing ROE, however, requires a strong Level 3 execution plan. Therefore, it is critical not only to call on business partners to help identify what success will look like, but also to design a cooperative effort throughout the learning and performance processes to maximize results.

Before training, learning professionals need to partner with supervisors and managers to prepare participants for training. Even more critical is the role of the supervisor or manager after the training. They are the key people who reinforce newly learned knowledge and skills through support and accountability. The degree to which this reinforcement and coaching occur directly correlates to improved performance and positive outcomes.

Kirkpatrick Foundational Principle #4: Value Must Be Created Before It Can Be Demonstrated

Up to 90 percent of training resources are spent on the design, development, and delivery of training events that yield the previously mentioned 15 percent on-the-job application. Reinforcement that occurs after the training event produces the highest level of learning effectiveness, followed by activities that occur before the learning event; yet each typically garners only 5 percent of the training time and budget.

Many learning professionals put most of their resources into the part of the training process that produces the lowest level of business or organizational results. They spend relatively little time in the pretraining and follow-up activities that translate into the positive behavior change and subsequent results (Levels 3 and 4) that organizations seek.

Formal training is the foundation of performance and results. To create ultimate value and ROE, however, practitioners must give strong attention to Level 3 activities. To create maximum value in their organizations, learning professionals must redefine their roles and extend their expertise, involvement, and influence into Levels 3 and 4.

Kirkpatrick Foundational Principle #5: A Compelling Chain of Evidence Demonstrates Your Bottom-Line Value

The training industry is on trial, accused by business leaders of consuming resources in excess of the value delivered to the organization. A chain of evidence includes data, information, and testimonies at each of the four levels that, when presented in sequence, demonstrate the value obtained from a business partnership initiative.

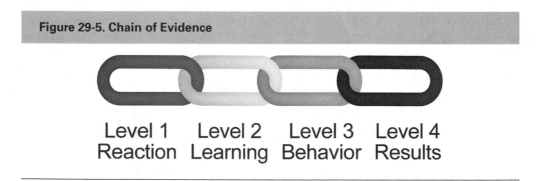

Figure 29-5. Chain of Evidence

Level 1
Reaction

Level 2
Learning

Level 3
Behavior

Level 4
Results

Following the Kirkpatrick Foundational Principles and using the Kirkpatrick Model will create a chain of evidence that demonstrates the organizational value of the entire business partnership effort. It consists of quantitative and qualitative data that sequentially connect the four levels and show the ultimate contribution of learning and reinforcement to the organization.

When workplace learning professionals work in concert with their key business partners, this chain of evidence supports the partnership effort and demonstrates the organizational value of working as a team to accomplish the overall mission. The chain of evidence unifies the learning and business functions. This unity is critical for Level 3 execution, where organizational value is produced.

When presenting a chain of evidence, keep in mind what is most important to the stakeholder audience. Generally speaking, data at Levels 3 and 4 are of most interest. Data related to Levels 1 and 2 should be limited unless a detailed report is requested specifically.

A Message From Don

When I developed the four levels more than five decades ago, I honestly had no idea where it would all go. I am so pleased that they have come far since then. I am officially retired, but that doesn't mean that I have lost interest in where the Kirkpatrick Model is headed.

Over the past several years, I have proudly watched Jim, my son, and Wendy, my daughter-in-law, along with global ambassadors of the New World Kirkpatrick Model, take the four levels to new heights. New applications of the model have occurred in enterprise evaluation, key policies and procedures, and individual goal achievement. Powerful enhancements have been made to each of the levels.

Some have asked me, "Don, are you pleased about the new directions Jim and Wendy are taking the four levels?"

Well, let me save you having to ask. The answer is a resounding yes. Any way the four levels can be applied that will help more people in more powerful ways, I am all for it!

Learn, enjoy, and apply!

—Don Kirkpatrick

Conclusion

The Kirkpatrick Model, when implemented correctly, is an effective and time-tested way to support learning transfer and evaluate training impact on the business. Consider each of the four levels throughout the training design and development process. Determine what information is required to show that the training improved job performance and key organizational results.

For mission-critical initiatives, focus resources on a strong Level 3 implementation plan and a Level 4 tracking and measurement strategy. Use evaluation time, money, and resources sparingly on Levels 1 and 2.

Following these guidelines will maximize your training results and create the most organizational impact with the resources invested. To help you in your efforts, a Hybrid Evaluation Tool Outline has been provided at the *Handbook's* website at www.astdhandbook.org. It gives you sample questions to develop your own hybrid evaluation tool for all four levels.

About the Authors

Jim Kirkpatrick, PhD, is the senior consultant for Kirkpatrick Partners. He is a thought leader in training evaluation and the creator of the New World Kirkpatrick Model. Jim trains and consults for corporate, government, military, and humanitarian organizations around the world. He is passionate about assisting learning professionals in redefining themselves as strategic business partners to remain a viable force in the workplace. Jim has co-authored three books with his father, Dr. Don Kirkpatrick, the creator of the Kirkpatrick Model. Jim can be reached at Jim.kirkpatrick@kirkpatrickpartners.com.

Wendy Kayser Kirkpatrick is the president of Kirkpatrick Partners. She is a certified instructional designer. Wendy draws on two decades of experience in training, retailing, and marketing to make her programs relevant and impactful with measurable results. Wendy can be reached at Wendy.kirkpatrick@kirkpatrickpartners.com.

Jim and Wendy have co-authored three books: *Kirkpatrick Then and Now, Training on Trial,* and *Bringing Business Partnership to Life.* They are proud to have the privilege of carrying on the landmark work of Don Kirkpatrick through their company, Kirkpatrick Partners. They attribute their success to the strong network of Kirkpatrick Community members around the world, who regularly apply the model and inspire them with success stories. Find additional information at www.kirkpatrickpartners.com.

References

ASTD. (2006). *State of the Industry Report.* Alexandria, VA: ASTD Press.

ASTD. (2009). *The Value of Evaluation: Making Training Evaluations More Effective.* Alexandria, VA: ASTD Press.

Brinkerhoff, R.O. (2006). *Telling Training's Story: Evaluation Made Simple, Credible, and Effective.* San Francisco: Berrett-Koehler.

Kirkpatrick, D.L., and J.D. Kirkpatrick. (1993). *Evaluating Training Programs: The Four Levels,* 1st edition. San Francisco: Berrett-Koehler.

For Further Reading

Kirkpatrick, D.L. (2010). *Evaluating Human Relations Programs for Industrial Foremen and Supervisors.* St. Louis: Kirkpatrick Publishing.

Kirkpatrick, D.L., and J.D. Kirkpatrick. (2005). *Transferring Learning to Behavior.* San Francisco: Berrett-Koehler.

Kirkpatrick, J.D., and W.K. Kirkpatrick. (2009). *Kirkpatrick Then and Now.* St. Louis: Kirkpatrick Publishing.

Kirkpatrick, J.D., and W.K. Kirkpatrick. (2010). *Training on Trial.* New York: AMACOM.

Kirkpatrick, J.D., and W.K. Kirkpatrick. (2010, August). ROE's Rising Star. *T+D*, pp. 34-38.

Kirkpatrick, J.D., and W.K. Kirkpatrick. (2013). *Bringing Business Partnership to Life: The Brunei Window Washer.* Newnan, GA: Kirkpatrick Publishing.

Chapter 30

The Basics of Return-on-Investment

Jack J. Phillips and Patti Phillips

················· **In This Chapter** ·················

- Explain ROI Methodology.
- Apply ROI Methodology to demonstrate the value of training and development programs.

" **S** how me the money." There's nothing new about the mantra. Organizations worldwide want to receive value in return for their investments—both the capital investments and the noncapital investments. In fact, about 85 percent of an organization's budget funds noncapital investments, which often places a greater focus on measures of value. These investments include training and development programs and projects. It is these types of programs for which the value contribution is often in question.

When executives call for training and development to show them the money, they are likely calling for ultimate measure of value, or the return-on-investment (ROI). Most organization leaders recognize that value lies in the eye of the beholder; therefore, the method to show the money must balance measures of value important to all stakeholders and generate information to help improve investment decisions. This chapter presents the basics of the ROI Methodology developed by Jack Phillips in the 1970s and initially described in detail in the first U.S. published *Handbook of Training Evaluation and Measurement Methods* (Phillips, 1983). It defines ROI and how to balance ROI with other types of measures. This chapter also describes a proven process for reliably generating six types of data that paint a complete picture of a program's success. It begins by redefining value.

Value Redefined

Do you see the value?

Shannon Ryan has been CEO for UA Mobility for the past year. She has a reputation for being aggressive in meeting goals, yet is pragmatic and fair. In her previous organization, Shannon increased profits and customer satisfaction ratings. In spite of having to reduce staff, there was an increase in employee engagement and the company landed on the national list of best places to work. Shannon is in the process of reorganizing UA Mobility, but before she makes any major decisions, she wants her leadership team to provide evidence of the value each function brings to the organization. Today she is meeting with chief learning officer (CLO) for UAM Academy, Earl Beuford.

Earl always receives rave reviews from participants after each program. He is ready for Shannon and plans to demonstrate to her what UAM Academy is accomplishing.

Shannon enters the room.

SHANNON: Hello, Earl. The place looks great and everyone seems really busy.

EARL: Hi, Shannon. Yes, we have several new programs under development. The last count was 12, primarily focused on soft skills.

SHANNON: Really? What do you mean by soft skills?

EARL: You know—programs such as the new communications program and a leadership development program like the one I attended three months ago. That was a good one. I enjoyed it and think the other managers will enjoy it as well. Oh, and there is the new neuroscience program that should help our coaches better support the managers.

SHANNON: How much time does it take to develop these programs?

EARL: Oh, not long—about a week for each day of training at the most. We have our four program developers working on three programs each. I estimate it will take a few months to develop all 12 programs.

SHANNON: I see.

EARL: Come on in the conference room, Shannon. I want to share our accomplishments thus far!

SHANNON: Great, I'd really like to see.

Earl brings up the Prezi presentation he created and hands Shannon a copy of the infographic describing the data he is about to present.

EARL: In the past nine months, we have developed 10 new programs, offered 750 hours of training, had 1,500 employees attend training, and received an average of 4.5 out of 5 on the program satisfaction rating. So, basically, we have developed new training, and offered some of the new programs as well as some of the old favorites, and the employees attending training seem to think we're moving in the right direction.

SHANNON: How do you know you're adding value?

EARL: Because of the feedback we receive. Many participants tell use they love the content and enjoy the networking opportunities we build into the courses.

SHANNON: How are participants using what they learn?

EARL: Well, we hear from time to time that the courses really meet their expectations and that they perceive the courses to be a valuable use of their time.

SHANNON: Do you have any formal information that describes how they are using what they learn and how it is helping them improve their department's key performance indicators?

EARL: Well, it's not a formal follow-up, but we do try to stay in touch with most of the participants.

SHANNON: I see. Thanks, Earl, for the overview. Let's reconnect next week to discuss more about your value contribution to the organization.

How are Earl's programs adding value?

The Value Shift

Historically, training and development's value was defined by the activity of learning. Training for training's sake was acceptable. Little consideration was given to the benefits of implementing learning activities, leaving those funding the activities with the question: So what?

Today, results reflect the true value of learning. The ultimate result of a learning investment compares the monetary benefits to the program cost, which is called return-on-investment (ROI).

Although the ROI Methodology to "show the money" had its beginnings in the 1970s, it has become the most comprehensive, documented, and applied approach to demonstrating the value of training and development. While many people posit that there is too much focus on economic value and ROI, it is economics, or money, that allows organizations and individuals to contribute to the growth and sustainability of the organization and all that the organization helps support in the community. Monetary resources are limited. We can underuse them, overextend them, or put them to best use. If the latter is the focus of choice, then stakeholders need a way to compare investment opportunities in terms that are meaningful to them. For many stakeholders, ROI provides the best comparison because it puts the benefits of programs in the same terms as the costs, and that is money.

The Show Me Generation

Today's leaders are asking training and development departments to show them value in the same terms as other business units. In the past, when stakeholders asked learning leaders to "show me," it implied that they wanted to see actual input data (that is, numbers, count) to account for program value. But years ago, this approach gave way to quantified measures of value, that is, the monetary value. This requires T&D professionals to convert the benefits of program to money and demonstrate a financial contribution. But, the assumption of making the leap from the program benefits to the monetary value was so great that a new set of stakeholders cried for training and development to show them the real money, meaning that they wanted to see a clear connection between the program and its monetary benefits. This connection requires that the measurement process include a step to isolate the effects of the programs. Today's generation of stakeholders takes the questioning one step further. While demonstrating monetary benefits due to the program is important, the real story only comes out when those monetary benefits are compared to the program costs. Stakeholders of today want training and development to show them the real money and make them believe it. Figure 30-1 illustrates the requirements of the new "show me" generation.

But even with the ultimate financial contribution evident, value must balance financial and nonfinancial as well as quantitative and qualitative data. The data sometimes reflect tactical issues, such as activity, as well as strategic issues, such as ROI. Value must be derived using different timeframes and not necessarily represent a single point in time. It must reflect the value systems that are important to the stakeholders. The data composing value must be collected from credible sources, using cost-effective methods; and value must be action oriented, compelling individuals to make adjustments and changes.

Figure 30-1. The "Show Me" Evolution

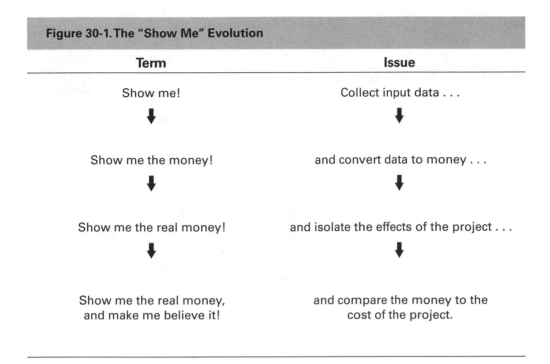

Term	Issue
Show me!	Collect input data . . .
Show me the money!	and convert data to money . . .
Show me the real money!	and isolate the effects of the project . . .
Show me the real money, and make me believe it!	and compare the money to the cost of the project.

The processes used to calculate value must be consistent from one project to another. Standards must be in place so that results can be compared. These standards must support conservative outcomes, leaving assumptions to decision makers. Acronyms most familiar to these decision makers must reflect their true meaning. This includes the financial acronyms with which business decisions are typically made such as those shown in Table 30-1.

Table 30-1. Financial Acronyms All Learning Professionals Should Know

Acronym	Definition	Description
ROI	Return-on-Investment	• Used to evaluate the efficiency or profitability of an investment or to compare the efficiency of a number of investments. • Calculation: Compares the net benefits of an investment by the cost of the investment, expressed as a percentage. • ROI = Net Benefits/Costs
ROE	Return on Equity	• Measures a corporation's profitability by revealing how much profit a company generates with the money shareholders have invested. Used for comparing the profitability of a company to that of other firms in the same industry. • Calculation: Compares net income to shareholder equity. • ROE = Net Income/Shareholder Equity
ROA	Return on Assets	• Compares how profitable a company is to its total assets. Measures how efficient management is at using its assets to generate earnings. • Calculation: Compares net income (annual earnings) to total assets, expressed as a percentage. • ROA = Net Income/Total Assets
ROAE	Return on Average Equity	• Modified version of ROA referring to a company's performance over a fiscal year. • Calculation: Same as ROA except the denominator is changed from total assets to average shareholders' equity, which is computed as the sum of the equity value at the beginning and end of the year divided by two. • ROAE = Net Income/Average Shareholder Equity
ROCE	Return on Capital Employed	• Indicates the efficiency and profitability of a company's capital investments. ROCE should always be higher than the rate at which the company borrows; otherwise any increase in borrowing will reduce shareholders' earnings. • Calculation: Compares earnings before interest and tax (EBIT) to total assets minus current liabilities. • ROCE = EBIT/Total Assets – Current Liabilities
PV	Present Value	• Current worth of a future sum of money or stream of cash flows given a specified rate of return. Important in financial calculations including net present value, bond yields, pension obligations. • Calculation: Divide amount of cash flows (or sum of money) by the interest rate over a period of time. • $PV = C/(1+r)^t$

NPV	Net Present Value	<ul><li>Measures the difference between the present value of cash inflows and the present value of cash outflows. Another way to put it is that it measures the present value of future benefits with the present value of the investment.</li><li>Calculation: Compares the value of a dollar today to the value of that same dollar in the future, taking into account a specified interest rate over a specified period of time.</li><li>$NPV = \sum_{t-1}^{T} (C_t/(1+r)^t) - C_0$</li></ul>
IRR	Internal Rate of Return	<ul><li>Makes the net present value of all cash flows from a particular project equal to zero. Used in capital budgeting. The higher the IRR, the more desirable it is to undertake the process.</li><li>Calculation: Follows the NPV calculation as a function of the rate of return. A rate of return for which this function is zero is the internal rate of return.</li><li>$NPV = \sum_{n=0}^{N} (C_n/(1+r)^n) = 0$</li></ul>
PP	Payback Period	<ul><li>Measures the length of time to recover an investment.</li><li>Calculation: Compare the cost of the project to the annual benefits or annual cash inflows.</li><li>PP = Project Costs/Benefits</li></ul>
BCR	Benefit-Cost Ratio	<ul><li>Used to evaluate potential costs and benefits of a project that may be generated if the project is completed. Used to determine financial feasibility.</li><li>Calculation: Compare project benefits to its costs.</li><li>BCR = Benefits/Costs</li></ul>

Source: Phillips, P.P. (2012). The Bottomline on ROI. *HRDQ*, 9-10.

The ROI Methodology meets all these criteria. It captures six types of data that reflect the issues contained in the new definition of value: reaction and planned action, learning and confidence, application and implementation, impact and consequences, return-on-investment, and intangible benefits. Five key components come together to make this approach work and ensure a sustainable practice of measurement and evaluation. Those five components are:

- evaluation framework
- process model
- operating standards
- case application
- implementation strategy.

Evaluation Framework

The richness of the ROI Methodology is inherent in the types of data monitored during the implementation of a particular program or project. The evaluation framework serves three purposes. First, the framework categorizes evaluation results. This is the most familiar use of the framework to training and development professionals. Second, it is the basis for developing program objectives. Third, it clarifies stakeholder needs.

Evaluation Results

An evaluation framework helps categorize evaluation data to ensure measures are taken from various stakeholder perspectives. This in turn ensures that results that resonate with all stakeholders will be reported, thereby becoming much more useful in decision making than results important to only facilitators and program owners.

Level 0 represents the input to a program and details the numbers of people and hours, the focus, and the cost. These data represent the activity around a program versus the outcomes of the program. Level 0 data represent the scope of the effort, the degree of commitment, and the support for a particular program. For some, this equates to value; however, commitment as defined by expenditures is not evidence that the organization is reaping value. It only reinforces what training and development costs the organization. Level 0 represents the investment in learning.

Reaction and planned action (Level 1) marks the beginning of the program's value stream. Reaction data capture the degree to which participants in the program react favorably or unfavorably. The key is to capture the measures that reflect the content of the program, focusing on issues such as usefulness, relevance, importance, and appropriateness. Data at this level provide the first sign that program success may be achievable. These data also present training and development leaders with information they need to make adjustments in design and delivery to help ensure positive results.

The next level is learning and confidence (Level 2). For every program, there is a learning component. For some, such as programs to implement new technology, systems, competencies, and processes, this component is substantial. For others, such as a new policy or new procedure, learning may be a small part of the process but is still necessary to ensure successful execution. In either case, measurement of learning is essential to success. The focus of measures at this level includes skill, knowledge, competency, confidence, attitude, and awareness. Measures may also reflect the number and quality of contacts met during networking sessions. Getting to know the right people can add big value to efforts attempting to make things happen in an organization.

Application and implementation (Level 3) measures the extent to which participants apply and implement various program components and learning outcomes. Effective implementation is a must if bottom-line value is the goal. This is one of the most important data categories, and most breakdowns occur at this level. Research has consistently shown that in almost half of all training and development programs, participants are not performing at desired levels following solution implementation. Results like these impede the opportunity to generate a positive ROI. Evaluation at the application level involves collecting data about measures such as the extent of new knowledge or information used, task completion, utilization rate, frequency of use of new skills, success with use, and actions completed—as well as barriers and enablers to successful application or on-the-job performance. Data at this level provide a clear picture of how well the organizational system supports the successful transfer of desired knowledge, skills, and attitude changes.

Level 4, business impact, is important for understanding the business consequences of the program. Here, training and development professionals collect data that attract the attention of the sponsor and other executives. This level shows the output, productivity, revenue, quality, time, cost, efficiencies, and level of customer satisfaction connected with the project. For some, this level reflects the ultimate reason the learning program exists: to show the impact within the organization on various groups and systems. Without this level of data, they assert, there is no success. When this level of measurement is achieved, it is necessary to isolate the effects of the program on the specific measures. Without this extra step, alignment with the business cannot occur.

The ROI (Level 5) is calculated next. This shows the monetary benefits of the impact measures compared with the cost of the program. This value is typically stated in terms of either a benefit-cost ratio, the ROI as a percentage, or the payback period. This level of measurement requires two important steps: First, the impact data (Level 4) must be converted to monetary values, and then the cost of the program must be captured.

Along with the five levels of results and the initial level of activity (Level 0), there is a sixth type of data—not a sixth level—developed through the ROI Methodology. This consists of the intangible benefits—those benefits that are not converted to money but nonetheless constitute important measures of success. By collecting data at all levels, program owners can report the full story of program success. Table 30-2 summarizes the levels of evaluation and the areas of focus at each level.

Table 30-2. Levels of Evaluation

Level	Measurement Focus	Typical Measures
0 = Inputs and Indicators	Inputs into the program including indicators representing the scope of the project	• Types of programs • Number of projects • Number of people • Hours of involvement • Cost of projects
1 = Reaction and Planned Action	Reaction of the project including the perceived value of the program	• Relevance • Importance • Usefulness • Appropriateness • Fairness • Motivation
2 = Learning and Confidence	Learning how to use the program, content, materials, and system including the confidence to use what was learned	• Skills • Knowledge • Capacity • Competencies • Confidences • Contacts
3 = Application and Implementation	Use of program content, materials, and system in the work environment including progress with implementation	• Extent of use • Task completion • Frequency of use • Actions completed • Success with use • Barriers to use • Enablers to use
4 = Business Impact	The consequences of the use of the program content, materials, and system expressed as business impact measures	• Productivity • Revenue • Quality • Time • Efficiency • Customer satisfaction • Employee engagement
5 = ROI	Comparison of monetary benefits from project to program costs	• Benefit-cost ratio (BCR) • ROI (%) • Payback period

Program Objectives

Objectives are statements of a program's expected outcomes. They are powerful because they provide direction and focus as well as create interest, commitment, and expectations. Training and development professionals are masters at developing instructional objectives. In recent years, however, the importance of higher levels of objectives has taken hold. These high-level objectives focus on organization needs. High-level objectives define the ultimate success of programs and projects. Additionally, they position programs to achieve that success by serving as a blueprint for designers and developers. They also ease evaluation efforts by identifying the measures to be taken and the criteria for success.

Using the five-level evaluation framework as the framework for developing objectives ensures that a program addresses all stakeholder expectations. As your program meets or exceeds the objectives set, you are by the same token meeting or exceeding stakeholder expectations.

Reaction objectives set an expectation regarding the desired perception participants have of a program. The critical issue with reaction objectives is to ensure you don't elicit behavior that offers a false sense of success. Objectives at the reaction level that focus on content measures and factors that enable the acquisition of knowledge, skill, and information provide some predictive value in terms of potential success with application. While reaction objectives only provide an indicator of what people think about a program and its content, the right objectives that include measures such as relevance, importance, and intent to use the content can provide indicators of potential success on the job.

Learning objectives set the expectations for what participants will learn or know from the content of a program. They may represent measures of knowledge, skill, information, attitude change, and awareness. Learning objectives are important, but they only direct what people will learn, not what they need to do with what they learn. That is the benefit of application objectives.

Application objectives describe what people *will* actually do with the content, information, or skills they gain from a program versus what they *can* do. They set the expectation that action will occur. By establishing application objectives, designers and developers can build into the program activities that relate to real-life use of the content. Facilitators will focus on post-program action discussions. Evaluators will know what questions to ask in a post-program follow-up. But to get to a positive ROI for a program, the issue is not about what people do with what they learn; the bigger issue is the consequence of what people do (or stop doing). This leads to the need for impact objectives.

Objectives at the business impact level tell stakeholders how much improvement will occur in measures of output, quality, cost, and time as well as customer satisfaction, job satisfaction, work habits, and innovation. Objectives at this level keep the ultimate result in mind at all times of the program development, delivery, implementation, and evaluation. But it is only by setting an ROI objective that we measure the extent to which we meet the ultimate expectation.

ROI objectives communicate to stakeholders the confidence that training and development professionals have in their programs and projects. They, along with the other levels of objectives, set the minimally acceptable target for success. Figure 30-2 provides guidelines for setting an ROI target.

Figure 30-2. Setting the ROI Target

There are a number of ways to set the ROI objectives. Four approaches are:

1. Set the ROI at the level of other investments.
2. Set the ROI at a higher standard.
3. Set the ROI at break-even.
4. Set the ROI based on client expectations

Stakeholder Needs

To develop powerful, relevant objectives and ensure your program aligns with organization needs, you must assess those needs. By using the evaluation framework as the basis for your needs assessment, you are ensuring that the right programs are in place, for the right reason, at the right time, involving the right people, at the right price.

As shown in Figure 30-3, stakeholder needs assessment begins with an examination of the potential payoff of solving a problem or taking advantage of a performance improvement opportunity. Is this a problem worth solving, or is the HPT project worthy of implementation? For some situations, the answer is obvious: Yes, the project is worthy because of its critical nature, its relevance to the issue at hand, or its effectiveness in tackling a major problem affecting the organization. A serious customer service problem, for example, is one worth pursuing.

The next step is to ensure that the program is connected to one or more business measures. Here you define the measures that must improve as a reflection of the overall success of the program. Sometimes the measure is obvious; at other times, it is not.

Next, you examine the job performance needs with the question, "What performance must change on the job to influence the business measures previously defined?" This step aligns the program with the business and may involve a series of analytical tools and questions to solve the problem, analyze the cause of the problem, and ensure that the program is connected with business improvement in some way.

After you have determined job performance needs, examine the learning needs by asking, "What specific skills, knowledge, or perceptions must change or improve so that job performance can change?" Every solution involves a learning component of some sort, and this step defines what the participants or users must know to make the program successful. The needed knowledge may be as simple as understanding a policy, or as complicated as learning new competencies.

The final step is to identify the design of the program. What is the best way to present the information to ensure that necessary knowledge, skill, or information will be acquired and job performance will change to solve the business problem? This level of analysis involves issues surrounding the scope, timing, structure, method, and budget for program implementation and delivery.

Figure 30-3. Business Alignment Process: The V-Model

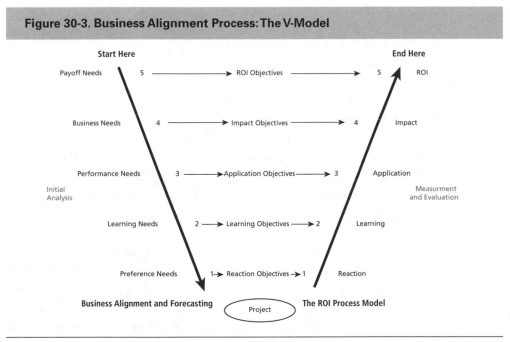

By using the evaluation framework to clarify stakeholder needs, develop program objectives, and evaluate the results of your programs, you will achieve alignment, mitigate risks of failed programs, and measure what matters to the organization.

The ROI Process Model

The next challenge for many program leaders is to collect a variety of data along a chain of impact that shows the project's value. Figure 30-4 displays the sequential steps that lead to data categorized by the five levels of results. This figure shows the ROI Methodology, a step-by-step process beginning with the objectives and concluding with reporting of data. The model assumes that proper analysis is conducted to define the need before the steps are taken.

Evaluation Planning

The first phase of the ROI Methodology is evaluation planning. This phase involves several procedures, including understanding the purpose of the evaluation, planning data collection and analysis, and outlining the details of the project.

Evaluations are conducted for a variety of reasons, such as, to:

- improve the quality of projects and outcomes
- determine whether a project has accomplished its objectives
- identify strengths and weaknesses in the process
- enable the cost-benefit analysis
- assist in the development of marketing projects or programs in the future
- determine whether the project was the appropriate solution
- establish priorities for project funding.

You should consider the purposes of the evaluation before developing the evaluation plan, because the purposes will often determine the scope of the evaluation, the types of instruments used, and the type of data collected. As with any project, understanding the purpose of the evaluation will give it focus and will also help gain support from others.

Three simple planning documents are developed next: the data collection plan, the ROI analysis plan, and the project plan. These documents should be completed during evaluation planning and before the evaluation project is implemented—ideally, before the program is designed or developed. Appropriate up-front attention will save time later when data are actually collected. The ROI Methodology Application Guide in the downloadable tools shows a sample data collection plan, ROI analysis plan, and the ROI project plan.

Data Collection

Data collection is central to the ROI Methodology. Both hard data (representing output, quality, cost, and time) and soft data (including job satisfaction and customer satisfaction) are collected. Data are collected using a variety of methods, including:

- **Surveys** are administered to determine the degrees to which participants are satisfied with the program, have learned skills and knowledge, and have used various aspects of the program. Survey responses are often developed on a sliding scale and usually represent perception data. Surveys are useful for Levels 1 and 2 data.

- **Questionnaires** are usually more detailed than surveys and can be used to uncover a wide variety of data. Participants provide responses to a variety of open-ended and forced response questions. Questionnaires can be used to capture Levels 1, 2, 3, and 4 data.

- **Tests** are conducted to measure changes in knowledge and skills (Level 2). Tests come in a wide variety of formal (criterion-referenced tests, performance tests and simulations, and skill practices) and informal (facilitation assessment, self-assessment, and team assessment) methods.

- On-the-job **observation** captures actual skill application and use. Observations are particularly useful in customer service training and are more effective when the observer is either invisible or transparent. Observations are appropriate for Level 3 data.

- **Interviews** are conducted with participants to determine the extent to which they have used the learning on the job. Interviews allow for probing to uncover specific applications and are usually appropriate with Level 3 data, but can be used with Levels 1 and 2 data.

- **Focus groups** are conducted to determine the degree to which a group of participants has applied the training to job situations. Focus groups are usually appropriate with Level 3 data.

- **Action plans and program assignments** are developed by participants during the training program and are implemented on the job after the program is completed. Follow-ups provide evidence of training program success. Action plans provide Levels 3 and 4 data.

- **Performance contracts** are developed by the participant, the participant's supervisor, and the facilitator who all agree on job performance outcomes from training. Performance contracts are appropriate for both Levels 3 and 4 data.

- **Business performance monitoring** is useful where various performance records and operational data are examined for improvement. This method is particularly useful for Level 4 data.

The important challenge in data collection is to select the method or methods appropriate for the setting and the specific program, within the time and budget constraints of the organization.

Data Analysis

Data analysis includes five specific steps: 1) isolate the effects of the program; 2) convert data to money; 3) tabulate program costs; 4) calculate the ROI; and 5) identify intangible benefits.

Isolate the Effects of the Program

An often-overlooked issue in evaluation is the process of isolating the effects of the program. This step explores specific strategies that determine how much of the business impact is directly related to the program. This step is essential because many systemic factors will influence performance data. The specific strategies of this step pinpoint the amount of improvement directly related to the program, resulting in increased accuracy and credibility of ROI calculations. An organization may use any of the following techniques to tackle this important issue:

- A **control group** is used to isolate training impact. With this strategy, one group receives training, while another similar group does not receive training. The difference in the performance of the two groups is attributed to the training program. When properly set up and implemented, the control group is the most effective way to isolate the effects of training.
- **Trend lines** are used to project the values of specific output variables if training had not been undertaken. The projection is compared to the actual data after training, and the difference represents the estimate of the effect of training. Under certain conditions, this strategy can accurately isolate the training impact.
- When mathematical relationships between input and output variables are known, a **forecasting model** is used to isolate the effects of training. With this approach, the output variable is predicted using the forecasting model with the assumption that no training is conducted. The actual performance of the variable after the training is then compared with the forecasted value, resulting in an estimate of the training impact.
- **Participants estimate** the amount of improvement related to training. With this approach, participants are provided with the total amount of improvement, on a preprogram and post-program basis, and are asked to indicate the percent of the improvement that is actually related to the training program.

- **Supervisors of participants** estimate the impact of training on the output variables. With this approach, supervisors of participants are presented with the total amount of improvement and are asked to indicate the percent related to training.
- **Senior management** estimates the impact of training. In these cases, managers provide an estimate or "adjustment" to reflect the portion of the improvement related to the training program. While perhaps inaccurate, there are some advantages of having senior management involved in this process.
- **Experts** provide estimates of the effect of training on the performance variable. Because the estimates are based on previous experience, the experts must be familiar with the type of training and the specific situation.
- When feasible, **other influencing factors** are identified and the impact is estimated or calculated, leaving the remaining, unexplained improvement attributed to training. In this case, the influence of all the other factors is developed, and training remains the one variable not accounted for in the analysis. The unexplained portion of the output is then attributed to training.
- In some situations, **customers** provide input on the extent to which training has influenced their decision to use a product or service. Although this strategy has limited applications, it can be quite useful in customer service and sales training.

Collectively, these techniques provide a proven, comprehensive set of tools to handle the important and critical issue of isolating the effects of projects.

Convert Data to Monetary Values

To calculate the return-on-investment, business impact data are converted to monetary values and compared with program costs. This requires that a value be placed on each unit of data connected with the program. Many techniques are available to convert data to monetary values. The specific technique selected depends on the type of data and the situation. The techniques include:

- **Output data** are converted to profit contribution or cost savings. In this strategy, output increases are converted to monetary value based on their unit contribution to profit or the unit of cost reduction. Standard values for these items are readily available in most organizations.
- The **cost of quality** is calculated and quality improvements are directly converted to cost savings. Standard values for these items are available in many organizations.
- For programs where employee time is saved, the **participants' wages and employee benefits** are used to develop the value for time. Because a variety of programs focus on improving the time required to complete programs, the value of

time becomes an important and necessary issue. This is a standard formula in most organizations.

- **Historical costs**, developed from cost statements, are used when they are available for a specific variable. In this case, organizational cost data establishes the specific monetary cost savings of an improvement.

- When available, **internal and external experts** estimate a value for an improvement. In this situation, the credibility of the estimate hinges on the expertise and reputation of the individual.

- **External databases** are sometimes available to estimate the value or cost of data items. Research, government, and industry databases can provide important information for these values. The difficulty lies in finding a specific database related to the situation.

- **Participants** estimate the value of the data item. For this approach to be effective, participants must be capable of providing a value for the improvement.

- **Supervisors and managers** provide estimates when they are both willing and capable of assigning values to the improvement. This approach is especially useful when participants are not fully capable of providing this input or in situations where supervisors need to confirm or adjust the participant's estimate. This approach is particularly helpful to establish values for performance measures that are important to senior management.

- **Soft measures are linked mathematically to other measures** that are easier to measure and value. This approach is particularly helpful when establishing values for measures that are difficult to convert to monetary values, such as data often considered intangible, like customer satisfaction, employee satisfaction, grievances, and employee complaints.

- **Staff estimates** may be used to determine a value of an output data item. In these cases, it is essential for the estimates to be provided without bias.

This step in the ROI model is important and absolutely necessary in determining the monetary benefits of a program or solution implementation. The process is challenging, particularly with soft data, but can be methodically accomplished using one or more of these strategies.

Tabulate Program Costs

An important part of the ROI equation is the calculation of program costs. Tabulating the costs involves monitoring or developing all the related costs of the program targeted for the ROI calculation. Among the cost components to be included are:

- initial analysis costs (usually prorated)
- cost to design and develop the program
- cost of all program materials
- costs for the training and development team (for example, facilitator, coordinator)
- cost of the facilities
- travel, lodging, and meal costs for the participants and team members
- participants' salaries (including employee benefits) for the time involved in the program
- administrative and overhead costs, allocated in some convenient way
- evaluation costs.

The conservative approach is to include all these costs so that the total is fully loaded.

Calculate the Return-on-Investment

The return-on-investment is calculated using the program benefits and costs. The benefit-cost ratio (BCR) is calculated as the program benefits divided by the program costs.

$$BCR = \frac{\text{Program benefits}}{\text{Program costs}}$$

The return-on-investment is based on the net benefits divided by program costs. The net benefits are calculated as the program benefits minus the project costs. In formula form, the ROI becomes

$$ROI \text{ (percent)} = \frac{\text{Net program benefits}}{\text{Program costs}} \times 100$$

This is the same basic formula used in evaluating other investments in which the ROI is traditionally reported as earnings divided by investment.

Identify Intangible Benefits

While all program benefits can be converted to money, it may be that the cost and the reliability of the data conversion technique prohibit us from doing so. If that is the case, the improvement in impact measures is reported as intangible benefits. Intangible benefits are Level 4 business impact measures that we choose not to convert to money. This does not mean they are less important than the ROI. On the contrary, for some programs intangible benefits hold just as much importance and balance the outcomes to help tell the complete story of program success. Intangible benefits may include items such as:

- increased job satisfaction
- increased organizational commitment
- improved teamwork
- improved customer service
- fewer complaints
- reduced conflict.

Reporting

The final step in the ROI process model is reporting results, a critical step that often lacks the attention and planning required for success. The reporting step involves developing appropriate information in impact studies and other brief reports. At the heart of this step are the different techniques used to communicate to a wide variety of target audiences. In most ROI studies, several audiences are interested in and need the information. Careful planning to match the communication method with the audience is essential to ensure that the message is understood and that appropriate actions follow.

Figure 30-4. ROI Methodology Process Model

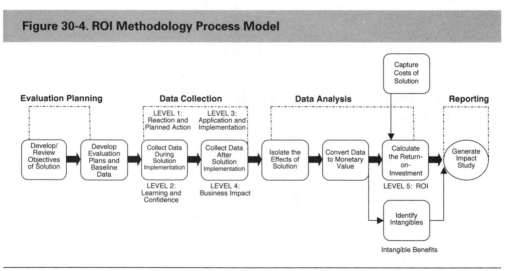

Operating Standards

Operating standards ensure consistency and replication of ROI studies. They serve as the decision-making rules that support implementation of the ROI process model. Based on sound research practices, 12 guiding principles ensure that evaluation results are valid and credible. Results of a study must stand alone and must not vary with the individual who is conducting the study. The operating standards detail how each step and issue of the process will be handled. The sidebar shows the 12 guiding principles that form the basis for the ROI Methodology operating standards.

---

12 Guiding Principles of ROI

1. When conducting a higher-level evaluation, collect data at lower levels.
2. When planning a higher-level evaluation, the previous level of evaluation is not required to be comprehensive.
3. When collecting and analyzing data, use only the most credible sources.
4. When analyzing data, select the most conservative alternative for calculations.
5. Use at least one method to isolate the effects of a project.
6. If no improvement data are available for a population or from a specific source, assume that little or no improvement has occurred.
7. Adjust estimates of improvement for potential errors of estimation.
8. Avoid use of extreme data items and unsupported claims when calculating ROI.
9. Use only the first year of annual benefits in ROI analysis of short-term solutions.
10. Fully load all costs of a solution, project, or program when analyzing ROI.
11. Intangible measures are defined as measures that are purposely not converted to monetary values.
12. Communicate the results of ROI methodology to all key stakeholders.

Case Application

Processes are only useful when they are put to use. A good theory is just a theory until it is applied. That is why so much effort has been put into publishing a variety of examples of the application of the ROI Methodology. Many of the case studies present first-time attempts at application; others demonstrate more advanced applications. In either respect, it is through the implementation of the process that training and development can demonstrate the value their programs bring.

Case studies tell a story using a balanced set of data; they show the results and tell how they came to be. Most important, the actual impact studies provide information that is useful in improving programs and processes. Evaluation without communication is useless—development of case studies puts good evaluation to use. You will find one of our favorite case studies, Nations Hotel, in the downloadable tools. This case study demonstrates how action plans were used to capture Level 4 impact data for an executive coaching initiative and the resulting ROI.

Implementation Strategy

To date, there are more than 7,000 individuals certified in the ROI Methodology. This excludes the thousands who have attended one-day and two-day workshops and those who are applying the process with support of books and other resources. The success of the ROI Methodology rests with the efforts of practitioners to implement and sustain this methodology. A variety of environmental issues and events will influence the successful implementation of the ROI evaluation process. That is why it is important to develop a strategy that addresses issues that can deter or support good implementation. These issues must be addressed early with specific topics or actions, including:

- a policy statement concerning a results-based program approved for training and development
- procedures and guidelines for different elements and techniques of the evaluation process
- formal effort to develop staff skills with the ROI process
- strategies to improve management commitment to and support for the ROI process
- mechanisms to provide technical support for instrument design, data analysis, and evaluation strategy
- specific techniques to place more attention on results.

Besides implementing and sustaining ROI use, the process must undergo periodic review. An annual review is recommended to determine the extent to which the process is adding value. This final element involves checking satisfaction with the process, and determining how well it is understood and applied. Essentially, this review follows an assessment with the five levels of data, including the ROI on the ROI.

Final Thoughts

The evaluation methodology presented here has been used consistently and routinely by thousands of organizations in the past decade. In some fields and industries, it has been more prominent than in others. Much has been learned about the success of this methodology and what it can bring to the organizations using it. It works because it provides a balanced set of measures and follows a step-by-step process. It bridges evaluation disciplines and balances research and reality. The process is flexible and presents a credible approach to developing data that stakeholders need. The key to remember is that while any program can be evaluated, not all should necessarily be evaluated to impact and ROI. Investment in evaluation is relative to investment in a program. On the *Handbook's* website, you will find a tool that lists the criteria for selecting programs for evaluation up to Level 4 business impact and Level 5 ROI. When you end this chapter, take inventory of your programs and identify how many are candidates for ROI.

To learn more about the ROI Methodology, download the tools provided with this *Handbook's* website at www.astdhandbook.org. You can also visit our website at www.roiinstitute.net.

About the Authors

Jack J. Phillips, PhD, is a world-renowned expert on accountability, measurement, and evaluation. Phillips provides consulting services for Fortune 500 companies and major global organizations. The author or editor of more than 50 books, he conducts workshops and presents at conferences throughout the world. His expertise in measurement and evaluation is based on more than 27 years of corporate experience in the aerospace, textile, metals, construction materials, and banking industries. Dr. Phillips has served as training and development manager at two Fortune 500 firms, as senior human resource officer at two firms, as president of a regional bank, and as management professor at a major state university. He is chairman of the ROI Institute, Inc., and you can reach him at jack@roiinstitute.net.

Patti Phillips, PhD, is president and CEO of the ROI Institute, Inc. A renowned expert in measurement and evaluation, she helps organizations implement the ROI Methodology in over 50 countries. She serves as Distinguished Principal Research Fellow for the Conference Board, as faculty on the UN System Staff College in Turin, Italy, and as Professor of Practice at the University of Southern Mississippi. She, along with her husband Jack Phillips, contributes to a variety of journals and has authored a number of books on the subject of accountability and ROI. In 2012, they celebrated their 40th title with ASTD. You can reach Patti at patti@roiinstitute.net.

References

Phillips, J.J. (1983). *Handbook of Training Evaluation and Measurement Methods*. Houston: Gulf Publishing.

For Further Reading

Phillips, J.J., and P.P. Phillips. (2007). *Show Me the Money: How to Determine ROI in People, Projects, and Programs*. San Francisco: Berrett-Koehler.

Phillips, J.J., and P.P. Phillips (2008). *Beyond Learning Objectives: Develop Measurable Objectives That Link to the Bottom Line*. Alexandria, VA: ASTD Press.

Phillips, P.P. (2012). *The Bottomline on ROI*. Prussia, PA: HRDQ.

Phillips, P.P., and J.J. Phillips (2007). *The Value of Learning: How Organizations Capture Value and ROI*. San Francisco: Pfeiffer.

Phillips, P.P., and Phillips, J.J. (2012). *10 Steps to Successful Business Alignment*. Alexandria, VA: ASTD Press.

Phillips, P.P., and J.J. Phillips (eds.). (2012) *Measuring ROI in Learning and Development: Case Studies From Global Organizations*. Alexandria, VA: ASTD Press.

Chapter 31

Building the Learning Transfer Competence of Participants

Calhoun Wick and Katherine Granger

·· **In This Chapter** ··

- ▉ Discuss eight ways to build training program participants' competence to transfer what they learn to work.
- ▉ Learn specific actions to help participants improve their capabilities, performance, and the business results.

We believe learning transfer is the key to creating value in training and development programs. Until participants actually transfer and apply what they learn in their work, the training has little value. Value is created when participants build new skills or use new knowledge in ways that lead to improved performance. When they do, participants experience the pride of accomplishment and their business benefits from improved results.

The core question in learning transfer is how to get participants to take action on what they learn in a way that improves their performance. Our research shows that a key element to activate learning transfer has been right before our eyes, but is one that training and development professionals have not clearly articulated and acted upon. That element is to turn participants into initiators of their own behavior change, rather than being passive recipients of content.

T&D professionals sometimes talk about "making learning stick." But making learning stick is not enough for successful learning transfer to occur. The fact that participants remember what they learned is not enough to ensure that they will put it into action in a way that improves performance. A better definition is contained in *The Six Disciplines of Breakthrough Learning* (Wick, Pollock, and Jefferson, 2010), which defines learning transfer as "the process of putting learning to work in a way that improves performance." To improve performance takes more than just knowing something, no matter how sticky the learning. Instead, "know-how," "know-do," and even "know-done" are all required if improved performance is to be accomplished.

This chapter will make the case that we need to increase the competence of participants to effectively transfer their learning. *Competence* is a powerful word. *Webster's* defines competence as "the ability to do something successfully or efficiently." Thus, if learning transfer is to be realized, participants need the ability to apply new learning to their work successfully and efficiently.

This chapter presents eight ways to build the competence of participants in your training programs to transfer what they learn to work. It will provide you with specific actions to help participants take what they learn and apply it in ways that improve their capabilities, performance, and the business results of your organization.

Eight Ways to Build Learning Transfer Competence

Ensuring that your learners apply what they learn is critical. These eight ways show you how to improve learners' competencies and performance.

1. Change the Mental Model to Learn, Apply, and Achieve

The first step to improving participant learning transfer competence is to change the mental model with which they approach learning. The current mental model for corporate learning is that when participants attend a learning program or take an e-learning module, they see the course itself as the finish line. It's a model of "learn and leave" rather than "learn, apply, and achieve."

Put in the context of a college academic setting, most corporate learning programs are classes to be "audited." Credit is given for just showing up. Most often there is little expectation on the part of participants that they will apply what they learn. Even more seldom do they attend with any expectations of needing to produce improved results by applying what they learn in their work.

We first discovered this many years ago at an executive development program delivered by an Ivy League university faculty. Toward the end of the program we asked those attending, "What percent of your classmates do you think will apply what they learned during this program in a way that will improve their results?" Their answers ranged from 3 to 40 percent.

Here was a group of high-level leaders attending an expensive, time-consuming leadership program—and most of them were operating under the mental model of "learn and leave" rather than "learn, apply, and achieve."

2. Contract Early to Apply Rather Than Just Attend

Rocky Kimball of Action Learning Associates said it best: "We need to be up front with our participants from the very beginning about what we expect from them. If we are going to expect that they will put to work what they learn and that improved performance is the deliverable, then we need to be explicit about this from the very beginning."

This contract needs to be clear about the kind of actions we want participants to take, the kind of results we want them to achieve, and the timeframe to accomplish both. Done correctly, this contracting can be quite motivating because participants can see the value that can be delivered as a result of their efforts.

This contract needs to be communicated *before* the formal learning—during the preprogram preparation phase—to participants and their managers. By doing so, you avoid the tension of participants being blindsided in the class with the expectation that they will apply new skills and achieve results.

We have seen the danger of not completing this contracting process before a program begins. For example, a senior-level group from a Fortune 50 company was attending a weeklong leadership development program with many expensive outside speakers in a posh location. At the end of the program, the facilitators moved to the final item on the agenda, which was to have participants write post-program action goals that they were to accomplish when they returned to their work. The goals were to reflect key competencies taught in the program and describe specific application in their leadership roles. The facilitators also said that the participants would be accountable for documenting the results and improvements that they accomplished.

Since neither application nor accountability for the delivery of results had been "contracted for" as part of the course setup, there was open rebellion by the participants. One senior leader stood up and said he would not do the goal setting because he had not "signed on" for anything after the week was over and that he would be too busy to do so. A second leader said post-program accountability was not going to happen, because their job as senior leaders was to hold others accountable, not be held accountable themselves. Those were the final words spoken before these participants packed up their program binders and walked out the door.

In addition to heading off a participant rebellion, effective contracting before the course has an added benefit. When the participants arrive knowing that application and achievement are part of their deliverables, they show up with a different level of commitment because they know they soon will have to take action on what they learn. The new contract causes participants to be far more than passive listeners. Instead they will be active learners who make multiple connections between what they experience in the program and what they do on the job.

The contract can be made more explicit by changing the finish line for a course. Glenn Hughes, senior director of Global Learning at KLA-Tencor, has changed the point at which participants get credit for participating in a learning program. Instead, of giving credit for showing up at the program, credit is only given once a participant is able to document the improved performance the course was designed to achieve. This makes very clear to participants that the learning contract includes both application and results.

3. Articulate the Program Outcome Goal

We need to clearly communicate with participants the improved performance they are expected to achieve by applying what they learn during their program. There are two approaches to creating strong program goals.

The best approach is to have the learning leader, or program manager, work closely with the line leader or sponsor to identify the desired business outcomes of the program. We call these "program outcome goals." They are based on "defining business outcomes," the first discipline in the learning design methodology of the *Six Disciplines of Breakthrough Learning*. The entire learning process begins by identifying the specific business needs that a learning initiative will address. Using what they call the Outcomes Planning Wheel™ (a four-step questioning process), the second step is to identify what participants will do better and differently in their work as a result of putting new learning into practice. This becomes the basis of a strong goal.

The challenge for the learning leader is to visualize the kind of application opportunities participants may have in their work, the kind of progress they can make, and results they can achieve within a specific timeframe. With this information, the learning leader can articulate a program outcome goal that can be shared with all participants. Here are two examples:

- By <date>, participants will apply new skills and planning tools from the Project Management Program by taking different and better action on their business projects and documenting at least two positive new milestones reached by doing so.
- By <date>, participants will use the concepts, models, and processes they learn in the Conversation Skills course with at least three people, get feedback from at least two people on ideas for improvement, and share an example of how the use of this learning enabled a better outcome.

The alternative approach is for participants to define goals that will be valuable to them and their business. The best outcome goals are those where participants can see immediate application for the learning in a way that addresses a need or challenge they want to address in their work. A key success factor is crafting a goal that has the right amount of stretch. A strong goal will challenge the participant to take both different and better action in their work and have the right scope so that it can be accomplished within a specified time (for example, 60, 90, or 120 days).

If you choose the second option, having participants write their own goals, you will need to provide two things for them. First, give them time to write strong, thoughtful, and effective goals. Writing valuable goals is more than a five-minute exercise as participants are about to walk out the door or complete an e-learning module. Most important, such goal setting needs to be done while the formal learning is taking place. People are too busy to write learning goals when they return to their work, especially since the emotional energy of goal setting is lost when the formal learning is over.

Another strategy to improve goal setting is to give participants examples of strong, challenging goals for their program. The first time a course is given, you can provide examples that you write. In repeating courses, you can share best-in-class examples of goals that participants have written in earlier sessions to apply what they learn. Here are two examples.

- By <date>, I will use new delegation skills from our management development program in my job by giving work currently on my plate to at least four other people so that I save myself five hours per week. I will use this time to focus on higher-value management tasks while providing others the opportunity to grow by taking on more challenging work. I also will give my manager a write-up describing at least one benefit to myself and one to our business by delegating more effectively.

- During the next 60 days, I will apply learning from our consultative selling course by putting it to work with two renewing customers and two new customers. I will prepare for meetings using the precall planning process we learned. I will take notes and reflect on my successes, problems, and questions after each sales call. My goal is to close one new account and renew one account in 60 days using these new skills effectively.

Takeaways From the Eight Ways to Build Learning Transfer Competence

1. Move from "Learn and Leave" to "Learn, Apply, and Achieve."

2. Move from a contract of "Credit for Showing Up" to "Credit for Achievement."

3. Move from "Goals Left to Chance" to "Goals That Deliver Desired Outcomes."

4. Move from "Ad Hoc Action" to "Strategic, Intentional Application."

5. Move from "Guessing What Success Looks Like" to "Providing Compelling Examples."

6. Move from "Blind to Opportunities" to "Seeing Many Valuable Opportunities."

7. Move from "Go It Alone" to "Recruit a Coaching Team."

8. Move from "Success Not Communicated" to "Success Shared."

---

4. Give Strategies to Link Learning and Work

When participants leave a training program, often with the best of intentions, they rarely have a clear strategy of exactly how to link what they have learned during the program to their work. They may have written an action plan, goals, or notes in their learning journal, but they often lack specific steps they can take immediately upon returning to their jobs. As a learning professional, you can provide participants with two strategies to link work and learning.

The first strategy is to recommend participants identify specific skills or knowledge in the program that they are energized to test out and put to work. Then have them look for opportunities in their work to use it to achieve the program outcome goal.

The second strategy is to have participants identify improvement opportunities they are energized to address on the job that are aligned with the program outcome goal. Then have participants identify what learning from the program can best accomplish this improvement.

Each of these strategies will build the competence of participants during their program to learn how to link what they are learning to their work. This is a great way to overcome what Teresa Roche, the chief learning officer of Agilent Technologies, sees as a major challenge in corporate learning: that many participants see learning as *apart from work* rather than *a part of work*.

5. Provide Examples of Success

An underutilized opportunity to improve the competence of participants is to share success stories from people in earlier programs. This has the benefit of teaching participants what success looks like and how to achieve success in a similar work environment.

An inventive use of this technique is evident at Emory University. On the website that presents the course catalog of its internal leadership programs, Emory's learning leader Wanda Hayes posts video case studies of past participants in each program. The participants talk about what they learned, how they used it in their work, and what results they accomplished postcourse. The inclusion of these videos communicates many important things to future participants. First, before the participants ever go to a program, they already know there is an expectation for application and effort. They see that colleagues who attended before them have achieved valuable results on the job. Many will see the kind of results they would like to accomplish as well. This gives participants a visual demonstration of the learning transfer competence in action.

Kimberly-Clark used an alternative in a leadership development program when the success of a participant who was a plant manager in one program was then presented in a classroom situation to participants who came later. Appearing in the January 2013 issue of *T+D*, the story told by the plant manager who attended a course on how to create a culture of accountability went like this:

I came into work the day after our plant had laid off 25 percent of the workforce. At the time, our costs were 10 to 20 percent higher than our competitors. For the first half hour, I listened to all the reasons why the leaders at the mill were victims. At that point, I told our leaders that we would not be able to control our destiny unless we stopped being victims. We needed to start seeing the problems, owning them, and doing something about them. I had the same exact conversation with the entire mill three days later.

Fast forward to today. We have already saved $3 million in less than one year—making us not only far more competitive, but also an industry leader. We have adopted a tag line of "Everyone in it to win it," and it's making a difference in how people act, think, and even feel. We are stronger, and by sharing daily success stories from every level of the organization, we're driving better results.

For me personally, without the culture of accountability training, and more important, being a role model, champion, and getting tough feedback, I would not be as successful in leading this transformation.

A third alternative is to share success stories with participants once they have left the formal learning program and have returned to work. These examples, sent via email, can cue participants with examples of actions they might be able to take as well. These stories can be sent to participants in a spaced learning fashion to reinforce program content and outcomes as participants are working through their own on-the-job change processes.

6. Show Where to Apply and How to Apply

A characteristic of participants who have a strong learning transfer competence is their ability to see opportunities for where and how to apply what they learn in their work. Here is an example:

A manager attended a one-day program on how to design and deliver more effective presentations. The focus of the course was on how he as an individual could use what he learned to improve the presentations he would deliver in the future. Instead of using what he learned to improve his own presentations, he went back to his team and taught them what he had learned, because in a week they were leaving for Korea to make a pitch to secure $40 million in new business. This manager had his team tear up the presentation they had planned to make and completely rewrite the presentation using the new approach he just learned. The new presentation was so strong that he said it saved his team two further trips to Korea to secure the business.

This example shows the three elements most often used by participants who are successful in putting what they learn to work in a way that improves their performance:

- They use their imagination to identify where the learning might be most valuable in their work, even if it goes beyond the bounds of the intent of the course.
- They teach others. They use what they learned to create value for others.
- They move from learning application as "make work" to "make work better."

Here are two ways to build the competence of where to apply and how to apply learning:

- Before the formal learning begins, in the precourse communications, ask participants to bring to the session specific priority work challenges they have that have the potential to be solved by what they learn. This way, they can be on the lookout for application opportunities that will create real value.
- During the formal learning program, stop from time to time to ask participants how they could apply what they just learned. There are several ways to create an engaging process to do this. Participants could meet in triads, pool their best answers, and do shout-outs with their recommendations. Or put everyone on the spot by tossing a ball to a participant and asking them to share how they might use what they just learned. That participant then tosses the ball to another participant and so on. In such a lightning round, four or five ideas can be shared in just a few minutes.

In e-learning, the design can include a question asking participants to identify how they might use what they just learned and provide an example.

7. Teach Participants How to Select Coaches

The application of learning is not an individual sport. It is a team sport. Participants who make the fastest and best progress are those who know how to reach out to others in the organization to help them. There are several types of people who can be most valuable to participants as they apply new learning.

- People who have real expertise using the skills and knowledge taught during a program. These subject matter experts can provide guidance in terms of how participants can apply similar learning in their particular situations. Examples of such subject matter experts could be people designated in call centers, manufacturing groups, or on sales teams as highly proficient in specific processes or techniques.

- People whose judgment participants trust and who can provide encouragement and support as they apply what they learn in a safe environment.
- Colleagues in the program can agree to peer coach each other to share their own experiences and offer ideas and feedback to their learning partners.
- Managers of participants are a particularly important coaching resource. Research shows that when managers are engaged in coaching, their direct reports make greater progress and are seen as more successful by their managers and others in the organization.

This is particularly true when participants engage their managers before the learning program even starts. What a great benefit for participants to be seen as having achieved higher performance and creating greater value in the eyes of their managers when it comes time for an annual performance review.

8. Equip Participants to Share a Success Story

If the whole purpose of the learning application process is to achieve a valuable outcome that benefits the participant and the business, then it is important that participants have an easy, effective way to share what they have accomplished. Sharing their success can benefit participants in several ways. It can give them a way to communicate positive change and outcomes with their managers at the end of the program. At the time of an annual performance review, the success story demonstrates the value they created out of the investment the company made in their development. Sharing a success story can provide an easy way to say thank you to a coach or supporter who helped them reach their achievement.

Success stories written by participants can be used by the learning organization in multiple ways. The stories can become effective teaching tools in future programs to communicate the kinds of outcomes that are possible when participants apply new skills and knowledge to create valuable results. The success stories can become the best testimonials for the learning organization to share the return on learning investment made by senior management.

A simple way to craft a success story is for participants to answer a question such as: "Can you share an example of the learning that you applied in your work, where you applied it, how your performance improved, and the benefits to you and your business?" Participants can respond to you via email and you can consolidate and share the best stories, anonymously, with the group.

If writing and submitting success stories is not a manageable process, another option is to have an in-person or virtual reconvene session with participants at some point after the program (for example, 60, 90, or 120 days). You can invite the participants and their managers to attend, and the "price of admission" is the success story that each person shares with the group.

Reconvening is an excellent way for participants to showcase their accomplishments with their managers, peers, and other leaders in the organization. It also enables you as the learning leader to highlight the business impact of the program you delivered to your internal clients and sponsors. It truly is a win for everyone involved.

The eight ways to build learning transfer competence can be used during design as well as delivery. A checklist of the eight ways can be downloaded on the *Handbook's* website at www.astdhandbook.org.

Equip Participants With Competence

The exciting opportunity for learning leaders is to design and deliver learning initiatives that teach competence as well as content. The new standard of excellence includes equipping participants to successfully and efficiently apply what they learn in their work immediately after the program. The payoff for participants is improved performance. The payoff for the company is improved results. And the payoff for the learning organization is to be recognized as the value-creating engine of the organization.

About the Authors

Calhoun Wick is the founder of the Fort Hill Company; co-author of *Six Disciplines of Breakthrough Learning*; inventor of ResultsEngine®, which is the first web-based learning transfer support system; and a passionate advocate for participants to put learning to work in ways that improve performance.

Katherine Granger, executive vice president of Fort Hill Company, has spent the last decade supporting successful learning transfer projects with a diverse global client base. Her thought leadership has contributed to significant improvements in how clients prepare and support their participants to apply their learning, as well as in the core functionality of ResultsEngine. With more than 25 years in the learning and development industry, she brings an experienced and pragmatic focus to her external client work and internal leadership of the Fort Hill Client Solutions team.

For Further Reading

Colvin, G. (2008). *Talent Is Overrated: What Really Separates World-Class Performers From Everybody Else.* New York: Penguin.

Coyle, D. (2009). *The Talent Code. Greatness Isn't Born. It's Grown. Here's How.* New York: Bantam Dell.

Lemov, D., E. Woolway, and K. Yezzi. (2012). *Practice Perfect. 42 Rules for Getting Better at Getting Better.* San Francisco: Jossey-Bass.

Wick, C., R. Pollock, and A. Jefferson. (2010). *The Six Disciplines of Breakthrough Learning: How to Turn Training and Development Into Business Results.* San Francisco: Pfeiffer.

Chapter 32

Linking Learning to Performance

Paul Elliott

······················· **In This Chapter** ·······················

- ▦ Create profiles of exemplary performers (PEP).
- ▦ Discuss how to link learning to performance.
- ▦ Optimize the link between training and performance.

A n underlying assumption held by the majority of learning professionals is that it is difficult, if not impossible, to demonstrate a definitive link between learning and performance. The problem is that most efforts to show the relationship attempt to do it retroactively. The training is designed, perhaps even developed, and then people ask the question, "How can we demonstrate the program's effect on key business metrics?" The fallacy with this approach is that the link between knowledge and performance can never be demonstrated retroactively.

Learning vs. Accomplishment

Thomas Gilbert (1978/1996) argued for a shift in focus in order to produce effective performance improvement; focus on what people *produce* in the work environment, not simply on what they *know* or *do*. Helping workers perform tasks more efficiently that don't produce the desired accomplishments won't improve a company's business results. Instead, you need to focus on and identify what a worker's major accomplishments are up front, and then determine how those accomplishments contribute to the company's business goals. Once you have this information, you can determine the tasks and support systems needed for workers to produce those accomplishments with a high level of competence and confidence.

Figure 32-1 illustrates Gilbert's point. The arrows that form the star on the left (the first column) represent what organizations provide to support individuals or teams in their performance. The next column represents the actions or tasks that individuals execute based on those influences. The third column represents the accomplishments or results that are produced as a result of the actions. The column on the far right represents the goals that are supported by those accomplishments or results. When we think about performance, we see the process unfolding from left to right.

Figure 32-1. Linking Exemplary Performance to Business Goals

PERFORMANCE UNFOLDS LEFT TO RIGHT

Influences	Job Behaviors	Job Outputs	Business Goal
✓ Expectations and Feedback	✓ Measuring Performance Against Plan	✓ Territory Plan and Scorecard	✓ Client Retention
✓ Rewards, Recognition, and Consequences	✓ Finding Qualified Leads	✓ Accurate/Compliant Admin. of Accounts	✓ Assets Under Management
✓ Motivations and Preferences	✓ Reaffirming Client Goals and Risk Tolerance	✓ Assets Allocations Aligned With Client Goals	✓ Time to Competence
✓ Skills and Knowledge			
✓ Capacity and Job Fit			
✓ Environments, Systems, and Resources			

ANALYZE PERFORMANCE RIGHT TO LEFT

However, if the purpose of your training is to improve performance, the analysis must proceed from right to left. By starting with the goals or strategy of the organization, you begin the process with a focus on which accomplishments are most critical to produce in order to achieve the organization's strategy and goals. This knowledge enables you to capture the critical tasks required to produce those accomplishments as well as identify the actions and activities that are not contributing directly to the desired results.

Thomas F. Gilbert

Thomas F. Gilbert is widely considered to be the father of human performance technology (HPT). Although close friends with B.F. Skinner, he came to believe that people should be judged by their accomplishments, not by the behavior they exhibit.

In his seminal book, *Human Competence: Engineering Worthy Performance* (1978), Gilbert developed a behavior engineering model that sought to define the barriers between individual and organizational performance. The model identifies three environmental factors (data, resources, motivation) and three human behavior factors (knowledge, capacity, and motives). Each of these factors can either contribute to or hinder an employee's productivity. Gilbert's model is significant because it identifies factors outside the individual that affect performance.

Another of Gilbert's major contributions to the field is his performance equation; he reasoned that "worthy" performance *(W)* is a function of the ratio between valuable accomplishment *(A)* and costly behavior *(B)*. The function reads $W = A/B$.

In 1996, the International Society for Performance Improvement named an award after Gilbert, the "Thomas F. Gilbert Distinguished Professional Achievement Award," which recognizes significant contributions to the field of human performance.

Leveraging Your Star Performers

When linking learning to performance, whose performance do you want to replicate? Which individuals or teams are consistently producing valued outputs at or above standard? The most effective and efficient way to capture expertise is to work with your existing accomplished performers—your internal benchmarks. These are the individuals who have established approaches to their work that produce the desired accomplishments at a consistently high level. They are often unconsciously competent, and so you will need to capture their expertise in a way that makes it explicit and transferable to other team members.

The process we use for capturing the exemplar's expertise is based on our work with hundreds of clients across multiple industries; the process must be context intensive and case based. For example, if you're working with a sales team that consistently wins competitive displacements, it's best to ask them to walk you through several recent wins in a detailed and methodical way. The questioning should address every step in the process, from the identification of the opportunity to closing the sale to full implementation of the product or service.

Capturing the expertise of high performers in your organization provides a rich repository of information that describes optimal work performance. We call this the profile of exemplary performance (PEP). The information in the PEP is useful to design and implement a wide range of performance interventions. You can think of the PEP as the DNA of your exemplars.

The PEP data includes such information as the accomplishments produced by the particular role or team, the success criteria for those accomplishments, the key activities or tasks that produce the accomplishments, and system facilitators and barriers that the stars have discovered.

Begin With the End in Mind

You can never link learning to performance unless you begin with the end in mind. You must take an accomplishment-based approach in defining the outcomes that will reflect business impact before beginning any other part of the analysis to determine the need for training.

- Generic training simply doesn't transfer.
- Context-intensive design is essential.
- There is always a transfer of training to performance when the training is linked directly to the job results for which the participants are accountable. Why? There is high relevancy.
- And, quite frankly, you will never be given credit for having a business impact after the fact if it wasn't defined before the initiation of the project.

Beginning with the end goal provides you with the information needed to analyze what intervention is required in order to affect performance. Well-designed training is an effective and efficient tool for transferring the requisite skills, knowledge, and information to add value to the organization's critical business metrics.

Figure 32-2. Driving Performance Through "LEAN" Training

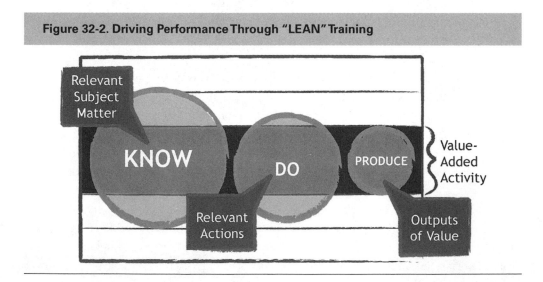

528

Teach only the knowledge (KNOW) and skills (DO) needed for people to produce valued results. Teaching anything outside the value-added band is potentially a waste of time and money.

Linking Learning to Performance: Performance Support

When analysis determines that performance is deficient, due to lack of skills or knowledge, you can ensure a strong and visible link to performance through the appropriate use of performance support. But first, you must decide which alternative for storing information is most effective for producing results. The options are to store the information in the memory of the performers or to store the information externally in what is referred to as performance support.

Performance support is a class of tools that provide requisite knowledge and information, just in time at point of need. Imagine visiting your local automated teller machine (ATM) to withdraw cash. But instead of finding the usual visual cues to help you select an account and indicate an amount, you had to attend a bank-sponsored training program until you could punch in a series of numerical commands from memory. To further illustrate the concept, imagine this familiar scenario *with* performance support that we all rely on nearly every day: leaving a voicemail message. Just imagine trying to leave an urgent message on a voicemail system without audio prompts to direct you, and your only option was to guess which numerical command was required.

Performance support is a storage place for information, other than memory, that is used *while* performing a task. It provides a signal to the performer of when to carry out increments of a task, which reduces the amount of recall necessary and minimizes error. Performance support can appear as simple instructions to assemble equipment or complex algorithms to analyze systems. This includes tools such as checklists, decision tables, performance-centric user interfaces, embedded help systems (such as the telephone example), job aids, and so forth.

Performance Support vs. Long-Term Memory

The decision whether to use performance support or long-term memory is a trade-off because each has advantages and disadvantages. Advantages of long-term memory include the following:

- Long-term memory allows performers to act quickly (within seconds), and this usually translates into higher productivity.

- The performer's hands and eyes are unencumbered.
- Performers are likely to be given more credit by other people (bosses, peers, customers) if they can respond without external aid. Often these people equate competence with speed and memory, rather than just the quality of the performance.
- In rare cases, memory storage is mandated by regulations.

The disadvantages of long-term memory storage include the following:

- Despite good teaching tactics, decline in retention begins within seconds and can be serious within hours. When the interval between learning and on-the-job practice is long, loss of retention often wipes out any performance improvement, unless performance support is used.
- There is greater variability of performance for memory-based activities.
- Variables such as task interference, personal problems, and prior learning can hinder job performers from accessing long-term memory.
- The instructional design and development of training materials takes much longer to produce than performance support, resulting in higher development costs.
- Training time for long-term memory storage is greater, resulting in higher delivery costs. The delivery cost of training typically exceeds all other costs combined.
- Higher retraining costs occur when there is a change in the work process. Unlearning then relearning is one of the more expensive problems faced by trainers and educators.

The following types of tasks are ideal for performance support:

- A task performed with relatively low frequency.
- A highly complex task. A task is complex if fine discrimination of stimuli is involved, such as a fighter pilot determining if an oncoming aircraft is friend or foe, or if there is a series of binary discriminations, such as inspecting or troubleshooting a complex electronic system.
- A task with criteria that, if not met, results in high consequence of error, such as high financial loss, injury, or loss of life (such as an engineer designing a chemical plant).
- A task with a high probability of change in the future; that is, the way in which the task is being currently performed is likely to change because of changes in technology, policy, or equipment. In such cases, other variables being equal, it is often not worth devoting time and other resources in the costly, time-consuming process of training. It is far more cost-efficient to update a performance support tool than to retrain a portion of the workforce.

- Characteristics of the task do not rule out the use of performance support. Some tasks have severe time requirements in which even seconds matter. For example, the initial actions of a pilot during an in-flight emergency must be immediate rather than guided by performance support. Note that pilots are trained to shift to performance support (flight procedures) immediately after taking the initial corrective actions. Why? These actions are infrequently performed, are highly complex, and could have devastating consequences.

- Another inhibiting factor might be the performance environment. For example, a surgeon might face the problem of how to ensure that a performance support tool is kept sterile. Social barriers might be another inhibiting factor in the use of performance support. For example, if more credit is given by bosses, peers, and customers for the use of long-term memory storage (such as knowing all product prices or order numbers), the job performer might not use performance support no matter how complex the task.

Figure 32-3 provides the logic for making the decision between performance support and training to memory. We have been using this tool for decades and find that it produces consistently valid results.

Figure 32-3. Job Aid vs. Memory Decision

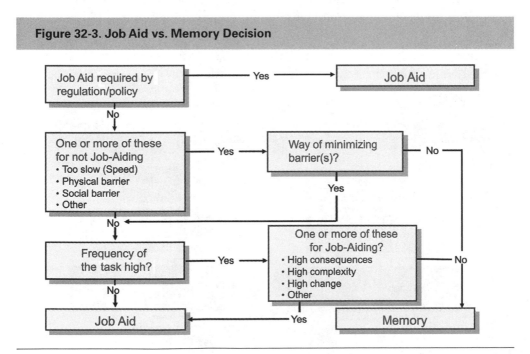

The most interesting aspect of this tool is the conclusion that performance support is the preferred option over training. This is the reverse of all the assumptions that most managers and training organizations have in regard to the most effective and efficient way to provide skills and knowledge to performers. We believe, however, that it is always preferable to provide performance support over training, when you have reached the conclusion to not use training based on data about the actual nature of the work. If this seems counterintuitive to you, remember that the costs of developing performance support are significantly less and are delivered in much less time than the equivalent training. You can locate tools to help you make decisions on the *Handbook's* website at www.astdhandbook.org.

How to Link Training to Performance (When Training to Memory Storage Is Required)

When training to memory is required, we are strong advocates for context-intensive training. The structure of the training is analogous to the actual work structure/process captured in the PEP. The examples and practices are role specific and include the current best approaches captured from exemplary performers and teams. Figure 32-4 shows the structure of a sales role on the left derived from the PEP and the corresponding curriculum model on the right. If one of the accomplishments for the role is *accurate forecast,* the corresponding course on the right would be titled How to Produce an Accurate Forecast. If a key task for producing accurate forecasts is *analyze competitive landscape,* you would need a module titled How to Analyze the Competitive Landscape. Since participants never have to ask how the training relates to their work, this design model drives measures of relevance and training transfer off the scale.

Figure 32-4. Relationship Between the Work Structure (PEP) and Curriculum Map

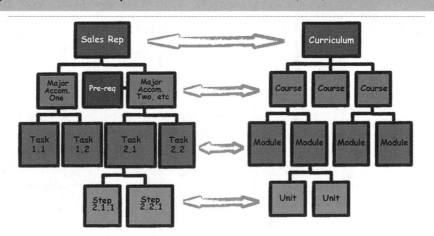

In effect, this means you should provide instruction and practice only in those skills and tasks not yet mastered and only as much training as is needed to produce the level of competence required for the role. This context-intensive model will enhance the trainees' motivation to apply what was learned to his or her world of work.

Profiles of Exemplary Performers (PEP)

The training should also be guaranteed to produce graduates who are able to perform to the level as described in the PEP and yet be flexible enough to avoid the enormous waste associated with a one-size-fits-all design approach.

Why do we stress the importance of designing the training based on the information captured from your exemplary performers? To do this requires a little background information as to the difference between declarative knowledge and procedural knowledge. Declarative knowledge is often described as "knowing what," and procedural knowledge is described as "knowing how."

If you know how to use a copier, you have procedural knowledge. If you know the underlying principles concerning how a copier works, you have declarative knowledge. There is significant evidence that declarative knowledge is different from procedural knowledge. You can learn everything there is to know about a subject, but still not be able to use that knowledge to do anything. For example, learning the rules of grammar may help you learn the Italian language, but being able to state the rules does not mean you can speak the language. Speaking requires procedural knowledge.

Experts aren't just faster and more accurate than novices or incumbents who are performing at a lower level; they know more and different things about the problem, and they have insights that the novice cannot yet fully understand. In fact, six major differences exist between experts and nonexperts that are important to consider in the design of instruction:

1. In general, experts have more specific declarative knowledge. They have more principles in their mental models, and those principles operate more automatically. This allows them to synthesize their declarative knowledge and apply it more systematically to the procedures that require it.
2. Experts have better links between their declarative knowledge (mental models) and their procedural structures. These links allow them to bring principles and procedures together to solve problems more efficiently.
3. Experts are really exceptional at organizing their mental models. Solving a new problem involves constructing and manipulating that mental model and making

more associations among the declarative and procedural knowledge structures. This ability provides them with mental shortcuts that make the experts highly efficient.

4. Experts categorize problems differently than less experienced performers. They are able to extract the abstract problem features from the surface symptoms they encounter and categorize those features based on their deep mental models.

5. Experts frequently generate heuristics (strategies) for solving problems by working forward from the initial condition or problem, generating a hypothesis for a solution, and then applying the new solution to see if it leads to the desired goal.

6. And finally, experts are more likely to persist if the first strategy doesn't work. A novice may give up after an initial failure.

Based on this research, the challenge for training is to assist learners with categorizing problems the way experts do and to build an appropriate mental model of the work that contains all the correct components in the right relationships with the right operating principles. This is the logic behind a context-intensive approach to training design.

How to Link Training to Performance (When Using On-the-Job Training)

Structured on-the-job training (SOJT) is an approach to training design and implementation that produces a rich, context-intensive approach. This is an approach we often recommend. But first, it is important to differentiate between SOJT and unstructured on-the-job training (OJT).

In North America, on-the-job training is most commonly used to refer to a haphazard and ineffective approach of pairing a novice with a more experienced performer. The hope is that through osmosis, the right information will pass at the right time from the more experienced performer to the less experienced performer. It is typically not systematic, replicable, scalable, or dependable. Unstructured OJT leads to trainees acquiring skills through the following means:

- Impromptu explanations and demonstrations by others, whether or not those providing the information are qualified performers. The research shows that when subject matter experts serve as ad hoc coaches, they leave out 70 percent of process steps that the novice requires to be successful.
- Self-initiated trial-and-error efforts.
- Random imitation of others' behavior, regardless of whether they are qualified to serve as examples.

In contrast, SOJT is defined as the planned process of developing task-level expertise by pairing an experienced employee with a less experienced employee at or near the actual work setting. The discrete job tasks that are documented and observed serve as the basis for the training content and objectives.

SOJT is only as effective as the experienced and knowledgeable employees who serve as the trainers. These SOJT trainers should demonstrate adequate competence in the work being presented and in the skills required to present that work to others. Therefore, in SOJT, the development of trainers is often a formal, extensive process in and of itself.

Regardless of the delivery method, context-intensive training provides multiple benefits.

Summary: Optimizing the Link Between Learning and Performance

Training with the following characteristics has been shown over and over again to have a direct and measurable impact on performance:

- The training structure should precisely mirror how your stars produce exemplary results.
- The content should align with actual work practices.
- Rich, role-specific examples and practices should be included.
- Sufficient practice is provided to support skills transfer to the work setting.
- An explicit decision must be made between storing the information in the memory of the performer and making it available through performance support.
- The training concludes with a simulation of the critical work processes at the highest level of fidelity that is practical.

When new hire training is designed and developed based on a PEP captured from your star performers, we consistently see impressive results. For example, ramp-up times for new hires are reduced by 30 percent or more. Concurrently, training design, development, and delivery times are all shortened by 20-40 percent. The combination of faster ramp-up times and reduced training cycles has a significant impact on the value that new hires produce in the early months of their employment.

Well-designed training is an effective and efficient tool for transferring the requisite skills, knowledge, and information to the organization's goal. When analysis determines that performance is deficient due to lack of skills or knowledge, you must look inside your organization for that star performer who consistently produces above standard. Then decide which alternative for storing information is most effective for producing the desired results. The options are to store the information in the memory of the performers or to store the information externally, in what we refer to as performance support.

When training to memory is required, we are strong advocates for context-intensive training. Context-intensive training is designed directly from the PEP. The structure of the training is analogous to the work structure/process. The purpose of designing the instruction is to prescribe instruction that will teach the learner to perform as the role requires and, at the same time, to adjust to the needs of the individual.

SOJT is a highly recommended approach to training design and implementation that produces a rich, context-intensive approach and is defined by its use of experienced and knowledgeable employees with the right skills who serve as the trainers. Regardless of the delivery method, context-intensive training is a relevant, efficient, lean, and effective approach to shifting your stars' expertise to the solid performers, thereby affecting the bottom line of the organization and shifting the performance curve.

Finally, performance support yields more accurate and reliable job performance, is less expensive to develop than instruction, and dramatically reduces formal training time. It should be considered in every project in which prior analysis shows a need for information.

About the Author

Paul H. Elliott, PhD, is president of Exemplary Performance LLC, based in Annapolis, Maryland. Dr. Elliott's expertise is in the analysis of human performance, the design of interventions that optimize human performance in support of business goals, and strategies for transitioning from training to performance models. Dr. Elliott assists organizations in performance analysis, instructional design, product and process launch support, design of advanced training systems, and design and implementation of integrated performance interventions. Co-author of *Exemplary Performance: Driving Business Results by Benchmarking Your Star Performers* (Jossey-Bass), Dr. Elliott offers business leaders, human resources professionals, and organization development practitioners the tools and processes to identify star performers, capture the high-performance attributes of these employees, and disseminate this valuable information throughout the organization.

References

Foshay, W. (2008). "Research in Learning: What We Know for Sure." *ASTD Handbook for Workplace Learning Professionals.* Alexandria, VA: ASTD Press.

Gilbert, T. (1978). *Human Competence: Engineering Worthy Performance.* New York: McGraw-Hill. Republished in 1996. Washington, DC: ISPI, and Amherst, MA: HRD Press, Inc.

Harless, J.H. (1989). *Accomplishment-Based Curriculum Development System.* Redwood Shores, CA: Saba.

Jacobs, R. (1999). "Structured On-the-Job Training." *Handbook of Human Performance Technology.* San Francisco: Jossey-Bass/Pfeiffer.

Rummler, G. (1972). "Human Performance Problems and Their Solutions." *Human Resource Management* 11(4):2-10.

This chapter is adapted from *Exemplary Performance: Driving Business Results by Benchmarking Your Star Performers,* with permission from the publisher, John Wiley & Sons, © 2013.

For Further Reading

Elliott, P., and A. Folsom. (2013). *Exemplary Performance: Driving Business Results by Benchmarking Your Star Performers.* San Francisco: Jossey-Bass/John Wiley & Sons.

Rossett, A., and L. Schafer. (2007). *Job Aids & Performance Support.* San Francisco: Bass/Pfeiffer.

Chapter 33

Results-Based Evaluation: Keeping the End in Mind

Karie Willyerd, Jenny Dearborn, and Sanchita Sur

··· **In This Chapter** ···

- Learn how to use a six-step process to design an evaluation strategy.
- Apply hard metrics to soft skills.

I magine your doctor has just told you that due to the changes in guidelines on cholesterol treatment, she now recommends that you take a statin drug. "Which one?" you ask.

"I have three for you to choose from," she replies. "Statin A has gone through the first level of evaluation and people really, really like it. It might be effective, but we just don't know yet because we have not progressed beyond that level of evaluation. But I promise, you'll love its teal, mint-flavored coating. Sometimes people even put a certificate up on their walls that says they've taken Statin A—they love it that much!"

She continues, "Statin B has gone through a bit more evaluation, and we know that it has reduced cholesterol levels for Caucasian men living in Missouri. Only a few people have had side effects."

"Um, I don't fit that patient category, and I'm a little worried about side effects," you reply.

"Yes, I know," she says, "but it might work for you. You never know."

"And the third?" you ask.

She replies, "The third has been evaluated with thousands of patients, has well-known, limited side effects, is quite effective, and best of all is entirely affordable. It's actually the one I recommend for you."

Now of course this is a silly conversation that would never happen with a reputable doctor, but you understand our point. What really matters when a treatment or solution is important is that first and foremost, it works. Results matter. Then, if it works, is it affordable to the patient or customer? Yet we rarely evaluate whether our learning solution works. Are we killing our learners? We don't really know most of the time, as shown in Figure 33-1. Most organizations measure less than half the courses beyond the reaction level, and by the time it gets to understanding behavioral change, only about a quarter measure that. In contrast, in clinical drug trials, each of the different phases is with increasing population sizes, with tests for effectiveness and efficacy—a predictor of effectiveness should the drug get to market.

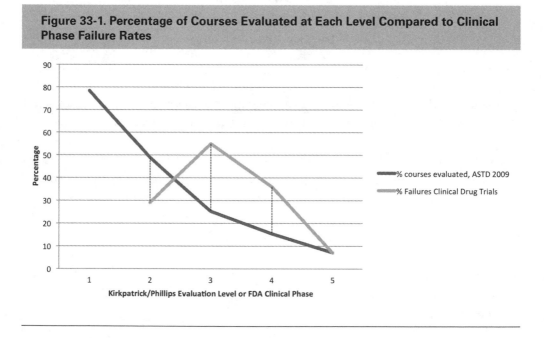

Figure 33-1. Percentage of Courses Evaluated at Each Level Compared to Clinical Phase Failure Rates

The levels and phases in Figure 33-1 are not at the same scale and do not overlay in methodology at all (DiMasi, 2010). What we do find interesting is that even though a thorough evaluation is done at every phase of clinical trials, as a drug is rolled out to an increasing population size, failure rates are perilously high. When a drug moves from Phase 2 to Phase 3, for example, which means moving from typically less than 100 participants to several hundred, the failure rate approaches 55 percent. In spite of thorough research and focused problem identification, the majority of drugs fail. It makes us wonder: Why aren't more training programs failing?

In contrast, the further along a training intervention progresses, the less likely it is to be subjected to anything beyond a cursory reaction evaluation (ASTD, 2009). We think training programs are failing and we don't know it because we are not measuring the results, especially in the long term with increasing population sizes. In other words, the programs are not improving performance or, even worse, creating the illusion of change but actually making things worse and we don't even know it. The placebo effect is in place for most of our evaluations actually administered, so we live under the secure feeling that somehow we made a difference. With complex problems that require a blended-learning solution, the challenge of evaluating results is compounded by the number of variables in play.

Our belief is that the only reason we should be spending the organization's money for training solutions is to deliver meaningful results. Therefore, we recommend that if there is only one evaluation that can be done, it should be one measuring results. Results-focused evaluation allows you to refine your solution over time to ensure both effective and efficient training. However, the evaluation should start with effectiveness and then continuously improve toward a more efficient solution. Measuring each of the components rather than the solution as a whole is pointless until we know whether a solution achieves its goal of achieving results. Separating program design from the goal results, where on the one hand we have a design process and on the other hand an evaluation process, is antique thinking in light of today's lean and agile processes.

When designing an evaluation strategy, our belief is that you must always start with the results, and then work backward to leading indicators of results. From there, head even further back to behaviors to identify what will affect the leading indicators. Finally, keep regressing to the performance interventions and how to measure them. This is almost exactly the opposite sequence of most evaluation designs we've seen, and it's why so many programs end at Level 1—participant reaction—evaluations.

Our approach used a six-step process that integrated our solution design and our evaluation methodology as one seamless approach. Although this reads as a linear process, it is really more of an approximation approach—get something out there, measure and get feedback, and keep approximating closer to the intended results. See Figure 33-2 for a high-level description of the six steps of our results-focused evaluation approach.

Figure 33-2. The Six Steps of the Results-Focused Evaluation Process

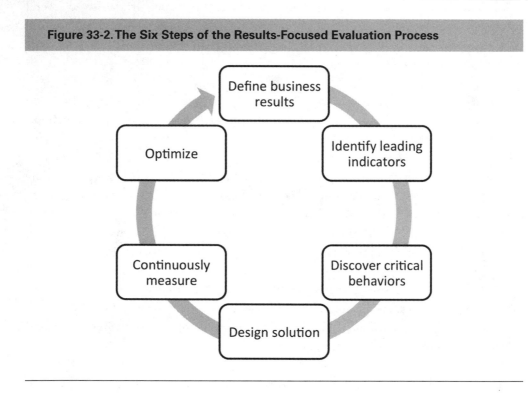

To move from the philosophical to the pragmatic, we would like to describe how we used these six steps to develop a complex, blended-learning solution for a sales program. At the end, we'll describe how we would evaluate an imagined leadership development training solution where measuring results might be seen as softer.

Background and Solution Formulation

Both the CEO and the president of the company had an itch: Can we be more effective in the training we are doing, especially in sales? The request was not terribly specific, as you might notice. "How do you know the training isn't effective?" we asked. "What are you trying to improve?" Wouldn't it be wonderful if executives responded with precise problem statements and recommended interventions that you can then tidy up, develop a blended solution, and evaluate with targeted, existing metrics? Newsflash: That never happens.

Instead, our executives had a gut feeling, correct as it turned out, that improvement was possible. It was up to us to define the problem, find the solution, and show that it made a difference. We talked to a couple dozen executives to get some understanding of the challenges they faced in fueling a young company in a high-growth environment. We reviewed the metrics that were already being measured by sales operations to understand what was important in the current environment. Before we could dive into deep analytics, the richest source of data was from our sales team members, especially those with less than a year's experience, as they had good comparison points to their most recent company.

From our own prior experience, we also knew there were sales operation measures that should be in place, but we could not find. Since this is not a chapter on front-end analysis, suffice it to say we did successive levels of front-end analysis throughout the project to refine problem statements and to understand what leading indicators would predict sales results. In the end, we came up with four big business results to address, the estimated improvement target with corresponding impact, and an approximate price point to significantly improve each business result. Note we didn't start with programs or solutions. We started with the business results we thought were the biggest pain points and asked the executive team which one or two they wanted solved the most. Since we were in rapid hiring mode, their choice was "decrease the time to quota for new salespeople by 50 percent in a two-year period."

"Starting yesterday," they added. The promised results were (increased revenue per new hire) × (the number of new hires). With more than 200 new hires anticipated in the next year alone, it's easy to see why this program was selected. From our six-step model, Step 1, define business results, was complete.

They approved our requested budget and, for the first time in our collective careers, offered to throw in more budget to accelerate results. We took them up on the offer for some of the extra budget, but we also knew that cutting down the timeline could have consequences, so we stuck to the two-year goal with a promise to at least achieve the midway mark at the end of the first year. The reduced time to quota assumption was baked into the company's business goals for the year, so we were now fully accountable for a lever that would drive results communicated to Wall Street. Our hearts beat a little faster knowing that the whole company was counting on us to deliver a solution that worked.

The Solution: Sales Academy

In order to communicate that change was afoot, we branded the initiative "Sales Academy." Although that name sounds like it might be just a collection of courses, it actually included several nontraining components. Like many companies, we have an annual sales kick-off early in the year. We were able to obtain one-and-a-half days of dedicated training at that event. We decided it was better to err in the direction of an intervention and refine than to wait and lose a prime opportunity for training, so we simultaneously worked on Steps 2, 3, and 4. Using a quick survey to ascertain current skill levels, we sorted people into one of four class offerings. With the quick start goal, we were able to put everyone through one of the four pilot offerings. These offerings ranged from off-the-shelf to a completely customized simulation and gave us a flash start. Over the next year, we modified the offerings based on our evaluation methodologies, editing or culling out some offerings and adding others. The key components were an intensive one-week program within the first month of being hired, a designated professional high-touch sales mentor for the first six months, a personalized training plan to direct to specialized skills courses, and ongoing support tools such as a social collaboration site, product sales enablement tools, a sales portal, and so on. All together there were dozens of courses, job aids, tools, and support methodologies that combined to make a solution.

Early Evaluations and Refinement

Like the drug approval process, an obvious problem with a results-focused evaluation is that it may take a long time to find out results. Thus for each component of the program, we also did a Level 1 reaction evaluation, largely to buy us time to get to actual results and to build buy-in and enthusiasm among the target audience. We think this is the most useful reason to do an evaluation on reaction to training—to buy a political grace period with executive sponsors until business impact could be measured. We could report back, early on, that the solution was well received by both new and existing salespeople, and we could report on the number of people attending, all measures that are typically reported and where most people stop.

Over time, we learned that there was no statistical relationship between Level 1 evaluation and performance results. None. Since we used the same content and same instructors for many courses around the world, we did learn that the biggest predictor of satisfaction variance in our courses was the quality of the classroom environment. If the classroom didn't have a view, had poor temperature control, or was suboptimal in any way, it negatively affected the ratings on every item in the Level 1 evaluation—not just classroom quality.

Two years is too long to wait to be able to report back results in most organizations and justify the next year's budget. In our Step 2 analysis, we looked for leading indicators of sales results as a predictor of future revenue results. Sorting our sales reps into top and bottom performers, we were able to compare more than 110 performance variables from our

CRM data. Using structural equation modeling techniques, we uncovered the early results that predicted top performance and then focused on these in as many components of our blended solution as we could.

One example was sales pipeline—the revenue opportunity each salesperson indicated they were working. We also had early behavioral feedback from the sales mentors, each of whom had, on average, 30 (at the peak, it was 40) new sales associates assigned to them. The mentors had a checklist they worked from to ensure consistency and to provide us early feedback on progress. The simplest of things, such as whether the salespeople were up and running on a computer with access to company resources, could make a big difference in how fast they could become productive. Did they clearly understand their territory? Did they know how to get in the door to a prospect? Did they understand our products and have a compelling value story? Were they connected meaningfully with their manager? The sales mentors were the support system to make sure these and more questions were solidly answered.

For every salesperson in the company, both existing and new, we tracked their tenure and comparison to when they achieved expected sales quota along with more than two dozen performance variables. As an aside, there were vigorous debates on the meaning of sales quota or sales ramp, ranging from the time someone first made a sale that achieved a quarterly quota to sustained quota over time. We learned to define our promised results well and ensure our stakeholders were in agreement with that definition. Without going into detail, we also had to enlist the support of several other organizations to ensure we could pull off our plan. These included sales operations, marketing, line management, the channel organization, HR, IT, and so on. The deeper our analysis continued, the more we found improvement opportunities across the company to improve the experience and time to productivity of the new salesperson and, by happy coincidence, all new hires. Fortunately, our partner organizations shared the vision and stepped in to help us with everything from collecting metrics to complete process improvement projects.

Delivering Business Results

The prime directive was to enable salespeople to achieve quota earlier, which we also called ramp. In Figure 33-2, the wide disparity of performance achievement of all salespeople can be seen. (Actual time to quota is not disclosed here for confidentiality reasons.) Note that some people with long tenure had never reached quota, while some people new to the organization were at nearly 500 percent of quota. Clearly, the quality of hiring could make a big difference, and our talent acquisition group paired with us to train managers to improve their hiring skills as well.

Upon deep dive, we learned that we needed to remove some outliers from the data set because there were typically extenuating circumstances, such as being a rehire. Also, a complexity we had to solve for was displaying the data in meaningful ways. We determined that the best way to show data was to plot quarterly by cohorts of new hires to make interpretation easy.

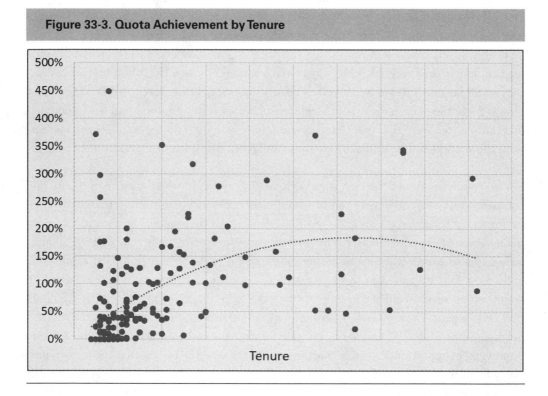

Figure 33-3. Quota Achievement by Tenure

With this kind of data view, we could look at what leading indicators were helpful in predicting that a salesperson was on track to achieve quota by targeted tenure date. Looking into historical data of top performers versus bottom performers, we could statistically determine through multivariate analysis which leading indicators the top-performing sales reps exceeded early in their tenure. See Table 33-1 for what we discovered are the top six indicators to predict sales performance and why those metrics mattered. Note that the predictors were identified purely through statistical methods and not through interview-based explicit knowledge documentation.

Table 33-1. Lead Indicators for Sales Success

Step 2: Identify Leading Indicators The Top Six Early Predictors of Sales Success	
Leading Indicator	**Why It Matters**
The number of opportunities created and logged in the CRM	The more opportunities created, the greater the possibility that some of them will come through. Volume matters!
The number of opportunities closed in the first three months	No matter how many opportunities, the salesperson needed to demonstrate the ability to close.
The close ratio (opportunities created/ opportunities closed)	This metric predicted a balance between qualifying opportunities and converting to revenue.
Average deal size	Typically, larger deal sizes meant bundling products together, making for an efficient sale.
Size of deals won versus size of deals lost	Indicated a win strategy for larger deals.
Time to close first deal	Velocity matters, and those out of the gate early tended to stay ahead.

The early predictors of success gave the mentors strong support for coaching their assigned new reps. They now had solid evidence on the size of the opportunity pipeline that a sales rep needed within the first three months, for example, and could nudge both the rep and the manager to ensure that territory and the resulting opportunities were well defined. The new reps received a report from their mentors on their progress against key early predictors and worked with their managers and mentors on shoring up any weaknesses. Eventually, we were able to use predictive analytics techniques like random forest and CHAID to predict whether a salesperson would meet quota or not based on CRM transaction patterns and deal characteristics. With early indicators identified, we could now chain backward to map the rep behaviors that would lead to early indicators. See Table 33-2 for our top 10 behaviors that were identified by analyzing the checklists kept by the mentors of new reps.

Table 33-2. Top 10 Differentiating Actions

Step 3: Discover Critical Behaviors The Top 10 Differentiating Actions	
Rep Action	**Why It Matters**
Build an internal network	Inside sales, presales, solution architects, partners, and so on can help improve deal size and sales cycle
Focus on bestselling products	Get wins on the board quickly and build success momentum
Target specific industries	Provides value to the customer as a thought leader and problem solver for industry-specific challenges
Prioritize accounts	Improves the number of high-quality prospects to drive pipeline predictability
Prospect with purpose	Uses time with potential customers optimally when discovery questions are well defined
Challenge the customer	Brings a differentiated expertise and value to the customer
Work the system	Understanding resources that are available and process flows minimizes administrative time
Keep existing customers happy	Improves renewal rates, upsell opportunity, referrals, and net promoter scores
Follow the playbook	Ensures consistency when others are brought in to help and shortcuts the time it takes to ramp up on a new product
Work around obstacles	Obstacles are everywhere, and only an attitude of "I will make this happen" ensures success

As mentioned, our Step 4 design process was successive and iterative—a solution with many moving parts. Our learning solutions included, as an example, a course on creating opportunities and closing deals, offered to both new and existing reps. In these cases, we could now look at the average number of opportunities created before training compared to the quarter after training, regardless of tenure and seasonal fluctuations. Translating the percentage improvements, as shown in Figure 33-4, into dollar amounts was a mere spreadsheet formula, as was return-on-investment. For courses and solutions that did not yield high returns, we either improved them until they did or eliminated them, completing Steps 5 and 6 for the first time through the cycle. Since not every rep took every course, we could also look for effects of reps who took certain courses versus others who did not—essentially what is called an A/B test in lean methodology—and determine overall effect.

Rensis Likert

Rensis Likert was a social scientist who spent much of his time researching human behavior within organizations. Likert is best known for developing the Likert scale, a linear scale used in data collection to rate statements and attitudes. An example of a Likert scale involves asking a participant to rate a statement on a scale of one to five:

1 = strongly disagree, 2 = disagree, 3 = neutral, 4 = agree, 5 = strongly agree.

Likert also developed the linking-pin model, which concerns the manager's role. The linking-pin theory suggests that a manager is a member of multiple groups, serving as a subordinate to upper management and as a superior to direct reports. The manager acts as the link between these two groups. For a manager to be effective in this position, he or she must be invested in the objectives, projects, and successes of each group.

In *The Human Organization: Its Management and Value* (1967), Likert developed a theory of business management that identified four types of organizational systems:

- System 1: Exploitive-authoritative
- System 2: Benevolent-authoritative
- System 3: Consultative
- System 4: Participative-group.

Likert argued that System 4, participative management, provided the best working climate. Participative management ensures that subordinates feel trust and support from management and are comfortable going to management with problems.

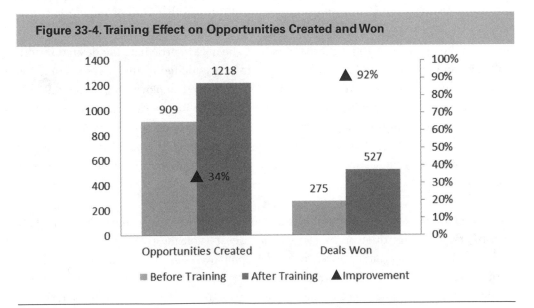

Figure 33-4. Training Effect on Opportunities Created and Won

For nonlearning solutions, we could readily sort into two groups of people—those who used the solution and those who did not. If we did not have the data available through system performance, we added a question to the mentors' checklist for them to ask their sales new hire mentee. Then by looking at leading indicators, we could tell whether a solution was making an impact or not. Still, our continued focus was on the end goal and helping the company to achieve it, and not just achieving a goal of showing proven return-on-investments.

More than two years after the program was begun, we have now cut the average time to quota by more than half. Yet we know we can improve even further to ensure most people achieve quota and not just that the average is achieved. We also know we can continue to make the program more cost-effective as we narrow down to the parts of the blended solution that yield the most results.

Hard Metrics Applied to Soft Skills

"That's all fine and good for sales, which is easily measured," you might be thinking. First, most of these metrics were not in place before we started, and it took a great deal of work and collaboration with other groups to make them happen. Second, we believe it is possible to apply the steps of results-based evaluation to soft skills as well. Engage with us in a brief thought experiment for a moment on how we might tackle a request to develop training for front-line managers for software engineers.

Perhaps you've had a request from a senior executive that starts out, "I need to train my managers. Can you put a course together for them?" Since that kind of request is all too familiar, experts in front-end analysis like Allison Rossett (2009) provide ample resources to guide you in helping the leader get to the point to be able to articulate the desired results. Following our six-step process, the first step is to clearly define results. Let's assume that two of the desired results are reduced attrition and increased employee engagement. Before we would commit to a training solution, we would work with the executive to understand what attrition and employee satisfaction are costing now. How does she know? How is it currently measured? Are there hard measures, such as number of lines of code created per group or number of bugs, which could be used to differentiate performance and therefore related productivity costs?

Next, what are the leading indicators of attrition and employee engagement that could help quantify the cost of attrition or disengaged employees? Typically, two types of surveys exist within companies that can supply some rich data: employee satisfaction surveys and manager quality surveys. A multiyear study at Google (Garvin, 2013) found these two data sources yielded a solid conclusion that manager quality was the strongest predictor of retention and employee satisfaction. For Step 3, to map behaviors, we would follow the Google approach and use additional double-blind interviews of top- and bottom-rated managers to find the behaviors best mapped to manager quality, which suggests the Step 4 design interventions. These may include training, but assuredly would include a manager personal feedback system and a communication plan on the importance of manager quality. The continuous measurement component of Step 5 cannot be understated. We know of one company that was able to improve manager quality by merely asking one question every quarter of every employee: "Did you have a meaningful discussion with your manager this quarter about your development?"

As fans of lean design, we favor the idea of small solutions iterated frequently using hard data to determine what works and what doesn't, improving often. Only those laser focused on results can maintain that target in view to optimize continuously and efficiently to achieve what really matters to the organization.

About the Authors

Karie Willyerd, PhD, is the co-author of *The 2020 Workplace*. She is also the vice president of Learning and Social Adoption at SuccessFactors, an SAP company, and the former CEO of Jambok, a social learning platform acquired by SuccessFactors. In 2009, while she was working as the chief learning officer of Sun Microsystems, her team won the ASTD BEST #1 designation. She holds a doctorate in management from Case Western Reserve University and a master's in instructional and performance technology from Boise State. Contact her at karie.willyerd@sap.com.

Jenny Dearborn, MBA, MEd, is chief learning officer and vice president of the award-winning Cloud Talent Success team for SAP's Cloud businesses (SuccessFactors, Ariba, and SAP Cloud). She has spent 20 years in corporate learning and development at tech companies such as Hewlett-Packard and Sun Microsystems. She is currently a member of the Board of Directors at ASTD. She holds degrees from the University of California, Berkeley; San Jose State University; and Stanford University. She can be reached at jenny.dearborn@sap.com.

Sanchita Sur, MBA, is the founder of Emplay, an award-winning business analytics company. Prior to Emplay, she worked at KPMG, Cable and Wireless, iGATE, and BTS in management consulting and sales management roles. A data scientist by profession and a salesperson at heart, she is passionate about developing advanced decision support systems for the sales community. She holds an engineering degree from Nagpur University and an MBA from NITIE in Mumbai. She can be reached at sanchita.sur@emplay.net.

References

ASTD. (2009). *The Value of Evaluation: Making Training Evaluations More Effective.* Alexandria, VA: ASTD Press.

DiMasi, J.A., et al. (2010). Trends in Risks Associated With New Drug Development: Success Rates for Investigational Drugs. *Clinical Pharmacology & Therapeutics* 87(3):272-277.

Garvin, D. (2013, December). How Google Sold Its Engineers on Management. *Harvard Business Review.*

Rossett, A. (2009). *First Things Fast: A Handbook for Performance Analysis.* San Francisco: Pfeiffer.

For Further Reading

Jordan, J., M. Teel, and M. Vazzana. (2011). *Cracking the Sales Management Code: The Secrets to Measuring and Managing Sales Performance.* New York: McGraw-Hill.

Ries, E. (2011). *The Lean Start Up: How Today's Entrepreneurs Use Continuous Innovation to Create Radically Successful Businesses.* New York: Crown Business.

Seley, A., and B. Holloway. (2009). *Sales 2.0: Improve Business Results Using Innovative Sales Practices and Technology.* Hoboken, NJ: John Wiley & Sons.

Chapter 34

Learning Analytics That Maximize Individual and Organizational Performance

Alec Levenson

································· **In This Chapter** ·································

▪ Explore the systems approach to evaluation.

▪ Review the steps to diagnose, evaluate, and improve the design of T&D programs.

This chapter covers analytics for evaluating the impact of training and development (T&D). There is literature on measuring T&D impact, starting with Kirkpatrick's classic model and return-on-investment (ROI) calculations promoted by Phillips and others. I take a different approach, using analytics of T&D to inform not just program measurement but also program design and implementation. The approach can be used to improve T&D impact even when direct measurement is impractical.

I recommend a systems approach, which recognizes that T&D is only one of a wide range of ways that HR and OD have an impact on organizational effectiveness. T&D is most effective when program designers evaluate the applicability of the entire HR and OD toolkit in any situation, not just T&D on its own merits. Doing so leads to approaches that use T&D where most appropriate, whether as a standalone activity or as part of a larger set of programs of which T&D is one component.

Incorporating T&D as Part of a Larger Organizational Approach

A fundamental goal of T&D analytics is understanding how to improve and maximize T&D's impact. Traditional models in the field can fall short of this goal by focusing solely on measuring the T&D program as designed; they do not consider other approaches that may enhance T&D when used as part of a coordinated approach or that may yield a better return as an alternative to T&D. To provide maximum actionable insights, the analytic approach should address whether and how the program design supports business impact. The scope needs to include the overarching objectives required by the strategy and organization design and the improvements in systems and processes needed for strategic success. It also needs to consider the role played by T&D alone, by T&D working in conjunction with other programs, and by other activities that are independent of T&D. Only with a broad systems view can the appropriate role for T&D activities be defined, designed, implemented, and measured.

Any model of organization design, such as Galbraith's Star model (Galbraith, 1977), can be used for a systems diagnosis. Figure 34-1 presents an organizational performance model that draws from organization design principles and that highlights capabilities that are the focus of most T&D programs. It separates capabilities into two levels: individual and organizational/group:

- Individual capability: the role competencies that are the focus of most T&D activities
- Organizational capability: the ability to accomplish organizational objectives at the group level, which lead to strategic outcomes such as cost reduction, margin improvement, quality, innovation, customer satisfaction, and so on.

Individual capability contributes to organizational capability but is defined separately from it because organizational capability depends on more than just having the right people in place. For example, effective R&D processes require competent scientists as well as the right organization design, incentives, and processes to support innovation. Market share depends both on having the right people in sales and marketing roles and on robust systems and processes that support a strong go-to-market strategy. High-performing manufacturing operations depend on having the right people in machine operator and supervisor roles and also the right equipment, processes, and supply chain to simultaneously support efficiency and quality. The interdependency between individual capability and organizational capability is one reason T&D cannot be evaluated in a vacuum, separate from considering what further contributes to organizational capability beyond T&D.

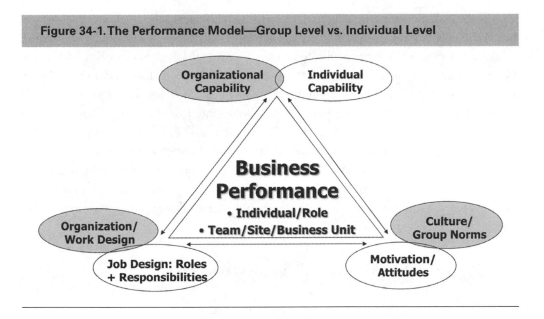

Figure 34-1. The Performance Model—Group Level vs. Individual Level

In addition to capability, the organizational performance model in Figure 34-1 has two other main components: organization design + job design and motivation/attitudes + culture/group norms, both of which span the individual and group levels:

- **Organization/work design:** How the organization is structured at the group level, including divisions, geographies, functions, departments, teams, and so on
- **Job design:** How individual roles and responsibilities are defined, evaluated, supported, and rewarded
- **Culture/group norms:** The cultures at the organization, unit, and team levels that shape how people act collectively, including establishing behavioral norms
- **Motivation/attitudes:** Individuals' attitudes about the work environment and motivation to do what is expected of them.

All these components, including individual and organizational capability, have to be aligned and working well in order for the organization to have successful business performance. It is possible for T&D programs to positively influence other components of the organizational performance model, but first and foremost, T&D improves individual capability. If the other parts of the organizational performance model are not designed and working optimally, the ability of T&D alone to improve business performance is limited.

This point is demonstrated in Figure 34-2, which shows a causal model of organizational performance. In Figure 34-2, the main components of the organizational performance model from Figure 34-1 are replicated in the Individual-Level Factors box and in the Group-/Unit-Level Factors box at the top center of the diagram. The HR/Human Capital Factors at the top left include programs such as T&D that help set the stage for improved performance. The Strategic Outcomes in the center flow from the Individual-Level and Group-/Unit-Level Factors, and in turn lead to Strategic and Financial Performance at the bottom of the diagram. Figure 34-2 shows clearly that T&D programs can contribute to improved organizational performance, but that they also are only one contributor in a highly complex system. It is the rare case when T&D alone will have a direct impact on improved business performance, which creates the flaw behind narrowly focused analytic approaches such as Kirkpatrick and ROI.

Figure 34-2. A Causal Model of Organization Performance

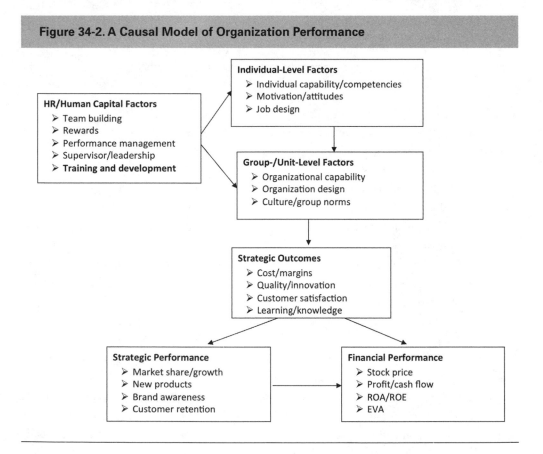

As an alternative to those narrowly focused approaches, the models in Figures 34-1 and 34-2, or their equivalents, can be used to diagnose, evaluate, and improve the design of T&D programs. The steps for doing so are outlined on the following pages.

Step 1: Refine Potential Programs Through Initial Assessment

The first step involves using a diagnostic such as the Performance Model in Figure 34-1 to assess the work design and identify the barriers to improved performance. Existing data on organizational performance and the insights of leaders and key stakeholders, gathered through interviews, usually are sufficient to identify the main potential barriers to improvement. Identifying the potential barriers is equivalent to articulating hypotheses about the drivers of organizational performance in Figure 34-1.

For example, a lack of cross-functional collaboration can hinder organizational effectiveness. Problems retaining key talent can diminish organizational capability. Compensation that is too stingy can retard talent recruitment. The product innovation pipeline may have dried up. Rapid expansion into new business lines or geographies may be going more poorly than expected. Identifying these and other potential barriers to improved organizational performance form the initial phase of the systems diagnosis.

The process of articulating the leading hypotheses about the drivers of organizational performance is a very important analytic step, even though no statistical analysis or complex calculations may be involved. Decades of social science research and practice provide a deep knowledge base about the drivers of motivation and behavior in organizations. This knowledge base can provide insights into the factors to be improved, even in the absence of conducting new data analysis (Levenson, 2014). That knowledge base should always be tapped during the initial assessment phase to reach preliminary conclusions about the drivers of organizational performance that are more versus less likely.

There are two important and related results that emerge from the initial systems diagnostic assessment: The most likely factors behind improved organizational performance are identified, and the least likely factors are also identified. For example, a competency gap among a small group of incumbent employees could be identified as a possible barrier to improved performance. The skills of a minority of people in that group might need to be improved to accomplish the organizational strategy, with the target employees to be helped comprising only 5-10 percent of the total employees in the group. Further investigation could reveal that those same employees already had been through extensive training, coaching, and attempts to provide developmental opportunities. This additional information would lead to the conclusion that T&D most likely is *not* a leading candidate for closing the competency gap among the target group; alternatives such as better performance management or recruiting a different set of people for those roles stand a much better chance of closing the competency gap. In this case, the conclusion of the initial assessment is that a T&D program most likely is not warranted, and other approaches should be considered instead.

Edward E. Lawler III

Edward E. Lawler III is an influential scholar in the fields of improving organizational performance, change management, and human resources development. In addition to being a well-respected scholar and professor, Lawler is a perennially popular consultant, author, and speaker on a diverse range of topics such as motivation, organizational change, high-performance organizations, strategic human resources management, reward systems and pay, organization design, corporate boards, and organizational effectiveness.

In 1979, Lawler founded the Center for Effective Organizations (CEO) at the University of Southern California's Marshall School of Business. The CEO conducts research on organizational design and effectiveness, and its academic theories and research inform and influence corporate practices worldwide. The CEO has a corporate sponsorship network of more than 60 major Fortune 500 corporations.

Lawler's research method, with its blend of theory and practice, appeals to both the mass market as well as scholarly journals. Some of his more popular works include *Motivation in Work Organizations* (Jossey-Bass, 1994), in which he theorized that an effective organization must motivate and encourage employees to perform well; *From the Ground Up* (Jossey-Bass, 1996), in which he completely rethought the old ways of organizational structure and formed six principles for organizing and managing a company based on a new logic intended to rebuild the organization from the ground up; and *Tomorrow's Organization* (Jossey-Bass, 1998), which offers solutions and guidelines for creating organizations that can compete successfully in the 21st century, including progressive ideas about customer product structures, design issues in networked organizations, and the structuring of global organizations.

As a different example, consider a much larger group of employees for which a competency gap is identified—a group comprising more than 50 percent of the total employees in the target population. If no previous attempts at T&D activities had been tried, the initial assessment might rule in T&D as a potential contributor to improve capabilities and performance. Yet if no other approach had been tried, the initial assessment likely would also identify other programs that could be tried at the same time as a T&D program. In this case, the conclusion of the initial assessment could be that an integrated approach combining T&D plus other programs is the right way to go.

As a third example, consider a similarly large group of employees with an identified competency gap, similar to the second case above, and for which the initial assessment also finds the following situation. Starting compensation for the role is set at below-market rates, in an effort to keep costs down historically, but is balanced by a dynamic work environment offering the opportunity to do interesting work and potentially progress into more lucrative jobs elsewhere in the organization. This work design leads to attracting and hiring people who have average to below-average initial skills needed for high performance in the role, but who have the aptitude for building the competencies needed for high performance. In this case, the initial assessment might reasonably conclude that a T&D standalone program may be all that is needed to improve organizational performance.

These three examples illustrate the range of possible conclusions regarding the suitability of a T&D program, which can be reached through the initial systems diagnosis using key stakeholder interviews and analysis of existing organizational performance data. This initial assessment can be used to optimize T&D program design before it is implemented, identifying whether T&D is among the categories of preferred programs and whether it should be considered on its own as a stand-alone activity or implemented as one part of a larger set of approaches. The ability to assess likely T&D impacts along with other activities is a strength of the systems diagnosis approach.

The other advantage of the systems diagnosis approach is it more clearly frames the role of individual competencies' contribution to business performance relative to other factors. It can always be argued that improved competencies help the organization to perform better. Yet just because improved competencies *might* help does not mean that the greatest return will come from closing the competency gap, as compared to other approaches.

As Figure 34-2 demonstrates, it can be hard to draw a direct link between increased competencies and improved organizational performance. This is especially true for managerial competencies where there is little documented evidence that increased competencies have a positive impact on the bottom line (Levenson, Van der Stede, and Cohen, 2006). Thus T&D programs for managers can have a hard time positively affecting business performance, even in cases where there may be a perceived managerial competency gap.

This brings us to the critical observation that any program, including T&D, that is designed to improve business performance should be focused on the true barriers to team/group performance. Whether increased competencies *can* help the business is less important than whether they *should* be the focus of efforts to improve organizational effectiveness. The latter can be answered only through a systems diagnosis that takes into consideration the full range of potential approaches or changes and how they can improve business performance.

Step 2: Identify the Business Outcomes That Matter and How Training Can Have an Impact on Them

As shown in Figure 34-2, there are many potential outcomes that are indicators, either directly or indirectly, of business performance. Financial measures such as ROI are not necessarily needed to demonstrate a positive business impact. If you can demonstrate a clear link between a T&D program and improvements in strategic outcomes, such as cost, margins, quality, innovation, customer satisfaction, and so on, that link alone may be sufficient to justify the investment in the program—without having to calculate a specific dollar value of the link.

What matters is identifying the specific strategic outcomes that matter for business performance and understanding the role they play in realizing the strategy. It is not sufficient to show that a T&D program can help boost revenue, or cut costs, or improve quality, or so forth. What is necessary is both showing a link to tangible outcomes that help the business and making sure those outcomes are strategically important.

For example, consider a lean manufacturing operation that uses a just-in-time (JIT) inventory management system for its suppliers. In a JIT system, the raw materials and other inputs needed for production are scheduled to be delivered with high frequency to minimize stockpiles held on site. Such a system keeps profits up by lowering the warehousing cost of holding the inventory on site and by reducing the risk of inventory overbuying in the event of a rapid and unexpected sales decline that requires a cutback in production. In this type of work setting, training workers in the principles of JIT inventory management can build skills that directly contribute to organizational success. The specific skills could include how to meet the dual and competing objectives of uninterrupted inventory availability (to avoid disrupting the manufacturing process) and low stockpiles (to minimize storage and excess purchasing costs).

In other settings that use inventories, though, training workers in JIT principles may help with cost reduction but may work at cross purposes with the strategy. For example, maintaining low inventories of surgical and cleaning supplies in a hospital can reduce inventory costs, but at the risk of a patient's surgery going wrong or increasing the chances of an infection. In a hospital, the potential benefits of JIT practices for managing the surgical and cleaning supplies inventory may be more than offset by costs that are unacceptable for the strategy.

The reason for the differential strategic importance of JIT inventory control in the two work settings is due to the nature of the product or service that is produced. In a manufacturing plant that produces durable goods, such as cars, electronic equipment, and so on, falling short on the inventory needed for production can introduce delays in the production process, but minor delays typically do not have a big impact on either product quality or sales. In addition, the inventory inputs into production (steel, rubber, plastic, circuit boards, semifinished parts, and so on) account for a relatively large portion of total production costs for durable goods; keeping inventory low can free up large amounts of cash that can be used for other purposes to support the strategy.

In the hospital setting, in contrast, falling short even once on the supplies needed to perform a surgery can substantially compromise patient safety and open the hospital to malpractice suits and loss of reputation that drives business elsewhere. In this case, the potential downside cost of falling short on surgical or cleaning supplies is proportionately much larger than the comparable costs in the durables manufacturing case. In addition, the proportion of total costs that the surgical and cleaning supplies account for is much smaller for the hospital—where employee compensation costs are a much larger fraction of total expenditures—than the comparable inputs to production are in durables manufacturing.

Thus a T&D JIT program to train employees in the durables manufacturing setting can be highly strategic, and the only benefit that may need to be demonstrated is that the employees improved their ability to operate a JIT inventory control system. If that benefit can be clearly demonstrated, senior executives likely would not call for an ROI or other financial calculation to justify continuing the T&D program. In the hospital setting, in contrast, even if a careful ROI calculation showed a direct link between JIT inventory management training and decreased holding costs of inventories, that evidence would not be sufficient to justify a JIT inventory T&D program. What matters is showing a direct link between the T&D program and outcomes that are important for strategic success, not just outcomes that have a financial benefit.

Step 3: Measure the Impact

The discussion to this point has highlighted the following tradeoff when it comes to T&D program design and measurement: the purest and cleanest statistical measurements are not necessarily feasible in cases where the T&D program is designed to have maximum business impact. This occurs because maximum impact may be achieved only through combining T&D with other activities or because the impact of T&D may be realized only through improving capabilities that indirectly have an impact on business performance.

It may be impossible to identify a direct and unique contribution of T&D to business performance, given all the other factors that contribute to performance. So the analytics, at best, might be able to show that the combined impact of T&D plus other activities have an overall business impact, and you may have to settle for that. It is not as clean as saying T&D had X percent ROI or contributed $Y to the bottom line, but it is usually much more accurate and credible. That also makes it much more useful as an aid to decision making.

When there are multiple programs or changes implemented at the same time, a pure measurement of T&D impact is not feasible. Yet that may not matter if the goal is to demonstrate a positive contribution of T&D to improved organizational performance and understand how to maximize the impact. What is needed is the information for accurate decision making: estimated economic impact may be an important component but certainly not the only basis for decision making.

It is important to keep in mind in these situations that the calculated unique impact of T&D can easily be an over- or underestimate. If other activities are needed at the same time, then it is easy to overstate the importance of T&D on its own merits. On the other hand, if only direct and clear impacts that are attributable to T&D are included in an ROI calculation, then the resulting figure likely understates the importance of T&D in improving business performance.

Thus the calculated economic impact of T&D can help inform decision making about its value but should be viewed with some caution. Estimated economic values of T&D's impact should never be the sole criteria used for determining whether a program's impact is positive, especially when deciding whether to continue, discontinue, or alter the program. It is impossible to clearly and accurately identify all the economic values of any HR or OD program on its own.

In conclusion, whatever method is used to estimate the business impact of a T&D program, the most important objective is to increase the information available for effective decision making, and this often requires a systems approach that measures the impact of many factors influencing performance.

About the Author

Alec Levenson, PhD, is senior research scientist at the Center for Effective Organizations at the University of Southern California. His action research with companies uses organization design, job design, human capital analytics, and strategic talent management to optimize organization performance and HR systems. Dr. Levenson's approach combines the best elements of scientific research and practical, actionable knowledge that companies can use to improve performance. He uses economics, strategy, organization behavior, and industrial-organizational psychology to tackle talent and organizational challenges that defy easy solutions. He has trained HR professionals from a broad range of Fortune 500 and Global 500 companies in human capital analytics.

References

Galbraith, J. (1977). *Organization Design*. Reading, MA: Addison-Wesley.

Kirkpatrick, D., and J. Kirkpatrick. (2006). *Evaluating Training Programs: The Four Levels,* 3rd edition. San Francisco: Berrett-Koehler.

Levenson, A. (2003). ROI and Strategy for Teams and Collaborative Work Systems. In *The Collaborative Work Systems Fieldbook: Strategies, Tools and Techniques,* eds. M. Beyerlein, C. McGee, G. Klein, L. Broedling, and J. Nemiro, San Francisco: Jossey-Bass/Pfeiffer.

Levenson, A. (2014). *Employee Surveys That Work: Improving Design, Use, and Organizational Impact*. San Francisco: Berrett-Koehler.

Levenson, A., and S. Cohen. (2003). Meeting the Performance Challenge: Calculating ROI for Virtual Teams. In *Virtual Teams That Work: Creating Conditions for Virtual Team Effectiveness,* eds. C.B. Gibson and S.G. Cohen. San Francisco: Jossey-Bass.

Levenson, A., W.A. Van der Stede, and S.G. Cohen. (2006). Measuring the Relationship Between Managerial Competencies and Performance. *Journal of Management,* 32(3).

Phillips, P., and J. Phillips. (2006). *Return on Investment (ROI) Basics*. Alexandria, VA: ASTD Press.

Section VI

Expanded Roles of the T&D Professional

Cobbler, What About Your Shoes? Career Contemplations for T&D Professionals

Luminary Perspective

Bev Kaye

As busy T&D professionals with multiple priorities, when do we take the time to stop and consider our own development needs? When do we stop to analyze our own wants? When do we figure out how to take action to move the needle on our own career satisfaction? The answer is usually "not often enough." We operate in overdrive, we balance so many balls, we serve so many clients, and we run so fast. It's no wonder we don't pause to think about our own careers and our own development.

This chapter points the finger at you to do some thinking about your own career. One of the strongest messages for today's workplace is the need to be accountable for your own career. The process begins with the self-assessment and moves to developing a strategic, realistic, and detailed development action plan that you can review with your manager.

Fit Is It!

The T&D field offers a wide variety of career options and choices. Self-awareness, or the lack of it, is critical because it affects every choice and decision you make. You need to know yourself in order to design and sustain a vital career. You need to become articulate about the person you are.

A good career fit happens when you find a job that matches your values, skills, and interests. All three are necessary for a productive and fulfilling working life. We gain feelings of commitment and purpose from our values. We gain feelings of competence from our skills. And we gain feelings of enjoyment and satisfaction from our interests.

Check out the latest information on skills and competencies required for our field. Pat McLagan has done the major competency work in our world and has published numerous articles in *T+D*. Most recently, Bill Rothwell and Ethan Sanders have also contributed to building these competencies. Stay up-to-date on her recommendations. Take advantage of all the ways that ASTD offers opportunities to learn from thought leaders and industry practitioners.

For starters, ask yourself:

- What have I always been naturally good at?
- What are my top three values or things I hold most dear?
- How would I spend my time if I didn't have to work?
- What tasks routinely get pushed to the bottom of my to-do list?
- What kinds of work settings/spaces help me do my best work?
- What skills do I see in others that I don't always see in myself?

Reputation Matters

Every workplace revolves around interactions with a wide variety of people. Their different perspectives have an effect on your career. Understanding how others see you provides you with information to assess yourself and to examine whether your reputation supports your career goals.

You can continually ask for feedback from people throughout your organization. You can use that knowledge to enhance skills, change performance habits, emphasize strengths, further develop your weaker areas, and create effective career plans.

Naturally, different people see you in different roles and situations. By comparing their views of your skills and potential with your own, you can test your self-image against reality. With that broad, accurate self-image, you will be able to set more realistic and more reachable career goals.

Understanding your reputation is a critical step in gaining this much-needed perspective. Your reputation consists of the stories others tell about you. These stories can take on a life of their own. Remember, rumors and anecdotes can enhance or limit your career opportunities. The further removed people are from firsthand experience of your performance, the more their assessments are based on their perception of your reputation.

T&D practitioners play to a huge career audience. Our brand is built by far more players than just the learners in our classrooms (wherever they are), including line management, other HR functions, senior leaders, our own peers, and those who report to us, to name just a few. Perspective from all audience members is critical.

For starters, ask members of your career "audience" these questions:

- What are my greatest strengths?
- Which of my skills are most valuable?
- What behaviors have you observed that might get in my way?
- How have I fallen short of expectations?
- In what settings or under what circumstances do I make the greatest contribution?
- Under what conditions have you observed me struggling?

The Landscape Changes

Understanding the world of work and identifying broad trends and challenges in your workplace environment is a critical next step. This allows you to weigh your options and make wiser choices. Understanding your job and your organization used to be enough. Today, marketability also demands foreseeing changes in your industry, organization, and profession.

Current and future trends, as well as challenges facing the industry, your organization, and your profession, can either create opportunities or limit your growth. The speed of information exchange, the "shrinking" of the world, and changes in technology, customer demographics, and increased competitiveness require a different kind of self-motivated, entrepreneurial mindset for every individual—not just leaders. Today, breadth of vision is essential for survival and marketability.

The faster the world is moving and changing, the more important it is to gain broad knowledge of these shifts. To master the realities of workplace challenges, every individual must continually follow workplace and professional trends. Reading material is everywhere. In additional to all the books, newsletters, journals, and whitepapers available through ASTD, there is additional data through SHRM, *CLO*, *Talent Management*, *HR Executive*, and *Training* magazine, just to name a few. Savvy careerists follow all of it. This empowers the smart career planner to maneuver more strategically, feel more confident about the direction they set for themselves, and contribute more effectively to the corporate objectives.

Consider these questions. Talk to your colleagues to gain their point of view:

- The most significant change I've seen in our industry is . . .
- I predict that the next big thing will be . . .
- I can imagine a time when . . .
- Our business would be turned upside down if . . .
- Everything will change with the obsolescence of . . .

Identify Multiple Options

Today, training and development professionals at all levels must pursue multiple career pathways. It was never really possible to think of career development as only moving up in your organization. If you are creative, open-minded, and willing to explore, there are a variety of choices that will provide opportunity and new ways to thrive in the changing world of work.

Taking responsibility for your own career requires learning to leverage your options. Often the biggest obstacle to career growth is not the lack of opportunity but inertia. If you are committed to actively pursuing multiple options, you will have a career strategy that will serve both your short-term and long-term goals.

It all used to be so simple. People selected a career area, educated themselves to pursue it, settled into an organization that could use their talents, worked to achieve higher rungs on the corporate ladder, and collected a retirement gift at the mandatory retirement age.

Today the picture has totally changed. Organizations are flattening and shrinking the number of management levels. Multidisciplinary teams and project groups are the new mode of work. Flexibility is the key—being ready to move to Plan B when Plan A is blocked. The more options you can pursue, the more likely it is that you will be successful.

Some questions to get you started:

- Where do you see yourself in one, two, or three years?
- What do you want to be doing?
- How do you want to be doing it?
- With whom and under what circumstances?

There will always be reasons to keep your options open—it's just smart planning. You can learn to explore six possible types of career moves by identifying career goals in each of these areas: lateral moves, enrichment opportunities, vertical promotions, exploratory actions, realignment options, and relocation prospects.

Lateral moves. Moving to new duties or areas, but at the same level and responsibility, can provide opportunities to expand your knowledge base. If you view your career as a rock-climbing wall as opposed to a ladder, you have a nearly unlimited combination of moves to help you grow, build your expertise, and learn something new. A lateral move may be more rewarding than you think. It makes you more valuable to your company and more attractive to promotions. For example, if you are in the training department, what positions might be available in the talent management shop or the organizational development group? Is there a position open in human resources such as hiring or benefits for which you could apply? Or consider a more dramatic shift to sales or marketing. Remember, every experience you gain and every position you hold will make you more marketable both within your organization and outside to other organizations.

Enrichment opportunities. Enhancing present skills and duties or adding new challenges and responsibilities creates potential for personal accomplishment and satisfaction. You can view this as growing on and in the job. Developing in place can become as attractive as other options. Look for opportunities within your organization such as leading a cross-functional team, volunteering to lead your annual charity drive, or taking on that new project that was just assigned to your department. Opportunities abound outside your organization as well. Consider taking on a leadership role in your local ASTD chapter, teaching a class at your local college, or providing pro bono work for a community, government, or nonprofit organization that has limited funds. Reflect on the skills you have and turn them into a personal enrichment experience. For example, if you help to conduct your organization's strategic planning session, you may be able to volunteer to conduct a strategic planning session for the board of a local university or nonprofit organization.

Vertical promotions. If you are seeking a promotion for more responsibility, beware that these positions may be in short supply. That does not mean you should not seek them out. Depending on your level in the organization, you may be waiting for your boss to retire—and that may be a longer time than you desire. Look beyond your immediate supervisor and consider positions being vacated by peers of your boss. Even if you are not selected, you are sending a message to your senior management that you are interested, want more responsibility, and desire opportunities that increase your value to the company. In addition, the act of applying for the job is an opportunity and an experience you should not ignore.

Exploratory actions. Testing change without permanent commitment by researching other options and identifying jobs that require your values, interests, skills, and style is both safe and satisfying. Ask your supervisor about rotational assignments. If this is not common in your organization, do a bit of homework before you meet with your supervisor to determine how your organization views rotational assignments, who has completed one, how it was managed, and how the results were measured. Your supervisor will be concerned about losing you, even if it is just a few weeks. Have a plan ready for your supervisor that includes how long you will be gone, how your work will be completed while you are gone, how you will stay in touch with your customers (internal and external), what you hope to learn during this rotational assignment, and how it will enhance your skills when you return. Often, as a T&D professional, you can rotate to a department that may be related to what you do, such as the internal consultant or the organizational development group. You could stretch even more, for example, by rotating to the graphic design shop to learn more about what goes into the services they provide to your department.

Realignment options. Starting over in a new but related area, or returning to a position with less status or responsibility, is a way to stay with the organization while starting a new career direction or reconciling the demands of your work with other priorities in your life. If you are looking for a career change or relief from the demands of the job you currently have, this may be an excellent move. For example, if you received your degree in a different profession but circumstances led you to the job you currently have, now might be the perfect time to revisit your original career path. For example, if you majored in business, would you consider a move to the finance, sales, or marketing department? If you majored in communications, is now the time to consider public relations or customer service? On the other hand, if you are just in the thinking stage, consider obtaining feedback before you make a final decision through a career assessment or even a 360-degree feedback instrument. Do you have a mentor? If not, get one. A mentor can provide you with insight about your future career, help you understand your organization's political climate, or lead you to others who can help you decide what you want to be when you grow up.

Relocation prospects. Looking outside the organization for a better career fit is a way to pursue a career goal not available in your current organization or to seize an entrepreneurial opportunity. If you are skilled and experienced, there is no end to where you might look for a position. Think about what parts of your job you enjoy the most and the least. Use that information to identify the best job for you. For example, if you like creating e-learning experiences the most, look for a high-tech company where you can excel. If you like delivery and wouldn't mind a bit of travel, check into companies that hire people to deliver training in various cities. Whether you are interested in more design or more delivery, remember to check some of the large training companies as well, such as The Ken Blanchard Company, DDI, Forum, or dozens of others. If you want to remain in the T&D world but test your entrepreneurial spirit, consider working for a local consulting firm as an employee or a sub-contractor. Ultimately, you might even consider starting your own training consulting firm.

Make Work Your Learning Lab

Successful career development requires a clear, viable plan of action that powerfully turns goals into realities. Planning involves action: writing things down, making connections with people who can help and support you, getting training or needed experience, identifying specific resources you can use, and taking advantage of upcoming opportunities.

You are responsible for your own learning and development. Learning to learn is one of the most essential competencies for the future. Organizations are lean and "doing more with less." Today, with the rate of change, it is harder to keep up with changing demands. Therefore, self-starting, self-learning professionals will have a competitive advantage.

Everyone needs to become a conscious and intentional learner. This is not only important for professional success and survival, but also for the survival of the organization. Nobody doubts that people must keep learning and growing in order to keep pace.

Learning comes in all shapes and sizes and is available in a variety of experiences. Which of these could provide the context for the learning you need? Consider combinations and permutations of:

- stretch assignments
- special projects
- events
- in-department rotations
- action learning projects and teams
- job shadowing
- community service.

The opportunity to leverage these experiences is limited only by you!

Time Well Spent

As a T&D professional, you should not allow yourself to be a "cobbler without shoes." You should be taking advantage of all the growth and learning opportunities available in your own organization and applying all those rich resources to your own career. This is important to you not only as a savvy careerist, but also because you are a role model for others.

Wondering where to start? Can't find the time? Here's one solid idea: Consider putting together a learning solution around career development for others in your organization. Select a department or division that had the lowest scores on those career-related questions on your last employee survey. Offer to scan the field for any off-the-shelf programs or design your very own. And, if you use yourself for all the examples, you'll be compelled and propelled to try this on for size.

Our field is changing rapidly and is ripe with new opportunities and new conundrums. It's a wonderful time for anyone with a thirst for continued learning. The T&D field needs your talent, your ideas, your energy, and your commitment. Invest. It will be time well spent.

Your Role

- Motivate yourself to begin working on your own development.
- Share your expectations, needs, and hopes for continued development.
- Broaden your skills and savvy to increase flexibility and offer added value to your organization.
- Participate in special assignments for enrichment and skill building.
- Gain a broader perspective of the industry and your organization.
- Set short-term and long-term goals.
- Build development plans to achieve your goals.
- Take advantage of opportunities for education, training, and development.

About the Author

Beverly Kaye, PhD, founder of Career Systems International, was named the 2010 recipient of the Distinguished Contribution to Workplace Learning and Performance Award by ASTD. Bev is recognized for her groundbreaking body of work and the significant impact she has had on learning and performance in the workplace. She is the author of *Up Is Not the Only Way*; co-author with Sharon Jordan-Evans of *Love 'Em or Lose 'Em: Getting Good People to Stay*, the *Wall Street Journal* bestselling book; and co-author of *Help Them Grow or Watch Them Go*. Career Systems International works with the Fortune 500 to invent, create, and design systems and strategies in development, engagement, and retention.

For Further Reading

Bolles, D. (2013). *What Color Is Your Parachute*. New York: Ten Speed Press.

Cleaver, J. (2012). *The Career Lattice*. New York: McGraw-Hill.

Kaye, B. (2003). *Love It, Don't Leave It: 26 Ways to Get What You Want at Work*. San Francisco: Berrett-Koehler.

Kaye, B., and J. Winkle. (2012). *Help Them Grow or Watch Them Go*. San Francisco: Berrett-Koehler.

Williams, C., and A. Reitman. (2013). *Career Moves: Be Strategic About Your Future*, 3rd edition. Alexandria, VA: ASTD Press.

Chapter 35

Designing an Economical and Effective Onboarding Process

Karen Lawson

Employees are an organization's most valuable resource. Yet the way organizations "welcome" a new employee creates the opposite impression. Bringing a new employee "on board" is a process, not an event. It involves providing information, training, mentoring, and coaching over a six- to 12-month period.

The Need for an Interactive Approach to Onboarding New Employees

The importance of a successful onboarding program is underscored by the following research:

- As many as 4 percent of new employees leave their new jobs after a disastrous first day (Moscato, 2005).

- New employees decide within the first 30 days whether they feel welcome in the organization (Friedman, 2006).
- One in 25 people leave a new job just because of a poor (or nonexistent) onboarding program (Owler, 2007).
- Forty percent of senior managers hired from the outside fail within 18 months of hire (Wells, 2005).

Doing Your Homework

Before you begin to design your new employee onboarding program, you need to spend time up front getting support, buy-in, and participation from others in the organization. You cannot design this program in a vacuum. You need to be clear about what the organization's top management wants to accomplish in a new employee onboarding program.

Purpose and Goals of Program

The purpose of a new employee onboarding program is to:

- Provide employees information to help them integrate smoothly and quickly into the organization.
- Introduce employees to the organization as a whole—its structure, philosophy, purpose, values, and so forth.
- Help new employees identify the importance of their roles within the organization and how what they do affects others.
- Introduce employees to their departmental goals and their roles in helping to meet those goals.
- Promote communication between the employee and management.
- Communicate expectations regarding policies, procedures, and performance.
- Make new employees feel welcome and assure them that they made the right decision to join the team.
- Get employees excited about being a part of the organization and motivated to do the best job possible.

Designing an Interactive Orientation Program

The first step in bringing a new employee into the organization is the formal orientation program. Many organizations approach this in a haphazard fashion. Others spend thousands of dollars and a great deal of time and effort on slick PowerPoint presentations, multiple guest speakers, and voluminous employee handbooks. Yet the new employee walks away from the session dazed, anxious, and overwhelmed. Why? For starters, the typical new employee orientation program is boring. Like many other training programs, it is presenter centered and lecture driven with little or no opportunity for participant interaction. This traditional approach is characterized by too many facts, figures, and faces packed into a few hours. Then when the new employee finally gets to his work site, it's obvious no one is prepared for his arrival.

The orientation program is really the employee's first exposure to the organization; therefore, it should be an enjoyable and memorable experience. Because it sets the tone, the new employee orientation program needs to be a priority. A thoughtfully planned and delivered program helps the employee's transition, helps him feel good about the organization, and ignites the employee's excitement and enthusiasm. The focus should be on helping to integrate the new employee into the organization and to begin to build relationships.

Organizations that "skimp" on orientation programs not only shortchange the employee, but also they miss the perfect opportunity to communicate and help the employee embrace and internalize the organization's philosophy, values, norms, and culture. Employees also need to understand how they fit into the big picture and that what they do is important and makes a difference. Thus it can help the new employee become more comfortable, confident, and competent.

Elements of an Effective Orientation Program

Ideally, the formal organization orientation session should provide an opportunity for the new employee to learn important information about the organization, and it should be conducted in a manner that reflects adult learning principles and active training practices.

A new employee orientation program should be handled no differently than any other effective training design. It needs to include specific learning objectives, "need-to-know" rather than "nice-to-know" content, active-training methods that focus on the participant and reflect adult learning principles, and ways to measure training effectiveness. The design should address all three learning domains: cognitive, affective, and behavioral.

Cognitive learning focuses on knowledge development, that is, the acquisition of information. In the case of our orientation program, you want participants to acquire knowledge about the organization such as its history, culture, structure, philosophy, policies, and procedures.

Affective learning addresses attitude development. It deals with attitudes, values, or feelings. You want your new employees to feel good about their decision to join your organization and to really get excited about being part of the team. You also want them to embrace your corporate values and be sensitive to issues such as sexual harassment and diversity.

Behavioral learning deals with skill development. Behavioral learning focuses on a person being able to perform a task or procedure. This, of course, becomes particularly critical once the employee is actually on the job; however, the new employee orientation program should give participants an opportunity to learn how to complete forms, answer the telephone properly, use the organization's intranet system, operate the copier and fax machines, and so on.

With these three learning domains in mind, the next step is to write specific, participant-centered learning objectives.

Setting Specific Learning Objectives

Objectives serve as a type of contract. If participants know the program or session objectives from the beginning, they will know what they will be learning. Objectives give participants a sense of direction. They know what to expect from you and what you expect from them.

Objectives serve as the basis for the design and development of the program, that is, the instructional plan. They help the trainer focus clearly on the desired outcomes and determine what the participants need to know and do in order to meet those objectives.

Objectives should be written from the participant's point of view, not the trainer's. The emphasis should not be on what you want to cover but what you want the participant to value, understand, or do with the subject, information, or skills after the training program is over.

Objectives are used to measure success. Because they describe what the participant will be able to do at the end of the training, the objectives automatically become the standard against which success is measured.

Orientation Program Content

Once you have determined the learning objectives or outcomes, the next step is to decide what specific content should be included. During the first few weeks on the job, new employees are overwhelmed. An effective new employee onboarding program will focus on what new employees absolutely need to know during the initial stages of their employment. It's tempting to want to give these folks everything all at once. Resist the "information dump" approach that creates cognitive overload and results in a high level of participant frustration.

Content flows naturally from the learning outcomes or objectives. The content driven by the objectives should determine the length of the program. There are, however, a number of factors to consider that may be outside your control and may limit the amount of time you would like to spend.

Standard Topics for a New Employee Orientation Program

Regardless of the program length, standard topics for a new employee onboarding program fall into the broad categories listed in the sidebar.

Standard Topics for an Onboarding Program

- Company History/Background
  - History
  - Organization profile
  - Culture
  - Philosophy
  - Mission, vision, values
  - Goals and organization direction
  - Logo/tag line
  - Senior management team/ department heads
  - Financial position
  - Locations/building layout
  - Structure
  - Products and services
  - Customers
  - Competitors

- Benefits/Compensation
  - Compensation/bonus
  - Insurance plans
  - Retirement/deferred compensation
  - Profit sharing

- Time off
- Paid overtime
- Workers' compensation
- Tuition reimbursement

- Policies/Procedures
  - Work hours
  - Standards of personal conduct
  - Ethics
  - Safety
  - Emergencies
  - Computer/Internet usage
  - Sexual harassment
  - Parking
  - Attendance/tardiness
  - Rest and meal breaks
  - Performance evaluation

- Programs/Services
  - Employee assistance program
  - Mentor program
  - Employee development
  - Service and recognition awards

Strategies and Methods

Once you have identified *what* you are going to include in the program, the next step is to determine *how* you are going to communicate the content. Instructional methods are the various means by which content or material is communicated. They include the use of activities (structured experiences) and a variety of cooperative learning or active training techniques.

Organization Orientation

Within three to six weeks, the employee should attend an organization orientation that addresses the company's history, philosophy and culture, and goals and direction. The purpose is to introduce employees to the organization as a whole and help them feel a part of it. This is also a good opportunity to elaborate on career opportunities and emphasize the importance of each person's role to the success of the organization. Members of senior management should participate as guest speakers, preferably in person or, at the very least, through a video presentation. A nice touch is to host a short reception either during a break or after the session during which members of management mingle with the newcomers, getting to know them on a personal level and answering any questions they may have but were afraid to ask in front of the group.

Depending on the size of the organization, "Breakfast With the President" could be another element of the orientation process. In this particular program, the president or another senior manager meets with new employees who have been on the job approximately three months, in small groups of 10-12. At this time, the senior member solicits feedback and answers questions employees may have regarding the organization as a whole. This is a good opportunity to identify and address potential problems before they become major issues and to help remove some of the mystique employees often associate with senior management.

Onboarding Materials

Printed materials are an important element of a new employee onboarding program. Each new employee should receive a three-ring binder with the materials they will need to be successful. New employees should also know where to locate this information on the company internal website. New employee information includes:

- mission, vision, values
- organization history
- organization structure
- products and services
- employee handbook
- resources and contacts
- helpful information
- "fun stuff."

Help the employee feel welcome by including organizational mementos such as logo pens, pins, mugs, product samples, and so on. You might also include the annual report, brochures, and maps. Create a fun, practical, and professional package that can also serve as important and useful reference material.

Creating the Environment

A major underlying goal of the new employee orientation program is to make it enjoyable and to show new employees how much you value them. To that end, put the time, energy, and money into making the actual training session a memorable experience. One way to accomplish this is by establishing a theme and creating the physical environment that reflects it. For example, you might choose a cruise ship theme. The cruise ship becomes the metaphor for the organization, and just like on a real cruise ship, you would throw a "bon voyage" party to celebrate the beginning of the cruise. In effect, the new employees are celebrating the beginning of their new jobs and career opportunities. Post a sign on the door of the training room that reads, "Welcome Aboard the SS (Your Company Name)." Greet each new employee with a Hawaiian lei and a "welcome aboard" packet of materials including some "fun stuff." Decorate the room with streamers and balloons. Play party music, and have each new employee pose for a picture as she enters the room (just like people do on a real cruise ship). You can expand the metaphor to include "ports of call" (learning about various departments) and "life rafts" (various resources to contact with questions). Of course, just like on a real cruise ship, you will have to have food! Now that the new employees are "on board," you can "set sail" for their exciting journey. Let your imagination and creativity run wild. Try out other themes such as outer space, the old west, races, sports events, and so forth.

Quality Control

Ensure that the onboarding process is successful by establishing it as a formal program with a program administrator. The most logical department to handle that responsibility is the training department or human resource department. In addition to providing the basic framework for the program, the training department can be very helpful by conducting onboarding training sessions for managers and supervisors. These sessions should include the following:

- the purpose and objectives of an onboarding program
- the importance of orientation and its effect on performance and turnover
- the supervisor's/manager's role
- the benefits of proper onboarding for the employee, the supervisor, and the company
- checklists and manuals to help guide managers and supervisors through the onboarding process
- follow-up and evaluation procedures.

Setting the Tone

New employee onboarding should begin even before the employee's first day on the job. It's important that the employee's supervisor make a personal telephone contact, welcoming her to the organization. Every effort should be made to make the new person feel a part of the team.

First Day—New Employee Concerns

It is important that the new employee feels comfortable in her new surroundings, whether the employee is an executive or an entry-level clerk, new to the company or just to a department. The new employee's comfort level should be a primary consideration, and it is the manager or supervisor's responsibility to aid the employee's adaptation to the work environment.

Onboarding the new employee goes beyond the company's formal orientation program. The first day is critical to the employee's success and for that reason should be planned and orchestrated carefully. Managers and supervisors need to take care of the basics and help employees adjust quickly so they can concentrate on doing what they were hired to do. Failure to orient employees properly will result in poor attitude, low morale and productivity, performance problems, and, in some cases, the loss of a valuable employee. The sooner employees adapt and feel comfortable, the sooner they become productive. Even before employees walk into the work area, efforts should be made to help them feel part of the organization and see themselves as part of the team.

New employees are filled with anxiety and confusion. In short, they are overwhelmed. They begin to question the decision they made. Did I do the right thing? Am I really qualified to do this job? Will I like my boss and the people I work with? Will I fit in? The way in which a person is treated on her first day will determine whether that person's fears and anxieties are warranted and, as a result, how she will approach this new experience.

New employees also have certain wants and expectations. They want to be treated like people. They want to know what is expected of them and how they will go about learning their new jobs. They want to know how they will be rewarded and how they fit into the total picture. It's easy to overlook or forget the fact that people begin a job with success in mind; they genuinely want to do a good job. This commitment and enthusiasm is either squelched or encouraged within the first few hours on the job.

Conducting a Departmental Orientation

The manager/supervisor plays a key role in the departmental onboarding process. The supervisor is usually the first one to have contact with the new employee and becomes the most influential person in developing the new employee's attitudes and impressions. The supervisor is responsible for giving the new employee the tools and resources to be successful in the new position.

A manager or supervisor will be on target in addressing the new employee's concerns if she approaches onboarding from the basic who, what, where, when, why, and how questions. These questions are presented in Figure 35-1.

Figure 35-1. Departmental Onboarding Checklist

WHERE
- ☐ Where will I find . . . ?
  - ☐ restrooms
  - ☐ lunch area
  - ☐ my work area
  - ☐ employee lounge
  - ☐ supplies
  - ☐ equipment
  - ☐ reference material
  - ☐ files/records
- ☐ Where should I park?

HOW
- ☐ How do I operate the . . . ?
  - ☐ telephone
  - ☐ photocopier
  - ☐ facsimile machine
  - ☐ postage meter
  - ☐ computer
- ☐ How do I fit in this department?
- ☐ How will I be trained?
- ☐ How will I be evaluated?
- ☐ How will I be compensated for overtime?
- ☐ How do I process the mail?
- ☐ How do I order supplies?
- ☐ How do I use email?

WHO
- ☐ Who is senior management?
- ☐ Who can I go to for help?
- ☐ Who do I report to?
- ☐ Who do I interact with?

WHEN
- ☐ When do I go to lunch and take breaks?
- ☐ When will I be paid?
- ☐ When will I be evaluated?
- ☐ When should I report for work each day?
- ☐ When can I expect to leave each day?

WHAT
- ☐ What are the job requirements?
- ☐ What are the manager's expectations?
- ☐ What are the standards of performance?
- ☐ What are the policies and procedures regarding . . . ?
  - ☐ coffeepot
  - ☐ lunchroom cleanup
  - ☐ smoking
  - ☐ dress
  - ☐ sickness
  - ☐ vacation
  - ☐ parties
  - ☐ call-in
  - ☐ travel and expense reports
- ☐ What is the structure of the department?
- ☐ What advancement/developmental opportunities are available to me?

WHY
- ☐ Why do we follow that procedure?
- ☐ Why do I have to do this?

Goals of the Departmental Onboarding Process

- Develop good communications with new employee from the start.
- Introduce new employee to departmental goals, policies and procedures, customs, and traditions.
- Convey responsibilities and expectations clearly.
- Provide new employee with information that will ease the transition to the workplace.

Preparation for the Employee's Arrival

- Inform the staff that a new employee will be joining the department. Tell them when the employee will arrive, what she will be doing, and where she will be located, and share some information about the employee such as previous job, background, and qualifications.
- Select a department member to be the newcomer's "buddy" or mentor whose responsibility will be to show the new employee around, make introductions, answer questions, explain why things are done a certain way, and, in general, help make her feel welcome and a part of the group. The person selected should be a high performer who demonstrates the behavior you want all employees to demonstrate, and should be respected, empathetic, well networked, and a good listener.

Employee's First Day

- **Employment processing.** As standard in most companies, the employee will report first to the human resource department to receive benefits information, sign the necessary employment processing forms, and be given an employee handbook or equivalent outlining the company's policies and procedures.
- **Department arrival.** Approximately mid-morning, the employee will leave the human resource department to report to his or her worksite. The supervisor should greet the new employee personally and set aside adequate time to introduce her to the work environment.

First-day orientation is not something a supervisor should delegate. It's too important. This initial interaction establishes lines of communication between the supervisor and new employee. The supervisor's responsibility is to set the tone and create an environment that helps reduce the employee's anxiety. The relationship between the supervisor and the employee is critical to the employee's success on the job.

The supervisor begins by getting acquainted with the employee and relating on a personal level. Ask the employee questions about her family and how the employee feels about starting a new job. The next step is to review the job duties and responsibilities, performance expectations and standards, and company policies such as sick time, vacations, hours, pay, dress code, overtime, smoking policy, and customs. In addition, the employee should receive a departmental information packet containing an organizational chart, department and organization telephone directory, manuals, safety rules, health regulations, and other helpful information such as company brochures, employee newsletter, annual report, and list of resource people. To ensure uniformity and consistency, the supervisor can follow a prepared checklist of topics to be addressed during the orientation period. Be sure to give a copy to the new employee so she will know what to expect. Since the organization orientation will cover personnel policies and practices as well as a more global view of the organization as a whole, this particular checklist addresses items peculiar to the department and the person's specific job.

An important and often overlooked area is an explanation of the unwritten practices within the department itself, the social norms such as kitchen cleanup, coffeepot, birthdays, parties, and other accepted behavior peculiar to that department. Failure to do so can result in a real disaster. These unwritten practices should be communicated to everyone new to the department—not just new hires. Often, people who have been with the organization and transferred to a new department are overlooked. Remember that this is a totally new environment for this employee as well.

With the preliminaries out of the way, the supervisor can begin acclimating the newcomer to the work unit itself by giving her a few minutes to settle into her own work space. This can be followed by a tour of the work area with the new employee, introducing her to co-workers, pointing out locations of restrooms, supply areas, lunch facilities, photocopy machine, bulletin boards, mail room, and adjacent departments. At this point, it would be appropriate to introduce the new employee to her "buddy" or mentor and break away to allow the two to get acquainted. This get-acquainted process could be facilitated by having the co-worker show the new employee how to operate the telephone system, photocopier, and other equipment; how to order supplies; and other operational details. The co-worker should also accompany the newcomer to lunch, taking care to introduce her to others in the organization.

At the end of the day, the supervisor should meet once again with the new hire to answer any questions, review important information, give encouragement, and reinforce how pleased everyone in the department is to have her on the team.

Employee's Second Day

On the second day, the on-the-job training process should begin with the designated trainer greeting the new employee first thing in the morning. The on-the-job training is structured and designed to get the employee working comfortably on her own as soon as possible. The employee's mentor should remain in the picture, arranging to go on breaks and lunches together and offering support.

Employee's First Week

At the end of the first week, the manager meets with the employee once again to check on his or her progress, answer questions, and provide additional information such as department goals and objectives, the performance planning and evaluation process, and career development opportunities. At this point, the manager may also want to review the company's mission statement and goals and explain how the department and the individual fit in the total organization. On the other hand, a discussion of "the big picture" might be more relevant and meaningful if delayed until after the employee's initial adjustment period.

Special Considerations

Today's workplace offers a variety of employment options, including a growing number of contract and temporary employees as well as telecommuters. These nontraditional employment arrangements require a different orientation approach.

Sometimes it just isn't cost-effective or practical to bring employees to a central location for an orientation session. People are often spread out among remote sites and locations. Bringing them to the corporate headquarters can be very costly. Some organizations, particularly small to midsize companies, have few new employees and, therefore, it could be a long time before there were enough new employees to hold a group session. Although situations such as those just mentioned may prevent you from conducting a traditional group orientation, you can still develop and administer a structured new employee orientation program.

Extra thought should be given to designing an initial orientation program for employees who may spend weeks (or even months) in training before placing them in their specific departments or branches. These circumstances may create a sense of isolation and disconnection; however, this lack of corporate identity can be greatly minimized through a new employee orientation program adapted to meet these special situations.

No matter what the format or venue, the orientation content does not change. New employees at remote sites still need the same information as those located at corporate headquarters.

Delivery Methods

Once you are clear on the information you want to include, the next step is to decide the method or methods you are going to use to deliver that information. You have several options depending on the resources and capabilities available to you and, more importantly, available to the new employee. Basically, the delivery methods fall into three broad categories:

- manager or supervisor facilitated
- technology based and computer based
- self-directed or self-study.

You may choose one of the delivery methods or any combination. Once again, your organization's unique circumstances and its management philosophy will drive those decisions.

Manager or Supervisor Facilitated

One fairly low-cost and low-tech delivery method is to develop a packaged program to be facilitated by the new employee's manager or supervisor. The program developer would prepare materials, a leader's guide, and perhaps a video and send the package to each site.

Design for a Small-Group Session

In this scenario, we are defining a small group as any number of people between three and 12. When designing a supervisor- or manager-facilitated program, you must be sensitive to the realities of the everyday business environment.

First of all, managers and supervisors have other responsibilities and, therefore, do not have a lot of time to prepare for and deliver a program. If they view this additional responsibility as an intrusion or inconvenience, they may not give it the attention it deserves. Even worse, they may decide to eliminate it altogether.

Second, because the new employees are already on the job and engaged in their specific job-related tasks and responsibilities, it may be difficult to pull them off the job for large blocks of time.

The solution to these potential problems is to scale down or chunk the program into manageable segments conducted over a period of weeks and months. The key is to make the process user friendly. With that in mind, here is a suggested design for a supervisor-facilitated program broken into one-hour segments:

Session 1	Objectives
	Getting acquainted
	Assessing needs
	Background/philosophy
Session 2	Organizational structure
	Products and services
Session 3	Policies and procedures
	Professional appearance
Session 4	Core values
	Ethics
Session 5	Resources
	Terminology

Design for a One-on-One Session

Even a one-on-one session can be interactive and fun. In most one-on-one sessions, the supervisor sits down with the employee and reviews information. The problem with this approach is that it can easily become an information dump, and the communication is primarily one-way, with the supervisor talking at the employee and then asking, "Do you understand?" followed by an equally dull, "Do you have any questions?" Both these questions result in "yes" or "no" answers and do little to promote two-way communication between the supervisor and the employee.

A more interesting and interactive approach would be to give information to the new employee to read on her own. Appropriate material would be the employee handbook, brochures describing products and services, and other critical pieces of information that you want the employee to know. It would be advisable to "chunk" the information and then to set up individual meetings to discuss the assigned material. During these one-on-one sessions, the supervisor could "test" the employee's knowledge or understanding of the material by asking open-ended questions. For example, the supervisor might ask, "What is our organization's mission statement, and what do you think it means?" The supervisor can also use some of the same activities normally used in a group session. Here are some activities the new employee could do individually:

- our heritage (video)
- organizational structure
- policies and procedures

- core values
- ethics
- resources.

Technology Based and Computer Based

The term "computer based" is used widely to include delivery via CD-ROM, intranet, or Internet. Organizations with video conferencing or teleconferencing capabilities may choose that venue to deliver their new employee orientation programs. Before you get excited about these state-of-the-art approaches, carefully consider the costs involved with the development as well as the resources necessary. Make sure that the new employees have access to a computer with the appropriate bandwidth.

Another consideration of any computer-based approach is the issue of updates. You need a program administrator to monitor the program and make sure the information is up-to-date and accurate. It's also important to select a delivery platform that lends itself to easy and cost-effective updates. Keep in mind, however, that all these technology-based delivery methods tend to be impersonal and thus defeat the purpose of making the new employee feel welcome and a part of the team.

Self-Directed or Self-Study

A self-directed program involves a combination of self-study activities to be completed by the employee on the job and frequent one-on-one meetings with the supervisor. Depending on the available resources, this approach could involve a combination of computer-based and supervisor-facilitated activities.

Onboarding as an Ongoing Process

The onboarding process does not end after the initial orientation activities. This ongoing six- to 12-month process involves giving the employee the skills and knowledge to do her job (training), integrating the employee into the organization's culture and community (mentoring), working with the employee to improve performance (coaching), and giving formal feedback (appraising performance).

Finally, you will need to monitor and measure the effectiveness of the onboarding process. At the end of 90 days, ask the employee to evaluate the first three months' onboarding experience. At six months, measure the new employee's total experience thus far. These evaluations should be a combination of written and one-on-one conversations with the employee's manager. On or near the employee's one-year anniversary, again have the employee evaluate his or her satisfaction with the company and the onboarding experience.

An effective new employee onboarding program takes time and effort but is well worth the investment. Studies show that a well-planned, comprehensive orientation program greatly benefits both the organization and the employees. A positive orientation experience results in a high level of engagement and commitment that leads to increased employee retention.

About the Author

Karen Lawson, PhD, CSP, founder and president of Lawson Consulting Group, is an international consultant, executive coach, speaker, and author of 13 books on the subjects of training, coaching, communications, and influencing. She holds a doctorate in adult and organizational development from Temple University and has presented at many national professional conferences in the United States, Europe, and Asia. She is currently an adjunct professor at Arcadia University, where she teaches Leadership for Effective Organizations in the international MBA program. She is one of only 400 people worldwide to have earned the designation of Certified Speaking Professional awarded by the National Speakers Association. She has received numerous awards for her contribution to the training and speaking professions and was also named one of Pennsylvania's Best 50 Women in Business, as well as one of the *Philadelphia Business Journal's* Women of Distinction.

References

Friedman, L. (2006, November). Are You Losing Potential New Hires at Hello? *T+D* 25-27.

Moscato, D. (2005, June/July). Using Technology to Get Employees on Board. *HR Magazine* 107-109.

Owler, K. (2007, June/July). The Art of Induction: A Process Not an Event. *Human Resources* 22-23.

Wells, S.J. (2005, March). Diving In. *HR Magazine* 55-59.

For Further Reading

Barbezette, J. (2001). *Successful New Employee Orientation,* 2nd edition. San Francisco: Jossey-Bass/Pfeiffer.

Bauer, T.N. (2010). *Onboarding New Employees: Maximizing Success.* Alexandria, VA: SHRM Foundation.

Lawson, K. (2002). *New Employee Orientation Training.* Alexandria, VA: ASTD Press.

Sims, D. (2010). *Creative Onboarding Programs: Tools for Energizing Your Orientation Program,* 2nd edition. New York: McGraw-Hill.

Stein, M., and L. Christiansen. (2010). *Successful Onboarding: Strategies to Unlock Hidden Value Within Your Organization.* New York: McGraw-Hill.

Chapter 36

Consulting on the Inside

Beverly Scott and B. Kim Barnes

In This Chapter

■ Review the differences between external and internal consultants.

■ Learn the different requirements, advantages, and challenges of an internal consultant.

■ Learn the process for internal consulting.

"I was reminded during my time inside that when you are in the system, you are part of the system—for better and for worse. Being inside inhibits your detachment. I think the main difference between internal and external consultants is that the internal consultant is more focused on task and the external on process. Neither is 'better' than the other: In order to have strategic change, you must have both."

—Amanda Trosten-Bloom, Corporation for Positive Change
(Scott and Hascall, 2002, 2006)

The term *consultant* often raises images of highly paid business consultants from large firms brought in by senior management to address problems that the organization cannot solve. External consultants from large or small firms bring the advantages of outsider status and expertise drawn from a wider base of experience—the basis for their perceived value to executives. It's also easier to understand their role as temporary advisors who help and influence management to address specific issues and then leave the organization. On the other hand, an "internal consultant" has different requirements, advantages, and challenges. See Table 36-1 for a comparison of internal and external consulting roles. This chapter explores the advantages and challenges of the internal consultant, the roles, unique competencies, and other success requirements.

Table 36-1. Comparison of Internal and External Consulting Roles

Similarities	Differences	
	Internals	**Externals**
Have knowledge of human systems, organization, and individual behavior	Are accepted as a member of the group and congruent with the internal culture	Sees culture and organization with outsider perspective
Understand the process of change	Have credibility as insiders	Have credibility as outsiders
Desire to be successful and recognized for the value they bring to their clients	Know organization and business intimately	Bring broader experience from other organizations
Make a commitment to learning	Build long-term relationships and establish rapport more easily	Confront, give feedback, take risks with senior management more easily
Have passion about their work	Coordinate and integrate projects into ongoing activities	Focus involvement on a project that ends
Are able to influence and lead	Have opportunities to influence, gain access, and sit at the table as insiders	Use broader experience to offer credibility, power, and influence
Have skills to analyze needs and design interventions	Leverage and use informal and formal organization structure	Can avoid or ignore the organization structure and move around organizations to achieve results
Possess credibility or authority	Lead from position and character (trust)	Lead from competence and personality (expertise)
	Know cultural norms that should not be violated	Can acceptably challenge or violate the informal rules of the culture
	Know the history, traditions, and where the bodies are buried	Are seen as objective and not part of the problem
	Can take an advocacy role	Bring more objectivity and neutrality
	May be expected to be broad generalists	Often seen as specialists with narrow expertise
	Have a lot more skin in the game	Can always move on to other clients

Advantages of Internal Consultants

The internal consultant offers unique benefits as an insider with deep knowledge of sensitive issues, cultural norms, and organizational history. External consultants are often engaged for their unique and specialized skills and knowledge, but the internal practitioner has the benefit of intimate, detailed, hands-on knowledge of the business, strategy, and culture of the organization (see Table 36-2 for when to choose an internal versus external consultant). Internal consultants understand organizational politics, webs of relationships, and details of past history to a degree that few externals can match. Internals can use inside jargon and language. Their deep, sometimes personal, relationships with clients and colleagues build trust and credibility over time. Consequently, internals have an enhanced ability to assess situations and use the right approach with a shorter ramp-up time on new projects.

A second advantage is that internal consultants participate in the life of the organization. They are aware of business challenges, customer issues, and management decisions and actions. External consultants often enter the system for a short time to implement a specific solution. The internal consultant remains in the organization long after the project is completed and can thus follow progress, identify challenges or barriers to the solution, and follow up quickly with members of the organization to support the effort or ensure that actions are carried out or adjusted as necessary. Insider knowledge allows internals to recognize potential linkages to allied initiatives in other parts of the organization, involve other functional staff, or expand an initiative to include other issues.

Third, internal practitioners are a ready resource to senior leaders, internal change partners, and employees. They collaborate across the organization, build commitment for change initiatives, and can give spontaneous coaching or advice. Immediate action may head off a potential problem, defuse a budding conflict, encourage a project leader, or provide needed support in developing new behaviors.

Table 36-2. When to Use Internal or External Consultants

When to Use External Consultants	When to Use Internal Consultants
To support development of strategy or facilitate corporate-wide initiatives or key priorities	To support implementation of strategic priority, or intervention as an operational focus
Internal expertise does not reside within the organization	Organization possesses the needed internal expertise
Deep expertise is needed	Broad generalist knowledge is needed
An outside, neutral perspective is important	Knowledge of the organization and business is critical
New, risky alternatives require validation from an outside expert	Speaking the jargon or the language of the organization and the culture is important
Internal does not have status, power, or authority to influence senior management or the culture	A sensitive insider who knows the issues is needed
CEO, president, or senior leaders need coach, guide, or objective sounding board	Need to sustain a long-term initiative where internal ownership is important
Initiative justifies the expense	Cost is a factor
Project has defined boundaries or limits	Follow-up and quick access are needed

Source: Scott and Hascall (2002, 2006).

Issues and Challenges

Internal consultants' intimate knowledge of the organization and the business makes them valuable business partners. It also challenges their role of neutrality and objectivity; they may be seen as too familiar, not capable of the objective outsider's worldview. They must stand at the edge, operate at the margins, and maintain distance. This delicate balance of having organizational knowledge yet keeping a marginal position defines the paradox that confronts the internal consultant. Belonging to the organization and finding acceptance helps internal consultants be congruent with their clients; yet they must be cautious and avoid collusion (such as failing to tell senior managers the truth.)

Internal consultants are often placed in a middle tier of the reporting hierarchy within the human resource function. Many organizations do not appreciate the value of a strong, skilled internal consulting function. Practitioners may find their status and reporting relationships a barrier to establishing competence and credibility. Sometimes their midlevel positioning makes it difficult to establish a consultant/client relationship with a senior executive. In addition, when senior leaders of the organization bring in external consultants to lead change initiatives, the success of these efforts will often depend on follow-up work by internal practitioners. Developing a professional relationship with external experts and a seat at the table for major initiatives can be difficult. The internal consultant has to show that he or she is more than a pair of hands to implement projects driven by an external firm. Table 36-3 describes the conditions that contribute to or undermine success.

Table 36-3. Internal–External Partnerships

Internal–External Partnerships
Success Conditions   • Flexibility and open communication   • Sense of being in it together   • Opportunity to leverage cost, efficiencies, knowledge, and credibility   • Strengths of internal recognized and valued   • Internal is open to learning   • Pairing insider knowledge with outsider perspective and credibility   • Appreciation and understanding of cultural differences
Undermining Conditions   • Internals may not be in position to have organizational influence to lead major change initiative   • Senior management may not understand the value of the internal's organizational ties and thus fail to support partnership   • Externals ignore or go around the internal function promoting themselves solely to senior management   • Internals left out of the contracting process may feel resentful, threatened, and marginalized, resulting in a lack of commitment   • Externals are often seen as arrogant, exclusive, judgmental; in turn, internals are perceived as ineffective, incompetent, and "poor losers"   • Weak internal functions that may be incapable of successfully leading change projects

Source: Scott and Hascall (2002, 2006).

Many internal consultants face pressure from senior-level clients to break confidences, take on unrealistic projects, or make inappropriate changes. Internal consultants often experience resistance and a lack of cooperation from their human resource peers. Successful internal consultants have access to and move throughout the hierarchy advocating and facilitating change. Human resource professionals are more focused on protecting and stabilizing the organization. These challenges and paradoxes create conflict and stress for the internal consultant who joins the organization unprepared for these challenges (Foss et al., 2005; Scott, 2000).

Developing collegial relationships within the organization may present difficulties, due to the confidential nature of much of the work that internal consultants undertake. Friendly colleagues may expect them to share inside information. They may have to look elsewhere in order to find others with whom they can discuss their concerns and issues in order to learn and gain new perspectives. They will have to find their best confidantes, mentors, and coaches outside their organization.

A key part of the role of the internal consultant in many organizations is educational—letting others know what they can expect and gain from developing a strong working relationship with him. This is a marketing challenge and may require the internal consultant to help clients and colleagues unlearn certain expectations (for example, that the consultant will fulfill his order as requested) and learn new ones (for example, that the client will be expected to provide resources including, but not limited to, his time, energy, and wholehearted support). Initial meetings with new clients offer opportunities to negotiate an effective working relationship, establishing realistic expectations of one another. There may also be other ways to promote a broader understanding in the organization of one's value proposition and how to best access and take advantage of it.

The role of a consultant, whether internal or external, is dependent on the ability to influence clients, colleagues, team members, and others in the organization. A strong set of influencing skills and a sophisticated ability to apply them in the service of important organizational or client goals is essential to success. These professionals do not have the luxury of waiting for the phone to ring or the message to arrive requesting their wisdom and expertise. Instead, they may be called upon to lead important change efforts and take an active role in moving the organization forward toward achieving key strategic goals. Perhaps the most important challenge any internal consultant faces is that of adding real value by influencing others to take actions they might not otherwise take. This may not win them recognition—in fact, if they are successful, as Lao Tzu once wrote, the people will say, "We did it ourselves."

Opportunities

Despite the challenges, internal consultants have a unique opportunity to exploit their position and have a long-term, significant influence on the organization. Internal consultants' holistic knowledge of the organization enables them to take a systems view, ensuring that linkages and processes support the change targets. When they partner with external consultants, they can be multipliers by disseminating and reinforcing expertise and cutting-edge concepts, integrating them into the culture of the organization through their day-to-day work. Using inside knowledge of the business and organization, they can be catalysts for needed change, ensure organizational alignment with the business strategy, prepare employees with skills to cope with forthcoming changes in a tumultuous business environment, and provide candid perspectives as confidential sounding boards for senior executives.

Internal Consulting Roles

The internal consultant, similar to the external consultant, uses expertise, influence, and personal skills to facilitate a client-requested change without the formal authority to implement recommended actions. The change usually solves a problem, improves performance, increases organizational effectiveness, or helps people and organizations learn. The role the internal consultant plays in the change initiative reflects four considerations: the characteristics of the consultant, the characteristics of the client, the client/consultant relationship, and the organizational situation. View Table 36-4 to review these considerations.

Table 36-4. Four Considerations in Choosing a Role

Characteristics of the Consultant
- What are my interpersonal strengths?
- What is my consulting competency?
- What is my technical expertise?
- How well do I grasp core business processes?
- How is my expertise relevant to the client?

Characteristics of the Client
- Who are the sponsor, primary client, and secondary clients?
- What support is there for the intervention at different levels in the organization?
- Is the client committed to be involved and participate in the project?
- What is the client's readiness for change?

The Client/Consultant Relationship
- Does the consultant understand the client's definition of success?
- Is there a commitment to help the client learn skills and insights?
- Have expectations been explored and clarified?
- Has client trust been established?

The Organizational Situation
- Are the organizational vision and strategy clear and understood?
- What are the key strategic needs of the organization?
- What are the effects of the current market and competition on the organization?
- What is the focus of attention?
- What resources are available to support the project?
- Are other strategic initiatives being driven in the organization, and how might they affect the current initiative?
- What are the cultural norms and mindsets that will influence the project?
- What are the organizational expectations of internal consultants?
- What organization needs are not being met?
- Is the expertise of the consultant relevant to the organization's needs?

Source: Scott (2000).

Discussions about consulting roles often reflect the tension between process consulting and technical or expert consulting (Marguilles, 1978). Technical consultation, or "expert" consulting as Block (1981) calls it, relies on the knowledge and expertise of the consultant to solve the client's problem. The expert approach uses data collection and analysis to determine solutions to recommend to the client. This is the traditional model of business consulting. Process consulting relies more on the intuitive awareness of the consultant who attends to and observes the emotional, nonverbal, perceptual, and spatial aspects of human behavior. Process consultants help the client understand what is happening, identify solutions, and transfer skills to the client to manage the ongoing process. Their focus is on the energy of the client system and a heightened awareness of the dynamics in the group or organization.

It takes both process and expertise. Internal consultants are expected to bring more than their presence, process, and observation skills. They also bring technical competence and expertise. Drawing on the four considerations, consultants may balance the process or technical roles or may emphasize one over the other. Table 36-5 lists some of the roles an internal consultant might choose, such as traditional organization development (OD) roles, classic business consulting roles, or new consulting roles. These descriptions were developed by one author in collaboration with Joseph Lipsey for the OD Network website (Lipsey and Scott, 2008).

Competencies

We have discussed the advantages, challenges, and roles of an internal consulting function. However, the competencies required to deliver the desired results are perhaps even more critical. Competency is the knowledge, skills, and attitudes (KSAs)—or the sum of everything—needed to be successful. Many basic competencies needed for external and internal consultants are similar: professional theories, techniques and methods, self-knowledge, and performance skills. However, internal consultants report that success as an internal does require *consulting* competencies that are different from external consultants. Table 36-6 shows the categories of internal consulting competencies and some of the descriptive behaviors developed from the results of interviews with internal consultants. In some cases, the descriptive phrase might seem to be the same as for external practitioners. Internal practitioners, however, demonstrate the competencies differently because the context of the internal practitioner is different. Foss et al. (2005) report that other competencies may be needed, but suggest that these are a starting point for discussion and future research.

Table 36-5. The Role Dilemma

CLASSIC CONSULTING ROLES

Doctor: The consultant's role is to make a diagnosis and recommend a solution. The client is dependent on the consultant to offer a prescription.

Expert: The client determines what the problem is, what kind of assistance is needed, and whom to go to for help. Then the consultant is asked to deliver the solution.

Pair of Hands: The consultant serves as an extra pair of hands, applying specialized knowledge to achieve goals defined by the client (Block, 1981).

TRADITIONAL ORGANIZATION DEVELOPMENT ROLES

Change Agent: This is the classic OD consultant role in which the consultant serves as a catalyst for change as an outsider to the prevailing culture and external to the particular subsystem initiating the change effort (French and Bell, 1999).

Process Consultant: The consultant provides observation and insights, often at a larger system level, which helps sharpen the client's understanding of the problem (Schein, 1988).

Collaborative Consultant: This is similar to both the change agent and the process consultant, but with the key assumption that the client's issues can be addressed best by joining the consultant's specialized knowledge with the client's deep understanding of the organization. The client must be actively involved in the data gathering, analysis, goal setting, and action plans, as well as sharing responsibility for success or failure (Block, 1981).

NEW CONSULTING ROLES

Performance Consultant: The demand for increasing organizational and employee performance has contributed to a role that transcends the traditional skills trainer description. This role combines the whole-system focus of organization development with the understanding and techniques of skills training. The performance consultant partners with the client to identify and address the performance needs within the organization and provides specialized services that change or improve performance outcomes.

Trusted Advisor: The rapid pace of change and the complexity of the environment place organizational leaders in unforeseen and unknowable challenges and dilemmas such as competitive global markets and rapidly changing technology; they must chart radically new strategic direction for their organizations. In the midst of this turmoil, they must focus internally on simultaneously maintaining cultural alignment and meeting the needs of customers, employees, and other stakeholders. Executives are often in lonely and isolated positions. The consultant who can serve as a sounding board, imparting insight into the human organization in the context of business demands can be valuable to top executives. The trusted advisor serves as a confidant and provides authentic communication and reaction based on awareness and understanding of the human organization, critical performance issues, business strategy, and pressures on the executives.

Change Leader: As organizations continue to cope with a rapidly changing business environment, efforts at organization-wide change require facilitators to guide the implementation and support of change or innovation initiatives. Many internal consultants are asked to both guide the process and be the driving force of a change initiative. This demand is based on the bottom-line business needs for expertise in change leadership and organizational alignment, as well as in certain technical competencies related to the change. The change leader becomes both an advocate and project leader for a change initiative. This results in the consultant being lifted from a neutral process role and becoming identified strongly with the project's success. This role is frequently associated with expertise in a specific arena, where the consultant is expected to initiate and guide the processes with or across organizational units.

Table 36-6. Competencies Critical to Internal Consultants

Competency	Behavioral Description
Collaborates With Others	• Ensures that interpersonal relationships with clients, peers, and others in the organization are collaborative, healthy, and team-based • Seeks balanced, win–win partnerships • Emphasizes follow-up and good customer service • Is humble, caring, compassionate, and capable of celebrating client's success
Establishes Credibility	• Establishes credibility and respect by doing good work, delivering value, and achieving results • Holds high ethical standards and maintains integrity through professionalism, ethics, and contracting • Provides a realistic picture to the client of what is achievable in the time available through clear expectations for the role of client and consultant partners, the degree of difficulty of change, and the approach used
Takes Initiative	• Is assertive in taking a stand, delivering tough messages, and pushing for decision and outcomes • Demonstrates entrepreneurial spirit • Acts to achieve results tied to the organization's goals • Understands, respects, and effectively uses power in the organization to assist clients in achieving their goals
Maintains Detachment	• Remains detached from the organization to maintain independence, objectivity, and neutrality • Is not only sufficiently aligned with the client organization to find acceptance, but also able to keep an external mindset to provide a more balanced perspective • Avoids getting trapped into taking sides or carrying messages
Markets the Value of Area of Expertise	• Helps clients and the organization understand the value of the work the consultant delivers to them and the organization • Works toward clarity of roles with other staff units (for example, human resource consultants, quality improvement, finance, or IT) • Offers clear statement of products and services as distinct from those offered by others in the organization • Clarifies products and services as distinct from external consultants and, at times, manages contracts with external consultants
Demonstrates Organizational Savvy	• Understands and knows how to succeed in the organization • Builds a relationship with senior leadership and develops an extensive network of contacts at all levels • Leverages insider knowledge to address organizational issues • Uses appropriate judgment, recognizing cross-functional interdependencies, political issues, and the importance of cultural fit • Recognizes the importance of systems thinking
Acts Resourcefully	• Uses imagination, creativity, and forward thinking • Is resourceful, flexible, and innovative in using methods and resources • Is not wedded to a specific approach • Takes advantage of windows of opportunity and most often functions with just-in-time approach to client needs
Understands the Business	• Knows what makes the business run and the key strategy • Thinks strategically and leverages support for critical strategic issues • Supports managers in aligning the organization with the strategy

Keys to Success

The most critical key to success for an internal practitioner is gaining the trust and credibility of both leadership and employees. Trust and credibility are based on both competency and personal integrity. The credibility of internal consultants, more than any other staff function, is influenced by the integrity, self-awareness, and self-management of individual practitioners. This strong foundation relies on developing authentic partnerships with clients and making careful judgments regarding the client's resistance, readiness to take the risk of change, need for support, ability to lead the organization through transition, and openness to tough feedback. To achieve the successful outcomes internal consultants envision with their clients, they must, because they live inside, also build strong relationships with their managers, other levels of management, and peers and colleagues in HR or other staff functions. Building strong relationships requires that internal consultants educate and prepare others to understand and appreciate the role of consultant; take the initiative to understand the others' perspectives; and be strong, clear, self-aware, and self-managing. Misunderstanding of behavior or agreements can quickly destroy many years of effort by the internal practitioner (Foss et al., 2005).

More than the external, who is often specialized in a limited area of practice, the internal consultant must be a generalist, familiar with and competent in a broad range of approaches and solutions. The internal practitioner has to master a wide range of potential initiatives. This also represents a potential pitfall. Internals cannot be successful trying to do everything, so they must be selective in offering their services to maximize the benefits of their efforts. By making conscious choices and aligning with organizational strategy and priorities, the internal consultant will add more value and better meet the needs of the organization.

The Process of Internal Consulting

The consulting process for the internal consultant is usually messy and organic; the steps are seldom linear, often overlap, or require cycling back to repeat or expand an earlier phase (see Figure 36-1). The consulting process does not begin with entry as it does for external consultants. It begins with the initial contact with the client and is heavily influenced by the consultant's reputation in the organization. That reputation is as valuable as a popular product brand name, and many internal consultants use it successfully to market themselves within the organization. Internal consultants can help to position their reputation by setting the stage at the time of hiring and negotiating their charter with their managers and their most senior potential clients. The ability to manage relationships and the dynamics of living inside the organization is a requirement for successful movement through the consulting process. (For more on the eight phases of consulting, see the sidebar.)

Figure 36-1. The Consulting Process

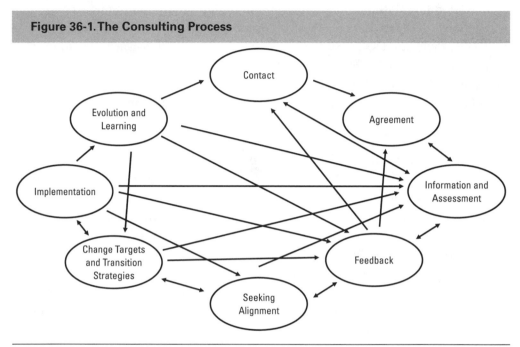

Source: Scott and Barnes (2011).

In some cases, the best action might be to partner with an external consulting firm. If the internal practitioner makes a judgment that an external practitioner can help, it is often because the internal practitioner has already laid the groundwork with the organization and knows that the external initiative has greater likelihood of being successful. This work in the trenches is rarely acknowledged. Another frustration occurs when the external consultant or consulting firm proceeds to work directly with senior leaders or with HR staff without the involvement of the internal function. Managers often lack the ability to prepare the organization for the coming change initiative and frequently have difficulty guiding the work of the external practitioners. Failure to involve the internal consultant can result in less than optimal outcomes for the external consultant's intervention (Foss et al., 2005; Scott and Hascall, 2002, 2006; also see Table 36-3).

Eight Phases of the Consulting Process

Contact: Seek an understanding of the client's organization or business need. Lay the foundation of the consultant/client relationship.

Agreement: Confirm the agreement on consultant and client roles, expectations, and the actions each will take. Define the need to be addressed and the goal or outcome to be achieved.

Information and assessment: Gather information about the issue, the business, performance, and the organization. Assess or analyze the data and information collected. Gain an independent view and interpretation of the issues.

Feedback: Provide the client with the information or data; seek acceptance or ownership of the data. Offer a consultant's analysis or interpretation.

Alignment: Seek alignment with the client on the desired outcomes or future state and the approach to be used to achieve it.

Change targets and transition strategies: Clarify which components of the system need to be changed, and identify necessary support and resources. Develop a transition strategy to navigate from the current state to the desired future.

Implementation: Complete the project by providing guidance, coaching, facilitation, and leadership to implement the planned change.

Evaluation and learning: Evaluate the success of the project with the client system by supporting the client's reflection and identification of learned skills, knowledge, and self-awareness. Explore enhanced knowledge, skills, and self-awareness.

Source: Scott and Barnes, 2011.

Summary

Internal consultants offer unique benefits to the organization with their deep and intimate knowledge of the organization. They are a ready resource to management and staff. Insider knowledge makes internal practitioners valuable partners to external consultants; however, being internal challenges the neutral and objective role of the consultant and requires him or her to manage a delicate balance of deep organizational knowledge with maintaining a position at the boundary.

Successful internal consultants cultivate trust and credibility as business partners to senior managers, supported by demonstrated competence. Competence includes their professional expertise as well as the unique capabilities required of internal consultants. Knowledge of themselves, their clients, and the organization allows them to choose appropriate roles.

The professional committed to successful outcomes for the organization, willing to step out of the limelight and remain humble and generous of spirit, can find reward and make a significant contribution to the organization to which he or she belongs.

Wondering how you rate on important competencies as an internal consultant? You can find out. The Internal Consulting Competencies Self-Assessment on the *Handbook's* website at www.astdhandbook.org will help you ascertain how you perceive your level of confidence and skill.

Parts of this chapter have been adapted from *Consulting on the Inside* (Scott and Barnes, 2011) and from the work of a team of internal consultants who conducted a research project on internal consulting (Foss et al., 2005).

About the Authors

Beverly Scott served as a consultant to organizations for more than 35 years. She served for 15 years as the director of organization and management development for McKesson Corporation in San Francisco. She is the co-author of the second edition of *Consulting on the Inside: An Internal Consultant's Guide to Living and Working Inside Organizations.* She has served on the faculty of Organization Psychology at John F. Kennedy University, and as chair of the OD Network Board of Trustees. Bev is currently focused on a new adventure of writing fiction, basing the story on uncovered family secrets in the lives of her grandparents.

B. Kim Barnes, CEO of Barnes & Conti Associates, Inc., has more than 30 years of experience in leadership and OD, working globally with organizations in many industries. A frequent speaker at professional conferences, Kim has published many articles and is the developer or co-developer of popular Barnes & Conti programs including *Exercising Influence, Managing Innovation,* and *Consulting on the Inside.* Her books include *Exercising Influence: A Guide to Making Things Happen at Work, at Home, and In Your Community; Consulting on the Inside: An Internal Consultant's Guide to Living and Working Inside Organizations,* 2nd edition, with Beverly Scott; and *Self-Navigation: A Compass for Guiding Your Life and Career* with Aviad Goz. She also writes mystery novels with an internal consultant as the protagonist.

References

Block, P. (1981). *Flawless Consulting: A Guide to Getting Your Expertise Used.* San Diego: Pfeiffer.

Foss, A., D. Lipsky, A. Orr, B. Scott, T. Seamon, J. Smendzuik, A. Tavis, D. Wissman, and C. Woods. (2005). Practicing Internal OD. In *Practicing Organization Development: A Guide for Consultants,* eds. W.J. Rothwell and R. Sullivan. San Francisco: John Wiley & Sons.

French, W.L., and C.H. Bell Jr. (1999). *Organization Development: Behavioral Science Interventions for Organization Development.* Saddle River, NJ: Prentice Hall.

Lipsey, J., and B. Scott. (2008). Consulting Skills Toolkit: Roles. OD Network, www.odnetwork.org.

Marguilles, N. (1978). Perspectives on the Marginality of the Consultant's Role. In *The Cutting Edge: Current Theory and Practice in Organization Development,* ed. W.W. Burke. La Jolla, CA: Pfeiffer.

Schein, E.H. (1988). *Process Consultation: Its Role in Organization Development,* 2nd edition. Saddle River, NJ: Prentice Hall.

Scott, B. (2000). *Consulting on the Inside,* 1st edition. Alexandria, VA: ASTD Press.

Scott, B., and B.K. Barnes. (2011). *Consulting on the Inside: An Internal Consultant's Guide to Living and Working Inside Organizations,* 2nd edition. Alexandria, VA: ASTD Press.

Scott, B., and J. Hascall. (2002). Inside or Outside: The Partnerships of Internal and External Consultants. In *International Conference Readings Book,* eds. N. Delener and C. Ghao. Rome: Global Business and Technology Association.

Scott, B., and J. Hascall. (2006). Inside or Outside: The Partnerships of Internal and External Consultants. In *The 2006 Pfeiffer Annual, Consulting,* ed. E. Biech. San Francisco: John Wiley & Sons.

For Further Reading

Barnes, B.K. (2006). *Exercising Influence: A Guide to Making Things Happen at Work, at Home, and in Your Community.* San Francisco: John Wiley & Sons.

Bellman, G.M. (1992). *Getting Things Done When You Are Not in Charge,* Fireside edition. New York: Simon & Schuster.

Henning, J.P. (1997). *The Future of Staff Groups.* San Francisco: Berrett-Koehler.

Lacey, M.Y. (1995). Internal Consulting: Perspectives on the Process of Planned Change. *Journal of Organizational Change Management* 8(3):77.

Ray, R.G. (1997, July). Developing Internal Consultants. *T+D* 30-34.

Schaffer, R.H. (1997). *High Impact Consulting.* San Francisco: Jossey-Bass.

Chapter 37

Building Extraordinary Internal Teams

Geoff Bellman and Kathleen Ryan

································· **In This Chapter** ·································

- Define what makes an "extraordinary group."
- Discuss what extraordinary groups do, and what motivates them.
- Learn how to help your teams become extraordinary.

···

The work of human resource development (HRD) increasingly involves teams, and we HRD professionals must know how to work with them—that's what this chapter is about. If anyone in the organization is going to be called upon to help develop internal teams, it is likely you. Plus, we are members of our own teams—another reason for us to learn how to work with them. This chapter offers you a model for working effectively with teams. It grew out of our consulting experience with teams, supplemented with what we learned from interviewing members of 60 extraordinary teams as we prepared to write *Extraordinary Groups: How Ordinary Teams Achieve Amazing Results* (2009).

Before diving into our model, here are a few of our underlying assumptions:

- Team performance is the path to organization performance—yes, teams, not individuals. Workplace success in this century is determined by team success. Consider the array of talents required on most projects today. Think about the worldwide connections now possible through the Internet. Teams make all that possible.

- Individual performance is best accomplished in the context of the work team. Focusing on the individual out of team context is much less effective. Those of us in HRD have spent years doing this with mixed success. We need to turn our eye more toward small group performance; we need to find ways of designing groups, growing groups, and rewarding groups. Small groups (two to nine members) are the platform for individual and organizational success.

- Extraordinary team results do not come through magic. We all love those moments when, with others on a team, we collectively realize huge success; we often speak of this as though it can't be replicated. The truth is that we hold that assumption because we haven't looked closely enough at what we did that made us great.

- Studying great teams can help our teams achieve better results, tangible and intangible. We need to plunge through the emotion and enthusiasm and mystery to find out what this great team actually did.

- Extraordinary teams have much in common, regardless of their purpose or expertise. The two of us came away from our work more reinforced in this assumption than we could have imagined.

- This chapter is about our current thinking on exceptional teaming. We hope that after reading about our theories and seeing our models, you'll be inclined to continue your own thinking and conversations about teams, and develop your own ideas and strategies.

With these assumptions in mind, we launched a study of 60 extraordinary groups in 2006. (We are using the word *groups* interchangeably with teams, committees, task forces, boards, and other designations for small groups.) We indulged our curiosity about what makes some groups fantastic while most of the groups are rather ordinary—or worse. Four years of work led to conclusions, a model, a book, and, later, a team assessment tool. We share highlights of what we learned here.

While reading this chapter, keep an extraordinary team in mind. Pause now to think of the best team you were ever part of—at work or outside work—then answer these three questions:

- What did that team do? Recall actual behaviors that contributed to team success.
- Why did you and others do what you did? What motivated you to act as you did?
- How did you and others feel about the team's performance?

Make a few notes on your answers so that you can compare your experience with what we learned in our study.

A Four-Year Field Study

Over four years, we focused on extraordinary groups of two to 20 people and what makes them so amazing. We interviewed members of 60 such groups. What a great source of the "secrets" of success! We collected stories from one or two members of each of these 60 great groups. We learned about what they actually did, what motivated them, and how they felt about their work.

Sixty percent of these groups were from the world of paid work, many coming from large organizations. The other groups came from people's community and personal lives. We interviewed organizational leaders, information technology professionals, motorcyclists, high school teachers, high school students, soldiers, trainers, human resource officers, community college counselors, nurses, basketball coaches, community activists, soccer players, moms, government contractors, whitewater rafters, board members, and small business owners. Almost half the teams we interviewed had no leader designated by some higher authority, and close to one-fifth of the teams were primarily virtual.

What Is an "Extraordinary Group"?

Based on what we learned from talking with people who were part of a group, we defined "extraordinary group" as *one which achieves outstanding results while members—individually or collectively—experience a profound shift in how they see their world.* Note our emphasis on results; the group needs to deliver for their own satisfaction and for the world they serve. A "profound shift" needs to be one they are aware of. And, their perspective, the way they see their world, needs to have changed. The shift is to seeing their world more realistically and full of opportunity.

We are now confident that any team member, leader, facilitator, or coach can move a team experience toward extraordinary. In your role as a T&D professional, you can move a team experience toward extraordinary. Don't get us wrong; we are not declaring that all teams can and should be extraordinary. We are declaring that all teams can learn from really great teams that a good team can become better, and a weak team can become stronger. With that in mind, let's get into the specifics of what we discovered.

What Do Extraordinary Groups Do?

Watch an extraordinary group in action and you will see behaviors related to these eight points:

1. **Compelling purpose** inspires and stretches members to make the group the top priority.
2. **Shared leadership** shows that each member feels responsible for group success.
3. **Just-enough-structure** is put in place to move the group forward.
4. **Full engagement** shows in member energy and enthusiasm.
5. **Embracing differences** pulls members to value and take advantage of their differences.
6. **Unexpected learning** takes the group where they did not expect to go.
7. **Strengthened relationships** bond members with each other.
8. **Great results** usually far exceed the expectations of the group.

We call these eight themes "performance indicators." Each is a magnetic center for an array of related behaviors. Watch an extraordinary team at work and you will see actions directly connected to these indicators. This will be true regardless of whether the team is for profit or not, volunteers or employees, face-to-face or virtual. As you read through our elaboration on each indicator, think back to your best team.

1. Compelling purpose. Watch an extraordinary team at work and you will see that their inspiring, compelling purpose surfaces constantly. Commitment to shared purpose is central to both individual and collective work. Members hold the purpose in their hearts; they post it on their walls; it's their primary guide for decisions; it shows in all they do—individually and collectively.

2. Shared leadership. Leadership comes from across the team, shifting with the subject at hand and the expertise required. Anyone can put forth a question, a task, an issue, or a proposal. Members share accountability for inputs and outputs. Designated leaders of extraordinary groups recognize they are one leader among many. They watch to see that the group is being led and do not insist on being the one single leader.

3. Just enough structure. A group with clear purpose and shared leadership will find practical, organic, and often chaotic ways of getting desired outcomes. Look in on an extraordinary team and you may have a hard time knowing what is going on. They know, but you may not! Members create just-enough-structure, just-in-time to support accomplishment. They are usually leery of formal structure, relying on it only when necessary. They guard against overstructuring or structuring too early or too long because they do not want to get bogged down by paying more attention to process than to their compelling purpose.

4. Full engagement. When fully engaged, members do not wait to be asked to contribute. In an extraordinary team, members often have trouble getting airtime. Intensity and excitement is more apparent than order. Extraordinary teams thrive on enthusiasm, spontaneity, and passion. Complicated group dynamics, conflict, and disagreement are characteristic.

5. Embracing differences. Members are intrigued by diverse perspectives, backgrounds, and ideas within the group. They know that creative solutions require a broad range of viewpoints and use those differences to spark creative breakthroughs. Respect for differences allows all members to bring their full selves to the group.

6. Unexpected learning. Our 60 extraordinary groups typically learned beyond their own expectations. Excited by the work before them, members individually stretch themselves and unite to learn together. The unexpected also comes when members learn not just new work skills and content knowledge, but team skills and life skills as well. They leave this team more confident and better able to contribute to their next team.

7. Strengthened relationships. Individuals feel respected for their contributions and this leads to tighter relationships within and loyalty to the team. When group members demonstrate commonly held values through working together, they become closer. When they routinely rely on one another, they exude loyalty, and friendships often result. Imagine the bonds forged through facing challenges together, through combining talents for a shared outcome.

8. Great results. Results—tangible and intangible—typically surpass members' expectations. The tangible results are valued by the team and often exceed the expectations of the sponsoring person or organization that created the team. Members are very proud of their tangible outcomes, but they treasure the intangible results: personal learning, new relationships, and profound shifts in how they see themselves and the world. Throughout the team's work, they experience small successes—both tangible and intangible. Those interim results feed members' motivation, their learning, and their engagement, and lead to more great results.

Attend to these eight performance indicators as a team and you will find yourself behaving differently. Use the indicators as a platform for improvement, for taking action on those indicators that need attention. The shared framework of the indicators promotes team discussion and decisions that encourage outstanding results and high performance. This chapter can help your team do that. The Extraordinary Teams Inventory, an assessment tool you can use with teams who want guidance to move toward great performance, can also do that.

What Motivates Extraordinary Groups?

As useful as it is to know what extraordinary teams do, you may still be faced with the challenge of team motivation: They know what to do, but they don't want to do it! A list of performance indicators is useless without an accompanying need to perform in ways the list suggests. In our field study, we did not stop at what extraordinary teams do; we wanted to know why members behave the way they do. We analyzed the stories we heard, searching for underlying patterns in motivation. We sorted through all we had learned and created the Group Needs Model, a lens through which to view teams. Just as there were patterns in team behavior, there are also patterns in the underlying reasons for that behavior.

Each of us comes to a team carrying a set of unexpressed needs, motivations, urges, longings, and wants that we hope to meet with this team. This is true whether we are part of a recreational sports team, a problem-solving group, a nonprofit board of directors, or a family gathered around the kitchen table. These core needs are central to being the social animal called humans and profoundly shape all we do. These are not passive needs; they are at work in each of us; they affect what we do moment to moment and are rooted in the long, successful struggle for survival of the human species.

We humans have been grouping for a very long time—hundreds of thousands, even millions of years. We have evolved interdependently; we have survived by facing the future together. We know it; our genes know it. Fast forward to the 21st century. We all come to groups with this long history of joining with others to survive. It's true in our families, workplaces, communities, and all our groups, regardless of our roles. These groups to a large extent define us, and we unknowingly hope important needs will be met through them.

The last two paragraphs describe our thesis and are the basis for what follows. Seeing team behavior through a set of identified human needs helps us understand why people do what they do. When we know what people need, we can more intentionally meet those needs. For example, if you know that a fellow team member has a great need for growing on the job, you can act to meet that need. If you don't know, your chances of meeting that need are much more random.

The stories gathered from our extraordinary groups study allow us to put forth three pairs of needs we humans have of groups:

- *Accep self* while moving toward one's *Potential.*
- *Bond with others* while pursuing a common *Purpose.*
- *Understand the reality* of the world while making an *Impact.*

In other words, in an ideal team, you would readily show your full self—both who you are and who you might become. You would be attracted to both being an integral part of the team and the team's reason for being. You would share the team's sense of the world around it while working to change that world.

In teams, we actively seek to meet these needs whether we know it or not, whether we can articulate them or not. These three pairs are in fact connected, intertwined, and overlapping, as shown in Figure 37-1 in this never-ending line in three loops. The model represents all six of the needs.

The Group Needs Model

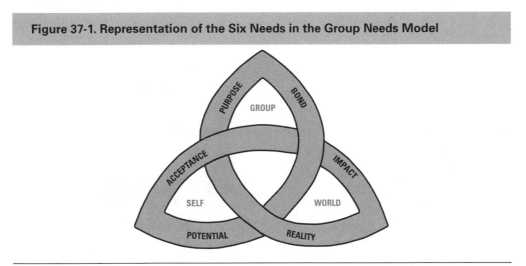

Figure 37-1. Representation of the Six Needs in the Group Needs Model

The model in Figure 37-1 represents how the six needs are related to each other and at work at all times. They provide motives for much of what we do. An overview of the three "loops" of the model follows.

Self: Acceptance and Potential

The two sides of the Self loop show the dynamic between our need to accept ourselves as we are and our need to reach toward the person who we could become. Check this against yourself and your own awareness of who you are and who you want to become. That dynamic, that tension, is important to this loop.

- Acceptance: knowing and accepting ourselves for who we are.
- Potential: sensing and growing into our fuller and better selves.

As we accept ourselves, we approach the present with more confidence, with an ability to look out at the world. We are more willing to risk. Our sense of our future selves allows us to initiate, to seek out situations where we might grow toward our potential. Our interviews were full of examples of this interplay of Acceptance and Potential. Team members talked easily about their reach for their finer, larger, better selves; they knew they were not done yet. And they liked being in a team where some of that potential could be realized. They also talked about their struggles of self-acceptance and feeling like they truly belonged on this team. Most of us want to live, work, and play in settings where our current and future selves are valued and supported. We bring our individual needs for Acceptance and Potential to our various groups.

Group: Bond and Purpose

Within the Group loop of the model, a team's purpose shapes the context for relationships among team members, and those relationships in turn shape the pursuit of purpose.

- Bond: the connections among us that create a shared sense of identity and belonging.
- Purpose: the reason we come together.

The team offers the possibility of a home—a safe place to be known, accepted, respected, and valued by others. This sense of "being on the same team," of belonging, is what Bond is about. When bonded members join to pursue a common Purpose, they commit to something larger than themselves and deepen their connection with one another. Shared purpose focuses their attention, energy, skills, and communication and unites them in a cause larger than their individual selves.

World: Reality and Impact

To understand the model's World loop, just imagine the larger context within which a team works and succeeds; imagine the people, the groups, the financials, and the politics that are all part of this larger world. The world this team lives in may be the marketing division, the city council, the parish, the statehouse, or the extended family. Whatever its world, a team's understanding of that world has a direct impact on team success in living in it.

- Reality: understanding and accepting the world as it is and how it affects us.
- Impact: our intention to make a difference and our readiness to act.

We humans are wired to survive; understanding our surrounding Reality is essential to that. As a species, our survival and success depend on our alertness to the world we live in. And so it is with a team; success depends on their alertness to and acceptance of their Reality. Understanding informs their strategies and actions; acceptance of Reality allows them to move forward.

Impact is about making a difference; it's about people coming together in teams to move their world a notch toward where they think that world ought to be. The creative dynamic between Reality and Impact is pragmatic: When group members understand and accept their Reality, they expand their options for truly making a difference.

Look at your best team experience in relation to what we've written here and the notes you took when you started reading this chapter. Notice especially how our ideas fit with your experience. Then imagine looking at team members through the lens of these six needs. Imagine asking questions related to what they might need or proposing action you think might satisfy those needs. Imagine watching for people's needs to be accepted, to grow, to join a group, to do things together, to understand what's happening around the team, to make a difference in their world. You can do just that by taking our model into your next meeting. Be quiet and watch your team through the model. You will be amazed at what you can see through these new glasses. Individual needs are everywhere, waiting to be recognized, waiting for action. And meeting those needs is key to extraordinary team success.

How Do Extraordinary Groups Feel About Their Work Together?

Needs determine actions; actions deliver outcomes; outcomes are accompanied by feelings. And that is how this third section on feelings relates to the eight performance indicators and six needs discussed earlier. The stories we heard from our great teams were laced with excitement, amazement, pride, exhilaration, joy, intensity, and more than 400 feelings noted in our study. We gathered those hundreds of words and phrases, stirred them together, and then sorted them again and again. We thought: Wouldn't it be nice if extraordinary groups shared feelings as well as performance indicators and needs? Well, they do!

Four feelings fit with individual and group transformative experiences, whether corporate planners, canoe trippers, ballplayers, software engineers, soldiers, college professors, or motorcyclists. As varied as their purposes and uniforms, tools, and rules might be, this diverse array of people shared the same satisfactions from working together. Thinking of your great team, note your response to the four identified feelings presented in these questions:

- Did this experience *energize* you? Yes!
- Did you feel more deeply *connected* to your group or the world around you? Yes!
- Did you feel more *hopeful* about yourself, your group, or the world around you? Yes!
- Did you feel *changed* by this experience? Yes!

Those four feelings ran through the hundreds we heard. Did everyone use these four words? No. Do we believe these four feelings represent their experience? Yes! Now we will elaborate a bit on each feeling.

Energized! The sense of vitality increases as members engage with the team and the world. The 60 people we interviewed were all energized in recalling their experiences. It was as if they were reliving it again in the interview. They became animated as they told their stories; they loved recreating the experience for us and for themselves. Just listening to them mirrored the high engagement and total investment they had experienced at the time. You have seen teams at work generating energy as they go. You have seen the aliveness, the vitality, in their interactions—that's what we are talking about. Vitality is a quick measure of where the team is in this moment, and can even be explored in the team with questions like, "Does this have life for us?" or "What about this project brings energy to you?"

Connected! People are often surprised at how connected they become to others on their team. They express being astounded by feelings of being tightly joined with other team members who, at the beginning, seemed so different from themselves. Some were more permanently joined and could put us in touch with team members they hadn't worked with in as many as 20 years. Connected obviously can mean not just in the moment, in the work, but for years beyond. We heard comments such as: "We bonded for life." "There was an informal heart-and-soul group made up of those who were willing to do whatever was necessary." "When I took this job, I thought I'd only be here for two years. The team and mission have kept me here for seven." Members personally connect to each other, to the group itself, to its purpose, and to the difference they make together.

Hopeful! People's stories of their work together had an underpinning of hope. Whether they say it or not, they did not exert themselves as they did without the hope for a better product, service, place, and world. They leaned toward the future with optimism; they believed they could make a positive difference on something important. Hopefulness is further fed by the fact that a uniquely capable group is doing this together. If there were more groups like this in the world, there would be less to worry about! Some examples of what we heard: "Each of us represented different nationalities. Somehow we met in the universe with different values, and we discovered that we speak the same language and have so much in common!" "I have experienced the power of our ability to positively influence kids who could go either way. They are ready and willing when we give them the skills. We see it in front of our eyes. It's quite incredible!" "I can help others by helping myself and utilizing all of my skills. This has made me feel relevant and useful. Together we have a sense of how it can be different." And the hope they have created here is contagious. It tells them what just might be possible in other realms of their lives.

Changed! All but one person we interviewed affirmed that they saw positive changes in themselves that could be tied directly to the group they told us about. For some, the change was dramatic and noticeable. For example: "It's made my life livable." For others, the change was subtle: "It confirmed what I have believed for some time." Some saw immediate impact: "I immediately knew that I was not alone. I had a global network of people I could call at any time—no matter what." Others sensed the power of the experience over time: "The work didn't seem like work anymore. My whole way of thinking about my work changed. I wanted to be the Charlie Parker of computer skills training. I wanted it to be like jazz—a bunch of really talented people working in chaos to make something beautiful." Each quote is testimony to how things will never be quite the same again.

Figure 37-2. Adding the Four Feelings to the Model

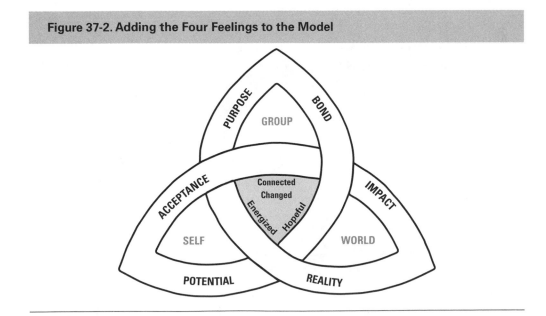

As a team meets more of the six core needs, more of the four feelings are evoked. There's a synergistic effect between needs and feelings—symbolized in our model (Figure 37-2) by placing the four feelings in the center of the model. These four feelings are the emotional evidence of exceptional events happening in an extraordinary group. And when your team feels them, you too are leaning toward extraordinary performance. Moving from a more predictable, ordinary view of your team is hinted at when members say this is fantastic, amazing, or life changing. At least that's what we heard in talking with people from 60 self-declared extraordinary groups. But it goes beyond this, beyond the feelings. There is the real possibility that in the process what the team is doing transforms the lives of individual team members.

What Is Transformation?

Transformation is a fundamental shift in individual perception that accelerates behavior change and personal vitality. It's an internal shift in how you see the world that results in you behaving differently and feeling more engaged. A small example: when a worker begins to understand that there is more to work than showing up on time and realizes that he or she wants to be there to be part of the team, or when a team leader discovers that he or she does not have to make every decision and realizes that the team members can decide together. These two examples show small shifts in perception that affect everything to come. No new skills, but a new way of seeing that profoundly influences immediate and future action: That's transformation.

The six core group needs are internal, and transformation is too. As important as needs and transformation are, we cannot grab hold of them. We can take visible action to try to meet needs; we can see evidence that needs are likely being met, or that transformation likely has occurred, but what we observe is the outcome of something unseen, of needs that motivated behavior.

And, it happens one person at a time. Occasionally it happens across an entire team, first one member then another and another. Because transformation is internal to each of us, we cannot see it; we can only see its effects. You can be transformed in one moment while teammates are oblivious. When you behave differently, others can see that. What they can't see is what motivated that difference.

You are more likely transformed when some or all of your core group needs are met. So if you want to be transformed or support the transformation of others, pay attention to meeting the group needs that you and your teammates share: self-acceptance and potential, bond and purpose, reality and impact. Though transformation cannot be guaranteed, it can be encouraged. When more of your needs are met, you can give fuller expression to who you are, bring more of yourself to your team, and help the team make a greater difference in the world. You will see the world differently, you will flourish, and you will flower. And all of that is at least fulfilling and perhaps transformative.

Help Your Teams Become Extraordinary

Whether we know it or not, we each hold theories about what makes teams work. And we act on those theories when making decisions in the workplace. The model you just read about was created by bringing forward our assumptions about teams. If teams are a major part of your life, we invite you to give time to figuring out how they work and how to work with them. Take notes on what you believe. Then, tell others what you believe and get their reactions. Table 37-1 can help you identify what to look for in yourself and in the team you support. For your convenience, this table is located on the *Handbook's* website at www.astdhandbook.org.

Table 37-1. Seeing Group Needs at Work

There are two ways to go about meeting the six group needs outlined in *Extraordinary Groups: How Ordinary Teams Achieve Amazing Results* (2009): 1) Take action to meet your own group needs, or 2) take action to help others meet their needs. To expand your ability to see group needs in action, what other examples can you add to the second column?

Group Needs—Definitions and Core Concepts	If Group Needs Were Being Met, You Might See Members . . .
Acceptance: Knowing and accepting myself for who I am. • I accept myself for who I am right now. • I know who I am and what I bring. • I can express who I am to myself and others.	• Share their relevant experience in group discussions. • Clearly state their beliefs on an issue. • Ask other members for assistance. • Give each other positive feedback for their contributions.
Potential: Sensing and growing into my fuller and better self. • I sense that I could be more. • I am drawn to my possibilities. • I want to learn and grow.	• Volunteer for assignments that require them to stretch or grow. • Share what they want to learn in this group. • Encourage others to take risks in order to gain new experience. • Ask each other questions in order to learn.
Bond: Our shared sense of identity and belonging. • We know who we are together. • We create a safe space for each other. • We each play our parts together.	• Express appreciation for being a member of this group. • Speak openly with one another, in self-disclosing ways. • Reference commonly understood values when making a decision. • Laugh together at "inside" jokes.

(continued on next page)

Table 37-1. Seeing Group Needs at Work (continued)

Group Needs—Definitions and Core Concepts	If Group Needs Were Being Met, You Might See Members . . .
Purpose: The reason we come together. • We influence each other. • We move in the same direction. • We count on each other.	• Give the group's work a very high priority. • Regularly remind themselves of the group purpose when making decisions. • Be fully present and engaged at meetings. • Set aside personal preferences in order to help the group move ahead with its work.
Reality: Understanding and accepting the world as it is and how it affects us. • We are alert to the world around us. • We are intrigued with that world. • We accept our reality.	• Actively survey the environment to understand the current reality. • Reach agreement on significant barriers or assets. • Shift plans to adjust to changes that affect the group. • Debrief actions to learn what worked well and what didn't.
Impact: Our intention to make a difference and our readiness to act. • We want to improve our world. • We need each other to make a difference. • We are powerful together.	• Talk specifically about how the group's purpose will make an important difference in the world. • Jump in to help each other out, regardless of role. • Express appreciation for the collective impact of all members. • Keep their commitments to one another.

Source: Bellman and Ryan (2009).

Get the conversation going! If you are a trainer or a consultant, convert your ideas to a form useful to others. Use the ideas in the table to expand on your ideas. Write about those ideas. Build a presentation around them. Test them on a team. By doing so, you will become more articulate, clear, and confident about how to engage people in teams—perhaps even helping them to become more extraordinary.

About the Authors

Geoff Bellman and **Kathleen Ryan** researched and wrote *Extraordinary Groups: How Ordinary Teams Achieve Amazing Results*. The book led to further research and a team assessment tool, *The Extraordinary Teams Inventory*. Their fieldwork for the book and the inventory inform this chapter. Kathleen has practiced organization development since 1984. Identified as "an organizational consultant with an instinct for translating complex human behavior into practical concepts," her work focuses on executive coaching and culture change. Geoff has worked with large organizations for more than 40 years—14 as an internal consultant and manager and the rest as an external consultant. They are founding members of the Community Consulting Partnership (www.ccpseattle.org), an all-volunteer organization that gives consulting to Seattle's not-for-profit community. For articles and exercises related to this chapter, go to www.extraordinarygroups.com. You can reach both authors through that site.

For Further Reading

Bellman, G., and K. Ryan. (2009). *Extraordinary Groups: How Ordinary Teams Achieve Amazing Results.* San Francisco: Jossey-Bass.

Bennis, W., and P. Biederman. (1997). *Organizing Genius: The Secrets of Creative Collaboration.* New York: Perseus Books.

Block, P. (2008). *Community: The Structure of Belonging.* San Francisco: Berrett-Koehler.

Briskin, A., S. Erickson, J. Ott, T. Callahan. (2009). *The Power of Collective Wisdom and The Trap of Collective Folly.* San Francisco: Berrett-Koehler.

Lawrence, P., and N. Nohria. (2002). *Driven: How Human Nature Shapes Our Choices.* San Francisco: Jossey-Bass.

Ryan, K., K. Coray, and G. Bellman. (2014). *The Extraordinary Teams Inventory.* King of Prussia, PA: HRDQ Press.

Chapter 38

Securing Executive Support: Presenting to the C-Suite

Dianna Booher

························· **In This Chapter** ·························

- Understand strategic and tactical thinking.
- Learn how to formulate a strategic message for the C-suite.
- Gain confidence to make recommendations rather than merely give reports.

N ow that you have your proverbial seat at the table, don't fall out of the chair. After two decades of talk about what it takes to earn respect and be asked for opinions about growing the business and improving profitability through improved performance and talent acquisition, we can't afford to fall on our faces when it comes to presenting ideas and information to the most opinionated population in the organization.

It's not enough to design economical and effective onboarding processes. You may successfully meet every challenge that internal consulting presents. You may have built, coached, and mentored strong internal teams from the ground up so that these groups work like a well-oiled machine. You may have led managers to relish developing their employees so that they see it as much their role as coaches grooming the next Olympic athletes. But if you and I cannot explain and gain support for all our work—the reasons behind it, the results achieved, the impact it has on profitability, and the opportunity it holds for the future—we have fallen out of the chair. We will have failed.

So let's talk about succeeding and securing support from your executive team.

Make Your Bottom Line Your Opening Line

"Once upon a time" opens many classic bedtime stories, but marks an amateur business presentation or document. If you are telling a joke, directing a screenplay, or writing a television sitcom, your audience will give you a few minutes to interest them before they nod off, flip the channel, or check their text messages.

Executives aren't always that patient. They want your bottom line up front for three reasons: It's difficult to understand the details if you don't have the big-picture message first. Second, they expect immediate relevancy. And third, let's face it, prioritizing their goals, budgets, projects, and time often equates to their paycheck and stock options.

If asked, many people would insist that they do just that—start their conversations, briefings, emails, and proposals to senior leaders with an executive overview. But having heard thousands of such briefings in sessions with our coaching clients, I disagree.

Instead, presenters start with a purpose statement—what I call a warm-up drill. They simply overview what they *intend* to say later. In other words, they promise to tell the executives something significant—later. Their opening is simply a prose table of contents, an agenda for the conversation or briefing. Instead, start strong. Spit it out. State your message. Then circle back and fill in the gaps with your elaboration.

Think Strategically

Strategic thinking sets you apart from the crowd. So what is strategic thinking versus tactical thinking, and how does it set you apart with your executive team? Consider the differences in Table 38-1.

The most significant of these differences has to be the central organizing statement: What is the goal, mission, message, lesson learned, benefit, conclusion, or plan?

Let me be more specific here about strategic thinking as it applies to formulating a strategic message or conclusion. See Table 38-2 to compare how a training message might be delivered to a midlevel manager versus a C-suite officer.

You will also find a tool on the *Handbook's* website at www.astdhandbook.org to help you define the value you deliver and to translate that value into a strategic message to deliver in the C-suite.

Table 38-1. Strategic Thinking Versus Tactical Thinking

Strategic Thinking	Tactical Thinking
Central common vision or organizing statement	Day-to-day actions or operations
Long-term concern	Short-term concern
Understanding why to do something	Understanding how to do something
Mental, conceptual	Physical, tangible
Doing the right thing	Doing things right
Focused	Scattered, many "balls in the air"
Road maps	Tools for the trip
Structure	Who and what gets placed into the structure

Table 38-2. Seven-Segment Format for Stating Strategic Messages in the C-Suite

HR Value Segment	
(time period) +	During the last 12 months,
(accomplishment/plans) +	the staffing of the Belco Center
has (action verb) +	has decreased
(organizational issue) +	overtime costs in the Widget division
(specific measurement of change)	by more than 80 percent.
Translated to Strategic Message for the C-Suite	
That (change/action/plan) has (action verb) +	That staffing plan has decreased
(financial measurement/quality metrics)	our total labor cost by 26 percent across the board.

Sort the Significant From the Trivial

Once you understand the overriding principle of *why*, other things from Table 38-1 fall into place: doing the right thing, focusing, and creating the road map. Sorting and sifting become second nature in day-to-day tactical tasks: designing and developing training programs, managing internal consulting projects, or selecting the right supplier partnerships.

Giving evidence of your ability to think strategically, you select appropriate information to pass on to others and forgo the urge to hit the "Send" button every time new stats hit your inbox. Squelch the urge to "speak your truth" in a meeting every time a thought flitters across your mind.

To gain buy-in from your executives, know how to sift the significant from the myriad bits of information you have at hand. Your reputation rests on what you choose to say, how you allocate your time, and what data you decide to distribute. Sort before you send. Your chances for later support of the significant depend on that action or inaction.

Learn to Zoom In and Zoom Out

Dr. Rosabeth Moss Kanter, professor of business administration at Harvard University, suggests an apt metaphor for two modes of strategic thinking: Consider the zoom lens on a camera. You can zoom in and get a close look at specific details—but be so close that you miss the bigger context and can't make sense of what you are seeing. Zoom out and see the big picture—but you may miss key details and subtleties that would prevent a bad decision. In her *Harvard Business Review* article, Dr. Kanter points out the virtues and drawbacks of both perspectives for leaders.

Like a camera with a malfunctioning zoom lens, some people get stuck in one mode of strategic thinking. That mode may be strategic in many ways, but still limiting.

If you have ever hired a professional photographer for an important occasion, like a wedding, family reunion, graduation, or your parents' 50th wedding anniversary cruise, then you know they'll shoot hundreds of photos to end up with 40 to 50 usable ones. Close-ups catch the emotion, excitement, and energy. Wide shots capture the context and relationships. You savor both.

When discussing an issue that interests your executive team, tactical thinkers will tell how they corrected a current situation or what is wrong with a vision, idea, or plan. Strategic thinkers, on the other hand, will tell how they plan to circumvent the problem altogether or take advantage of opportunities the problem created. The book *Flash Foresight*, by entrepreneur Dan Burrus, outlines seven strategic thinking principles and examples for doing just that.

My point is not that tactical thinking is unnecessary. On the contrary, goals demand tactical execution. Tactical thinking is critical. It's just that strategic thinkers typically get projects approved, budgets funded, and visibility increased.

Ask Thought-Provoking Questions

Executive management teams insist that a key value advisory board's offer is asking the right questions to guide thinking and prevent missteps. Effective internal consultants provide their clients the same service. They go into an organization, listen to the situation and plans, analyze data, and ask questions. Their value most often lies not in the answers they provide but in the questions they ask.

Inventors stumble on new processes and new products because they have great curiosity and continually ask others or themselves provocative questions—and then go discover or develop the answers.

The more provocative your questions, generally the stronger others consider your contribution to the outcome. Your presence of mind showcases your distinct way of thinking in a manner just as recognizable as your body language.

Consider how you could pique executive interest in the value of your training initiatives: What research would you need to show evidence of improved performance after your coaching program? What dissertation study done in a different industry would tempt your executive to sponsor a rollout of the same training in your organization? What "what if" scenarios would spur interest to extend financing for evaluation of a key program you already have in place? What would be the results in five years if your proposal writers could increase their closing ratios by 5 percent, and could you trace those closes directly to the unsolicited proposals? What if . . . ? You get the picture; so will your executives.

Take a Point of View

Recommend rather than simply report. Those in staff positions frequently argue, "But nobody asked me to make a recommendation; they just asked me to answer a question." Think again. In most such cases, the reason someone has asked the question is that you are the expert—the go-to person with the appropriate expertise. They don't want "just the facts, thank you, ma'am." They want your expert opinion. In light of the context, their goal, the question they've asked, and the question they *should have* asked, what is your recommendation to accomplish the organization's goals—improve performance, acquire the best talent, develop your leaders, improve morale, build bench strength?

When you go to see a medical doctor, do you expect an opinion along with your lab reports and x-rays? When you go to see your CPA, do you expect only the numbers or an opinion about what's deductible and what's not? When you talk to your financial advisor, do you want only a report on the effective yields of your portfolio, or would you like the firm's opinions about various investments options?

Whether you are walking into the executive's office or the internal client's office, be ready to state a viewpoint or offer a recommendation. Consider that a key value you can contribute.

Make Your Facts Tell a Story

When a C-suite officer calls our organization about training employees in presentation skills, one of the key complaints that officer expresses is this: "They do a data dump. They need to learn to make their information tell a story."

The only thing worse than filling up your presentation, emails, proposals, or reports with fact after fact is not shaping them to tell your story. Where do the facts lead? How does the story need to end?

Tell how the RTC division exploded with the introduction of the new widget, and your headcount climbed from three sales representatives to 48 sales representatives and 12 customer service agents in the first two years you were in business. Then tell how you grew lax in your quality control. Tell about how your reject rates and customer complaints mounted. Show how the customer satisfaction numbers plummeted. Show how orders started dropping off as fast as they were logged on the computer. Then circle back to the layoff of 14 employees three years later. Then, out of the ashes, came the new training program with a mere investment of X dollars. Today, without increased headcount, profitability in the RTC division has grown to. . . . Well, you get the picture. Drama. Dialogue. Climax. Denouement. Facts alone will never feed the executive mind—at least not for long.

Make Your Points Memorable

Analogies lead to a conclusion based on a specific comparison. Jeff Bezos, founder and CEO of Amazon.com, used this analogy in a recent report to shareholders:

> *Long-term thinking is both a requirement and an outcome of true ownership. Owners are different from tenants. I know of a couple who rented out their house and the family who moved in nailed their Christmas tree to the hardwood floors instead of using a tree stand. Expedient, I suppose, and admittedly these were particularly bad tenants, but no owner would be so short-sighted. Similarly, many investors are effectively short-term tenants, turning their portfolios over so quickly they are really just renting the stocks that they temporarily "own."*

We talk about prime real estate in referring to the home page of a website or placement above the fold in a newspaper or product catalog. Many HR managers talk about cafeteria benefits to their employees. With just one word, this analogy implies that employees have a menu of benefits to select from, that a parent has agreed to cover the total invoice up to a certain amount, and that employees select according to taste or preferences from that menu.

Such comparisons as these don't exactly solicit an emotional response; they simply clarify a complex concept. Metaphors, on the other hand, imply a comparison and typically evoke an emotion and a mindset. Both types of comparisons can be succinct yet powerful ways to manage how your executives think about a performance problem that needs to be corrected or see potential to be gained with a new training initiative. Certainly you use analogies, metaphors, anagrams, quotations, and slogans to illustrate key points in your training programs. But have you considered their value in your executive presentations?

General Kevin Chilton, a former command astronaut responsible for U.S. nuclear forces, effectively illustrated his message to the Pentagon, Capitol Hill, and the press about the need to modernize the U.S. military. He likened current nuclear warhead technology to maintaining a 1957 Chevrolet in the 21st century. General Chilton pulled out a prop: a glass bulb about 2 inches high. "This is a component of a V-61 nuclear warhead," he said. "It was one of our gravity weapons—a weapon from the 1950s and '60s. It's a vacuum tube. My father used to take these out of the television set in the 1950s and '60s and go down to the local supermarket and test them. That is the technology we have today."

How do you know if you have been successful? Is your executive using your phrasing or illustration at the next all-hands meeting? Have your heard your slogan bandied about in a follow-up staff meeting? Did your presentation title get tweeted—and retweeted? Did someone else quote you in their presentation to motivate others to action?

Executives are typically lifelong learners. Otherwise, they would not be at the top of the organization. To gain their support, engage at their point of interest with a clear, succinct, strategic message.

About the Author

Dianna Booher's research in the field of business communication serves as the foundation for her 46 books, published in 26 languages, many providing communication skills training. Her latest titles include *Creating Personal Presence: Look, Talk, Think, and Act Like a Leader* and *Communicate with Confidence!* Founder of Booher Consultants, Dianna has received the highest awards in the speaking industry, including induction into the Speaker Hall of Fame®. *Good Morning America, USA Today, Wall Street Journal, Forbes*, NPR, Bloomberg, *Investor's Business Daily, Washington Post, New York Times*, Fox, CNN, and *Entrepreneur* have interviewed Dianna for opinions on workplace communication. Read her blog at www.Booher.com/BooherBanter.

References

Burrus, D. (2011). *Flash Foresight: How to See the Invisible and Do the Impossible*. New York: Harper Business.

Kanter, R.M. (2011, March). Zoom In, Zoom Out. *Harvard Business Review*.

For Further Reading

Booher, D. (2001). *Speak With Confidence: Powerful Presentations That Inspire, Inform, and Persuade*. New York: McGraw-Hill.

Booher, D. (2012). *Communicate With Confidence: How to Say It Right the First Time and Every Time,* revised and expanded edition. New York: McGraw-Hill.

Booher, D. (2012). *Creating Personal Presence: Look, Talk, Think, and Act Like a Leader*. San Francisco: Berrett-Koehler.

Hogan, K. (2013). *Invisible Influence: The Power to Persuade Anyone, Anytime, Anywhere*. New York: John Wiley & Sons.

Chapter 39

Mentoring: Building Partnerships for Learning

Chip R. Bell

··· **In This Chapter** ···

- Define mentoring.
- Learn why mentoring is important to the T&D professional.
- Consider the challenges of mentoring.
- Learn how to create a partnership for learning.

···

Mentoring is a lot like panning for gold. It is not always easy. Panning for gold works like this: First, you put a double handful of sand in a heavy-gauge steel shallow pan and dip it in the water, filling it half full of water. Next, you gently move the pan back and forth as you let small amounts of yellow sand wash over the side of the pan.

The objective is to let the black sand sink to the bottom of the gold pan. This is the point where panning for gold gets really serious. Impatience or strong-arming the way the pan is shaken means the black sand escapes over the side along with the yellow sand. Once black sand is the only sand left in the pan, you are rewarded with flecks of gold. The gold resides among the black sand.

Mentoring can be like panning for gold among the sand. Insight is generally not lying on top ready to be found and polished. If it were easy pickings, the help of a mentor would be unnecessary. It lies beneath the obvious and ordinary. It is lodged in the dark sands of irrational beliefs, myths, fears, prejudices, and biases. It lurks under untested hunches, ill-prepared starts, and unfortunate mistakes.

Helping the protégé extract insight takes patience and persistence. It cannot be rushed and haphazardly forced. And, most of all, it cannot be strong-armed with the force or wisdom of the mentor. It must be discovered by the protégé with the guidance of the mentor. Learning is a door opened only from the inside.

As a mentor, you are in charge of getting the protégé to properly shake the pan. You help the protégé learn to recognize the real treasures of insight and understanding and not be seduced by "fool's gold"—achieved by rote and temporarily retained only "until the exam is over." The way you help the protégé handle the dark sand is central to the acquisition of understanding and its ultimate manifestation: wisdom.

What Is Mentoring?

The concept of mentoring has had a checkered past in the world of work. The usual mental image has been that of a seasoned corporate sage conversing with a naïve, wet-behind-the-ears young recruit. The conversation would probably have been laced with informal rules, closely guarded secrets, and "I remember back in '77 . . . " stories of daredevil heroics and too-close-to-call tactics. And work-based mentoring has had an almost heady, academic sound, reserved solely for workers in white collars whose fathers advised, "Get to know ol' Charlie."

In recent years, the term *mentor* became connected less with privilege and more with affirmative action. Organizations viewed enabling minority employees through a mentor as part of its responsibility to expedite the employees' routes through glass ceilings, beyond old-boy networks and the private winks formerly reserved for WASP males. Such mentoring sponsors sometimes salved the consciences of those who bravely talked goodness but became squeamish if expected to spearhead courageous acts. These mentoring programs sounded contemporary and forward-thinking. Some were of great service, but many were just lip service.

Mentoring in its rawest form is simply helping another learn. Conducted in a one-to-one format, it employs a relationship as the primary vehicle on a learning journey. That relationship might be between peers, protégé with someone senior, or protégé with someone outside his or her chain of command. It might also be reverse mentoring—a junior person mentoring a senior person. Fundamentally, the possession of confident competence is not sufficient to make the journey fruitful. It requires a relationship laced with authenticity, curiosity, safety, and encouragement. It is best conducted as a partnership.

Why Is Mentoring Important to the T&D Professional?

Organizations scramble to attract and retain skilled employees. Since T&D professionals are charged with facilitating organizational competence, mentoring can be a powerful weapon useful in winning the war for talent. T&D professionals are expected to be change agents. As organizations have flattened, the span of control of most leaders has widened. This has triggered the transformation of the role of boss, leaving many managers in a bit of an identity crisis. Having risen up the hierarchy by virtue of their command and control skills, they must change to a world where bossing is now more about coaching, mentoring, and partnering.

Organizations have always operated in a competitive arena. Whether vying for a share of an economic market, a share of the customer's loyalty, or a share of the resources doled out by some governing body, most organizations operate in a contest mode. In today's race, the winners are those that prove themselves more adaptive, more innovative, and more agile. These are the organizations populated by employees who are perpetually learning, led by managers who are always teaching.

This new landscape has put "helping employees grow" near the top of the list of critical success factors for all leaders. As mentoring has grown in importance, so have the specifications for mentoring tools. Leaders today want proficiency without having to buy into a program. They seek helpful resources and techniques, not hindering rules and policies. Explorations of philosophy and theory might be tolerated after hours, but in the middle of the challenge and the heat of the contest, leaders shun any instruction not immediately transferable to their everyday practice.

Organizations cannot afford to rely on mentoring programs as the tool to equip people with all the competence they need. Mentoring has to be an everyday event performed by people with the skills to facilitate growth. In the words of author and consultant Arie De Geus, "Your ability to learn faster than your competition is your only sustainable competitive advantage." Every professional (leader and nonleader) must become a mentor.

How Is Mentoring Different From Coaching?

There are clearly skills employed by both mentor and coach. Great mentors and great coaches strive to be good role models, bolster confidence, provide advice, deliver feedback, and offer affirmation. Watch a great athletic, dance, or work coach, and you witness a commitment to bringing out the best in the target of their attention. Watch an effective mentor—whether reverse mentoring, leader to follower, or peer to peer, and you observe a devotion to protégé discovery, insight, and understanding. But, the greatest difference lies in the intent or primary focus. The goal of the coach is primarily to nurture and sustain performance; the goal of mentoring is learning. Granted, the raison d'etre for learning is enhanced performance; it is the immediate focus that most differentiates coaching and mentoring.

There are other differences. Table 39-1 is crafted to characterize the primary differences.

Table 39-1. Coaching and Mentoring Comparison

	Coaching	Mentoring
Primary Goal/ROI	Enhanced performance	Increased learning
Target Audience	Individual or group	Individual only
Source of Influence	Position	Expertise/experience
Primary Methodology	Instruction and role model	Discovery
Relationship	Comes with the job	Generally self-selecting

The Three Challenges of Mentoring

Archeologists excavating the pyramids discovered wheat seeds that dated back to around 2500 B.C. As in the tradition of antiquity, the seeds were there for the dead pharaoh to eat if he got hungry. The find was important because it would enable scientists to determine what variety of wheat was in use in the ancient world and could be invaluable for engineering new types of wheat. Out of curiosity, the scientists planted the 4,500-year-old wheat seeds in fertile soil and an amazing thing happened. The wheat seeds grew!

"No one can teach anyone anything of significance," wrote the legendary psychologist Carl Rogers in his classic work, *On Becoming a Person*. The purpose of mentoring is to help another remember, renew, and make ready to use. Mentoring is facilitating a bridge between knowledge from the mentor and understanding inside the mind of the protégé. That bridge is insight—the spark that fires the engine of wisdom; the "aha" that turns confusion and uncertainty into understanding and confidence. The first challenge of mentoring is enabling the insight to happen in the mind of the protégé. It is the process of awakening, nurturing, and blossoming—just like the wheat seeds.

The second challenge is coping with the recognition that protégé learning is a door only opened from the inside. In a brain-based work world (as opposed to a brawn-based world), learning involves much more than rote and practice. Effectiveness relies on comprehension and understanding, not simply proficiency and recollection. Such higher-level competence can only be achieved if the protégé invites in the mentor's wisdom.

Learning requires moving from novice to mastery. Rarely does this occur without mistake and error. The third challenge of mentoring is creating the type of relationship that encourages the protégé to take the risk to publicly make mistakes. Taking an online course is quite different from showing one's inadequacy in front of his mentor. This is exacerbated by the fact that most protégés enter the relationship feeling a bit one-down. Even if mentoring is peer to peer, the protégé must begin with the realization that the mentor has expertise the protégé lacks and needs. It is for this reason that a partnership relationship is most like to bring the equalitarian approach needed to foster a safe setting for risk taking.

How to Create a Partnership for Learning

Mentoring from a partnership perspective is fundamentally different from the classical "I'm the guru; you're the greenhorn" orientation. Mentoring from a partnership perspective means "We are fellow travelers on this journey toward wisdom." Stated differently, the greatest gift a mentor can give his or her protégé is to position that protégé as her mentor. However, a learning partnership does not happen; it must be created. And, the mentor must take the lead in crafting it.

The main event of mentoring entails giving learning gifts—advice, feedback, focus, story, and support. However, such learning gifts may not be readily seen by the protégé as a desired present. Gifts, no matter how generously bestowed, may not always be experienced with glee. Recall the last time someone said to you, "Let me *give* you some advice" or "I need to *give* you a little feedback." You probably did more resisting than rejoicing! Protégés are no different.

Smart mentors create a readiness for the main event of mentoring. Protégés are more likely to experience the benevolence of gifts if they are delivered in a relationship of safety, advocacy, and equality. Mentoring from a partnership perspective entails four stages: 1) leveling the learning field, 2) fostering acceptance and safety, 3) giving learning gifts, and 4) bolstering self-direction and independence. The first two stages are aimed at creating a readiness for the main event, gifting. The final stage is all about weaning the protégé from any dependence on the learning coach.

Stage 1: Leveling the Learning Field

The first challenge a learning coach faces is to help the protégé experience the relationship as a true partnership. Leveling the learning field means stripping the relationship of any nuances of mentor power and command. It requires creating rapport or kinship and removing the mask of supremacy.

The word *rapport* comes from its French derivation, which literally means "connection renewed." Think of it as creating kinship, much like a host welcomes a visitor. The success of a mentoring relationship can absolutely hang on the early mentor–protégé encounters; good starts affect good growth. The tone created in the first meeting can decide if the relationship will be fruitful or fraught with fear and anxiety. Quality learning will not occur until the shield has been lowered enough for the learner to take risks in front of the mentor. Rapport building expedites shield lowering.

Rapport begins with the sounds and sights of openness and authenticity. Any normal person approaching a potentially anxious encounter will raise her antennae high in search of any clues that would give an early warning regarding the road ahead. Will this situation embarrass me? Will this person take advantage of me? Will I be able to be effective with this encounter? Is there harm awaiting me?

Given this pioneering search for signals by the protégé, it is crucial the mentor be quick to transmit responses with a welcoming tone and feel. Open posture (such as no crossed arms), warm and enthusiastic reception, eye contact (some might say eye hugs), removal of physical barriers, and personalized greetings are all gestures communicating an attempt to cultivate a level learning field. Mentors who rely on the artifacts of power (peering over an imposing desk, making the protégé do all the approaching, tight and closed body language, a reserved manner or facial expressions that telegraph distance) make grave errors in crafting early ease important to relationship building.

Stage 2: Fostering Acceptance and Safety

Great mentors who are effective at fostering acceptance avoid testing tones, judgmental gestures, and parental positions. Great mentors show acceptance through focused and dramatic listening. When listening is their goal, they make it *the* priority. They do not let *anything* distract. A wise leader said, "There are no individuals at work more important to your success than your associates . . . not your boss, not your customers, not your vendors."

When your protégé needs you to listen, pretend you just got a gift of five minutes with your greatest hero; for me, it is Abraham Lincoln. What a great concept! Think about it. If you could have five minutes, and *only* five minutes, with Moses, Mozart, or Mother Teresa, would you let a call from your boss, your customer, or *anyone* eat up part of that precious time? Treat your protégé with the same focus and priority.

Listening done well is complete absorption. Ever watch Piers Morgan on CNN or Charlie Rose on PBS? Their success as a superb interviewers lies not in their questions, but in their terrific listening skills. They zip right past the interviewee's words, sentences, and paragraphs to get to the interviewee's message, intent, and meaning. The mission of listening is to be so crystal clear on the other person's message that it becomes a "copy and paste" execution command from one brain's computer screen to another's.

Protégés feel the relationship is safe when mentors demonstrate receptivity and validation of their feelings. The goal is empathetic identification. The "I am the same as you" gesture promotes kinship and closeness vital to trust. Empathy is different from sympathy. The word *sympathy* comes from a Greek word that means "shared suffering." Relationship strength is not spawned by "misery loves company." Strength comes through the "I have been there as well" type of identification.

Mentors do not just listen, they listen dramatically. They demonstrate through their words and actions that the words of their protégés are valued and important, not just heard and understood. Feeling valued, they are more likely to take risks and experiment. Only through trying new steps do they grow and learn. The bottom line is this: If your goal is to be a great mentor, start by using your noise management skills to help you fully use your talents as a great listener.

Stage 3: Giving Learning Gifts: Advice and Feedback

Leveling the learning field and fostering acceptance and safety are the stages that lay the groundwork for the main event: giving learning gifts. Great mentors give many gifts: support, focus, courage, story, and affirmation. But, two crucial learning gifts are advice and feedback. We will look briefly at each, starting with advice.

Begin your advice giving by letting the protégé know the focus or intent of your mentoring. For advice giving to work, it is vital you be very specific and clear in your statement. Make certain the protégé is as anxious to improve or learn as you are to see him or her improve or learn.

Ask permission to give advice. This is the most important step! It can sound like: "I have some ideas on how you might improve if that would be helpful to you." The goal is to communicate in a way that minimizes the protégé feeling controlled. State your advice in the first person singular. Phrases like "you *ought* to" quickly raise listener resistance. By keeping your advice in the first person singular, such as "what I've found helpful" or "what worked for me," helps eliminate the "shoulds." The protégé will hear such advice without the internal noise of resistance.

Because advice is about adding information, feedback is about filling a blind spot. And, the "blindness" factor makes protégé feedback a tricky gift. Because the issue with advice is potential resistance, the issue with feedback is potential resentment. How does a mentor bestow a gift that by its basic nature reminds the protégé of his inability to see it? How do you fill a perceptual gap and have the recipient focus on the gift, not the gap—to focus on the filled side of a filled hole?

The mentor's goal is to assist the protégé's receptivity for feedback by creating a climate of identification. Seek comments that have an "I'm like you, that is, not perfect or flawless" kind of message. This need not be a major production or overdone, just a sentence or two.

State the rationale for your feedback. This is not a plea for subtlety or diplomacy as much as a petition for creating a readiness for gap filling. Help the protégé gain a clear sense of why the feedback is being given. Assume you are giving *you* the feedback. We know that we more accurately hear feedback delivered in a fashion that is sensitive and unambiguous. However, there is another key dimension to effective feedback giving. It should possess the utmost integrity. This means it is straight and honest. Frankness is not about cruelty; it is about ensuring that the receiver does not walk away wondering, "What did he *not* tell me that I needed to hear?" Think of your goal this way: How would you deliver the feedback if you were giving *you* the feedback? Take your cue from your own preferences.

Stage 4: Bolstering Self-Direction and Independence

Effective mentoring relationships are rich, engaging, and intimate. As such, ending them is not without emotion. No matter how hard we may try, there is a bittersweet dimension. However, healthy mentoring relationships craft separation as a tool for growth. Effective adjournment of the present mentoring relationship paves the way for effective inauguration of the next mentoring relationship.

Celebrate the relationship with fanfare and stories. Celebration need not be a big party with band and banner. Celebration can be as simple as a special meal together, a drink after work, or a peaceful walk in a nearby park. The point of celebration is that it be clearly an event associated with the closure of the mentoring relationship. The rite of passage is a powerful symbol in gaining closure and moving on to the next learning plateau. Celebration should include compliments and stories. Make the celebration woven with laughter and joy.

Your protégé now needs your blessing far more than your brilliance, and your well-wishing more than your warnings. Avoid the temptation to give one last caution. Your kindest contribution will be a solid send-off rendered with confidence, compassion, and consideration.

Lace your final meeting or two with opportunities to remember, reflect, and refocus. Let your recall questions bridge the discussion toward the future.

As rapport building was crucial to a successful beginning of a mentoring relationship, adjournment is equally important. Letting go is rarely comfortable but is always necessary to enable the protégé to flourish and continue to grow out of the shadow of a mentor to become a self-directed learner. In the final analysis, the upper end of growing is "grown," which implies closure and culmination. Mark the moment by managing adjournment as a visible expression of achievement and happiness.

There is an expression in golf of "playing over your head." It means that a golfer is playing at an unexplained level of excellence in which serendipity and the extraordinary seem the momentary norm. Effective mentoring is a relationship of a learning coach and protégé who seek to honor their alliance by "learning over their heads." Such an occurrence is practiced at its most harmonious level when the two operate as a partnership.

Interested in how you are doing as a mentor? A Mentoring Competence Assessment is available at the *Handbook's* website at www.astdhandbook.org.

Mentoring Support

You will likely be both a mentor and a protégé at some point in your life, given that you are a T&D professional; however, it is also likely that you will be asked to assist with establishing a mentoring culture in your organization. What might that entail?

Successful mentoring is not a program; it is a process. Programs typically die because they are perceived as add-ons, not culturally integrated into the DNA of the organization. Add-on focus tends to amplify the means and forget the end. For example, most organizations don't want diversity programs; they want diversity. Successful churches focus on promoting a culture of stewardship rather than relying on an annual stewardship drive. Mentoring is similar. If your mentoring program comes laden with policies and forms, you can expect the death knell. So, how do you support the sustainability of mentoring, the outcome rather than mentoring, the program? Three things come to mind.

Emotional worth. Mentoring is sustainable when there is a clearly perceived link between mentoring effort and some outcome that employees (mentors and protégés) believe has emotional worth. Worth comes in many forms: economics, affirmation, growth, status, or power. However, the root of worth lies in the degree to which it has emotional grounding.

That is, it matters deeply to the person. When mentors are affirmed for their mentoring work, it sends a signal to the rest of the organization that mentoring is important.

Relevant anchors. Mentoring is sustained when it has relevant anchors. This means that mentoring is deliberately hardwired into the norms, values, mores, and symbols of the organization. Relevant means the anchors are those that capture the attention of employees and are deemed important. When the incentive system is altered to reflect affirmation of mentoring, when effective mentors are the people getting the best assignments or promotions, or when executive leadership frequently asks for status reports on mentoring, such actions telegraph relevance.

Success resources. Finally, mentoring is sustained when the mentor and protégé are given the success resources of time, training, and support to be effective. One major organization crafted a training program that provided learning opportunities for both mentor and protégé to together learn ways to enrich their relationship. Another organization provided all mentor–protégé pairs with a coach (shadow mentor) whom they could call on if their mentoring relationship was not being as successful as it needed to be.

As for practical advice, the sidebar offers several tips to ensure a successful mentoring effort in any organization. But, remember: The mentoring that occurs in your organization will be sustained if employees perceive emotional worth, mentoring is anchored to the organization, and adequate resources are available for success.

A Dozen Ways to Ensure a Successful Mentor Process

By Elaine Biech

Confirm leadership support. Executive support is required to ensure success. The best way to demonstrate support is to have leaders who model mentoring send a signal to the rest of the organization. Yes, even your CEO should have a protégé or two. Identify a senior leader who can act as a champion and advocate for the mentoring process and ensure that it is a part of the organization's culture.

Identify a passionate manager. Select a program manager who has energy and is excited about the possibilities of mentoring. The manager will need to train and coach mentor–protégé partners, solve problems that may arise, and market and promote the effort. The manager will also need to ensure that mentoring is culturally integrated into the organization and, as Chip states, has the "relevant anchors" to sustain it.

Make it an easy sell. It is easier to encourage mentors to volunteer if you put the responsibility on the protégés for scheduling. Conduct special events, such as guest speakers or learning events, that are open only to mentors and protégés, to encourage others to get involved. Formally recognize mentors for their contributions, ensuring that there are incentives for their efforts. Eliminate all paperwork for mentors and almost all for protégés. All of these provide what Chip calls the "success resources."

Match mentors and protégés. Web-based mentoring tools exist for matching protégés to mentors, but they are by no means required. This may mean that someone needs to become a matchmaker. Expect protégés to complete a simple application that requires them to identify their key objective(s) for having a mentor. Then identify the best mentor to meet the objectives. Include protégés in the decision-making process.

Implement partnership agreements. A partnership agreement that is discussed and signed by both parties ensures that both understand the expectations. The partnership agreement covers topics such as objectives, roles, responsibilities, expectations, time commitment, confidentiality agreement, and how to resolve conflict. Partners should revisit the agreement at the end of one year whether they continue on or not.

Orient partners. Deliver an orientation event for mentors and protégés. Conduct activities that clarify roles, identify objectives, address potential issues, and discuss expectations. This is a good time to introduce the partnership agreements. Hold brown bag events between orientations to allow new pairs to get started without waiting for the next orientation. Or have the mentoring manager meet with partners to get them started.

Establish simple guidelines. Clarify your objectives and keep guidelines simple. Establish few rules. Two guidelines that seem to work well are: 1) the mentor should not be in the direct supervisory line (to eliminate any hint of favoritism), and 2) the mentor should not be more than two levels above the protégé (to ensure practical advice). Another guideline might be that all mentor–protégé partnerships are reviewed for continuation at the end of one year.

Ensure flexibility. Because you are meeting individual needs, mentoring requires the flexibility to be successful. Build in flexibility around areas such as the mentoring format you use, how the partners interact, duration of the partnerships, how often they should meet, and other things. Determine early what flexibility is required for your organization's success.

Develop a mentoring handbook. A mentoring guide or handbook includes whatever you believe will ensure success for the mentor–protégé partnership. Suggestions include roles and expectations, why mentoring is important for your organization, potential communication topics, time commitment expectations, successful mentor and protégé characteristics, exercises for building the relationship, and communication skills and techniques.

Provide conversation starters. Provide tips and topics to the mentors and protégés. These can be in the form of articles, self-assessments, controversial issues, career options, or any current topics such as leadership, technology, office politics, goal setting, life–work balance, or others.

(continued on next page)

A Dozen Ways to Ensure
a Successful Mentor Process (continued)

The conversation starters can be emailed monthly, and the partners can choose to use the conversation starters or not.

Fine-tune the process. This requires that you ask for feedback and measure the process. Survey the mentors and protégés to determine if mentoring is meeting their needs and what ideas they have for improvement. In addition, determine if it is meeting the organization's objectives. All of these ensure that your mentoring efforts have what Chip calls "emotional worth."

Market for ongoing success. Demonstrate the benefits of mentoring. Include articles in your corporate communication vehicles. Encourage current and past participants to share their success stories. Broadcast mentoring events as benefits of the program. Provide ongoing recognition to mentors. Find ways to keep mentoring in front of everyone in your organization.

Closing Lessons From the First Mentor

The word *mentor* comes from *The Odyssey*, written by the Greek poet Homer. As Odysseus (Ulysses, in the Latin translation) is preparing to go fight the Trojan War, he realizes he is leaving behind his one and only heir, Telemachus. Since "Telie" (as he was probably known to his buddies) is in junior high and since wars tended to drag on for years (the Trojan War lasted 10), Odysseus recognizes that Telie needs to be coached on how to "king" while Daddy is off fighting. He hires a trusted family friend named Mentor to be Telie's tutor. Mentor is described by Homer as being both wise and sensitive—two important ingredients of world-class mentoring.

The history of the word *mentor* is instructive for several reasons. First, it underscores the legacy nature of mentoring. Like Odysseus, great leaders strive to leave behind a benefaction of added value. Second, Mentor (the old man) combined the wisdom of experience with the sensitivity of a fawn in his attempts to convey kinging skills to young Telemachus. We all know the challenge of conveying our hard-won wisdom to another without resistance. The successful mentor is able to circumvent resistance.

Homer characterizes Mentor as a family friend. The symbolism contained in this relationship is apropos to contemporary mentors. Effective mentors are like friends in that their goal is to create a safe context for growth. They are also like family in that their focus is to offer an unconditional, faithful acceptance of the protégé. Friends work to add and multiply, not subtract. Family members care, even in the face of mistakes and errors.

Superior mentors know how adults learn. Operating out of their intuition or on what they have learned from books, classes, or other mentors, the best mentors recognize that they are, first and foremost, facilitators and catalysts in a process of discovery and insight. They know that mentoring is not about smart comments, eloquent lectures, or clever quips. Mentors practice their skills with a combination of never-ending compassion, crystal-clear communication, and a sincere joy in the role of being a helper along a journey toward mastering.

Just like the first practitioner of their craft, mentors love learning, not teaching. They treasure sharing rather than showing off, giving rather than boasting. Great mentors are not only devoted fans of their protégés, but also they are loyal fans of the dream of what their protégés can become with their guidance.

About the Author

Chip R. Bell is a customer loyalty consultant and the author of several national bestselling books, including *Managers as Mentors* (with Marshall Goldsmith), *The 9½ Principles of Innovative Service, Take Their Breath Away* (with John Patterson), and *Managing Knock Your Socks Off Service* (with Ron Zemke). He was formerly director of management development and training for NCNB (now Bank of America) and served as a guerilla tactics instructor on the faculty of the U.S. Army Infantry School. A frequent contributor to *T+D* magazine, he authored a chapter for the previous edition of the *ASTD Handbook.* He is a past president of the Charlotte Area ASTD chapter.

References

Bell, C.R. (2013, February). How Leaders Grow Innovation. *T+D.*

Bell, C. (2013). Mentor Your Employees. *MWorld* (AMA).

Bell, C.R., and M. Goldsmith. (2013). *Managers as Mentors: Building Partnerships for Learning.* San Francisco: Berrett-Koehler.

Bell, C.R., and M. Goldsmith. (2013, Summer). Mentor-Leaders: Making Learning a Competitive Strategy. *Leader to Leader.*

Rogers, C. (1961). *On Becoming a Person.* New York: Houghton Mifflin.

For Further Reading

Bell, C.R., and M. Goldsmith. (2013). *Managers as Mentors: Building Partnerships for Learning.* San Francisco: Berrett-Koehler.

Chapter 40

Helping Managers Develop Their Employees

Wendy Axelrod

In This Chapter

- Promote managers' role expectations, and clarify the roles everyone plays.
- Assist managers to embed development in work and pinpoint the skills they need.
- Help managers see developmental opportunities and just-in-time resources.

Years ago, in a high-powered management meeting in Philadelphia, all eyes were on me. The division leaders were discussing the considerable skill gaps among the professional staff, and as their learning and development manager, they said it was all up to me to ensure employees were fully developed. Squirming in my chair, I gulped hard before responding. Ever find yourself in a similar situation?

The fact is, it is not up to the training and development (T&D) manager to get the workforce fully developed; actually, it is up to their direct managers. A great deal of research supports this. What is our responsibility? Helping managers become highly proficient at developing their workforce every day. Yes, managers do face many obstacles: lack of know-how, lack of time, and, often, lack of their leaders' support. Many managers even believe they are already doing it, yet research tells us most managers operate at a cursory level, bypassing the deeper developmental actions. As a T&D professional, your efforts can be spot-on for helping managers overcome what seems insurmountable: learning what it really takes to provide significant development *in* the job.

What Managers Focus on to Accelerate Talent Development

In the practical and research-based book *Make Talent Your Business: How Exceptional Managers Develop People While Getting Results,* Jeannie Coyle and I (2011) describe a model for manager-driven, performance-centered talent development. Based on research with exceptional development managers (EDMs) from dozens of companies, this approach is used to improve the way organizations prime their managers to accelerate talent development (TD). With this approach, many have met impressive business objectives, such as quickly adapting to global changes in customer response strategies, bolstering weak bench strength, and addressing significant national expansion of operations. Rather than sending employees off to training, T&D professionals in these companies partner with managers to grow the workforce, and that workforce then takes on the new business demands.

What's behind their success? These managers implement this simple yet profound principle: intertwining work, performance, and development on a daily basis to achieve significant workforce development. These managers also understand that employees' learning is not true development until it is applied, and they are in the best possible place to ensure this application occurs. To do this effectively, our research points to five practices used regularly by EDMs:

1. Make every day a development day.
2. Tap the psychological side of development.
3. Connect people with development partners.
4. Teach skills to navigate organization politics.
5. Shape your environment to drive development.

These practices focus on the manager, but what can you do to help managers become exceptional at developing others? The rest of this chapter will give you a head start toward supporting your managers' abilities to develop their people.

Promote Managers' Developmental Role Expectations

If an engineering department head thinks his daily job is designing the most efficient operation, or the director of accounting believes her daily work is getting the books straight, they are on the wrong track. Their jobs are all about helping their people achieve increased performance in line with the department objectives. Managers should be doing far less hands-on work and far more equipping of their people. Shifting from their long-held role expectations is a journey—maybe as much for you as it is for them—and will require collaboration, discovery, and patience. Here are several suggestions, based on the actions of T&D leaders who help managers become more skilled at developing others.

Assess Your Company's Current Situation

The larger organizational context shapes managerial behavior. Identify, modify, and potentially eliminate HR policies that are obstacles for encouraging managers to be more developmentally savvy (for example, performance management that emphasizes twice-yearly development planning rather than ongoing developmental actions).

Create a Compelling Picture

Hook managers with success stories. Find a story in your company similar to this one: A vice president of retail operations, faced with huge expansion and an equally daunting skill shortage, regretfully planned an enormous effort to hire scores of supervisors externally. But, he found another way. Instead, he invested in his middle managers' ability to make every day a developmental day for their teams. They rapidly grew the needed supervisory talent from within, saving time and resources, while increasing performance.

Show Them the Money

Provide some straight statistics on the impact of developmental managers from the myriad of current research studies (for example, managers who are highly developmental with their teams have a significant impact on engagement, retention, and productivity).

Invite Their Involvement

We know that managers' buy-in increases substantially if they are part of the process. Collaborate with managers in brainstorming or conduct focus groups; learn about their objections, carefully consider their suggestions, and provide them feedback on the impact of their recommendations.

Make It Part of the Company Plan

Include growing managers' TD role as a pivotal element of the strategic HR/T&D plan. Specify actions your function will take (for example, T&D professionals work with management teams to address the shift in managers' roles and to provide tools), as well as targets and measures.

Clarify the Roles Everyone Plays

A colleague who is a corporate HR business partner with a strong T&D background heard one of her line manager clients say, "If you are asking me to conduct development on a daily basis, then what is the employee's responsibility, and why do we even have a T&D department?" My colleague understood that this overwhelmed manager was not trying to neglect his responsibilities; he just needed to know how all the role responsibilities fit together.

Start with this sample for providing a clearer image of where managers' efforts fit into the picture.

Senior Management

Because talent is the main differentiator in business today, senior leaders establish a workplace focused on continuous manager-driven development. Top leaders must take on several responsibilities in their roles:

- demonstrate the company's commitment to prioritizing the key role managers play in TD
- lead and model the manager-as-developer role through decisions, actions, and priority given (for example, in budget, effort, and staff meetings)
- regularly track progress against metrics and support accountability at all levels
- collaborate with HR and T&D leaders to enhance planning and execution of managers' TD process.

Training and Development Team

T&D professionals serve as the company's deep expertise on what policies and programs will fuel the engines for managers in the talent development role:

- Partner with senior management in establishing and enhancing TD policies and practices.
- Address the important gaps that limit the execution of manager-as-developer.
- Further develop managers' competence in the practices of EDMs.
- Ensure road maps and tools are well communicated, accessible, and understood.

Employees

Employees take accountability for their own development and willingly lean into efforts that go beyond the stated job descriptions:

- Proactively seek opportunities to build new skills; know how to extract the most targeted learning from work experiences.
- Strengthen developmental relationships with their managers, asking for feedback and being responsive to managers' delegation and coaching.
- Understand the more sophisticated components of taking skills to the next level (for example, political savvy, intricate interpersonal exchanges).
- Build a trusted network of experienced peers and willing mentors; know who is the best resource for the targeted learning.

Managers

Managers act as the general contractor for employees' growth in the job, so that learning is efficient, goal driven, and applied. Several practices will enhance employee development:

- Know each employee's proficiencies and continually use obvious and subtle opportunities in the workplace to take them to the next level.
- Use other members of the team and experts to serve as development partners, yet stay close by to ensure employees apply the learning effectively.
- Provide high-quality feedback, inquiry, and coaching with an emphasis on employee learning rather than teaching (for example, less "telling" and more "asking" thought-provoking questions).
- Fill the work environment with continuous development actions for the team, such as after action reviews, coffee breaks for brainstorming, and shifting work assignments around to various members of the team.
- Respond to company requirements and HR programs, and offer suggestions to make the processes more productive for manager-driven, performance-centered development.

Figure 40-1. Organization Roles in Manager-Driven Talent Development

Senior Management
Demonstrate the company's commitment to prioritizing managers' key role in talent development every day.

Training & Development Team
Provide deep expertise on policies and programs, which accelerate managers' role in talent development.

Organization roles in manager-driven talent development

Managers
Act as general contractors for employees' growth *in* the job, so employees' learning is efficient, goal driven, and applied.

Employees
Take accountability for own development and willingly lean into efforts that go beyond the stated job description.

Steer Managers to Embed Development Right Into the Work

Can you imagine an IT quality assurance manager who neglected to include the change management protocol in a major client project in order to meet the intended release date? That would be totally ill-advised. She would need to build in that protocol as part of the deliverable; otherwise, her ongoing work with this client would be doomed. It is the same for managers; they can tie their efforts of employee development right into the performance results they expect. So, when managers tell you they can barely get on top of managing all the work, let alone provide development to their employees, graciously guide them with some of these ideas:

- Help managers think development as they plan and manage work assignments. It's a mindset shift that takes the manager out of the immediate to-do list and onto the long view of what can be accomplished in the next six months, especially once his or her staff has a broader and deeper set of skills.
- Managers need to clearly connect what's to be learned with what's to be accomplished, turning the work itself into a dynamic development tool. EDMs require employees to be accountable for both the targeted development, and the performance outcomes, and help employees see the value in this. One finance

manager tells his staff members that every project has one finish line but two ribbons: one ribbon for results and one for development.

- Work with managers to analyze which skill improvements of employees would best ratchet up the ability to achieve department objectives. Make sure managers select developmental assignments that fully align with anticipated department results, not simply stretch assignments that are expedient.

- Much of embedding development occurs in the delegation of work. Managers must learn to reshape or add to the everyday work assignments so that it has a developmental component for that particular employee. EDMs break big deliverables into new, smaller stretch tasks that will expand employees' expertise.

Guide Managers to Pinpoint the Skills They Need

In a major assessment of their talent development practices, a large Midwestern firm with highly regarded TD practices desired to uncover why they were not getting the increased skill levels they anticipated. They discovered that despite the myriad of tools offered to the workforce, managers were not asked to be part of the TD process, nor did they know how to provide hands-on development. Yet, those managers wanted to be part of the action. Truly, that lack of managers' involvement was a broken link in the company's development chain. In an effort to turn things around, the TD department looked at what skills managers needed. Based on observing EDMs, we know that the manager must have skills well beyond those necessary in a typical coaching scenario or required in managing performance.

T&D professionals can help managers understand their levels of capability with the skills listed in Table 40-1. Many of these may already be included as part of your managerial assessment and development tools. If not, consider adding them.

These are the skills that managers need for the manager-as-developer process. Why not take a few minutes to consider what competencies would support your work with them, such as those recently identified by Dave Ulrich (Ulrich, Younger, Brockbank, and Ulrich, 2012): change champion, strategic positioner, and credible activist.

Table 40-1. 12 Skills Used by Exceptional Development Managers

Type of Capability	Skills
Deep Interpersonal Connection	*Emotional intelligence:* Being self-aware and transparent; managing your own emotions and tuning in to others' interests
	Discovery learning: Guiding people to discover their own lessons versus telling them what to do
	Building trusting relationships: Demonstrating honesty, credibility, and caring in the relationships you build with others; doing what you have said you will do
Broad and Long-Term Outlook	*Strategic thinking:* Adapting a mindset that takes into account the broader, longer view of the business and your department's bench strength to obtain results
	Perspective setting: Helping others understand the larger context; diminishing the drama that comes with a narrow, immediate view
Deliberate and Decisive Communications	*Enhanced listening:* Being able to read others; taking into account both people's words and the feelings behind their words
	Productive inquiry: Asking tailored, thought-provoking questions that make people reflect and discover new ways of thinking and acting
	On-point articulation: Sharing sufficient detail (beyond general comments) in nuanced explanations to ensure your message is readily grasped by others
Conviction and Character	*Tenacity:* Maintaining forward momentum and a positive attitude despite prevailing challenges
	Risk taking: Willingness to move out of your comfort zone and beyond the status quo; having the courage and the wisdom to take considered chances
	Adaptability: Operating effectively with ambiguity or in less than ideal conditions; being willing to take the heat
	Passion about development: Consistently showing a zeal for developing others and yourself

Open the Door to Developmental Opportunities and Just-In-Time Resources

"The medium is the message" is the powerful and evocative phrase coined by Marshall McLuhan (1964) 50 years ago. It certainly applies here. We cannot ask managers to learn how to make every day a development day for their people by sending them to a classroom. For managers, learning the deeper skills of becoming an EDM needs to be integrated with their work.

Training and development professionals can challenge managers to increase their employees' skills in targeted areas (for example, working with an employee to quickly move from the role of marketing analyst to that of marketing consultant, or increasing the entire team's capacity to shift from a domestic client base to one that is global). Several excellent companies use these approaches for growing managers' developmental capabilities:

- Provide ongoing action learning forums where peers learn about an EDM practice, followed by implementing specific developmental actions with targeted employees. Then, these same managers meet as a group to report on successes and challenges and receive counsel from peers and T&D professionals.
- Have senior leaders champion the EDM approach and model these developmental practices with managers who report to them.
- Put managers in new challenging roles that require them to be developmental managers.
- Package your company's resources, such as articles, videos, tools, and diagnostics, under a user-friendly framework for exceptional developmental managers. Provide needed explanation about the positioning and impact of company TD programs, so managers can maximize their value. Complement these tools with accessible options such as lunchtime peer discussions and open call hours to you.
- Enlist the EDMs you already have in the company to work with other managers as a development partner for an established amount of time.

Partner With Managers for Success

The next time leaders tell you it is your job to address all the skill gaps in their workforce, make it a partnership; your approach will be a big factor in the success. You can help managers establish the corporate expectation; clarify the role as a developmental manager; embed development right into the work itself; identify the skills managers require to do the job well; and tap into company resources to become exceptional at developing people every day. By taking these steps, you multiply your own impact on and accelerate development for the entire workforce.

About the Author

Wendy Axelrod, PhD, is an expert in manager-driven, performance-centered people development. During 30 years as a corporate executive, consultant, and executive coach, she has helped organizations drive substantial development of people in practical, yet often unexplored ways. She has worked with thousands of managers and leaders through both workshops and leadership coaching. She is co-author of *Make Talent Your Business* and numerous articles and speaks regularly to professional and corporate audiences. She is also passionate about her work as an executive coach and as a volunteer mentor. Her website can be found at www.TalentSavvyManager.com.

References

Axelrod, W., and J. Coyle. (2011). *Make Talent Your Business: How Exceptional Managers Develop People While Getting Results.* San Francisco: Berrett-Koehler.

Institute for Corporate Productivity. (2012). *Building a Change Ready Organization: Critical Human Capital Issues: 2013.* Seattle.

McLuhan, M. (1964). *Understanding Media: The Extensions of Man.* New York: McGraw-Hill.

Right Management. (2013). *How Leaders Drive Workforce Performance.* Philadelphia.

Ulrich, D., J. Younger, W. Brockbank, and M. Ulrich. (2012). *HR From the Inside Out: Six Competencies for the Future of HR.* New York: McGraw Hill.

For Further Reading

Axelrod, W., and J. Coyle. (2011, August). Grow Your Talent; Make Daily Work Developmental. *Leadership Excellence.*

Kaye, B., and J. Winkle Giulioni. (2012). *Help Them Grow or Watch Them Go.* San Francisco: Berrett-Koehler.

Kent Hayashi, S. (2012). *Conversations for Creating Star Performers: Go Beyond the Performance Review to Inspire Excellence Every Day.* New York: McGraw Hill.

Chapter 41

Knowledge Management: An Introduction for T&D Professionals

Marc Rosenberg

·· **In This Chapter** ··

- ▪ Learn the basics to using knowledge management (KM) as a training and development professional.
- ▪ Explore the misconceptions and challenges of KM.
- ▪ Understand the three components of KM and how to get started.

··

The critical intellectual assets in your organization are referred to as *knowledge assets*. One of the emerging tools we have for managing organizational knowledge is knowledge management (KM). It is an increasingly important tool for learning, but beyond that, it is becoming a critical organizational capability to manage intellectual property and make the right information available to the right people, at the right level of detail, and at the precise moment of need.

Knowledge workers spend vast amounts of time searching for information needed to perform their jobs. Often searches yield poor, few, or no results. The costs associated with such inefficiency include lower productivity, higher business expenses, and slower marketplace response time, among others. However, these costs can be reduced if organizations learn to better create, share, and manage organizational knowledge.

Organizational knowledge can be defined as the collection of critical intellectual assets within our organizations. Knowledge sharing is being used increasingly to boost customer service, decrease product development time, and share best practices. How do we define knowledge management? ASTD's definition is: "Knowledge management captures, distributes, and archives intellectual capital in a way that encourages knowledge sharing in the organization" (Arneson, Rothwell, and Naughton, 2013).

Knowledge sharing occurs in both formal and informal ways, from document storage on the intranet to conversations around the water cooler. This chapter provides a primer to get you started on what you need to know about KM as a training and development professional.

Information Challenges

The rate of knowledge growth is increasing exponentially, while the half-life of knowledge is shrinking dramatically. In other words, we need to know more and more all the time, but the useful "shelf-life" of what we know is shrinking. "Getting information off the Internet is like taking a drink from a fire hydrant," claims Mitchell Kapor.

There are five key information challenges we face (Beasley et al., 2011):

- **Information overload,** where there is too much information for the performers to organize, synthesize, draw conclusions from, or act.
- **Information underload,** where they can't find enough information to confidently act.
- **Information scatter,** where the needed information is in multiple locations, placing it at high risk of being overlooked or ignored.
- **Information conflict,** where information is duplicated and different, creating the challenge of trust (also positioning information at high risk of being overlooked or ignored).
- **Erroneous information,** where the information is misleading or outright wrong, creating high risk of failure wherever there is a critical impact.

What KM Is Not

There are several different misconceptions about what knowledge management is and is not. Table 41-1 outlines what knowledge management is not.

Table 41-1. What KM Is Not

Training	Training is about instruction—a refined and focused approach to moving learners through specific, predefined content. KM deals with information, where workers decide for themselves when, how, and to what depth they will explore the content.
Data mining	We are awash with data, but we don't know what to do with it. KM transforms data into information, which we use to build our knowledge.
A website	KM is not a place on the web; it's about what you do with the web and how the web is organized to make organizational learning and performance improvements happen.
A search engine	Finding information is easy; it is finding good, relevant information, at the right level of detail and at the right moment in time, that is hard.
Technology	Do not confuse the means with the ends. Technology is an enabler of KM.

Some see KM as primarily a technological solution to managing intellectual capital, while others simply use the term as an umbrella for a variety of other approaches to foster knowledge sharing and collaboration. There are those who do not like the term *knowledge management* and prefer *knowledge exchange, knowledge sharing,* or another similar term.

How Does KM Address These Challenges?

KM helps address these challenges and achieve several key goals within your organization (see Table 41-2).

Can your organization benefit from some form of KM? An assessment to help you discover the answer can be downloaded from the *Handbook's* website at www.astdhandbook.org.

Table 41-2. KM Can Achieve Organizational Goals

Goal	Goal Description	Benefit
Better tracking of intellectual capital	Inventory, manage, and find key technical and business knowledge	Enhanced business speed responsiveness, ability
Reduced redundancy of work	Recognize opportunities for consolidation of redundant projects	Lower costs and better use of resources
More reliable information	Level of uncertainty about the accuracy and validity of information will be reduced	Better decision making
Precise knowledge distribution	Target the right information, at the right time, to the right people, and at the right level of detail	Higher user value and learning
Knowledge/expertise sharing	Sharing knowledge across distance and organizational boundaries	Greater teamwork and collaboration
Increased knowledge asset security	Define access and entitlements by organization, level, content, and so on	Protection of intellectual capital
Enhancing customer value (marketing, sales, service)	All organizations have access to the same complete set of customer information	Enhanced customer satisfaction
Promote innovation	Allow new ideas to surface and develop into best practices at a faster rate	Generation of new knowledge
Retool workforce	Prepare workforce for constant change and new challenges	Better use of human assets

Getting Started With KM

Like any new effort, several guiding principles will help you initiate your KM effort effectively. A well-planned KM strategy should include:

- a unified, virtual, and secure library of knowledge that is accurate, relevant, and authentic
- the capability for each individual and organization to choose resources of greatest importance and to organize those choices in a personalized view
- accountability to ensure that resources are kept relevant and up-to-date
- the capability to share ideas through collaboration
- the capability to find information across all resource types and sources, both technological and human
- a common single point of access to knowledge
- scalability and flexibility to accommodate growth, geographical dispersion, and new uses.

Three Components of KM

The three major components of knowledge management (KM) include information repositories, communities of practice, and access to experts and expertise. What are their critical characteristics and the implications for the training and development function?

Information Repositories

An information repository is an online information resource created by codifying the collective knowledge of the organization and making it readily available. Information that could go into a repository may include:

- research and development
- installation, care, use
- customer service, troubleshooting records
- new product updates
- training courses
- support for transaction systems

- product knowledge
- recommended resources
- corporate messages
- policy and procedures
- field support documentation
- best practices
- competitive intelligence.

Figure 41-1 depicts how raw data is coded into certain domains of knowledge and fed into a knowledge base or repository. There the information is channeled into multiple portals, depending on the needs of the unique users, and delivered on demand.

Figure 41-1. How Raw Data Is Coded Into Domains of Knowledge for Multiple Users

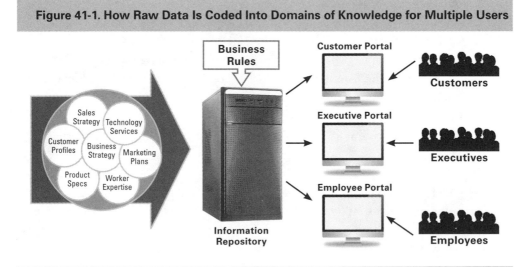

Communities of Practice

The second component of KM is communities of practice or groups of people who share a concern or interest for something they do and interact in order to learn to do it better. Communities of practice can be organized either vertically or horizontally. Vertical communities are structured similarly to the way organizations are structured and are usually based on reporting relationships. Think of business units and departments as a good example. Members throughout a certain unit might be involved as a community and discuss topics related to specific goals of the unit. Most communication in vertical communities is top-down, and sometimes, bottom-up.

Horizontal units are based more on common interests and needs rather than reporting relationships. These communities are focused more on sharing knowledge than accomplishing specific tasks. Think of ASTD membership as a good example. Communication is more likely to be collaborative and multidirectional at the same time.

Several factors ensure the success of the communities of practice:

- **Peer identification:** Group members by common interest or need.
- **Value to user (purpose):** Make sure the community content and conversations are relevant, fresh, and focused on the users' needs.
- **No pain:** The community should not be difficult to use or take unwarranted time away from users' jobs.
- **Make it special:** Consider making membership available only through approval or as a reward for excellence.
- **Community leadership:** Appoint a facilitator to help keep the community focused and maintain momentum.
- **Tools:** To foster effective communities, make sure they have the right tools.
- **Support from the top:** It is crucial to have top-level leadership endorsement and actual participation.
- **Minimal oversight:** Avoid excessive monitoring of the group by management.
- **The right environment:** Take care to develop a trusting knowledge-sharing culture.

Social media has the potential to significantly advance our capabilities here. A community will use numerous collaboration tools to enhance its ability to share knowledge more effectively, including email, chat rooms, web conferencing, blogs, wikis, texting, and a variety of social networks.

Access to Experts and Expertise

Historically, people learned skills by studying under a master through a formal apprentice-ship program. Today, access to true experts in an organization is much more difficult and leveraging experts across organizations or business units is challenging. Although experts are often called on to conduct training or write whitepapers, they simply do not have time to impart their knowledge to those who need it when they need it most: in the process of doing their work. Managers and peers do not always have all the knowledge and wisdom necessary to adequately coach their subordinates in skills or domains needed.

So how can you promote the sharing of expertise? Here are eight things you can consider.

1. **Reduce the workload.** Experts are generally very busy and already have many requests for their expertise. To avoid resentment and possible burnout, include sharing expertise as part of their job description and allocate work time to the task.
2. **Use the right incentives.** Provide incentives, such as organizational perks or professional development opportunities, for true experts who share their knowledge.
3. **Rotate your experts.** If you have enough experts, rotate them so that no single person is giving too much time.
4. **Manage the demand.** Do not allow an onslaught of demands on the expert's time to become discouraging. Consider specific time parameters on when the expert is available.
5. **Publish expertise as it becomes more stable and repeatable.** Documenting and storing expertise in a searchable format helps eliminate redundancy.
6. **Point to where the information can be found.** Sometimes experts are most helpful when showing others where or how to find information, rather than giving direct answers.
7. **Use different knowledge-capture techniques.** Because it is not always easy for an expert to document his or her knowledge and wisdom, think of a variety of creative knowledge-capturing techniques to get at the essence of the expert's knowledge. Examples include interviews, recording of storytelling, apprentice/mentor relationships, and, of course, training.
8. **Bring in your trainers.** Consider using your trainers as experts.

Knowledge Management Development Framework

A knowledge management development framework is a matrix of primary KM development activities. The framework adopted by every organization will likely be different; however, several of the key components will remain the same. The key components generally found include:

- **Organizational knowledge strategy:** This includes a vision and mission, a current- and future-state analysis, and a business case.
- **Implementation strategy:** Thinking about implementation early prevents failure later and includes training and support, communication, and how you will manage change, how you will manage the project, and how you will keep all stakeholders informed and involved.
- **Web strategy:** Three primary focus areas include mobility, social networking and messaging, and content creation and access.
- **Governance:** This is required to ensure that the function is organized and managed for peak efficiency; for example, clarifying the organizational structure, roles, responsibility, leadership representation, issue resolution, and program management.
- **Tools and applications:** There is an increasing array of sophisticated tools and applications that make KM systems work. Choosing the right tools can bring together a complex set of information and make it accessible to the right people.
- **Technical infrastructure and architecture:** This includes things such as assessing how well KM will integrate in your IT infrastructure through linking the system to existing business processes as seamlessly as possible. It is here where you must work very closely with IT, since that department is most likely responsible for the technical systems that make KM work. Think of it this way: Training and development may own the "cars" (the content), but IT owns the "road" (the infrastructure). Neither will be successful without the other.
- **Procedures:** Everything from help systems and training to features and functionality is considered to ensure the KM system will be easy and effective to operate.
- **User expertise:** Making systems easy to use and user friendly is essential if users are to buy in to the KM system as making their life easier, not more difficult.
- **Content:** In a knowledge management system, the organization of content in the system is key to its effective use. Finding a structure for organizing content is essential to KM success.

This list provides a summary of the areas that are required and demonstrates that KM is much more than collecting and posting documents.

Your Role as a T&D Professional in KM

You might be wondering about your role as a T&D professional in all this. Let's explore how KM and organizational learning work together, some new skills you may need for working on a KM system, and how to get started with implementing KM in your organization.

How KM and Organizational Learning Work Together

Although KM and training and development may appear to be mutually exclusive, they are in fact more yin and yang—mutually compatible. Using both KM and training and development tools wisely and appropriately can result in a powerful learning system. The key to maximizing the use of both tools is being able to differentiate between skills that must be performed automatically (often from memory) and information that can be accessed or referenced as needed (Rosenberg, 2001). How much of your classroom content is basic knowledge that could more easily be delivered through a well-designed KM strategy? And, if you can take some of the basic content out of your courses, what types of higher-level learning strategies can you replace them with? In other cases, by moving the basic content to KM, you might be able to shorten your formal training sessions, which can be a huge cost saver.

Skills You May Need for Working on a KM System

Working in the training and development field, you have probably developed these skills and competencies:

- evaluation
- instructional design
- needs assessment
- project management
- teaching.

While these skills are very important to training and development, and knowledge management, in order to enhance your career in training and development and become more advanced in KM, you will need to develop the following skills and competencies or find the right people with these skills for support:

- business analysis
- change management
- community building and collaboration strategies
- content analysis
- information design
- knowledge architecture design
- library and information science
- performance analysis
- software development
- user interface design
- vendor/outsourcing management
- workflow.

Why develop these skills? Even if your organization does not currently have a KM system, it most likely will in the future. Remember that not everyone must be an expert in all these areas, but you should make sure that they are all covered, in depth, somewhere in your organization. As mentioned earlier in this chapter, information overload for everyone needs to be managed. KM is likely to become a bigger part of your world. An innovative, forward-reaching attitude will be required of all successful T&D professionals. This attitude encompasses how to view and serve the new learner:

- The employee/learner is viewed as a knowledge seeker, with constantly changing learning needs and timeframes.
- Online and offline services enable greater access to the total set of knowledge, learning, and performance resources.
- On-demand learning in the workplace, at the moment of need, becomes essential.

There are many disruptions at work; training may be one of them. If we can embed knowledge and learning into the flow of work, there would be fewer disruptions and more efficiency. There is still a role for training, but it will be different.

Implementing KM in Your Organization

Figuring out how to get started may seem like a daunting task, but a KM project does not have to be huge, especially for your first KM project. While creating a KM system for the entire organization is a worthy goal, if you don't have the resources, experience, or support, do not attempt to develop a solution so large. Instead, look for smaller KM opportunities within your work area. A small project will be more manageable as you are developing your KM skills. In addition, within your organization, small successes will be much more desirable and appreciated than a big failure (Rosenberg, 2001).

For example, the techniques for sharing information commonly used by online university courses can be applied to your organization. Professors of online university courses generally use an online classroom management system to communicate information to students and provide them with supplemental reading and project templates. In addition, these systems allow students to share information with each other through chat rooms, discussion boards, and document-sharing capabilities included within the system.

Similarly, you can look for opportunities in your organization in which KM would help people better share information or work collaboratively on a project. You can add the review and use of selected knowledge assets as precourse or postcourse activities. You can use knowledge resources to supplement and enhance what is learned in class. You can create a community of practice for your learners, adding new learners to the community as they complete their training. You can also look for opportunities in which KM can be added to or replace an existing training and development program to make learning more effective and efficient. The key thing to remember when getting started is not the size of the project, but whether KM solutions are right for your particular learning and performance issue.

There is also the issue of whether you should tackle KM alone or seek the assistance of qualified vendors and consultants. This all depends on your specific KM capabilities and strategy, but most organizations find that they will use vendors and consultants at least for part of the process. Preparing RFPs (requests for proposals), managing the bidding process, and contracting with a KM provider is just as important as effectively managing that provider once the work begins. If you are inexperienced in this area, check with your purchasing or procurement department for guidance and appropriate procedures, and be sure to involve IT, your client, and other stakeholders in the process.

There is much more to know about knowledge management; this chapter serves as a primer to get you started. As you think more about KM, consider these three critical challenges:

1. What happens when people seek information but can't find it? How does constant searching for content, which should be readily available, impair performance?
2. What happens when people find the information they are looking for, but, unknown to them, it is incomplete or inaccurate? When we get information from what we mistakenly believe are reliable sources, and then we take actions based on that information and those sources, the consequences can be devastating.
3. Finally, what happens when we send learners back to their jobs without adequate on-the-job resources to continue and confirm what they learned in training? Our responsibility for keeping people up-to-date does not end at the classroom door. It is a continuous, workplace-based process, one that is necessary to our key goals of continuous learning and performance improvement.

Knowledge management is nothing new. We've used textbooks and libraries throughout our schooling, and encyclopedias, dictionaries, cookbooks, travel guides, instruction manuals of all sorts, and product catalogues throughout our lives, just to name a few sources. Organizations are no different; processes and procedures, policies, product information, manufacturing know-how, marketing and sales strategies, financial and human resource data, and technical specifications, for example, are critical to any enterprise.

Now, these resources are quickly moving online. The technology is changing and the amount of information instantly available is almost incomprehensible. But the bottom line remains the same: to efficiently get knowledge from where it is to where it's needed, exactly when it's needed. Training, even e-learning, cannot possibly meet this challenge alone. We must put knowledge management into the mix.

About the Author

Marc Rosenberg, PhD, is a management consultant in training, organizational learning, e-learning, knowledge management, and performance improvement. He has written two books, *E-Learning* and *Beyond E-Learning*. His monthly column, Marc My Words, appears in the eLearning Guild's *Learning Solutions* online magazine. Marc is past president and honorary life member of the International Society for Performance Improvement and an eLearning Guild "Guild Master," has spoken at The White House, debated e-learning's future at Oxford University, keynoted conferences around the world, authored more than 50 articles and book chapters, and is frequently quoted in major trade publications. He is the subject matter expert and lead facilitator of ASTD's Knowledge Management certificate program. Learn more at www.marcrosenberg.com.

References

Arneson, J., W. Rothwell, and J. Naughton. (2013). *ASTD Competency Study: The Training & Development Profession Redefined.* Alexandria, VA: ASTD Press.

Beasley, J.W., et al. (2011). Information Chaos in Primary Care: Implications for Physician Performance and Patient Safety. *Journal of the American Board of Family Medicine,* 24(6):745-751, www.ncbi.nlm.nih.gov/pubmed/22086819.

Rosenberg, M. (2001). *E-Learning: Strategies for Delivering Knowledge in the Digital Age.* New York: McGraw-Hill.

For Further Reading

Rosenberg, M.J. (2006). *Beyond E-Learning: Approaches and Technologies to Enhance Organizational Knowledge, Learning, and Performance.* San Francisco: Pfeiffer.

Dozens of blogs are available; here are just a few for additional information:

- **ASTD's Learning Circuits**, www.learningcircuits.blogspot.com
- **Clark Quinn's Learnlets**, http://blog.learnlets.com
- **Harold Jarche,** www.jarche.com
- **Internet Time Alliance**, www.internettime.com
- **Jane Hart's Pick of the Day** (UK), www.janeknight.typepad.com
- **Marc My Words** (column in *Learning Solutions* magazine), www.learningsolutionsmag.com/authors/219/marc-j-rosenberg
- **Will at Work Learning** (focus on what research tells us), www.willatworklearning.com

Section VII

Managing the Business of Training

Section VII

Tying Training to Business Needs

Luminary Perspective

William C. Byham

Many senior leaders feel their organization's training efforts are not operated in the same businesslike way as other parts of the organization such as distribution or sales. It's their observation that development programs don't align with the business's needs and organizational ROI is hard to calculate.

Learning and performance managers reply, "What?" and further offer:

- "We continuously use data gathered in job analyses to determine what new training programs to offer."
- "Before selecting a solution, we evaluate training needs more than ever before. Our goal is to put learners into the right competency-based training programs and help them to leverage their assessment feedback to understand what parts of the program (key actions) they should give special attention."
- "We have adjusted our training to meet the changing needs of our trainees, for example, Millennials, more individual contributors who need to lead, and so forth."
- "We offer web-based training, virtual classroom, and training broken down into smaller pieces to allow less continuous time off the job and more independent learning."
- "10/20/70 is our motto. Training is just the beginning. We skill up managers to act as coaches before, during, and after training and ensure further skill growth before participants start to independently use skills on the job."
- "We measure the success of our training programs in terms of real, on-the-job behavior change. Those new skills lead to real business results such as increased engagement, productivity, and employee retention."

Then they ask, "What are we *not* doing?"

I respond, "You're doing many things right, but you may not be focusing training on what the CEO and top management are really interested in—the accomplishment of the organization's business strategy."

Then I ask, "Can you name your organization's current business strategies—particularly recent changes? Can you make a solid business case for how your training or development initiatives directly and meaningfully have an impact on specific organizational business strategies?" Unfortunately, many training and development professionals can't.

Far too many choose training topics based on "what's hot" in the training business—areas people are writing articles and books about this year—or out of habit. Few organizations look to their organizational strategy for guidance.

Training and development for an organization should be selected based on three factors:

- **Job analysis:** Identify exactly which competencies are important for job success in key roles.
- **Assessment:** Clearly pinpoint who needs to be developed in each competency.
- **Organizational business strategy:** Establish the priority of individual or group skills that need to be developed based on where the business needs to go.

Table A shows examples of common business strategies paired with leadership and interpersonal skills training topics that would give people at various organizational levels the skills and knowledge needed to execute a strategy.

Table A. Leadership and Interpersonal Skills Training Topics That Would Aid in the Accomplishment of Business Strategy

Business Strategy	Skills Topics
Drive innovation	• Empowerment/delegation • Coaching and developing others • Influence—selling the vision • Emotional intelligence
Increase global focus	• Global acumen • Building organizational talent • Emotional intelligence

The choice of specific training topics would depend on where each organization sees gaps in its leaders' and associates' ability to implement the strategy.

Connecting to Business Strategy Is Just the Start— Everyone Needs to Know What You're Doing

Once training programs are aligned with an organization's strategy, the alignment has to be communicated. Trainees and their managers won't necessarily get the connection. For that reason, we strongly recommend that every competency-based training program, including basic programs, start off with the facilitator explaining why one or more targeted organizational strategies are important and how the training or other development activity in which they are about to participate will positively affect those strategies. Following this with a brief discussion to emphasize the business connection gives each learner a clear link to his or her role in making the organization and themselves successful. Once back on the job, the learner and manager will make even clearer links to skill application and business impact through coaching discussions, assignments, and performance management.

Such an approach aligns training to what is important to the organization and to the individual. All associates want to know that they will make a difference. Knowing that their new skills are tools that will help them, drives faster and more effective application. The training now has a real business purpose (besides general self-development).

Top managers also should be reminded about the connection of training and development initiatives and business strategies. A good way to do this is to show the connection when lists of course offerings are compiled, clearly linking courses to key business strategies.

Aligning Programs With a New Business Strategy Is Particularly Important

In the past, organizations may have had a set of strategies they followed for 10 or more years. As we know, that's not true today! Businesses are constantly changing their strategies to adapt to business and competitive pressures. These frequent changes make the change implementation that HR and training professionals need to address more difficult. People get "change fatigue," which may lead to thinking that a new strategy can be ignored because it will probably be replaced by a newer one in a year or two.

CEOs constantly tell us that their biggest problem isn't coming up with the right strategy— it's execution. Given the importance that senior management places on strategy, more than anything they want people at all levels to get behind the strategy and make it work. They need all the help they can get, and that includes the training organization giving associates the skills to move strategy forward through execution.

Think Vertically Rather Than Just Horizontally

Training organizations often think horizontally in aligning with strategic priorities. Most focus on building strategic priorities into "first-line leader" or "customer-service" curricula. For real change in strategy to happen at an organization-wide level, the integrated learning and performance curricula at all levels need to be the focus of the efforts, and the message should be coordinated.

Align All HR Activities With Business Strategy

To get buy-in and ongoing support from top management, all areas of HR need to be connected to business strategy. This means that recruiting, selection, performance appraisal, and promotion decisions should be focusing on the same set of business strategy–related target competencies. Too often a new business strategy does not get translated into an HR strategy for a year or more. This is particularly bad when the hiring system is still bringing in people with the skills needed to implement the old strategy rather than the new one.

Aligning With a Major Change in Strategy

When a senior team decides on a major strategy shift, many parts of the organization will need to decide how they will align and support the change. This is where a training organization can truly make its mark helping the organization execute by building knowledge, skills, and role awareness. Think about what your training team would do if your CEO decided to:

- spin-off part of the organization
- totally change how the organization markets
- become a center for creativity overnight
- adjust to new ownership
- become more "green."

Here are two areas that you could consider when a big change happens at your organization.

1. Help the Change Be Understood and Accepted at All Levels

For large organizations, this is a huge challenge. Training such as the following is often needed to set the stage for how management wants all levels to view the change and to provide them with the skills to understand how they can support it.

- **Embracing change:** To help employees focus on the role of the individual performers in implementing change in the workplace. Participants discover their "change IQ," learn about the phases of change that many people experience, and are introduced to best practices that will enable them to tackle and overcome the new business challenges of today and tomorrow.
- **Driving change and building and sustaining trust:** To help frontline leaders have the skills and resources they need to accelerate the process of implementing change with their team members and to create an agile work environment where people are more open to change.
- **Making change happen:** To help managers and directors gain the ability to drive change by understanding the importance of stakeholders, multiple viewpoints, communication, and buy-in.

Naturally, some people will already be good at these skills, but most won't. Everyone will benefit from these training topics when they are specifically focused on the new business strategy. Also, the training provides a forum for people at each organizational level to discuss the change among themselves, and to counsel and coach each other—a very valuable trigger for their personal acceptance. These programs are most effective when participants are able to pull into the classroom real-life situations they are currently facing that will require a change in behavior for themselves or people they lead.

The biggest obstacle that we have seen is being able to deliver these programs extremely rapidly. Organizations don't want to wait for six months or even six weeks. They want to complete the training in two or, at the most, four weeks after the announcement of the change—a major effort, as you can imagine. When done at the right time, the skills acquired are appreciated by everyone, even the people who don't believe in the strategic change. The training can help the nonbelievers be good soldiers and do their part to make the change work. I know of several situations where thousands of employees and managers were trained within two weeks after a new initiative was announced, and in all cases, the training was widely acclaimed as one of the best parts of the rollout.

2. Provide Ongoing Training to Help People Rapidly Gain Skills Needed in Their Changed Jobs

Most of the time, a major organizational change will surface new training needs for many people. Meeting these needs must be a high priority so that individuals will rapidly feel comfortable and be successful in their new positions. Often, both new and refresher training will be needed.

The message sent by quickly offering specialized training help is that the organization is concerned about its people and will do everything necessary to help them succeed. (This is particularly important if there are layoffs involved.)

How to Prepare for Strategy Changes of All Types

The big thing training professionals can do to handle strategy changes is to make sure that managers at all levels are well grounded in basic interpersonal competencies: leadership, communication, delegation, empowerment, and programs that develop emotional intelligence or "interaction essentials." These will likely be key parts of any competencies selected to support a new strategy.

What About ROI?

All the trainers I know want to measure their impact, but few can follow through with real action. Generally, they blame this on the lack of management support and money. I find that when top management is asked to fund research on the effectiveness of training interventions relative to a change in organization strategy, they are more interested because the data from the measurement will provide a clear understanding of the impact of the training intervention showing them what will work the next time strategy changes.

A Partner for the Business

The focus for top management relative to small or large strategy change is to get everyone onboard and moving toward execution. If training professionals can play a meaningful role in this and measure their impact, I guarantee they will be viewed as business partners and that top management will start to bring them to the table earlier when future changes are being planned.

About the Author

William C. Byham, PhD is chairman and CEO of Development Dimensions International, Inc. (DDI).

For Further Reading

Byham, W.C., A.B. Smith, and M.J. Paese. (2002). *Grow Your Own Leaders: How to Identify, Develop, and Retain Leadership Talent.* Upper Saddle River, NJ: FT Press.

Smith, A.B., R.S. Wellins, and M.J. Paese. (2011). *The CEO's Guide to Talent Management: A Practical Approach.* Pittsburgh, PA: DDI Press.

Chapter 42

Developing a Strategy for Training and Development

John Coné

·· **In This Chapter** ··

- Develop a strategy for learning in your organization.
- Review a sample learning philosophy.
- Determine how to communicate your strategy.

···

Throw a ball at a target a few feet away, and if your aim is off by a couple of degrees, you'll likely still hit it. Send a capsule to the moon and be off by a thousandth of a degree at launch, and you could miss by miles. Training, done right, is strategic. It doesn't just react to the problems of today; it prepares for (and at its best *avoids*) the problems of the future. Sure, some training programs pay off quickly, but a training department is a long-term investment.

A Strategy for the Learning Function Is a Learning Strategy for the Organization

Fostering a learning organization is everyone's responsibility, but the learning professional is singularly charged with the relentless pursuit of that ideal. Your strategy is much more than a statement of your long-term intent. It is a blueprint to guide your actions for years to come. It doesn't happen in a vacuum. Learning is already happening. Most often, a training department already exists, so a new strategy often means change—change that is not incremental.

It is not optimization, process improvement, or visioning, although all those things come into play. Developing the strategy for your learning team must be a thorough, thoughtful, and analytic process aimed at making the training function the best possible resource for the organization it serves.

Building according to any blueprint takes time. Adjustments get made along the way. But without a complete strategy in place—one that is supported by the leadership of the organization you serve—there's no way to know if what you create will be what you need, or even if it will survive.

There are innumerable books, workshops, webinars, and articles that talk about strategy. Several of my favorites are listed at the end of this chapter. ASTD provides instruction, tools, and examples in its Managing Learning Certificate program. All of these resources ask core question such as: Who are we? What do we do? And, where are we going? Every good strategy must address those questions. But few of the resources I've found consider the requirements of developing a solid strategy for a function inside a larger organization, and fewer still focus on the learning function. My experience suggests a few more questions to add:

- Why are we developing a strategy (now)?
- Who are we?
- Whom do we serve?
- How do we serve?
- Where are we now?
- Where are we going?
- How will we get there?
- How will we know we are getting there?

Let's look at each of these in more depth.

1. Why Are We Developing a Strategy (Now)?

Chances are, neither the training function nor the organization it serves is brand new. Something has led to this moment. Something has changed. It's a good idea to document the background and context that has inspired (or required) you to develop a strategy. Whatever the cause, there is likely a sense of a need for change. Document it. One way you'll be able to evaluate the quality of your strategy is by assessing the extent to which it addresses the conditions that led to its creation.

2. Who Are We?

Who you are is often documented in the form of mission, vision, and values. But at a fundamental level, your training strategy must be consistent with the culture of the organization and meet the obligations for training and development implied by that culture. I call this consistency of purpose. Consistency of purpose requires an understanding of the organization's beliefs about employee development. How is learning connected to decision making, business planning, and budgeting? Is training regarded as an investment, a cost, or even a competitive advantage? Is learning used proactively or in response to problems? What are the unspoken obligations of employees and managers when it comes to learning? Is training shared with customers, partners, or suppliers? Is self-development rewarded, punished, or ignored?

> *Your training strategy must be consistent with the culture of the organization.*

We could spend an entire book just contrasting various cultural archetypes. But ultimately, the work product of aligning learning with your organizational strategy is the creation of a philosophy of learning. Let me illustrate by example. Take a look at the Sample Learning Philosophy below.

Sample Learning Philosophy

Our business environment will continue to be dominated by rapidly changing and growing customer demands, increasing competitive pressures, requirements for continuous improvement in all areas of endeavor, and the creation of vastly more sophisticated business processes. These factors and others will expand and change success requirements for employees throughout the organization. Therefore, continuous development of all employees will remain essential to our business success.

Because it is the way we run our business, the model for learning must be aimed at putting organizational resources close to our businesses while minimizing cost. Decentralized resources sharing a common strategy and common core processes will achieve this balance.

In our organization, *people are a resource to be developed.* They are responsible for managing their own development, and we will put them in a position to *control their own development.* The *organization shares with all employees a responsibility* to ensure that development occurs. Development *must be a planned and managed part of the strategy* for the success of the organization; a marriage between the development needs of the employee and the demands of the business. Our success depends not only on what we can do now, but also on what we are able to learn.

Development should be concerned with developing the whole person, facilitating all aspects of their mental development. Employees will have opportunities to participate in organization-sponsored

(continued on next page)

685

Sample Learning Philosophy (continued)

development *and be encouraged to take advantage of other external opportunities.* Our organization must be able to count on our people to help us to build a great organization, and we intend for them to be able to count on our organization to build great people.

Development is business-issue based, and should be supported by a *corporatewide development planning* process that is integral to our business planning. It should also be tightly linked to the individual development process and integrated with recruiting, performance appraisal, career planning, and job design.

To meet our obligations to our customers, stockholders, and employees, the following priorities should guide us in planning all development:

1. development required for the survival (continued business success) of the organization/department
2. development required for the survival (continued employability) of the individual
3. development that will take the organization/department to the next level of competency
4. development that will move the individual to the next level of competency.

Development is an investment; therefore, each business should *clearly identify the level of investment required* for the continued success of our organization, and the return on that investment should be measured. We accept the responsibility to plan and budget strategically for development.

How we develop employees *shapes our culture.* It should deliver key messages about our expectations concerning behavior. Training should provide the skills needed to excel at new behaviors that enable change and should also reinforce those things about our organization that should not change, such as our values.

Employee development is also *a competitive weapon* and should produce a workforce that can surpass our competitors and exceed our customers' expectations. *Renewal and improvement of skills and knowledge will be a constant activity.* Development should be *broadly based* and *widely available,* and its availability well communicated. Our efforts should balance immediate and long-term needs and be as concerned with creativity and innovation as with continuous improvement. At our organization, *development should extend beyond the (virtual) classroom* and into the workplace, using the tools and methods that are most effective and efficient.

Management should be champions of development for the organization—and be teachers, coaches, and mentors. Our best employees should play a major role in our organization's developmental process as instructors, facilitators, mentors, and subject matter experts. As an organization, we must have in place policies and processes that provide timely developmental feedback, create actionable development plans, ensure that development opportunities are available, and recognize when they have been achieved.

The learning function must ensure that developmental tools are available and that employees have the means to find and select the most efficient and beneficial options for them.

It would probably not be too difficult to reverse-engineer this learning philosophy to delineate the organizational culture it supports. It may not be your culture, so your philosophy will be different. But developing one and getting top leadership to agree to it will guarantee consistency of purpose and help you create your mission.

If you've already documented your mission, vision, and values, check them. They should be consistent with why you exist, what you believe in, and how you will behave. Although a good strategy is more specific than a vision statement, it should always move you toward the vision of what you want to be someday. And sometimes the greatest value of that part of the strategy is that it exposes the things you are not. If you are expected to be the employee communications function, the employee survey group, an integral part of the HR function, or the driver of the entire talent management process, say so. But what you don't say, you don't do.

3. Whom Do We Serve?

At first blush, this might seem obvious: the organization. But in most cases, the learning function charter is not that broad—or that clear. Perhaps you serve corporate management, but not the divisions. Or you serve everybody except sales and IT. Or you serve those whose needs are common to the organization-wide curriculum, but not those with special needs. You must make clear who your true customers are. If there is a hierarchy, you should delineate it. If it really is first-come, first-served, you should say so.

4. How Do We Serve?

This is where you begin to document our portfolio of products and services. But products and services are just a part of the business model. The business model addresses the broader issues of:

- What is the agreement you have with the organization you serve?
- What is your business model?
- Your financial model?
- Your organizational/operational model?

Your Deal

Every organization has a deal with its learning function, a set of expectations about what you will deliver. Different kinds of deals set different expectations and require different responses. Here are five types that I have experienced:

1. **Administer the medicine.** Customers regard the learning function as an unfortunate necessity, much like a trip to the dentist. Training is needed, maybe even

a good thing, but they'd rather being doing anything else. The repertoire of the training group is heavily weighted to safety and compliance training, doing whatever is necessary to avoid lawsuits, fines, or other bad outcomes. Training keeps us out of trouble and away from bad publicity. When this is the deal, the primary criteria used to judge the learning function is *ease*. What we provide should be almost invisible. What is visible must be quick, nonintrusive, and painless.

2. **Deliver basic capability.** Here the big organizational need is new talent. People need to be trained on how to do all the things the business requires. Often, the emphasis is on creating common practices, processes, and even common language. It's about basic skills and information needed for job success. With this deal, we are measured on *responsiveness*. Organizations don't excel at anticipating talent needs, so by the time they recognize them, time is short. We may be the ones who clarify and codify what is actually needed.

3. **Replicate our success model.** Over time, organizations invent or discover preferred ways to get things done. Especially at times of growth or retrenchment, the most important work of learning is to replicate those models of success. This may be through ongoing development programs or though episodic interventions, when new locations or divisions are in startup mode and whole systems must be replicated. In these circumstances, the critical measure of us becomes *consistency*.

4. **Provide tactical support.** If the learning function does the basic jobs well, it may be called on to aid in the pursuit of key goals. Learning is integrated into critical processes and into action plans. (Opening a new plant, implementing a new payroll system, or sales process are examples.) The deal is one of providing tactical support. Here the organization is apt to measure us first on *immediacy*. Our work is integral to goal attainment, so whatever results we promise have to happen now. Development cycle time and on-schedule delivery are now critical.

5. **Partner strategically.** Most learning professionals aspire to a fifth type of "contract"—that of supporting broadly based strategic initiatives. (Globalization, TQM, and leadership development may be examples.) Being a strategic business partner is the way this deal is most commonly expressed. We have the "seat at the table"—we are part of the planning process and a key driver in the plan for success. Under this deal, we are most often measured by *comprehensiveness*. Leading-edge resources are more important, partnerships are complex, and this type of contract will usually require the full repertoire of our capabilities, all in sync and there on demand.

Learning functions usually have a deal that is a complex combination of two or more of these types. In large organizations, one division may have different expectations from another. Most organizations go through cycles, changing the deal to meet the times. But usually the deal is implied, not stated. It has evolved over time, is not well understood, and is not being managed.

You have a deal with the organization you serve. You may be able to change it, but if you are not living up to that deal, you won't be around to change it. Whatever your strategy requires for learning to be in the organization, it has to start from where you are.

Your Business Model

Your business model defines how your training function will deliver value to your customers and how you will entice them to be your customers. While there are often "givens," based on the operating requirements of the organization you serve, there is always a lot of room for choice. The model you choose is based on your hypothesis about what your customers want, how they want it, and how training can organize to best meet those needs and be funded to do so. The implications of your business model are wide ranging. They operationally define your purpose, offerings, strategies, infrastructure, organization, and practices.

A comprehensive business model outlines the key activities necessary to fulfill your deal and defines the resources you will need to create value for your customers. It makes clear where your competition exists and the alliances you will need. It drives staffing, outsourcing, technology, marketing, and fulfillment.

Your business model includes:

- Your value proposition: What you offer, how you will differentiate yourself from your competitors, and the reason customers buy from you and not them.
- Customers/customer segments: The target audience for your products and services.
- Channels: The means by which you will deliver products and services to customers. This includes your marketing and distribution strategy.
- Customer relationships: The links you establish between you and your various customers (and stakeholders).
- Finally, your business model outlines your product/service portfolio, including what it will feature and what it will *not* include.

Your Financial Model

The only thing harder than building the training budget is justifying it. It doesn't help that, by the end of the year, what you spent doesn't look much like what you planned. Nothing solves that headache entirely, but the right financial model will enable you to pursue your strategy. Making the right choice between overhead allocation, strategic financing, fee for service, or even the profit center approach can create synergy between strategy and the funds that support it.

The right financial model also helps you to deal with ongoing program maintenance, broad-based analysis, capital outlays, outsourcing, and even the professional development of your own staff.

It informs how you deal with economic downturns, unanticipated requests, and vexing issues such as establishing the value of training interventions, dealing with no-shows, and calculating ROI.

Your Organizational Model

A strategy cannot succeed if you are not organized to pursue it. You need to know if you have an organization that can deliver on your strategic intent. What should be the balance between centralized and distributed resources? Does the organization you serve, by its very nature, make demands on how you must operate? Will your portfolio require dedicated resources in key areas?

In addition to your organization chart, you must determine the key policies, procedures, and processes that you will need for your strategy to succeed. How important will administrative systems be? Needs analysis? Annual planning and prioritization? Contract management?

You may need policies on budgeting for learning, development planning, or decision making regarding priorities for education.

W. Warner Burke

W. Warner Burke is a leading figure in the organization development and change fields. Burke is known for his emphasis on organization development as a change process designed to bring about a specific end result. Burke believes that organization development should involve such steps as organizational reflection, system improvement, planning, and self-analysis. Using a combination of theory and research to bolster his case, Burke stresses that organization development should be a deliberate, radical change instead of the gradual process typically exercised in organizations. Burke is a professor of psychology and education at Teachers College, Columbia University. He has served as executive director of the OD Network. Burke is a one of the top 50 executive coaches and has consulted with a variety of organizations in diverse industries. Burke is the author of more than 130 articles and book chapters in organizational psychology, organization change, and leadership. He has authored, coauthored, and edited 14 books. In 1993 Burke was awarded the Lippitt Memorial Award (the Organization Development Professional Practice Area Award for Excellence) from ASTD.

Your decisions on structure and key systems will drive other decisions regarding the experience and competencies you'll need on your team. Will you require specializations in analysis, assessment, contracting, consulting, evaluation, or administration? Will use of technology be critical? Instructional design? Facilitation? And you will also need to determine the broader competencies that will be the hallmark of your team based on your value proposition.

You may need to emphasize collaboration, organizational agility, sales or marketing ability, systems thinking, attention to detail, initiative, creativity, or technical or market knowledge. As managers, we want every one of our team members to possess all those attributes, but since reality always steps in, we must be ready to make the choices that will support our strategy.

5. Where Are We Now?

Your strategy is designed to take you where you want to go, starting from where you are. That requires an objective and thorough assessment of the current state. A good format for such a review includes a SWOT (strengths, weaknesses, opportunities, and threats) and PEST (political, economic, social, and technical) environmental analysis. Consider using this simple tool to cover particular concerns of the learning function. You may also find this tool on the *Handbook's* website at www.astdhandbook.org.

Figure 42-1. Tool for Environmental Analysis

The current state of our training product/service portfolio?	◯ WEAK	◯ AVERAGE	◯ STRONG
The current staff mix of skills presently needed or needed soon?	◯ POOR	◯ IFFY	◯ A MATCH
The current reputation of the learning function?	◯ POOR	◯ MIXED	◯ GREAT
How is training considered?	◯ COST	◯ INVESTMENT	◯ STRATEGY
Does the organization think its training needs are being met?	◯ POOR	◯ AVERAGE	◯ WELL
Is the learning function tied to the business?	◯ NO	◯ POORLY	◯ STRONGLY
Can we prove our worth?	◯ NO	◯ ANECDOTES	◯ ROI

Obviously, a lot of selections in the first column mean that the first phase of your strategy may be recovery. The right strategy must include how you will get through average and to strong. Having many selections in the last column suggests a strategy to take things to an even higher level.

6. Where Are We Going?

A strategy takes years to achieve. Three to five years is a common timeframe. This component of the strategy is the set of initiatives you plan to implement over that period. In addition to the products or services that you will deliver, it can include initiatives in operations, information technology, finance, and marketing.

These are the plans that guide your focus and resource allocation. If your strategy is specific enough, you will have detailed plans in all these areas. To check yourself, look to see if you have included:

- changes or improvements to current products and services
- implementation of new offerings
- adding service to new customer groups
- implementing new learning modalities or administrative systems
- changes or enhancements to key systems or processes
- enhancing the financial model
- improving governance
- developing new staff competencies
- cost reductions and productivity improvements.

The specific initiatives depend on your circumstances, but here are some ways to think about the quality of your initiatives:

- Are they linked to the organization? All your strategies should be clearly in support of the critical issues of the organization you serve. The stronger the connection, the better the initiative.
- Are they practical? You should have the capabilities, funding, and information you need for the strategy to succeed. If not, there should be a clear and likely way to get them. And though the timeframe may be a stretch, it should still be reasonable.
- Are they likely to succeed? Your strategies should be logical. They should make economic sense. The risks should be clear, and there should be specific plans to avoid or minimize them. They should fit with and not conflict with the strategic

direction of other major players in the organization. And they should be clearly linked to measures that can be used to prove their success.

- Are they politically acceptable to the organization? If you've linked your strategies to critical organizational issues, then the outcomes they produce will be politically acceptable. But the strategies themselves must also be OK with your stakeholders. They must accept the risks, participate in the strategies, and support them politically. That means the stakeholders have to be clear on and supportive of the expected benefits of the strategy.

7. How Will We Get There?

Much of the "how" is probably already clear from the strategic initiatives; however, there are some broader considerations worthy of attention.

Choose an overall strategic approach that will support your initiatives. Yours may be a growth strategy (increasing utilization of your offerings), a market penetration strategy (serving a greater percentage of potential users), a consolidation strategy (bringing together disparate training groups), a harvesting strategy (making the most of popular services), or a divestment strategy (transferring programs or services to other departments or training groups so that you can focus on a few key areas).

You might also decide that a particular set of resources will form the foundation of all your initiatives. It might be a set of strategic alliances, the implementation of a particular technology, the acquisition of a particular set of competencies, or even the creation of a new set of adjunct or outsourced resources.

The "how" portion of the strategy is a great place to add detail to your value proposition. What the learning function will do differently from or better than others (or your own function in the past) is what truly defines the means by which you will achieve your stated objective. It explains why your strategy is going to work.

This section of your strategy is also where (if they have not appeared elsewhere) you can document any major operational actions you have planned or structural changes you intend to make. In addition, you can list any critical dependencies that could radically alter your strategy.

Finally, and perhaps most important, you can detail the financial plan that forecasts what it will cost to implement your strategy and the monetary results you expect to get from it. The first year of your strategic plan can't be separated from your annual budget. In most organizations, if it's not in the budget, it isn't going to happen. That's why you'll want both your boss (who approves your budget) and a senior financial person to review the early drafts of your strategy. The entire strategy, but especially the financial plan, needs to earn the approval of your organization's management and should be reviewed on a regular basis to track results and make refinements.

8. How Will We Know We Are Getting There?

It has been said that no battle plan survives the first encounter. When any strategy meets reality, adjustments get made. But without the right metrics, how can you know if the strategy is working? Can you be sure that you are still on track? A great strategy includes a clear view of how you will know you are making progress.

Measuring effectiveness is about each of your individual offerings, the aggregate of all those solutions, and therefore the learning function. Done well, it describes how you will routinely answer the question: What measurable business results will be evidence of success? The best measures are those already used by the organization. They need to be accurate, valid, reliable, easy to use, and hard to manipulate and, most of all, must lead to the right results.

Although the impact of your training is the most important measure, how efficiently you do your job is also critical. The right strategy makes clear how you will continuously improve the training group. Evaluating efficiency usually assesses processes, costs, cycle time, consistency, quality, and utilization of resources. Since most strategies call for the evolution of the organization, you'll need to know how efficiently you are adding and upleveling critical skills in your group.

As an additional tool, the Strategic Planning Template may serve as a simple template for documenting your learning function strategy. You may download it from the *Handbook's* website at www.astdhandbook.org.

Finally, What's the Point of Having a Strategy if It Is a Secret?

You'll need to determine how you will communicate your strategy and to whom. Clearly, your team needs to understand and be on board. The leadership of the organization you serve has to sign up. But who else? Are there strategic partners? Critical stakeholders? Suppliers? Contractors? The when, who, and how of communicating your strategy are worthy of a full marketing plan. (But that's a subject for another chapter.)

It may seem that these keys to a best-in-class learning function strategy sound more like things to worry about when you are *implementing* your strategy. Precisely. A strategy may be the most powerful tool any leader can possess. It allows you to be proactive, to engage and involve your team, your peers, and every key stakeholder you serve. It is the basis for critical decisions about staffing, budgeting, and operations and makes the political argument for each. It legitimately sells the learning function. And it enables you, as the leader of learning, to coordinate your efforts and maintain focus on what is truly critical. Since needs and circumstances change, a good strategy allows you to change with them consciously and effectively. You will make better decisions, get better buy-in, and get better results.

About the Author

John Coné consults, teaches, and writes on issues of organizational learning, with emphasis on strategy and operations. He works with CLOs and others to create great learning functions and learning organizations. He was one of the founders of Motorola University, vice president of HR and CLO for Sequent Computer Systems, and was creator and VP of Dell Learning. He also served briefly as interim president and CEO of ASTD. John served as chair of the board of ASTD, on the board of ASTD's e-learning certification institute, the Editorial Board of Strategic HR Review, and the board of SumTotal Systems.

For Further Reading

Aaker, D.A. (2001). *Developing Business Strategies*, 6th edition. San Francisco: John Wiley & Sons.

Barksdale, S., and T. Lund. (2006). *10 Steps to Successful Strategic Planning*. Alexandria, VA: ASTD Press.

Horwath, R. (2009). *Deep Dive: The Proven Method for Building Strategy, Focusing Your Resources, and Taking Smart Action*. Austin, TX: Greenleaf Book Group Press.

Israelite, L. (2006). *Lies About Learning: Leading Executives Separate Truth From Fiction in a $100 Billion Industry*. Alexandria, VA: ASTD Press.

Johnson, G., K. Scholes, and R. Whittington. (2008). *Exploring Corporate Strategy: Text and Cases*, 8th edition. Upper Saddle River, NJ: Prentice Hall.

Phillips, J., and P. Phillips. (2005). *ROI at Work: Best-Practice Case Studies From the Real World*. Alexandria, VA: ASTD Press.

Rummler, G., and A. Brache. (2012). *Improving Performance: How to Manage the White Space on the Organization Chart*. San Francisco: Jossey-Bass.

Schooley, C. (2008). *How to Create a Comprehensive, High-Impact Learning Strategy*. Cambridge, MA: Forrester Research.

Chapter 43

Building Your Business Acumen

Kevin Cope

.... **In This Chapter** ....

- Explore the importance of building business acumen for career development.
- Introduce seven steps an individual can take to build business understanding.

....

When I first got out of college, I began my career in banking. I remember my enthusiasm and desire to excel in my first job, to set the organization on fire with the sheer brilliance of my performance.

Well, as it turned out, I created more smoke than fire. I quickly began to realize how little I had actually learned in school. I struggled even to keep up a stumbling pace with my associates who had spent a few years in the real world.

I remember how there was nothing more discouraging than being dressed for success and feeling like a failure—sitting in a meeting with managers and senior executives, totally in over my head, trying to follow basic concepts of the financial discussion.

I was usually at a loss to make any intelligent comments, much less any meaningful contribution. I regularly found myself hoping that no one would call on me for anything important, in case I actually had to say something and reveal that I had only faint clues as to what they were talking about.

So early in my career, the embarrassment of ignorance compelled me to make a commitment to competence.

There is no more empowering feeling in business than to be in the company of experienced leaders and to be able not only to follow the flow of their discussion, but to make intelligent contributions to it. To sit in important meetings with professional colleagues, peers, and managers and have everyone nod their heads in acknowledgment of your insightful comments and recommendations.

Believe me when I say, "If *I* can do it, *you* can do it!" Really! *Anyone* can build business acumen. The key will be to move forward, adopting Nike's slogan at face value. *Just do it!* Whatever your background, schooling, or experience, there is nothing about business that is beyond your grasp. As a workplace learning and performance professional, make a commitment to build your business acumen through ongoing study and action.

Securing Your Seat at the Table

A Fortune 500 CEO says, "When I walk into a meeting, I want to see people surrounding me who are smarter than I am."

Securing your seat at the table means developing and continuing to exercise your ability to influence decisions and decision makers within your organization. You must study business generally, your business specifically, and then make and act on sound decisions.

Your application of business acumen requires a focus on the chief concerns and goals of your boss or CEO. You'll need to develop and apply continued insights concerning market trends, competitor analysis, partner relationships, strategic choices, financial markets, consumer trends, technology, and more. You'll need to effectively communicate strategic goals if you want to contribute to your company's growth and to your own.

As you grow in your influence at the decision table, you'll need to stretch yourself, move outside your comfort zone. It can be challenging to find the time and energy, but the rewards will be worth it. Your knowledge, contributions, and impact on your company and career will be obvious. I challenge you to move forward with a commitment to *do it*. In pursuing your worthy personal or business objectives, you must never omit the hard work of preparation.

An admiring audience member said to the virtuoso concert pianist, "I'd give my life to play like that." The predictable response: "I have."

Seven Steps for Building Business Acumen

The seven practical ideas in this sections will encourage and support your ongoing development and application of sound bushiness acumen.

1. Commit the Time to Study and Research

Set aside time for regular study and research. Your days are already full, crowded with professional and personal activities. Find opportunities to carve out the time to advance your career and your business. How much time do you spend watching television? Can you chat with co-workers less and read industry information more? Can you use your lunchtime more productively? An hour of preparation, even once a week, will yield a great payoff.

Whether you can spend an hour a week or a half-hour daily, set aside time for study and preparation regularly—and then do it!

Devote time to learning how your company is organized and operates: its organization and internal structure; key officers; primary products and services; and present and future goals. Understand the important priorities, values, and strategies of your CEO, division head, and direct supervisor.

Do you know how your company is doing financially or what its financial goals are? Go deeper than the big picture of your company and explore the financials of each division or department if you can.

You can learn this by reading the annual report; email and other communications from your boss and company officers; company press releases; all materials on the company website; information about your company on the Securities and Exchange Commission (SEC) website; quarterly Form 10-Q filings and annual 10-K filings; and other resources about your company, including interviews of your senior leadership in all media. Ask your supervisor how to access internal operating data if it isn't publicly available.

Also, if possible, listen to your CEO's quarterly conference calls with Wall Street analysts. Or get a summary from your public communications department or company website. This quarterly call provides a current report on your company's operations, financial performance, and your CEO's priorities and future plans. You should also know who your company's three to four most important competitors are and learn about their basic financial data, organizational structure, strategies, products and services, and strengths and weaknesses. Read their annual reports, their websites, and information about them in the media.

Finally, learn what is happening in the external environment that might affect your company. Read or listen to financial, economic, and business news from websites, print and broadcast media, books, magazines, or the *Wall Street Journal* or the business section of any large metropolitan daily paper.

As Harold S. Geneen, once CEO of ITT and father of the international conglomerate, once said, "When you have mastered numbers, you will in fact no longer be reading numbers any more than you read words when reading books. You will be reading meanings."

2. Talk With Key Company Managers

Build relationships with key company leaders and managers. Start with your boss or supervisor. Talk regularly with peers or teammates in different departments who have specific expertise. Ask questions that reveal your own research. Share your helpful insights in return. Talk with your boss or supervisor about the big picture of your organization and how your work team or department, and you personally, can have a more significant impact.

Learn the key measures and dashboard metrics that your boss and division or company senior management is focused on. Discuss with your boss or supervisor how to better achieve these targets so you know how your team and your job function fit in.

Meet people for lunch; set brief appointments in their office. Let your reasons be known: You want to become more knowledgeable in order to make more effective contributions.

Build relationships!

3. Be Proactive—Contribute and Follow Through

Whenever an assignment or opportunity for action results from your study, discussions, or meetings, follow through and *do it.* Report back in a timely way to the appropriate parties so others will realize you have *done it.*

When realistic or appropriate, put your comments and questions into succinct, meaningful, and timely emails or memos addressed to appropriate personnel; however, don't overwhelm people with a flood of ideas or recommendations. Use a targeted approach.

Write a brief action list. Link your actions to results that move the needle in areas important to your boss and senior management, and that support the key measures they have identified. Identify in writing how your learning and performance initiatives affect the business. Give a copy to your boss or supervisor and discuss.

4. Attend Industry Meetings and Make Outside Contacts

If your company provides any occasion for you to attend industry or major customer conferences or meetings, take the opportunity. Network with those you meet there. Read the literature available. Grow your own database of contacts. Keep in touch with them over time as possible. Gain your own direct sources of helpful industry, economic, or business information. Stay in communication with those you meet.

5. Use a Buddy for Accountability and Mentoring

Use the buddy system. Ask a co-worker—maybe a fellow training and development (T&D) professional or senior manager—to work with and mentor you. At least identify someone to whom you can make a commitment regarding your business acumen action plan and to whom you can be accountable. Perhaps that person would want to further his or her own knowledge, and you can help and support each other. *Being* a mentor to someone else will help you both.

Above all, accept an assignment from and be accountable to *yourself* to continue to develop your business acumen.

6. Influence Management

To influence senior management, you have to follow all of the above recommendations to prepare yourself to present an idea or opportunity.

Then, when asking a leader to consider seriously your views or recommendations, follow these four important suggestions—principles that have worked for thousands of employees across many industries and types of companies:

- **Listen to understand:** Listen first. Your sole purpose in listening? To *understand* where the individual or management team is coming from, to get what's important to *them*. In every meeting, listen carefully for opportunities to ask insightful questions to learn even more. If you deeply understand *their* point of view, *their* needs and priorities, it will first influence you. Then you'll better be able to influence them.
- **Present their case and needs to them:** Once you have deeply listened, in classic consultative form, make a "my understanding of your needs and objectives"

summary before making your own proposals. Once managers know that you really do understand their perspective, they will be more open to listening to your analysis and proposals. You'll have built greater trust.

- **Talk their language:** Once you've established mutual understanding, connect your analysis and recommendations to management's strategic goals, concerns, needs, and mindset. Link your message to what's important to them in financial language they understand. Demonstrate the impact of your proposal or analysis on those drivers important to them. Remember that every department or function has somewhat differing priorities.
- **Use return-on-investment (ROI) analysis:** As a T&D professional, I don't have to tell you how important ROI analysis is. Ultimately, every business decision boils down to determining how best to use capital for maximum ROI. Make a convincing case for a favorable ROI through your recommendation.

7. Increase Your Value

Your ultimate ability to become a more valuable and valued employee is primarily up to you. Your contribution to the success of your department, division, or company at large will add to your own career success. Helping others along the way will add dimensions of experience, knowledge, and insights that will benefit both them and you.

As you become better known for your insightful business acumen, you will become more visible as a contributor and a more valued member of your company team. Wherever you go in your future professional career, your ability to understand the keys that drive business and to exercise the acumen associated with them will lead to sustained profitable success.

Get Started Today

I encourage your continued commitment and hard work. You can begin by turning to the online tools that accompany this book (see the *Handbook's* website at www.astdhandbook .org) and use the worksheet aligned with this chapter to consider what you need to do. Persevere. I'm confident it will pay off. The ultimate keys to success? To *engage* and to stay with it!

About the Author

Kevin Cope is the founder and CEO of Acumen Learning, the leader in business acumen training (business savvy/business intelligence) and ISA's 2012 Training Company of the Year. Kevin is a keynote speaker and the author of *Seeing the Big Picture*, a number one *Wall Street Journal* and *New York Times* bestseller. Kevin's clients include some of the most respected and profitable companies in the world, including 17 of the Fortune 50; he's been recognized as a top-rated speaker at national conventions including SHRM and ASTD; he's been a guest on NPR and *Business Insanity Talk Radio*; and has been featured in *Chief Executive Magazine* and *Industry Week*. Kevin's ideas and message will resonate with anyone who runs or works for a business. You can reach Kevin at info@acumenlearning.com or visit the website at www.acumenlearning.com.

For Further Reading

Christensen, C.M. (2012). *How Will You Measure Your Life?* New York: HarperCollins.

Collins, J. (2011). *Good to Great: Why Some Companies Make the Leap...and Others Don't.* New York: HarperCollins.

Cope, K. (2012). *Seeing the Big Picture: Business Acumen to Build Your Credibility, Career, and Company.* Austin, TX: Greenleaf Book Group Press.

Covey, S.M.R. (2006). *The Speed of Trust.* New York: Free Press.

Covey, S.R. (2005). *The 7 Habits of Highly Effective People.* New York: Free Press.

Tracy, J.A. (2009). *How to Read a Financial Report.* Hoboken, NJ: John Wiley & Sons.

Chapter 44

Managing From the Middle: Challenges and Opportunities as a T&D Manager

Tacy M. Byham

·· **In This Chapter** ··

- Examine the concerns and issues facing middle managers.
- Understand the role T&D can play to develop midlevel managers' leadership skills.

The midlevel of any organization holds the key to long-term business success. The leaders at this level link strategy to execution and corporate vision to customer experience. While economic realities have created a flattening of middle-manager ranks, organizations suffer from overstretching these people whose success as leaders has a direct impact on the business. Learn how organizations can capitalize on the potential these managers bring to the business by closing their leadership gaps and accelerating their development gaps.

Middle management is an awful phrase. No child has *ever* dreamed of growing up to be a middle manager.

That doesn't mean middle management has always been denigrated. For most of the history of large companies, middle managers were seen as vital—indeed, they were the people who basically ran the place. Rising up the corporate ladder, rung by rung, offered opportunities for increased responsibility and, importantly, put countless businessmen and their families on a path to the upper middle class.

But in the delayering efforts of recent decades, authors and consultants depicted supervisors as superfluous bureaucrats whose jobs consisted of putting roadblocks in the way of frontline workers, and organizations responded by firing whole swathes of midlevel leaders. Of course, workers still need supervision and direction and management, so companies still have middle managers, and as before, they're the ones who make everything happen. Organizations lean heavily on their midlevel leaders to execute strategy, drive results, and get work done. As MIT's Jonathan Byrnes rightly observed, "Regardless of what high-potential initiative the CEO chooses for the company, the middle management team's performance will determine whether it is a success or failure."

In fact, it's not a reach to say that as organizations vie for market share, profitability, and even viability in an ever-increasingly competitive global economy, their middle managers symbolize these challenges. In *What the Dog Saw and Other Adventures*, Malcolm Gladwell (2009) makes a strong case for why midlevel leaders are a direct reflection of their organization's frenetic state: "You don't start at the top if you want to find the story. You start in the middle because it's the people in the middle who do the actual work in the world."

What of that story to which Gladwell refers? It's one of stress, neglect, and struggling to adapt to changing roles and expectations, as supervisors work to do more with less in an increasingly complex and demanding environment. It's also one that's fraught with risk for those very organizations that lean so heavily on their middle managers.

The Neglected Level

How bad is the pressure-cooker environment in which middle managers operate today? Just ask them. One manager I know has 72 direct reports and is responsible for conducting performance reviews for all of them. Another told me that being insanely busy is a "badge of honor" in her organization and that, in conversation, midlevel leaders try to one-up one another by cataloging their back-to-back meetings, international conference calls in the middle of the night, and hundreds of daily emails.

Then there's the colleague of mine who was one of a group of middle managers in an organizational function. Over time, repeated downsizings thinned the ranks of this group until she was the only manager left to handle all the work that previously had been entrusted to many. The demands were so great and the expectations so unreasonable that she *asked* to be downsized.

The discontent in the midlevel ranks isn't just anecdotal. In a 2007 Accenture study, midlevel managers identified their top "headaches" as insufficient compensation, having too much work to do while getting too little credit, poor work–life balance, and lack of a career path. A 2010 study by DDI and Human Capital Institute describes the emerging phenomenon of the "Gloom Spiral," which results from midlevel leaders growing increasingly stressed as they struggle to do more with fewer staff and their staff, in turn, growing more stressed and less engaged. This same study offered evidence: 41 percent of HR leaders indicated that the engagement level of their organization's midlevel leaders had dropped noticeably during the previous 18 months against just 14 percent who said that midlevel leader engagement levels had increased either noticeably or substantially.

Even following a quarter century of underappreciation, this decline is notable. And though organizations have begun to understand the critical importance of their midlevel leaders, this newfound focus arrives against a legacy of neglect. Traditionally, scarce training dollars have flowed toward maximizing the performance of large populations of frontline leaders, and senior-level retirements have driven a sustained focus on the need for executive development. The middle, meanwhile, has tended to be overlooked.

How Did We Get Here?

During the past several decades, two important trends have shaped middle management. One is the flattening of organizations, a phenomenon that has been in motion for decades. Where once multiple management levels defined organizations, downsizings, re-engineering efforts, and reorganization have pruned management to a bare-bones structure in which middle-management roles are defined by a greater span of control and more responsibility. This has made the middle manager's job more difficult than at any time in the past. (Attempts at fully understanding the middle manager's plight face a further complication: Those classified as middle managers can fall across a wide swath, from a general or district manager, leading just a handful of frontline leaders, to an operational leader managing multimillion-dollar budgets and several hundred employees—and all points in between.)

Despite its outward appearance of corporate inefficiency, the organizational structure of old, with multiple leadership levels between the front lines and the executive suite, represented a favorable system in many ways. Consider the rising leader of decades ago who would progress slowly and purposefully up the organizational ladder. From an initial frontline leadership position, he or she would be promoted to a slightly higher-level leadership job with more responsibility. The junior executive would be in this position long enough to master it and build a toolbox of leadership skills. When the time was right and a position was open, the leader would move upward yet again to another job that offered more

---

Warren Bennis

Warren Bennis is an important figure in the behavioral science movement and is regarded as a pioneer in the field of leadership studies. He is distinguished professor of business administration at the University of Southern California and a founding chairman of the Leadership Institute at the University of Southern California.

Bennis began his groundbreaking work on leadership as one of Douglas McGregor's protégés, and he was greatly influenced by McGregor's interest in exploring and explaining the characteristics of effective leaders. Bennis was one of the first scholars to note the distinction between managing and leading, based on his observations that many organizations are managed well but have poor leaders. Bennis found that there is no one approach to becoming a successful leader, but after interviewing more than 90 top leaders in different fields, he identified some common characteristics or competencies among successful leaders:

- the management of attention—the need for a vision to focus minds
- the management of meaning—the need to communicate the vision
- the management of trust—the need to be consistent and honest
- the management of self—the need to be aware of one's weaknesses.

Bennis also acknowledged that successful leaders must be able to accept valid criticism and then decide whether it is best to change or to stick to their guns.

Later in his career, Bennis began to study group dynamics, and he worried that his earlier work neglected the role that collaboration plays in the role of the successful individual leader. He now believes that leadership is increasingly becoming a shared task, which he has termed partnership instead of leadership.

In addition, Bennis served as an advisor to four presidents of the United States and has written voluminously on leadership; his book *An Invented Life* (2004) was nominated for a Pulitzer Prize.

---

responsibility and more opportunities to grow, build capability and competence, and properly prepare for the next promotion when the time arrived.

This structure, with its multiple levels, which in time many would come to see as wasteful and unnecessary, was, in fact, an effective approach for preparing leaders for the executive suite. Not everyone advanced that far up the chain of command, of course. But those who did, by the time they rose to the top, usually had developed a strong base of skills, experience, and knowledge.

Those days are long over. In their place are flatter organizations in which leaders too often are promoted in sink-or-swim fashion and are expected to begin producing results quickly. Meanwhile, expectations remain sky-high for the amount and complexity of work that needs to be done by the leaders operating at the amorphous, wide-ranging midlevel—even though organizations provide little in the way of additional development or support.

Predictably, as this arc of development and growth has been removed, today's midlevel leaders themselves are pessimistic about leadership skills in their organizations. In DDI's Global Leadership Forecast 2011 study, only 34 percent of respondents rated leaders in their organization as good or excellent. This was lower than ratings provided by senior leaders (43 percent) and executives (46 percent), who viewed their organizations' leaders in a far more positive light.

Then there's the second trend: the ever-increasing complexity characterizing organizations as they strive to compete, grow, manage costs, innovate, and, in some cases, even survive. Gone are the days of tight centralization, straight-line supply chains, and stable markets impervious to advances in technology and globalization. Midlevel leaders are now called upon to lead increasingly geographically dispersed teams, operate within a matrix with blurred accountabilities and dotted-line reporting relationships, and take on a greater share of the work required to execute strategy and meet customer needs. That means their organizations are counting on them as never before.

As one senior HR manager told me, "Middle managers have a high organizational impact. We expect a lot from them: They need to understand a P&L statement, be proficient in certain processes and procedures, lead and manage people effectively, and if needed, roll up their sleeves and do the work themselves. We require them to execute organizational strategy, develop new leaders, and produce bottom-line results. Often resources are limited, but the expectations remain just as high."

The convergence of these two trends has put the squeeze on midlevel leaders. And this represents a significant risk for organizations. Midlevel leaders who feel overwhelmed, overworked, and underappreciated may become disillusioned with their jobs and disengaged from their teams and fail to do all the important things they are counted on to do. Inevitably, when middle managers become disengaged, there is a higher risk of them turning over. In fact, in a *McKinsey Quarterly* survey, a minority of middle managers—just 36 percent—said they were very or extremely likely to be with their current employers in two years.

Even those loyal to their organizations aren't necessarily loyal to their jobs. In a DDI global survey of 2,001 midlevel leaders, 54 percent said they would take a demotion to a nonleadership role for the same amount of money. What's more, a significant portion of midlevel leaders apparently have had enough: 16 percent said they would take a demotion to a non-leadership role even if it meant taking a cut in pay.

The bottom line is that given the flatter organizational structures and the demands of a complex and competitive global economy, the need for strong, effective middle managers has never been greater. Yet, even if a midlevel manager is committed to staying in the job, that doesn't mean he or she is effective.

Understanding the Skill Gap

To understand what we need our midlevel leaders to be, we need to be specific about what we are asking them to do. Midlevel leaders operate in a sort of organizational limbo: They are too low on the organizational totem pole to formulate or set strategy, and in many cases, they also lack a clear line of sight to the front lines and the ability to monitor and fully understand customer needs and preferences firsthand. This isn't to suggest that what middle managers are expected to do isn't important—it is, as they do much of the managerial grunt work required for execution. Their jobs often entail critical responsibilities, such as driving results, allotting resources, staffing, negotiating with vendors and partners, troubleshooting, promoting efficiency, and keeping a close eye on costs.

In this way, middle managers serve as the linchpin between where the organization wants to go and what it takes to get there. What is expected of them confirms this. And those expectations are changing. As organizations look to boldly move forward into an uncertain future, they need their midlevel leaders to be innovators and change agents. Specifically, midlevel leaders must be able to address four key challenges: drive performance in a changing world, manage horizontal integration in a complex organization, lead and develop talent, and make tough decisions.

When the midlevel leaders in the DDI survey were asked about the responsibilities on which they spend most of their time, what emerged was a contrasting picture. Among the roles to which they devoted the most time were resource allocator, negotiator, executor, and navigator. Talent advocate, one of the most important roles organizations are looking to their leaders to fill, finished a distant eighth. The Big Disconnect sidebar displays the results.

Big Disconnect

Multiple studies have identified the most critical skills that leaders need now and for the future. Comparing this list against the hats midlevel leaders say they wear most frequently reveals a big disconnect between the strategic roles that organizations need their midlevel leaders to fill and the tactical roles they actually are spending most of their time doing.

The Skills Leaders Need Now and for the Future

- Managing change
- Fostering innovation
- Developing talent
- Executing strategy
- Coaching and developing others

The Hats Middle Managers Wear Most Frequently

- Resource allocator: 19%
- Negotiator: 17%
- Executor: 15%
- Navigator: 10%
- Change driver: 9%
- Innovator: 9%
- Global thinker: 7%
- Talent advocate: 3%

Further evidence that leaders are out of sync with what their organizations need them to do comes from DDI's 2011 leadership forecast. The five skills that leaders identified as the ones needed most to drive business success over the next three years were driving and managing change, identifying and developing future talent, fostering creativity and innovation, coaching and developing others, and executing organizational strategy. Yet, when asked to rate their own effectiveness in each of these leadership skills, 40 percent or more of leaders conceded ineffectiveness in at least one skill.

Why the disconnect? One reason is that organizations are driving midlevel leader behavior by continually trying to do more with less. In the DDI survey of midlevel leaders, nearly 70 percent said that their work stress had increased over the previous 18 months due to larger personal workloads and increased pressure to succeed.

And it would appear that they lack the skills to take it all on. When these leaders were asked if they feel they have the leadership skills they need to succeed in their roles, just 10 percent said they feel "well prepared."

How to Turn the Tide

The good news is that organizations are waking up to both the criticality and the difficulty of leading at the midlevel. A vice president in organizational effectiveness at a financial services institution captured this growing awareness perfectly when she told me, "We must provide [our midlevel leaders] with support, resources, and the development they need to deliver. We know if we don't do this, we won't be able to deliver on our business strategy."

But what about providing that support, resources, and development? While some of the steps that organizations need to take and the things they need to consider may be clear, others may be less obvious. As a T&D professional, you can support your organization in several ways.

Differentiate Between High Potentials and High Performers—Invest in Both

High-potential leaders, of course, represent the organization's strategic future. But a far larger and arguably more important population is those midlevel leaders who can be classified as high performers. These are the middle managers on whom the organization counts to excel in their roles indefinitely, not as a means to preparing them to step up to the next level.

While high-performing middle managers typically won't be good candidates for the limited number of special development opportunities that must be reserved for high potentials, they do warrant a holistic development approach to make them optimally effective.

This differentiation also needs to extend to assessment. While high potentials may require the deep assessment that can be provided only by a day-in-the-life assessment center, high performers also will need to be assessed to determine their strengths and development needs, but in less depth. Multirater (360-degree) tools are a good solution, as they can be administered to a large population of leaders at a relatively modest cost. Regardless of how the data are gathered, what matters is that the company is assessing middle managers to provide the data and insights needed to guide development planning for the individual as well as the midlevel leader population.

Take a Business/Role/Self Approach to Development

While midlevel leaders, like frontline leaders, must develop strong leadership skills, their development should be grounded in a business/role/self approach that emphasizes both personal growth and business contribution. Such an approach takes into account the need for a comprehensive understanding of the business; total clarity about the leader's role within the organization and the contribution he or she needs to make to support the organization's strategic priorities; and a realistic understanding of oneself in terms of relevant experiences, capabilities, and personality factors.

This means that while a comprehensive, competency-based leadership-development curriculum is a great start, it won't be enough to address the entire business/role/self dynamic. Especially important is emphasizing the view of development as a "learning journey" that treats the job as a practice and experimentation lab, where skills and knowledge are paired with deliberate practice and translate into sustainable behaviors. (The 70/20/10 formula is a good rule of thumb, where 70 percent of learning happens on the job, 20 percent comes from coaching or mentoring relationships, and 10 percent results from formal development programs.) Of course, leaders need to learn and practice the right skills, whether they are those required to coach, challenge others' thinking, partner with other business units, or drive team member development.

Mentoring is another approach that can support development, and when the mentor is a senior leader within the organization, the business and role aspects can be emphasized. (Note that midlevel roles have changed so much, so fast that a veteran top executive may be out of touch with the day-to-day reality of the contemporary middle manager.)

And don't sell short all that middle managers can learn from one another, whether it's finding out how a peer in another part of the organization deals with a similar challenge or engaging in team "action-learning" experiences in which leaders work together to solve a problem or innovate a new approach or solution for an improved process or product. The networks they build and the connections they make with their peers can help to promote middle managers' own job engagement and morale, while also giving them a valued chance to interact and work with counterparts with whom they may not come into contact on a regular basis.

It's critical to give midlevel leaders opportunities to step away from their daily rigors in order to reflect. Self-insight tools, such as the Index of Emotional Intelligence or the Change Style Indicator, can make middle managers more aware of their own personal leadership styles. These insights help individuals to focus on specific areas for development and can motivate them to take action or seek support from their manager, peers, or team, as well as from individuals and resources outside the organization.

Driving Success: A Role for Everyone

Organizations that are finding success in developing and supporting their midlevel leaders rely on some common best practices. For one, senior leadership not only acknowledges the importance of strong middle managers, it provides budget dollars and sends the clear message that the organization can't execute if its leadership pipeline is prohibitively empty in the middle. Executives also are visible in their support, taking the time for activities such as kicking off formal learning sessions or serving as mentors.

HR best practices include designing and executing the right development initiatives for both high-potential and high-performing midlevel leaders. As discussed above, these initiatives integrate assessment and development and take a business/role/self approach to ensure that middle managers are getting the full range of learning and growth they require. In many organizations, HR also takes the lead in constructing meaningful career paths for midlevel leaders in which the career ladder of the past is recast as a career "lattice," with skills, knowledge, and experience gained through lateral career moves as well as through promotions.

Midlevel leaders themselves also play a role by taking ownership of their own development and, ultimately, of their own careers. They manage their own development plans and take accountability not only for acquiring the skills, knowledge, and insights they need to target but also for changing their behavior in order to be more effective in their roles.

The current state of middle management is not only bleak—it's unsustainable. No one is suggesting relieving pressure by reinstating layers, but organizations, starting at the top and stretching down to the leaders themselves, need to be more aware of the challenges facing midlevel leaders and be more active in addressing them. If these people really are the ones responsible for actually executing key plans, they deserve consideration, resources, and recognition.

No efforts, however ambitious and well executed, will make middle management cool; kids will never yearn to emulate Grandpa and forge a career as a midlevel supervisor. But corporate initiatives can make things better—for both middle managers and the organizations that count on them.

The T&D Manager's Opportunity

Whether you are a T&D middle manager or you help develop middle managers throughout your organization, you have an opportunity to make a difference. You can start by using the benchmarking tool on the *Handbook's* website at www.astdhandbook.org to compare and rate your organization to determine how it stacks up against some of the world's leading organizations when comparing best practices in midlevel leader assessment and development.

- **Recognize that your business success is tied directly to the leadership abilities of all midlevel leaders.** Their roles are more complex than ever, and your organization's future rests on their ability to successfully meet the challenges confronting them. In short, your midlevel leaders need to develop because the business needs them to develop.
  Are you devoting the focus and resources necessary to develop your midlevel leaders?

- **Midlevel development methods continue to evolve, and those changes have distinct implications for the HR function and the organization as a whole.** If the development methods you are using for your midlevel leaders remain stuck in time, you are likely to be left behind—and so will your midlevel leaders.
  Have you made or are you willing to make the necessary adjustments to your development methods to effectively stay competitive?

- **70/20/10 isn't just a clever catchphrase, but rather a foundational best practice that has direct application for midlevel leaders.** If you expect to see meaningful results from your midlevel development efforts, none of these three components can be left out.
  If your midlevel leaders aren't as actively engaged in their development journey as you need them to be, which of these components have you shortchanged?

- **Without the proper and consistent use of assessment tools, your development program starts out with "one arm tied behind its back."** There are useful assessment tools available to aid you in making sound development decisions about your midlevel leaders, both individually and as a group. How you use them is up to you, but not using them should never be an option.
  Do you have a consistent assessment strategy for your midlevel leaders that optimizes the use of 360s and assessment centers?

- **Assessment center results can provide powerful insights for predicting the success of midlevel leaders in future roles.** Don't forget that those same results can inform many of your talent management decisions, including selection and succession. This is a great opportunity to improve your success rates. Wouldn't it be nice to know in advance if your leading candidate will succeed or fail?
  Are you using your assessment results for everything you can, including development, selection, and promotions?

■ **Measurement isn't easy, but it is necessary.** Midlevel leaders in different organizations typically find themselves on different development journeys, but in any case the journey needs to begin with the end in mind. Measure what you can. Look to industry leaders or come up with an alternative definition that works for your organization. Don't worry about whether it's perfect; just do it.
Do you have a clear vision of what you are trying to accomplish with midlevel leader development?

Organizational success depends on middle managers' success. And T&D has a role to fill to ensure that middle managers have the skills and knowledge required to be successful.

About the Author

Tacy M. Byham, PhD, DDI's senior vice president of Leadership Solutions, brings her expertise in assessment centers, 360s, development planning, and customized leadership solutions to maximize growth for individuals across the leadership pipeline. Tacy is an energetic, thought-provoking presenter for industry conferences and events, such as the ASTD International Conference, Conference Board, SIOP, and the annual International Congress on Assessment Center Methods. Also a published author, Tacy wrote a chapter, titled Leadership Development Strategy, in *The ASTD Leadership Handbook* (ASTD, 2010) and received the national ASTD Dissertation Award (2006). Tacy holds a PhD and an MS in industrial/organizational psychology (University of Akron).

References

Accenture. (2007). *Strengthening the Critical Core,* http://www.accenture.com/Global /Consulting/Talent_and_Organization/Human_Resources_Mgmt/R_and_I /Critical_Core.htm.

Boatman, J., and R. Wellins. (2011). *Global Leadership Forecast 2011: Time for a Leadership Revolution.* Pittsburgh, PA: Development Dimensions International.

Byham, T.M., K. Routch, and A. Smith. (2010). *Put Your Money in the Middle: A Meta-Study and Talent Management Guide for Mid-level Leaders.* Pittsburgh, PA: Development Dimensions International.

Bynes, J.L.S. (2005). *Middle Management Excellence.* Cambridge, MA: Harvard Business School Working Knowledge.

Change Style Indicator [change management assessment program]. (1995). Greensboro, NC: Discovery Learning, Inc.

DeMarco, M., A. Mellish, and R. Wellins. (2010). *Mid-level Managers—The Bane and Salvation of Organizations*. Washington, DC: Human Capital Institute.

Donahue, J., K. Routch, and N. Thomas, N. (2011). *Strengthening the Middle: Global Challenges and Best Practices in Mid-level Leader Assessment and Development*. Pittsburgh, PA: Development Dimensions International.

Gladwell, M. (2009). *What the Dog Saw and Other Adventures*. New York: Little, Brown.

Index for Emotional Intelligence [survey]. (2003). Belle Vernon, PA: Adele Lynn Leadership Group.

McKinsey & Co. (2010). *Global Survey Results: Building Organizational Capabilities*. New York: Author.

A version of this chapter was published in *The Conference Board Review* (April 2012).

For Further Reading

Bossidy, L., and R. Charan (with C. Burck). (2002). *Execution: The Discipline of Getting Things Done*. New York: Crown Business.

Byham, W.C., A. Smith, and M. Paese. (2002). *Grow Your Own Leaders: How to Identify, Develop, and Retain Leadership Talent*. Upper Saddle River, NJ: Prentice Hall.

Goleman, D. (2006). *Emotional Intelligence: Why It Can Matter More Than IQ*, 10th anniversary edition. New York: Bantam Dell.

McCall, M.W. (1998). *High Flyers: Developing the Next Generation of Leaders*. Boston: Harvard Business School Press.

Osterman, P. (2009). *The Truth About Middle Managers: Who They Are, How They Work, Why They Matter*. Boston: Harvard Business Press.

Chapter 45

Project Management for T&D Professionals: Five Steps to Increase Your Effectiveness

Lou Russell

In This Chapter

- Learn the five steps of project management.
- Understand your greatest project constraint.

Why are you reading this? Aren't you too busy to read? I'm impressed that you are taking this time to grow your competence. As a person who helps deliver learning for performance improvement to people, you are a member of a community to which I am proud to belong. We are the only people in organizations whose job it is to help people be better. Think about it. Human resources (HR) is primarily responsible for protecting the organization *from* the people, but you help. You really want learning to drive behavioral change in others. That's the metric you're personally passionate about, and that's why you are reading this chapter.

Project management is perfect for you. The world of work is moving faster and faster. An emergency room worker is expected to run through the halls, instantly figuring out how to triage the situation, and leap to save the most seriously ill. Thanks to a recently tough economy, job loss, and ever-present technology, we who work exhibit similar behavior. Whether this is the best way to work or not, it is the new norm and it is the world in which we must learn to deliver our value regardless of the delivery constraint (voice, live, webinar, coaching, e-learning, games, or smoke signals).

It is impossible to deliver value (complete a project) alone. We depend on multiple people (stakeholders) to help us get our projects done. These stakeholders already have too much to do because they are juggling their own piles of projects. All work is highly matrixed.

In haste and complexity, critical questions are difficult to answer and tempting to skip. Questions like: "Who will approve this design?" "Who can make changes once we produce the videos?" and "When will this e-learning project end!?" are often ignored at the peril of the organization because there's no time to discuss anything except emergencies.

Enter *realistic* project management. To add value by growing people *and* work in the chaos requires a flexible structure. At all times, you've got to be able to "see" what you're up against to contribute value to the organizational strategy. At all times, you've got to be able to adapt your strategy to what you see is reality.

Projects are literally flash mobs today. People come together temporarily through virtual communication (like texts or email) to collaborate and hopefully deliver something of perceived value. They then disperse. Yes, I'm saying that our pile of projects is actually a pile of flash mobs, not the dancing or singing kind, but flash mobs nonetheless. How do you "project manage" a flash mob? That's what this chapter is about. Why do you manage a flash mob? Because it's the only way to get things done in matrixed chaos and the only way to help people grow through learning.

Over the last 30 years, I have boiled down complex and sophisticated project management techniques and processes created by brilliant thought leaders, many who came from information technology. Some of my favorites are Tom DeMarco, Randy Englund, Jim Highsmith, Joan Knutson, Michael Mah, and Rob Thomsett, to name a few gifted authors. Less known outside of T&D but equally brilliant are Elaine Biech, Lindsay Blamire, Courtney Kriebs, Nadine Martin, Richard Sites, Trish Uhl, and Gary VanAntwerp. I know I have missed teachers of mine in this list because there are brilliant and flexible project managers everywhere we look, most not famous outside their immediate circles. My work has stayed aligned to the standards of the Project Management Institute (www.pmi.org) supported by the Project Management Body of Knowledge (PMBOK). Everything you'd ever need to do a project is in the PMBOK. You could never, and should never, do it *all*, so that's where my boiling down begins.

In my first book, *The Accelerated Learning Fieldbook* (1999), I boiled down how people learn. If you don't keep up with how people learn, please don't develop learning solutions. The first goal of all T&D work is to begin with this core question: "What will the learners be able to do after this learning experience that they aren't able to do now?" If your focus is on anything other than changing and growing performance through learning, stop the project. Forget about all the cool things you'll teach and the really cool tools you'll leverage. Focus clearly on the performance gap that is preventing your organization from being awesome.

The Accelerated Learning Fieldbook led to my next book, *Project Management for Trainers* (2000), which was requested by ASTD Press to help trainers successfully build learning solutions. This and all books that followed emphasized the criticality of a "lean, mean project charter." In this first boil, I wrote about how to estimate tasks. My next ASTD book, *10 Steps to Successful Project Management* (2007), replaced estimating tasks with working back from the fixed end-date. In my latest project management book, *Managing Projects* (2012), I include and emphasize what I now consider the secret sauce of flash mob management—influencing skills. Parts of all my books are combined into my five steps below. The mantra remains "Bad news early is good news."

In this chapter, you will see my current boiled-down brew of project management. Although it's a wonderful ego boost for you to use all my tools and processes, it is important that you adapt mine to create a boil of your own. This chapter includes:

- Step 1: Build a common language (fight the Tower of PM Babble).
- Step 2: Define a project (why?).
- Step 3: Plan a project (how?).
- Step 4: Manage a project (adapt).
- Step 5: Review a project (learn).

Step 1: Build a Common Language

Let's begin by defining a project and project roles.

What Is a Project?

I challenge you to start by clearly defining what you mean by the term *project*. It may seem obvious, but at this very moment, you have tasks on your to-do list that aren't tasks at all. They're projects. Until you treat them like projects, they'll continue to sit undone on your to-do list, driving the stress and frustration I predict you leave with every day.

A project has a distinct beginning and end. For example, developing a new course is a project. There is a day you start it, and there is a day that the course is built. That's not to say that there won't be an ongoing set of activities to deliver, maintain, and enhance this course as it lives its useful life. That is not a project, but a maintenance *process*. Ongoing activities without a specific end-point are called processes. They repeat over and over again. Here are a few examples of the difference:

Projects	Processes
Creation of a one-day workshop	Mentoring an employee
Creation of a web-based training registration system	Training administration
Creation of a competency model	Performance review
An organizational needs analysis	Contracting with a vendor

A project and process should not be on your to-do list because it takes a long time to check them off. If they stay on your list, it will trigger guilt and frustration. Projects belong in a project folder and processes belong on your calendar, with time held to do what needs to be done every month (or whatever period of time the repeated process happens).

Tasks are the only thing that should be on your to-do list. Tasks have a beginning and an end but they are small bits of work, easier to define. A task by definition takes less than a day, but in today's chaos your tasks may be bigger. To determine whether it's a task or a project, ask yourself this question: "What are the steps to get this thing done?" If you come up with multiple steps (or tasks), it's a project. Otherwise, it's a task. The tasks from your projects to be done today should be on your to-do list.

What Are the Project Roles?

For projects or flash mobs to be successful, all people involved have to be clear about what they are supposed to be doing. When people are unsure, they duplicate each other's efforts or miss work that they thought someone else was doing. Both are costly, expensive, and sure to happen if you haven't defined the roles.

Just to be clear, one role (for example, instructional designer) can belong to multiple people (three instructional designers with different learning content to design). One person (for example, you) can have multiple roles on a project (project manager, developer, and subject matter expert). In fact, both of these rules are true in a project or a flash mob due to the matrixed workflow. Everyone has a pile of projects that they are managing, and each project needs the help of other people who have their own piles of projects. Clarity of role is the best way to make sense of this. Role clarity drives accountability, which drives trust, which drives high performance.

There are three primary roles in project management that are critical to success.

Project Sponsor

The project sponsor is responsible for delivering the business value that the project is predicted (hoping) to bring to the organization. He or she keeps an eye on whether the project, as it unfolds, will drive increased revenue or costs from the business. It's possible that once the project begins, it may not do what everyone thought it would. The project sponsor is responsible for canceling a project if that is the case. The sponsor is usually an executive who owns the strategy that drove the need for the project. A sponsor should be responsible for governance (approving deliverables and changes, if needed) and communicating to other leaders how things are going. Many, if not most, sponsors have no idea that this is their role, so the project manager may have to help them define their roles with great care.

There should be *one and only one* project sponsor. Unclear governance due to multiple sponsors adds rework. If you have no sponsor, you have no project. Stop doing it and see if anyone asks you about it. Sometimes you politically do not have access to the project sponsor and have to work through your boss or others up the hierarchy. This "game of telephone" is a risk because it increases the chance of poor communication and rework. Insist on regular meetings with the sponsor and constantly nurture that relationship.

Project Manager

The project manager is like a quarterback. He or she leads and manages the project but does not own it. The company owns it. The project manager is passionate about the project and knows when to escalate to the project sponsor when the business case isn't working out. Since the project manager is involved with day-to-day project activities, he or she has a clearer view of problems and possible solutions, which must be pushed up for sponsor decisions. The project manager sees the weeds clearly, while the project sponsor sees the strategy and the future clearly.

There should be *one and only one* project manager. Over the years, the experiment of paired project managers has never really worked. Best case, the project gets done but it takes twice as long. Project manager is not a promotion or royal position; it's just a role. Separate ego from what it takes to get the project done. Team members are equally as important and the project manager should consider them peers, not servants.

Team Member/Stakeholder

The team members perform the tasks needed to get the project done. Years ago, there were dedicated team members on projects. Today this is not the case. A stakeholder is someone who will get something from the project or give something to the project (to help get work done), but the project is not his or her only responsibility. Most team members are really stakeholders. They have real jobs. They don't have to do what you ask them to do when you ask them to do it.

A critical challenge of being a project manager is to nurture the stakeholder roles to keep them interested and involved. The project charter (in the define step in Figure 45-1) is the document or picture that helps everyone maintain the same view of who the stakeholders are and what part of the project they deliver or receive. The project plan (in the plan step in Figure 45-1) is the schedule that informs stakeholders when their help is needed.

Now that you understand the difference between a project, process, and task, and you know the three critical roles of projects and flash mobs, you're ready to learn about a simple and PMBOK-aligned process for minimal and effective flash mob project management—Dare to Properly Manage Resources. Figure 45-1 shows the flow of the processes. Each phase will be discussed. You can download this resource on the *Handbook's* website at www.astdhandbook.org.

Figure 45-1. Steps to Great Projects

Dare to **P**roperly **M**anage **R**esources!

START → **Define** *initiate*	→ **Plan** *plan*	→ **Manage** *monitor*	→ **Review** *close*	→ END
1. Set Business Objectives	1. Determine Milestones	1. Control Work in Progress	1. Close the Project	
2. Establish Project Scope	2. Schedule Task Dependencies	2. Provide Status and Feedback	2. Turn Over Deliverables	
3. Set Project Objectives	3. Adjust for Resource Dependencies	3. Leverage Governance	3. Hold Project Review	
4. Mitigate Risks	4. Create a Budget	4. Resolve Conflict	4. Celebrate Accomplishments	
5. Establish Constraints				
6. Plan Communications				
7. Establish Governance Plan				

Source: © Russell Martin & Associates www.russellmartin.com

Step 2: Define a Project (Why?)

This step answers the business question: "Why is the company doing this project instead of spending the money on something else?" The project sponsor is responsible for the answer to this question. The project manager creates the project charter as the deliverable of this phase. This visual document becomes a common language for everyone to have a shared understanding of the project, including its business purpose. It provides the critical context of the project.

You can find blank templates for a project charter at www.russellmartin.ning.com under Free Resources.

Here are the critical success factors for creating a project charter:

- Start with the business objective. There is one most important need for each project—either increased revenue or cost avoidance. You can sometimes achieve both, but one has to be the priority. The project sponsor chooses this.
- Spend most of your time on the project scope diagram. If you do it correctly, it should look like a sun with all the arrows emanating from or to the middle. This critical document does the following: communicates the actual complexity of the project to all, identifies the stakeholders needed, predicts tasks that need to be done, and lays the groundwork for communication and governance. See more details in Figure 45-2. You can download this resource on the *Handbook's* website at www.astdhandbook.org.
- One of the biggest complaints about projects is scope creep. Projects continually grow bigger and bigger as stakeholders add more needs. This is the organization's project, not yours. Project managers don't say, "No," they say, "Yes, and the impact will be this. . . ." Every change adds new work, which will take more time and resources or you'll have to cut something else to keep the project on track. The ultimate decision, however, rests with the owner—the business—represented by the project sponsor.
- In T&D, project objectives are learning objectives plus whatever other deliverables you need: LMS interfaces, e-learning software, hardware, and so forth. The project objectives are "your promise" to the business. Create strong, measurable objectives that can be used at the end to jointly determine when the project will end and if it is a success. Clarity here will drive your ability to close down the project at the end, versus messing with irritating changes forever. You've been warned.

Figure 45-2. Project Charter for a Volunteer Day of Caring

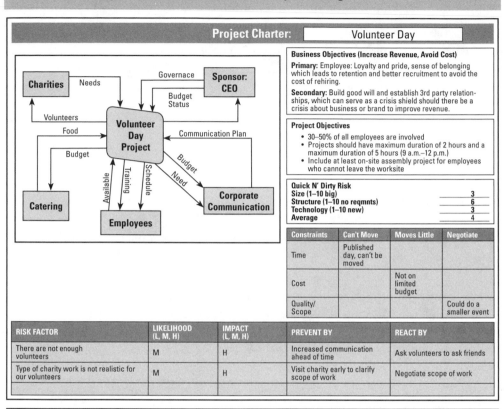

Project Charter: Volunteer Day

Business Objectives (Increase Revenue, Avoid Cost)

Primary: Employee: Loyalty and pride, sense of belonging which leads to retention and better recruitment to avoid the cost of rehiring.

Secondary: Build good will and establish 3rd party relationships, which can serve as a crisis shield should there be a crisis about business or brand to improve revenue.

Project Objectives

- 30–50% of all employees are involved
- Projects should have maximum duration of 2 hours and a maximum duration of 5 hours (9 a.m.–12 p.m.)
- Include at least on-site assembly project for employees who cannot leave the worksite

Quick N' Dirty Risk

Size (1–10 big)	3
Structure (1–10 no reqmnts)	6
Technology (1–10 new)	3
Average	4

Constraints	Can't Move	Moves Little	Negotiate
Time	Published day, can't be moved		
Cost		Not on limited budget	
Quality/ Scope			Could do a smaller event

RISK FACTOR	LIKELIHOOD (L, M, H)	IMPACT (L, M, H)	PREVENT BY	REACT BY
There are not enough volunteers	M	H	Increased communication ahead of time	Ask volunteers to ask friends
Type of charity work is not realistic for our volunteers	M	H	Visit charity early to clarify scope of work	Negotiate scope of work

Project Charter: United Way

Communications Strategy

Stakeholder	Goal	Frequency	Medium	Comments
Project Sponsor	All is well	Weekly	Email	Status Report
Project Sponsor	All is well	Weekly	Visit	Pop In . . .
Construction	Schedule	Weekly	Email	Status Report

Governance Strategy

Type of Change (requirements, budget, scope, etc.)	Final Decision Makers	Consulted	Comments
Change in budget, schedule	Project Sponsor	Project Manager	
Change in requirements	Subject Matter Expert	Project Manager	Assumes no change in budget, schedule
Quality issues	Project Manager	Functional Area	

- Risk is a big deal. Spend some time anticipating risks and deciding whether you can do anything to prevent them. If you can, make sure these ideas show up as tasks on the project plan (next step).
- Creating a clear plan for communications (status and organizational change) and governance (who approves what) will save you hours of rework and stress.
- Spend less than an hour on the project charter. Seriously. Do a sketch and keep improving it. The project charter is a draft until the project ends. It is organic and will change. If it doesn't, you aren't doing a project that really matters.

Step 3: Plan a Project (How?)

There is confusion around the use of the words *project plan*. Many companies use this term to mean the schedule for the project tasks. The Project Management Institute (www.pmi.org) calls this the project schedule, and project plan means both the project charter and the project schedule. Figure out what it means in your organization. Whatever you call it, it's time to build out who is going to do each task by what date.

With the project charter, you and all your stakeholders understand what you are up against so you're ready to build a schedule. Your schedule is done when you have one task, one owner, and one date. Creating a schedule is hard. Again, if you think it's easy, you didn't dive into enough detail or you are doing a project no one wants. Scheduling is like sudoku: You have to juggle tasks, which will have to happen in a certain order; people, who will be needed to get them done and who also have date conflicts; and dates, because you likely started with the due date before you knew anything else. You can't get a schedule done in an hour, but like a project charter, it will not be done until the project is over.

Rather than starting with the whole project, it's easier to manage if you break it into groups of tasks. These are represented by milestones. Each milestone is just a date indicating when a group of tasks will be done. It's a nice way of figuring out and later tracking project tasks at a higher level. You can use milestones to work back from the due date. You can also build the plan by moving forward from a start date to recommend a due date if you've been asked to do that. I find that's rare today.

Milestones and tasks can be discovered by using a methodology. A training example is AD-DIE. A methodology provides a list of milestones and tasks that other people have already worked out for you to use. You can use this as a starting point for your project; however, you'll never use all the tasks. SAM (Allen Interactions) is another example, as are agile approaches. Each methodology has strengths and weaknesses, and your project objectives and constraints determine which is best to use. There is no silver bullet here.

Figure out the tasks that need to be done by brainstorming. People struggle with thinking up the tasks. Whether you use a mind map, sticky notes, a hierarchy/work breakdown structure, a timeline, or something else, find a tool that works well for you. Since we all have brains that prefer to process different ways, don't feel locked in to a brainstorming technique that doesn't work for you. There is no standard tool for this, although someone may tell you there is.

Once you figure out the tasks, the puzzle solving begins. That's why using sticky notes can be helpful. Sometimes, tasks have to go in a certain order (the example my students made up is "pillage, then burn"). Sometimes tasks can be done in parallel if you have other people to work on them.

In today's world where there is no dedicated project team, your stakeholders defined on the scope diagram in the project charter will have tasks assigned to them. Many of these tasks can be done in parallel to save time since different people are working on them. In project management, you can't schedule multitasking. You know, and research has confirmed, that when you multitask, all the tasks take more time.

Your "minimal" project schedule is done when you have figured out the tasks and the order, and have assigned a due date and single owner to each—one task, one date, one name.

This is where my method veers away a bit from more traditional processes. I don't spend much time estimating how long a task will take. It's a wild guess and a lot of work to do this for every task. Talk with each person who will be playing a stakeholder role, and find out how to get to the intersection of when they can do it and when you have to have it by. Work at a due date level if possible.

Instead of thinking, "How long will this task take?" I think, "How much time on my calendar will it take to get this task done?" The difference between the two is significant. For example, writing this chapter will likely take me eight hours, but I will work on it for a couple of months around my other responsibilities.

If you are a vendor or charging back inside a company, you will have to estimate the cost of the project, which will require that you calculate hours for each task and an hourly rate. If you are asked to track hours for timesheets and charge back, you'll count hours after they've occurred, which is different. There is an important difference between "planned" hours and "actual" hours. As you know, these are never the same.

Once your Project Plan is drafted, you'll need to store it someplace that is easy to update. The best place to start is Excel, which allows you to sort, communicate tasks, and track project progress easily. For more difficult projects and more experienced project managers, there are Cloud-based tools available. One of the most used and complex is MS Project. This is a powerful tool for those who know it. It is a huge time eater for those who do not.

Here are the critical success factors for creating a project plan (or schedule):

- Use the arrows from the scope diagram (see project charter) to discover the tasks you need and help you brainstorm the tasks in the first place. The project charter and plan must always tell the same story.
- If you determined that you need to do risk mitigation (prevent risks from occurring) in the project charter, tasks need to be put in the project plan to do these.
- Tasks should be included for communicating with the stakeholders (the communication plan), and decision making and approval (the governance plan).
- Do a final check to make sure everything you need to do to deliver your project objectives is being done by someone.

Step 4: Manage a Project (Adapt)

Once you have the project charter and project plan done—for now (they will change as you go)—you'll almost feel like the project is done. It hasn't even started yet. The most difficult and courageous part of the project is about to begin.

There are lots of artifacts you can create to manage that all have to do with tracking the project well. Ultimately, you want the project to stay on track (assuming the customer wants it to stay on track). You also want to know when to escalate to the project sponsor when the project no longer makes sense from a business objective perspective. For example, you are working on e-learning modules for a new product roll out and find out that the new product isn't testing well and may not roll out. There are insane but true situations where these projects continue on and finish even though there was no need. Clearly in these cases, not even communication was occurring.

Fancy software and toolkits will not save you during the manage step. In fact, they are tempting to hide behind when things start to get dicey. The best things a project manager can do are know what people are supposed to be doing and help get things out of their way. Communication is critical. Influencing skills are imperative. As a project manager, you are negotiating constantly. The levers you have to negotiate with are money, time, and scope. You'll adjust these as needed to push the project to completion.

One of the challenges of the manage step is that it is very likely that you play other roles on the project in addition to project manager. For example, people doing course development can be the project manager, the developer, the videographer, the tester, and the LMS loader. In the thick of the project, it's easy to get sucked into these other critical roles and neglect project management.

Remember these critical success factors for managing a project:

- Schedule time on your calendar. Based on the risk of your project, hold time on your calendar to "think about" your project. The higher the risk, the more frequently you'll need this time. Grab a quiet spot with a cup of coffee and update your project charter and/or project plan on a regular basis. "It's Monday morning; do you know where your project is?" Keep the time sacred.
- Bad news early is good news. Do not try to *control* the project (you will at some point). Control influences your brain to focus entirely on short-term nagging, and the purpose of the project can get lost. When you focus on control, your stress level prevents you from being adaptive.
- Ask, ask, ask. Resist the urge to hide from the customer so that you can frantically build a thing before they change it again. When you are most stressed, talk to the most people. Your choices and decisions will be more aligned to the need.
- Frustration is the normal state of a project. The brain seeks to resolve things that are undone (cognitive dissonance); for example, if I promise you five bullet points and deliver four, your discomfort will force you to ask me for the fifth. Projects are the same; you want them to be simple and done. Every day, the reality is that there are barriers preventing that.
- A little stress is good. Leverage your frustration like an elite athlete. These athletes are both satisfied with their improvement and yet know they can do better. The same can be true with projects.

Step 5: Review a Project (Learn)

There are three critical parts for this step: transition the project, end the project, and review the project.

Transition the Project

Lack of transition is one of the biggest reasons that projects fail to launch. Projects are finished, and tragically, no one uses the results. IT systems are built, and no one takes the time to learn how to use them. Courses are created at the request of the business, and no one registers to attend them. New products are created, but the marketing materials are never created so sales can't start selling them. If this is happening in your project, the transition plan was not done well and not approved prior to the end of the project. Following is a checklist of how to transition a new e-learning course into use:

- Who will take over the marketing, registration, and maintenance processes of the new e-learning course?
- Who will load the new e-learning modules into the LMS?
- Who will you train on the e-learning module artifacts (for example, authoring package, graphics) so maintenance can occur?

End the Project

This is the question I get most often from frustrated project managers: "How can I end the project when the customer never stops changing things?" If this is happening late in the project, there will be conflict as you resolve the issues.

In the project charter (the first deliverable), one of the deliverables is a governance plan. This plan specifically determines who will approve the final result, which is how the end happens. The governance plan builds the base for ending a project well, the scope diagram quantifies what is in and out of scope, and the project objectives define the measurable deliverables of your project. If the scope, project objectives, or governance plan has changed, the charter gives you the base to negotiate the change. Getting sloppy in keeping the project charter and plan up-to-date will create this hard-to-end situation. Your only recourse is to go back, get agreement on the project charter again, and create clarity around what *end* means.

Review the Project

Post-project review is the easiest and quickest way to grow your project management competence. Although you learn the most when the stakeholders also participate, doing the review by yourself is still powerful.

The tough part of review is that you have other projects to get to since this one is complete. It's tough to take the time to stop and review before jumping into other work. My team and I struggle with this as well. It helps to stop periodically during the project and do a mini review rather than wait for the whole thing to be over.

Here is a simple and powerful set of questions for reviewing a project:

- Name a negative emotion you had on the project. Rank it 1 to 10 (high) in terms of intensity.
- List three things that happened that triggered the negative emotion.
- Name a positive emotion you had on the project. Rank it 1 to 10 (high) in terms of intensity.
- List three things that happened that triggered the positive emotion.

Starting with the emotion and establishing a rating helps your brain to replay project memories, not just the last thing that happened. This makes it easier to identify what happened that was most significant (the triggers). Ending with the positive emotion reinforces the fact that all projects have good as well as bad. These questions can easily be adapted to an online survey or email.

Here are the critical success factors for ending a project:

- You can see the end and you are so close. Now will be when you have your most difficult conversations with your stakeholders because they can see the end as well. I recommend the book *Fierce Conversations.* Stay the course unless the customer is willing to increase the time or budget to make new scope changes.
- The review step of project management should include lessons learned from the project management process as well as an evaluation of the quality (and return-on-investment) of the project deliverables. You need both, whether done in parallel or separately. They may require different audiences.
- Another useful thing in the end and review step is to identify reusable project artifacts that can be used to jump-start future projects. If you've just finished a large e-learning project, reusing your project charter and project plan (schedule) can be helpful for future projects. Sharing the charters and plans in your team is even more powerful. Of course, some tweaking will have to be done when you reuse them. Take the extra time to archive your project charter and plan so you or someone else can use it to jump-start the next project.
- Celebrate. Remember to thank everyone involved with a formal or informal recognition, even if it takes just a few minutes. The best way to help your next project go smoothly is to build your relationship network, because no one gets a project done by him- or herself.

Your Greatest Project Constraint

There's an old fable I learned from Alan Colquitt years ago and used in my *10 Steps to Successful Project Management* (2007) book. It's a great illustration of the reality of projects.

A group of pigs lived happily together in a small kingdom, surrounded by water. Slowly but surely, they began to run out of food. As the pigs discussed what to do, they realized there were few solutions. They decided that the best option was to build a boat out of their remaining food and set sail across the uncharted waters in hopes of finding a land with food across the water. They elected their best and brightest pig to be in charge of the project. This project manager's critical responsibility was not to build the boat, or chart the course, or lead through conflict and fear. The critical responsibility is the same one that you have, and the most dangerous: You must keep the pigs from eating the boat. As always, *insanity is just a project constraint*. Manage it.

About the Author

Lou Russell is the CEO/Queen of RMA, an executive consultant, speaker, and author whose passion is to grow companies by growing their people. Through speaking, training, and writing, Lou draws on 30 years of helping organizations achieve their full potential. She inspires improvement in leadership, project management, and individual learning. Lou's upbeat style and humorous stories with on-the-ground experience provide you enthusiasm and tools to improve the bottom line. You will be moving, laughing, participating, inspired, and challenged. Most important to Lou, you will learn.

For Further Reading

Allen, D. (2002). *Getting Things Done: The Art of Stress Free Productivity*. London: Penguin.

Allen, M., and R. Sites. (2012). *Leaving ADDIE for SAM*. Alexandria, VA: ASTD Press.

Biech, E. (2007). *The Business of Consulting*. San Francisco: Jossey-Bass.

Bion, W. (1991). *Experiences in Groups*. Oxford: Routledge.

Bridges, W. (2009). *Managing Transitions: Making the Most of Change*. Cambridge, MA: Da Capo Lifelong Books.

Brooks, F.P. (1995). *The Mythical Man Month*. Reading, MA: Addison-Wesley.

Campbell, J. (2008). *The Hero With a Thousand Faces*. Novato, CA: New World Library.

Englund, R., and A. Bucero. (2006). *Project Sponsorship: Achieving Management Commitment for Project Success*. San Francisco: Jossey-Bass.

Feldman, J., and K. Mulle. (2007). *Put Emotional Intelligence to Work*. Alexandria, VA: ASTD Press.

Russell, L. (1999). *The Accelerated Learning Fieldbook*. San Francisco: Pfeiffer.

Russell, L. (2000). *Project Management for Trainers*. Alexandria, VA: ASTD Press.

Russell, L. (2007). *10 Steps to Successful Project Management*. Alexandria, VA: ASTD Press.

Russell, L. (2012). *Managing Projects*. San Francisco: Pfeiffer.

Scott, S. (2004). *Fierce Conversations*. New York: Penguin.

Chapter 46

Managing Relationships With Universities, Vendors, and Consultants

Rita Bailey

·············· **In This Chapter** ··············

- Explore the essentials of relationship fundamentals.
- Define win–win partnerships.
- Identify best practices for creating and maintaining long-term relations.

The basis of any good relationship is predicated on fundamental principles of trust, respect, mutual benefit, fairness, and honesty. While these foundational values seem rudimentary, they are often minimized in business relations. Although simple in concept, execution of building and managing sustainable, collaborative relations requires commitment, focused effort, and communication skills. The reality is that business relationships are like any other relationship because you must be willing to share and support, not just take or dictate. To quote Covey's Habit 5, "Seek first to understand and then to be understood" (Covey, 1989). Organizations that take a "what's in it for us" versus "what's in it for me" attitude are more likely to grow and prosper.

The key to stability and growth in today's dynamic global marketplace is long-term customer relationships. Companies differentiate themselves through superior, personal service as a competitive advantage. Customers no longer represent just a sales transaction; they are now considered relationships that will generate business over many years. Customer relationship management (CRM) is the most efficient and effective approach in creating and maintaining relationships with customers. Relationship management requires a balance of emotional intelligence and structured methodologies and systems to organize all the components involved. Workplace learning professionals who adopt this concept with university, consultant, and vendor partners also experience the benefits of having processes that help build, manage, and maintain multiple relations.

Finding Compatible Business/University Partners

While businesses and higher education have operated relatively autonomously in the past, relationships are steadily evolving due to the importance of education in our knowledge-intensive society. The workplace is in a period of transition where employers expect employee skills to continue to develop after being hired. With 95 percent of businesses financially supporting employee education, and some companies offering up to $15,000 or more in individual education benefits, this is clearly an area where employers are willing to support and eager to grow.

Higher education providers have the opportunity to play a major role in this shift toward career-focused training and development education. However, only a minority of employers say colleges have specialized offerings to suit their needs or that new partnerships with higher education institutions are easy to form. Although employers are willing to spend money on employee training and find formal learning methods to be more effective, huge amounts of workforce development spending is being spent outside higher education institutions. The reason for this discrepancy appears to be a lack of relevant and available programming offered by accredited higher education institutions.

Universities are an integral part of the skills and innovation supply chain to business. However, this supply chain is not a simple linear supplier–purchaser transaction; it is not the acquisition of a single product or service. This supply chain is multidimensional; it has to be sustainable; and it has to have quality, strength, and resilience. These attributes can only be secured through close collaboration, partnership, and understanding between business and universities. Higher education has much to offer business—mainly expert faculty and graduates for the workforce. They also have much to gain from businesses that provide serious, mature students who want and need additional formal study. These students bring real work experience to the classroom, which tends to create a richer and more rewarding learning experience for the other students and faculty. While many one-on-one relationships are forming between businesses and universities, other resources that focus on accelerating and expanding collaboration between higher education and business are listed in the sidebar.

Resources for Collaboration
Between Higher Education and Business

- Business Higher Education Forum (BHEF) is dedicated to advancing solutions to U.S. education and workforce challenges.
- American Society for Higher Education and Accreditation (ASHEA) envisions and articulates agendas for change as education and business move together in an era of digitized education.
- International University Consortium for Executive Education (UNICON) is a global consortium of business school–based executive education organizations focused on the development of leaders and managers to enhance performance in public and private organizations.
- International Consortium for Executive Development Research (ICEDR) is the world's premier network for companies developing talent around the globe.
- National Centre for Universities and Business (NCUB) promotes collaboration in the UK.
- IP Publishing Ltd is a leading journal for all involved in university–business collaborations.
- The College Board, known for administering SAT testing, also has programs to help identify the needs of adult learners, especially those without postsecondary credentials or degrees. Unemployed or underemployed populations cause reduction of state revenues and taxes, so several foundations and organizations are funding research to identify ways to better prepare adults with skills to advance in the workplace.
- National Council for Continuing Education and Training (NCCET) is committed to continuous quality improvement and to quality service as change agent for lifelong learning.
- Network of Academic Corporate Relations Officers (NACRO) strengthens academic /corporate relations.

Historical University Relations

Universities and industry have been collaborating for more than a century, but the rise of a global knowledge economy has intensified the need for strategic partnerships that go beyond the traditional funding of discrete research projects. World-class research universities are at the forefront of pioneering such partnerships. They are designed to run longer, invest more, look farther ahead, and hone the competitiveness of companies, universities, and regions. In short, they transform the role of the research university for the 21st century, anchoring it as a vital center of competence to help tackle social challenges and drive economic growth.

Until the late 1980s, many companies provided significant financial gifts and in-kind donations in support of research, scholarships, and student activities in ad hoc, nonstrategic ways. Research sponsorship or donations were often provided to obtain preferential access for recruiting purposes. As a result, corporate relations programs traditionally focused on generating philanthropic dollars from industry.

Donors to Investors

In an environment of fluctuating economies, deregulation, global competition, ever-changing tax codes, and increased financial accountability, corporate philanthropy to academia has been in transition from an ad hoc activity to a long-term business strategy. As corporations have moved from donors to investors, priorities for their academic relationships have evolved. The emphasis is now on working with those universities that provide holistic value—student recruiting, executive education, faculty consultants, sponsored research, licensing opportunities, joint government proposals, and so forth. Another approach corporations are taking is to decrease the number of universities with which they work, and many now select only a handful of institutions. For example, over the last four years, one Fortune 500 company moved from a three-tier structure of 35 universities to a more refined list of just 15 schools. Another Fortune 500 company has restricted its university interactions to a small group of schools that have been willing to sign a master agreement with them.

One challenge facing all U.S. universities is that companies have begun establishing academic relationships globally, particularly because they seek the growth potential, abundant R&D personnel, and more favorable IP terms of foreign universities, leaving fewer resources for U.S. universities.

Transitions

In 2010, the Network of Academic Corporate Relations Officers (NACRO) conducted a survey, polling corporate relations officers from 45 research universities, to assess how universities are adapting to the new corporate paradigm. The survey confirmed that the university corporate relations function is in transition as universities try to "figure out" how to best conduct corporate relations in the current environment and anticipate what these trends mean for the future.

The Five Essential Elements for Long-Term University Relationships

NACRO members representing 21 research universities overwhelmingly identified five essential elements to develop successful, long-term relationships with industry. For the purposes of this discussion, a "successful" program is one that maximizes the flow of resources in support of the university's teaching and research missions, whether those resources are generated as gifts, research grants, royalty payments, executive education tuition, or gifts-in-kind.

1. **Institutional support:** The commitment of the university leadership to corporate relations.

2. **Mutual benefit:** A successful university/industry collaboration should support the mission and goals of each partner. Table 46-1 provides a comparison.

Table 46-1. Benefits for the University and the Corporation

University Gets	Corporation Gets
Jobs/internships for students; fellowships	Future employees/recruiting
Executive education participants	Executive education for employees
Expanded research capacity; access to real-world problems	Campus research collaborations
Licensing revenue	License patents
Equipment/facility fees	Access to specialized equipment
Event funding	Event sponsorship/publicity

3. **One-stop shopping:** Universities are complex entities, and companies want a single point of entry where they can be guided to campus resources relevant to their needs. The corporate relations office, whose goal is to increase corporate interactions throughout campus, is uniquely positioned to serve as this central hub, working with external and internal partners to overcome barriers to corporate engagement. Corporate relations professionals, as representatives of the university with no bias toward any single campus unit, can provide personalized services tailored to the needs and interests of each corporation. The corporate relations office is not a gatekeeper; rather, it facilitates access to the entire university.

Figure 46-1. Services Provided by Corporate Relations

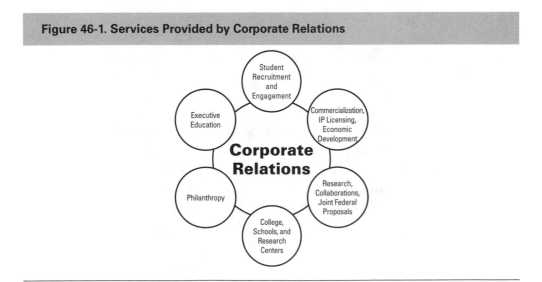

4. **Integrated approach to research development:** Negotiating research agreements to include a philanthropic component and identifying companies with sponsored research needs. According to a senior VP for medicine and technology at Medtronic, "Increasingly, our R&D budget is weighted to the development side as we vigorously compete in public markets. We must look more and more to universities to be partners in the R side of this balance."

5. **Campus coordination:** Unlike the philanthropic corporate relations model, a successful 21st-century corporate relations program is not only dependent on the corporate relations office, but also it is dependent on its ability to find willing partners across the campus:

   ■ Chancellors, presidents, provosts: provide institutional support
   ■ VPs of research: leverage federal funding opportunities with corporate partners
   ■ Deans: serve as a bridge to various academic programs
   ■ Development leadership: coordinate approaching corporate alumni
   ■ Office of licensing/technology transfer: negotiate corporate IP terms
   ■ Research administration: negotiate corporate-sponsored research agreements
   ■ Career center: facilitate positive student recruiting experiences

Building Solid Relations

If you decide that colleges and universities are potential resources for your company's education and training needs, you will want to identify an institution that has compatible values, goals, and resources.

Research the key players in the academic communities you are considering. Executives from your organization and the university should be involved in the initial meetings to discuss the business needs and to establish a mutual partnership agreement. It is important to consider and address the typical concerns in collaborating with external resources: quality, flexibility, delivery, and price.

The resulting product is largely a function of the chemistry between the representatives and the ability to compromise and think about how to create win–win outcomes. The strongest partnerships are based on compatibility, trust, commitment to shared goals, motivation, a sense of adventure and fun, innovation, and recognition that the outcome of the relationship and the impact of the work can transform individual lives and organizational performance.

Consider this view from a business school.

IMD, International Institute for Management Development in Lausanne, Switzerland, consistently ranks at the top of the list compared to other business schools worldwide. In 2012 and 2013, *Financial Times* ranked it first in open programs.

In a whitepaper written by IMD Executive Director Michael Stanford, he referred to the relationship with corporate universities as *beautiful friendships*. He said that those who predicted the downfall of business schools at the hands of corporate universities usually based their reasoning on two assumptions: that corporate universities would only want highly customized development experiences for their participants, and that business schools would always be too focused on their academic agendas to provide such customized support.

Corporate universities are attractive to us for primarily three reasons. First, corporate universities reflect a serious commitment to organizational capability building. When an organization develops a corporate university, it almost always does so because it believes that organizational learning is worthy of serious investment. Since it is not always clear to business schools where organizational learning sits on a CEO's agenda, or the extent to which a successful partnership with the client will depend on convincing important internal stakeholders that learning and development can be a powerful competitive tool, the existence of a corporate university can be a reassuring sign of commitment.

Second, most corporate universities have a clear sense of purpose and have created a set of learning and development activities that are consistent with that purpose. When we work with a corporate university, we understand quickly what the university's agenda is and how our partnership with the university serves that agenda. The organizational landscape within which we are working is usually clear and obvious, and so we aren't unduly distracted from building outstanding development experiences by an uncertain environment.

Third, corporate universities are expected to add value to the organization in real and measurable ways. This expectation puts pressure on the corporate university to focus only on the most influential activities and to search always for new ways to help the business perform better. Corporate universities understandably transfer this pressure to their partners, which mean we must also always innovate to serve them more effectively. Corporate universities force us to innovate, and innovation is a healthy thing for the business school world.

Now consider this view from the business.

Dow Chemical

At Dow Chemical, the journey toward innovation is enhanced through collaboration. That's why they develop relationships in academia and invest in universities all over the world, working with the brightest minds to transform research into solutions.

In addition to existing academic programs, in 2011, Dow bolstered its commitment at 11 leading U.S. universities with an investment of $25 million annually over 10 years. These investments support faculty, students, and infrastructure, enabling a critical mass of resources to address some of the world's leading challenges.

As a result, they are seeing a paradigm shift in the value generated from academic relationships, ensuring long-term partnerships focus on cutting-edge technology research.

Sandals Corporate University Chooses Educational Institute as Academic Partner

Another example of a successful partnership was announced in January 2013. The American Hotel and Lodging Educational Institute signed a Global Academic Partner agreement with Sandals Corporate University (SCU) in Montego Bay, Jamaica, to deliver courses, hospitality training, and professional certification to 20 properties in the Caribbean. Launched in March 2012, SCU is Sandals Resorts International's adult education program for Caribbean nationals employed by Sandals Resorts, Beaches Resorts, and Grand Pineapple Beach Resorts, in an effort to continuously elevate the skill level of its more than 10,000 employees across the Caribbean. "This is a phenomenal opportunity for both of our organizations to help our team members to grow and develop through educational development and through certification," said Philip Brown, PhD, Sandals's Group director of human resources, training, and service standards. "The partnership represents something that will be together for five years and probably beyond that. More important, it brings the lives of other people in this region to a place of understanding about the importance of why it is we do the things we do."

Partnering With Consultants

You work for a large global organization. You've worked hard and landed in a position of influence and authority. You've recently been given a significant project to implement. Can't fail. Has to be done on time. Don't have internal expertise or staff to implement. Have to find a consultant. You look far and wide, and you find the *perfect* consulting organization. They really look like they can handle the job. Their presentation was great. Their bid was 30 percent lower than all the others. They seem eager—they want the job. You sign on the dotted line, and things go downhill from there. The project takes longer. Suddenly, the project cost is now creeping higher and higher. Your users are starting to whisper among themselves. The rising star of the company (you) is now crashing and burning, they say. You respond by getting tough with the consultant, enforcing the contract you signed. The project keeps getting delayed. Costs are now ridiculously high. Your boss is now getting involved. You're reading want ads for a house sitter, which has to be less stressful than this.

Have you heard or experienced this story before? How about this one?

You are project manager for a consulting company. The client from heaven approaches you with the world's greatest project. The one you've been waiting for! You've got the bandwidth. Things look good. You're so eager to get the project, you make sure your estimate is as competitive as you can manage. The client sounds nice. If it works, your staff will thank you forever for the great project. The deal is signed. You begin work. You deliver the first prototype. The users are bewildered. It looks nothing like what they expected. You try again. The users are even more confused. After six attempts at an acceptable prototype, you call your client contact and inform her that there is no way the project will get done on time and within cost. Suddenly, the client is in your face. You're spending even more money and more time trying to make the client happy, but you're bleeding to death. Project costs are so out of control there is no way you'll ever break even. You are now reading want ads for pet sitters, which has to be less stressful than this.

Outsourcing application development is frequently like this. In fact, cynical consultants love to follow other consultants around, calling on the other consultant's clients about three-fourths of the way through the project.

Outsourcing doesn't have to be like this. If you stop to think about it, the interests of the consultant and the interests of the client are remarkably close. Both sides want to get done on time and within budget. Both sides want less stress. But why doesn't it happen that way?

Why Client–Consultant Relationships Go Awry

Most client–consultant relationships have problems for largely nontechnical reasons, including:

- lack of effective communication about how the project will proceed
- improperly setting expectations too high or too low
- lack of follow-through on small yet important details
- underestimating project complexity or scope
- failing to understand user requirements.

The client is usually preoccupied (and rightfully so) with the business side of the project. Will the project meet organizational goals or objectives? Will the return-on-investment be realized? Will the software be easy for employees to use? Will the consultant be responsive (or available) for fixes and changes? The consultant is usually preoccupied with technical (and rightfully so) concerns. How can we implement the request for a fancy user interface? How long will it take us to figure out how to query and combine the data for the export that the user has requested? Why are the users concerned with inconsequential interface issues instead of the more complex data relationships that need to be ironed out?

Because both sides have different orientations, both sides are blind to each other's issues. The way out of this mess is for both sides to consider each other's concerns. In fact, good client–consultant relationships are sort of like marriages: both sides want the other to be happy. In fact, most problems with client–consultant relationships can be solved if both sides communicate with each other clearly and effectively.

Why Use Consultants?

There are many reasons to use consultants—the need to expand capability when time is short and stakes are high, the need for specialized expertise, the need for intangibles of objectivity or corporate leverage to get a job done. This is usually a political reason, because using an outside consultant whose neutrality or credibility is an asset in terms of seeing the problem from a fresh perspective. As you identify the appropriate consultant, determine whether to use a specialist or generalist. It is important to select the type of consultant who can best meet your needs and to agree on how to integrate them into your current staffing structure.

Qualities to Seek

- Trust and confidence obviously are the most important. Be aware if you have any concern about sharing information, honesty, or transparency. You want someone who has a desire for a long-term relationship rather than a pattern of one-time engagements.
- A solid understanding of your problems or needs. The questions they ask are a good indication. Do they test your assumptions relating to the need? Do they tend to use one approach or tool as a solution to every need? Professionals know that their objectivity is a major part of their value.
- The ability to reduce uncertainty. When addressing or solving one problem or need, how do they propose to reduce the risk of generating another problem in the process? What controls or checkpoints are used to measure progress? Table 46-2 offers a number of factors to consider when comparing several consultants. You will also find this tool on the *Handbook's* website at www.astdhandbook.org.

Table 46-2. Consulting Firms to Consider

Desired Qualities	Rating 1–10	Firm #1	Firm #2	Firm #3
1. Trust and confidence				
2. Quick to understand				
3. Industry experience				
4. References				
5. Capability				
6. Desire to help us				
7. Prior similar work				
8. Writing and organizational skills				
9. Needs analysis skills				
10. Project management skills				
11. Can meet time requirements				
12. Charges are within budget				

Other Factors to Consider

Invest time considering other factors as well. Some can be measured, while others may be a personal gut-check for you and your colleagues.

- Are they genuinely interested in making you or your organization successful or using your organization to serve their own egos?
- How quickly do they grasp the cultural norms or political climate of the organization?
- How are they perceived by managers, staff members, and others in the organization?
- How much time will the consultant or their colleagues spend with your team?
- What is their professional and business acumen?
- What type of prior clients have they worked with, and do they have credible references?
- How do you know if they are sincerely interested in your business?
- What is their process for organizing and managing the project?
- Will they customize their programs to meet your needs?
- Have you considered more than one consulting option and compared services and fees?

Consultant engagements are more than purchasing expertise. It requires the development of a mutual relationship between client and consultant. Turner (1982) proposed a continuum with eight categories of client–consultant relations:

1. providing information to the client
2. solving the client's problem
3. making a diagnosis, which may necessitate redefining of the problem
4. making recommendations based on the diagnosis
5. assisting with implementation actions
6. building a consensus and commitment around a corrective action
7. facilitating client learning
8. permanently improving organizational effectiveness.

The best relationships occur when all parties know exactly what is expected of them. This includes responsibilities, objectives, costs, timeframes, and less obvious things such as access to information and individuals; use of company facilities, equipment, and resources; and what expense policies are. Once all the details are communicated in writing and everyone is clear, the relationship should be able to progress smoothly.

Managing Vendor Relations

There are many facets of vendor or supplier relationships to consider when negotiating terms. What's in it for me? This seems obvious, but many a businessperson has launched into a deal where they did not fully understand the total benefits that a vendor gave them. What's in it for them? A mutually beneficial relationship requires both parties to understand what the other brings to the partnership. What really matters to the business? Sometimes it's price, and other times it's turnaround time. Understand how each vendor or supplier contributes to your business and how that plays into your core business objectives. Can they deliver? Vendors and suppliers can promise a lot and not deliver. Avoid making the process about price; consider your real needs and go with the deal that really meets your business needs.

Conflict Avoidance and Resolution

All relationships have conflict no matter how good they are. A good relationship is able to withstand some amount of conflict as long as both parties want to resolve it in a productive way. Some of the most common vendor/supplier conflicts include late payments, product returns, specification misunderstandings, and poor product performance. Conflict resolution can be tough, but avoiding is even tougher.

Parting Ways Is Never Easy

After exhausting every possibility of resolving the conflict, you still end up severing the relationship (nearly 50 percent of strategic vendor/provider relationships end in failure). Follow these steps to protect your job, your sanity, and your organization:

- Be sure you need to terminate. Sometimes renegotiating the relationship could be effective and less risky.
- Make the case for termination—benefits versus risks. Terminating should be treated as a significant project, which requires a business case SWOT analysis.
- Determine what will replace the services you are terminating.
- Plan your exit and how you will make a successful transition.
- Prepare your evidence, and determine if the evidence is strong enough to proceed.
- Choose the right forum—negotiations, mediation, expert determination, arbitration, or litigation.
- Manage the exit process; determine whether to use technical experts.

Take the time up front to select carefully and build solid partner relations with consultants and vendors, and hopefully you will have a long-term relationship.

Figure 46-2. Best Practice Checklist for Long-Term Relationships

☐ Explain the business goals so the vendor understands what is important.
☐ Assign a dedicated manager to keep track of each vendor.
☐ Put everything in writing.
☐ Request progress reports.
☐ Plan in advance to respect vendor's time and resources, provide adequate lead times.
☐ Train vendors to meet your needs.
☐ Avoid the drama triangle or blame game.
☐ Be reasonable—don't lowball quotes or expect something for nothing.
☐ Show good will—balance demanding requests, give referrals, offer more business.
☐ Don't be afraid to be friendly—the more comfortable they are, the more likely they will be to reciprocate.
☐ Be a model client—just as you want a model vendor.
☐ Show that you trust them if they have earned it.
☐ Give thanks and recognition.
☐ Share information and priorities.
☐ Balance commitment and competition.
☐ Allow key vendors to help you strategize.
☐ Build partnerships for the long term.
☐ Seek to understand the vendor's business too.
☐ Create a healthy competitive environment and seek credible alternatives.
☐ Focus on value, not price.
☐ Always pay on time.

Figure 46-2 provides you with a list of best practices to build long-term relationships. Use it to prevent conflicts. You can download this list on the *Handbook's* website at www .astdhandbook.org.

About the Author

Rita Bailey served for 25 years at Southwest Airlines in several leadership positions prior to starting her own consulting practice and co-authoring *Destination Profit: Creating People-Profit Opportunities in Your Organization.* She travels worldwide, speaking, presenting, and coaching leaders on the value of creating people-centered cultures. She has served on advisory boards in multiple industries and was 2005 National ASTD board chair. As founder of Up To Something Partners, Rita designs, develops, and facilitates custom transformational leadership and entrepreneur programs. She is also co-founder of ExpoSkill, an online content portal for professional development.

References

Barbazette, J. (2008). *Managing the Training Function for Bottom-Line Results.* San Francisco: Pfeiffer.

Biech, E. (2008). *ASTD Handbook for Workplace Learning Professionals.* Alexandria, VA: ASTD Press.

Covey, S. (1989). *The 7 Habits of Highly Effective People.* New York: Free Press.

Craig, R.L. (1987). *Training and Development Handbook,* 3rd edition. New York: McGraw-Hill.

Destiny Solutions. (2011). *The Voice of the Employer on the Effects and Opportunities of Professional Development.* A research paper based on 200 NA interviews investigating perceptions of continuing higher education.

Network of Academic Corporate Relations Officers Benchmarking Committee. (2011). *Five Essential Elements of a Successful 21st Century Corporate Relations Program* whitepaper.

Peterson, M.W. (2000). *Managing Institutional Change and Transformation Project.* Ann Arbor, MI: Center for Study of Higher and Postsecondary Education.

Turner, A.N. (1982), Consulting is More Than Giving Advice. *Harvard Business Review* 60(4).

Watton, A. (2013, July). Making Service Provider Partnerships Work Blog. www .bestpracticegroup.com.

For Further Reading

Guth, S. (2007). *The Vendor Management Office: Unleashing the Power of Strategic Sourcing.* Raleigh, NC: Lulu Press, Inc.

Lendrum, T. (2011). *Building High Performance Business Relationships.* Milton, Queensland, Australia: John Wiley & Sons.

Section VIII

Developing and Leading Organizations: T&D's Role

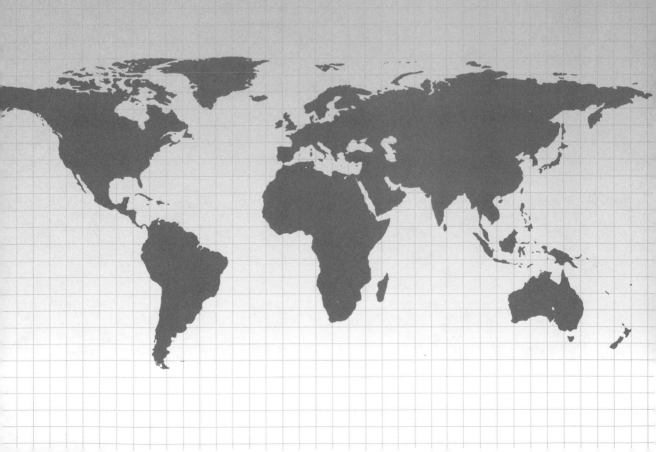

Training and Development's Role in Developing and Leading Organizations

Luminary Perspective

Ken Blanchard

The great organizations I know and have had the privilege of working with over the years—Chick-fil-A in quick service restaurants, Nordstrom in retail, Ritz-Carlton in hospitality, Southwest Airlines in transportation, Synovus in financial services, and WD-40 Company in sales and marketing—understand that training and development is essential to leading and developing an organization. Why do I say that? Because the leaders of great organizations recognize that their most important customer is their people. These leaders believe that if they care for their people—train, develop, empower, and love them—their people will become fully engaged and excited about their work and will reach out and take care of the organization's number two customer—the people who use their products and services. If people do a good job with these folks, the customers will brag about the company and want to do more business with it, which will satisfy the third most important customer—the owners and stockholders.

Unfortunately, Wall Street–focused companies have these three priorities reversed. They think their number one customer is their stockholders. As a result, they act like the most important reason for being in business is to make money. Their customers come next in importance, followed by their people, whom they consider least important. Wall Street–focused companies view their people as disposable parts—when they need them, they hire them; when they don't, they downsize and get rid of them.

The great companies I mentioned all recognize that profit is the applause you get for creating a motivating environment for your people that excites them about taking care of your customers. I like to visualize this as a three-legged stool. The reason I love the three-legged stool analogy is that all three legs are important. The first leg is gung ho people, the second leg is raving fan customers, and the third leg is financial strength. If any of these three legs is weak, the stool falls down. I say this to emphasize that financial strength is important in business. You have to make money to survive in the long run. But making money—profit— is the outcome of taking care of your people and your customers.

The seat that holds the three legs together is vision and direction. A compelling vision tells you who you are (your purpose), where you're going (your picture of the future), and what will guide your journey (your values). Direction involves establishing goals that help people determine what they should focus on right now. Vision and direction are important, because a river without banks is a large puddle. Vision and clear direction are the banks that allow the river—the company—to flow and thrive.

The Leader's Role in Managing Performance

If the number one customer of great organizations is their people, what is the role of training and development? My wife Margie, who co-founded our company with me, contends that every leader/manager has three roles. First, they must do their own job. Everyone has someone to whom they report, responsibilities to fulfill, and goals to accomplish. The second role is to train and develop their people. The third is to be concerned about the career aspirations of their people. In exploring the role of training and development in leading and developing organizations, I will focus on the last two.

If you're concerned about developing your people, one of your main roles is managing their performance—in other words, helping them accomplish their goals and be effective in their jobs. There are three aspects of managing performance: performance planning, performance coaching, and performance evaluation. When I ask people around the world which aspect most organizations spend the greatest amount of their time on, the universal answer is performance evaluation. Why is that? Because that's when they have to sit down, fill out all kinds of forms, and have performance review discussions. Yet if you're going to really develop your people, the real action is performance planning and performance coaching. It's in these two roles where servant leadership comes into play at the operational level.

The Role of Servant Leadership in Managing Performance

When I mention servant leadership, most people think I'm talking about the inmates running the prison, pleasing everyone, or some religious movement. This is because they don't understand that in managing people's performance, there are two parts of servant leadership. The first is goal setting. All good performance starts with clear goals. That's why the first secret of *The One Minute Manager* is one-minute goal setting; it is a key aspect of performance planning. Setting clear goals in performance planning is the responsibility of the traditional hierarchy. While leaders/managers should involve their people in this process, it's the leader's responsibility to make sure that clear goals are established. That's the *leadership* part of servant leadership.

Once people are clear on their goals and understand what they're being asked to do, it's time to implement performance coaching, the second aspect of managing performance. Here's where the *servant* part of servant leadership comes into play. During performance coaching, the traditional hierarchy must be turned upside-down. Now you work for your people, and your job as the leader/manager is to help them win.

If performance planning and performance coaching are done well, performance evaluation provides the chance for both the leaders/managers and their direct reports to celebrate the wins during the year. Unfortunately, performance planning and performance coaching are not done well in most organizations.

Some organizations do a good job on performance planning and set very clear goals. However, after goal setting, what do you think happens to those goals? Most often they get filed and no one looks at them until they are told it's time for performance reviews. Then everybody runs around bumping into each other, trying to find the goals.

Of the three aspects of an effective performance management system, which one do people spend the least amount of time on? The answer is performance coaching. Yet this is the most important aspect of managing people's performance, because it's during performance coaching that feedback—praising progress and redirecting inappropriate behavior—happens on an ongoing basis.

Helping People Get an A

To illustrate my thinking in this area, let me tell you about my 10-year experience as a college professor. I was always in trouble. What drove the faculty crazy more than anything was that at the beginning of every course, I gave students the final exam. When the faculty found out about that, they asked, "What are you doing?"

I said, "I thought we were supposed to teach these students."

The faculty said, "You are, but don't give them the final exam ahead of time!"

I said, "Not only will I give them the final exam ahead of time, what do you think I'll do throughout the semester? I'll teach them the answers so that when they get to the final exam, they'll get As. You see, life is all about getting As—not some stupid normal distribution curve."

Do you hire losers? Do you go around saying, "We lost some of our worst performers last year, so let's go out and hire some new ones to fill those low spots"? No! You hire either winners or potential winners. You don't hire people to fit a normal distribution curve. You want to hire the best people possible, and you want them to perform at their highest level.

Giving people the final exam ahead of time is equivalent to performance planning. It lets people know exactly what's expected of them. Teaching direct reports the answers is what performance coaching is all about. If you see people doing something right, you give them an "attaboy" or "attagirl." If they do something wrong, you don't beat them up or save your feedback for the performance review. Instead, you say, "Wrong answer. What do you think would be the right answer?" In other words, you redirect them. Finally, giving people the same exam during the performance review that you gave them at the beginning of the year helps them win—get a good evaluation. There should be no surprises in an annual or semiannual performance review. Everyone should know what the test will be and should get help throughout the year to achieve a high score on it. When you have a forced distribution curve—where a certain percentage of your people have to be average or less—you lose everyone's trust. Now all people are concerned about is looking out for number one.

After learning about this philosophy, Garry Ridge, president of WD-40 Company, implemented "Don't Mark My Paper—Help Me Get an A" as a major theme in his company. Garry and I wrote about this in our book, *Helping People Win at Work*. WD-40 calls its company "the WD-40 tribe." To put the "Don't Mark My Paper—Help Me Get an A" philosophy into action, at the beginning of the fiscal year every tribe leader sits down with each of their tribe members, and after reviewing the company's goals, together they set four or five observable, measurable goals for the tribe member. Once goals are established using Situational Leadership® II, together the leader and tribe member analyze the tribe member's development level (competence and commitment) to accomplish each goal without supervision. After goals and development levels are determined, the leader and tribe member agree on the appropriate leadership style (amount of direction and support) the tribe member needs to accomplish each goal.

Once performance planning is complete and both leader and tribe member understand the goals to be accomplished, development level, and appropriate leadership style, the process moves to performance coaching. Peter Drucker often said, "Nothing good ever happens by accident; you have to put some structure around it." At WD-40 Company, they did two things that ensure effective performance coaching takes place. First, all tribe leaders hold one-on-one meetings at least once every two weeks for 15-30 minutes with each of their tribe members. The tribe leader schedules the meeting but the tribe members set the agenda. Tribe members can talk about anything they want—a sick child, how they are doing on a particular goal, the need for a different leadership style, and so on. If you met with each of your people for 15-30 minutes 26 times a year, would you know what they needed from you? Of course you would.

Finally, with one-on-one meetings set every two weeks, not only do tribe leaders have the information they need to do effective performance coaching, but also they have a chance to talk to their tribe members about their career aspirations. Some people wonder why leaders would be concerned about their people's career development. Organizations like WD-40 Company realize that most people aren't going to work in the same position forever. By encouraging the career development of their people, tribe leaders boost morale, strengthen relationships, and increase the overall talent within the company.

In addition to bi-weekly meetings, tribe leaders hold quarterly meetings with each tribe member. At these meetings, tribe leaders and members do three things:

First, they agree on whether the final exam is still relevant. In a lot of organizations, people set goals at the beginning of the year and are evaluated on those goals at the end of the year, even if something like a tsunami or economic downturn has happened and they are no longer working on the original goals. At WD-40 Company, tribe members can change the final exam goals up until the beginning of the fourth quarter.

Second, tribe members individually grade themselves on their goals with an A+, A, B, C, or L. L stands for "I'm still learning, so I shouldn't be evaluated yet on this goal." One of the powerful things about WD-40 Company's "Don't Mark My Paper, Help Me Get an A" philosophy is that tribe members only fill out one performance review—their own. I think there's nothing more stupid than managers sitting around filling out performance review forms while their people are outside wondering how well they'll do.

Third, after the tribe members have graded themselves, the tribe leader agrees or disagrees with the tribe member's grades. The goal for a tribe leader is to help each tribe member get an A average. Garry is so emphatic about this concept that he will fire a poor performer's manager rather than the poor performer when he finds out that the manager has done nothing to help that tribe member get an A.

Does WD-40 Company's performance system work? You'd better believe it does. In 2013, WD-40 Company had its finest stock performance on Wall Street in the history of the company. Furthermore, in 2012, an internal employee satisfaction survey received a 90 percent return rate with an employee engagement score over 90 percent. The survey revealed that:

- 98.5 percent said they felt free to contact others at WD-40 Company for help whenever it was necessary to get the job done.
- 98.5 percent said they knew the goals that were expected of them.
- 98.2 percent said their supervisor respected them.
- 97.9 percent said the WD-40 Company treated them with dignity and respect.
- 97.9 percent said they were encouraged to strive for quality and take the initiative to improve the quality in their area.

When you treat your people as your number one customer, they take care of your external customers, who take care of your stockholders. Duh! Why isn't common sense common practice?

In this section of the *ASTD Handbook*, you will receive excellent information on the key role training and development plays in leading a great organization. Pat McLagan addresses training and development's role in guiding change; Marcus Buckingham discusses training and development's role in strengths-based performance management; Jean Leslie and Nick Petrie present training and development's role in developing leaders for the future; and finally, my son, Scott Blanchard, discusses how training and development can help those with high potential be successful.

Enjoy! Recognize that great organizations depend on their T&D professionals to serve many and varied roles. Great organizations act on the belief that training and developing their people is fundamental to success.

About the Author

Ken Blanchard, one of the most influential leadership experts in the world, is the co-author of the iconic bestseller, *The One Minute Manager,* and 60 other books whose combined sales total more than 21 million copies. Ken is also cofounder and chief spiritual officer of The Ken Blanchard Companies, a global management training and consulting firm headquartered in San Diego, California. The College of Business at Grand Canyon University bears his name.

For Further Reading

Blanchard, K., K. Cuff, and V. Halsey. (2014). *Legendary Service: The Key Is to Care*. New York: McGraw-Hill.

Blanchard, K., and G. Ridge. (2009). *Helping People Win at Work*. Upper Saddle River, NJ: FT Press.

Blanchard, K., P. Zigarmi, and D. Zigarmi. (2013). *Leadership and the One Minute Manager*. New York: HarperCollins Publishers.

Chapter 47

The Training and Development Professional's Role in Guiding Change

Patricia A. McLagan

································· **In This Chapter** ·································

- Learn the keys to implementing successful change.
- Understand T&D's role in addressing organizational change.

Training and development professionals are change agents in their enterprises, for their focus is on the core resource of the business: people's knowledge, skills, and energy. However, their larger change influence is often either minor or marginalized, even though the potential for larger impact is increasing. To help position the T&D professional for a larger change role, it is important to understand 1) the keys to successful change implementation today, and 2) what the T&D professional can do to help address the larger change needs of the organization.

Keys to Successful Change Implementation

Change may be the only constant. But scholars and practitioners have only recently begun to understand change dynamics in and around our institutions with the intent to influence their direction and impact. The following five lessons about successful change management reflect findings across a spectrum of studies focused on what works to make deliberate changes successful. If you heed them, the chances of costly failures and organization trauma significantly diminish.

Kurt Lewin

Kurt Lewin is recognized as the father of social psychology. He was one of the first researchers to study group dynamics and organization development and was influential in the study of group dynamics and experiential learning. Lewin may be best known for his three-step change model, which he developed in 1947 and which maintained its fundamental integrity through several iterations for nearly 50 years. The three steps in the model are unfreezing, changing, and refreezing.

Unfreezing refers to the work that is required to move people out of their safe and comfortable status quo. To do this requires an understanding of forces that drive change as well as those that stand in the way of change. Lewin's force-field analysis identifies and measures the strengths of these forces. Driving forces are listed and given a value from one to four, and restraining forces are listed and given a value of negative one to negative four. This analysis helps the decision maker to assess the forces acting on a proposed change.

Changing is the process of doing all that is required to effect change. An important idea that Lewin put forth in this context is that change takes time and may involve several iterations of moving forward and sliding back before it begins to stick. Finally, refreezing involves institutionalizing the change and getting comfortable with the new status quo.

Lewin was also famous for his field theory, which emphasized how individuals' relationship with their environment affected their work. Lewin found that human behavior (b) was a result of an individual's activity (p) and the environment (e) in which the person works, or $b = (p, e)$. This was one of the first attempts at creating what is now known as a human performance equation.

---

1. Be Sure the Change Will Add Value

There are many, many instances of changes that occur because they are the latest fad, someone's pet project, technically brilliant or seductive, or promise benefits that can't be achieved with the proposed solution. There are several questions to ask in order to test the potential real value of a change.

- *"Will this change make us more successful in our environment?"* If the environment doesn't require and won't support major new directions, then making *core* changes (in strategy, core competencies) will fail.
- *"Will this change improve things?"* Will it make work more successful while reducing the effort required? Will it provide truly better customer service or product quality? Will it have a positive impact on people at work—their status, the meaning of their work, the ease of work, the elimination of barriers to success? It's not

enough that on the surface the change is a good technical, financial, or political idea. That may matter to executives and technical people. But, if the change complicates things for customers or for people at work, reject it unless you are willing to spend vast extra resources supporting and getting compliance with the change.

■ *"Will this change really improve performance for our overall organization?"* A change that is positive for a part of the organization may not be positive for the organization overall.

Many change projects should not be introduced at all. The savvy change agent questions the need and potential impact before jumping on the train.

2. Match the Change Process to the Challenge

Some changes are complex and unpredictable (like managing the organization as part of a global supply chain versus as a single organization). Other changes are relatively simple (shifting from one word processing software package to another). More complex and dicey changes generally call for new roles and power relationships and require changes in a variety of systems and processes. Simpler changes leave roles and relationships intact and just call for a few behavior, knowledge, and skill changes.

Complex and unpredictable changes require more resources for trial and error and for learning. They call for multiple changes in systems and processes and require lasting and visible commitment from leaders who must provide vision and optimism until results occur and the change is sustainable. These more difficult changes also require more attention to communication and the human side of change. Simple and predictable changes don't need all this extra attention.

Think of changes as transactional, transitional, or transformational. *Transactional* changes (for example, making a software switch) only require a few minor interventions such as training or changing the incentive system. *Transitional* changes are complex changes that shake up roles, power, relationships, and systems, but where there is a good chance of success because you can draw on precedents, expertise, and guidelines from similar implementations (for example, installing a comprehensive but well-tested new software system or opening a plant in another country that is similar to others you have established). Transitional changes require a much higher investment in change management than transactional changes because there are many secondary effects that have to be addressed. If you want success, you have to set up detailed project plans, do innovation in phases, address the emotional side of change, and take many of the other actions listed in this chapter.

Transformational change differs from transitional change: It is multifaceted and has no or few precedents. It is difficult, at the outset, to prescribe exactly how the change will evolve, but it requires a redesign of virtually everything in the organization—especially the fundamental beliefs and norms that guide decisions and actions. An example from my own experience was South African Breweries expansion into Eastern Europe and Asia. It was a breakthrough that had to be designed during implementation. No one had done it before.

The level of investment in the change escalates with the complexity and uncertainty of the change process: low for transactional, moderate to high for transitional, and very high for transformational changes.

3. Provide Management Support

Managers and leaders are very important for the success of change. Leadership can and often does come from people without formal management responsibility. But successful changes are more likely than unsuccessful changes to be well supported by formal leaders. They:

- **Are guided by clear goals and feedback.** This is true even if and when goals must change based on learning and feedback.
- **Have a structure that optimally balances plans and flexibility.** Physicists talk about the "edge of chaos" as the point of optimal performance—the place that balances order and innovation/experimentation. Deliberate changes are more successful if they have the right amount of structure for alignment and focus but enough freedom for learning and quick self-correction. Poor implementations tend to either be too highly controlled and structured or have no structure at all.
- **Receive enough resources for success.** The lesson is "don't scrimp on the resources you need." If you need to boil water, you turn the dial on the stove up to nine, not three; you put in the necessary energy to achieve the goal. Many initiatives fail because there were not enough resources to bring the change to a boil.
- **Publicize frequent wins.** Some changes take a long time and involve difficult personal and organizational transitions. Things may also get worse before they get better. In this environment, it is easy to give up before the change can get traction. Thus, it is important for change leaders to keep up optimism and energy by finding and publicizing the little steps forward. When people see improvements, it inspires them to more action.

4. Prepare the System for Change

A recurring theme in successful change is the importance of adjusting various aspects of the organization so the change can take root and thrive. A change may require minor or radical shifts in processes, technology, tools, information flows, skills, structures, facilities, and so on. Here are the important lessons:

- **Be sure work processes are supportive.** One common feature in change failures is the lack of coordination of process changes between departments. For local changes to succeed, the larger processes they are part of may have to change. The questions to answer include, "What, if any, work processes will be directly or indirectly affected by this change? How can we get them aligned?"
- **Create change-enabling managers.** It's obvious but important to emphasize: Be sure that managers and supervisors actively support the change. When supervisors personally use the change practices taught in training, employees are more likely to use new methods. Beyond this, as the Gallup organization's ongoing studies of millions of employees and managers repeatedly discover, the *supervisor* is a key factor in the success of any effort. It makes sense to focus on managers. They are a key part of the glue that keeps the organization together. They can also keep people's feet stuck in the past. The lesson? Ask, "What do managers at all levels need to do to support this change, and how can we support them in their role and actions?
- **Align the HR system.** Human resource practices, such as selection, career movement, performance management, pay, and reward, are critical success factors in change. They must support it, or long-term success is unlikely. An early and seminal study (Pil and MacDuffie, 1996) concluded that when changes in HR practices accompany technical changes, there is significantly greater performance improvement than when technical changes occur alone. Success requires asking, "How do our HR practices support or impede this change, and what can we do to get the HR system alignment we need for success?"

It's also important to ask, "What organizational barriers could defeat this change, and what will we do about them?" and "As we review our change plans, how confident are we that we are making enough supportive changes to successfully birth and grow the change?"

5. Help People Align

The first four lessons relate primarily to the technical aspects of the change. Focusing on this alone may be enough for *transactional* (simple and predictable) changes. But for any other kind of change, it's the people side that makes or breaks success. Thus it is important to:

- **Honor the psychological contract.** This is the implicit and explicit agreement about the organization's and employees' commitment and behaviors toward each other. There may be agreements about employment continuity, development, being a "family," the relationship between performance, and continued work. The traditional relationship focused on loyalty from both sides. Some of the newer contracts just focus on the immediate exchange of work for pay. *How* you implement change must be consistent with the psychological contract, or you will pay a high price of prolonged "survivor" bad feelings and general ill will. If you find you want to manage the change in ways that break the contract, be ready to deal with the consequences—and plan to change the contract for the future.

- **Be scrupulously just, fair, and trustworthy.** People can accept changes that adversely affect them *if* they believe the change is right *and* they feel there is "procedural justice" (no unfair discrimination). This means that decision makers must work hard to be objective and just for all affected people. And, they must communicate about both the change and their decision process. It's important to answer the questions, "What decisions may affect people adversely, and how can we make these decisions in a fair and just way?"

- **Find the positives.** The first lesson ("Be sure the change will add value") tells us how important it is to pick changes that will make a difference. Here, the emphasis is on *communicating* the value of the change. People will support changes that make sense—that make work easier and more effective, that make customers happier, that improve product quality. They also have to believe that the change is achievable. The key question here is, "What are the key short- and long-term positives of this change for the organization and its people?"

- **Involve opinion leaders.** Some people have more influence on what employees do than others. These opinion leaders are often not the formal leaders in the organization. Successful change efforts draw on their expertise and energy. Success with change may hinge on the answer to the question, "Who are the opinion leaders that people listen to, and how can we get them involved?"

- **Communicate effectively and over the long term.** Sadly, by the time executives approve a change project, they have often lost interest in it. Perhaps they have spent months looking at the pros and cons and making the decision. They are ready to move on to something new at the very time when they must visibly and continuously show their support for the change. The decision to make a change is the beginning of an intense and ongoing communication process that may last for years. It is important for managers to find the mental and emotional stamina to keep talking about the same message over and over again. This is especially true in organizations where people's trust levels are low. Successful managers keep this question in front of them: "What are the main messages I need to stand for—over and over again—until this change is fully implemented?"

■ **Appropriately involve people.** When people are involved, they are more committed. Also, it is clear that decisions in today's complex business world require broader involvement and input. But, involvement will not save a change that doesn't add value or a change that is implemented unfairly. Involvement must have a purpose, too. If it's just a way of manipulating people—and has no potential impact on decisions—don't go through the motions. Such involvement only increases cynicism. People don't always need to participate in order to be committed. They do need to trust the people setting the goals, believe that the goals will lead to great performance, have access to feedback, and have control and ownership of the steps and actions for achieving the goal. In other words, there needs to be participation at the level of getting things done! Successful changes always implement the answer to the question, "Where do people affected by the change need to be involved because they have something important to contribute to defining or implementing the change?"

Chris Argyris

Chris Argyris is a leader in the field of organizational learning. His early research concerned the effects of organizations on individuals. He found that traditional organizational structures caused individuals discomfort, damaged creativity, and reduced productivity. Instead of being free to work, employees have to expend energy navigating communication channels, levels of power, and performance goals. Because the needs of the organization are put before the needs of the individual, neither ends up being met.

Argyris and co-author Donald Schön wrote *Theory in Practice: Increasing Professional Effectiveness* (1974). In this book, they developed the classic theory of action, which focused on the difference between what people say and believe they will do and what they actually do. The former became known as espoused theory and the latter theory-in-use. Argyris felt that people were most effective when their espoused theory and their theory-in-use were similar.

From the theory of action, Argyris and Schön developed the concepts of single- and double-loop learning. Single-loop learning involves finding a problem and correcting it without altering the organizational model. Double-loop learning seeks to correct a problem by looking for the values or practices that might be causing the problem in the first place.

Argyris and Schön also identified two models of behavior. Model I behavior is evident in many people. People who exhibit this kind of behavior tend to work in ways that cannot be judged by others. This is seen as defensive behavior. People who exhibit model II behavior illustrate how they have achieved results and look for the input of others; this model of behavior facilitates double-loop learning. Both models of individual behavior can then apply to the organization as a whole if many employees exhibit the same type of behavior. Argyris found that model I behavior could actually inhibit organizational growth because employees act only in their own interests, while model II behavior promotes productivity and organizational learning.

Other change considerations include being sure that people have the skills they need for implementing and sustaining the change and aligning the incentive and pay system, especially if the change is not naturally rewarding and motivation to act is low. You will find these five lessons for creating a successful change strategy accompanied by a list of questions you might ask in preparation for your next change effort on the *Handbook's* website at www.astdhandbook.org.

How T&D Professionals Can Meet the Larger Change Needs of the Organization

The training and development professional has skills and perspectives that are critical for success in the areas above. They have many of the basic skills and knowledge, although some may need to be expanded, updated, or repackaged.

T&D Professional Skills That Support Change Efforts

Capabilities we associate with the T&D professional that are valuable for facilitating change include:

- **Analysis and synthesis skills.** These include the abilities to identify ideal and current states and gaps in system support as well as skills, determine where to put energy, and to truly listen for deeper issues and meaning.
- **Knowledge of what it takes to support personal change.** The T&D practitioner understands how to help people acquire new knowledge, develop and entrench new skills, and examine and even change attitudes and perspectives.
- Ability to **teach and facilitate** group.
- Ability to **track and evaluate** changes over time.
- Appreciation of and the **value and contribution of learning** to personal and organizational success. This value is fundamental to the creation of a "learning organization."
- **Design skills.** The T&D professional's basic toolkit includes the ability to create learning experiences and organize them into powerful programs that change perspectives and behavior. This design capability can extend to more complex interventions.

These capabilities are part of the T&D professional's skill portfolio. However, they may need to be repackaged and broadened for use in the larger organizational change management arena. Big organization changes—such as implementing a big new global strategy, executing an organization-shaking and enterprise-wide IT implementation, or transitioning to operating as a value-network/supply chain—require advanced versions of all these capabilities.

Additional Skills Required

There are additional requirements of systems thinking and perspective, business and cross-functional understanding, emotional intelligence, and understanding of how complex systems change.

- **Systems thinking and perspective.** Major changes are affected by and are the product of external and internal, organizational, and personal factors. The change management professional needs to be able to notice and act with awareness of these factors—riding the waves that are positive for the organization and its strategic impact, while learning from, adapting to, and helping to manage the rest. Specifically, it's important for change agents to understand and describe the interplay of strategy, structure, systems, processes, skills, culture, and external environment. Changes may need to occur in one or several organization design elements. The change agent's role is to help identify problem and opportunity areas and to help bring all these elements into better alignment.

- **Business and cross-functional understanding.** Change agents, such as CEOs, are integrators. This requires an understanding and appreciation of how business works and knowledge of what various functions bring to the table. My personal view is that change agents must spend some time in all the functions as part of their preparation to lead or assist change programs. People who understand the parts of a business from the inside out are better able to communicate across functional lines. They are more likely to interact with empathy, credibility, and trust that make it easier for others to constructively participate in change processes.

- **High emotional intelligence.** Change projects are difficult and require constant balancing of a variety of agendas in the midst of uncertainty. Conflict, confusion, resistance, politics, gamesmanship, sabotage, and other emotional and ego-driven reactions are part of the process. The change agent has to be able to ride the waves, sit in the fire, and separate self from what is going on. The challenge and exposure are greater when there is a multifaceted change process going on versus a change being driven inside a training framework.

- **Understanding how complex systems change.** We are learning a lot about how change happens in individuals, organizations, society, and the universe itself. Change is an inbuilt dynamic of living systems. Most programs on change management focus on very limited issues: How do we deal with (that is, "control") resistance? How do we ensure our plans turn out the way we want them? How do we communicate in ways that convince people the change is good? This mindset is rational and intellectual and is part of the solution set. However, for many changes we face, the "how to control" has to be balanced with "what are we learning and what does it mean for how, and even *if*, we proceed on the planned path?" Sometimes, in the interest of longer-term success with change, we have to (see the previous point) "sit in the fire" of polarization, dissent, and confusion rather than being defensive and sorting it out right away. It is only possible to do this if we have a bigger-picture view of how change actually happens and how it can be facilitated. We have to go way beyond the control-oriented approaches of the past.

Richard Beckhard

Richard Beckard was one of the founders of the field of organization development and is responsible for creating its standard definition: "an effort planned, organization-wide, and managed from the top, to increase organization effectiveness and health through planned interventions in the organization's 'processes,' using behavioral-science knowledge." This definition was published in his seminal work, *Organization Development: Strategies and Models* (1969).

Beckhard also worked in the field of change management. He helped develop the Formula for Change (also known as Gleicher's formula) with David Gleicher. The formula is used to determine how successful a change is likely to be, indicating that dissatisfaction (D) times vision (V) times first steps (F) is greater than resistance to change (R), or $D \times V \times F > R$.

Conclusion

The training and development professional has many important capabilities that are transferable to the larger organization change arena. However, success as a large system change agent requires a deeper understanding of change dynamics and a willingness to repackage existing skills and learn new ones. Even if the professional's work stays focused on individual and team training and development, having the bigger perspective and broader change skills described in this chapter will make the professional a more powerful and influential contributor during these rapidly changing times.

About the Author

Patricia A. McLagan's life focus is on understanding and facilitating change—individual, organizational, and societal. She has worked with all levels in government and business in the United States and globally, including in South Africa during the transformational time of the 1980s and 1990s. She authored many articles and books, including *On the Level, Performance Communication That Works, The Age of Participation: New Governance for* *the Workplace and the World, Change Is Everybody's Business,* and *The Shadow Side of Power: Lessons for Leaders.* She has served in leadership roles for ASTD, the United Way (Minneapolis Cabinet), and the Desmond Tutu Peace Foundation.

References

McLagan, P.A. (2002, December). Success With Change. *T+D.*

Pil, F., and J. MacDuffie. (1996, July). The Adoption of High-Involvement Work Practices. *Industrial Relations.*

For Further Reading

Argyris, C., and D. Schon. (1995). *Organizational Learning II: Theory, Method and Practice.* New Jersey: FT Press.

Conner, D. (2006). *Managing at the Speed of Change: How Resilient Managers Succeed Where Others Fail.* New York: Random House.

Kotter, J., and D. Cohen. (2013). *The Heart of Change: Real-Life Stories of How People Change Their Organizations.* Boston: Harvard Business Review Press.

Lewin, K. (1964). *Field Theory in Social Science: Selected Theoretical Papers.* New York: Harper Torchbooks.

McLagan, P.A. (2002). *Change Is Everybody's Business.* San Francisco: Berrett-Koehler.

McLagan, P.A., and C. Nel. (1996). *The Age of Participation: New Governance for the Workplace and the World.* San Francisco: Berrett-Koehler.

Chapter 48

Strengths-Based Performance Management

Marcus Buckingham

······· **In This Chapter** ·······

- Understand the evolution of performance—how we measure it, train it, teach it, and reward it.
- Review the current struggles with rating the strengths and skills of others.
- Build your own strengths-based performance management system.

·······

In 1850, it took the average piece of mail five weeks to travel from St. Joseph, Missouri, to the California coast. This was frustrating, since in 1848 gold had been discovered in the California hills and the wild and crazy rush was on. America was moving west and needed a much more efficient, streamlined way to communicate with its West Coast, full of riches.

The Pony Express was the answer—400 horses; 150 short, wiry riders; 200 stations; and the innovation of lightweight, leather cantinas to carry the mail itself. It was a fantastically complicated arrangement, requiring careful forethought, detailed planning, and not inconsiderable daring. And, having woven together this complicated system, the inventors managed to streamline the process so well that, on its very first journey, what was once a five-week trek turned into a 10-day sprint from St. Joe to Sacramento. Speeches were made, fireworks fired, a great innovation was celebrated. And then, Baron Pavel Schilling destroyed it all.

He didn't do it deliberately, of course. But he did invent the telegraph. And with that one invention, that one concept, he created a new worldview, one that rendered obsolete the entire system that they had worked so hard to streamline.

Our current performance management systems are akin to the Pony Express—time-consuming, labor-intensive, complicated systems designed to add a little speed to an already difficult and cumbersome process.

And the telegraph? We will argue that strengths-based performance management can serve as the telegraph to this particular Pony Express. The telegraph was actually an innovative combination of a new technology (electromagnetic signal cables) and a new language (Morse code). In the same way, the strengths-based system is the combination of a new technology (your smartphone) and a new language (the language of strengths). These combine to create the blueprint for a lighter, faster, more outcome-focused system. Our hope is that, guided by this blueprint, you'll be able to begin implementing a system for your company that truly accelerates performance.

Before we describe this blueprint, let's lay bare once and for all why our current systems struggle to deliver any meaningful return on all the time and money we spend on them.

Trouble With the Curve?

"No more curve," said Lisa Brummel, Microsoft's EVP of HR recently, curtly ditching Microsoft's iconic practice of ranking each team member on a forced distribution. This was big news, the lead of many a business section. After all, this practice of "stack ranking," of being forced to rate every single one of your team on a bell curve from excellent to poor (even if the whole team had, in fact, performed excellently) had been singled out by everyone from *HBR* to *Vanity Fair* as one of the reasons for Microsoft's inability to foster high-performing teams, a major cause of its "lost decade."

It wasn't just big news, but welcome news for anyone who has ever struggled to keep a straight face while telling a direct report that a "3" really isn't that bad, that it truly does mean "meets expectations," that, sorry, but next year will have to be "your year," and that, hey, 60 percent of the company gets that rating, so don't be too down on yourself.

But ditching stack ranking, as welcome as it may be, wasn't even the most forward-thinking thing that Microsoft announced—after all, according to a Corporate Executive Board (CEB) survey, only 29 percent of companies use a forced curve in their performance management systems. No, the really shocking part came in the next paragraph of Lisa's email:

"And no more ratings," she said.

No more ratings? According to the CEB study, more than 90 percent of all companies surveyed use some kind of rating system to measure performance. Every single one of the big human capital management (HCM) software platforms uses ratings as its lynchpin. These ratings—of overall performance, and of the many competencies that apparently combine to create overall performance—are the raw material for everything else that the company does to and for its people. These ratings pinpoint performance gaps and then trigger the necessary training and learning interventions. They feed compensation. They guide succession planning. These ratings are the lingua franca of performance, and are so central to performance management that HCM software providers are competing with each other to see who can help managers generate them faster, explain them better, and display them ever more graphically. All systems are designed to produce something. For HCM systems, that something is ratings.

So, if Microsoft is ditching ratings, if they are saying that ratings hinder performance rather than help it, what does that mean for the 90 percent of us who labor every six months to generate them for our teams? And what does it mean for the software providers whose systems compel us to do so?

Hard to say, of course—after all, on the day Microsoft announced its rejection of ratings, Yahoo! was publicly struggling with the fall-out from its botched relaunch of stack rankings. Nonetheless, when Microsoft throws out ratings, and on closer scrutiny one discovers that in the last year, many other companies such as Adobe, Kelly Services, NY Life, and Juniper have done the same, it's time to pay attention. Performance—how we measure it, train it, teach it, and reward it—is changing. And so now is an excellent time to ask ourselves: "What is the world we are leaving behind, and where, precisely, are we headed?"

False Precision

The world we are leaving behind is the falsely precise. All current HCM systems are based on the notion that a manager can be guided to become a reliable rater of another person's strengths and skills. The assumption is that, if we give you just the right scale, and just the right words to anchor that scale, and if we tell you to look for certain behaviors, and to rate this person a "4" if you see these behaviors frequently, and a "3" if you see them less frequently, then, over time, you and your fellow managers will become reliable raters of other people's performance. Indeed, your ratings will come to have such high inter-rater reliability (meaning that two managers would give the same employee's performance the same rating) that the company will use your ratings to pinpoint low performers, promote top performers, and pay everyone fairly.

Unfortunately, there is scant evidence that this happens. Instead, a large body of research reveals that each of us is an unreliable rater of another person's strengths and skills. It appears that, when it comes to rating someone else, our own strengths, skills, and biases get in the way and, rather than rating the person on some wonderfully objective scale, we end up rating them on our own scale. The result? Our rating measures us, not the person we are rating.

The most comprehensive research on what ratings actually measure was conducted by Mount, Scullen, and Goff. In their study, 4,492 individuals were rated on a number of different performance dimensions by two bosses, two peers, and two subordinates. A little fewer than half a million ratings were produced. The researchers then analyzed these ratings and found that 62 percent of the variance in the ratings could be accounted for by what they called "idiosyncratic rater effects"—namely, the peculiarities of each individual rater's perception. Only 21 percent of the variance in ratings could be explained by the ratee's actual performance. All of this led the researchers to the following conclusion:

> *Although it is implicitly assumed that the ratings measure the performance of the ratee, most of what is being measured by the ratings is the unique rating tendencies of the rater. Thus ratings reveal more about the rater than they do about the ratee.*

Some companies have tried to neutralize this effect by training the manager to look for specific clues to the desired strength or skill. This may result in managers becoming more observant, but it doesn't turn them into better raters. This inability to rate reliably is so entrenched that even when organizations spend millions of hours and dollars training up a roster of experts whose *only* job is rating, they still don't get the reliability they seek.

As an example, over the last few years, every U.S. state has done precisely that. Each state created a cadre of experts to evaluate, in extraordinary detail, the performance of teachers. One would have expected variation, some good teachers, some not so good, and some differently good, reflected in a range of ratings from the experts. But as the *New York Times* reported in 2013, the results of these ratings have revealed alarmingly little variation. These expert raters are simply not very reliable.

Scour the literature and you will discover similar studies all confirming our struggles with rating the strengths and skills of others. Our ratings of others certainly *look* precise. They look like objective data. But they aren't. They offer precision, but it is a false precision. So when we decide to promote someone based on that person's "4" rating, or when we say that a certain choice assignment is open only to those employees who scored an "exceeds expectations" rating, or when we pay someone based on these ratings, or suggest a particular training course based on them, we are making decisions on faulty data.

In a spirited defense of the forced curve in *The Wall Street Journal*, Jack Welch advocated rating people on lists of competencies so that you can, in his words, "let them know where they stand." This is a worthy sentiment, but competency ratings will never achieve it. Given how poor we are as raters, competency ratings will only ever serve to confuse people as to where they stand. As they say in the data world: "Garbage in, garbage out."

The Wrong Practice, Streamlined

Even if we could somehow train our managers to become objective raters, our current performance management systems would still be hamstrung. Why? Because, as many of us realize when we try to implement them in our own teams, they are designed to streamline a practice utterly unfamiliar to great managers.

We know how great managers manage. They define very clearly the outcomes they want, and then they get to know the person in as much detail as possible to discover the best way to help this person achieve the outcomes. Whether you call this an individualized approach, a strengths-based approach, or just common sense, it's what great managers do.

This is not what our current performance management systems do. They ignore the real person and instead tell the manager to rate the person on a disembodied list of strengths and skills, often called competencies, and then to teach the person how to acquire the competencies he lacks. It's not just the rating part of this that's hard to pull off. The teaching part is supremely tricky—after all, what *is* the best way to help someone learn how to be a better "strategic thinker" or to display "learning agility"? In recognition of just how hard this is, current performance management systems attempt to streamline the process by supplying the manager with writing tips on how to phrase feedback about the person's competencies, or lack thereof, and then by integrating the competency rating with the company's learning management system so that it spits out a training course to fix a particular competency "gap."

The problem with all this is not just the lack of credible research proving that the best performers possess the entire list of competencies, or any research showing that if you acquire competencies you lack, your performance improves—or even that, as we described earlier, managers are woefully inaccurate at rating the competencies of others. No, the chief problem with all of this is that it is not what the best managers actually do.

They don't look past the real person to a list of theoretical competencies. Instead, actual people, with their unique mix of strengths and skills, are their singular focus. They know they can't ignore it. After all, the person's messy uniqueness is the very raw material they must mold, shape, and focus in order to create the performance they want. Cloaking it with a generic list of competencies is inherently counterproductive.

Some say that we need to rate people on their competencies because this creates "differentiation," a necessary practice of great companies. Of course, they are right, in theory—companies need to be able to differentiate between their people—but the practice is off. Differentiation cannot mean rating people on a preset list of competencies. These competencies are, by definition, formulaic and so they will actually serve to *limit* differentiation. True differentiation means focusing on the individual: understanding the strengths of each individual, setting the right expectations for each individual, recognizing the individual, putting the right career plan together for the individual. This is what the best managers do today. They seek to understand and capitalize on the whole individual. This is hard enough to do when you work with the person every day. It's nigh on impossible when you are expected to peer at her through the filter of a formula.

Six (and a Half) Characteristics

Obviously, we need a new system. What do we know about this new system? Well, the specifics of your system will depend on your company, but we do know that it must have the following six (and a half) characteristics, each of which follows logically from the one preceding. These characteristics should provide you a blueprint to guide you in building your own strengths-based performance management system.

First, and most obviously, it must be a *real-time* system that helps managers give in-the-moment coaching and course correction. The world we live in is unnervingly dynamic: We are on one team one week, another the next; goals that were fresh and exciting at the beginning of Q1 are irrelevant by the third week of Q1; and the skills, relationships, and even strategies necessary for success have to be constantly recalibrated. In this real-time world, batched performance reviews delivered once or twice a year are obsolete before we've even sat down to write them. We need much more frequent check-ins—weekly, or at most monthly.

Luckily, we now live in a world where most of us are armed with a device that knows exactly who we are, and into which we can record pretty much anything we want. This device—your mobile phone—will enable you, the employee, to input what you are doing this week and what help you need; and, because it knows you, it will be able to serve up to your manager coaching tips, insights, and prompts customized to your particular set of strengths and skills.

Second, it must be a system with a *light touch*. If we expect our employees to share their weekly or monthly focus, and if we expect our managers to react to and adjust this focus as needed, then there can be no complicated forms to complete, no narrative sections requiring writing wizards to supply the right words, no conversation guides, no input from a requisite number of peers—none of that. For this performance system to be as agile as it needs to be, it must be wonderfully simple. Just two questions answered by the employee—"What are you going to get done this week, and what help do you need from me?"—and a chance for the manager to speak into these answers. Counterintuitively, the simpler the form, the richer the coaching.

Third, it must feel to the individual employee that it is a system *about me, designed for me*. Even if a system uses a light touch and is in real time, managers will reject it if they have to initiate. Instead, the employee has to be the one to drive it. And the only way to achieve this is to make its starting point and ongoing focus: me, my strengths, where I am at my best, and how I can get better.

At present, we don't do this very well at all. We talk about it a great deal—we're all familiar with the mantra that "you have to be responsible for your own development"—but we struggle to execute. For example, most companies' employee profile pages are clearly a company tool, not a "me" tool, and as such are updated infrequently and inauthentically, and wind up reading like a computer-generated resume. With a little creativity, there is every reason to believe that we can design for each employee a place—let's call it her "standout" page—to positively present her strengths, skills, accomplishments, and aspirations. Although current "profiles" are clinical, superficial, and out of date, it is entirely in the company's interest that they not stay this way.

And besides, given that we live in a world where we expect all content, from our news, to our entertainment, to our healthcare, to be aware of our individual needs and desires, this "start with me" positioning is the least we will expect.

Fourth, and centrally, it must be a *strengths-based* system. Current systems are explicitly remedial, built on the belief that to help people get better you must measure them against a series of competency bars, point out where they fall short, and then challenge them to jump higher. While this feels practical and rigorous, even "tough," it is also depressingly inefficient. Although we label weaknesses "areas of opportunity," brain science reveals that we do not learn and grow the most in our areas of weakness. In fact, the opposite is true: We grow the most new synapses in those areas of our brain where we have the most pre-existing synapses. Our strengths, therefore, are our true "areas of opportunity" for growth.

More to the point, if we want each employee to take responsibility for his own performance and development, what better place to start than with his particular strengths? The new performance system must help each employee pinpoint his strengths in detail, and then find myriad ways to challenge him to contribute his strengths more intelligently over time. (To be clear, this does *not* mean ignoring his weaknesses. It simply means acknowledging that his weaknesses are actually his "areas of least opportunity" for growth.)

Fifth, it must be a system focused on *the future*. Our current systems are fixated on feedback about the past. You are asked to write a review on yourself, your manager writes her review, often being required to sit with her peers to calibrate your review with others at your level, sometimes even your peers will be called upon to share their insights about your personality and performance, and then your manager will be trained on how to deliver this feedback to you so that you will see it as "developmental" rather than overly "critical."

The new performance system will dispense with all of this, on one level simply because these feedback systems are plagued by a terrible signal-to-noise ratio: Managers are, and will always be, highly subjective providers of feedback; peer feedback when anonymous is just gossip, when public is sugarcoated; your own self-ratings are more than likely generously distorted; and calibration sessions merely turn up the volume on the noise.

On another level, though, we will dispense with it because future-focused coaching about performance is a better use of time than past-focused feedback. To accelerate my performance tomorrow, don't try to grade my personality with feedback from all sides—it will always be hard to give, hard to receive, and net a disproportionately small performance return. Instead, coach me on the few specific work-related activities that I could usefully add to my strengths repertoire tomorrow. Or tell me what skills I should go acquire next week. Or advise me which specific contacts I should seek out next month. None of these will necessarily be easy for me to do, but at least they will be something that I *can* do—because they are in the future. In the new performance system, this is where most of our time and creativity will be focused.

Finally, it must be a *local* system. Current performance management systems are centralized. Their express purpose is to cascade the defined company strategies and values down through all levels. But this flies in the face of the previous characteristics—a fixed, cascaded strategy prevents the company from being agile, even if, ironically, one of the company values is "agility"; I care a great deal more about my own success and strengths than I do about "alignment"; and allocating each of my goals to one of the company values or strategies is inevitably both heavy-handed and retrospective. And if you dig into your HCM data, you'll discover that many of us end up retroactively shoving our goals into one of the company's buckets only *after* the goals have been completed.

But more significantly, most of the company's best intelligence about the future of its products, people, and customers can be found in each local team. If you want to know what is relevant to your customers, what trends are happening in the marketplace, and which employees are truly most valuable, look inside each local team. So in place of cascading down, the new performance system must be designed to capture this local intelligence, and then aggregate it up. Goals should be set at the team level and aggregated up; compensation should be allocated by local leaders directly and then aggregated up; employee opinion surveys should be triggered by the local team leader and aggregated up. Only then will the company be agile and smart enough to stay relevant.

If those are the six characteristics, what's the half? Well, the entire system must have *data integrity*. Our clients often tell us that their performance management system is an unhappy mix of IT's views on managing people combined with HR's view of data. The result? A system with all the humanity of an Excel spreadsheet underpinned with squishy data. We can invert this. We can ask HR to speak loudly into designing a system that reflects what the best managers actually do, and we can demand that the data in our system are collected credibly and reliably.

Take the thorny issue of variable compensation. Currently we collect ratings (squishy data) and then use these to figure out compensation (real data). We can't learn much of anything from this because the ratings data are so unreliable (you may remember from your statistics class that you can't run any correlations when your reliabilities are low). Instead, in the new system, we can bypass the squishy data, allocate a pot of dollars to each team leader—dollars are real data—and then ask each one to divvy up the dollars as they see fit. Will some of them divvy it up better than others? Perhaps. And over time, we will learn what "better" actually means, and who is doing it "better." For example, we will learn: Is there a measurable pattern to how the best managers distribute their dollars? Do the dollars you receive predict your likelihood to be promoted? Or to leave the company? Do the highest-performing teams have a narrow range of pay within the team, or a broad range? Does range in pay predict the team's level of engagement?

These are the sorts of real-world discoveries you make when you build your system on real data.

So, that's a blueprint for a better system—lighter, more creative, more flexible, strengths based, and ultimately more human. With current technologies, you can start designing your version of this in your company. And, frankly, you can do this even before your HR department has retired your existing corporate performance management system. Current systems are thankfully so infrequent, and a strengths-based system so light touch, that the two can co-exist before the former are phased out.

About the Author

Marcus Buckingham's groundbreaking ideas about how to turn strengths into performance have changed the business world. Beginning with *First, Break All the Rules*, his books have sold more than four million copies, and he has been profiled in the *Wall Street Journal*, the *New York Times*, *Fortune*, and *Fast Company*. His leadership development firm, The Marcus Buckingham Company (www.TMBC.com), works with organizations worldwide, including Facebook, Kohl's, Hilton, Accenture, and The Gap, to achieve a straightforward but impactful mission: Instill at scale the very few practices shared by the world's best leaders. TMBC's strengths-based performance platform, StandOut, launched in 2011, reinvents performance management by providing team leaders with a light-touch, in-the-work tool to accelerate and evaluate employee performance.

References

Kropp, B. (2013, November 15). *Is the Performance Management System Dead or Creating Zombies?* Corporate Executive Board (CEO Blogs), www.executiveboard .com/blogs/is-the-performance-management-system-dead-or-creating-zombies.

For Further Reading

Buckingham, M. (1999). *First, Break All the Rules: What the World's Greatest Managers Do Differently*. New York: Simon & Schuster.

Buckingham, M. (2011). *Standout: The Groundbreaking New Strengths Assessment From the Leader of the Strengths Revolution*. Nashville, TN: Thomas Nelson.

Chapter 49

Developing Leaders
for the Future

Nick Petrie and Jean Brittain Leslie

--- **In This Chapter** ---

- Learn the key trends currently influencing leadership development.
- Explore the role T&D professionals play in developing leaders for the future.
- Identify the skills that T&D professionals will need to develop leadership skills.

W e can't predict the future. No one can. What we can do, however, is apply research, emerging practices in the field, and our client experience to predict what we believe will be needed to develop leaders for the future. Many methods—such as content-heavy training—that are being used to develop leaders for the 21st century have become dated and redundant. While these were relatively effective for the needs and challenges of the last century, they are becoming increasingly mismatched against the challenges leaders currently face. We may be arriving at a point where we face diminishing returns from teaching managers what good leadership looks like and how to mirror those behaviors, all the while neglecting to help managers understand what is required for their own development. Our challenge is no longer just one of preparing leaders; it is a development challenge.

This chapter presents an overview of the key trends, knowledge, and examples T&D professionals can use to make the future of leadership development happen.

Trend 1: Focus on Vertical Development

For a long time, we have thought about leadership development as working out which competencies a leader should possess and then helping individual managers to develop them. This type of development, referred to as horizontal development, concerns the acquisition of new skills, abilities, and behaviors. While horizontal development (and competency models) will remain important as one method for helping leaders develop, in the future it cannot be relied on as the only means. As one expert pointed out to us, "It is time to transcend *and* include the leadership competency mentality so that in future, we are able to grow our leaders simultaneously in both horizontal *and* vertical directions."

Vertical development, in contrast, refers to the stages that people progress through and how they make sense of their world. We find it easy to notice children progressing through stages of development, but conventional wisdom assumes that adults stop developing at around 20 years old—hence the term *grown up* (you have finished growing). However, developmental researchers have shown that adults do, in fact, continue to progress (at varying rates) through predictable stages of cognitive development. There are various frameworks researchers use to measure and describe levels of cognitive development. Table 49-1, for example, presents three levels adapted from Robert Kegan's (1995) model of adult development. At higher levels of development, adults make sense of the world in more complex and inclusive ways—their minds expand.

Table 49-1. Three Levels of Adult Development

Level 3: Socialized mind	At this level, we are shaped by the expectations of those around us. What we think and say is strongly influenced by what we think others want to hear.
Level 4: Self-authoring mind	We have developed our own ideology or internal compass to guide us. Our sense of self is aligned with our own belief system, personal code, and values. We can take stands and set limits on behalf of our own internal voice.
Level 5: Self-transforming mind	We have our own ideology, but can now step back from that ideology and see it as limited or partial. We can hold more contradiction and opposition in our thinking and no longer feel the need to gravitate toward polarized thinking.

Research shows that managers at higher levels of development perform better in complex environments. A study by Keith Eigel and Karl Kuhnert (2005) looked at 21 CEOs and 21 promising middle-level managers from various companies, each with annual revenues of more than $5 billion. The study showed that across a range of leadership measures, there was a clear correlation between higher levels of vertical development and higher levels of effectiveness. Eigel and Kuhnert conclude that managers at higher levels of cognitive development are able to perform more effectively because they can think in more complex ways.

The Role of T&D

The methods for horizontal development are very different from those for vertical development. Horizontal development can be learned from an expert, whereas vertical development must be learned for yourself. Developmental movement from one stage to the next is usually driven by limitations in the manager's current stage. Summarized below is what researchers (Kegan and Lahey, 2009) have learned in the last 75 years about preceding conditions to vertical development:

- The person feels consistently frustrated by a situation, dilemma, or challenge in his or her life.
- It causes the person to feel the limits of his or her current way of thinking.
- It is in an area of life that he or she cares about deeply.
- There is sufficient support that he or she is able to persist in the face of the anxiety and conflict.

When managers are confronted with increased complexity and challenge that can't be met with their current levels of knowledge and ability, they are pushed to take the next step (McGuire and Rhodes, 2009). In addition, development accelerates when people are able to surface and test the assumptions that are holding them at their current levels of development. John McGuire and Gary Rhodes describe vertical development as a three-stage process, as shown in Table 49-2.

Table 49-2. Three Stages in the Vertical Development Process

Stage 1: Awaken	The person becomes aware that there is a different way of making sense of the world and that doing things in a new way is possible.
Stage 2: Unlearn and discern	The old assumptions are analyzed and challenged. New assumptions are tested out and experimented with as being new possibilities for one's day-to-day work and life.
Stage 3: Advance	This stage occurs when, after some practice and effort, the new idea gets stronger and starts to dominate the previous ones. The new level of development (leadership logic) starts to make more sense than the old one.

You may wish to download an interview with Nick Petrie on the topic of the vertical development process at the *Handbook's* website at www.astdhandbook.org.

Example of a Vertical Development Process: The Immunity to Change

The Immunity to Change process was developed over a 20-year period by Harvard professors and researchers Robert Kegan and Lisa Lahey (2009). The process uses behavior change and helps people discover what's stopping them from making the changes they want.

How It Works

Leaders choose behaviors they are highly motivated to change. They then use a mapping process to identify the anxieties and assumptions they have about what would happen if they were to make those changes. This uncovers for the person their hidden immunity to change (that is, what has held them back from making the change already). The participants then design and run a series of small experiments in the workplace to test out the validity of their assumptions. As people realize that the assumptions they have been operating under are false or at least partial, the resistance to change diminishes and the desired behavior change happens more naturally.

Why It Accelerates Development

The method accelerates people's growth because it focuses directly on the four conditions of vertical development (an area of frustration, limits of current thinking, an area of importance, and support available). Many leadership programs operate on the assumption that if you show people how to lead, they can then do it. However, the most difficult challenges people face in their work are often associated with the limitations to the way they make meaning at their current level of development. When people surface and question their assumptions about the way the world works, they begin to make meaning at a more advanced level. For example, a manager may have difficulty making decisions without his boss's direction, not because he lacks decision-making techniques, but because of the anxiety that taking a stand produces from his current level of meaning making (the socialized mind).

How This Is Used

The method is currently being used in the leadership development programs of a number of leading banks, financial services firms, and strategy consulting firms. It is best suited for leaders who already have the technical skills they need to succeed but who need to grow the capacity of their thinking in order to lead more effectively.

Trend 2: Close the Leadership Gap Throughout the Whole Organization

Studies over the past decade have shown concerns about a shortage of leaders. Despite efforts to thwart the impeding situation, concerns about the deficit remain. Many studies have looked for possible solutions at the individual competency/skill level (for example, strategic planning, change management), but few have looked at solutions from an organizational standpoint until now. A recent survey of more than 500 managers found four key tendencies underlying the leadership gap in organizations: outdated leadership development practices, current business challenges require different leadership styles, leaders are resistant to changing their leadership styles, and organizations are underinvesting in leadership development. This research further reveals that organizations that report the smallest leadership gaps are employing cultural initiatives that promote leadership capabilities in all employees. The higher the priority the organization places on leadership development, the lower the concern managers report about a leadership gap in three to five years and in five to 10 years from now.

The Role of T&D

The Center for Creative Leadership (CCL) is expanding beyond the individual leader programs to partner with senior leadership teams to build leadership cultures. A powerful approach to developing a new leadership culture is to work with the most senior leaders first so they can model the new way. CCL's approach is to have the senior leadership team diagnose the current culture and then determine what is needed for a new leadership culture to execute the strategy. Rather than then communicating their conclusions to the organization, the senior team sets out to transform their own thinking and acting so they can embody the new culture. For the first six to 12 months, the team focuses on their own development in order to embed the new ways of thinking and acting into their working behaviors. This is not for the fainthearted. If they are not prepared to do the hard work to grow their leadership culture at the top, there is little hope that the rest of the organization can make the shift.

Once the leadership team has successfully grown their own leadership capabilities such that they can model the new approach, the developmental tools are cascaded out into the organization, but with a twist. Rather than rely on outside experts, it becomes a process of leaders developing leaders. Each of the senior leaders becomes responsible for taking and applying the process and tools back with their team. The aim is that the new leadership culture takes hold both within and between teams. Once the top 50 leaders can start leading collectively across boundaries, the culture starts to spread throughout the organization.

Trend 3: Transfer Developmental Ownership to the Individual

Many of the leadership experts we interviewed believe that the training model common in organizations for much of the last 50 years has bred dependency, inadvertently convincing people that they are passengers in their own development journeys. Even as methods have evolved, such as performance feedback, action learning, and mentoring, the sense for many still remains that it is someone else's job to "tell me what I need to get better at and how to do it." The challenge is to help managers get into the driver's seat for their own development. One company we worked with, for example, changed its leadership programs from content events to development processes in which managers took ownership of their own development. All senior managers engaged in a six-month process in which they learned the principles of development, then put those principles into practice on themselves. Only after they had experience developing themselves with the new tools did they start coaching their team members to start using them.

The Role of T&D

Leadership development can become democratized if managers get a better understanding of what development is, why it matters for them, and how they can take ownership of their own development. The leadership experts suggest the following factors be present in organizations for managers to take greater ownership of their development:

- recognition from senior leaders that in complex environments; business strategies cannot be executed without highly developed leaders (and that traditional horizontal development won't be enough)
- buy-in from senior leaders that new methods for development are needed and that, as agents of change, the senior leaders will go first and lead by example
- education for staff on the research of how development occurs and what the benefits are for them
- understanding among staff that development works better when they own it
- realignment of reward systems to emphasize both development and performance
- use of new technologies (such as Rypple) that allow people to take control of their own feedback and gather ongoing suggestions for improvement
- creation of a culture in which it is safe to take the risks required to stretch your mind into the discomfort zone programs.

Kegan and Lahey (2009) suggest that you would know an organization had people taking ownership of their ongoing development when you could walk into the organization and any person could tell you:

- what one thing they are working on that will require them to grow to accomplish it
- how they are working on it
- who else knows and cares about it
- why this matters to them.

Example of a Development Process That Increases Ownership: Feedforward Coaching

What It Is

The feedforward process is a behavior change process designed for busy, time-poor people who like to see measured results. In the feedforward process, an individual engages trusted colleagues in a peer-coaching process, asking each colleague to do three things: focus on the future, give only suggestions, and make the suggestions something positive and attainable.

How It Works

Participants choose one or two areas they want to improve and five to eight internal people they trust who become feedforward coaches. With the support of an internal or external coach, the leaders gather monthly suggestions from the feedforward coaches as to how they can improve in chosen areas and progress reports on how much they are changing. At the six- and 12-month points, participants can take a minisurvey that measures the level of their behavior change (information on the minisurvey is courtesy of Chris Coffey).

Why It Works for Development

It is extremely time efficient, taking only two to three hours per month, involves the people who know the coachee best to help him or her change, measures results, holds the coachee accountable over time, and acknowledges that behavior change is a process, not an event. Feedforward puts responsibility for development into the hands of individuals and lets them determine who will be involved, what they will work on, and how conversations will take place. In addition, the structure of the process ensures continuous support and account-ability conversations with a coach, which helps people to continue to follow through on their actions.

Trend 4: Leadership as Collective Social Process

The story of the last 50 years of leadership development has been the story of the individual. The field of leadership has long held up heroic individuals as examples of great leaders who could command and inspire organizations. This idea resonated with the public, as it did with business audiences who sought to glean leadership secrets from these leaders' books and speeches. However, complex, chaotic environments are less suited to the problem solving of lone, decisive authority figures than they are to the distributed efforts of smart, flexible leadership networks. These collectives, who often cross geographies, reporting lines, and organizations, need to collaboratively share information, create plans, influence each other, and make decisions.

The Role of T&D

The transition from thinking of leadership as a lone, heroic figure to understanding that it is a dynamic process of influence between groups of people may not come quickly or easily to many people. A starting point is to redefine what is meant by the term *leadership*. There has been a major trend among organizational theorists to shift the focus from leadership as a person or role to leadership as a process. For example:

- the process of mobilizing people to face difficult challenges (Heifetz, 1994)
- anyone and everyone who puts in place and helps keep in place the five performance conditions needed for effective group functioning (Hackman, 2002)
- leaders are people in the organization actively involved in the process of producing direction, alignment, and commitment (McCauley and Van Velsor, 2004).

A key distinction in the definitions above is that leadership can be enacted by anyone; it is not tied to a position of authority in the hierarchy. Heifetz, in fact, believes it is far easier to exercise leadership from a position outside of authority, without the constraints that authority brings. More important, these definitions do not tie the act of leadership to an individual. Leadership becomes free to be distributed throughout networks of people and across boundaries and geographies. Who the leader is becomes less important than what is needed in the system and how we can produce it.

If leadership is thought of as a shared process, rather than an individual skill set, senior executives must consider the best way to help leadership flourish in their organizations.

Leadership spread throughout a network of people is more likely to flourish when certain conditions support it, including:

- open flows of information
- flexible hierarchies
- distributed resources
- distributed decision making
- loosening of centralized controls.

In order for organizations to become more effective at using networks of leadership, experts such as CCL's Phil Willburn and Kristin Cullen suggest a number of changes that would need to occur. First, at the collective level, the goal for an organization would be to create smart leadership networks, which can coalesce and disband in response to various organizational challenges. These networks might be comprised of people from different geographies, functions, and specializations, both within and external to the organization. Just as brains become smarter as the number of neural networks and connections increase, organizations that connect more parts of their social system to each other and build a culture of shared leadership will have greater adaptability and collective capacity.

Second, organizations would use their leadership development programs to help people understand that leadership is not contained in job roles but in the process that takes place across a network of people to continuously clarify *direction,* establish *alignment,* and garner *commitment* (DAC) of stakeholders. While leadership may sometimes be enacted by an individual, increasingly it will be a process that happens at the group level, with various people's contributions influencing the DAC of the collective. As these changes happen, the distinction between who is a leader and who is a follower becomes less clear or relevant; everyone will be both at different times.

Both the Center for Creative Leadership and the Bertelsmann Foundation (a German research and publishing foundation) are exploring new ways to think about leadership development at the collective level. Both advocate looking at different strata at which leadership could take place. CCL outlines four levels, which it calls SOGI (society, organization, group, and individual). At each of these levels, they are innovating different practices specifically designed to enhance this strata's level of development.

Grady McGonagill and Peter Pruyn (2010), in their comprehensive study of leadership development best practices, suggested that in the future, organizations could choose to invest their leadership development efforts to improve capacity at one of five different levels:

- individual capacity
- team capacity
- organizational capacity
- network capacity
- systems capacity.

Depending on the area in which increased capacity was desired, organizations will target different group sizes and use different development practices (see Table 49-3). Not all types of organizations will need to adopt this new paradigm of thinking. For traditional companies, in stable environments, requiring little creativity from staff may well be more effective if they stick to traditional, individualistic command and control management styles. However, organizations that expect to operate in VUCA (volatility, uncertainty, complexity, and ambiguity) environments will quickly need to develop the types of networks and cultures in which leadership flows through the system. Complex environments will reward flexible and responsive, collective leadership, and the time is fast approaching for organizations to redress the imbalance that has been created by focusing exclusively on the individual leadership model.

Trend 5: Enhance and Accelerate Leadership Development Through New Practices and Feedback Loops

There are no simple existing models or programs that will be sufficient to develop the levels of collective leadership required to meet an increasingly complex future. Instead, an era of rapid innovation will be needed in which organizations experiment with new approaches that combine diverse ideas, theory, and practice in new ways. The challenge for organizations is to discover and cultivate methods that develop leaders and leadership as effectively and efficiently as possible.

Technology and the web will both provide the infrastructure and drive change. Grady McGonagill and Tina Doerffer (2011) describe three stages of technological innovation that have already occurred:

- Web 1.0 (1991-2000), in which tools for faster, cheaper, and more convenient forms of communication (such as email) became available and widely used.
- Web 2.0 (2001-2010), in which the use of another set of new tools for communication (such as wikis and blogs) began enabling interaction and communication in transformative ways.
- Web 3.0 (2011-), in which powerful new computing platforms (the Cloud), a second generation of search tools, and meta-level methods for managing knowledge (such as tags and folksonomies) are beginning to realize the web's potential to generate more immediately and personally useful knowledge from archived information.

McGonagill and Doerffer go on to argue that leaders have no choice but to begin to accept the future as the present. Organizations and individuals need to decide to what extent they want to cultivate the culture, mindsets, skills, and knowledge that make it possible to leverage the enormous potential of the tools of the evolving web to better realize their purposes.

Table 49-3. Bertelsmann Stiftung Leadership Development

	Individual Capacity	Team Capacity	Organizational Capacity	Network Capacity	Systems Capacity
Individuals	Develop capacity of individuals for self-awareness, ongoing learning, and exercising initiative	Develop capacity of individuals to work together in groups and lead teams	Develop capacity of individuals to understand and lead organizations	Develop capacity of individuals to cultivate and leverage peer relationships	Develop capacity of individuals to see the big picture, understand root causes, and influence systems
Teams	Develop capacity of teams to develop and elicit the full potential of all team members	Develop capacity of teams to define and attain purposes	Develop capacity of teams to enhance organizational performance	Develop capacity of teams to align their goals and activities across boundaries	Develop capacity of teams to prototype systems change
Organizations	Develop capacity of organizations to support staff, volunteer, and board member development	Develop capacity of organizations to support effective teamwork	Develop capacity of organizations to foster internal collaboration to effectively adapt to challenges	Develop capacity of organizations to collaborate with one another	Develop capacity of organizations' coalitions to lead systematic change
Communities	Develop capacity of communities to support reflective learning and encouragement of community members	Develop capacity of communities to foster and support inclusive group initiatives	Develop capacity of communities to sustain organizations that promote community well-being	Develop capacity of communities to learn together and align efforts toward common goals	Develop capacity of communities to advocate systems change
Fields of Policy and Practice	Develop capacity of fields to cultivate innovative thought leaders and practitioners	Develop capacity of fields to organize around shared interests and goals	Develop capacity of fields to organize and disseminate knowledge and field best practices	Develop capacity of fields to find synergies across functional silos and disciplinary boundaries	Develop capacity of fields to generate policy solutions and transform institutional practices and culture

The Role of T&D

A different skill set is required for many training and development specialists who must transfer from creating the programs for the executives to becoming the social facilitators of a construction process that involves all the stakeholders in the system. Given this, the greatest challenge for the T&D community may be the ability to manage the network of social connections, so that the maximum number of perspectives can be brought together and integrated. The great breakthrough for the transformation of leadership development may turn out to be not the practices that are created but the social networking process that is developed to continuously innovate new practices to be distributed throughout the network.

While it will be easy for organizations to repeat the leadership practices that they have traditionally used, this continuation makes little sense if those methods were created to solve the problems of 10 years ago. Instead, an era of innovation will be required.

The creation of new development methods will be a process of punctuated progress. Transformations are most likely to begin with small pockets of innovators within organizations, who sense that change is either needed or inevitable. These innovators will need to be prepared to experiment and fail in order to gain more feedback from which to build their next iterations. T&D innovators will need to look to find partners within and outside their organizations with whom they can join to create prototypes that push the boundaries of the existing practices.

Conclusion

If you believe that the future will present leaders with an environment that is more complex, volatile, and unpredictable, you might also believe that organizations that attempt to address the trends suggested in this chapter will be prepared. They will:

- focus on vertical development, not just horizontal
- develop leaders at all organizational levels
- transfer greater ownership of development back to the people
- build more collective rather than individual leadership in the network
- experiment with new practices.

About the Authors

Nick Petrie is a senior faculty member at the Center for Creative Leadership's (CCL) Colorado Springs campus, where he facilitates customized programs for senior-level executives and writes extensively about future trends in leadership development. His current focus is working with CEOs and their teams to transform organizational cultures. A New Zealander with significant international experience, Nick has worked and lived in Asia, Europe, and the Middle East. Industries in which he has worked include government, law, accounting, engineering, construction, and telecommunications. He holds a master's degree from Harvard University in learning and teaching and undergraduate degrees from New Zealand's Otago University.

Jean Brittain Leslie is a senior fellow and director of applied research at CCL's Greensboro campus. In this role, she manages a global research team that designs and delivers a variety of research services and products. Jean has published more than 70 pieces on leadership, derailment, 360-degree feedback, political skill, and cross-cultural issues in the form of peer-reviewed articles, popular press articles, book chapters, and books. Jean has also presented more than 50 papers at professional conferences. She received a BA in sociology from Elon University and an MA in sociology from the University of North Carolina at Greensboro.

References

Eigel, K.M., and K. Kuhnert. (2005). Authentic Development: Leadership Development Level and Executive Effectiveness. *Monographs in Leadership and Management* 3:357-385.

Hackman, J.R. (2002). *Leading Teams: Setting the Stage for Great Performances*. Boston: Harvard Business Press.

Heifetz, R.A. (1994). *Leadership Without Easy Answers*, volume 465. Boston: Harvard University Press.

Kegan, R. (1995). *In Over Our Heads: The Mental Demands of Modern Life*. Boston: Harvard University Press.

Kegan, R., and L. Lahey. (2009). *Immunity to Change: How to Overcome It and Unlock Potential in Yourself and Your Organization*. Boston: Harvard Business School Press.

McCauley, C.D., and E. Van Velsor (eds.). (2004). *The Center for Creative Leadership Handbook of Leadership Development*, volume 29. San Francisco: John Wiley & Sons.

McGonagill, G., and T. Doerffer. (2011, January 10). *The Leadership Implications of the Evolving Web*, www.bertelsmann-stiftung.de/cps/rde/xchg/SID-6822B895 -FCFC3827/bst_engl/hs.xsl/100672_101629.htm.

McGonagill, G., and P. Pruyn. (2010). *Leadership Development in the U.S.: Principles and Patterns of Best Practices*, www.bertelsmann-stiftung.de/cps/rde/xbcr /SID-F91CB766-44B3F71F/bst_engl/xcms_bst_dms_30465_31367_2.pdf.

McGuire, C., and G. Rhodes. (2009). *Transforming Your Leadership Culture*. San Francisco: Jossey-Bass.

For Further Reading

IBM. *Capitalizing on Complexity: Insights from the Global Chief Executive Officer Study*, http://public.dhe.ibm.com/common/ssi/ecm/en/gbe03297usen/GBE03297USEN.PDF.

McCauley, C.D., and E. Van Velsor (eds.). (2004). *The Center for Creative Leadership Handbook of Leadership Development*, volume 29. San Francisco: John Wiley & Sons.

McGonagill, G., and T. Doerffer. (2011, January 10). *The Leadership Implications of the Evolving Web*, www.bertelsmann-stiftung.de/cps/rde/xchg/SID-6822B895 -FCFC3827/bst_engl/hs.xsl/100672_101629.htm.

Petrie, N. (2011). *Future Trends in Leadership Development. Center for Creative Leadership Whitepaper*, www.ccl.org.

Chapter 50

How Training and Development Can Help High Potentials Be Successful

Scott Blanchard

···················· **In This Chapter** ····················

- Identify three key topic areas for a leadership curriculum.
- Gain specific insight into how T&D professionals can coach future leaders.

When people join companies, especially young employees trained in specific skills, they usually start as individual contributors. They are assigned specific key responsibility areas directly linked to their areas of expertise. They may be part of the team but contribute as individuals.

As individual contributors grow and develop, they frequently are promoted into management roles by demonstrating that they have the skills, intelligence, and determination to be a leader in the organization. But the skills that high-potential leaders use early in their careers don't necessarily translate to success as they move into the next leg of their leadership journeys.

For this next level of achievement, high-potential leaders will benefit from taking a second look at the traits that have made them successful in the past to reassess if there are any overused behaviors that might be holding them back from even greater success in the future.

This type of honest self-assessment can be a challenge for high potential leaders. Many have well-developed blind spots that make it difficult to look at their own behavior subjectively. Training and development professionals can help by providing assessments, analysis, and a well-thought-out development curriculum.

Fast Track Leadership Development

In their book, *Coaching in Organizations*, master certified executive coaches Madeleine Homan Blanchard and Linda Miller (2008) identify that in the past, developing leadership capability was done on the job. Wisdom came, at least in theory, over time—although often employees moved into leadership positions simply as a function of seniority. Those days are gone. Young people today are being thrust into leadership positions that require wisdom and maturity far beyond what one could expect from them, given their age and experience level. Typically, they are fast tracked for leadership positions because they show specific competencies that organizations need now, as rapid growth is forcing these companies to rely on the much younger and more inexperienced workforce.

Often, however, these high potentials have no management experience and limited interpersonal skills, especially if their fields are highly technical.

At the higher levels of an organization, the high-potential leader has to learn how to shift his or her focus and delegate, as his or her primary role is to oversee a larger group's success or failure. This level of responsibility is what sets executives apart from other employees in the organization. Executives are charged with leading others to excellence so that the entire organization succeeds. If they try to do too much by themselves, progress will stall. They must be willing and able to work through others.

This is a stretch for many highly successful individual contributors. And while there are many reasons why people initially choose to seek a leadership position—power, prestige, money—going into it with a clear-eyed view helps.

As Harvard professor and business author Linda Hill (2007) points out from her work studying star performers making major career transitions to management, most novice bosses don't recognize the realities of managing in today's organizations:

> They assume the position will give them more authority and, with that, more freedom and autonomy to do what they think is best for the organization. No longer, in the words of one, will they be 'burdened by the unreasonable demands of others.'

New managers nursing this assumption face a rude awakening. Instead of gaining new authority, those I have studied describe finding themselves hemmed in by interdependencies. Instead of feeling free, they feel constrained, especially if they were accustomed to the relative independence of a star performer. They are enmeshed in a web of relationships—not only with subordinates but also with bosses, peers, and others inside and outside the organization, all of whom make relentless and often conflicting demands on them. The resulting daily routine is pressured, hectic, and fragmented.

It's important that training professionals make it clear what it actually looks like to be a manager.

A lot of being a good manager is administrative. It's budget. It's performance review. It's using an online performance management system that seems like you need a graduate course in computer programming. It's about depending on others to get the work done instead of doing it yourself.

And many times, it is managing a team that will all be having a bad day on the same day. The people you depend on the most will quit—when you need them the most. You're going to have to work with team members who don't like working with each other, don't get along, and come whining to you about it. You're going to talk to people about the length of their breaks, or that they've been caught in a lie, or that they're not compliant with the dress code.

As a training and development professional, ask aspiring leaders what they want from a leadership career. One client we work with has a class called So You Think You Want to Be a Manager. What a great idea! In our experience, many aspiring leaders often get caught up with ambition and pursuing that next shining star, which is fine—you just don't want to have them end up reaching the top of the corporate ladder only to find it's leaning against the wrong wall.

Three Learning Objectives for a Leadership Development Curriculum

Once you have a good grounding in the big-picture vision of what leadership really looks like, you can begin to define the key components of a leadership development program. In our experience, working with hundreds of high-potential leaders over the years, we've found that succeeding at the next level requires developing skills in three areas:

1. **Increasing self-awareness.** Who are you? What do you value? How do you come across to others? What strengths can you lean on to be successful? What strengths are you potentially overusing to the point that they have become weaknesses?
2. **Building relationships.** Who are the key people in the organization who can help you and your team? Who are your allies? Who are the potential roadblocks? How can you be on good terms with all the important people in your life?
3. **Producing results.** What are the key objectives for your team? How does each person fit in? What are team members' current levels of competence and commitment on their assigned tasks? What do individual team members need in terms of direction and support?

We've also found that prior to conducting any development, it's important to set some ground rules. Because of the personal—and interpersonal—nature of the content typically discussed during development sessions, it's important to define how information will be shared among everyone involved.

Often the T&D professional acts as a coach. As Homan Blanchard and Miller (2008) explain,

> To instill trust between the coach and executive, the executive must be confident that anything said during a coaching session will be kept confidential. Establishing communication agreement ensures that everyone understands who will talk with whom, about what, and when.

> Expanded communication within the organization is encouraged between the person being coached and other senior leaders, colleagues, or team members, but it is the responsibility of the person being coached to share feedback about the process and the coaching conversation to his or her manager, HR professional, and/or others who need to be kept informed.

> To that end, it is useful, prior to the start of coaching, to set up a conference call involving the person to be coached, his or her manager and/or an HR representative, and the coach. The purpose of the meeting is to discuss what will occur during the coaching; clarify goals and objectives for the organization; and address confidentiality issues, the coaching agreement, and expected results from the coaching.

Homan Blanchard and Miller (2008) go on to recommend that the objectives for the coaching and the desired end results be identified at this time as well. These typically will line up with the organization's competencies and strategies. Examples of objectives they've seen include increasing levels of communication among team members, improving retention of key employees by a certain percentage, identifying specific sales data or targets, and increasing leadership effectiveness as evidenced by a particular promotion. Focusing on these areas is part of the agreement process before coaching begins and ensures that the coach and leader are starting "on the same page."

Start by Increasing Self-Awareness

High-level leaders need to have a keen self-awareness, knowing their strengths as well as their weaknesses. There are several assessments that training and development professionals can use with high-potential leaders to help them understand this key aspect of who they are—the Myers-Briggs Type Indicator and Keirsey Temperament Sorter are two of the better known.

In their book, *What Makes You Tick & What Ticks You Off: How the Basic Elements of Temperament Will Lead You to a Happier Life*, co-authors Jim Harden and Brad Dude (2009) look at dominant temperament—the innate traits and behaviors each of us feels most comfortable with and are the most natural to use—along with shadow temperament—the ones that least describe us and are difficult to identify with.

The challenge for training and development professionals is in helping high potentials understand what their dominant temperament is, how they can take ownership of it, and how they can have empathy for people who may come from a different perspective.

Without a theory, framework, and understanding of temperament, people tend to judge others in comparison to themselves. For example, if a potential leader's dominant temperament craves variety, action, and a freedom to act without hindrance, he or she may devalue and see as obstacles people who are peacekeepers and more team focused, collaborative, and harmonious.

While one leader may be comfortable with change, and open to it, and even drive it most of the time, there are other temperaments that come from a place that is more cautious and wary of change. There is nothing wrong with either disposition—they are just different. Still, it's easy for someone who is more "change able" to judge others who are not as ready. Conversely, it is easy for someone who is more careful and guarded to turn around and judge someone who likes change as being less than rigorous in his or her thinking and not very respectful of achievements in the past. Without an understanding of temperament, it is easy to judge other people and to feel judged in return.

Recognizing the way you are helps you to understand how you are different from other people. Using this as a starting point, you can begin to modulate your communication style to be more effective with people who are different from yourself. It also keeps you from defaulting to a lazy, "Well this is the way I am, I can't change," attitude.

Getting the Complete Picture

Assessments such as 360s can be used to identify what's working and what needs to be changed in order for a leader to succeed. Another process we use extensively with the leaders we coach is the Three Perspectives exercise, which Madeleine Homan (Blanchard) and I (2004) describe in our book, *Leverage Your Best, Ditch the Rest*. The Three Perspectives are questions that provide a simple and straightforward framework to help leaders understand who they are, how others see them, what drives them, and, finally, what to do about it.

The Three Perspectives exercise provides high potentials with an opportunity to review and make choices that are consistent with what they are trying to achieve in life personally and professionally. People don't always like everything they see, but going through the process always provides an opportunity to improve effectiveness in all areas of your life.

Perspective #1: How Do You See Yourself?

It's important for leaders to first get a sense of what they like about themselves and what they do not like—who they are from the inside out. This is important because your opinion of yourself is a crucial piece of your personal operating system. No matter what you accomplish, who your friends and family are, or how fast, how smart, how beautiful, or how nice you are, if you do not have a healthy image of yourself, nothing else matters. Understanding how you see yourself is the first powerful step to getting the most out of life.

Questions for an aspiring leader to answer include:

- What am I trying to accomplish?
- What do I know to be true about myself in this role?
- What drives me in this role? What are my motivations?
- What qualities, skills, or traits do I possess that will make me successful in this role?
- What qualities, skills, or traits do I possess that will get in my way?

Perspective #2: How Do Others See You?

No man or woman is an island. We live our lives in relation to others—at work, at home, in our communities. Everyone has at least one relationship that is troubling him or her. This second perspective can provide a leader with valuable insight into the way he or she comes across to others.

The second perspective can get tricky. We all know folks who put too much weight on what other people think—that certainly isn't a great way to go either. So what we are talking about here is simple, reliable information. You can't be all things to all people, but you do need to understand how people see you so you can find the best way to be effective with them. If we want to change and grow, we have to understand how we are seen.

Questions for an aspiring leader to answer include:

- Do I know how people see me in my current role?
- If not, how can I find out how each person sees me?
- If yes, do I care how others see me?
- Is there any point of view about me that I disagree with or ignore?
- Am I sure how others see me? What evidence do I have?
- What do I think people say about me when I am not around?

Perspective #3: How Do You Want to Be Seen?

Human beings possess an extraordinary capacity to fool themselves. It's standard fare for stand-up comedians on Comedy Central. Who hasn't laughed at a bad toupee or an outfit that is ill-advised for a figure? These are some common examples of what happens when a person confuses how they see themselves with how they want others to see them. It's the adult equivalent of one-year-olds who believe that if they hide their eyes, no one will be able to see them either.

Questions for an aspiring leader to answer include:

- What do I wish were true about me that I'm not sure is true?
- What do I wish others would think about me?
- Are the people who are important to me proud of me?
- If so, what are they proud of?
- Is it something I am also proud of?
- If not, what do I wish they were proud of?
- How do I consistently disappoint others?
- How do some of these inconsistencies get in my way?

The Final Crucial Question: So What Do You Do Now?

After your high potentials consider the first Three Perspectives, there is one final question to ask: So what do I do now?

Coaching is ultimately about action. The Three Perspectives are only useful if they cause aspiring leaders to take new or more effective action to change the situation they are dealing with. The Three Perspectives exercise forces you to stop and think about what is going on so you can make conscious choices about how you spend your time and how you treat people.

One important element of the discussion is to pay special attention to the overall congruence among the four questions. Very few people see themselves the same way others do; they rarely see themselves as they wish they were completely. We've yet to meet someone who doesn't feel they could be more effective in some way.

Identifying and Communicating Your Personal Values

Many high-potential leaders make decisions early in their careers without the benefit of clearly determined values to help with the process. As a result, they sometimes find themselves acting in ways that, when they look back in hindsight, they would have acted differently with a little forethought. Values guide our behavior when the choices are many or when the areas are gray.

Training and development professionals can guide high potentials through this process by helping them to identify personal values and their leadership point of view. The benefit of this is twofold. One, high-potential leaders gain additional understanding of themselves and what drives them. Second, high-potential leaders have a way to communicate information about themselves and to create some transparency with others in the organization.

We first learned about this concept through Noel Tichy's (1997) book, *The Leadership Engine* (co-authored with Eli Cohen). The authors' extensive research has shown that effective leaders have a clear, teachable leadership point of view and are willing to teach it to others, particularly the people they work with.

There are seven questions training and development professionals can ask to help high-potential leaders identify and share their personal values.

1. *Who are the influencers (leaders) in your life?* When we ask people who had the most impact on their lives, seldom do they mention bosses or other organizational leaders. Don't be surprised to hear people talk about their parents, grandparents, friends, coaches, or

teachers. It is surprising to see where leadership values originate. Ask, "How did their influences help your leadership point of view evolve?"

2. *Think of your life purpose.* Ask high potentials, "Why are you here, and what do you want to accomplish?" This question can be tied back to earlier discussions of why individuals are seeking leadership positions to begin with.

3. *What core values will guide your behavior as you attempt to live your life "on purpose"?* Some people value wealth and power, while others are more concerned with safety or survival. In trying to determine what their values are, people might start with a long list. Remind high potentials that fewer is better; trying to evaluate against too many values can immobilize your behavior.

4. *Given what you've learned from past leaders, your life purpose, and your core values, what are your beliefs about leading and motivating people?* These should flow naturally from the people who were identified earlier as having influenced the high potential's purpose and values.

5. *What can people expect from you?* Leadership is not something you do to people; it's something you do with people. When leaders let people know what they can expect from them, it underscores the idea that leadership is a partnership.

6. *What do you expect from the people you work with?* Because leading is a partnership process, it is perfectly reasonable—in fact, it's essential—that you let people know what you expect from them in return.

7. *How will you set an example for your people?* Ask your high-potential leaders to share what people will see on a daily basis. Leaders must walk their talk.

Using the questions above, new leaders have an opportunity to share information about themselves personally and open up dialogues with those they lead and work with.

Building Relationships

Everyone needs to build relationships with others—unless you have a special technical skill that no one else can do and that will never change in the future. If you have that, and you've got a job for life, then you don't have to worry about building relationships.

For the rest of us—even high potentials—you need to learn how to build relationships.

Even so, it is surprising how many people completely underestimate the importance of building relationships with immediate peers and people who are immediately relevant to helping high potentials in achieving goals.

For example, most high potentials will eventually find themselves in an onboarding situation where they are stepping into a new role. Much of the focus of onboarding involves the identification of essential resources, networking, and developing a strategy for the new position that aligns with the company's vision, mission, and goals.

To onboard successfully, leaders must be able to read the landscape, identifying who could help them succeed, whom they can trust, who are key influencers, and who can guide them through key processes. Getting to know these people and developing strong working relationships with them is critical when moving to a new position within an organization.

Relationship Mapping

One of the ways that training and development professionals can help high potentials develop skills in networking is by having them practice mapping out all the important relationships present in their current work environment for each of the projects they are working on. In *Leverage Your Best, Ditch the Rest*, Madeleine Homan (Blanchard) and I (2004) outline the steps that a training and development professional can recommend to a high potential to accomplish this.

- To get started, take a large piece of paper, find a whiteboard, or use mind-mapping software.
- Have the high potential identify one prime objective. What exactly are you trying to accomplish? What is the goal? (The high potential may have several; recommend a separate map for each objective.)
- Now have the high potential draw a space for each person who might be affected by what the high potential is doing. Include senior leaders, colleagues, peers in other departments, direct reports, functional reports, and dotted line team leads—anyone who might matter. Don't worry about going overboard—you can always scale back—but you might be surprised at what you find when you get the big-picture perspective.

Once you have identified all the possibilities, have the high potential think about each person he or she has listed and identify the following:

- What are that person's main goals/objectives? How will it serve him or her if you succeed? Fail?
- What do you need from that person? How can he or she help you? Hurt you?
- What is that person's style? How will you need to communicate in order to influence him or her? Does this person like a lot of detail or just want the executive summary?
- What regard does this person have for you? Does he or she like, respect, or trust you?
- How do you feel about him or her? Do you harbor judgments about this person that he or she might be picking up on? What assumptions might you be making about this person that you haven't checked out?
- Next, create a mini action plan around each person. What are some of the things you can do to build relationships and better understand the people who are crucial to your success?

Action plans can include spending time together, going to the person to ask for advice, or picking up the phone simply to get his or her opinion about something. You can also plan to go to lunch, drop by occasionally to chat, or include key people in relevant emails.

No Excuses

One of the common reactions we hear from high potentials when we first discuss building relationships in this manner is that we are asking them to play office politics or engage in "it is not what you know, but whom you know."

Our recommendation? Get over it.

You can't let excuses such as, "I'm shy," "I'm introverted," or "I don't like to play office politics" get in your way. Leadership is the act of influencing others. As a high-potential leader, you don't have the luxury of not participating.

Even though no one likes to think of him- or herself as a political animal, we have yet to meet a leader who can afford to be politically naïve about work relationships. Taking the time to map relationships and understand how these may or may not be serving your aims allows you to maximize your potential and the potential of others.

Producing Results—Strategic and Operational Leadership

Young leaders need to be educated about the dynamics of how an organization is run most effectively and how leadership interacts with that. The purpose-driven organization is the model that is the most desirable and lasting these days. That basically means aligning around a vision, identifying where the company is headed, and helping the company identify and reinforce a shared set of values with employees.

Our research into the Leadership-Profit Chain has shown that leadership can be divided into two main categories: strategic and operational. Coaching can help leaders assess both their strategic and operational abilities to identify gaps and strengthen areas where they can improve.

Strategic leadership includes vision, culture, and strategic imperatives. Coaches can help leaders strategize more effectively by:

- Articulating the organization's vision to ensure that everyone in the company is working toward the same goals.
- Defining and building the culture. The strategic leader defines the culture of an organization according to company values, priorities, expectations, and goals and objectives.
- Setting strategic imperatives for any given time. Ensuring that all resources are deployed for the purpose of achieving company goals to achieve the established strategic imperatives.

Operational leadership includes management practices that drive policies, procedures, and systems. Leaders at the operational level are responsible for strategy as well as operation. Coaching can help these leaders:

- Understand group dynamics and how they affect the implementation of strategies. Once policies have been set, operational leaders are in charge of ensuring that they are followed.
- Establish procedures for communicating, making decisions, managing conflict, responding to emergencies, and solving problems.
- Create and employ goal setting, performance management, and performance review systems that make it easy for people to do their jobs, for others in the company to interact with their team, and, overall, make the company customer friendly.

Assumptions and Limiting Beliefs

In our experience, aspiring leaders have more opportunity to grow in the operational leadership area than the strategic.

For example, Homan Blanchard and Miller (2008) identify that a leader might assume that his or her employees are not capable of making good decisions, and so tend to micromanage to make sure the "right" decisions are being made in the department. The inability to partner with others, or the desire to remain a "Lone Ranger," may be rooted in this assumption. Many leaders also assume that their employees need constant oversight, when in fact they are fully competent and would work more effectively without their boss "standing over their shoulder."

An effective executive coach will bring this misguided assumption to a leader's attention and then help him or her to explore the beliefs underlying it, with the goal of replacing it with one that is more useful.

Providing Direction and Support

A proven leadership model can help with this transition. In our work with aspiring leaders, we introduce Situational Leadership II® at this stage in their development because it teaches managers how and when to use the two most important categories of influencing behavior. Fundamentally, managers need to know how to do two things: They need to know how to prioritize and direct action. Those are directive behaviors. They need to address feelings, concerns and motivations, and issues of commitment related to the work. And those are supportive behaviors. Situational Leadership II® teaches people how to use directive behaviors, how to use supportive behaviors, and when to use those behaviors and in what combination.

Using a framework and a model teaches managers how to focus first on the needs of their employees through a process of diagnosis. Leaders learn to diagnose what the employee needs, and to deliver the appropriate direction and support for that individual. The model is based on the idea that people need different styles and approaches to leadership based on where they are.

Self Versus Other Orientation

Making the jump to leadership requires a focus on serving others and letting people flourish under your leadership.

Our ongoing research into the ways that leaders can create engaging, passionate work environments has identified that one of the factors that leads to a greater sense of employee well-being are perceptions individual employees have about their immediate supervisor being an "others-focused" leader.

What we have found is that leaders who are "others focused" are much more likely to create a sense of connection with their direct reports, which leads to increased well-being and subsequent intentions to perform at a high level.

High potentials need to remember and recognize that the quality of the relationships you create with people follow you throughout your career. People want to do business, cooperate with, and follow people with whom they have a productive win–win relationship. Recognizing that is important for a young leader. Many people approach relationships with a zero sum, win–lose approach. This clouds and colors their decisions.

Despite the good intentions of the self-oriented leaders, others may perceive their focus as being self-serving. It may seem that the self-oriented leaders are set on a personal agenda even when they may be trying to accomplish something for a larger good.

Training and development professionals can help by recommending a simple variation of the Golden Rule if a new leader is being perceived as too self-oriented. Ask the high-potential leader the question, "How would I respond to the influence and behavior that I am engaging in with this person?" We have found that in taking a moment to answer that question, it gives people time and a chance to change the tone of their approach.

In *Good to Great: Why Some Companies Make the Leap and Others Don't*, author Jim Collins (2001) writes about Level Five Leaders, those leaders who demonstrate a rare combination of two traits: fierce resolve combined with humility. To describe this, he uses an analogy of a window and a mirror to describe the way that a Level Five Leader responds to success and failure. When everything is going well, a Level Five Leader looks out the window to consider all the other people who contributed to the accomplishment. When things are going badly, that same leader looks in the mirror and takes full responsibility for it. A poor leader does this in reverse—taking credit for the good and blaming others for the bad.

If bosses are unable to create effective relationships with their direct reports, they won't encourage the employee passion and engagement required for a department, team, or business unit to succeed. Research by Marcus Buckingham and Curt Coffman (1999) in *First, Break All the Rules: What the World's Greatest Managers Do Differently* shows that one of the contributors to job satisfaction is the quality of the relationship between an employee and his or her manager.

Create a Motivating Environment for Your People

Managers produce better results when they create an environment where people are intrinsically motivated and see meaning in their work. Great leaders of today need to learn how to create the optimal environment for employees so they can motivate themselves individually and work together.

Meaningfulness requires a collective effort toward a goal that is bigger than something an individual puts forward. It requires an others focus, whereas happiness is something you can experience independent of the larger goal of doing something together and creating something better for a larger group of people. When you look at pursuit of meaning, that's where you're trying to create a culture where people feel that they are part of something bigger than just themselves.

Build on a Good Base

High potentials are those individuals who have the raw ingredients to be great leaders— usually the educational background, intelligence, charisma, or some other factor that makes them attractive candidates for leadership.

That's a great place to start, but it isn't enough to guarantee, or even predict with any amount of certainty, that those raw ingredients will translate into a successful leadership career.

A solid process for developing high potentials begins with a curriculum that examines the following points:

- How can your personality work for you in your career?
- How can you use this knowledge to hire and build a strong team?
- How can you chart your own career path by identifying where you are today and where you want to be long term?

Leadership development works best when it is structured as a series of events, conducted over time to let people learn new ideas, use the skills on the job, and then come back on a regular basis to interpret what is going on and integrate it into their approach.

Leadership Development as a Journey

In their book, *Great Leaders Grow*, Ken Blanchard and Mark Miller (2012) offer a formula using the acronym GROW that young leaders can use as a road map along the way:

- **G is for Gain knowledge.** Stay up-to-date on what is happening in your industry and within your profession. From an internal standpoint, make sure that you are learning more about yourself through behavioral, personality, and temperament assessments. Know yourself!

- **R stands for Reach out to others.** The idea of one person, toiling alone, to accomplish something of lasting importance is largely a myth. The best, most influential ideas come from a team of individuals working together toward a common goal. It's hard work, but it's worth it. As a leader, you need to develop the skills that bring people together.

- **O stands for Open your world.** The best leaders are constantly searching the perimeter, examining the boundaries of their knowledge. What can be learned from a neighboring industry? What can you learn from a customer or a supplier? What can you learn from something completely unrelated to what you do? Explore and open up the possibilities.

- **W stands for Walk toward wisdom.** Once you set your mind to making a change and continuing to grow, take your first step. If five frogs are sitting on a log and one decides to jump, how many frogs are left sitting on the log? It's still five until that one frog actually leaps.

Help your aspiring leaders take that leap.

About the Author

Scott Blanchard is principal and executive vice president of The Ken Blanchard Companies, the company co-founded by his father, bestselling business author Ken Blanchard. An accomplished author in his own right (co-author of *Leverage Your Best, Ditch the Rest* and *Leading at a Higher Level*), Scott represents the next generation of pioneering thought leadership on management issues. Scott's personal philosophy is based on what he sees as a fundamental shift that is occurring in the discipline of leadership—the movement away from a limited focus on individual goal attainment toward getting things done with, and through, others.

References

Blanchard, K., and M. Miller (2012). *Great Leaders Grow: Becoming a Leader for Life*. San Francisco: Berrett-Koehler.

Blanchard, S., and M. Homan. (2004). *Leverage Your Best, Ditch the Rest: The Coaching Secrets Top Executives Depend On*. New York: William Morrow.

Buckingham, M., and C. Coffman (1999). *First, Break All the Rules: What the World's Greatest Managers Do Differently*. New York: Simon & Schuster.

Collins, J. (2001). *Good to Great: Why Some Companies Make the Leap and Others Don't*. New York: HarperCollins Publishers.

Harden, J., and B. Dude. (2009). *What Makes You Tick & What Ticks You Off: How the Basic Elements of Temperament Will Lead You to a Happier Life*. Sarasota, FL: Snow In Sarasota Publishing.

Hill, L.A. (2007, January). Becoming the Boss. *Harvard Business Review*.

Homan Blanchard, M., and L. Miller. (2008). *Coaching in Organizations: Best Coaching Practices from The Ken Blanchard Companies*. Charleston, SC: CreateSpace Independent Publishing Platform.

Tichy, N., and E. Cohen. (1997). *The Leadership Engine: How Winning Companies Build Leaders at Every Level*. New York: HarperCollins Publishers.

Zigarmi, D., S. Blanchard, V. Essary, and D. Houson. (2005). *The Leadership-Profit Chain: Defining the Importance of Leadership Capacity*. San Diego, CA: The Ken Blanchard Companies.

For Further Reading

Blanchard, K., and M. Miller. (2012). *Great Leaders Grow: Becoming a Leader for Life*. San Francisco: Berrett-Koehler.

Blanchard, S., and M. Homan. (2004). *Leverage Your Best, Ditch the Rest: The Coaching Secrets Top Executives Depend On*. New York: William Morrow.

Harden, J., and B. Dude. (2009). *What Makes You Tick & What Ticks You Off: How the Basic Elements of Temperament Will Lead You to a Happier Life*. Sarasota, FL: Snow In Sarasota Publishing.

Section IX

Contemporary Challenges

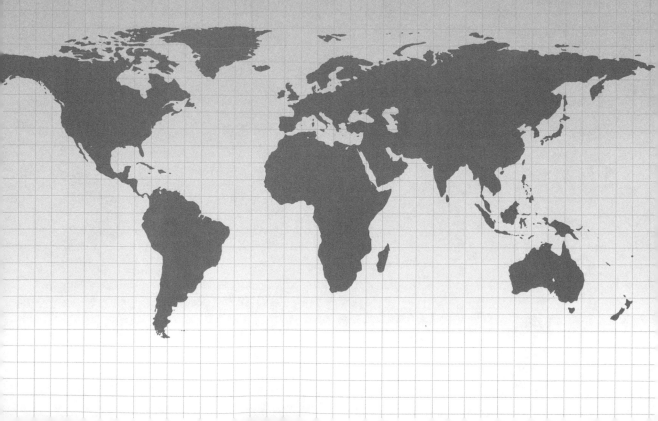

Section IX

Learning Challenges of the Future: Personalization and Control Shifts

Luminary Perspective

Elliott Masie

After 40 years in the learning field, I find myself facing a future where our content, processes, technology, and learner expectations are radically shifting. In a nutshell, the future of learning will focus on personalization and control.

These shifts are not originating from a cool new book by a consulting company, nor are they arising because of a new set of features in a learning management system. The move toward richer learning personalization and control shifts is coming from large-scale changes in how our workers experience, consume, and interact with media outside of work. Let's look at how Pat, a midlevel supervisor, has changed her consumption of media at home:

Pat and TV 20 years ago: She watched TV based on a network schedule. She watched on her TV in the living room or bedroom. She watched shows at the same time as her friends did, across town or across the country. She watched the whole show—without a fast-forward option. And, she could only control the TV process by turning it off or switching to the two dozen channels on her TV. Pat watched TV based on the equivalent of an instructional designer's best guess at what she needed or wanted.

Pat and TV today: She watches almost everything on demand. She watches on her laptop, her tablet, and sometimes even her mobile phone. When she watches on the big TV in the living room, she is often simultaneously using a second screen on her lap. She fast-forwards past the commercials and sometimes skips to the ending of a show. She can choose from more than 10,000 shows, live or on demand, and recently became a "marathon watcher," consuming all 13 episodes of *Orange Is the New Black* during a stay-at-home weekend. Pat personalizes her viewing, and she is in control.

The shift in media use is radically changing our (and our learners') expectations and assumptions. I grew up buying albums of songs, knowing that I might only love two or three on any given album, but they were packaged as 12 songs for many dollars. Today, I check out all the songs online, with free samples and ratings from others. Then, I purchase just one song for about 99 cents and can access that from the Cloud, listening to it on any device from anywhere. At home, we have rapidly come to expect media personalization and almost complete control of the what, how, when, duration, and even style of content that we consume.

When we go to the workplace, learning is nowhere near that level of personalization or control. Let's face it: The learning field has grown up creating resources that were hopefully "one size fits all" or at least "one size fits many." Then we offer remedial or coaching assistance to those who did not succeed with the mass offering.

As I taught instructional designers, the goal was for them to:

- access the expertise of several subject matter experts
- survey the needs of learners through needs assessment
- select content and activities that mapped to the desired learning outcome(s)
- narrow or widen the content to the correct "scope" given the objectives and background of learners and time allocated to the program
- select the correct "sequence" of content to guide the learner through a logical and orderly flow
- create an end-of-learning assessment or quiz to provide outcome results to both the learner and the organization.

It worked. And, it was supplemented by great teachers, coaches, managers, and peers who provided the personalization or cleared up confusion for a learner who was confused, frustrated, or not ready to perform after taking a course. Learning, particularly in the classroom, was congregational, with the assumption that we wanted people to have the same shared flow through the content. Even when webinars and e-learning were introduced, we still designed with the "one-size-fits-all" model in mind.

But, times are changing rapidly and radically. It starts with the assumption of control. Ask a group of learners about learning control, and this is what you might hear:

Learners: "Why do I have to learn content that I already know? Why do I have to learn content that I will not use for months (or ever)? Why do I have to learn content that I can easily look up on our intranet? Why do I have to wait until the class is scheduled to start learning the content? Why do I have to sit in a lecture and listen to content from slides if I can just watch it online at an ideal time and location? And, why do I have so little control over the duration, style, sequence, format, social collaboration, and more?"

The learner wants "one-size-fits-one" options! (I borrowed that phrase from Stu Crabb at Facebook.)

My old reaction would have been moderate: "I understand, but given budget, technology, compliance requirements, and corporate culture, we can't come close to this model. Sorry!"

My new reaction is radical: "Let's change the fundamental assumption of learning personalization and control with new processes for learners, designers, managers, and even compliance officers. Let's find a way to honor the learner's words with increased efficiency, evidence-based effectiveness, and perhaps decreased learning/training budgets."

To be even more blunt, we don't have a choice! Learners and their managers are already voting with their time, travel budgets, and preferences, driving the learning organization to make changes. Here are a few of the shifts that I am observing in the 230 member companies of our Learning CONSORTIUM:

- **Compression:** The duration of courses and digital learning activities is getting shorter. For example, five-day programs are shortened to three days. Three-day classes are shortened to one day. One-day programs become webinars. Webinars become shorter video clips.
- **Attendance shifts:** Only 40 to 45 percent of learners who register for webinars actually participate. Only 65 percent of those who start a webinar stay until the end. And, almost 85 percent of webinar attendees do at least one, and sometimes a few, other tasks during the webinar. We are watching overall attendance in many programs drop as alternative approaches become available.
- **Great content versus learning programs:** Many organizations now brand their best content as "TED Talks" and make them available on pages that are not

branded as "training." Instead, they are shifting away from a school model brand to one of knowledge on demand.

- **Test before teaching:** There is a rising desire to have learners take in-depth pretests before starting a class. In many instances, the learner already knows 70 percent of the content. Managers can then either exempt them from the program or allocate targeted learning experiences to close any gaps. Follow the game design model, where there are continuous assessment gates, and let the learner try, fail, and learn multiple times on the path to success.

Learning personalization is also going to be driven by changes in the world of advertising. I believe that there must be a picture of Elliott Masie somewhere on a wall at Amazon. Why? Because I get these perfect emails from them, suggesting a product that I need, don't have, and would want to order that minute. They must know Elliott! And, to their delight, I often press the purchase button—if the offer is based on data about Elliott and timed in a way that I find it helpful versus annoying. This use of big data and personalized data is driving a radical shift in how we experience advertising. It is also helping to establish a parallel expectation in the workplace.

Soon, many organizations will use the data that is now in learning management systems, in talent systems, in search requests from learners, in performance reviews, and more to provide a short, personalized "ad" that might trigger a learning behavior. For example:

- Matt has just received an assignment to travel to Atlanta for a meeting with a customer at Coca-Cola. His organization hopes to sell a new product to the soft drink company. The travel system knows that Matt has never been to Coca-Cola or gone to Atlanta on a business trip. The product management system knows that Matt has never sold the latest version of the product. And, Matt's manager has indicated that he is working on developing his ability to close deals. Imagine that Matt would receive some small "ads" from his company suggesting short videos, a PDF to read, and even a telephone call with a salesperson who used to work at Coca-Cola as part of his prep.

Amazon would do that in an instant; yet, most learning functions do not have the technology, perspectives, or permissions to drive this. Matt is not going to take three courses before this trip. But, Matt does need the learning resources that exist—outside the traditional box—to succeed in his pitch to Coca-Cola.

Ironically, the sales manager may understand this better than the learning manager. The sales manager is not interested in how much training Matt has, but does want to see him succeed, grow, and make the sale. And, the sales manager's preference will be for shorter, more targeted, more personalized, and more continuous resources for Matt.

One warning: I am not saying that Matt gets to control the entire process. In fact, I am suggesting a shift in control. Matt must be able to demonstrate readiness to do tasks and be held accountable for assessments—and clearly for performance. But, we want to empower and leverage Matt's behaviors to drive toward success. This is not about moving toward a great and widespread informal learning model. This is about providing targeted learning assets to Matt, monitoring his activities, and working together to make him competent.

To be honest, most of us in the learning field are already there when it comes to our own learning approaches. Most trainers, instructional designers, and learning managers I know rarely go as students to long-duration classes. We rarely take the full e-learning programs that we advocate and produce for others. And, we often ask, "Do you have anything shorter that I might take when I have time?" As learners, we get it and want increased personalization and control. As learning leaders, we sometimes ignore our own choices as we create strategies for others.

In order to get to increased learning personalization and control shifts, the learning function needs to make some key changes and competency gains:

- **Tired and lazy learning management system:** Many of our learning management systems (LMSs) are built for the "one-size-fits-all" model. We need to enhance, replace, or work around our LMS, which must become able to drive personalization and track learner control in a very different manner.
- **Big and small learning data:** We must embrace the ability to leverage big learning data to allow the learner to operate from small data (focused on one's history and needs). We must add analytics and usability data competencies to the repertoires of our designers and producers. And, we must experiment with split models of teaching the same content: compare the sales of learners who took the class versus the sales of learners who watched eight video clips.
- **Branding shifts:** It is time for us to think about branding that does not reflect the words of schools, which are rarely about personalization or learner control. NBCUniversal shifted its learning brand to TalentLab. Let's leverage brands from the changing media world. For example, leverage the iTunes brand and create

iLearn. A rating system for learning assets might leverage the Trip Advisor brand to create TipAdvisor.

- **Experiment as learners:** Please don't be chefs who won't eat their own dishes! We must include ourselves, as learning leaders, in the process as learners. Start experimenting as learners with new and divergent learning modes. Reflect on your experience as you enroll for a MOOC, take on a mentor in another part of the world who works with you for 15 minutes a week via Skype, or teach a class where the learners—rather than you as the instructor—are the sages on the stage.

- **Control shifts for line managers:** The other side of this shift in control is the increasing ability of line managers to assemble digital assets that can support learners, without working through or with learning departments. Accept the growing pattern of work groups driving the control, and build an open resource relationship to share best practices. Don't struggle over control. They will win!

Finally, don't focus on what learning invention is getting venture funding or might someday be a hot IPO in the market. True learning innovation is not going to be mapped to a single company or be bought from a booth at a learning trade show. Follow the learners' changing behaviors outside of work and find low-cost, simple ways to experiment with workplace learning.

The future is already here. Learning personalization and control shifts will be part of today and tomorrow's learning experience!

About the Author

Elliott Masie is the CEO of The MASIE Center and Chair of The Learning CONSORTIUM. Elliott has provided leadership, research, and convening for the learning field for more than 40 years. He is credited with helping to introduce the term and approaches for e-learning in the mid-1990s and provides a dynamic vendor-neutral approach to the changing learning field. His CONSORTIUM includes 230 global companies. He is the author of more than 12 books, including the recent title, *Big Learning Data*. Elliott believes in an evidence and lab approach to learning innovation. He is the host of the annual Learning Conference. Contact him via www.masie.com.

Chapter 51

Developing Leadership Around the Globe

Bill Wiggenhorn and Renie McClay

With Global Contributors

L eadership has been a topic of study, discussion, and practice for thousands of years. Cyrus the Great in 540 B.C. and Confucius in 470 B.C. were two early students of leadership who defined leadership in great detail. Both built on the premise that leaders develop trust, serve as role models, create an environment for their followers to perform, and operate at the highest level of integrity.

In this chapter, our contributing authors explore the challenges, opportunities, tools, and techniques for developing the leaders necessary to support the growth in their regions as well as to have their leaders lead in a globally integrated world.

To maintain authenticity of the authors' original submissions, spelling preferences have been maintained to reflect the region each author represents.

Today's world requires global leaders who have the ability to lead in stagnant, mature, and high-growth markets. Leaders are expected to foster environments that support innovation and quality at the same time; to be strategic and excellent at execution of strategy; to create an organizational environment that is exciting and collaborative; and to provide feedback to their team members so that the performance of the organization can continue to remain competitive.

Successful organizations are more diverse today than ever before in history, fostering myriad skill sets and high levels of knowledge. This requires the leader to be better prepared to face the challenges of the marketplace, government agencies, or the NGO/volunteer organizations. Various CEO surveys in the last several years have identified the need of future leaders to have digital skills, agile thinking, interpersonal and communication skills, global operations experience, and multilingual language capability.

Changes in technology, business models, and investor expectations are occurring at an ever-increasing pace, forcing leaders to be as aware of the external world as they are of their own organizations. Top of mind is the need for leaders who can foster collaboration, pursue organic growth, and globalize while localizing. It is this concept of recognizing the global requirements for leadership worldwide, while at the same time honoring the differences in regions around the world, that embodies the spirit of this chapter. Our contributors, whose experiences span the globe, offer suggestions for developing the leadership skills the world needs at this dynamic time in history.

In the pages that follow, our contributors offer suggestions for developing leaders in their respective regions: Africa; Australia; China; Europe; India; Korea, Japan, and Southeast Asia; Latin America; the Middle East; and North America. While reading the various authors' perspectives, you will be amazed at the many similarities of leadership development needs around the world. Read each entry carefully, however, and you will also be intrigued by the nuances and differences—no matter where you are located as your read this *Handbook*. The contributors explore the challenges, opportunities, tools, and techniques they are using to develop leaders who will succeed both in their regions and around the globe. All of these can assist you in your own development and the development of others as leaders. The global voices in this chapter describe how leaders must foster environments that support innovation and quality so that their organizations remain competitive. At the same time, they report that leaders must embrace strategy and create organizational cultures that are exciting, collaborative, and interactive.

Read on, learn on, and travel your world with my mentor, Bob Galvin's, advice: "Take two suitcases with you . . . one filled with knowledge to share and one empty to fill with what you will learn from others." My suitcase bulges with what I have learned from others. I wish the same for all of you as we continue our journeys.

The Perspective From Africa

Africa is the second largest continent in the world, comprising 53 countries, with a few disputed areas. Population exceeds 1 billion people. The largest desert in Africa, the Sahara, spans 3.5 million square miles. Nigeria is the most populated country in Africa, with a population of more than 140 million, whereas Cairo in Egypt is the most populated city. Africa has more than 3,000 ethnic groups, and more than 200 languages are spoken. In 2010, one of the most successful FIFA soccer World Cups ever was held in South Africa, with a cumulative TV audience of 30 billion and more than 4 million spectators.

Leadership Development

Interaction fundamentals remain the most basic and fundamental challenges of effective solutions across the African continent. Interaction here means the ubuntu concept where people communicate and collaborate at all levels. Even the old tribal kings used to get their tribes together and listen to input from the most junior participants before making decisions. The emerging economies in Africa are gradually building globally savvy executives who need to move from transactional leadership to transformational leadership but without forgoing the concept of servant leadership, which, like ubuntu (the concept of fellowship, loosely translated as "you are who you are through other people"), is an integral part of the cultural system.

The war for talent in African countries is fierce, especially at the senior executive level, where the name of the game is finding individuals with leadership potential. In countries like South Africa, one of the more progressive economies in Africa, much emphasis is placed on Affirmative Action programmes (Broad-Based Economic Empowerment) due to past inequalities. This has developed strong and economically powerful upper-class black executive millionaires.

Education and Unemployment

Two of the biggest challenges facing countries in Africa, due to lack of facilities and distance issues, are the lack of education for all and the poverty issue. According to recent UNESCO statistics, 29.8 million children in Sub-Saharan Africa did not attend school in 2011 (one in every three children). In contrast, 40,000 laptops were issued to 375 primary schools in

Ghana in 2013. Some schools in South Africa have done away with textbooks, and teaching is done digitally via tablets.

Mobile learning is flourishing in many parts in Africa, and local e-learning developers are increasingly focused on apps as the most effective way to deliver learning content. E-learning and mobile is an excellent solution for the African market because of its cost-effectiveness, flexibility, and accessibility.

African Cultural Value Systems

It is clear from studies by E.S. Van Zyl, Khosa, Shonhiwa, and Van Rensburg that the effective cross-cultural manager should have an in-depth understanding of the African cultural value system, which also determines the behavior of manager versus subordinate.

Here is a summary of the value system:

- Africans prefer spiritual collectivism to individualism. Spiritual guidance is expected and respected.
- There is an inclination toward consensus in problem solving, rather than dissention.
- Humility and helpfulness are expected instead of wanton criticism that describes the ubuntu philosophy (servant leadership principles feature strongly).
- There is an inherent trust and belief in fairness of those in leadership, hence a lack of criticism.
- African moral standards are based on ancestral precedents, and thus history plays a prominent role in guiding future conduct.
- Society is a structure in which an inclusive system of hierarchy plays an important role. This inspires orderliness and acceptance of authority.
- Perpetual optimism and a belief in superior forces underlie the African sense of being and attitude towards life. This explains why young people can become guerrilla fighters by having fanatical allegiance instilled in them.
- There is a tactical expectation that those who are in a superior position will display sound leadership and to not disappoint their subordinates. They expect leaders to exhibit sound ethics, fairness, transparency, and accountability.

Unfortunately, many fail to uphold these values, and we often find that those, especially in high governmental positions, enjoy the luxuries and exorbitant fringe benefits.

Training and Development Challenges

In many countries in Africa, corruption was accepted as part of everyday life. There is a strong move to introduce legal consequences for corruption. Nepotism in business has seriously damaged the ethics of organisations.

Governance in business institutions is gaining more prominence, and countries like South Africa have produced the King report; Ghana, a manual for corporate governance; and Zimbabwe, principles of corporate governance. Research conducted by Shonhiwa in 11 countries across Sub-Saharan Africa revealed how African managers can lead to achieve success:

- Have respect for seniors and elders.
- Ensure consultation on all issues.
- Exercise patience backed by cultural knowledge.
- Have compassion and respect the ubuntu principles.
- Community takes precedence over personal wishes.
- Nurture a sense of objectivity and equality.
- Be generous and helpful.
- Use a people-oriented approach to problems.
- Be eager to learn new things.
- Be decisive and assertive.
- Show a desire for justice.
- Recognise diversity.
- Maintain accountability.

There is a chronic shortage of well-qualified and trained managers. Many have come up the ranks using home-bred management styles and often progress through political appointments and will soon be challenged by a better educated younger generation. Many first-world theories and management practices are widely adopted but need to be fine-tuned to fit the local cultural climate.

Summary

The African style of leadership is often epitomised by the dichotomy between leading through the espoused capitalistic business ideals and leading through the real socio-economic constraints in which organisations must operate. Therefore, learning needs to address both the modern qualities and the practical competencies of leadership. We often find that great westernised theories and practices are advocated, and leaders are open to new learning opportunities, but when it comes to practical application, we often miss the boat.

Africa is hungry for transformation and innovation, and with the next highest population growth imminent, the opportunities for progress can only outstrip the rest of the world—but it needs to overcome the challenges of education, poverty, and job creation.

The Perspective From Australia

Enterprising Nation (1995), the first Australian government–commissioned national report on the status of leadership in Australia in relation to the preparedness of Australian managers to meet the challenges of the Asia-Pacific century, identified two key indicators of best practice:

- ability to be at ease working outside Western parameters (and by implication became proficient in an Asian language)
- ability to work in highly ambiguous and uncertain environments.

These themes have, over the past 20 years, informed leadership development in Australia, providing leaders with the framework for action in an increasingly chaotic business, economic, and social environment.

Unique Leadership Practice

Alongside *Enterprising Nation*, a series of cultural archetype studies identified that the Australian culture, influenced by democratic and highly egalitarian norms, did not relate effective leadership to hierarchical position, but rather that effective leaders "lead" their teams while also being team players. This work led to the formation of the Captain/Coach Model of leadership—a unique Australian addition to leadership practice.

As with most developed economies, responsibility for leadership development has become divided between organization-specific leadership models and internal cultural change programs on one hand, and the preferred leadership models and customised interventions of business schools on the other.

Within their organizations, leaders need to build personal presence and emotional intelligence, develop individuals, engage their teams and their organizations through a clear sense of purpose, and open up opportunities for creativity and innovation.

Strategically and globally, leaders need to apply systems and integral thinking to understanding global trends and the effect they have, as well as the entrepreneurial opportunities that arise as a result of these trends.

Challenge

One of the key challenges in Australia is how to contextualize the twin themes of virtualization and multiculturalism for businesses. The next generation of leaders is actually more comfortable learning and communicating through social media than face-to-face and more likely to have different cultural expectations in regard to leadership.

Leadership development has also focused on reflection and self-awareness: the leaders' deep understanding of themselves and of the ways their drivers, choices, and blind spots shape their thinking.

Once a theory-driven discipline, leadership development is now a field that involves both accessing the best research available and applying it in the work environment. In this context, leaders in Australia need a clear line of sight between the theory and the practice of the craft of leadership. In addition to stretch projects, development practices increasingly recognise a need to include job rotation opportunities, scenarios, mentoring, and coaching. Other helpful development practices are secondments (temporary transfers to another job in the same company) and the opportunity to work in other sectors such as the government and not-for-profit arenas.

Summary

The key success factors for Australian leaders are the ability to execute effectively in the short term while concurrently finding a way forward through the multiple realities that surround them.

Above and beyond what we already know, the growing focus on intergenerational equity positions leadership development at the core of our ultimate responsibility to ensure future generations will be able to achieve their potential.

The Perspective From China

Leadership development is in the early stages in China. The Chinese government implemented a socialist market economy, and firms gradually became independent players in the market in 1992. At that point, leadership development became important. China's most prestigious business school, Tsinghua SEM (School of Economy and Management), and eight other business schools launched the first MBA program in 1991. Tsinghua SEM delivered the first leadership course for MBA students in 1999 and the first leadership development program for executive education in 2003.

Recent Changes

Changes in leadership needs are occurring rapidly. In more recent years, with increased competition and globalization, leadership development became a crucial piece for managers and leaders in China. More and more companies established a leadership competency model. Building a leadership pipeline is becoming more common. Many of the big companies have established corporate universities.

The global expansion has created the need for improved cultural self-awareness in leaders. They need to be able to get results through developing relationships. They need knowledge of global business drivers and to be effective in a diverse environment. They need to have core values and to demonstrate flexibility as they influence across boundaries.

The top three factors for successful leadership in China are being broad minded, forward looking, and competent in the role. When comparing China to North America, the two unique characteristics for China are being broad minded and ambitious. Also, although honesty heads the list for North American respect, it is number six in China. Table 51-1 shows a comparison of respected leadership qualities between China and North America. These differences require understanding of how to best develop leaders.

Table 51-1. Characteristics of an Admired Leader

	North America	China
1	Honest	*Broad minded*
2	Forward looking	Forward looking
3	Competent	Competent
4	Inspiring	Fair minded
5	Intelligent	*Ambitious*
6	Fair minded	Honest
7	Broad minded	Inspiring

Source: Kouzes & Posner LPI workshop in China, based on approximately 1,000 questionnaires.

Top Organizational Leadership Needs

China's companies have numerous requirements to be successful. Organizations need to learn how to increase employee engagement, build a leadership pipeline, define and integrate a competency model, provide training and coaching on skills, and integrate talent management with business strategy. When developing leaders, they need to leverage specific Chinese best practices and use case studies.

Challenges

Leadership development practice is highly situational; senior executives must change the value and mindset of the business first. This includes spending more time on leadership development, having enough patience to allow for change and learning, using appropriate assessment tools and training programs, and developing coaching skills.

Changing the leaders' values and mindset is the biggest challenge. Leaders are very busy and don't want to spend time developing their people. There is often a lack of patience because change needs time.

Women in leadership roles is a new phenomenon in China. About 60 years ago, Chairman Mao Zedong said that women hold up half the sky. From that point, women have been given an increasingly important role in work and life. About 30 percent of managers are women in business and government. Leadership development for women has become more and more important in China.

Summary

For organizations to make progress, first leaders at all levels must understand the organization's challenges and have an urgent need to improve their leadership. Second, top leaders must engage in leadership development practices and align these practices with business strategy. Third, organizations must establish a model and tools they can use to create leadership development programs. Fourth, scholars and experts should develop more effective leadership development practices and best practice cases for Chinese leaders at all levels.

The Perspective From Europe

Leadership development in Europe is as heterogeneous as Europe itself. Based on differences in cultural values, leadership is like shoes—no one size fits all. The cultural differences in Europe have brought forward various styles of leadership and different expectations (Brodbeck, 2000) that people have of leaders. Similarly, companies create different leadership competency models that are aligned with their unique strategies. However, a few common denominators are emerging due to the volatile, uncertain, complex, and ambiguous business environment that all of Europe faces: Leaders are more and more demanded to show high adaptability, are comfortable with being uncomfortable and can lead through uncertainty (Johansen and Ryan, 2012), and are able to span boundaries across departments, geographies, cultures, organizational levels, and stakeholder groups, so that implementation processes are accelerated (Ernst and Chrobot-Mason, 2010).

The positioning of leadership development (LD) also varies strongly from country to country. The examples of the UK, Germany, and France showcase the variety of approaches, challenges, and methods needed for LD in this complex region.

Country Challenges

The most sophisticated region for LD in Europe is Great Britain, where focus on worker welfare since 1850 led to a long tradition of industrial psychology, which has morphed to comprise organisational psychology and organisational science. The Chartered Institute for Personnel and Development (CIPD), with more than 130,000 members, provides standards and guidelines in all areas of talent management. CIPD chartership is practically required for any HR professional in the UK. The economic crisis has slashed spending in the UK on individual development that cannot articulate direct strategic necessity for the company. Many companies ask themselves rigorously what kind of leadership they need in order to execute their strategies. More and more, leadership development initiatives are linked with business strategy and organisational change.

Germany, Austria, and German-speaking Switzerland have a different tradition, in that the dominant source of leadership lies in leaders' technical expertise. Only slowly, companies are realizing that operational excellence alone will not provide enough of a global competitive advantage for them. Thus, they focus more on excellence in people. Investments in LD, however, are still often individual focused and competency based, even mechanistic, with little spillover into collaborative team working and team building. While academic models are welcome as an intellectual challenge, any good LD initiative in Germany is highly tangible and grounded in workplace reality.

In France, a country that still prides itself on its egalitarian value system, LD used to be the privilege of a privileged group: Many company leaders have been groomed through an elite system of universities dedicated to developing national leaders. This has led to a somewhat paradoxical approach to leadership that contains extremely hierarchical and highly collaborative elements. Effective LD initiatives usually show strong interactive and team-focused features and few formal assessments, and are aligned with company values as much as with their strategy.

So even though leadership development in Western Europe is highly diverse and based on different traditions, it relies on relatively sophisticated talent management processes. In other parts of Europe, particularly Eastern Europe, the labour market dynamics require a different approach. Young talent is more often focused on vertical career advancement; thus, their organisational tenure is relatively short. We see high potentials often reaching senior positions at a relatively young age, with relatively little work and life experience to draw on. Leadership development is still a relatively young area, often focusing on specific skill development or networking rather than holistic person development. Being sent to leadership training is seen as much as a reward and recognition for good work as it is seen as a development opportunity; thus, learner engagement can vary tremendously and is sometimes challenging to maintain.

An important common challenge for leadership development across Europe is demographics. In most parts of Europe, population is aging, which results in huge societal challenges: public pension schemes risk collapsing, costs for healthcare and social care are increasing, and economic competitiveness is weakened. One important lever to counteract this development is the wider inclusion of diverse populations in the labour market, particularly in high-value positions. Women are a promising population for this endeavour as they are often underemployed compared to men and underchallenged compared to their education and talents. Thus, many countries are considering and implementing quota systems to increase the number of women leaders in business and the public sector. The EU itself is even considering a gender quota. Scandinavia, particularly Norway, is leading the list for women in senior management positions and is an example to many other countries. Initiatives for women leadership within companies are on the rise as well, ranging from cross-mentoring schemes to network-based development and women leadership programs. However, these will only be successful if they are accompanied by organisational culture change towards more inclusiveness, flexibility, and work-life balance, and if they are embedded in changing values on a societal level towards more gender egalitarianism.

Summary

Maximising learning for such a diversity of audiences is tricky—particularly as many organisations are not monocultural anymore. Finding a common language for development in itself is a first hurdle. Particularly for highly emotional and personal development methods, such as coaching, delivery in participants' native language is essential. An ever higher degree of interdependence and connectedness among Europeans, however, provides the opportunity to develop aligned approaches to common problems, such as shortage of engineering talent, development of women leaders, and harnessing the benefits of a diverse workforce.

The Perspective From India

While there are many similarities to growing leaders elsewhere, Indian leaders often have different areas of need. Until 25 years ago, India was a socialist country where individual initiative and productivity were not valued. The demands of the growing economy have changed, but the education system and social institution are tragically out of date. The challenge for Indian leaders is to perform to global standards while working within the constraints of the local context. The success of leaders in India rests in their ability to ethically shape change by aligning culture, skills, and resources.

Context

Unique to India is its diversity—arguably the most diverse country in the world. Larval leaders grow up in an extremely diverse setting where friends and neighbours are from different religions, castes, and in some cases socio-economic backgrounds. In this area, India offers lessons to the rest of the world's leaders about tolerance and peaceful co-existence.

Indians constantly cope with the reality of the tsunami of corruption and unethical behaviour that batters Indians on a minute-by-minute basis. In this area, Indian leaders need to learn deeper levels of moral reasoning about the long-term role of leadership needed to courageously combat nearly every government employee, including the police, who are chronically corrupt. Practitioners who wish to participate in making a big difference in India need to learn greater levels of patience, thrift, and resilience in a country where processes and products rarely work as promised, including those required to develop leaders.

What to Grow

Indians are great at bouncing back and adapting in the face of change. On a daily basis, they will have malfunctioning power, water buffalo interfering with their commute, and corrupt police. This doesn't dishearten them. But it does discourage any form of planning. The mindset is that if nothing will work out as you plan, then why bother? This is a helpful mindset in the early-stage start-up forms of entrepreneurial leadership, but a liability as the firm grows and requires systematic processes and repeatable sources of competitive advantage. On average, Indian leaders are less proficient with medium- and long-term strategic planning, perhaps because they are so overpracticed with short-term tactical change management.

India is also an extremely competitive place. Children study hard to get into a good school, with a tiny fraction of seats, so that it is possible to get a good job and a good arranged marriage. Only the best of the best can actually get a good education outside the country or a coveted expat assignment. At all levels, but especially at the board level, leadership is about teamwork, both leading and following. Such individual competitiveness can undermine relationships with others with whom one must work to realize shared goals and subordinate personal preferences for the greater good. These are not skills and values that are fully developed in some Indian leaders.

Key areas to develop in Indian leaders:

- Strategic thinking: inventing approaches that are hard for global competitors to copy
- Innovation: new solutions to wicked problems
- Self- and team leadership: finding, growing, and leveraging a team that is better than them in one or more areas relevant to the business strategy
- Market value: quality and cost rather than just a "cheap and best" mentality
- Moral compass and a leader's role in the team, business, and society.

Whom to Grow

India is a young and crowded country with economic growth and abundant entrepreneurial enthusiasm. Young leaders compete fiercely for jobs and promotions. Larval leaders grow up in an environment where they have to fight and claw to get ahead, and those who make it into an organization are extremely ambitious. There is a high focus on gaining advanced but often meaningless degrees but not enough focus on what people can actually do at the end of their education. Often they don't have well-developed notions of who they are, what they want to stand for, or the importance of moral and ethical values in leadership. There are also many social pressures that hurt women's leadership development, including social expectations about staying home with the children, as well as overt sexism and less overt cast/culture-ism about who is acceptable to consider for promotion. Key themes include:

- median age of 25
- young leaders often placed in leadership roles before they are ready because of the growth of the country and highly ambitious leaders
- growing recognition for more support for women, people with disabilities, and ethnic groups.

How to Grow

Just as is true elsewhere, Indian leaders need a portfolio of investments to grow. Their ability to systematically secure experiential assignments, jobs, or projects that stretch them is important. Given the corruption, and difficulty in thinking for the long term, Indians can especially benefit from mentoring from senior leaders in their industry and coaching from specialists, particularly industrial/organizational psychologists.

Also, given the need to build relationships, Indian leaders can especially benefit from systematic training in the science of persuasion, as taught by Robert Cialdini, the world's foremost expert. Key takeaways include:

- Role modeling: Development needs to move from classroom training to having exposure to great leaders.
- Organizational practices: Create a culture with clear expectations on the desired behaviors and actively extinguish behaviors that are misaligned. This is harder in the Indian context because of greater tolerance and cultural norms of not giving negative feedback.
- Redundancy: In an economy with plenty of opportunities and scarce talent, turnover at all levels tends to be high.

The Perspective From Korea, Japan, and Southeast Asia

Many corporations of all sizes are searching for the best ways to develop their leaders. Some companies have senior leaders who are able to articulate their key business challenges and developmental needs. Some have consultants (internal or external) who are able to design and develop interventions to produce the expected business and behavioral results. For a few of them, leadership development is sending them to listen to talks given by "celebrity" leaders and academicians. Most companies adopt the strategy of "the more courses I send you to, the better leader you will become."

Common Cultural Trait

In many regions and countries in Asia, one cultural trait influences the way managers lead their organizations. Paternalism is ingrained in the culture. This cultural trait cuts across ethnic groups, be they Chinese, Koreans, Japanese, Malays, or Thais. Some believe that it has its roots in Confucianism, but the Malays, Indonesians, and Thais have a similar influencing trait. Paternalism leads to a paternalistic leadership style.

Being a manager in a paternalistic environment has its advantage. Direct challenges to leadership decisions are rare. This doesn't mean that there is agreement among their people. They just don't challenge it openly and directly. This is also exemplified even in a democratic environment. Frequently, incumbent presidents and deputy presidents of political parties are returned unopposed. In meetings, the "boss" dominates the "airtime" while others nod their heads in apparent agreement. Subordinates shy away from making decisions and, in a sense, "delegate" it up to the leader or manager. Leaders, in some cases, begin to think and believe that they are the only ones who are capable of making decisions.

Additionally, the leader or manager rarely gets ideas from the team. Depending on the trust they have in their leaders, ideas may be cautiously provided. So, if the leader is effective, there is progress.

Challenges to Address Paternalistic Leadership

Breaking this paternalistic system is difficult. Trust is critical to reverse the situation. Additionally, they need to find different ways to seek information and put the owners of finding solutions back to their subordinates. The leaders need to be skillful in communication such that it does not appear that they have abdicated their roles. Finding a good coach will help the manager make the required changes. However, it will be even better if the coaching is integrated with the leadership developmental system.

Many good models of leadership development are available. The combination of education (learning a new concept), action learning (applying the concept), and coaching (guiding the application of concept) is a powerful model. The concepts must originate from the strategies and expectations of the senior leadership. This developmental model works in all regions and countries.

Paternalistic leadership styles are common across Southeast Asia, Greater China, Korea, and Japan. While it can be addressed and modified, it is tremendously difficult. This cultural trait is ingrained not only in the work but also in the home. The juniors and subordinates constantly "reinforce" this style with agreement. This change requires a strong commitment and positive behavioral modeling from senior leaders. Training must cascade down from the most senior. The education and action learning projects provide a framework for the managers to test out their modified behaviors. Consequences must also be in place for those who can't and those who will not want to. It has to be a systematic and holistic change system.

Japan's Leadership Landscape

According to a research report by the Japan Management Association, "Corporate Management Issues 2013," there are three focus areas of leadership development in Japanese companies:

- leading change and innovation
- global leadership development for Japanese expat and local management
- middle manager and next-generation leader development.

Popular leadership development programs include:

- MBA type of leadership development course combined with the action learning over a period of several months
- new business development workshops as an innovation leader development course
- cross-industry (company) exchange program

- the overseas experiential training in emerging countries such as in the Philippines, Vietnam, and India for several weeks
- leadership courses for women managers that target only women.

The employment system of Japan is a problem that is affecting leadership development. For many companies in Japan, there is a distortion of the population pyramid. There was the mass employment in the late 1980s and early 1990s. Following that, the recession caused the decline of employment of the younger generation. The mass employed population, now in their mid-40s, are the current middle managers. Due to the traditional seniority system, there are many middle managers without subordinates. Many of them lack leadership and management skills. This is affecting the execution of the next generation of leadership development.

The top three capabilities required for the leadership are to be able to:

- demonstrate the ability to initiate organizational change and build an environment to lead innovation
- promote the advantage of the organizational diversity that goes beyond gender, generations, and the country
- communicate the company vision and mission clearly across the organization, and show the specific strategies for the realization of the vision.

Both senior management and human resources departments are aware of the importance of the next-generation leadership development. However, some companies are not able to actively implement a selective leadership development program for the younger generation. It is said that the side-by-side consciousness of the seniority system (or lock-step mentality) is causing a sense of resistance to the selection of the younger generation for leadership development. Some leaders and HR professionals are concerned that selecting only a small percentage of people for leadership development is unfair and will demotivate the other people who were not selected.

Leadership development programs are being seen as "personal development." They are not seen as a talent management strategy or as an "organizational strategy." As a result, the practice of leadership and independent personal capacity has become a major issue.

Summary

Systematic and holistic changes need to occur throughout the region. Paternalistic leadership must be addressed and discussed. Implementing special global leadership training courses and selection of young leaders for the future must also be addressed.

The Perspective From Latin America

Think of leadership development as the Latin America leadership rainbow. A successful leadership development program in Bogotá and Medellin may be an utter failure in Venezuela. We often say that even though the leadership colors might seem similar in our region, they are different—very different. We cannot train all in the same way. Even when using accepted educational principles, the latest research, and the best practical cases, those working in Latin America must be sure to complete their "cultural due diligence" prior to designing and facilitating content

Assuming that all Latin American leaders are the same, even in the case of Colombia and Venezuela, countries with similar national cultures and extremely identical historical backgrounds, can jeopardize the success of any human capital development initiative.

Generalizations are irresponsible when they are made using wrong assumptions. The designers and facilitator can use some traits and characteristics that could be transversally found in Latin leaders, but they need to be fully aware that those "common" qualities can be completely absent when they move from one country to another, and even more when they move from one company to another.

Leadership Development Guidelines for Latin America

In order to provide some useful information that a designer or a facilitator can use in order to effectively and successfully train, coach, and do business with Latin leaders, we combined our experience with scientific literature and the result of interviews to c-level executives about the profile and best practices in nurturing a new breed of leaders in the region. Some guidelines emerged:

1. Vertical and horizontal. Latin leaders come with a history of hierarchical mandates where the leaders lead their people in a vertical way, imposing ideas and giving orders that need to be followed as they are said. This leadership modality has been transformed in the past 15 years thanks to a new generation of leaders educated mainly in American, European, and Latin American top business schools, changing it toward a more horizontal democratic and situational leadership modality in

which the leaders co-create the vision through collaboration, allowing more room for a shared effort in leading and managing the human teams.

2. Affiliation and education. Relations are as valued as preparation. Latin leaders increase their effectiveness thanks to a strong human relations capital both internally and externally. The perception of belonging and being part of a greater collectiveness is radically important among Latin American leaders.

3. Process and product. Business results can be the main focus of top-level leaders but the intentions, desires, and emotional commitment of team members despite the final outcomes can be positively taken into account when judging performance. Here, a balance between the goal and the way to reach it is the key to successfully develop better leaders.

4. Here and there. National or regional subcultures might take the cultural quotient of your leadership development program back to zero. Assuming a Peruvian leader gives the same importance to the financial, commercial, operational, and human aspect of business as a Bolivian leader just because they look alike and have a common ethnic and historical background is like saying that Texans and Californians are the same because they are both from the United States and are close to the Mexican border. A proper due diligence to identify hidden different and similar cultural attributes needs to be done before designing and delivering any leadership training across cultures.

5. Your and ours. Local leaders might be as respected as international leaders. Latin senior executives, even though they might respect and appreciate the achievements of business, political, and scientific leaders from the United States and other developed countries, feel very proud of their own national and local leaders. Including real cases of top successful Latin leaders both in the content and the activities is a smart decision that can lead you to the success of your learning initiative.

Summary

The combination of the right knowledge, attitudes, and skills build better leaders no matter their culture. Studying, respecting, and including the different colors and tonalities of the ideal model of Latin American leaders of the company or public office for which you are going to be designing and training will ensure that your program will address the specific strategic or tactical need you seek to cover with the training initiative, making you a master of the Latin American leadership rainbow.

The Perspective From the Middle East

With the current challenging growth and structural changes taking place in many major Middle Eastern corporations today, the search for leadership talent is ever growing and represents a key component in these organizations' strategic plans.

Companies in the Middle East have recognized effective leadership as a key success factor because it is leadership that plays a pivotal role in achieving their short- and long-term business goals. Accordingly, one finds an increasing number of publications and formal initiatives that attempt to explain the complexities (cultural and behavioural) of leadership in Middle East companies based on a variety of approaches. Examples include the Aspen Institute's Middle East Leadership Institute; INSEAD's research into Women-Focused Leadership Development in the Middle East; and the recent publication of *Leadership Development in the Middle East* (Beverly Metcalfe and Fouad Mimouni, editors), one of the first publications to draw upon both Arabic and English scholarship on the subject.

Complexities of Leadership in Middle East Companies

While leadership is a complex process with multiple dimensions that can be looked upon from different perspectives, it becomes even more complex in multinational and global companies in the Middle East, depending on their size and cultural diversity, as well as the traits or characteristics of their employees and leaders.

Similarities Throughout the World

In the Middle East, those who can competently coach, influence others, inspire trust, and model open communication are more likely to be considered successful in their leadership positions by those they lead as well as those to whom they report in their organizations. These key characteristics, competencies, and principles are as valued in the Middle East as they are throughout the world.

Accordingly, from the perspective of many major Middle Eastern organizations, the five top challenges to leadership success include:

- the inability to create and communicate a vision for the future
- reluctance to challenge existing circumstances that could lead to improvements and innovation
- inability to empower others
- failing to be a role model,
- inability to motivate and inspire others.

In fact, recent corporate-sponsored research into leadership derailment factors link closely to not meeting or addressing one or more of these challenges head-on.

In many companies in the Middle East, leadership development programs and processes for women and men are for the most part the same. However, there are situations where some leadership programs are tailored to a specific role depending on the role itself and the gender composition of the team being led.

To meet the regions' leadership challenges, many medium to large organizations in the Middle East are investing heavily in leadership development and capacity building. It is now, and more than ever, that leadership development is considered a major initiative in the strategic plans of successful organizations. And more targeted leadership development is being provided to those in need of a variety of skills such as communication, decision making, interpersonal relationship building, problem solving, and planning skills. As a result, it has become increasingly common to see both in-house and external leadership development programs in medium to large organizations. Such programs and processes are being managed to be culturally relevant, timely, and take into account a diverse audience in order to ensure the growth and sustainability of large populations of participants.

Summary

Historically, several key process components have been identified to ensure regional leadership development programs remain relevant and sustainable in the Middle East. They include:

- having guiding principles for the program based on the program's goals and expected outcomes
- building the program's foundation incorporating a defining (learning) philosophy with a conceptual framework and strategy
- determining the competencies that need to be developed
- incorporating diagnostic tools for program participants to identify which competencies need to be developed
- ensuring all participants have an individual plan for learning and development.

The Perspective From North America

Today, social networks are filled with definitions of leadership, references to both good and bad leaders, and assessment tools to help individuals identify their strengths and gaps as leaders. With all these resources, there is still no one right model or no one right approach to leadership development.

Many Leadership Development Approaches Work

Many approaches work. The key is to develop the one approach that works for your company. This does not mean that everything is unique to the organization or the culture. For example, all organizations define the specific leadership competencies and behaviors their executive teams endorse to support their organizational cultures and implementation of their strategies.

One company uses a three-category definition to explain the role of the leader:

1. Leading others: Leaders who lead individual contributors.
2. Leading managers: Leaders who lead other leaders or who lead a global function.
3. Leading a business: Vice presidents or directors who report to the CEO.

In each category, the competencies become broader and more complex, but they also retain consistency across, such as being a role model for the company's core values and demonstrating integrity.

A second company defines the seven talents of a leader: relate to others, energize, continue to develop yourself, coach others, communicate clearly, deliver on time and in style, and innovate.

Both of these companies and dozens of others we work with built robust leadership models to inspire and grow their leadership benches. Multiple generations of institutional leaders are held accountable for performing against the standards of the defined competencies and behaviors of their individual companies. The company size is irrelevant when it comes to needing a model that guides leadership development.

Develop a Leadership Development Model

Several elements are required to ensure a successful leadership model. Most organizations consider some of these to shape their leadership development and the strategy: engage their leaders in the development; determine the competencies required in the future; define a leadership development philosophy; ensure that leadership development integrates with other corporate systems; incorporate development plans and feedback; create a selection process; and link the value of leadership development to the organization's bottom line.

Even with excellent leadership models in place, many challenges face U.S. organizations.

Leadership Challenges in the United States

In the United States, we face similar problems to other organizations around the world. Many organizations in the United States acknowledge that they face a shortage of leaders prepared for the future. Some of the current challenges facing the multiple generations of leaders in the United States include the need to:

- lead remote global teams
- use technology as a communication and feedback tool
- influence outcomes without direct control or authority
- overcome biases
- effectively lead a workforce that is a blend of older and younger associates
- select and groom the next generation of gender and culturally diverse leaders
- interface with both external and internal customers
- recognize that leadership is perishable and must be continuously nourished
- push individuals and organizations into thinking and acting outside established or familiar patterns of learning in both what they learn and how they learn.

Summary

Like many countries, we face challenges in developing leaders. We continue to use our ingenuity to uncover new approaches and answers to leadership development. One of those is to design effective and efficient methods to develop all employees. Several tools are available to download on the *Handbook's* website at www.astdhandbook.org. One of them is a list of self-development tools and techniques that you can incorporate into your leadership development program or use to develop your own leadership competencies.

Call to Action

This chapter is a nod to the concept of "saving time in a bottle." During the 40+ years we have dedicated to designing and refining leadership programs, we know that thousands of you have been following the same dream. We have attempted to shape and refocus leadership studies to inspire and define the most critical leadership elements for leaders in every corner of the world.

It is humbling to reflect on how long leadership has been a topic of study, discussion, and practice. It is neither a new art nor a breakthrough science. As we stated at the start of this chapter, the very basic tenets of leadership that we believe in today were carved out by Cyrus the Great and Confucius. These two early thinkers defined leadership in great detail, based on the premise that leaders must develop trust, serve as role models, and create an environment in which their followers are inspired to perform and operate at the highest level of integrity.

Information abounds. Research papers are published daily defining the leader of today and describing the need for transactional, results-oriented leaders who are also transformational leaders, capable of creating and building collaborative organizations. The continuing challenge for all of us is to use that information to develop moral leaders who respect the wisdom of the past and uncover the issues of the future.

Although there are many differences around the world, there are also many commonalities. Leading multiple generations and multiple cultures, leveraging changing technology, and navigating challenging business landscapes all contribute to the need for dynamic and skilled leadership in companies all over the world. We hope this chapter leaves you with more to ponder about leadership and to recognize that there is no one right way, though there are several underlying principles that are valued the world over: those of trust, integrity, and inspiration.

We appreciate the two whitepapers researched and written by associates of the Center for Creative Leadership (CCL), titled *The Challenges Leaders Face Around the World: More Similar Than Different* and *Crafting Your Career: Cultural Variations in Career-Relevant Relationships*. Both will help you to understand and address developing leadership around the globe. You will find these resources on the *Handbook's* website at www.astdhandbook.org.

About the Authors

A. William (Bill) Wiggenhorn is a principal of Main Captiva, LLC. Bill is responsible for custom-designed executive development strategy, systems, and programs, as well as talent management strategies and systems. He is an acknowledged expert in the fields of training and development, executive and leadership development, e-learning, marketing, and business strategy, working with clients in 60 countries. He was a senior learning and development executive at Xerox and chief learning officer at Motorola and Cigna. Perhaps best known for establishing Motorola University (MU) as the benchmark corporate university, Bill expanded MU's international reach to encompass 101 education offices in 24 countries. He developed two corporate museums, several corporate customer briefing centers, the archives of the corporation, a university, a secondary-education relationship team, and an externally focused consulting team for key Motorola customers and suppliers.

Renie McClay, MA, CPLP, has been a performance improvement professional for more than 20 years. Founder of Inspired Learning, LLC, she brings her passion and practical approach to her work. She has authored books on training global audiences, creating engaging training, building high-performing sales teams, and team building. She facilitates workshops in North America, Europe, Africa, Latin America, Asia, the Middle East, and Australia—in person and virtually. She is a certified online instructor. Renie is adjunct professor for Roosevelt University and Concordia University, and facilitates for the American Management Association. She is an honoree for the International Business Awards, the Stevie Awards for Women, and past president of the Professional Society for Sales and Marketing Training.

Regional Contributors

Africa: Robin Probart, president/CEO, African Society for Training and Development, South Africa.

Australia: Christopher A. Bell, PhD, director, The Sanciolo-Bell Group, past CEO of The Leadership Consortium, and a founder of Telstra Centre for Leadership.

China: Bin Yang, PhD, senior associate dean, School of Economics and Management; director of Tsinghua Center for Leadership Research and Development. **Zhong Xu,** PhD, director of Excelland Center for Leadership Development; secretary of the Party Committee in School of Economics and Management, Tsinghua University.

Europe: Gina Eckert, PhD, senior research faculty EMEA, Center for Creative Leadership, Brussels, Belgium.

India: Matt Barney, PhD, founder and CEO of LeaderAmp. **Shreya Sarkar-Barney,** PhD, president of Human Capital Growth Inc., located in the United States and India.

Korea, Japan, and Southeast Asia: Koko Nakahara, president of Instructional Design, Inc., in Japan. **KL Cheah,** founder of his own company and a seasoned leadership developer and coach.

Latin America: Fernando Sanchez-Arias, director general of MEJORAR International, a global business and human strategy firm with operations throughout Latin America and the United States.

Middle East: Moutaz M. Mashour, vice president, Industrial Relations, Aramco Sinopec Refining Company, Saudi Arabia. **Patrick Carmichael,** vice president, Senior Executive Board, Best Practice Institute, Aramco, Saudi Arabia.

North America: Bill Wiggenhorn, a principal of Main Captiva, LLC. **Renie McClay,** founder of Inspired Learning, LLC.

References

Brodbeck, F.C. (2000). Cultural Variation of Leadership Prototypes Across 22 European Countries. *Journal of Occupational and Organizational Psychology* 73(1):1-29.

Ernst, C., and D. Chrobot-Mason. (2010). *Boundary-Spanning Leadership*. New York: McGraw-Hill.

Johansen, B., and J. Ryan. (2012). *Leaders Make the Future: Ten New Leadership Skills for an Uncertain World*. San Francisco: Berrett-Koehler.

For Further Reading

Barney, M. (2013). *Leading Value Creation: Organizational Science, Bioinspiration and the Cue See Model*. Hampshire, England: Palgrave Macmillan.

Biech, E., ed. (2010). *The ASTD Leadership Handbook*. Alexandria, VA: ASTD Press.

Gentry, W., R.H. Eckert, S.A. Stawiski, and S. Zhao. (2013). *The Challenges Leaders Face Around the World: More Similar Than Different*. Greensboro, NC: Center for Creative Leadership.

Johansen, B., and J. Ryan. (2012). *Leaders Make the Future: Ten New Leadership Skills for an Uncertain World*. San Francisco: Berrett-Koehler.

Kouzes, J.M., and B.Z. Posner. (2012). *The Leadership Challenge: How to Make Extraordinary Things Happen in Organizations*. San Francisco: Jossey-Bass.

McClay, R., and L. Irwin. (2008). *The Essential Guide to Training Global Audiences*. San Francisco: Pfeiffer.

Zenger, J., J. Folkman, and S. Edinger. (2009). *The Inspiring Leader: Unlocking the Secrets of How Extraordinary Leaders Motivate*. New York: McGraw-Hill.

Chapter 52

Challenges and Solutions for a Multigenerational Workforce

Alexandra Levit

······································· **In This Chapter** ·······································

- ■ Define the four generations of the American workforce.
- ■ Discuss challenges and solutions for older and younger employees.
- ■ Fine-tune training and development programs for a multigenerational audience.

The American workforce is getting older and younger at the same time. According to recent census data, the percentage of people 65 and older in the labor force increased from 12.1 percent in 1990 to 16.1 percent in 2010. As the Baby Boomers (born 1946–1963) age, this number is expected to increase every year until 2028, when the last of them retire and leave the labor market. Meanwhile, nearly half of the 80-million-strong Millennial generation (born 1980–1995) is in the workforce already, and by 2028, this generation will make up roughly three-quarters of the working population. However, the number of middle-aged workers is shrinking due to the relatively small size of Generation X (born 1964–1979).

These shifting demographics leave us with four generations working closely together for the next several years. So far, the adjustment has not been easy. When I receive an SOS call from a VP of human resources, it's usually because the organization's Baby Boomers are frustrated by having to manage and train the Millennials and the Millennials are equally frustrated by having to be managed and trained by the Boomers.

One recent story crystallized the tensions between these two groups. At a Fortune 500 client of mine, a 27-year-old woman named Jennifer had graduated from a top university and tried to make her mark immediately. As a result of her accomplishments, Jennifer was named the youngest manager in her division's history. Jennifer's new 54-year-old boss, however, perceived Jennifer to be irreverent and disrespectful. The company experienced mass layoffs, and due to the clashes with her boss, Jennifer was worried she'd be a casualty. She frantically tried to change her boss's perception of her, but the damage was done.

Some say that people are people, and that the differences between generations are just flimsy stereotypes. But while stereotypes aren't true for every individual, research supports some generalizations with respect to the attitudes and behaviors of the four generations. If you wish to build an inclusive and successful culture, you must be attuned to generational differences and adapt your approach to suit your unique employee mix.

In this chapter, we'll broadly outline the four generations and discuss challenges and solutions for the older and younger camps. We'll also provide practical advice for fine-tuning your training and development programs to resonate with a multigenerational audience.

Talking About Whose Generation?

Bruce Tulgan, the founder of Rainmaker Thinking, is a generational workplace expert who has authored books such as *Winning the Talent Wars*, *Managing Generation X*, and *Managing the Generation Mix*. In *Managing the Generation Mix*, a book he co-authored with Carolyn Martin, he defines the generations as follows:

- Traditionalists: Born before 1946. Their strengths are loyalty, dependability, responsibility, altruism, and a strong work ethic. Other generations can count on these seasoned workers for everything from historical perspective to an important document. Their attitude is: Take charge and do what's right.
- Baby Boomers: Born 1946–1963. The huge Baby Boom generation experienced a child-centered upbringing, a focus on individuality and youth, and a distrust of authority. Older Boomers admit they're competitive and self-centered but have a strong commitment to the mission of their organizations. Younger Boomers see themselves as cautiously loyal and more realistic about life and work.

- Generation Xers: Born 1964–1979. These independent, ambitious go-getters are accustomed to taking care of themselves. Not obsessed with climbing the corporate ladder, these free agents are energetic, creative, and adaptable as they make lifestyle choices that contribute to their wellness, happiness, and health.
- Millennials: Born after 1980. The Millennials are the most outspoken and empowered of all the generations. Influenced by education-minded Boomer parents and fueled by their facility with technology, Millennials are poised to be lifelong learners. They're socially conscious, have high expectations of organizations, and are constantly looking for ways to improve how things are done.

Generational Challenges and Solutions

There are two sides to every story, so it's useful to acknowledge the potentially toxic attitudes the younger and older contingents have toward one another before identifying solutions. In all likelihood, you have heard about or personally experienced many of these before.

Traditionalist/Boomer/Xer Gripes About Millennials

- Millennials have been raised on the "everyone gets a trophy" phenomenon and expect to be handed a career. They don't deserve it; they have to earn it. My role in life is not to be at their beck and call.
- Organizations have survived this long without the Millennials. They don't know everything and should defer to colleagues with years of experience.
- I don't want to hear from Millennials' parents that they are unhappy about their career situations.
- Millennials need to learn how to assimilate into our culture. This means following spoken and unspoken rules and dressing appropriately. I don't care how hot it is—no tanks and flip flops—and when Millennials are meeting with me, they need to stop multitasking and turn off their phones.
- Millennials are not very diplomatic in asking for what they want. We're glad they want to contribute and make suggestions, but too much empowerment and aggressiveness is annoying. They also need to stop complaining.

Millennial Gripes About Traditionalists/Boomers/Xers

- Older colleagues do things a certain way because that's the way they've always done it, and they are so siloed that one hand doesn't know what the other is doing!
- Tenured employees don't know more just because they've been here longer. We have a fresh perspective and want to use it to make a meaningful contribution right away.

- Older managers often aren't accessible and don't offer us clear channels of career progression.
- Older colleagues are slow to adapt new technology and other current methods to do business better. We want to implement more customized, streamlined approaches to internal and external problems, and they hold us back.
- Older colleagues play political games and insist on a rigid schedule. We prefer a comfortable culture that feels like family and want to do work on our terms as long as we get satisfactory results.

Influencing the Generations

Whether you are a manager, trainer, or both, there are several things to keep in mind as you seek to motivate and influence members of the Traditionalist, Baby Boomer, X, and Millennial generations. Here are some recommendations to that effect.

Traditionalists

- Empower Traditionalists to make their own decisions by encouraging them to trust their instincts and supporting them in whatever they determine is the best course.
- Have deference for their years of experience and listen. After all, what has happened in the past is the best predictor of what will happen in the future.
- Talk to Traditionalists about their learnings and their long-term plans. Don't assume they have one foot out the door just because they're approaching what was once the standard retirement age.
- Provide constructive feedback as you would to any other employee—they can and should learn new tricks.

Boomers

- Give recognition whenever possible. Acknowledge Boomers' contributions and be cognizant about implementing their suggestions.
- Encourage them to mentor younger colleagues and learn new skills and technologies so that they can continue to hone their potential.
- Allow them to experiment with their jobs. Many Boomers are getting antsy and want to do work that's different and more personally meaningful.
- Respect the status quo. Boomers feel that if it ain't broke, don't fix it. Don't insist on change for its own sake.

Xers

- Share your unique expertise. Xers are interested in amassing as much training and knowledge as possible.
- Look to Xers as team leaders. They have been chomping at the bit to be out of the Boomers' shadow and are ready for their time to shine.
- Use technology to make team meetings easier. Many Xers have families to think about, and they appreciate you keeping their necessary work–life balance in mind.
- Don't block their path to decision makers. Xers just want to get the work done and can get impatient with turf wars and too many bureaucratic channels.

Millennials

- Take Millennial employees out to lunch and inquire about their career goals and aspirations. They want to feel that you care.
- Explain to Millennials why things are done a certain way in your organization, educate them on who they need to talk to to get things done, and spell out unwritten rules to ensure compliance.
- Have an open-door policy in which you are available for Millennial team members to ask questions and receive guidance. Provide constructive feedback in real time.
- In the event of a crisis, don't shut them out. Millennials love the apprenticeship approach and will learn much from having the opportunity to work by your side.

Members of all generations should be educated about the performance benefits of diversity so that they will view it as a plus rather than a minus. For example, according to a study by the National Urban League, companies with effective diversity practices generate an average productivity increase of 18 percent beyond that of the overall U.S. economy. There's no doubt about it: Diversity is good for business and prompts everyone to do their best work.

Your training programs can also bring people together by focusing on the similarities between generations rather than the differences. All employees, for instance, are motivated by inspirational leaders, need to understand expectations and objectives, want to receive consistent feedback, and prefer to do work that's creative and makes a difference. All employees like to be treated as individuals rather than unceremoniously dumped into a generational category. At the end of the day, we're all human, and employees should be prompted to relate to each other at this most basic core.

As a T&D professional, think about the various generations you train. How do they exemplify the experiences, attitudes, behaviors, and expectations of their generations? What challenges do they provide you? Ask yourself how you can address these challenges to become a more effective trainer. You will find a worksheet at the *Handbook's* website at www.astdhandbook.org to capture your ideas.

What Demographic Shifts Mean for Training

Within the next decade, retiring workers will need to be replaced at an unprecedented rate, yet there will be fewer midlevel individuals available to meet the labor market's growing demands. This will require Millennials to move into leadership roles sooner—and at a younger age—than prior generations. And, as confirmed by a Cass Business School study, 59 percent of executives do not think their organizations are ready for the upcoming power shift.

According to a 2013 survey I conducted with Deloitte, an incredible 50 percent of currently employed Millennials are already serving in leadership positions. Forty-four percent of them have only three to five years of experience, yet 41 percent have four or more direct reports. By contrast, at the same age, most Baby Boomers and Gen Xers were still in junior-level positions.

Organizations haven't adequately trained these young professionals to be managers, and it shows. Of current Millennials who are leaders, only 36 percent said they felt ready when entering the role, and 30 percent still do not feel ready today—citing managing difficult people or situations, lack of experience, and dealing with conflicts as their top concerns upon entering a leadership role.

This lack of preparedness echoes what has been reported in prior research. A recent survey by ASTD reported that two-fifths of Millennials don't think their cohort is entering the workforce with sufficient skills to become future leaders, and *Harvard Business Review* claimed that the average age to receive leadership training is 42, more than a decade away for the average Millennial leader.

Over half of ASTD's respondents felt that Millennials require specialized leadership development programs, but only 15 percent said their organizations offer such programs, although the business case is clear. For instance, higher-performing organizations are 57 percent more likely than low-performing organizations to have a Millennial leadership development program in place.

Therefore, if I had to pick one area in which to focus your training and development initiatives, I'd suggest Millennial leadership. There is simply the greatest need here, as well as the most significant gap between where most organizations are and where they need to be.

Multigenerational Development Techniques

Most organizations that do emphasize training and development of their multigenerational workforces do so via traditional classroom training. Unfortunately, classroom training is proving to be less effective with 21st-century employees for the following reasons:

- Training cannot be immediately applied to real-world situations.

- Training induces enthusiasm while in the classroom, but participants forget about it as soon as they leave.
- Training is often done as a one-off session with an outside facilitator, which does not help participants learn to work better with their individual peers and managers.
- Training is not as effective with individuals who are not outspoken in a group setting.

Instead of relying on classroom training, training and development professionals should perhaps consider more innovative techniques for skill building.

E-Learning

Led by the Millennials, who prefer online delivery for most of their information, employees are increasingly receptive to e-learning. Cisco estimates that by 2017, 69 percent of data for both businesses and consumers will be video based, and it's easy to search websites like YouTube, TED, and Howcast for content to add to your programs, as long as you follow copyright laws. You can also use in-house video and IT resources to create visually appealing, straightforward pieces that can be reused and repurposed over time.

Create an ongoing learning experience by delivering sequenced video lessons on a predetermined schedule. Your participants can interact with the lesson at their convenience, apply the lesson to their real-world work, get feedback and advice from their multigenerational colleagues and managers, and report back on the outcome. The on-demand nature of e-learning makes it simple for new hires to catch up to the rest of the group.

When it comes to e-learning, digestibility is also extremely important. It is notoriously difficult to get people to pay attention to an online training course for more than a few minutes at a time. If your offering is longer than that, participants zone out or simply click through the content until they can check a box saying they've completed the course. This is the last thing you want after you've invested your time and resources in a training solution. Just as with traditional classroom training, the central challenge is to capture participants' attention and sustain it until you can spur them to action.

Gamification

Gamification, which can be online or offline, is about taking the essence of games—fun, play, transparency, design, and challenge—and applying it to real-world objectives rather than pure entertainment. These real-world objectives might involve skill acquisition in the areas of project management, conflict resolution, and risk taking. The common denominators of successful games are the use of challenges and evolving narratives to increase task completion, a system of feedback and rewards, social connections that provide support, and a sophisticated graphical interface and user experience.

To assess whether gamification is a valid option for your team, first articulate the problem the game needs to address, and speak to others who have tried gamification for similar reasons. Understand what worked, what didn't, and whether the gamification strategy was worth the investment.

Mentor-Based Learning

In my 2013 research with Deloitte, young professionals shared that organizations need to provide training opportunities outside of formal job titles so they can master decision making and problem solving. Mentor-based learning is a form of development in which employees master skills through regular interaction with experienced senior leaders via traditional mentoring relationships, reciprocal relationships, and project-based partnerships or apprenticeships.

The younger generations value the apprenticeship model, in which they are allowed to work alongside senior leaders during a typical project or atypical crisis situation. Apprenticeship is beneficial in anchoring new and soon-to-be leaders in tangible responsibilities and real-world scenarios with reduced risk. This, along with reciprocal mentor relationships (which pair more experienced and less experienced colleagues together for the purpose of learning specific skill sets from one another), are also terrific motivators for Traditionalists and Boomers who still want to contribute meaningfully to the future of the organization.

Many forward-thinking organizations have adopted project-based mentorship. At its core, project-based mentorship puts employee development into the hands of many instead of relying on a busy primary supervisor. Each employee has the opportunity to work on assignments with a diverse group of team members, all of whom are aware of that employee's strengths and career goals. In the context of the individual project, employees may be placed in situations that are out of their comfort zones (for example, a board meeting) and mentored actively on appropriate preparation, actions, and behaviors.

Intrapreneurship

Intrapreneurship was first defined in 1978 by Gifford and Elizabeth Pinchot and referred to free market entrepreneurship within a corporation. Lately, however, this practice of entrepreneurial development of a new product, process, or service in the context of an established organization has become a critical means for companies of all sizes to ignite innovation within their ranks and effectively develop employees of diverse ages and backgrounds.

Intrapreneurship is easier said than done. After all, the post-recession business climate is risk-averse and the priority is to keep the organization afloat, sometimes at the expense of driving new growth. Fortunately, there are ways that you can infuse your team with the spirit of intrapreneurship without overhauling your organization's existing structure.

HR and training professionals can create program elements that encourage employees to pinpoint fresh opportunities and utilize cutting-edge tools. Your content may include creativity building exercises from a website like www.creativitygames.net. They can be as simple as developing a story from a list of random words or building a new product from a box of matches.

Work with your executive management team to set up formal innovation committees and establish processes for vetting and funding the most promising initiatives that arise from your participants' efforts. You will see the greatest results if employees are able to bring their ideas to life with reassurance from senior leaders that their jobs are not in jeopardy if an initiative fails.

Several new training techniques that are available include e-learning, gamification, mentor-based learning, and intrapreneurship, all of which can more readily address the requirements of your multigenerational workforce. The trouble is, most of them are not yet being implemented on a wide scale. As either a consultant or an internal professional, how can you be a pioneer? An innovative tactics worksheet on the *Handbook's* website at www .astdhandbook.org may help you plan for this change.

The key to successfully developing your multigenerational workforce is to realize that circumstances are different today and the old ways won't work. By taking one small step at a time and evangelizing those around you, you will diffuse tension, facilitate collaboration, and sustain a vibrant learning culture.

About the Author

Alexandra Levit is a consultant who builds better relationships between organizations and top talent. A former nationally syndicated columnist for the *Wall Street Journal* and a current writer for the *New York Times*, Alexandra has authored six books, including the bestselling *They Don't Teach Corporate in College*. She has designed and implemented Millennial leadership development and multigenerational employee engagement programs on behalf of the Obama administration and more than 20 Fortune 500 companies. A *Money Magazine* and *Forbes* career and workplace expert of the year, Alexandra has appeared in more than 1,000 media outlets to discuss issues facing modern organizations and their employees.

References

American Society for Training and Development. (2013). *Leadership Development for Millennials: Why It Matters*. Alexandria, VA: ASTD Press.

Cass Business School. (2012). *After the Baby Boomers: The Next Generation of Leadership*. London, United Kingdom: Odgers Berndtson.

Cisco, Inc. (2013). *Visual Networking Index: Forecast and Methodology, 2012-17*. San Jose, CA: Cisco Systems, Inc.

Howard, D., and B. Kromer. (2013). *Labor Force Participation and Work Status of People 65 and Older. American Community Survey Briefs*. Washington, DC: Bureau of the Census.

Lamoureux, K. (2010). *Experiential Learning for Leadership Development: Approaches, Best Practices, and Case Studies*. Bersin by Deloitte.

Levit, A. (2014, forthcoming). *Leadership Now: Are Millennials Ready to Take the Reins?* Deloitte Development LLC.

Levit, A., and S. Licina. (2011). *How the Recession Shaped Millennial and Hiring Manager Attitudes About Millennials' Future Careers*. The Career Advisory Board, http://careeradvisoryboard.org/research/the-future-of-millennial-careers-research.

Martin, C., and B., Tulgan. (2006). *Managing the Generation Mix*. Amherst, MA: HRD Press.

Millennial Inc. (2010). *What Your Company Will Look Like When Millennials Call the Shots*. New York: Mr.Youth and Intrepid.

National Urban League. (2005). *Diversity Practices That Work: The American Worker Speaks.* New York: National Urban League.

Pinchot, G., and E. Pinchot. (1978). *Intra-Corporate Entrepreneurship*. New York: Tarrytown School for Entrepreneurs.

Zenger, J. (2012). We Wait Too Long to Train Our Leaders. *Harvard Business Review*.

For Further Reading

Drucker, P. (2006). *Innovation and Entrepreneurship*. New York: Harper Business.

Haneberg, L. (2010). *Coaching Up and Down the Generations*. Alexandria, VA: ASTD Press.

Levit, A. (2008). *Success for Hire: Simple Strategies to Find and Keep Outstanding Employees.* Alexandria, VA: ASTD Press.

Levit, A. (2009). *MillennialTweet: 140 Bite-Sized Ideas for Managing the Millennials*. Silicon Valley, CA: Superstar Press.

Martin, C., and B. Tulgan. (2006). *Managing the Generation Mix*. Amherst, MA: HRD Press.

Chapter 53

The Neuroscience of Learning

Susan Goldsworthy and Walter McFarland

·· **In This Chapter** ··

- ▪ Understand the essentials of neuroscience and their importance in workplace learning.
- ▪ Know how the 21st-century workplace environment affects the ability of the brain to learn and the implications for workplace learning.
- ▪ Explore a neuroscience perspective on familiar elements of workplace learning: the environment, the facilitator, and the learner.

···

The competitive environment of the 21st century is causing organizations everywhere to adapt and change more, faster, and differently than ever before. One implication of this is an unprecedented demand for workplace learning. This learning must be delivered more quickly, effectively, and at lower costs. In addition, organizations must also be able to create new kinds of learning needed to cope with increasingly complex organizational problems. Simply said, workplace learning professionals are under more pressure to perform—and to assume their role as learning leaders—and as business leaders. In this chapter, we pose the question: Can neuroscience help?

A hallmark of ASTD in the 70 years since its founding has been its ability to help workplace learning remain constantly relevant to the changing business environment. In doing this,

ASTD has encouraged a multidisciplinary approach to workplace learning. Over time, a growing number of fields have increased our understanding of how workplace learning unfolds. These include psychology, sociology, instructional systems design, adult learning theory, management science, organizational development, and organizational theory, to name but a few. Each new field or approach added more insight into workplace learning and enabled it to provide increased value to people and organizations.

In the past three decades, the field of neuroscience has grown in impact and popularity (Ringleb and Rock, 2008). In the last few years, neuroscience has begun to affect numerous other fields as divergent as economics and agriculture—and with good results. The purpose of this chapter is to explore the role of neuroscience in workplace learning. The chapter is organized in three parts: introduction to neuroscience, implications of neuroscience for workplace learning, and recommendations for action.

Introduction to Neuroscience

The scope of neuroscience is immense. The Oxford Dictionaries define neuroscience as "any or all of the sciences, such as neurochemistry and experimental psychology, which deal with the structure or function of the nervous system and brain."

Our brains contain around 100 billion neurons and 100 trillion synapses (at which electrical or electrochemical signals can be transmitted from one cell to another); they consist of thousands of distinguishable substructures, connected to each other in synaptic networks whose intricacies have only begun to be unraveled. A recurring theme of this chapter is the need for more neuroscience research—particularly in the area of workplace learning.

Neuroscience is being aided by the advent of brain imaging technologies such as functional magnetic resonance imaging (fMRI), positron emission tomography (PET), and brain wave analysis techniques such as quantitative electroencephalography (QEEG). These technologies, combined with computer analysis of results, have enabled a better understanding of how the brain functions and have facilitated the integration of psychology (the study of the mind) and neuroscience (the study of the brain) (Kleiner, 2011). As a result, the neuroscience world has become vast, with more than 30,000 scientists worldwide studying a variety of issues affecting multiple fields, including neuroeconomics, neuroaccounting, and neuromarketing—among others (Ringleb and Rock, 2008).

With reference to workplace learning, early neuroscience research appears to be validating some previously held assumptions and contradicting others. For example, some research is suggesting that features of the current organizational environment can affect the ability of the brain to learn more than previously thought. An environment characterized by continuous adaptation and change can affect multiple systems in the brain, eliciting behaviors to avoid or actively resist new learning (Kleiner, 2011). This suggests that a neuroscience perspective could further advance our understanding of how learning unfolds in today's complex, fast-paced workplace. The next section explores some potential implications of neuroscience for workplace learning.

Implications of Neuroscience for Workplace Learning

In this section, we explore a neuroscience perspective on three familiar elements of workplace learning: the role of the learning environment, the role of the learning leader, and the role of the individual learner.

Neuroscience and the Learning Environment

We began with a discussion of how much the competitive environment has changed and suggested that one implication of the new environment is higher levels of confusion and stress for the workforce. In our research, executives, managers, and the workforce highlighted the increasing turbulence inside their organizations (McFarland and Goldsworthy, 2013). They told us that before one change has ended, new changes have begun, and some described being in a permanent state of flux. In describing the internal environments of their organizations, people often use words such as permanent whitewater (Vaill, 1996), chaos (Wheatley, 1992), and VUCA (Johansen, 2012). It is clear that many people feel adversely affected by the new environment. What is less clear is whether the new environment affects the brain's ability to learn and, if so, how.

Traditionally, workplace learning acknowledges the environment as a factor in learning— but only in a general way. For example:

- Bandura's (1986) social learning theory suggests that learning occurs entirely in a social context as the result of an interaction between people and their environment.
- Kolb (1984) stated that experience is a key factor in how adults learn—and that their environment helps determine the nature of that experience.
- Schein (1983) stated that a key factor in adult learning is reflection—and that organizational context can help or hinder this reflection.

However, little is known about how the current organizational environment is affecting the social environment, the quality of workplace experiences, or the ability to reflect on learning. In short, little is known about the specific effects of the current workplace environment on learning.

Great workplace learning is often portrayed as a function of great design, great delivery, and great content—with the learning environment only a minor consideration. Neuroscientists are suggesting that great workplace learning in the 21st century must recognize—and account for—the turbulent organizational environment as a significant factor in learning because such environments affect multiple brain systems.

This section focuses on three specific areas of the brain and one brain reaction that neuroscientists are connecting to learning. The three areas are working memory, basal ganglia, and the hippocampus, while the reaction is the threat response.

Working Memory

When it comes to learning, working memory is an important region of the brain to access. Working memory is the brain's initial holding area for new perceptions and ideas and is associated with the brain's prefrontal cortex, a small, energy-intensive region behind the forehead. When we activate working memory, we are processing or "working on" incoming stimuli, or internal stimuli, to find meaning, make value judgments, or manipulate data in some way. Working memory is essential in learning something new. The challenge is that working memory is quite limited—we can't process very much information at any one time (McFarland and Goldsworthy, 2013). Constant environmental distractions can divert the brain's focus and use working memory—leaving less capacity for learning. Constant distractions can overwhelm working memory, causing physical discomfort and reducing the brain's ability to learn. This is why we can feel exhausted after a day's training, even if it has been enjoyable. It is also the reason that neuroscientists are suggesting that designers of learning interventions ensure new information is presented in relatively brief "chunks" of time. Developing the ability to consciously focus the brain on learning—in the midst of distraction—could be an important new learning competency.

Basal Ganglia

As workplace learning professionals know, modern learning tasks often require a significant change in learner behavior—something the brain can actively resist as part of its normal functioning. Activities that we do repeatedly are referred to the basal ganglia, thus freeing up processing power in the prefrontal cortex (McFarland and Goldsworthy, 2013). The basal ganglia are associated with a variety of functions, including voluntary motor control; procedural learning relating to routine behaviors or "habits" such as bruxism, eye movements, and cognitive; and emotional functions (Davachi, Rock, and Rock, 2010). The basal ganglia form a low-energy, high-capacity part of the brain that doesn't tire like the prefrontal cortex. We use this region for physical habits and activities we can do without too much conscious thinking. If we have practiced doing something for long enough, then it becomes "second nature." We all know that once formed, habits are notoriously difficult to change. Even so, neuroscientists are learning how new ways of thinking—often referred to generally as "mindfulness"—can help people learn how to change their own habits more easily and effectively.

Hippocampus

The hippocampus is vital for learning, as it is a part of the brain that plays an important role in the consolidation of information from short-term to long-term memory. Neuroscientists have discovered that activation of the hippocampus during encoding tasks plays a significant role in whether people can recall what they have learned. In the workplace, much learning is declarative, or explicit, meaning information that needs to be recalled (Davachi, Rock, and Rock, 2010). This kind of learning involves encoding information for easy retrieval. Recent neuroscience research demonstrates that by building in the right amount of attention, generation, emotions, and spacing (AGES), learners can intensely activate their hippocampus, creating deep circuits for easy retrieval (Davachi, Rock, and Rock, 2010).

Attention requires the minimizing of distractions and placing focus on what is being learned. *Generation* involves the individual taking ownership for the content and working out what it means for him or her as an individual. It should be noted that generation is seen as more than self-directedness but as an expression of Dewey's notion of the learner actively teaching him- or herself how to learn. *Emotions* refers to the fact that memory can be enhanced because, first, emotion grabs the attention and, second, it can create a stronger ability to recall an experience. Finally, *spacing* refers to the fact that distributing learning over a longer period of time leads to better long-term memory than cramming learning into one session (Davachi, Rock, and Rock, 2010). It is easy to imagine how the modern workplace might affect all four elements of AGES.

It is important for learning professionals to support others to generate their own insights. The hippocampus plays an important role in the creation of insight as it is involved in both memory formation and retrieval. Insight matters because the moment of insight changes the brain in a way that linear problem solving does not. Neuroscience research is also demonstrating that learning through insight is more memorable, with new networks created in the brain that help us to see a situation in a totally new way (Whiting et al., 2011).

Howard Gardner

Howard Gardner is best known for his multiple intelligence theory, a reappraisal of the long-held belief that there is one single human intelligence by which everyone processes information. Gardner claims that each person has a unique, multifaceted blend of intelligences that traditional psychometric instruments, such as intelligence quotient (IQ) tests, cannot accurately gauge. In his groundbreaking book, *Frames of Mind: The Theory of Multiple Intelligences* (1983), Gardner initially formulated a list of seven intelligences: verbal-linguistic, logical-mathematical, visual-spatial, bodily-kinesthetic, musical-rhythmic, interpersonal, and intrapersonal. Since publication of the book, Gardner expanded the list of intelligences to include emotional, naturalistic, and existential. Gardner's research suggests that most learners are comfortable with three to four intelligences and are likely to avoid the other intelligences, greatly affecting knowledge acquisition. Although multiple intelligence theory was not immediately accepted by the psychological community, educators have embraced it, integrating the theory into curricula ranging from nursery school to adult education.

Gardner is the John H. and Elisabeth A. Hobbs Professor in Cognition and Education at the Harvard Graduate School of Education. For the past 20 years, he and colleagues at Harvard University's Project Zero have been working on the design of performance-based assessments, education for understanding, and the use of multiple intelligences to achieve more personalized curriculum, instruction, and assessment.

Threat Response

In a turbulent, ever-changing environment, the ability to be creative and innovative is often lost as the brain focuses on more basic needs such as minimizing uncertainty and reducing threat. If we feel threatened in some way, either physically or emotionally, it may trigger a response in the amygdala, an almond-shaped set of nuclei linked to both fear and pleasure. The fight-or-flight response was first described in the 1920s by American physiologist Walter Cannon, who realized that a chain of rapidly occurring reactions inside the body help mobilize the body's resources to deal with threatening circumstances (Cherry, 2013). Once triggered, the threat response moves the brain's focus away from learning, dialogue, and solutions and switches it quickly to survival mode. It can take the body 20 to 60 minutes to return to its pre-threat arousal levels (Cherry, 2013). In a workplace full of frequent change with constant distractions creating potential uncertainty and doubt, it becomes vital that the learning professional creates an environment where the threat response is minimized and contained.

External distractions are on the increase, thanks to the advances in technology and also the way we live in increasingly open-plan spaces, be it at home or at work. Today, we can receive an e-mail, text message, FaceTime request, and many other "distractions" at any time, in any place, day or night. It can be increasingly difficult to stay focused and stay productive. And our internal distractions, those voices in our heads that help our minds to wander off track, add to the challenge. Not only can distractions be frustrating, but also they can be mentally exhausting as the brain has to keep switching between both competing external tasks and competing internal thoughts, remembering where it was before it became distracted. A set of slides that can assist you in sharing some of the basics of essentials of neuroscience and their importance in workplace learning is located at the *Handbook's* website at www.astdhandbook.org.

Even if distractions are relatively minor, they have been shown to interfere with the ability of the brain to produce insight. And without insight, connections, ideas, and creative connections are less likely to be made. The ability to forge a learning environment that enables greater focus—and insight—may be useful in solving the current generation of complex problems and increase the value of learning.

In summary, neuroscientists are suggesting that the current environment in modern organizations can impede the ability of the brain to learn. This environment can overwhelm short-term memory, require the constant changing of habits, rob the hippocampus of the focus required to create insight, and threaten the brain so that learning anything is harder.

Neuroscience and the Learning Leader

In the previous section, we noted that from a neuroscience perspective, the workplace environment is a more important factor in learning than previously thought. In this section, we focus on the neuroscience perspective on the role of leadership in workplace learning.

The role of the "learning leader" in the workplace learning lexicon varies greatly, but is often described as a fairly passive one. In the adult learning literature, for example, the role of the learning leader is described as more of a facilitator who brings adult learners together in the workplace and guides their learning experiences via artful questions and guided interactions with other learners (Knowles, 1990). Little attention is focused on how the leader helps learners focus their brains and effectively navigate in turbulent learning environments.

Some neuroscience research indicates that leadership may be a much more important factor in workplace learning than previously thought. Neuroscience is suggesting that specific actions by a leader can create better learning environments by calming and focusing the brain. In this section, we highlight three such actions: actively modeling positive behavior, creating a learning environment that considers the brain, and helping learners positively reframe uncertainty.

Actively Modeling Positive Behavior

According to neuroscientists, the actions of the learning leader can have an impact on the learning state of others due to the social nature of our brains. In 2004, brain researchers in the Italian town of Parma made an amazing discovery. A neuron that fired when a monkey actually picked up a peanut also fired when the monkey saw someone else pick up a peanut. Originally called "monkey see, monkey do" neurons, these special brain cells are now called mirror neurons because they fire whether one is doing the action or watching someone else do the action. Further research with humans has shown that mirror neurons lead to the ability to learn through imitation. You watch someone do something, and you imitate it. The more you copy an activity from someone else, the easier it becomes, and eventually you can do it almost without thinking. The mirror neuron system provides scientific validation of the need for empathy and authenticity in order to engage and inspire others. It is central to "emotional intelligence," the ability to be self-aware and to be socially aware, to connect with and empathize with those around them by managing their own emotions and influencing the emotions of others (Kohlrieser, Goldsworthy, and Coombe, 2012). Finding ways to engage the "social brain" during learning can increase the ability to retain what is learned.

Our mirror neurons provide an explanation as to why it is so important for a leader to remain calm during a crisis. If the person in a position of authority panics, it can elicit panic in others. Research has shown that the ability to remain calm is a key leadership characteristic (McFarland and Goldsworthy, 2013). By remaining calm, the leader can provide a "model" for lessening the negative emotions associated with change and helping others to access the conscious, thinking part of their brains. In other words, the leader's positive behavior sets the stage for improved workplace learning.

Creating a Learning Atmosphere That Considers the Brain

One of the key ways for leaders to create a learning atmosphere is by implementing a feedback culture. It is through the process of receiving and integrating feedback that people can develop and grow. Research indicates that specific, positive feedback that treats individuals as valued members of the organization may activate reward systems in the brain that promote stronger learning of those behaviors (Street, 2010). However, for the comments to be accepted, it must be perceived that the deliverer of the feedback is being fair.

Neuroscientists have suggested that fairness and equity are extremely important motivators in organizational settings (Mobbs and McFarland, 2010). A feeling of fairness is essential in focusing our brain on the potential and the gain, and away from the threat and the pain that is experienced when people feel they have been treated unfairly. The perception of fairness in the workforce is believed to be a fundamental requirement for high levels of motivations and performance (Mobbs and McFarland, 2010). From the perspective of the brain, great workplace learning environments are fair.

Neuroscience research suggests that by enabling people to express any feelings of unfairness, inequity, and frustration, they can actually reduce the amount of negative emotion in the amygdala (Lieberman, 2009). Rather than suppressing an initial negative reaction to a workplace event, the learning leader creates an environment where people can express their frustrations, let them go, and then refocus on those things that they can influence or control, thereby releasing more productive energy.

Neuroscientists are studying the impact of how a leader shapes the environment as well as the minds of those in that environment and a number of concepts are proving useful for application in the workplace. One such example is the SCARF model from the Neuro-Leadership Institute (Rock and Christine, 2011). The SCARF model involves five domains of human social experience: status, certainty, autonomy, relatedness, and fairness. **S**tatus is about relative importance to others. **C**ertainty concerns being able to predict the future. **A**utonomy provides a sense of control over events. **R**elatedness is a sense of safety with others, of friend rather than foe. **F**airness is a perception of fair exchanges between people.

Helping Learners Positively Reframe Uncertainty

Changes in the working environment may create a sense of the unknown for employees who fear the potential impact. As noted earlier, when threatened, the brain may focus more on areas of concern, where fear, uncertainty, and doubt reside, rather than on the areas that they can positively influence or control. If a threat response is elicited, employees may disengage and become passive, defensive, or aggressive. The challenge for learning leaders is to create an environment where people can move toward this positive mental state that enables thinking that is more innovative, creative, and solution focused. The brain learns better when it is free from anxiety and can be curious, exploratory, and even playful without fear of ridicule. To neuroscientists, a key goal of the learning leader is to actively create environments that minimize engagement of the brain's aversive system and attempt to best engage the motivational system (Mobbs and McFarland, 2010). Neuroscientists suggest that by better understanding how the brain works, learning leaders can ensure that they actively shape the learning environment to minimize disruption and distraction and to maximize dialogue and discovery.

Neuroscience and the Individual Learner

In conventional workplace learning, although the individual learner is considered "self-directed" (Houle, 1992; Tough, 1967), it often falls to the learning leader to craft learning interventions that cater to the unique learning characteristics of adults—and increase their "readiness to learn." For example, workplace learning interventions are expected to be immediately and clearly job relevant, build on the experience of adults, encourage interactions among learners, understand that adult learners are self-directed, and build in the opportunity for "critical reflection" (Schein, 1983; Marsick, 1988).

Neuroscientists are suggesting that the tumultuous workplace environment is demanding more of learners than self-directedness and reflective practice. Learners must possess the skills necessary to keep themselves constantly "ready to learn." This ability to become more agile, faster, and more effective in learning is demanding that people adapt new behaviors and discard old ones. It is demanding that learners develop the ability to embrace and lead change in themselves. Said another way, today's learners need to take Dewey's (1916) advice literally and teach themselves how to learn.

How can neuroscience help adult learners become better at learning? Ironically, to move forward in this area, neuroscience is looking back to a practice several thousand years old. The words *Know Thyself* were carved above the entrance to the temple of Apollo at Delphi, rebuilt after an earthquake in 373 B.C. Neuroscientists refer to the process of knowing yourself as mindfulness. Mindfulness is defined by the Oxford Dictionaries as "a mental state achieved by focusing one's awareness on the present moment, while calmly acknowledging and accepting one's feelings, thoughts, and bodily sensations, used as a therapeutic technique."

Numerous studies have shown that mindfulness meditation can improve our ability to sustain the focus and attention that are key to learning. Four days of mindfulness training for just 20 minutes per day can help on a battery of cognitive tests. In one study, mindfulness meditation practitioners performed particularly well on tasks with time constraints, suggesting that mindfulness could be useful for helping us to work to deadlines. The more mindful people are, the more activation they have in the right ventro-lateral prefrontal cortex, referred to as the brain's braking system (McFarland and Goldsworthy, 2013). Through practice, people can learn to actively intervene in their own thought processes and choose the way they act, as opposed to reacting mindlessly to the incoming stimulus. By introducing simple mindfulness techniques into the workplace, learners can equip themselves to increase their ability to focus their attention, and thereby increase their ability to learn. Research is also showing that mindfulness practitioners seem to avoid generating aversive responses during episodes of unfairness (Kirk, 2011).

Mindfulness, as the definition suggests, is about focusing on "how" a person thinks as he or she goes about his or her daily business. A related concept in neuroscience, metacognition, is defined by the *Oxford Dictionaries* as "awareness and understanding of one's own thought processes." It is about thinking about your thinking in order to improve that thinking. It is known that metacognition helps people to perform many cognitive tasks more effectively (Metcalfe and Shimamura, 1994). Ways of practicing metacognition include self-questioning techniques such as asking yourself, "What do I know about this topic? What experience have I had? How may I have solved problems like this before?" It can also be helpful to "talk yourself through" a task by speaking out loud and by using graphical representations of your thoughts. Research also has shown that the simple act of writing things down can play a large part in both developing metacognitive skills and in helping the learner to remember what he or she has just learned (Gammil, 2006).

Neuroscientists suggest that by introducing reflective practice and mindfulness into the workplace, people can improve the ability to learn at both the individual and group levels, and it has also been seen that any behavior that encourages people to quietly reflect can be helpful for insight and, therefore, learning (Beeman, Collier, and Kounios, 2008). Building in the discipline of debriefing after projects is a practical tool to capture learning and stimulate a greater emphasis on reflection and mindfulness in the moment.

Finally, neuroscientists suggest that by increasing our awareness and understanding of how our own brains work, we are then better able to take conscious actions that will support our ability to learn, as both individuals and teams, thereby further enhancing the value of learning to the organization. The end goal may be a lofty one, but it is the small daily steps that we consciously choose to implement that build our ability to individually take greater control of our collective impact.

Conclusion

We believe that the emerging field of neuroscience will be able to contribute much to improved workplace learning. Better understanding of how the modern organizational environment is affecting the ability of the brain to learn is a critical and largely overlooked consideration. Neuroscientific findings offer important new insights into how learning unfolds in the 21st-century workplace; and they should be better integrated into the workplace learning lexicon. We also believe that much more research and practice are needed before this integration can occur. ASTD's leadership will be essential in guiding this research and practice to ensure that workplace learning professionals have continuing access to the best emerging thinking.

About the Authors

Susan Goldsworthy is CEO of Goldswolf & Associates, specializing in leadership development, executive coaching, and change communications. A former Olympic finalist with more than 20 years' management experience in large multinationals, Susan works with executives, global companies, and a number of the world's leading business schools. Susan is co-author of *Choosing Change* (2013, with Walter McFarland), co-author of the award-winning *Care to Dare* (2012), and a contributing author to *New Eyes* (2013). She holds an MSc, Coaching & Consulting for Change from HEC/Oxford University, and an Executive Masters in the Neuroscience of Leadership from the NLI.

Walter McFarland is founder of Windmill Human Performance and the 2013 board chair of ASTD. He was previously a senior vice president at Booz Allen Hamilton, leading the global business in HR, learning, and change. Walter teaches in the Summer Leadership Institute of Columbia University, the NeuroLeadership Institute, and at HEC Management School, Paris. He recently served on President Obama's 2013 Rank Award Council. Walter writes and speaks frequently on the topics of organizational change, leadership, and learning and is co-author (with Susan Goldsworthy) of *Choosing Change* (2013, McGraw-Hill).

References

Bandura, A. (1986). *Social Foundations of Thought and Action: A Social Cognitive Theory.* Englewood Cliffs, NJ: Prentice Hall.

Beeman, M., A. Collier, and J. Kounios. (2008). How Insight Happens: Learning from the Brain. *NeuroLeadership Journal* 1:20-25.

Cherry, K. (2013). What Is the Fight-or-Flight Response? About.com Psychology, http://psychology.about.com/od/findex/g/fight-or-flight-response.htm.

Davachi, L., K. Rock, and L. Rock. (2010). Learning that Lasts Through the AGES. *NeuroLeadership Journal* 3:53-63.

Dewey, J. (1916). *Democracy and Education.* New York: Macmillan.

Gammil, D. (2006). Learning the Write Way. *The Reading Teacher* 59(8):754-762.

Houle, C.O. (1992). *The Literature of Adult Education: A Bibliographic Essay.* San Francisco: Jossey-Bass.

Johansen, B. (2007). *Get There Early: Sensing the Future to Compete in the Present.* San Francisco: Berrett-Koehler.

Kirk, U. (2011). Neural Substrates of Corporate Decision-Making. *NeuroLeadership Journal* 4:77.

Kleiner, A. (2011). *The Neuroscience of Leadership.* Halifax, Nova Scotia: The Alia Institute.

Knowles, M. (1990). *The Adult Learner: A Neglected Species,* 4th edition. Houston: Gulf Publishing Company.

Kohlrieser, G., S. Goldsworthy, and D. Coombe. (2012). *Care to Dare: Unleashing Astonishing Potential Through Secure Basel Leadership.* Warren Bennis Signature Series. London: United Kingdom: John Wiley & Sons.

Kolb, D.A. (1984). *Experiential Learning: Experience as the Source of Learning and Development.* Englewood Cliffs, NJ: Prentice Hall.

Lieberman, M. (2009). The Brain's Braking System (and How to Use Your Words to Tap Into It). *NeuroLeadership Journal* 2:9-14.

Marsick, V.J. (1988). Learning in the Workplace: The Case for Reflectivity and Critical Reflectivity. *Adult Education Quarterly* 38(4):187-198.

McFarland, W., and S. Goldsworthy. (2013). *Choosing Change: How Leaders and Organizations Drive Results One Person at a Time.* New York: McGraw Hill.

Metcalfe, J., and A. Shimamura. (1994). *Metacognition: Knowing About Knowing.* Cambridge, MA: MIT Press.

Mobbs, D., and W. McFarland. (2010). The Neuroscience of Motivation. *NeuroLeadership Journal* 3:43-52.

Ringleb, A.H., and D. Rock. (2008). The Emerging Field of Neuroleadership. *NeuroLeadership Journal* 1.

Rock, D., and C. Christine. (2011). SCARF in 2012: Updating the Social Neuroscience of Collaborating With Others. *NeuroLeadership Journal* 4:129-142.

Schein, E. (1983). *The Reflective Practitioner: How Professionals Think in Action.* New York: Basic Books.

Street, C. (2010). Application of Neuroscience in Executive Team Coaching: The WSR Case. *NeuroLeadership Journal* 3:64-77.

Tough, A.M. (1967). *Learning Without a Teacher: A Study of Tasks and Assistance During Adult Self-Education Projects.* Toronto: Ontario Institute for Studies in Education.

Vaill, P.B. (1996). *Learning as a Way of Being: Strategies for Survival in a World of Permanent Whitewater.* San Francisco: Jossey-Bass.

Wheatley, M.J. (1992). *Leadership and the New Science: Learning About Organization from an Orderly Universe.* San Francisco: Berrett-Koehler.

Whiting, J., et al. (2011). Lead with the Change in Mind. *NeuroLeadership Journal* 4:112.

For Further Reading

Eisenberger, N.I., M. Lieberman, and K. Williams. (2003). Does Rejection Hurt? An fMRI Study of Social Exclusion. *Science,* 302(October):290-292.

McFarland, W., and S. Goldsworthy. (2013). *Choosing Change: How Leaders and Organizations Drive Results One Person at a Time*. New York: McGraw Hill.

Rock, D., and A. Ringleb. (2013). *The Handbook of Neuroleadership*. The NeuroLeadership Institute. Charleston, SC: CreateSpace Independent Publishing Platform.

Schwartz, J., P. Gaito, and D. Lennick. (2011). That's the Way We (Used to) Do Things Around Here. *Strategy + Business*, 62 (Spring).

Chapter 54

The Persistent Classroom

David Powell

·· **In This Chapter** ··

- Review the contemporary challenge of adult learning.
- Redefine the traditional classroom.
- Review the steps behind the evolution of the Persistent Classroom™.

If you go into an Apple retail store on any given Saturday, it is likely that you will see three-year-old children playing a game on an iPad. At home, they will use the iPad one moment to video call their grandparents who live in another state, and then in the next moment, use an app to learn how to read. Just like their parents, they use their fingers to navigate the iPad, but unlike their parents, they haven't learned that there are multiple user interfaces, so it's funny to watch their faces when they touch a laptop computer screen and nothing happens. These children will grow up in a world that stops using touch to control computers. They will grow up in a world where computers, phones, and other digital devices are no longer external to things. They will live in an "always on" web of smart objects, with multiple avatars—incarnations of the self—inhabiting multiple digital domains.

They will work and learn in a world where there is no longer a distinction between what is analog and what is digital, where "the empirical 'reality' of the 'virtual' is never in doubt" (Drohan, 2013). Thirty years from now—when these three-year-olds are in positions of power, leading groups and organizations in an extremely mobile, radically connected global community, where presence is unbound by physical location and time, and the office is your GPS coordinates—will we be able to look back and say our education and training systems have kept pace with advancing times and prepared them to excel in what has become the new normal?

This now decades-old digital society is changing us. The United States Postal Service (USPS) is an exemplar of this change. The contemporary challenge for the USPS is that it is mandated by Congress to physically deliver mail, yet the demand for mail delivery has dried up. People no longer write letters; they send email. People no longer send postcards on vacation; they send photos from their smartphones. With more and more companies moving to online bill payment systems, invoices are no longer being mailed. Even catalog delivery, a staple of the USPS, is shifting from print to online. Without the constitutional mandate, would the USPS exist in five years? This shift from print literacy (Cole, 2011) to "digital literacy" has already had an impact on primary education. As cursive instruction is being replaced by "keyboarding" instruction, digital communication is becoming the new "paper"—the dominant mode of asynchronous communication in education.

The channels of communication are increasing, creating new "virtual learning spaces" that heretofore did not exist—whether it is blogging on your personal website, Skyping, texting on Facebook, building your professional network on LinkedIn, tweeting, posting to Pinterest, or sending self-destructing data through Snapchat. Teenagers today use texting (a.k.a. instant messaging) significantly more than email and voice telephony. Texting has replaced letter writing as the dominant mode of asynchronous communication. It is a unique form of asynchronous conversation in that people are having parallel continuous conversations they move in and out of at will. Instant communication has spawned the wisdom of crowds. Today's college students dwell and think in the virtual learning spaces they inhabit. As an example, college students today make decisions to physically attend a specific class or simply view the lecture online at a later date based on "crowdsourced" knowledge about professors posted on university websites. If the crowd determines the professor's lectures are "non-engaging," then they watch the lecture on their computer, at the time of their choosing. In addition to watching the lecture video, this personal virtual learning space may include concurrent web research or paper writing, along with texting with fellow students.

Many assert that our fragmented presence in multiple domains of digital interaction inhibits our ability to sustain our attention, let alone apply what we've learned, whether borne of experience or training. This thinking is the learning paradigm of the past, reacting to change that has already happened. There has always been competition for attention in the classroom. This digital shift has empowered people (learners) to connect in new ways, creating virtual learning spaces that are more engaging than the "concrete" classroom. This contemporary human condition of multiple digital channels, and the multiple virtual learning spaces that these channels enable, challenges the preeminence of our concrete learning institutions.

In the Phaedrus (370 B.C.), Plato wrote of writing:

> *If men learn this, it will implant forgetfulness in their souls; they will cease to exercise memory because they rely on that which is written, calling things to remembrance no longer from within themselves, but by means of external marks. What you have discovered is a recipe not for memory, but for reminder. And it is no true wisdom that you offer your disciples, but only its semblance, for by telling them of many things without teaching them you will make them seem to know much, while for the most part they know nothing, and as men filled, not with wisdom, but with the conceit of wisdom, they will be a burden to their fellows.*

Technology has always evoked fear for the future. Writing has not proven to be an impediment to learning; it is simply a tool. Learning technology, like all methods, materials, and devices used to solve problems, do not impart wisdom. Wisdom is the result of the application of knowledge through the crucible of experience. Wisdom is learned, and when we learn, we are changed. In the following pages, we will explore how the traditional training classroom will need to change to effectively address the current challenges facing adult learners in this evolving culture of multiple learning spaces.

A Brief History of the Classroom

In the United States, by the time you are 18 years old, you have likely spent 15 years in a classroom. If you matriculate college and graduate school, add another six to 10 more. By the time you reach the age of 25, the majority of your life—the vast majority—will have been spent seated in rows of chairs facing the front of a four-walled room. In the front will stand an authority figure (that is, a teacher, instructor, professor, facilitator, or trainer) who is responsible for, among other things, rating your performance (that is, grades, completion certificate, diploma, and so forth). Your day will be segmented into units of time, and you and your fellow students, regardless of nature or interest, will engage in subject-based activities at the same time.

This makes sense if you consider schools as "normalizing institutions" (Foucault, 1975), that is, that they are organized around educating, socializing, and acculturating vast numbers of children in a highly structured, regimented, rigid, and hierarchical way. Our current educational system historically reflects our work systems, mirroring the change that happened during the industrialization of the west as workers migrated from farms to work in urban factories. It's about replication of information, control, and authority more than it is about knowing and thinking. This view of education reflects the Latin root of the English word *education—educare,* which means to train or to mold. When children graduate the education system, they have been socialized and acculturated to, and are ready to participate in, organizational life—they are ready to work. One has to merely look back on the intensity of their primary, secondary, and collegiate learning experiences, or measure the years of on-the-job training it took to get to a level of job mastery, to appreciate how long it takes to learn something with the ability to successfully apply that knowledge.

The Contemporary Challenge of Adult Learning

In many ways, the executive education classroom of today is much like the classroom of the past. Learners sit in a four-walled room and receive instruction from the authority figure at the front of the room, follow a time-based daily agenda, and are periodically asked to work with their fellow participants. Executive education continues this paradigm, but often without the benefit of time, repetition, and ongoing feedback that were the foundation of a person's almost 20 years of classroom practice.

While executive education classrooms look a lot like the classrooms of the past, the level of temporal investment pales in comparison to the commitment it took to get there. Yet there is an expectation that the executive learner will be able to take what he or she has learned and creatively apply that learning to known problems at work. This issue of learning transfer, or lack thereof, is industry wide. Houde suggests the lack of transfer reflects that the training and development classroom evokes "a repertoire of [classroom] practices for the context that may be contrary to desired learning and behaviors in the work context." In addition, he suggests it may be the "lack of correspondence between the classroom context and the work context . . . [that] an analogical comparison of the deep structure of a classroom and any given work context is likely to reveal no similarities" (Houde, 2007). The problem is that learning transfer presupposes that learning has occurred. What do we expect participants to learn in a two-, three-, or even five-day training program?

Maybe the job of executive education is "readying them [students] to create solutions to problems yet unknown and requires questioning, thinking, and creating" (Bass and Good, 2004). This is also in line with a Deleuzian view of learning as Bogue writes: "By 'learning' Deleuze clearly does not mean the mere acquisition of any new skill or bit of information, but instead the accession to a new way of perceiving and understanding the world. To interpret signs is to overcome 'stock notions,' 'natural,' or 'habitual' modes of comprehending reality. What often passes for learning is simply the reinforcement of commonsense notions, standard codes, and orthodox beliefs. But the commonsense, conventional, orthodox world is ultimately illusory. Genuine learning, the learning through signs, takes us beyond the illusions of habit and common sense to the truths of what Proust calls 'essences' and Deleuze labels 'differences'" (Bogue, 2008).

If learning is simply about the "reproduction of the same" (Deleuze, 1994), then according to Deleuze, "We learn nothing from those who say: 'Do as I do.' Our only teachers are those who tell us to 'do with me' and they are able to emit signs to be developed in heterogeneity rather than propose gestures for us to reproduce" (Deleuze, 1994). According to Semetsky and Delpech-Ramey (2012), "Experience is thus paramount for learning, for creating novel meanings embedded in what Deleuze called the pedagogy of the concept. Experiential education will have paid attention to places and spaces, to retrospective as well as untimely memories, and to those dynamic forces that are capable of *affecting* and *effecting* changes thus contesting the very identity of subjects participating in this dynamical process." These ideas on experience-driven learning seem to reflect the other Latin root of the word *education—educere,* meaning to "bring out, lead forth." This educational tension, between educational production and learning-as-becoming, is endemic throughout the entire field of contemporary education.

In December 2013, Penn GSE released a study on MOOCs (massively open online courses) showing "that massive open online courses [MOOCs] have relatively few active users, that user 'engagement' falls off dramatically—especially after the first one to two weeks of a course—and that few users persist to the course end [with] course completion rates, averaging 4 percent across all courses and ranging from 2 percent to 14 percent depending on the course and measurement of completion" (Penn GSE, 2013). Those in the media who saw this as an indication of the failure of MOOCs to grasp what the "democratization of education" truly means. May and Semetsky assert that education is a collaborative process between teacher and student. "For Deleuze, education would begin, not when the student arrives at a grasp of the material already known by the teacher, but when the teacher and student together begin to experiment in practice with what they might make of themselves and their world" (May and Semetsky, 2008).

MOOCs represent a tectonic shift in contemporary education, whereby education is not measured by production, by the value to the system (certificates, diplomas, and so on), but by the value to the end-user—the student. Students have equal agency as teachers, completing as much or as little of a course based on their definition of value. This value may or may not be aligned with any aspect of the education system. "Deleuze emphasized that students were not required to take in 'everything, [yet] everyone took what they needed or wanted, what they could use' indeed defying the necessity of some superior educational aim which imposed from without" (Semetsky, 2007; Deleuze, 1995). In many ways, MOOC-based education is not unlike the shift from letter writing to texting. Like letter writing, texting is asynchronous, with bursts of seemingly synchronous dialogue. People drop in and out of the texting conversation to the extent that it provides value in the moment. Like texting, in the MOOC "classroom," students drop in and out, skim material, and take deep dives depending on their unique learning habits and goals. In this way, "it makes learning not a rationally deduced abstraction but a meaningful encounter expressed in terms of students' literally making sense out of their own experiences" (Semetsky, 2007).

The experiential learning executive education classroom faces the same drive for change as seen in higher education. Today, executives who attend leadership development and other training programs continue to sit in the same seat every day and become disoriented when they return to the classroom and find the tables and chairs have been moved; they expect daily agendas, and many become agitated or anxious when one is not posted. They expect certificates of completion and are disappointed when they do not receive one. Yet the goals of experience-driven learning are about acting together in the world, reflecting on that action to develop and transform oneself. As Cameron Duff writes, "Learning is a process of becoming sensitive to signs and events; how to be affected by them and to affect them" (Duff, 2013). The goal of the experience-driven executive education classroom in 2014 is no different than what John Dewey said of education in 1916: "What [one] gets and gives as a human being . . . is . . . a widening and deepening of conscious life—a more intense, disciplined, and expanding realization of meanings. . . . And education is not a mere means to such a life. Education is such a life" (Dewey, 1924). Like the MOOC experiments at Stanford, UPenn, and other institutions, executive education is poised for change. What is called for is a redefinition of the classroom.

The Persistent Classroom

The definition of the office has remained unchanged. The office is where you are located. With the rapid proliferation of the smartphone in work life, what has changed is that the walls you inhabit no longer define your location. Your location is the GPS coordinates in your smartphone. Just as the office walls are giving way to a networked, mobile workforce, walled learning spaces are giving way to networked mobile learning . . . the classroom is wherever you are. As dramatic as this might sound, it is important to remember "all learning is virtual in that pedagogues, pedagogical institutions, and pedagogical technologies impart signs to students who in turn must interpret and make sense of them in both thoughts and actions. The process is 'virtual' because the significant pedagogical program must be transmitted to some degree through insignificant signs. The student then interprets these into their own significant understandings, so as to create a new image or thought and action from the essence of what is taught" (Drohan, 2013).

People will continue to come to training programs, but in this connected future, the majority of experiential learning is likely to come from these un-walled "virtual" learning spaces. If experience-driven executive education is about learning-as-becoming, then the physical classroom is the place where the participants experiment with and on themselves (Delueze, 1994) and discover (or rediscover) a new connection, a new direction, or a new path to follow. But these discoveries do not bear fruit in the training room; learning (that is, change) has yet to occur. "We learn by means of multiplying and intensifying connections" (Semetsky, 2007) and for these classroom discoveries to turn into new knowledge and actions-in-the-world, the participant must take the classroom (trainer, other participants, created objects, and thoughts) with them when they return to work. For learning to occur, they must enfold the experience into work, and merge the training and development context with their work context.

The Innovation Lab at the Center for Creative Leadership (CCL) has been experimenting with the transition from the analog classroom to the digital classroom over the past several years. Like many in our field, we are faced with the same three fundamental questions: How can we successfully deliver leadership development in this increasingly mobile, hyper-connected world? Like in the MOOC example, how do we create ongoing value-based relationships with our end-users that are not production based (certificates for corporate development plans)? Lastly, what needs to change in current IT systems and workflows to promote the regular and consistent engagement that is required to enchant our user base and establish a loyal following among our participants and alumni?

As trainers, it is gratifying to know that we have had a significant impact on the lives of our customers; in order to thrive in 2014 and beyond, we must maintain a persistent presence—a continuous connection, in the learning lives of executives. To do this, CCL has reimagined the classroom as no longer bound by a date or a physical space; rather, executive learning will be both synchronous and asynchronous, local and distant, primarily defined by an ongoing, value-based relationship with the center. We call this "the Persistent Classroom."

Developing the ideas for the Persistent Classroom first began in 2009, when CCL began to experiment with porting some of its leadership development curriculum into Second Life, one of the early Internet-based, 3D immersive virtual environments (Torres, Brodnick, and Powell, 2009). Van Velser, McCauley, and Ruderman (2010), in the CCL *Handbook of Leadership Development*, identified the potential benefits of leadership development in 3D immersive environments when they wrote, "This platform may allow individuals to participate fully with others in a leader development program without leaving their home or office. Individuals use avatars (virtual representations of themselves) in Second Life classrooms and could potentially receive feedback on their assessments, participate in experiential exercises, receive confidential feedback in a one-on-one session with a trained coach, and accomplish their end of program goal setting all in a virtual world, while being an active but remote participant."

In May 2009, supported by a grant from SHRM, CCL partnered with George Mason University to evaluate the efficacy of "Executive Coaching in Technology Supported Environments." In this study (Chen, et al., 2013), 28 participants in CCL's Leadership Development Program (LDP™) received their 3.5 hours' assessment for development feedback session in Second Life. The participants never physically met their executive coaches, and at the end of the coaching session, the average rating for the experimental group was 4.4/5.0 versus the control group, which was 4.8/5.0.

An interesting finding was that people had physiological and psychological responses to what their avatars were encountering in the virtual world. As an example, a participant's avatar stopped moving and talking after stepping on a rickety bridge 200 meters above the "virtual" ground. When the coach asked her to follow him, she responded that she couldn't move, stating with a rapid breath that she was afraid of heights. This is in line with a study by Fox, Bailenson, and Ricciardi (2012), which found the "virtual self causes physiological arousal."

Subsequently, CCL built a virtual campus and held conferences and experimented with "virtualized" versions of its leadership development curriculum.

You can view a video of Tool 1, CCL's experiments in Second Life, at www.youtube.com/watch?v=e0f-ZSj-fBA&hd=1&wide or download the video and the other two tools mentioned in this chapter on the *Handbook's* website at www.astdhandbook.org.

While there were many issues with using Second Life or any other open 3D platform for corporate clients, we discovered that learning and development curricula could be reimagined for this unique digital learning environment. We learned that we could create a high-fidelity 3D virtual learning space and have similar learning impact with our participants' avatars as we were having with our traditional participants. This is consistent with the research on virtual reality: "research suggest[ing] that stronger levels of presence in virtual reality are more likely to affect behavior in the real world" (Rosenberg, Baughman, and Bailenson, 2013).

The next step in the evolution of the Persistent Classroom was the introduction of iPads in LDP in 2012. While this first effort successfully replaced paper and pen with its digital counterpart, the next phase of building the Persistent Classroom will be creating a technology-enabled version of the entire curriculum.

The Persistent Classroom is being designed to facilitate a continuous learning relationship with its end-users. One of its functions is to broker leader relationships and leadership knowledge between and among all people who touch this ever-expanding network and build a thriving community of learning. In this vision of the Persistent Classroom, CCL participants never leave CCL once they enter its doors. It is in this Persistent Classroom that the relationship to CCL is established and the initial value created. One function of the Persistent Classroom is to inaugurate participants' connection to the learning community, establish their presence in the classroom's social network (for example, Yammer), connect them to other leaders and just-in-time knowledge, and orient them to the classroom's "digital hallways, bookshelves, and other virtual learning spaces."

Figure 54-1. CCL's The Persistent Classroom

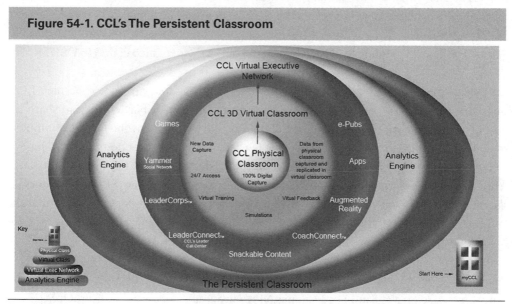

Source: Powell, D. (2013). CCL Persistent Classroom Graphic. Greensboro, NC: Center for Creative Leadership.

This digital shift will necessitate the digital capture of the user-generated content in a program. Once a participant leaves a CCL campus, this content will "live" inside their virtual 3D classroom and be accessible via LeaderConnect™, a gamified app under development. At the end of their programs, participants are able to download LeaderConnect and continue to use it to access their data, add and manage their goals, participate in their CCL social networks (program level and all alumni), search for an executive coach, and access the "Ask Leaders" help center. The "Ask Leaders" help center searches all CCL social network feeds, publications (books, guidebooks, and whitepapers), podcasts, and LeaderCorps videos (two- to four-minute leader stories as told by leaders). If your search does not yield the results you were looking for, with a touch of a single button, your question is posted to the CCL social network(s) of your choosing. Participants accrue points and badges as they use the app, and their standing relative to other participants is displayed on the app leaderboard. Points are redeemable for additional CCL products and services in the app store.

As we make this transition, the classroom as a physical plant will change. With all participants having iPads, which can serve as monitors, there is no need to have an LCD projector and screen. Since participants will no longer have eyes facing front, the "proscenium arch"– based classroom can morph into a "theater in the round" classroom. The physical space will be open, unadorned by furniture and infinitely reconfigurable. Fixed tables and chairs will give way to movable furniture that will be stored in the "prop room" and available for use by the class. The classroom will no longer reflect the static learning environments of the past, but will be the blank canvas on which the class creates itself anew.

View Tool 2, a video example of reconfiguring space, at http://vimeo.com/34647917.

Instead of paper-based flipcharts, each classroom will have four networked 55-inch LCD monitors mounted on movable stands. This way, any trainer or participant can share his or her iPad screen on the classroom monitors. No matter where anyone is in this infinitely reconfigurable space, they only need look a few feet in any one direction to see a "shared" screen. Small groups can be designated to any one "shared" screen. A participant can record the group's ideas, drawings, and photos and mirror it to the group or class monitors for large group discussion and debrief. Each breakout room will also reflect this configuration. When video recording is required in a classroom or breakout room, iPads will be used for recording and mirrored on the 55-inch monitors for discussion and debrief.

View Tool 3, an animation of what the concrete learning space of the Persistent Classroom might look like on the San Diego campus, at www.youtube.com/watch?v=Z8rhOpMJK2k& feature=youtu.be&hd=1&wide.

Classroom roles will also need to change. With the proscenium stage gone, the trainer as "authority" will give way to the trainer as "collaborator." Program coordinators will become classroom producers. They will be responsible for managing the a/v capture across all feeds and working with the trainers to feed images to the classroom in real time as well as preliminary marking of feeds for later editing. They will spend the majority of their time in the main observation room, which will look much like a video production control room. A great deal of data will be generated, and working with it in effective ways will require us to add a whole new job category. We will place feeds on participants' personal CCL webpages, and we will use parts of feeds for LeaderCorps (short videos of leader stories as told by leaders), e-pubs, and other digital offerings.

In the Persistent Classroom, curricula will be reimagined with an eye toward continuous learning unbounded by time and the four walls of the classroom. One can imagine CCL programs as modified MOOCs, where the lectures exist in the CCL Cloud. Participants complete modules attached to a specific program, and their progress through this "prerequisite program" is tracked though an LMS. Once the prerequisite coursework is completed, they are automatically registered for the "concrete" classroom portion of the program.

The venue for their continued learning after they leave a campus is their class-specific 3D virtual classroom. Everything participants create as a class, peer-learning group, or individual will have been digitally captured and replicated in the virtual classroom. Their concrete classroom persists in the digital realm, where their avatars continue to engage with their classmates, faculty, and the greater CCL network.

The Persistent Classroom creates the opportunity to become far more immersed in alumni's lives, and with the use of video and digital capture, user-generated content, and big-data analytics, we have the opportunity to collect research data on a regular basis and use the data collection and analytics to increase the value to the user, develop future products, research projects, and for custom services. This conception of the Persistent Classroom, merging the physical classroom with the virtual classroom, will empower faculty and participants to interact and collaborate across time and through communities built around vertical markets, industries, professions, aspirations, and leadership topics. Through the use of virtual worlds, mobile devices, digital content, and social networks, we will establish a new type of classroom that creates an immersive experience for its users, which provides a continuous space for discovery, creativity, and learning that persist over time. This is the future of learning, yet our goal as learners has never changed. T.S. Elliott points to it in his poem *Little Gidding* (1968):

> *We shall not cease from exploration*
> *And the end of all our exploring*
> *Will be to arrive where we started*
> *And know the place for the first time.*

The Classroom of the Future

The Persistent Classroom is the beginning. Integrating tools that exist today to create a persistent presence in the lives of executives creates the possibility of continuous learning and development in this increasingly connected world. The business landscape is evolving into a vast, digitally connected, multichannel world where the boundaries between analog and digital experiences, between concrete and virtual learning spaces, are rapidly dissolving. In the future, Bailenson and Blascovich (2011) predict that "when people interact with others for substantial periods of time, much as they do now on Facebook but with fully tracked and rendered avatars, entirely new forms of social interaction will emerge." The field of training and development will and must adapt to these emerging forms of communication, identity, and presence.

The research in augmented reality and other virtual learning spaces is exploding. The MIT Media Lab is developing augmented reality collaboration systems that "foster a real-time interaction for user-generated contents on top of the physical environment" (Kasahara, Heun, Lee, and Ishii, 2012). They are exploring the boundaries of the human machine interaction, proposing the concept of tangible user interfaces (TUI) that is based on physical embodiment of digital information and computation. "TUIs [will] expand the affordances of physical objects, surfaces, and spaces so they can support direct engagement with the virtual world" (Lakatos and Ishii, 2012).

In 2013, we saw research in state-changing 3D user interfaces introducing "sublimation and deposition as metaphors for transitions between physical and virtual states" (Leithinger, et al., 2013) and for "including proprioception and embodied interaction into an environment for remote collaboration [exploring] how remote collaborators can 'reach into' a shared digital workspace where they can manipulate virtual objects and data" (von Kapri, et al., 2013). This year, we will see biometric sensors, once the sole domain of medicine, become fashion accessories. Point-of-view cameras will become ubiquitous. By 2017, people will be wearing contact lenses that are personal HUDs (heads-up displays) with bone-conducted spatial audio and 3D projected imagery. They will simultaneously walk through a world of corporeality and virtual reality where the multiplicity of learning spaces blend into one that is defined simply as "learning space."

Just as it is normal for the three-year-old of today to masterfully engage with an iPad, the three-year-olds of the future will grow up in a world where there are no computers, just smart-networked objects. Everything will be connected, and they will receive a continuous queryable stream of data about people, places, and objects as they interact with the world.

These three-year-olds, the leaders of the future, will grow up in a radically connected world where the notion of embodied space (Low, 2003) includes the digital self. They will work in a world where personally curated experiences are expected. In this possible future, augmented and virtual reality will lose their meaning, as they will no longer be seen as different or distinct from reality, and the classroom will be a continuous presence in their lives.

About the Author

David Powell, PhD, is senior faculty and a founding member of the Innovation Lab at the Center for Creative Leadership. The goal of the Innovation Lab is to "find, create, and validate groundbreaking leadership development innovations for new products, services, and business models to advance CCL's business and mission worldwide." David is part of a team responsible for crafting future scenarios that guide CCL's strategies and product/service development investments and creating a culture of innovation at CCL. David also manages a variety of technology-driven projects to validate innovative concepts. He creates prototypes, simulations, and other experiential demonstrations that guide CCL's thinking and decision making.

References

Bailenson, J.N., and J. Blascovich. (2011). *Virtual Reality and Social Networks Will Be a Powerful Combination: Avatars Will Make Social Networks Seductive.* IEEE Spectrum, http://spectrum.ieee.org.

Bass, R.V., and J. Good. (2004). Educare and Educere: Is a Balance Possible in the Educational System? *Educational Forum* (68)2:161-168.

Bogue, R. (2008). Search, Swim and See: Deleuze's Apprenticeship in Signs and Pedagogy of Images. In *Nomadic Education: Variations on a Theme by Deleuze and Guattari,* ed. I. Semetsky (pp. 1-16). Rotterdam: Sense Publishers.

Chen, T.R., S. Zaccaro, T. McCausland, D. Powell, and C. Torres. (2013). Coach and Client Cognitive Characteristics Match in Executive Coaching Relationships. Poster presented at the 2013 APA Annual Conference, Honolulu, HI.

Cole, D.R. (2008). Deleuze and the Narrative Forms of Educational Otherness. In *Nomadic Education: Variations on a Theme by Deleuze and Guattari*, ed. I. Semetsky. Rotterdam, The Netherlands and Boston: Sense Publishers.

Cole, D.R. (2011). Matter in Motion: The Educational Materialism of Gilles Deleuze. *Educational Philosophy and Theory*, volume 44, Issue Supplement s1, Pages 3-17, May 2012 (first published online April 14, 2011).

Deleuze, G. (1994). *Difference and Repetition*, Paul Patton (trans.). New York: Columbia University Press.

Deleuze, G. (1995). *Negotiations 1972–1990*, Martin Joughin (trans.). New York: Columbia University Press.

Dewey, J. (1924 [1916]). *Democracy and Education*. New York: Macmillan.

Drohan, C. (2013). Deleuze and the Virtual Classroom. In *Deleuze and Education*, eds. I. Semetsky and D. Masny. Edinburgh, Scotland: Edinburgh University Press.

Duff, C. (2013). Learning to Be Included. In *Cartographies of Becoming in Education*, ed. D. Masny. Rotterdam, The Netherlands and Boston: Sense Publishing.

Elliot, T.S. (1968). *The Four Quartets.* New York: Mariner Books.

Foucault, M. (1975). *Discipline and Punish: The Birth of the Prison*. New York: Vintage.

Fox, J., J. Bailenson, and T. Ricciardi. (2012). Physiological Responses to Virtual Selves and Virtual Others. *Journal of CyberTherapy & Rehabilitation* 5(1):69-72.

Houde, J. (2007). Analogically Situated Experiences: Creating Insight Through Novel Contexts. *Academy of Management Learning & Education* (6)3:321-331.

Kasahara, S., V. Heun, A. Lee, and H. Ishii. (2012). Second Surface: Multi-User Spatial Collaboration System Based on Augmented Reality. In SIGGRAPH Asia 2012 Emerging Technologies (SA '12). ACM, New York, Article 20.

Lakatos, D., and H. Ishii. (2012). Towards Radical Atoms—Form-Giving to Transformable Materials. In Proceedings of Cognitive Infocommunications (CogInfoCom), 2012 IEEE 3rd International Conference, Kosice, Slovakia.

Leithinger, D., S. Follmer, A. Olwal, S. Luescher, A. Hogge, J. Lee, and H. Ishii. (2013). Sublimate: State-Changing Virtual and Physical Rendering to Augment Interaction With Shape Displays. In Proceedings of the 2013 ACM Annual Conference on Human Factors in Computing Systems (CHI '13). ACM, New York, 1441-1450.

Low, S. (2003, February). Anthropological Theories of Body, Space, and Culture. *Space & Culture* (6)1:9-18.

May, T., and I. Semetsky. (2008). Deleuze, Ethical Education, and the Unconscious. In *Nomadic Education: Variations on a Theme by Deleuze and Guattari*, ed. I. Semetsky. Rotterdam, The Netherlands and Boston: Sense Publishers.

Penn GSE. (2013). www.gse.upenn.edu/pressroom/press-releases/2013/12/penn-gse-study-shows-moocs-have-relatively-few-active-users-only-few-persisti.

Plato. (370 B.C. [1961]). Phaedrus. In *The Collected Dialogues of Plato*, eds. E. Hamilton and H. Cairns. Princeton, NJ: Princeton University Press.

Rosenberg, R.S., S. Baughman, J. Bailenson. (2013). Virtual Superheroes: Using Superpowers in Virtual Reality to Encourage Prosocial Behavior. *PLOS One* 8(1):1-9.

Semetsky, I. (2007). Towards a Semiotic Theory of Learning: Deleuze's Philosophy and Educational Experience. *Semiotica* 164(1/4):197-214.

Semetsky, I., and J. Delpech-Ramey. (2012). Jung's Psychology and Deleuze's Philosophy: The Unconscious in Learning. *Educational Philosophy and Theory* (44)1:69-81.

Torres, C., R. Brodnick, and D. Powell. (2009). Leader Development Gets a Second Life. In *Leadership in Action,* (29)3.

Van Velsor, E., C. McCauley, and M. Ruderman. (2010). *The Handbook of Leadership Development,* 3rd edition. San Francisco: Jossey Bass.

von Kapri, A., K. Wong, S. Hunter, N. Gillian, P. Maes. (2013). InReach: Manipulating 3D Objects Remotely Using Your Body. International Conference on Human Factors in Computing (CHI 2013), workshop paper in Blended Interaction: Envisioning Future Collaborative Interactive Spaces.

For Further Reading

Blascovich, J., and J. Bailenson. (2011). *Infinite Reality: Avatars, Eternal Life, New Worlds, and the Dawn of the Virtual Revolution.* New York: William Morrow.

Doorley, S., and S. Witthoft. (2012). *Make Space: How to Set the Stage for Creative Collaboration.* New York: John Wiley & Sons.

IEEE Spectrum: http://spectrum.ieee.org

McCauley, C., D. DeRue, P. Yost, and S. Taylor. (2013). *Experience-Driven Leader Development.* San Francisco: Jossey-Bass.

MIT Media Lab: www.media.mit.edu.

Semetsky, I., and D. Masny, eds. (2013). *Deleuze and Education.* Edinburgh, Scotland: Edinburgh University Press.

Virtual Human Interaction Lab at Stanford: http://vhil.stanford.edu.

Chapter 55

Learning Is Not Optional: A CEO's Perspective

Douglas R. Conant

Although it has been said many times throughout history, I'm going to echo the sentiment: Times are tough.

The rapidly changing business landscape is deeply competitive and unforgiving. What is common practice today may be obsolete tomorrow. What is innovative this week may be old-hat the next. In my many years of experience as both a leader and a follower, I have found that you owe it to all your stakeholders to do everything in your power to remain competitive, to succeed in the face of adversity, to deliver quality results in an enduring way, and to do so with integrity. As a leader, committing to meeting the challenges of today's marketplace is crucial to serving your people and your organization. What does that mean? It means that you must work tirelessly to develop an adaptive leadership approach to all aspects of your business. The demands of the marketplace require it. This translates to an indisputable need for the fierce pursuit of learning and growth. This requirement remains a constant in the face of the staggering changes we are encountering in the 21st century.

Grow or Die

The global marketplace requires a tough-minded commitment to setting and meeting high standards. Businesses must constantly strive to meet customer needs faster, better, and more completely than their competitors. It is a very Darwinian environment. Innovation is essential. You either adapt and prevail or you cease to exist, crushed under the weight of mediocre performance. So how do you arm yourself, and the people you serve, with the tools to thrive in the face of the challenges of an ever-changing landscape? First, you must ensure quality growth. You must demand it as part of your organizational DNA. As Darwin observed, those who thrive and survive are not the strongest or the smartest, but the most *adaptable*. Those who are most able to change and grow are best equipped to meet the rapid-fire changes encountered in the workplace, the marketplace, and the world at large. Growth is essential to remaining afloat.

How do you grow? You learn! Growing demands learning. You learn by constantly seeking new ways to leverage your ability to contribute, by learning new skills, and by voraciously consuming the advice of people with valuable expertise. You really have no choice. Everyone around you, including your competitors, is striving to attain the necessary growth to survive—if you do not, you are at risk. Given the choice of growth or death, growth surely beats the grim alternative.

Does this mean ruthlessly pursuing growth at the expense of deeply held values and relationships? Absolutely not. A misconception often associated with Darwinian business examples is the idea that one must embrace brutality to survive. The opposite is true. While tough standards are integral to business success, a commitment to learning and development allows for a practical and rewarding way to meet those standards. It is a win–win. A company that embraces learning in a quality way has met the demands for growth while visibly demonstrating that it values its employees. This has the potential to make you wildly competitive. Indeed, in my experience, the most effective companies and leaders understand that the key to success begins and ends with people. *It is all about the people.* You get the right people "on the bus." Then, you invest in the growth and development of those "right" people. Give them the tools and energy to do their jobs with distinction and they will do the same for you and your company. And, you will have meaningfully improved your potential to thrive.

Be the Change

To take this notion a step further, I've found that purposefully embracing growth and learning is so crucial to effective leadership and success of any kind that it bears constant repeating. But, it is not enough to say the words. You can't just pay the idea lip service. Gandhi famously said that you have to "be the change" you want to see in the world. His words are remarkably applicable here. Creating a company that champions learning and development in a meaningful way begins with leadership, at the top. While it is important to declare your commitment, there has to be quality alignment between your words and your actions. If you say, "I believe a learning culture is essential to growth," you have to physically show it and help create it. This means walking the talk every day with your own conduct. There are two important ways to manifest this commitment to creating a culture of learning.

At the Individual Level

A quality learning culture in any organization needs to be led by people who are visibly learning and growing. It is essential to model the behavior as an individual. People should be able to perceive your efforts in plain sight. My office is lined with books from floor to ceiling. It is no accident. I love to read, I hunger to learn, and I enjoy sharing that enthusiasm with my friends, family, and colleagues. If we've spent any meaningful time together, chances are I've handed you a book (or two). I am clearly committed to learning and personal growth as I endeavor to be the change that I want to see in the world.

At the Group Level

The idea of growth extends beyond the individual and becomes even more paramount when you are pursuing this notion in order to move a whole company forward. Then, it becomes about creating a community that is learning and growing together. Most necessary here is that your leadership must foster an approach that both celebrates learning and demands it.

When you are working to build a community that values growth, it is helpful to note a push/pull dynamic in play. The principle works like this:

> Pull: Celebrate learning so that people are inspired to pursue it and want to do it.

> Push: Make the expectation clear. Leaders must articulate clearly that they expect members of their organization to be learning and growing.

When deployed effectively, the dynamic works harmoniously, creating a tandem push and pull in which people are challenged to learn and increase their ability to contribute, and are celebrated for doing so. Everybody wins. And everybody gets better.

Talent Is Overrated

You know the demands of doing business require growth. And, you know that you have to embody growth and precipitate the desire for it through your own behavior. So, what's the next step? How do you actualize the effort? Vital to accomplishing essential training and development initiatives is the idea of *deliberate practice*. In Geoff Colvin's (2008) celebrated book, *Talent Is Overrated,* he makes the powerful assertion that neither talent nor experience can explain extraordinary performance. In fact, they are poor predictors of success, time and time again. What really makes the difference between "average" and "extraordinary" is hard work. Sure, it sounds obvious. The harder you work, the better you get. But Colvin is not referring to merely putting in the hours. *Deliberate practice* refers to a calculated and studious approach to improving and practicing, to identifying specific areas for growth and pursuing them tirelessly, often working through discomfort and a strong urge to throw in the towel. Only through this arduous process can you achieve superior progress.

What's the lesson here? There are no shortcuts to exemplary performance. And there are no excuses. If you're not great in one area that is crucial to your success at the individual or organizational levels, it is simply inadequate to say, "Well, that's just not something I'm good at. I'll keep focusing on the strengths I do have." No! This is where the importance of training and development becomes so riveting. With a fierce resolve for improvement, you can and must identify the precise areas you want to develop and pursue a way to progress in those *specific areas*. A shortcoming or lack of experience is no longer a pretext for complacency. It becomes an exciting opportunity to leverage the resources that are available to make you better. How empowering! I find it deeply inspiring that you don't have to be born with any special set of talents or predilections but can work to manifest them through steadfast training. I believe that part of serving a great company in a leadership capacity means providing the necessary resources for ongoing growth, while also championing the high standards that are required to deliver that growth in an enduring way. It boils down to this mantra: **To win in the marketplace, you must first win in the workplace**. To win in the workplace, you must commit to training and development in a meticulously purposeful way.

Jack Zenger

Jack Zenger is a pioneer in leadership training as well as a renowned author and speaker. He has co-authored numerous books on leadership, including *The Handbook for Leaders: 24 Lessons for Extraordinary Leaders* (2004, with Joseph Folkman and John Zenger), *The Extraordinary Leader: Turning Good Managers Into Great Leaders* (2002, with Joseph Folkman), and *Results-Based Leadership* (1999, with David Ulrich and Norman Smallwood). Zenger's research on leadership resulted in the identification of five clusters of leadership competencies, which include character, personal competence, interpersonal competence, driving for results, and leading change.

A Mastery Model

During my tenure as CEO of Campbell Soup Company, I had the privilege of applying my personal passion for training and development to our CEO Institute. This was a comprehensive, two-year program that I created and taught with my chief human resources officer, Nancy Reardon, and my friend and co-author of *TouchPoints*, Mette Norgaard (2011). We focused on leadership because we identified it as a specific area we needed to develop—not just to improve things today, but also to be proactive about creating a tangibly fulfilling experience for our future employees. We chose leadership as a distinct area to conscientiously nurture in accordance with the idea of deliberate practice. We emphasized leadership training because we were well aware that people will join a great company, but they will abandon poor leadership. In order to build Campbell into a company that would be great in an abiding way, we needed to ensure that there was a generation of leaders in place who would be competent enough to profoundly inspire people and deliver exceptional results for generations to come. Crucial to bringing this notion to fruition was the idea of a mastery model for leadership.

I do not believe great leaders are born, as some popular thinking suggests. Rather, they are made. In Jim Collins's (2001) seminal leadership work, *Good to Great*, he concluded (after analyzing an enormous amount of compelling data) that what distinguishes the very best leaders from the merely good leaders are the traits of humility and fierce resolve. Not humility *or* fierce resolve, but both. This means that great leaders recognize the need to get better (humility) and are determined to do whatever it takes to achieve that growth (fierce resolve). This supports my own observations of the leaders I admire.

Great leaders view leadership as a craft, not a congenital birthright. Like any craftsman, they do the painstaking work necessary to hone their skills. This was the mastery model concept we applied to the CEO Institute. Once we had the right participants in place—

people who were highly competent and visibly committed to bettering their craft—we were able to work closely with them as they "apprenticed" in our leadership institute. First, they were exposed to the six expectations of the Campbell Leadership Model that we created, as displayed in Figure 55-1.

Then, in the pursuit of ownership of their own mastery, they were urged to do the careful reflection necessary to developing their own leadership models—personal models that would work for them in their unique cultures and contexts. I've included the Campbell Leadership Model in Figure 55-1 because I think it is helpful to note that each component requires ongoing growth.

Figure 55-1. The Campbell Leadership Model

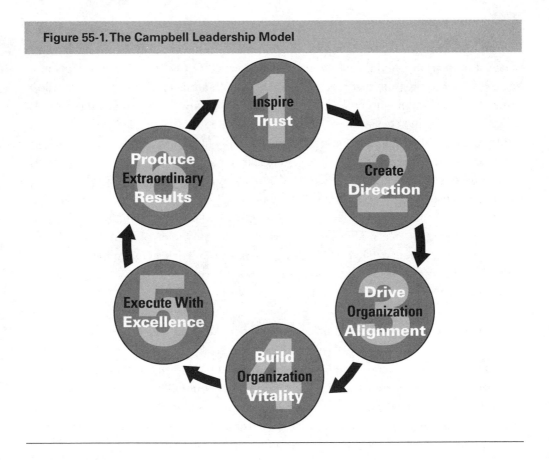

Expanding on the idea of deliberate practice and a mastery model, it is important to advocate accumulated wisdom. A training agenda that asks participants to simply attend a class and take some notes is highly unlikely to get traction with anyone. One class will not do the trick. Maybe this should be obvious, but regrettably it is not. Deliberate practice and a mastery model are designed to leverage accumulated knowledge over the long term. This includes three essential components:

1. **Experiential learning:** Learning through real-life experiences; applying and practicing principals and tools in the real world and workplace.
2. **Classroom learning:** Structured learning led by knowledge experts in the field; assigned reading and written work; case exercises.
3. **Personal development time:** Pursuing further knowledge; internalizing and reflecting on acquired skills and principles; fostering a process for perpetual personal improvement.

When all three components work in concert, only then can you begin to realize your full potential as a leader—or anything else you seek to become: a painter, a linebacker, a litigator, a poet. No matter what discipline you choose, you have to put in the work on all three fronts. And when you are leading change at the organizational level, and endeavoring to advance a culture of learning companywide, it is imperative you understand this notion intellectually, viscerally, and wholeheartedly.

Abundance Is Best

An idea that inspires all my thinking about leadership is that of an abundance mentality. The abundance idea anchors my behavior in each and every interaction. I use it as a compass to keep me on track and help me contribute in the most useful way at the time, and I think it is highly relevant to training and development. Without an abundance mentality, your learning and personal growth will be limited.

What does an abundance mentality entail? It means profoundly changing your thinking to reject the tyranny of the "or" and embrace the genius of the "and." From a leadership perspective, that means being tough-minded on standards *and* tenderhearted with people—not one or the other. Both. It's the only way to create a sustainable model that works and thrives in the face of adversity. This circles back to the idea of personally valuing people by giving them the resources to succeed and grow, which in turn allows them to meet the tough standards necessary to keep your company on top in an ever-challenging marketplace. Provide all your employees with a training agenda and give them an opportunity to grow. You will be amazed at what you can do. From a training perspective, the abundance mentality principle applies to the humility *and* fierce resolve needed to carry out the actual learning. You need both to fulfill the mandate of radical progress in the face of constant change.

The mission of advancing the training and development profession is a pressing one. I've seen firsthand how powerful learning and the pursuit of mastery can be. Personally, I humbly consider myself an eternal student, always studying the art of leadership, always trying to do better. It is my belief that fostering an enthusiasm for learning and underlining its importance are critical directives. In my opinion, it is truly the most effective way to keep your promise of excellence to all stakeholders. If you are not providing employees with the resources to improve, you are missing the mark. If you invest in people and provide them opportunities for development, the more engaged they will become, the better they will perform in their roles, and the better growth potential of your organization in the marketplace. Remember, it is all about the people. Your challenge as a leader is to recognize that your company's only sustainable competitive advantage is the ability of your people to innovate, adapt, learn, and create new value for your customers. Every single day, there is the choice to grow or die. I suggest growth. It is by far the most rewarding, and effective, choice of all.

About the Author

Douglas R. Conant serves as chairman of Avon Products and chairman of the Kellogg Executive Leadership Institute (KELI) at Northwestern University. He is also the founder and CEO of ConantLeadership, a company dedicated to improving the quality of leadership in the 21st century. From 2001 to 2011, he served as the president and CEO of Campbell Soup Company, where his mission to achieve superior employee engagement levels was a crucial contributor to the company's exemplary performance during his tenure. A *New York Times* bestselling author, Conant speaks widely to organizations on effective leadership practices for the 21st century.

This chapter was possible with the help of Amy Federman.

References

Collins, J.C. (2001). *Good to Great: Why Some Companies Make the Leap—and Others Don't*. New York: Harper Business.

Colvin, G. (2008). *Talent Is Overrated: What Really Separates World-Class Performers From Everybody Else*. New York: Portfolio.

For Further Reading

Beer, M., R. Eisenstat, N. Foote, T. Fredberg, and F. Norrgren. (2011). *Higher Ambition: How Great Leaders Create Economic and Social Value*. Boston: Harvard Business Review Press.

Collins, J.C. (2001). *Good to Great: Why Some Companies Make the Leap—and Others Don't*. New York: Harper Business.

Colvin, G. (2008). *Talent Is Overrated: What Really Separates World-Class Performers from Everybody Else*. New York: Portfolio.

Conant, D.R., and M. Norgaard. (2011). *TouchPoints: Creating Powerful Leadership Connections in the Smallest of Moments*. San Francisco: Jossey-Bass.

Appendix A

Glossary

A

Accelerated Learning (AL) is the practice of using a multimodal, multisensory approach to instruction to make learning more efficient. It's accomplished by honoring the different learning preferences of each learner and using experiential learning exercises (such as role plays, mnemonics, props, and music).

Accomplishments refer to the specific outputs a performer is asked to achieve.

Active Training is an approach that ensures that participants are actively involved in the learning process. Active learning is based on cooperative learning, in which participants learn from each other in pairs or small groups. Some examples of active training include group discussions, games, simulations, and role plays.

ADDIE is an instructional systems development model composed of five phases: analysis, design, development, implementation, and evaluation.

- **Analysis** is the process of gathering data to identify specific needs—the who, what, where, when, and why of the design process.
- **Design** is the planning stage.
- **Development** is the phase in which training materials and content are selected and developed based on learning objectives.
- **Implementation** occurs when the course is delivered, whether in person or electronically.
- **Evaluation** is the ongoing process of developing and improving instructional materials based on feedback received during and following implementation.

Adult Learning Theory encompasses the collective theories and principles of how adults learn and acquire knowledge. Popularized by Malcolm Knowles, adult learning theory provides the foundation that learning and development professionals need to meet learning needs in the workplace.

Affective Learning is the acquisition of knowledge based on Benjamin Bloom's taxonomy in which he identified three learning domains: cognitive, affective, and psychomotor. Affective refers to the learner's outlook, attitude, or mindset.

Affinity Diagrams (also referred to as affinity maps) gather large numbers of ideas, organize them into logical groupings based on the natural relationships among items, and define groups of items. The outcomes of affinity diagrams are large groups of ideas that are grouped into related clusters of ideas, each with a clear title and with the relationship among the clusters clearly drawn. (See also *Interrelationship Digraphs*.)

After Action Review (AAR) was first developed by the U.S. Army to allow individuals to learn for themselves after an action what happened, why, and how to improve performance.

Alternate Reality Game is a story-like game that manifests in the real world, spread over time and space, using varied media.

Analysis is a systematic examination and evaluation of data or information that breaks it into its component parts to uncover their interrelationships. Common analyses in training and development include these.

- **Audience Analysis** is conducted to understand a target population, demographics, and other relevant information prior to job analysis, training, or other solution.
- **Gap Analysis** identifies the discrepancy between the desired and actual knowledge, skills, and performance, and specifies root causes.
- **Job Analysis** identifies all duties and responsibilities and the respective tasks done on a daily, weekly, monthly, or yearly basis.
- **Root Cause Analysis** identifies the true cause(s) of the gap between desired and actual knowledge, skills, or performance.
- **SWOT Analysis** is a matrix analysis of strengths, weaknesses, opportunities, and threats, usually addressing an organizational analysis, but can be used by an individual.
- **Task Analysis** is the process of identifying the specific steps to correctly perform a job function.
- **Training Needs Analysis** is the process of collecting and synthesizing data to identify how training can help an organization reach its goals.

Analytics is the discovery and communication of meaningful patterns in data. Talent management analytics refers to the use of HR and talent data to improve business performance.

Andragogy (from the Greek meaning "adult learning") is the adult learning theory developed by Malcolm Knowles based on five key principles that influence how adults learn: self-concept, prior experience, readiness to learn, orientation to learning, and motivation to learn.

Appreciative Inquiry (AI) is an approach to large-scale organizational change that involves the analysis of positive and successful (rather than negative or failing) operations. The AI 4-D cycle (discovery, dream, design, destiny) includes identifying areas for improvement, analyzing previous successes, searching for solutions, and developing an action plan.

Areas of Expertise (AOEs) are specialized, functional knowledge and skill sets needed for a particular job or industry. In the current Competency Model, 10 AOEs were identified for the T&D profession.

Assessment Center is a catch-all term for a variety of exercises, including oral exercises, counseling simulations, problem analysis exercises, interview simulations, role-play exercises, written report or analysis exercises, and group exercises.

ASTD Competency Model is an occupation-wide model that identifies the knowledge, skills, and behaviors necessary to be a successful performer in the T&D field.

ASTD HPI Model is a results-based, systematic process used to identify performance problems, analyze root causes, select and design solutions, manage solutions in the workplace, measure results, and continually improve performance in an organization.

Asynchronous Communication is a communication that occurs outside real time.

Asynchronous Training or Learning is learning in which the trainer and the learner do not participate simultaneously; for example, asynchronous e-learning.

Audio refers to the electronic or digital reproduction of sound waves. Used most broadly to refer to sounds we hear. On its own, it is a method of communication that is used in radio and in multimedia applications. Audio is also a component of video communication that combines both pictures and audio.

Audio Editing is the process of cutting out unwanted content from an audio recording. Traditionally performed by literally cutting tape, it is now performed using audio editing software where "umms" and "ahhs" and other elements can be cut from the audio. Audio editing also includes adding music, sound effects, and processing the audio elements with tools such as the graphic equalizer and compressor.

Augmented Reality uses digital technology to add information to a real-world environment whose elements are augmented or supplemented by computer-generated sensory input such as sound, video, graphics, or GPS data.

Authoring Tools are software programs that allow a content expert to interact with a computer in everyday language to develop courseware.

Avatar is a graphical representation of the computer user or the user's alter ego or character.

B

Baby Boomer refers to the generation born from 1946 to 1963 in the U.S. who are typically characterized as competitive and loyal to their employers.

Behaviorism is an approach to psychology focused on observable and measurable behavior. It is usually associated with psychologist and author B.F. Skinner.

Benchmarking is an evaluation of one's own practices and comparison with other companies' practices.

Best Practices are techniques that are believed to constitute a paradigm of excellence in a particular field.

Blended Learning is the practice of using several media in one curriculum. It typically refers to the combination of classroom instruction and any type of training that includes use of online resources.

Blog (weblog) is an extension of a personal website consisting of journal-like entries posted on a webpage for public viewing. Blogs usually contain links to other websites along with the thoughts, comments, and personality of the blog's creator.

Bloom's Digital Taxonomy is an update to Bloom's Revised Taxonomy that attempts to account for the new behaviors and actions emerging as technology advances and becomes more ubiquitous.

Bloom's Taxonomy, developed by Benjamin Bloom, consists of the three learning outcomes based on three domains: cognitive (knowledge), psychomotor (skills), and affective (attitude)—sometimes referred to as KSAs.

Brainstorming is a group process for generating ideas in an uninhibited manner.

Breakout Rooms are private meeting sub-rooms where participants have private discussions and collaborate on tasks. In a virtual classroom, the facilitator creates a breakout room as a whiteboard or chat; in an instructor-led in-person classroom, the facilitator identifies additional space, often located in a separate room.

Burden of Evidence is the degree to which an evaluation must be able to isolate the effects of the interventions, and to provide compelling proof on a solutions impact.

Business Acumen is the understanding of how a company makes money in order to make prompt and wise business decisions that are likely to lead to a good outcome.

Business Awareness is the understanding of key factors affecting a business, such as its current situation, influences from its industry or market, and factors affecting growth. Having business awareness is essential to strategic involvement with top management.

Business Case is the justification of value added for any organization, program, project, or initiative.

Business Intelligence (BI) Tools are tools and systems that play a role in strategic planning and help organizations make decisions.

Buzz Groups are small groups of learners assembled to discuss specific issues, problems, or situations within a short, stated timeframe.

C

Career Advisors, also called career coaches, are those professionals responsible for career advising.

Career Development is a planned process of interaction between an organization and an individual that allows the employee to grow in an organization.

Case Study is a learning method in which a real or fictitious situation is presented for analysis and problem solving.

Cause-and-Effect Analysis is a diagram-based exercise (sometimes called a fishbone diagram) to identify all the likely causes of a problem.

Certification is the validation of competencies, usually through testing, which typically results in a designation. The designation is typically earned by an individual for the purpose of assuring one's qualifications to practice.

Chain of Evidence refers to the data, information, and testimonies at each of the four evaluation levels that, when presented in sequence, act to demonstrate value obtained from a business partnership initiative.

Chat Room is a synchronous process in which the learners and trainer are online at the same time. Chat rooms are similar to electronic bulletin boards, but bulletin boards are asynchronous.

Coaching is a process in which a more experienced person, or coach, provides an employee with constructive advice and feedback with the goal of improving performance.

Cognition is a group of mental processes that includes attention, memory, producing and understanding language, learning, reasoning, problem solving, and decision making.

Cognitive Dissonance Theory states that when contradicting cognitions exist, this conflict compels the human mind to acquire or invent new thoughts or beliefs or to modify existing beliefs to minimize the amount of dissonance between cognitions.

Cognitive Load refers to mental work imposed on working memory that may help or impede learning.

Cognitivism is a theory that attempts to answer how and why people learn by attributing the process to cognitive activity. It is the "tell" approach to learning, based on the theory that learning occurs through exposure to logically presented information, usually involving lecture. It can also include diagrams, videos, films, panels, class presentations, interviews with SMEs, readings, debates, and case studies.

Collaborative Learning is an instructional approach in which learners and instructors share the responsibility for learning and work together to determine how a session should progress.

Commentary is a media term used to describe narration in audio or video. In video, commentary provides additional information that has not been conveyed by picture.

Community of Practice (CoP) is a group of people who share a common interest in an area of competence and who share the experiences of their practice.

Competencies include the knowledge, skills, and behaviors necessary to successfully perform key work functions in a job, industry, or occupation.

Competency Model refers to the knowledge, skills, and behaviors necessary to successfully perform key work functions in a job, industry, or occupation. A competency model is usually represented graphically.

Computer-Based Training (CBT) encompasses the use of computers in both instruction and management of the teaching and learning process. Computer-aided instruction and computer-managed instruction are also included under the term CBT.

Concurrent Validity is the extent to which an instrument agrees with the results of other instruments administered at approximately the same time to measure the same characteristics.

Conditions of Learning refers to Robert Gagné's theory of nine events of instruction that ensure learning occurs.

Consultant is a person who uses expertise, influence, and personal skills to facilitate a client-requested change or improvement. Consultants may be employees of an organization (internal) or under contract with the organization (external) due to needed help, information, or perspective.

Content Management System (CMS) is a computer software system for organizing and facilitating collaborative creation of documents and other content. A CMS is frequently a web application used for managing websites and web content, though in many cases, CMSs require special client software for editing and constructing articles.

Control Group is a group of participants in an experiment that is equal in all ways to the experimental group except for having received the experimental treatment (for example, a group that has undergone training versus a group that has not).

Correlation is a measure of the relationship between two or more variables; if one changes, the other is likely to make a corresponding change. If such a change moves the variables in the same direction, it is a positive correlation; if the change moves the variables in opposite directions, it is a negative correlation.

Cost-Benefit Analysis is a type of return-on-investment analysis used to prove that an initiative either paid for itself or generated more financial benefit than costs.

Counseling helps people evaluate their behaviors and discover and learn more productive behavior patterns.

CPLP (Certified Professional in Learning and Performance) is a professional credential offered by the ASTD Certification Institute to training and development professionals.

Criterion Validity is the extent to which an assessment can predict or agree with external constructs. Criterion validity is determined by looking at the correlation between the instrument and the criterion measure.

Critical Behaviors are the minimum, key behaviors that employees require to consistently perform on the job in order to bring about targeted outcomes.

Crowdsourcing is the practice of obtaining needed services, ideas, or content by soliciting contributions from a large group of people, and especially from an online community, rather than from traditional employees or suppliers.

CSS stands for cascading style sheets, a standard for separating out how information looks from what it says, supporting flexible content delivery.

Current Capability Assessment measures an organization's talent and how current skills match the needs of the organization now and in the future.

D

Data Collection refers to the collection of all facts, figures, statistics, and other information that is used for various types of analyses and assessments. Some examples of data-collection methods or tools are examinations of in-house or external written sources, questionnaires, interviews, and observation of trainees or jobholders.

Decorative Graphic is a visual that is added for aesthetic or humorous effect.

Delivery is any method of transferring content to learners, including instructor-led training, web-based training, CD-ROM, and books.

Design is the planning stage of a learning initiative.

Development is learning or other types of activities that prepare a person for additional job responsibilities and enable him to gain knowledge or skills. It may also refer to the creation of training materials or courses. (See also *ADDIE*.)

Discovery Learning is the process of learning by engaging in an activity.

Distance Learning is an educational situation in which the instructor and students are separated by time, location, or both. Distance learning can be synchronous or asynchronous.

Double-Loop Learning is to change underlying values and assumptions as decision making progresses. People often refer to this act as reframing or changing the context.

Drivers are processes and systems that reinforce, monitor, encourage, and reward performance of critical behaviors on the job.

Dyads consist of two learners working together as a team to conduct discussions, role plays, or other experiential activities in a training session.

E

Effect Size is a way of quantifying the difference, using standard deviation, between two groups. For example, if one group (the treatment group) has had an experimental treatment and the other (the control group) has not, the effect size is a measure of the effectiveness between the two groups.

E-Learning is a term covering a wide set of applications and processes, such as web-based learning, computer-based learning, virtual classrooms, and digital collaboration. Delivery of content may take place via the Internet, intranet or extranet (local area network [LAN] or wide area network [WAN]), audio- and videotape, satellite broadcast, interactive television, CD-ROM, and more.

Electronic Performance Support System (EPSS) is software that provides just-in-time, on-demand information, guidance, examples, and step-by-step dialog boxes to improve job performance without the need for training or coaching by other people.

Embodied Interaction occurs during human-computer interaction in physical and social spaces emphasizing practical engagement over abstract reasoning and situated meaning over generalization.

Embodied Space is the location where human experience and consciousness takes on material and spatial form.

Emotional Intelligence is an "eighth intelligence" based on Gardner's multiple intelligence theory, which suggests an ability to accurately identify and understand one's own emotional reactions and those of others and is related to personal qualities,such as self-confidence and motivation. The theory was popularized by Daniel Goleman in the 1990s in his book, *Emotional Intelligence.*

Enabling Objectives, also called supporting objectives, support terminal objectives by breaking them down into manageable chunks. Enabling objectives are the building blocks that provide additional concepts or skills needed to meet a terminal objective. (See also *Terminal Objectives.*)

Engagement is a heightened emotional connection that an employee feels for his organization that influences him to give greater discretionary effort to his work. Higher engagement levels yield higher productivity and retention rates.

Environment is the setting or condition in which an activity occurs. Environment is a factor that affects performance and it can include tools, equipment, furniture, hardware and software, and physical conditions, such as light, heat or cold, ventilation, and so forth.

Evaluation of training is a multilevel, systematic method for gathering information about the effectiveness and effect of training programs. Results of the measurements can be used to improve the offering, determine whether the learning objectives have been achieved, and assess the value of the training to the organization.

Evidence-Based Training is a process of making decisions regarding the design, development, and delivery of training on data rather than opinion or tradition.

Experience-Centered Instruction focuses on the learner's experience during instruction and the production of fresh insights.

Experiential Learning occurs when a learner participates in an activity, reviews the activity, identifies useful knowledge or skills that were gained, and transfers the result to the workplace.

Experiential Learning Activities (ELAs) are a way of learning that emphasizes experience and reflection and uses an inductive learning process that takes the learner through five stages: experiencing, publishing, processing, generalizing, and applying.

Explanatory Graphic is a visual that illustrates qualitative or quantitative relationships among lesson content elements.

Explicit Knowledge is information that has been documented or can be shared with someone.

Extant Data are archival or existing records, reports, and data that may be available inside or outside an organization. Examples include job descriptions, competency models, benchmarking reports, annual reports, financial statements, strategic plans, mission statements, staffing statistics, climate surveys, 360-degree (or upward) feedback, performance appraisals, grievances, turnover rates, absenteeism, suggestion box feedback, and accident statistics.

Extraneous Cognitive Load refers to irrelevant mental work imposed on working memory that impedes learning.

F

Facilitation in the training field refers to the work of the person or trainer who guides or makes learning easier, both in content and in application of the content to the job.

Flipped Classroom is a form of blended learning in which new content is learned independently online, by watching video lectures, or reading, followed by more personalized guidance and interaction with the trainer instead of lecturing.

Force Field Analysis is a diagnostic tool developed by Kurt Lewin to assess two types of forces related to introducing change in organizations: driving and restraining. Driving forces are those that help implement the change, whereas restraining forces are those that will get in the way of the change.

Forecasting Models are used to isolate the effects of training. With this approach, the output variable is predicted with the assumption that no training is conducted. The actual performance of the variable after the training is then compared with the forecasted value, which results in an estimate of the training impact.

Formal Learning is planned learning that derives from activities within a structured learning setting.

Formative Evaluation (from a training impact perspective) is an assessment of the effectiveness of a training program while the program materials are being developed or "formed." Examples of formative evaluation include pilots as well as technical and production reviews.

Foundational Competencies are the clusters of competencies needed for success across most occupations. In the ASTD Competency Model, they are the bedrock upon which to build more specialized, T&D-specific competencies.

Front-End Analysis is a term credited to Joe Harless that refers to performance analysis. It includes carrying out a business analysis, identifying performance gaps, completing a task analysis, performing a cause analysis, and usually identifying a key performer or exemplar.

G

Gagné's Nine Events of Instruction were developed by Robert Gagné, a pioneer in the field of instructional design. His nine events of instruction are meant to help ensure that learning occurs.

Gamification applies the essence of games: fun, play, transparency, design, and challenge to real-world objectives in scenarios that can be conducted online or offline.

Gantt Chart graphically displays the time relationships of a project's steps and key checkpoints or deliverable dates, known as milestones.

Gap Analysis is a critical activity carried out during performance analysis that defines driving and restraining forces, current state versus desired state, and methods for change.

Gardner, Howard developed the Multiple Intelligence Theory, which states there's no single way in which everyone thinks and learns. Gardner devised a list of intelligences: linguistic/verbal, logical/mathematical, spatial/visual, bodily/kinesthetic, musical, interpersonal, intrapersonal, naturalistic, existential, and emotional. These intelligences in different combinations make up a person's learning style.

Generation X refers to those born from 1964 to 1979 in the U.S. who are typically characterized as independent free agents accustomed to taking care of themselves and making lifestyle choices that contribute to their happiness and health.

Generation Y, also called Millenials, are the members of the generation born after 1980 in the U.S. who are the most outspoken and empowered. They are socially conscious, self-centered, and have high expectations of organizations.

Gilbert's Behavior Engineering Model identified six factors that can either hinder or facilitate workplace performance: information, resources, incentives or consequences, knowledge and skills, capacity, and motivation. Thomas F. Gilbert was a psychologist who lived from 1927 to 1995.

Goals refer to end states or conditions toward which human effort is directed.

Governance is the oversight of process, such as strategy or content life cycle, including policy and management.

H

Hard Data are objective, quantitative measures commonly stated in terms of frequency, percentage, proportion, or time.

Harless's Front-End Analysis Model is a diagnostic model designed by Joe Harless to identify the cause of a performance problem; the model is based on the belief that the cause should drive the solution.

Heads-Up Display (HUD) is any transparent display that presents data without requiring users to look away from their usual viewpoints.

Herrmann Brain Dominance Instrument is a method of personality testing developed by W.E. (Ned) Herrmann that classifies learners in terms of preferences for thinking in four modes based on brain function: left brain, cerebral; left brain, limbic; right brain, limbic; right brain, cerebral. (See also *Learning Styles*.)

Horizontal Development refers to adding more knowledge, skills, and competencies. It is about what you know and is measured through 360-degree feedback.

HTML5 is the fifth revision of the markup language for the World Wide Web, standardizing a variety of advanced features supporting animation and interactivity across web applications' responsive design.

Human Capital describes the collective knowledge, skills, competencies, and value of the people in an organization.

Human Performance Improvement (HPI) is a results-based, systematic process used to identify performance problems, analyze root causes, select and design actions, manage solutions in the workplace, measure results, and continually improve performance in an organization. It is based on open systems theory, or the view that any organization is a system that absorbs environmental inputs, uses them in transformational processes, and produces outputs.

Human Resource Development (HRD) is the term coined by Leonard Nadler to describe the organized learning experiences of training, education, and development offered by employers within a specific timeframe to improve employee performance or personal growth. Also, it is another name for the field and profession sometimes called training or training and development.

I

Icebreakers are activities conducted at the beginning of training programs that introduce participants to one another, may introduce content, and in general help participants ease into the program.

Implementation occurs when a course is delivered, whether in person or virtually.

Independent Variable is the variable that influences the dependent variable. Age, seniority, gender, shift, level of education, and so on may all be factors (independent variables) that influence a person's performance (the dependent variable).

Individual Development Plans (IDPs) are plans for improvement in a current job or for job advancement. These plans may or may not be tied to a performance appraisal system; however, a good plan usually is integrated with a performance appraisal.

Informal Learning describes learning that occurs outside a structured program or class. It happens in everyday life and on the job through observing others, trial-and-error, and talking and collaborating with others. The broad category of informal learning can include social learning, but some instances of informal learning are not social—for example, studying and reading.

Instant Feedback is a feature that allows participants to communicate with facilitators at any time throughout a virtual classroom by selecting from a menu of feedback options such as: raise hand, agree, stepped away; may also be referred to as a raise hand feature, emoticons, or status changes.

Instruction is imparted knowledge as well as the practice of instructing. Instruction or training is used to fill a learning need. In the workplace, it covers many types of content and can be delivered in many formal and informal ways.

Instructional Designer is a person who applies a systematic methodology based on instructional theory to create learning content.

Instructional Strategies, sometimes called presentation strategies, are the mechanisms through which instruction is presented.

Instructional System is the combination of inputs, such as subject matter and resources, and outputs, such as curriculum and materials, to build a training course.

Instructional Systems Design (ISD), sometimes referred to as instructional systems development, is a systems approach to analyzing, designing, developing, implementing, and evaluating any instructional experience based on the belief that training is most effective when it gives learners a clear statement of what they must be able to do as a result of training and how their performance will be evaluated.

Integrated Talent Management (ITM) is a series of HR processes that are integrated for competitive advantage. ITM builds an organization's culture, engagement, capability, and capacity through the integration of such processes as talent acquisition, employee development, retention, and deployment; it ensures that these processes are aligned to organizational goals and strategy. ITM is sometimes described as putting the right people with the right skills in the right jobs at the right time.

Interrelationship Digraphs are follow-ons to affinity diagrams. They chart cause-and-effect relationships among groups of ideas. (See also *Affinity Diagrams.*)

Interval Variables make it possible to rank order items being measured and to quantify and compare the sizes of differences between them.

Intranet is a computer network that's accessible only to authorized users; for example, to employees of an organization.

Intrapreneurship was defined in 1978 by Gifford and Elizabeth Pinchot and refers to free market entrepreneurship within a corporation; currently is used as a means for organizations to ignite innovation within their ranks and effectively develop employees of diverse ages and backgrounds.

J

Job Aids provide guidance about when and how to carry out tasks and steps. Job aids, also known as performance support, reduce the amount of recall needed and minimize error. Tasks performed infrequently, or tasks that are highly complex or likely to change, or involve a high probability of error, are good candidates for job aids. Job aids often take the form of checklists, video demonstrations, or audio instruction.

Job Analysis identifies all duties and job responsibilities and the respective tasks done on a daily, weekly, monthly, or yearly basis that make up a single job function or role.

Just-in-Time Training is instruction delivered when it's needed and used on a job.

K

Kirkpatrick, Donald, a pioneer of training evaluation, first postulated his evaluation model in the 1950s. The model has four levels of evaluation: reaction, learning, behavior, and results. (See also *Evaluation.*)

Knowledge relates to the cognitive abilities a person needs to be able to carry out a job. Knowledge involves the development of intellectual skills.

Knowledge Exchanges, also known as knowledge exchange networks, enable different groups in an organization to share documents and information, create lists of links in simple webpages, and discuss issues of mutual interest.

Knowledge Management (KM) is the explicit and systematic management of intellectual capital and organizational knowledge as well as the associated processes of creating, gathering, organizing, disseminating, leveraging, and using intellectual capital for improving the organization and the individuals in it.

Knowledge Mapping is a process for identifying and connecting the location, ownership, value, and use of knowledge and expertise in an organization. Examples of knowledge maps are network charts, yellow pages of experts, or a matrix relating knowledge to key processes.

Knowledge Repository is the storage location of knowledge in a knowledge management system.

Knowles, Malcolm is considered the father of adult learning theory. He defined six assumptions about adult learning and published *The Adult Learner: A Neglected Species* in 1973.

Kolb's Learning Style Inventory, developed by David Kolb, is an inventory of four learning styles or modes (concrete experience, reflective observation, abstract conceptualization, and active experimentation) and learners' orientation to them. Kolb categorizes learners as convergers, divergers, assimilators, or accommodators.

KSA is an abbreviation standing for two different things, depending on who is using it: 1) Knowledge (cognitive), skills (psychomotor), and *attitude* (affective) are the three objective domains of learning defined by Benjamin Bloom's taxonomy in the 1950s. Bloom's classification of learning objectives is used in education and training to determine the goals of the educational process. 2) Knowledge, skills, and *ability* are the KSAs used by the U.S. federal government and some private hiring agencies to distinguish qualified from unqualified candidates.

L

Leadership Development is any activity that increases the leadership ability of an individual or the leadership capability of an organization. It includes activities such as learning events, mentoring, coaching, self-study, job rotation, and special assignments to develop the knowledge and skills required to lead.

Leading Indicators are short-term observations and measurements suggesting that critical behaviors are on track to create a positive impact on desired results.

Learning is the process of gaining knowledge, understanding, or skill by study, instruction, or experience.

Learning Content Management System (LCMS) is software technology that provides a multi-user environment where developers, authors, instructional designers, and subject matter experts may create, store, reuse, manage, and deliver digital e-learning content from a central object repository. An LCMS focuses on the development, management, and publishing of the content that will typically be delivered via a learning management system (LMS).

Learning Environment is the physical and emotional surroundings and setting in which learning takes place.

Learning Information Systems are complementary networks of hardware and software used to create, deliver, and administer learning. LMSs and LCMSs are examples of such tools.

Learning Management System (LMS) is software technology for delivering online courses or training to learners while performing learning management functions such as creating course catalogs, keeping track of learners' progress and performance across all types of training, and generating reports. An LMS is not used to create course content. That work is performed using an LCMS.

Learning Modalities (See *Learning Styles.*)

Learning Objectives are clear, measurable statements of behavior that a learner must demonstrate for training to be considered a success.

Learning Objects are self-contained chunks of instructional material used in LCMSs. They typically include three components: a performance goal, the necessary learning content to reach that goal, and some form of evaluation to measure whether or not the goal was achieved.

Learning Styles describe individuals' approaches to learning that involves the way they behave, feel, and process information. Learning styles are the basis for a number of assessment models. (See also *Herrmann Brain Dominance Instrument* and *VAK Model*.)

Learning Transfer refers to how individuals transfer learning in one context to another similar context.

Level 1: Reaction is the first level of Kirkpatrick's Four-Level Evaluation Model. It measures participants' reaction to and satisfaction with a training program.

Level 2: Learning is the second level of Kirkpatrick's Four-Level Evaluation Model. It determines whether participants learned what was intended for them to learn as a result of a training session. It measures the participant's acquisition of cognitive knowledge or behavioral skills.

Level 3: Behavior is the third level of Kirkpatrick's Four-Level Evaluation Model. It measures the degree to which training participants are able to transfer their learning to their workplace behaviors.

Level 4: Results is the fourth level of Kirkpatrick's Four-Level Evaluation Model. It measures the effect of the learning on organizational performance.

Likert Scale is a linear scale used in data collection to rate statements and attitudes; for example, respondents receive a definition of the scale from 1 to 10.

M

Mager, Robert developed behavioral learning objectives with three elements: what the worker must do (performance), the conditions under which the work must be done, and the standard or criterion that is considered acceptable performance.

Maslow's Hierarchy of Needs was introduced by Abraham Maslow in 1954 in his book *Motivation and Personality*. Maslow contended that people have complex needs, which they strive to fulfill and which change and evolve over time. He categorized these needs as physiological, safety/security, social/belongingness, esteem, and self-actualization. Maslow contends that basic needs have to be satisfied before a person can focus on growth.

Mean Score, or the average of a group of numbers, is the most robust, or least affected by the presence of extreme values (outliers), of the three measures of central tendency because each number in the data set has an effect on its (mean) value.

Measures of Central Tendency are three statistical averages: mean (the average of a group of numbers), median (the middle of a distribution where half the numbers are above the median and half are below), and mode (the most frequently occurring value in a group of numbers).

Media is a term traditionally used to describe the radio, television, and print industries; however, in a broader context it includes anything that facilitates transmission of a message such as the web, instructional workbooks, and radio or television.

Median is the middle of a distribution arranged by magnitude; half the numbers are above the median, and half are below the median.

Mentoring is the career development practice of using an experienced person or group to share wisdom and expertise with a protégé over a specific period of time. There are three common types of mentoring: one-on-one, group, and virtual.

Meta-Analysis is a statistical review technique that synthesizes the results of many experimental studies.

Milestones are the indicators of an event within a process, usually placed at the end of a phase to mark its completion. They are used to ensure that a deliverable or project can be completed on time.

Millennials (See *Generation Y*.)

Mobile Learning is learning that takes place via such wireless devices as smartphones, tablets, or laptop computers.

Motivation Theory is based on the idea that when people have the right environment to work in, they will be motivated to grow and become connected to that environment. This theory is important to coaching.

Multimedia is a term used to describe the convergence of audio, video, animation, images, text, and interactive content into one medium such as the web. Multimedia content is associated with digital technologies and enables users to control various aspects of online learning such as content sequence.

Multiple Intelligence Theory, popularized by Howard Gardner in *Frames of Mind* (1985), describes how intelligences reflect how people prefer to process information. Gardner believes that most people are comfortable in three to four of these intelligences and avoid the others. For example, for learners who are not comfortable working with others, doing group case studies may interfere with their ability to process new material.

Multi-Rater Feedback is another name for **360-Degree Feedback Evaluation,** which is feedback from superiors, direct reports, peers, and internal and external customers on how a person performs in any number of behavioral areas.

Multisensory Learning engages the learner and increases retention. Audio and video can often convey feelings and subtle contexts of learning more effectively than other tools.

Multi-Tracking is the editing process where multiple audio tracks are combined to play simultaneously. Each individual track has its own controls for volume and effects, such as graphic equalization; it was traditionally used as a technique to record pop music where each track would feature a different instrument.

Myers-Briggs Type Indicator (MBTI) is an instrument that helps determine personality type based on preferences for extraversion or introversion, intuiting or sensing, thinking or feeling, and judging or perceiving. It's used in career development and team building.

N

Needs Analysis is the process of collecting and synthesizing data to identify how training can help an entity reach its goals.

Neurolinguistic Programming (NLP) is an approach to communication, personal development, and psychotherapy created by Richard Bandler and John Grinder in California in the 1970s. The title asserts a connection between the neurological processes ("neuro"), language ("linguistic"), and behavioral patterns learned through experience ("programming") that proponents speculate can be changed to achieve specific goals in life.

Neuroscience is any of the sciences, such as neurochemistry and experimental psychology, that deal with the structure or function of the nervous system and brain.

Noise Removal Technology attempts to identify background noise when you are recording and then remove it.

Nominal Data is a number or variable used to classify a system, as in digits in a telephone number or numbers on a football player's jersey.

Normal Distribution is a way observations tend to pile up around a particular value rather than be spread evenly across a range of values.

O

Objective is a target or purpose that, when combined with other objectives, leads to a goal.

- **Behavioral Objectives** specify the particular new behavior that an individual should be able to perform after training.

Objective-Centered describes a theory of instruction that concentrates on observable and measurable outcomes. It is based on behaviorism, the primary tenet of which is that psychology should concern itself with the observable behavior of people and animals, not with unobservable events that take place in their minds.

Observation occurs when participants are directed to view or witness an event and be prepared to share their reflections, reactions, data, or insights. This is also a methodology for data collection.

Onboarding, sometimes called *new employee orientation,* refers to the process by which new employees acquire the necessary knowledge, skills, and behaviors to become effective members in their organizations.

Open Space Technology is an approach for facilitating meetings, conferences, symposia, and so forth that is focused on a specific purpose or task—but starting without any formal agenda beyond the overall purpose or theme. Open space meetings ensure that all issues and ideas that people are willing to raise are discussed.

Open System is one that continuously interacts with its environment. In organizations, an open system is said to allow people to learn from and influence one another because of their interconnectedness and interdependence within the system.

Open Systems Theory, also known as living or general systems theory, is based on the idea that an open system continuously interacts with its environment. Organizations can be viewed as open systems.

Ordinal Data is a number or variable that allows ranking order of importance from highest to lowest.

Organization Development (OD) is the process of developing an organization to be more effective in achieving its business goals. OD uses planned initiatives to develop the systems, structures, and process in the organization to improve effectiveness.

Organizational Culture is the unspoken pattern of values that guide the behavior, attitudes, and practices of the people in an organization.

Outlier is a data point that's far removed in value from others in a data set.

Outsourcing Training refers to using resources or products external to an organization to meet its learning requirements.

P

Pedagogy is the art or practice of teaching and often refers to teaching children. Pedagogy focuses on the skills teachers use to impart knowledge and emphasizes the role of the teacher. It is contrasted with andragogy, the teaching of adults. In andragogy the focus is on the learner, who is assumed to be self-directed and motivated to learn in order to perform a task. (See also *Andragogy*.)

Performance describes the execution and accomplishment of some activity; it is not an adjective that describes the action itself.

Performance Analysis measures the gap between desired and actual performance.

Performance Gap Analysis identifies and describes past, present, and potential future human performance gaps.

Performance Support is a storage place for task-specific information, other than memory, that is available just in time at the point of need and may also be called a *job aid*.

Personal Learning Network (PLN) is an informal network of people seeking knowledge or willing to share knowledge in a particular subject area. Members of a PLN enjoy a mutually beneficial relationship. They may be inside or outside each other's work group or company.

Phillips, Jack and Phillips, Patricia developed a model for measuring the return-on-investment or ROI of training programs.

Podcast is a series of digital-media files distributed over the Internet using syndication feeds for playback on portal media players and computers. The term *podcast*, like *broadcast*, can refer either to the series of content itself or the method by which it is syndicated; the latter is also called podcasting. The term derives from the words *iPod* and *broadcast*—the Apple iPod being the brand name of the portal media player for which the first podcasting scripts were developed.

Poll is a virtual classroom feature that allows the facilitator to post questions to participants and show poll results in real time or after all responses have been received.

Process Consulting refers to helping a client understand what is happening based on attention and observation of the emotional, nonverbal, perceptual, and spatial aspects of human behavior; it identifies solutions and transfers the skills to the client to manage the ongoing process.

Producer refers to the virtual classroom technology expert who partners with the facilitator to deliver virtual classroom training.

Professional Development Plan (PDP) is a working document or blueprint for career goals and the strategies for achieving them.

Professional Niche is a marketing statement bundling personal expertise and capabilities spotlighting a candidate's individualized qualified background.

Program Evaluation assesses the effect of a training program on learning.

Program Evaluation Review Technique (PERT) Chart is a diagramming technique that enables project managers to estimate a range of task durations by estimating the optimistic, pessimistic, and most likely durations for each task.

Project Life Cycle is everything that happens from the beginning to the end of a project.

Project Management is the planning, organizing, directing, and controlling of resources for a finite period to complete specific goals and objectives.

Project Scope is what will or won't be done on a project. Project scope management includes the processes needed to complete all required work (and only the required work) so that the project is completed successfully.

Project Work Teams are groups of employees from various departments or backgrounds who work together to identify and resolve workplace issues or problems.

Proprioception is the sense of the relative position of neighboring parts of the body and strength of effort being employed in movement.

Pull Learning allows learners to select what they want, is self-directed, and may be called informal learning.

Push Learning is directed by others, requires learners to accept knowledge and skills as presented, and may be called formal learning.

Q

Qualitative Analysis involves looking at participants' opinions, behaviors, and attributes and is often descriptive.

Qualitative Data are information that can be difficult to express in measures or numbers.

R

Random Assignment is the process of assigning a sample to different groups or treatments in a study.

Random Sampling means that each person in a population has an equal chance of being chosen for the sample. Choosing every tenth person from an alphabetical list of names, for example, creates a random sample.

Random Selection is the process of drawing a sample of people from a population for a study.

Rapid Instructional Design (RID) is a collection of strategies for quickly producing instructional packages to enable a group of learners to achieve a set of specific instructional objectives.

Reliability is the ability to achieve consistent results from a measurement over time.

Results refer to the goals an organization strives for.

Results-Based Approach is driven by a business need and a performance need and must also be justified by the results of the cause analysis.

Return-on-Expectations (ROE) is the measure of satisfaction by key business stakeholders that demonstrates the degree to which their expectations have been met.

Return-on-Investment (ROI) is a ratio of the benefit or profit received from a given investment to the cost of the investment itself. ROI calculations are used to show certain benefits of training programs.

Role Play is an activity during which participants act out roles, attitudes, or behaviors that are not their own to practice skills or apply something they have learned. Frequently, an observer provides feedback to those in character.

Root Cause Analysis is used to determine why a performance gap exists and identify the contributing factors.

Rummler-Brache's Nine Box Model is a matrix approach to performance management based on three levels of performance (organization, process, and performer) and three dimensions of performance (goals, design, and management).

S

Schein's Career Anchors Theory is a concept developed in 1961 by Edgar Schein. A career anchor is one's self-concept about one's talents and abilities, basic values, and motives and needs as they pertain to career.

Scope Creep refers to work or deliverables that are added to a project but were neither part of the project requirements nor added through a formal change process.

Screen Text is written text that is reproduced on the screen of a media device such as a computer monitor, mobile telephone, tablet, or e-book reader. It is read 25 percent slower than text on paper and does not always conform to traditional grammar.

Self-Directed Learning (SDL) is learning in which the learner determines the pace and timing of content delivery. SDL occurs through a variety of media, ranging from print products to web-based systems. It also refers to informal learning in which a person seeks information or guidance from others, for example, through social media.

Semantic Web is a mechanism of adding information about information, supporting machine processing and recombination so that content can be assembled by rules, not by hand.

Significant means probably true (not caused by chance) in statistics.

Simulation is the act of imitating the behavior of some situation or some process by means of something suitably analogous. In training situations, simulations range from simple live exercises to complex computer software. Simulations allow people to learn by performing and repeating an action in a safe environment. Simulations are popular for teaching decision making.

Single-Loop Learning refers to a type of learning in which people learn and use new skills for necessary but incremental change.

Six Sigma Methodology is a disciplined, data-driven methodology for eliminating defects (driving toward six standard deviations between the mean and the nearest specification limit) in a process. The fundamental objective of the Six Sigma methodology is the implementation of a measurement-based strategy that focuses on process improvement and variation reduction.

Skills refer to proficiency, facility, or dexterity that is acquired or developed through training or experience.

Smile Sheet is a nickname for the form used in Level 1 evaluation of instructors and training classes.

Social Learning refers to learning that occurs through interacting with and observing others. It is often informal and unconscious, and often happens as an organic result of living and moving in the world.

Social Media are electronic communication tools used to extend social interactions and learning across organizations and geography.

Soft Data are qualitative measures. They are intangible, anecdotal, personal, and subjective, as in opinions, attitudes, assumptions, feelings, values, and desires. Qualitative data cannot be objectified, and that characteristic makes them valuable.

Sound Effects are audio recordings of common day noises such as a door closing or car starting. Sound effects are individual elements usually saved as individual files that can be combined to create an audio picture and are powerful for grabbing attention and conveying information fast.

Split Attention is the mental load that is caused by separation of related instructional content causing working memory to hold parts of the information while viewing other parts.

Stakeholder is any individual or group who has an interest in the outcome of a project, program, or general success.

Standard Deviation is a common measure or indicator of the amount of variability of scores from the mean. The standard deviation is often used in formulas for advanced or inferential statistics.

Storyboard is a visual plan of each shot a videographer plans to shoot in order to convey a message. It features a drawing of how the shot should look with additional instructions such as shot size, camera positions, movements, and angles.

Strategic Planning is the process that allows an organization to identify its aspirations and future challenges, clarify and gain consensus around a business strategy, communicate the strategy throughout the organization, align departments and personal goals with the overarching organizational strategy, and identify and align strategic initiatives. This process is often combined with long-term (five- to 10-year) planning initiatives.

Structured Mentoring is a time-limited process focused on a protégé's acquisition of a particular skill set and on specific behavioral objectives.

Subject Matter Expert (SME) is a person who has extensive knowledge and skills in a particular subject area.

Succession Planning is the process of identifying key positions, candidates, and employees to meet the challenges that an organization faces in the short and long term.

Summative Evaluation assesses and summarizes the development of learners at a specific point following training. Summative evaluation may also be used to diagnose weaknesses.

Surveys collect the type of information employees have as well as the type of information they need to do their jobs.

Synchronous Training occurs when the trainer and the learner participate in the training at the same time. It is most often used when discussing web-based training, which can be synchronous or asynchronous.

Systems Thinking is a conceptual framework that encompasses the whole, making patterns (and ways to change them) more understandable.

T

Tacit Knowledge (as opposed to explicit knowledge) is the kind of knowledge that is difficult to transfer to another person by means of writing it down or verbalizing it. It is personal knowledge gained through experience.

Talent Development Reporting Principles (TDRp) establishes internal reporting standards for planning and collecting human capital data and defining and reporting critical outcomes, effectiveness, and efficiency measures needed to deliver results and contribute to organizational success. TDRp is an industry-led, grassroots initiative.

Task Analysis examines a single task within a job and breaks it down into the actual steps of performance.

Technical Consulting relies on the knowledge and expertise of the consultant to solve the client's problem.

Teleconferencing is the instantaneous exchange of audio, video, and text between two or more people or groups at two or more locations.

Terminal Objectives are the final behavioral outcomes of a specific instructional event. The designer must state an objective clearly and describe the intended exit competencies for the specified unit, lesson, course, or program for which it was written.

Texting is the act of composing and sending a brief, electronic message between two or more mobile phones or fixed or portable devices over a phone network. Term originally referred to messages sent using the Short Message Service (SMS).

Theory X is a theory of human motivation about work developed by Douglas McGregor in the 1960s. It assumes that employees are inherently lazy, dislike work, and will avoid it if they can. Belief in Theory X leads to close supervision and tight control of employees by their managers.

Theory Y, also developed by Douglas McGregor, postulates that most people are self-motivated and enjoy working and will work to achieve goals to which they are committed, especially if rewards result from the achievement of those goals.

360-Degree Feedback Evaluation is feedback from superiors, direct reports, peers, and internal and external customers on how a person performs in any number of behavioral areas.

Traditional Mentoring focuses on career development and overall career performance over the short or long term.

Traditionalists refer to the generation born before 1946 in the U.S. who are typically characterized as loyal, dependable, responsible, altruistic, and hard working.

Trainers are people who help individuals improve performance by teaching, instructing, or facilitating learning in an organization.

Training Needs Assessment is the process of collecting and synthesizing data to identify how training can help an organization reach its goals.

Training Objective is a statement of what an instructor hopes to accomplish during the training session.

Training Transfer Evaluation measures the success of the learner's ability to transfer and implement learning on the job.

Trend Lines are used to project the values of specific output variables if training had not been undertaken. The projection is compared to the actual data after training, and the difference represents the estimate of the impact of training. Under certain conditions, this strategy can accurately isolate the training impact.

Triple-Loop Learning refers to a type of learning in which people make fundamental shifts about how they view themselves and willingly alter their beliefs and values about themselves and about the world (a transformational act).

Tuckman Group Development Model is a team-maturing model that depicts five stages: forming, storming, norming, performing, and adjourning.

V

VAK Model, developed by Neil Fleming, is a division of learning styles into three categories: visual (learners need pictures, diagrams, and other visuals), audio (learners need to hear information), and kinesthetic (learners need hands-on learning). Some people learn primarily through one learning style, others through a combination of the three.

Validity describes how well the evaluation instrument measures what it is intended to measure.

Variance is a measure of how spread out a distribution is. It's calculated as the average squared deviation of each number from the mean of a data set.

Vertical Development refers to advancement in a person's thinking capability or how one thinks. The outcome of vertical stage development is the ability to think in more complex, systemic, strategic, and interdependent ways.

Video refers to the electronic or digital reproduction of moving pictures and is a key method of online communication. It is generally combined with audio to create a final message although it does not have to include an audio track.

Video Editing is the process of assembling video footage in a video editing software program, cutting out redundant elements of the footage and trimming them so they are run naturally together. Music, sound effects, and special effects are combined during the edit process to create a final video file.

Video Script is written text of a video that includes all spoken word content plus a visual description of each shot along with camera moves, positions, and angles. Factual scripts such as those used in industrial video tend to follow a two-column format. In the left column the shot is described visually and any monologue, dialogue, or commentary is included in the right column. Any audio such as music is also noted in the right column.

Virtual Classroom is an online learning space where learners and instructors interact.

Virtual Reality (VR) is computer-based technology that gives learners a realistic, three-dimensional, interactive experience. This powerful tool enhances learning by allowing students to perform skills in a realistic, engaging simulation of a real-life environment.

W

Web 2.0 is the use of Internet technology and web design to enhance information sharing and, most notably, collaboration among users. These concepts have led to the development and evolution of online communities and hosted services such as social networking sites, wikis, and blogs.

Web Portals are websites that brings information together from diverse sources in a uniform way.

Web-Based Training (WBT) refers to the delivery of educational content via a web browser over the Internet, a private intranet, or an extranet.

WIIFM is Internet slang for "What's in it for me?" Also used by trainers and facilitators at the start of a training program to promote learners' interest in its content.

Wiki is a collection of webpages designed to enable anyone who accesses it to contribute or modify content using a simplified markup language. Wikis are often used to create collaborative websites and to power community website.

Work Breakdown Structure (WBS) is the primary tool in project management used to begin planning and documenting project deliverables.

Workforce Planning is the process that ensures that an organization can meet its goals and objectives within a given business environment by having the right workforce capability. It is part of integrated talent management, which involves having the right people with the right skills in the right jobs at the right time.

Workplace Learning and Performance (WLP) is a term for the professions of training, performance improvement, employee development, and workplace education. Collectively, this profession is more commonly known as training and development (T&D).

X

XML is a markup language specifically designed to support separating out content structure in in web pages supporting different delivery of the same content to different devices.

Appendix B

List of Tools

Contributors to the *ASTD Handbook* provided tools to help you implement the concepts you learned in each chapter throughout the book. The tools are available for downloading at www.astdhandbook.org. As long as you maintain the copyright information and the "used with permission" designation on the tool, you will be able to use it in your daily work.

Section I: The Training and Development Profession

Luminary Perspective, Shaping the Future of the Training and Development Profession
William J. Rothwell
- Tool I-1: A Worksheet on Issues Affecting the Training and Development Profession

Chapter 2: ASTD's New Competency Model
Jennifer Naughton
- Tool 2-1: Using the New ASTD Competency Model: Action Planning for Individuals

Chapter 3: The Importance of Certification
Kimo Kippen, Coline T. Son Lee, and Jeff Toister
- Tool 3-1: Value of Certification
- Tool 3-2: Develop a Study Strategy
- Tool 3-3: Gap List
- Tool 3-4: CPLP Candidate Self-Assessment
- Tool 3-5: Create a Countdown CPLP Planning Calendar

Chapter 4: Take Charge of Your Career: Breaking Into and Advancing in the T&D Profession
Annabelle Reitman
- Tool 4-1: Set Employment Priorities

About the Editor

Elaine Biech is president and managing principal of ebb associates inc, an organizational and leadership development firm that helps organizations work through large-scale change. Her 30 years in the training and consulting field include support to private industry, government, and nonprofit organizations.

Elaine specializes in helping people work as teams to maximize their effectiveness. Customizing all her work for individual clients, she conducts strategic planning sessions and designs and implements corporatewide systems such as change management, re-engineering of business processes, and mentoring programs. She facilitates topics such as fostering creativity, creating leadership development programs, time management, speaking skills, coaching, consulting skills, training competence, conducting productive meetings, managing corporatewide change, organizational communication, and effective listening. She is particularly adept at turning dysfunctional groups into productive teams.

She has presented at dozens of national and international conferences. Known to many as the trainer's trainer, she custom-designs training programs for managers, leaders, trainers, and consultants. Elaine has been featured in dozens of publications including the *Wall Street Journal, Harvard Management Update, Washington Post, Investor's Business Daily,* and *Fortune* magazine.

She is the author and editor of more than 50 books, including two that have received national awards: *ASTD Leadership Handbook*, 2010 (*Choice Magazine's* Outstanding Academic Title, 2011) and *90 World-Class Activities by 90 World-Class Trainers,* 2007 (Training Review Best Training Product, 2007). Her books have been translated into Chinese, German, and

Dutch. She was the consulting editor for the prestigious Pfeiffer Training and Consulting Annuals for 16 years and designed five ASTD certificate programs.

Elaine has her BS from the University of Wisconsin-Superior in Business and Education Consulting, and her MS in Human Resource Development. She is active at the national level of ASTD, is a lifetime member, served on the 1990 National Conference Design Committee, was a member of the National ASTD Board of Directors and the Society's Secretary from 1991 to 1994, initiated and chaired Consultant's Day for seven years, and was the International Conference Design Chair in 2000. In addition to her work with ASTD, she served on the ISA Board of Directors.

In 2001, she received ISA's highest award, the ISA Spirit Award, and in 2012 was recognized as ISA's Outstanding Contributor. Elaine is on the Board of Governors for the Center for Creative Leadership. Elaine is the recipient of the 1992 National ASTD Torch Award, the 2004 ASTD Volunteer-Staff Partnership Award, and the 2006 ASTD Gordon M. Bliss Memorial Award. She was selected for the 1995 Wisconsin Women Entrepreneurs' Mentor Award. In 2012, ASTD awarded Elaine the inaugural CPLP Fellow Program Honoree from the ASTD Certification Institute.

About ASTD

ASTD Vision: Create a world that works better.

ASTD Mission: Empower professionals to develop knowledge and skills successfully.

ASTD (American Society for Training & Development) is the world's largest professional association dedicated to the training and development field. In more than 100 countries, ASTD's members work in organizations of all sizes, in the private and public sectors, as independent consultants, and as suppliers. Members connect locally in 120 U.S. chapters and with 10 international strategic partners.

ASTD started in 1943 and in recent years has widened the profession's focus to align learning and performance to organizational results, and is a sought-after voice on critical public policy issues. For more information, visit www.astd.org.

What We Do

ASTD provides resources for training and development professionals—research, analysis, benchmarking, online information, books, and other publications. These include:

- ***State of the Industry* report:** providing annual analysis of training investments and practices, plus additional research reports on critical topics and trends in learning.
- **ASTD Forum:** convening private and public sector organizations from around the world.
- ***T+D magazine:*** keeping readers up-to-date on the latest ideas, trends, and best practices.
- **ASTD Press:** publishing and distributing the best titles on training, learning technologies, and performance improvement.

- **ASTD Online Library:** providing access to nearly 3,000 articles, business books and summaries, and select content from major newspapers and regional news sources.
- *Infoline* **series:** giving short, practical "lifelines" on a range of subjects.
- **ASTD's Buyer's Guide:** providing a searchable database of products and services.

We also bring people together in conferences, workshops, and online:

- **Communities of Practice:** focusing on key areas of the training and development field; led by community managers whose in-depth knowledge will ensure that the content, offerings, and resources serve your needs.
- **International Conference & Exposition:** serving the needs of the worldwide community of training and development professionals.
- **ASTD TechKnowledge® Conference & Exposition:** focusing on e-learning and the use of technology.
- **Other conferences and events:** focusing on key topics in the field.
- Connecting locally in 120 **U.S. chapters** and globally with 10 **international strategic partners**.

We offer professional development opportunities for training and development practitioners:

- **ASTD Job Bank** and the online **Career Center** provide career resources.
- **Certified Professional in Learning and Performance™** (CPLP) credential is available for individuals in the training and development field to pursue and achieve certification in the field.
- **ASTD's Master Trainer™** and the **Master Instructional Designer** programs are assessment-based certificate programs covering training delivery and instructional design.
- More than 50 face-to-face and online workshops and programs aligned with the Areas of Expertise in **ASTD's Competency Model** are available through ASTD Education.

We recognize excellence and set the standards for best practices:

- Advancing **ASTD's Vision Awards:** recognizing individuals and teams for their contributions to the goals and vision of ASTD.
- Advancing **Workplace Learning Awards:** honoring individuals' thought leadership in and advocacy for the profession.

- **ASTD BEST Awards:** honoring organizations that demonstrate enterprise-wide success as a result of employee training and development.
- **Excellence in Practice Awards:** recognizing results achieved through practices, interventions, and tools from the entire field of workplace training and development.
- **ASTD Certification Institute Awards:** recognizing thought leaders and organizations that support the profession through the Certified Professional in Learning and Performance (CPLP) credential.

How to Contact ASTD

Website: www.astd.org

Phone: 703.683.8100 or 800.628.2783

Email: customercare@astd.org

Mail: 1640 King Street, Box 1443
Alexandria, Virginia 22313-1443 USA

Index

A

abundance mentality, 895–896

Accenture, 707

accomplishment, learning versus, 525–526

action, theory of, 767

activities
    See also content and activities
    learning, 81

ADDIE model, 182–183, 188, 202–203, 206, 368, 727

Adobe Connect, 402, 775

adult development, 784

Adult Learner: A Neglected Species, The (Knowles), 24

adult learning theory, 24, 28, 193–195

Africa, 825–828

AGES (attention, generation, emotions, and spacing), 863

aggregation, 277, 278–279

Agile, 727

Allen, C.R., 14

Amazon.com, 298

American Hotel and Lodging Educational Institute, 742

American Intellectual Property Law Association, 292, 298

American Petroleum Institute, 15

American Society for Training & Development. *See* ASTD

American Society of Training Directors. *See* ASTD

analysis
    front-end, 127

performance, 92–93
    SAM, 206

analytics and systems approach, 553–562

Analyzing, 227–228

andragogy, 24, 338

animations, 317–318

Anti-Cybersquatting Consumer Protection Act (ACPA), 296

application, content curation, 277, 280

Applying, 226–227

Apprenticeship Act (1961) (India), 11

apprenticeships, 11

apps at ASTD, 421, 427

areas of expertise (AOEs), 38, 39, 40

Argyris, C., 21, 23, 767

Asia, 836–839

assembly line, 14

assertiveness training, 25

assessments
    of barriers to improve performance, 557–559
    bottom alignment and needs, 109–122
    mentoring, 643
    reassessment, need for, 71–72
    self-, 345, 567–574
    self-awareness, 801–805
    techniques, validating, 222–223
    of your current career situation, 62–63
    of your current work situation, 62

ASTD (American Society for Training & Development)
    See also Competency Model
    apps at, 421, 427
    code of ethics, 288